1,000,000 Books

are available to read at

---◇---

www.ForgottenBooks.com

---◇---

Read online
Download PDF
Purchase in print

ISBN 978-0-282-40234-1
PIBN 10847790

1 MONTH OF
FREE
READING

at

www.ForgottenBooks.com

By purchasing this book you are eligible for one month membership to ForgottenBooks.com, giving you unlimited access to our entire collection of over 1,000,000 titles via our web site and mobile apps.

To claim your free month visit: www.forgottenbooks.com/free847790

THE

LIFE

OF

JAMES THE SECOND

KING OF ENGLAND, &c.

COLLECTED OUT OF MEMOIRS WRIT OF HIS OWN HAND.

TOGETHER WITH

THE KING'S ADVICE TO HIS SON,

AND

HIS MAJESTY'S WILL.

PUBLISHED FROM THE ORIGINAL STUART MANUSCRIPTS
IN CARLTON-HOUSE,

BY THE REV. J. S. CLARKE, LL.B. F.R.S.

HISTORIOGRAPHER TO THE KING, CHAPLAIN OF THE HOUSEHOLD,
AND LIBRARIAN TO THE PRINCE REGENT.

―――――――

IN TWO VOLUMES.

VOL. I.

LONDON:

PRINTED FOR LONGMAN, HURST, REES, ORME, AND BROWN, PATERNOSTER-ROW;
FOR PAYNE AND FOSS, AND BUDD AND CALKEN, PALL-MALL.

1816.

TO

HIS ROYAL HIGHNESS

GEORGE PRINCE REGENT

OF THE UNITED KINGDOM OF

GREAT BRITAIN AND IRELAND

AND OF

THE KINGDOM OF HANOVER.

SIR,

IN obedience to Your Royal Highness's
most gracious Command to me, as

Historiographer to His Majesty, I have selected and prepared for the press the most valuable of the Private Manuscripts of JAMES THE SECOND; whereby the Public may be enabled to form an opinion of the Principles and Motives, which influenced, in his own apprehension at least, the Counsels and Conduct of that Monarch.

In the execution of this important trust I have spared neither care, nor labour, to fulfil the liberal intention of Your Royal Highness; yet I do not presume so much on my diligence, as to imagine that no errors may have occurred, and that no historical illustrations may have been omitted in the course of so long a work:

Your Royal Highness may still, I fear, perceive omissions that have escaped my observation. But encouraged by a Benignity which conspicuously appears amidst the brilliant Events of THE RE-GENCY, I venture, SIR, to indulge the hope, that Your Royal Highness will accept of this discharge of my Duty with your accustomed goodness and condescension.

I have the Honour to remain

With unfeigned Respect and sincere Attachment,

SIR,

YOUR ROYAL HIGHNESS'S

Most dutiful and most devoted Servant

JAMES STANIER CLARKE.

CARLTON HOUSE,
August 12, 1815.

PREFACE.

———

THE Nation is indebted to the zeal and unremitting exertions of His Royal Highness the PRINCE REGENT, for the preservation of these Historical Documents, from the destruction with which they were menaced by the events of the French Revolution.

During the year 1804, Sir John Hippisley, by command of H. R. H. the PRINCE OF WALES, communicated in a Letter from Mr. Fox, dated Oct. 5. concluded a negotiation with the Abbé Waters, Procurator General of the English Benedictins, respecting all the Original Papers of the Royal House of Stuart, which had come into his possession after the death of Madame D'Albany, generally styled Dutchess of Albany, according to the last will of that Lady. Mr. Fox in the above-mentioned Letter to Sir J. Hippisley had said, That it was the wish of His Royal Highness to have the Stuart Papers consigned to the care of Mr. H. Elliot, Lord Minto's brother, who was then at Naples, and added, " If the Papers are not mere duplicates, *they must at any rate be extremely valuable,* though not particularly so to *me,* unless they relate to the period between 1672 and 1690, or thereabouts."

Mr. Pitt, having previously obtained information of the existence of these Stuart Papers, had authorised Mr. Jackson, His Majesty's Minister at the Court of Sardinia, to treat for them in the name of His Majesty's Government; but on Sir John Hippisley's representation to Mr. Pitt, that he was far advanced in his Negociation on account of His Royal Highness, Mr. Pitt authorised Mr. Long to write to Sir John Hippisley, that, in deference to His Royal Highness, he had countermanded his instructions to Mr. Jackson.

Before the memorable departure of the ever to be lamented Lord Nelson from Portsmouth, in the autumn of 1805, Sir John Hippisley had requested, in consequence of a Letter from Lord Dundas, that the noble Admiral would endeavour to obtain these invaluable Manuscripts, which had been removed from Rome to Civita Vecchia, and had been deposited in the hands of a British merchant at that Port: " The Prince of Wales," said Lord Dundas, " expresses great anxiety for the safety of the Commission, and requests that Lord Nelson will keep it on board his own ship until he returns, unless he has the opportunity of some safe and sure conveyance to send it home."

Subsequent to the Victory of Trafalgar, Lord Collingwood on the 11th of January 1806, in thanking Sir John Hippisley for his condolence on the death of a Friend, whose loss could never be replaced, informed him, That the strictest regard should be paid to the subject of his Commission; and on the 31st of October, in the same year, his Lordship also wrote as follows, " From the length of time it is since I had the honour to write to you, on the subject of communicating with Mr. Bertram at Civita Vecchia, you will conclude there has been difficulty; which I am sorry to say has been such as has prevented any intercourse with that gentleman, or even obtaining any information of him — except a report that he is in prison, seized on and confined by the French.

" I sent a Sloop of war up early in July, for the purpose of carrying your letter, and receiving any box or parcel which Mr. Bertram might have to send to me, and in a letter to Mr. Bertram desired him to send off a confidential person to receive your letter. Captain Raitt made several attempts to communicate with the shore — his boats were not permitted to land, and his Ship was fired at. In a second attempt in September he took with him a Sicilian officer, who it was thought could make his way to Mr. Bertram, and as the letter was supposed to be on a subject relating to the Fleet, those officers took a great interest in getting it delivered, and I am exceedingly sorry they were not successful.——Should any change of circumstance give more hope of obtaining the Papers which His Royal Highness is desirous of possessing, I will not fail to take advantage of it."

In 1810 THE PRINCE OF WALES not discouraged by these obstacles, and impelled by a consideration for the Stuart * Family, which His Royal Highness had previously shewn in assuring the Cardinal York of a continuance of his Pension even if it were to be paid out of the Privy Purse of His Royal Highness, was pleased to authorise Sir John Hippisley to confide the commission for obtaining the Stuart Papers to Mr. Bonelli; who at length, though with considerable risk, and through the assistance of the Rev. Mr. Macpherson President of The Scotch College, succeeded in shipping off the Cases for Leghorn, and having there concealed them from the vigilance of the Custom House Officers, they were with great difficulty embarked on board a Tunisian vessel bound to Tunis, and thence forwarded to Malta and finally to London, when the whole were placed in the Library at Carlton House. Sir John Hippisley, to whose care they had previously been consigned on their arrival, had frequently when at Rome from 1792 to

---

* The HOUSE OF BRUNSWICK from the first displayed a noble regard for the feelings of The Stuart Family. See a Letter from the Princess Sophia of Hanover to King WILLIAM, (Vol. ii. p. 362.)

1795˹ examined the whole Collection, and was perfectly
satisfied respecting their authenticity.

The Procurator General, *Abbé James Waters,* died at Rome
soon after he had received the first payment of his annuity,
which he had requested to be allowed him from His Royal
Highness in preference to any other mode of remuneration.
The following is an extract from the Abbé Waters' Account
of the Stuart MSS., which he sent to Sir John Hippisley from
Rome, January 12th, 1805, giving an opinion of the Biographical Manuscript in four volumes, which forms the principal
part of the present work :

" Hon^d Dr Sir,

" It would be difficult to give you in the small compass of
a letter, all the elucidations you seem to require. The Papers
in my possession were left me by the late D. of Albany, who
found them in her Father's Library in Florence, from whence
I myself brought them to Rome and lodged them in the
Chancery till her death ; when I brought them in consequence
of her Will to which I was sole executor to my own house.
I here enclose a List of them as you desired. I shall observe
in the 1st place, that the four Volumes first mentioned of THE
LIFE OF K. JA^s 2^d, do not seem a collection of scattered
papers with intervals of time or place, but form an Historical
uninterrupted Acc^t of the principal events private and publick
of his life and connections, from his first Campagnes in

France and Spain, his return to England, his residence, employs, persecutions at Court, his exile in Scotland, his conversion, marriage, and accession to the Throne; viz. from his Birth in October 1633, to his Death in Sept' 1701. All these contents are * asserted to have been collected from Memoirs written in his own hand, to which they bear continual references, citations, and long extracts. The King before he left England collected all his papers together, which in confusion and hurry he put in a box and entrusted to the Count of Therese, the Duke of Tuscany's Envoy. By his means they were sent to Leghorn and Florence, and by the G. Duke to Paris, where they were deposited in the Scotch Colledge. These papers made in all a Collection of nine †

---

* See Vol. 2. Page 242. for a most satisfactory attestation of the Original Sources, whence the following Life was composed.

† Lord Holland, in his prefatory address to the Reader of Mr. Fox's History of JAMES THE SECOND, has subjoined the following note: " Among Mr. Fox's papers was found a List of *The Works which were placed in the Scotch College at Paris, soon after the death of James the Second, and were there at the time of the French Revolution.* It is as follows:

Four Volumes folio, six Volumes quarto,	Memoirs in JAMES THE SECOND's own hand-writing, beginning from the time that he was sixteen years of age.
Two thin quarto Volumes,	Containing Letters from CHARLES THE SECOND's Ministers to James the Second (then DUKE OF YORK) when he was at Brussels and in Scotland, MS.
Two thin quarto Volumes,	Containing Letters from CHARLES THE SECOND, to his Brother, JAMES DUKE OF YORK, MS.

Vols, all written with his own hand. What access were
given to these Original Papers I cannot say; but sure the
Author of the four Vols. by me, whoever he was, saw
them, since he copied and cites so much from them. I have
never seen the work published by a Mr. Macpherson in
Edinburgh, entitled Memoires of K. Ja^a 2^d, so cannot say if
it be taken from these Vols. *I am however assured the totality
of their contents never was published.* A Copy of these four
Volumes by me was taken by a Secretary of the King, and
put into the hands of Mr. Gordon, Superior of the House at
Paris; this Copy your friend Paul Macpherson, now here as
agent for the Scotch Clergy, took to England in 1788, and
showed it to a Mr. Chambers who was writing The History of
Scotland, he wished to borrow it as useful to his work, but
it was refused. This Copy is now in Scotland, *and has
nothing to do with the Papers printed by Macpherson author of
Ossian.*"

" This is all I can say of the MS. in four Vols. in my
possession, which Mr. Lock some years ago Consul at Naples
praised, and the Rev^d Mr. * Gunn admired, as well as Mr.
Jackson now here. At all events if the Original Memoires
of the King have been destroyed or burnt at St Omers, as
the Hon. Mr. Fox seems to believe, and was printed in the

---

* It is difficult to make out this name correctly.

Monthly Reviser (*Review*) of last June, these Copies will become interesting if not already printed."

An Extract from a Letter of Dr. Cameron to Lord Holland, dated March 2, 1808, inserted in his Lordship's Prefatory * Address, gives some further interesting information respecting the fate of The Original Biographical Notes written by KING JAMES himself, and extending to nine volumes.

" Before Lord Gower, the British Embassador, left Paris, in the beginning of the French Revolution, he wrote to Principal Gordon and offered to take charge of those valuable Papers, (KING JAMES's Manuscripts, &c.) and deposit them in some place of safety in Britain: I know not what answer was returned, but nothing was done. Not long thereafter the Principal came to England, and the care of every thing in the College devolved on Mr. Alexander Innes, the only British Subject who remained in it. About the same time, Mr. Stapleton, then President of the English College of St Omer, afterwards † Bishop in England, went to Paris, previously to his retiring from France, and Mr. Innes, who had resolved not to abandon his post, consulted with him about the means of preserving the Manuscripts. Mr. Stapleton

---

* Page 28.　　　† Catholic Bishop.

thought if he had them at St Omer, he could with small risk convey them to England. It was therefore resolved that they should be carefully packed up, addressed to a Frenchman, a confidential friend of Mr. Stapleton, and remitted by some publick carriage. Some other things were put up with the Manuscripts. The whole arrived without any accident, and was laid in a cellar. But the patriotism of the Frenchman becoming suspicious, perhaps upon account of his connection with the English College, he was put in prison; and his wife, apprehensive of the consequences of being found to have English Manuscripts richly bound and ornamented with Royal arms, in her house, cut off the boards and destroyed them. The Manuscripts thus disfigured, and more easily huddled up in any sort of bundle, were secretly carried, with papers belonging to the Frenchman himself, to his country house and buried in the garden. They were not, however, permitted to remain long there; the lady's fears increased, and the Manuscripts were taken up and reduced to ashes.

" This is the substance of the account given to Mr. Innes, and reported by him to me in June, 1802, in Paris. I desired it might be authenticated by a *procès verbale*. A letter was therefore written to St Omer, either by Mr. Innes, or by Mr. Cleghorn, a lay gentleman, who had resided in the English College of St Omer, and was personally acquainted with the Frenchman, and happened to be at Paris at this time. The answer given to this letter was, that the good man, under the pressure of old age and other infirmities, was alarmed by the proposal of a discussion and investigation, which revived in his memory past sufferings, and might, perhaps, lead to a renewal of them. Any further correspondence upon the subject seemed useless, especially as I instructed Mr. Innes to go to St Omer, and clear up every doubt in a formal and legal manner, that some authentic document might be handed down to posterity concerning those valuable Manuscripts. I did not foresee that war was to be kindled up anew, or that my friend Mr. Innes was to die so soon.

" Mr. Cleghorn, whom I mentioned above, is at present in the Catholick seminary of Old-Hall Green, Puckeridge, Hertfordshire. He can probably name another gentleman who saw the Manuscripts at St Omer, and saved some small things, (but unconnected with the Manuscripts,) which he carried away in his pocket, and has still in his possession.

" I need not trouble your Lordship with my reflections upon this relation; but I ought not to omit that I was told sometimes, That all the Manuscripts, as well as their boards, were consumed by fire in the cellar in which they had been deposited upon their arrival at St Omer."

It is difficult to ascertain with certainty who was the person employed in drawing up the following. LIFE OF JAMES THE SECOND, but it seems to be the general opinion, which Lord * Holland has noticed as being also that of the Catholick Bishop Cameron, (in whose possession is the other Copy of the Manuscript which the Abbé Waters mentioned as having been taken,) That this Life was compiled from those Original Documents which appear to have been consumed at Sᵗ Omer, " by *Thomas Innes,* one of the Superiors of the Scotch College, and author of a work entitled, *A Critical Essay on the ancient Inhabitants of Scotland.*" " The Narrative," says Mr. Fox in his letter † to Mr. Laing, " was said to have been revised and corrected, as to style, by *Dryden* the poet, (meaning probably Charles Dryden, the great poet's son,) and it was not known in the College whether it was drawn up in JAMES'S Life, or by the direction of his son, the Pretender."

Others on the contrary who have inspected the Stuart MSS. in the Library at Carlton House are inclined to think, that the person employed in drawing up the Life was *Mr. Lewis Innes,* styled by Voltaire *Le Jesuite Innès,* who with Lord Caryll (the nobleman to whom Pope was ‡ indebted for the first idea of the Rape of the Lock) had been associated in the

---

* Lord Holland's Prefatory Address to the Reader.   † Ibid.

‡ Dr. Warton informs us, in his Edition of Pope's Works, That a *Mr.* Caryll, who was Secretary to Queen Mary, wife of JAMES THE SECOND, was the person who originally proposed to Pope the subject of The Rape of the Lock. *Lord* Caryll continued after JAMES's death to act as Secretary to the Queen.

service of JAMES after his withdrawing into France. Into the custody of this gentleman THE ORIGINAL MEMOIRS OF JAMES were given by a Warrant, dated March 24, 1701, to be preserved in the Archives of the Scotch College of Paris. This Warrant is inserted in one of the * Books of Entrys, Certificates and other Papers signed by JAMES THE SECOND, and his Son, which are preserved with The Stuart Manuscripts in Carlton House.

" JAMES R.

" James the Second by the Grace of God King of Great Britain, France and Ireland, Defender of the Faith, &c: To our Trusty and Wellbeloved Mr. Lewis Jnese, Almoner to our deerest Consort the Queen, and Principal of our Scotch Colledge at Paris Greeting. WHEREAS WEE are well assured that our Originall Memoires writt in our own hand can be no wher more safely kept then in Our Scotch Colledge of Paris, wher ther has been formerly severall papers of Our Royall Predecessors depositated and preserued by the great care and fidelity of those who have had the Government of Our said Colledge, And whereas wee have particular knowledge of your zeal discretion and affection for Vs and our Seruice, Wee have thought fitt to charge you with all the foresaid Originall Memoires as a Testimony of Our Trust and confidence in you, And wee do hereby authorize you to take into your care and custody these our s^d Memoires to be preserv'd in the Archiues of our said Scotch Colledge at Paris, and ther to remain as a lasting mark of our trust in you, and our affection for our said Colledge. And for so doing this shall be to you and your successors in the Government of Our said Colledge a sufficient Warrant. Given at our Court at S⸱ Germains the 24ᵗʰ day of March 1701 And in the 17ᵗʰ year of our Reign.

By his Maᵗⁱᵉˢ Command

CARYLL."

The knowledge which JAMES herein professes to have had of the Zeal, Discretion and Affection of this his faithful Servant, rendered Mr. Innes peculiarly fit for being the confidential Secretary of that Prince; and the Chevalier St. George, if the Life commenced under his auspices after his Father's Death, would probably prefer the ability of such a biographer before that of any other. The hand-writing throughout appears to be the same, and is remarkable for its clearness and uniformity, but the mode of composition seems to vary in the different volumes, of which the reader will judge for himself. The endless variation of the orthography has greatly increased the labour of editing the work, since it demanded a continued attention, not only to words and sentences, but almost to every letter throughout the Manuscript. The Writer of it, whoever he may have been, continually spells the same words in different ways even in the course of only a few lines, and this when printed as it has been to preserve a similarity with the Manuscript, may frequently appear to the reader as errors of the press. There are also some omissions which both the writer of the Life and the Son and Grandson of JAMES THE SECOND have neglected to supply, and, when these have tended to perplex the sense of the Narrative, the Editor has been advised to supply the words, that appear to have been wanting, by printing them in Italics between crotchets; it seems also to have been the practice of the writer of the Life to use capitals in the beginning of any words on which he wished particular emphasis to be placed. The whole of the biography, if not begun before the death of JAMES, was probably written (and this is the prevailing opinion of those persons who have had access to the MSS.) during the first ten or fifteen years of the Eighteenth Century: the following passage, already marked by a Note, (Vol. 2. p. 195.) would fix the date, at least of the composition of that part of the Life, after the death of James and his Queen: " Never Child had a greater resemblance of his Parents both in body and mind than his present Majesty, of the late King his Father and the Queen his Mother."

If the leading object of JAMES, in continuing Memoirs of what had passed under his own eyes, were to form materials for his own Life at a subsequent period, the following Biographical Narrative might possibly have been begun under his direction and by Mr. Lewis Innes, to whom the private papers had been entrusted before the death of his Royal Master. After that event a large portion of The Manuscript, perhaps the third and fourth Tomes, which seem to have been composed much later than the former ones, were probably completed under the direction and eye of his own Son, the Chevalier St. George: Accordingly we find in * one of the Books of Warrants, Certificates, &c. an Order, dated Jan. 12, 1707, addressed " to Our Trusty and Wellbeloved Lewis Jnese, to transport some of his late Majesty's papers from the Archives of the Scots College to St. Germains to be inspected:

" JAMES R.

" Whereas by a speciall Warrant of the late King Our Royal Father of blessed memory, his Mat^ies Memoires and other papers written in his own hand are depositated in the Archives of our Scots Colledge of Paris there to be kept, And whereas none of the s^d papers are to be lent out from thence on any pretext whatsoever without our positive order or Warrant, We do hereby require and authorize you to transport for some months to our Court at St Germains so many of the fores^d Royal Papers as relate to the year 1678, and downwards, to be inspected and perused by such persons as We shall appoint for that effect, And afterwards to carry back and repone them with all care and safety in the s^d Archives there to be kept conforme to the s^d Warrant of Our Royal Father. And for so doing this shall be your Warrant. Given at Our Court at St Germains the 12th day of January 1707. And in the 6th year of Our Reign.

By his Mat^ies Command,

CARYLL."

---

* Vol. 4. p. 28.

Lord Hardwicke (in his State Papers Vol. 2. p. 304.) appears to have considered that a work like the present, in which The Memoirs of King JAMES could be given unmutilated by those who had the power over them, would be a very valuable addition to Historical Literature: " It is perhaps," says he, " more to be wished than expected that King JAMES's Memoirs might be given entire to the world by those who have the power over them; as it would be far more satisfactory to review them in their original state, than in such imperfect and hasty extracts as have hitherto been allowed to be taken. And to speak fairly, the prudential motives, which might formerly have rendered their publication improper, seem no longer to exist. *A greater treasure of anecdotes for the perusal of an Englishman, one's imagination can hardly form an idea of; and it would be very material to combine and compare the whole historical mass, as it came, at different times, from the pen of that exact and diligent Prince,* whose application to business may justly be proposed as a pattern to those of his rank, though his Principles and his Judgment were erroneous, and exceptionable, in the highest degree."

That the treasure of historical anecdote and information is great in these volumes, cannot be doubted : The commencement of CHARLES THE SECOND's Secret Negociations with France, is therein more fully given than by any historian that has yet appeared. The loss of the decisive fight at Marston Moor has usually been imputed to * Prince Rupert's impetuosity and rashness, but the compiler of the ensuing Life of JAMES THE SECOND, alludes (Vol. 1. p. 23.) to a positive Order sent by King CHARLES THE FIRST to that Prince, as the cause of his hazarding the action. At page 29 the striking fact is recorded, That of all the Parliamentary Officers introduced to THE DUKE OF YORK, when under the peculiar circumstances of calamity that attended the surrender of Oxford and the total depression of the Royal Cause, Cromwell was the only person who rendered to that Prince the homage of kneeling when presented : There occurred probably in those stormy and intriguing times more than one moment, in which Cromwell, before more daring views were opened to his ambition, might have been won over to the Royal Cause ; as *Sir John Reresby* observes in the beginning of his Memoirs, Cromwell was doubtless the deepest dissembler on earth. — In page 290 of the same volume, the reader will find a curious passage, which proves, That the Right of Search, which Foreigners have thought fit to challenge as an Innovation exercised in an unprecedented manner by British Men of War, was

---

* *Mr. A. B. Lambert* was so obliging as to favour the Editor with a List of some Stuart MSS. in the possession of John Benet, Esq., of Pyt House, a relation of his, amongst which is a MS. Life of Prince Rupert. Mr. Benet's ancestor was Secretary to Prince Rupert. Mr. Benet's Collection of Stuart MSS. and papers relative to these times, is extremely rich and extensive. The Editor also found some other Historical MSS. relative to the times which these volumes illustrate, in the Library of the Earls of Leicester, at Penshurst, which seemed not to have been noticed by Collins in his publication of the Sidney Papers; and were therefore recommended to be published.

practised in 1657, as an old acknowledged privilege, without being the subject of either resistance or remonstrance. The reader will also find, under the year 1650, in addition to the account in the Harleian Miscellany of the Actions that took place before Dunkirk, much interesting information (p. 334.) respecting that transaction.

It were endless to dwell on the valuable addition which His Royal Highness THE PRINCE REGENT has made to the history of this nation, by directing those Manuscripts to be published which form the substance of the following volumes. This Life of JAMES bears also a striking analogy with those events which have so recently convulsed and demoralised a considerable. part of Europe: *Few Princes*, as Campbell observed, *have struggled with greater Difficulties than King* JAMES THE SECOND, *and few ever sustained a greater load of trouble afterwards.* Yet the Difficulties he had to struggle with have not always been sufficiently considered by Historians, nor does it appear, that the essential and lasting service which JAMES rendered to this Country, in compacting and as it were building up its Naval Power, has been sufficiently weighed : It is not generally known, that the Naval Regulations now in force are taken almost verbatim from those which he established, or that when lately the Board of Naval Revision wished to add to and improve the Naval Regulations, they sent for the Papers of Pepys, the Marine Secretary of JAMES, as being the best materials whence they could obtain the object they had in view. As Campbell frankly acknowledged, *James* *thoroughly understood.the whole business of the Admiralty,. and knew also the disorders which had crept into the whole œconomy of the Fleet, in the six years immediately preceding his Accession.* This fact is amply corroborated by the honourable testimony of Mr. Secretary Pepys in his Memoirs; the excellent methods there recorded, by which J A M E s regenerated the Naval Power, clearly shew how well he understood it in all its bearings. The following were the * Qualifications which during that Monarch's reign were required from every one, who occupied a place in any branch of his Naval Department:

I. *A Practiced Knowledge in every part of the Works and Methods of your Navy, both at the Board and in your Yards. The not discerning of which and the others that follow,* (adds Mr. Pepys in addressing James the Second,) *appears to have cost your Royal Brother and You within the fore-mentioned five years, above half a million.*

II. *A General Mastery in the business of Accounts, though more particularly those incident to the Affairs of Your Navy.*

III. *Vigour of Mind, joyn'd with approv'd Industry, Zeal, and Personal aptness for Labour.*

IV. *An entire Resignation of themselves and their whole time to this Your Service, without lyableness to Avocation from other Business or Pleasure.*

---

* Pepys' Memoirs relating to the State of The Royal Navy of England, p. 45.

V. *Lastly, Such Credit with your Majesty for Integrity and Loyalty, as may (with the former conditions) lead both Your Self and my Lord Treasurer, to an entire confidence of having all done that can be morally expected from them, in the Advancement of your Service, and the circumspect and orderly Dispensing and Improving of your Treasure.*

And to the above judicious Qualifications, which cannot be too much attended to in the present day, may be subjoined what PEPYS termed, HIS THREE TRUTHS ESSENTIAL TO THE SEA ŒCONOMY OF GREAT BRITAIN, as corollaries from the premises:

1. *That Integrity, and general (but unpracticed) Knowledge, are not alone sufficient to conduct and support a Navy, so as to prevent its Declension into a state little less unhappy than the worst that can befall it under the want of both.*

2. *That not much more (neither) is to be depended on, even from Experience alone and Integrity, unaccompanyd with Vigour of Application, Assiduity, Affection, Strictness of Discipline, and Method.*

3. *That it was a strenuous Conjunction of all these (and that Conjunction only) that within half the time, and less than half the charge it cost the Crown in the exposing it, had (at the very instant of its unfortunate* LORD's *Withdrawing from it) rais'd the* NAVY OF ENGLAND *from the lowest state of Impotence, to the most advanced step towards a lasting and solid Prosperity, that (all circumstances considered) this Nation had ever seen it at.*

II

AND *yet not such, but that (even at this its Zenith) it both did and suffered sufficient to teach us,* THAT THERE IS SOMETHING ABOVE BOTH THAT AND US THAT GOVERNS THE WORLD, TO WHICH (INCOMPREHENSIBLE) ALONE BE GLORY.

Such were the Principles and Maxims which JAMES THE SECOND established, whose interesting Commentaries on what had passed before him both as a Prince and a Sovereign, are now given in these Volumes to the Public through the liberal condescension of His Royal Highness THE PRINCE REGENT.

There yet remains to the Editor one duty to be performed, which it is very difficult to discharge: He might indeed be blamed, and with some degree of justice, if he attempted to thank, though he will ever gratefully remember, the countenance and assistance he has received from every individual. Yet is it his duty and pride to declare, that the progress of the work, though tedious and protracted, has been uniformly honoured by the interest which both Her Majesty the Queen, and His Royal Highness the Prince Regent have continued to take in the perusal of the sheets as they came from the press. The able assistance of Mr. Walter Scott came when the Editor least expected and most required it, like the cheering radiance of an autumnal evening after days of anxiety and labour. The Editor's thanks are also due to Colonel Johnes of Hafod, for the information he early transmitted to

Carlton House; and the zealous friendship and literary talents of Dr. Bain demand some acknowledgement from one who has so much benefited by their exertion, and who in dating this Preface from the hospitable mansion in which the labours of the Editor were concluded, laments that he possesses no other means of acknowledging his obligations and of expressing his gratitude.

Heffleton, Dorsetshire.

** It may be of service to some readers of the following Life to be reminded, that much valuable information, with many interesting anecdotes respecting the leading men in the Courts of CHARLES and JAMES THE SECOND, may be found in Mr. Walter Scott's Edition of Dryden, particularly in his notes to the Poem of *Absalom and Achitophel,* under which names the poet represented the Duke of Monmouth and Lord Shaftsbury. In the following lines Dryden delivered his sentiments respecting the DUKE OF YORK, whose exclusion as a Catholick, adds Mr. W. Scott, was warmly urged in the House of Commons:

> " His Brother, though oppressed with vulgar spite,
> Yet dauntless, and secure of native right,
> Of every Royal Virtue stands possest,
> Still dear to all the bravest and the best:
> His Courage foes, his friends his Truth proclaim,
> His Loyalty the King, the world his Fame;
> His Mercy even the offending crowd will find,
> For sure he comes of a forgiving * kind."

* Vol. 9. p. 228.

CONTENTS

OF

VOLUME THE FIRST.

The Marginal Notes throughout the Life are given verbatim from the Original MS. — ORIG. MEM. and OR. MEM. on references to King JAMES's ORIGINAL Memoirs noticed in the Preface, pag. 14.

TOME I. OF THE MS.

Oct. 1633—1642.

*** This event is thus noticed by the industrious Izacke in his *Memorials of the City of Exeter*, 1681. — " The King in person coming to this city, being in pursuit of the Earl of Essex, ... lodged here in *Bedford* House two days, and having defeated his enemies, returned hither again, and was pleased to bestow the dignity of Knighthood on the Mayor; Prince Charles attended his Father in all this march, and lodged here in the Dean's house. The Queen likewise resorted hither for safety, *Bedford* House was prepared in readiness for her reception, where during her abode, *sc.* 16 *Junii*, Her Majesty was delivered of a young Princess, who was baptized in the Cathedral Church here by Dr. Burnell Chancellour and a Canon residentiary of the said Church on *Sunday* 3 *Julii* then next following. In the body of the Church a Font was erected on purpose, under a rich Canopy of Estate, and Sir *John Berkley*, then Governour of the said City, the Lady *Poulett*, and the Lady *Dalkeith* (the said Princess's Governess) were her witnesses. . . . . This City presented the King's Majesty with 500*l.* the Queen with 200*l.* and Prince Charles with 100*l.* more." (*Page* 158.)

*** The King's Messages from Oxford during the years
1643 and 1644, are given at length in the folio edition of
the Works of CHARLES I. the second edition of which was
printed in 1687.

The Duke, soon after his arrival at Paris, hears of his Father's
being put to death by the Republicans   -   -   - 46
Charles II. arrives in France from Holland, and both pass the
Summer at St. Germains   -   -   -   - ib.
Expedition of that King, and the Duke, to Jersey   - 47
Ill state of Affairs in Ireland, which induced the King not to
go thither   -   -   -   -   -   - ib.

1650.

Charles II. returns again to France, and thence to Holland
and Scotland   -   -   -   -   -   - 48
The Duke of York in obedience to the King returns to Paris,
and thence to Brussells, where he received an account of the
death of his Sister the Princess Elizabeth   -   - 49
Death of the Prince of Orange, and birth of the succeeding
Prince   -   -   -   -   -   - ib.

1651.

The Duke of York is reduced to great hardships, and to avoid
the sight of the English Ambassadors at the Hague, where
he had continued all the winter with his Sister, he goes to
Breda   -   -   -   -   -   - 50
He arrives at Paris in June, in consequence of a Letter from
the King   -   -   -   -   - 51
Goes to meet Charles II. at Magny, after the perils which he
had experienced in escaping from the Battle of Worcester   52
Generous offer made to Charles II. by Cardinal de Retz   - ib.
Proposal of Marriage with Charles II. and the eldest daughter
of the Duke of Orleans, and with the Duke of York and
Mademoiselle de Longueville   -   -   -   - 53

THE DUKE OF YORK'S SECOND CAMPAIGN UNDER M. DE TURENNE.

Page

TOME II. OF THE MS.

f

1666.

1667.

** *Pennant,* in his Account of London, (page 123.) thus
answers one of the many Calumnies that prevailed against
this accomplished Statesman: " The virtuous Chancellor,
the Earl of Clarendon, had a house facing the upper end of
St. James's-street, on the site of the present Grafton-street.
It was built by himself, with the stones intended for the re-
building of St. Paul's. He purchased the materials; but a
Nation, soured with an unsuccessful war, with fire and with
pestilence, imputed every thing as a crime to this great and
envied Character: his enemies called it *Dunkirk House,*
calumniating him with having built it with the money arising
from the sale of that Town, which had just before been
given up to the French, for a large sum, by his master."

1668.

Page

1669.

lvi

Page

lxvi

lxvii

h 2

Page

The Duke narrowly escapes being convicted of recusancy - 675
Fresh obstacles to the Duke's return - - - 676
Extract from the King's private Letter to the Duke - 678
His Reflections on what had passed—" Had I affected
  Popularity, or considered only my own well-being in the
  world, I had not trodden the paths which I now am
  so intangled in" - - - - - 679
Mr. Churchill is sent to Court, to beg leave that the
  Dutchess might go to Bath - - - - ib.
The Duke, finding every expedient fail for his return, oc-
  cupies himself entirely with the business of Scotland, and
  the PRINCESS ANNE comes to him - - - 682
The Duke, in consequence of the wishes of many of the chief
  men in Scotland, writes to the King to desire that a
  Parliament might be called there - - - 683
The Scotch Parliament is in consequence appointed to meet,
  July 28th, and the Duke is named as the King's Com-
  missioner in it - - - - - 684
Fitzharris is tried - - - - - ib.
Attempt made by Lord Shaftsbury to keep up the credit of
  the late Plot - - - - - 685
Some Machinations of the Dutchess of Portsmouth against
  the Duke of York are brought to light by the trial of
  Fitzharris—" So now His Royal Highness saw, what a
  special friend she had been to him all along" - 686
Lord Howard of Escrick sent to the Tower, and Bishop
  Plunket, the Catholick Primate in Ireland, is executed - 687
Lord Shaftsbury committed to the Tower, and hooted at for
  a Traitor as he went through the City - - 688
The Character of that Nobleman, " Who had the cunning
  to keep the wind on his back and to swim continualy with
  the tide, so that in all changes from the year fourthy to
  sixty, he came sailing down before it" - - ib.

11

*** Pennant informs us, in his Account of London, (page 117.) that the DUKE OF MONMOUTH lived in the center house in Soho Square, facing the Statue. " Originally the Square was called, in honour of him, *Monmouth Square ;* and afterwards changed to that of *King Square.* I have a tradition, that, on his death, the admirers of that unfortunate man changed it to *Soho,* being the word of the day at the field of *Sedgemoor.* The House was purchased by the late Lord Bateman, and let by the present Lord to the *Comte de Guerchy,* the French Ambassador. After which it was leased on building leases. The name of the unfortunate Duke is still preserved in *Monmouth Street."*

*** *Mr. Walter Scott,* in his valuable Notes to Dryden's Historical Poem of Absalom and Achitophel, has given much attention to the Character of *Lord Shaftsbury,* the leading Enemy of CHARLES THE SECOND. (Vol. IX. p. 222.)

> " For close designs, and crooked Counsels fit,
> Sagacious, bold, and turbulent of wit.
> In Friendship false, implacable in hate,
> Resolved to ruin or to rule the State."

" The *Earl of Shaftesbury,*" says Mr. Scott, (page 326) " was at the head of the Cabal, which advised the measures of repealing the Test, of shutting the Exchequer, of breaking the Triple Alliance, and uniting with France to the destruction of Holland. .... Lord Shaftesbury (page 297) in the Parliament of 1679, insinuated an accusation against the Duke, (of Ormonde) on account of the alleged favour he shewed to Papists. From this charge he was vindicated by the *Earl of Ossory,* with an uncommon degree of spirited eloquence. After pleading his Father's services against the Roman Catholic Rebels, the danger of assassination from them which he had repeatedly escaped, and the active share he had in preventing the perversion of the DUKE OF GLOUCESTER from the Protestant Faith, he thus retorted upon Shaftesbury : *Having spoke of what he has done, I presume with the same truth to tell your Lordship what he has not done. He never advised the breaking the Triple League ; he never advised the shutting up of the Exchequer ; he never advised the Declaration for a Toleration ; he never advised the falling out with the Dutch, and the joining with France ; he was not the Author of that most excellent position,* DELENDA EST CARTHAGO ; *that Holland, a Protestant Country, should contrary to the true interest of England, be totally destroyed. I beg your Lordship will be so just, as to judge of my Father, and of all Men, according to their Actions and Counsels.*" This great and distinguished Nobleman the Faithful Friend of CHARLES II. is described by Dryden, under the name of *Barzillai*, (page 241) when speaking of the Friends of that Monarch.

> " Friends he has few, so high the madness grows;
> Who dare be such must be the people's foes:
> Yet some there were, even in the worst of days,
> Some let me name, and naming is to praise.
> In this short file *Barzillai* first appears,
> *Barzillai*, crowned with honour and with years."

ERRATA IN THIS VOLUME.

Preface, page x. l. 20. *For* " these" *read* " those."
Page 225. *Dele* in the first Line the repeated words " the Count."
Page 738. l. 5 *For* " seized in" *read* " seized in to."

*** The Extract in French from this Life relating to the Wars of M. de Turenne, which King JAMES sent to the Cardinal de Bouillon, and which has been occasionally referred to in the notes by the Editor, (particularly at pages 144 and 379) will be found at the end of the Life of Turenne by Ramsay, 2 vols. quarto, Paris.

THE LIFE

OF

H.R.H. JAMES DUKE OF YORK,

LORD HIGH ADMIRAL OF ENGLAND,

COMPILED

BY HIS ROYAL HIGHNESS'S PRIVATE SECRETARY

OUT OF MEMOIRS WRITTEN BY THAT PRINCE.

THE LIFE

OF

JAMES THE SECOND,

KING OF ENGLAND, &c.

COLLECTED OUT OF MEMOIRS WRIT OF HIS OWN HAND.

THE FIRST PART.

To. I.

JAMES Duke of York son of Charles the First King of Great Britain, and of Henrietta Maria daughter to Henry the 4th, King of France, was born at the palace of St. James on the 14th of October in the year 1633, and till the time that the King his father left London in the year 1641, he was there educated with the rest of the King's children.

P A R T I.

The Duke's birth, 14thOct.1633

But when by reason of the tumults, the King, Queen and Prince of Wales, were in a manner forced out of London, the Duke went also with them, together with the Princesse Mary his eldest sister (then newly marryd to the Prince of Orange) first to Hampton-Court and afterwards to Windsor; where his Majesty, hearing that the disorders in the city still increased, took the resolution of sending the Queen with the Princesse Mary into Holland; and accordingly carryd them to Dover, without passing thorow London: and at the same time he sent the Duke of York to St. James's, to stay there with his brother the Duke of Glocester and the Princesse Elisabeth.

1641.
The King forced out of London, the Duke go's with him to Windsor.

The disorders increasing, theQueenand the P^{sse} Mary are sent into Holland and the Duke is sent to St. James's.

Orig. Mem. Part 1. p. 1.

VOL. I.   B

PART
I.

1642.
The King go's
with the P᷎ of
Wales to York.

He sends for
the Duke.

The Duke
arriues at
York where
he is made
Knight of the
Garter.

The King
makes use of
his Royall H:
to get posses-
sion of Hull.

Or. Mem.
Part 1. p 2.

The King
misses of gain-
ing Hull, and
how.

S᷎ Jo : Ho-
tham confines
the Duke to
his lodging.

His Majesty after having seen the Queen and the Princesse of Orange on ship board, taking the Prince along with him, went immediatly to York: soon after which, still finding differences growing to that higth between him and the Parliament, that there was litle probability of agreement, he sent order a litle before Easter to the Marquess of Hertford, to bring the Duke of York to him; of which the Parliament having notice, sent a message to the Marquess forbidding him to do it: notwithstanding which to [he] obeyd the King, and upon Easter Munday setting forth from London, he conducted the Duke to York, where his Royall Highnes being arriued, he was made Knight of the Garter; And not long after, the King made use of him (as young as he was) to get possession of the town of Hull; having reason to suspect that the governour S᷎ John Hotham might refuse to admitt his Ma᷎ in his own person, out of fear of displeasing the Parliament, wherefore he sent the Duke thither, as if it were only out of curiosity to see the place.

With the Duke there went the Prince Elector Palatin, and severall lords and gentlemen; and his Ma᷎ resolv'd to follow the next day together with the Prince, beleeving that if the Duke were once in the town, accompanied as he then was, it would not be in the power of the governour to keep them out, thō he should endeavour it.

But the event did not answer his expectation, for the next morning, the Duke being then on the platforme, accompanied by the governour, Sir Lewis Dyves came in and told his Highness that the King was coming, then turning to the governour, he acquainted him from the King, that he would dine with him that day. At which news Hotham suddenly turn'd very pale, struck himself on the breast, and return'd no answer to him, but immediatly desir'd the Duke with his company to retire to his lodging, which was accordingly done.

3

Then causing the gates to be shutt, he commanded the garrison to stand to their armes. Presently the King came to the gates, which finding shutt against him, and soldiers appearing upon the walls, he demanded to speak with the governour, who accordingly appearing, endeavour'd to excuse himself for refusing to admitt his Ma^ty into the town, alledging that he was intrusted with that government by the Parliament ; after which he fell upon the old common place of declaiming against evill Counsellors with such canting expressions as were generally in use amongst that party. To all which his Majesty replyd with a moderation of a Prince who had no other means of reducing him to his duty, but perswasions and arguments ; vrging to him what a good subject and an honest, ought to do in his case and how undutyfull and criminall it was, according to the known law of the land, for a subject to deny his Soveraign entrance into his own town ; and by such an open act of Rebellion begun by him, he would make himself guilty of all the evills and blood-shed that might therupon insue.

But all these reasons had no effect upon Hotham ; for besides his being peringaged in the faction of the Parliament to confirm him in his refractorines, he had newly receiv'd an advertisment from Mr. William Murray a groom of the King's bed chamber, that it was resolved so soon as the King was master of the town, first to secure him, and then by a court martiall to try him for his life. This intelligence thō wholy void of truth, had nevertheless the effect malitiously intended of keeping out the King. So that all perswasions proving unsuccessfull, his Majesty at last told him, that he hoped thō he would not give him entrance, he would at least suffer his son, and his nephew with the rest of their company, to come out to him ; which indeed he did, but with this caution, that he sent them out one by one, that so it might not

PART I.
1642.
And refuses the King's entrance into Hull. Ibid.

The Duke being let out of Hull, go's back with the King to York. Or. Mem. Part i. p. 3.

B 2

be in their power to attempt any thing. So soon as they were all out of the town, his Majesty went directly to Beverley wher he lay that night, and from thence to York.

Thus having miss'd of gaining Hull, he not only left a strong place (at least so reckon'd in those days) in the hands of the Parliament (which afterwards prov'd very ruinous to his affairs, by the unsuccessfull seige which was layd to it by the Marquess of Newcastle) but therby was almost put out of capacity of raising an army; for in that town ther was a plentifull magazin of armes and ammunition for a body of above twenty thousand men, with a train of artillery proportionable to it, his Majesty at that time not being otherwise furnished wherwithall to arme a hundred men.

Hull missed
of by ill
managem'.
Ibid.

And certainly this Place was not only miss'd of by the disloyalty of the governour, and treachery of him who sent the message, but more particularly by the ill management of the whole affaire: For had the King, instead of sending Sir Lewis Dyves, surpriz'd the governour by an unexpected visite, and without warning of his coming, in all probability he had been master of the place, for the inhabitants at that time were very affectionat to his service; and besides he was attended by so many gentlemen of that country, and others, that how disaffected soever the garrison had been, they could haue made no considerable resistance. Neither did it appear that the soldiers themselves were ill intention'd; the generalty of them throwing down their armes, when they were call'd on, so to do, by some who attended his Majesty without the wall, when they heard Sir John Hotham refuse him entrance; in so much that the officers with swords in their hands compell'd them with threatnings, before they would take them up again.

Another great errour in this conduct was, that the King did not instruct some one bold and vigourous man of their number who were sent before with the Duke, with a commission to

secur the person of Sir John Hotham, in case he should prove
refractory, and with a positiue order for the rest to obey the
person so intrusted upon his producing the commission.
This might easily have been effected, either when Sir Lewis How easy it
had been to
secur the
person of Sir
John Hotham.
Dyves first brought the message from the King to the gover-
nour, or a litle after when Hotham came in to the room unat-
tended by any of his officers, wher he had confin'd the Duke Or. Mem.
Part 1. p. . .
N.B. *The*
number of the
page has been
cut out by the
binder.
and all his company: And many since have wonderd at it,
that amongst so many noblemen and gentlemen who attended
the Duke, no one of them should think of making use of
such an oppertunity of doing the King so considerable a seruice.   True it is, that Hotham was no sooner out of the room,
then Sir Lewis Dyves, and Mr. William Murray (one of the
grooms of the Duke's bedchamber, and a much honester man
then his name-sake) without imparting their design to any
one, made a shift to get out after the governour, with a firm
resolution either to throw him over the walls, or to kill him.
But he seeing them approach at the same time when he was
in conference with the King, immediatly ordered them to be
seiz'd, and a guard to be sett on them, which was accordingly
executed, and they detained prisoners, till such time as the
Duke departed out of the town; and then they were dismiss'd,
because he was not able to prove any thing against them.

   Thus it pleas'd God, that this governour should not then A remar-
quable punish-
ment of God
upon Hotham
for his disloy-
alty.
receiue his punishment; but it appear'd afterwards, that he
was reserved by the justice of Providence, in a more extra- *Ibid.* p. 5.
ordinary manner, to receiue his due reward and to lose his
head; for they wer the instruments of the Divine Vengeance,
for whose sakes and in whose quarrell, he then began the rebellion: It so happening that the Parliament afterwards put
both him and his son to death on the same day, for designing
to deliver that very garrison into the hands of His Majesty,
and that the father and the son accus'd and betrayd each the

PART
I.

1642.
The King be-
gins to raise
an Army for
his own secu-
rity. *Ibid.*

The Queen
sends a supply
of arms and
ammunition
from Holland
to the King by
one Captain
Straughan
a Scotsman.

A particular
account of
this Captain's
great conduct
and bravery
in executing
his commis-
sion.
Or. Mem.
Part 1. p. 7.

other, whilst both had hopes given them of saving their lives by a separate confession.

His Majesty being come to York, thought it high time for him to endeavour his own security by raising an army, as the Parliament already had given him the example, but he wanted both mony and armes: Of the first he had no other supply but what the Loyall Lords and Gentlemen about him did voluntarily furnish; and as for armes, it was impossible for him to get any sufficient quantity but from beyond seas, which also was exceeding difficult to do, the Parliament having all the Navy at their disposall, except a ship or two of those that conveyd the Queen to Holland; one of which called the Providence, commanded by Captain Straughan a Scotsman, her Majesty dispatch'd back fraught with armes and ammunition, about the time when the King had been refused entrance into Hull; without which seasonable assistance, it had been impossible for his Majesty to have rais'd any body of an army. The captain ran such hazards in his passage and incounter'd with so many difficulties in executing his commission, that these passages deserve to be related as they were taken out of his Journall in manner following.

Captain Straughan being commanded by her Majesty to carry over to the King a quantity of armes, and to convoy over a ketch loden with pouder; and being inform'd that the coast all along was layd to intercept him, or any other ships or vessells, that should be design'd to bring over armes or ammunition to his Majesty (the Parliament knowing the great want he had of them) chose, as the best way of performing his commission, to saile directly for the Humber, wher he beleev'd they never would expect him; and ther at a place by him appointed, to run his ship a shore, and land what he brought over; having to this purpose sent before, to give notice to his Majesty of his intention, and to desire that

some might be in a readines at the place agreed on, to receive
the armes and ammunition; and that upon his coming near
the place, and making such a signall, they should answer him
with the like, by which he might understand they were there
attending him: Accordingly he set sayle from the Brill, and
came into the Humber, and made the signall which was
appointed, but was not answer'd, for which reason he did
not adventure to run in, where he first intended; but the tyde
being spent, was forced to come to an anchor, with his ketch
by him, that it might not be driven out to sea. He was no
sooner at an anchor, but there came down from Hull a Parliament ship of 54 guns, which came to an anchor near him; and
another of their ships which was in Grimsbey-road, which
had weigh'd as he past by her, and stood up after him, came
likewise to an anchor, a stern of him, and immediatly sent
their boat to command him on boord of them; which he
refused, as being in one of his Majesty's own built ships, and
that therfore it was their duty to come on boord of him; yet,
upon his refusall they did not stir, as thinking it more proper,
and time enough to do their busines at the tyde of flood. The
Captain was then under great hardships what to do; he could
not possibly go out to sea, for besides that their two ships
waited on him, his own was in so ill a condition, that he durst
not venture out; he therfore resolved to weigh anchor with
the tyde of flood, and to turn up as far as he could above the
town, and then run his ship a shore, where he hoped some
might come into his rescue. Having fixed on this expedient,
he sent on board the Parliament ships, desiring them to lend
him a couple of cables and anchors, he being in great want of
them, and that it was the custome of men of war to be helpfull
to each other in such extremitys. But they refusing this, he
sent them word (the better to disguise his intention) that so
soon as the tyde serv'd he would go for Hull, and complain

to the governour of their denyall ; being assur'd he would
check them for it, and furnish him with what he wanted. In
the mean time he caus'd his ketch which rode by him, to
yeere on board him upon his quarter, which was from their
ships; and cutt a hole in his own quarter, through which
passage he took in all the pouder which was on board the
ketch, and stowed it in his own ship: After which, so soon as
the tyde serv'd, he weigh'd and stood up towards Hull, the
two Parliament ships doing the like, and keeping a good
distance, a starn of him, to make sure that he might not get
out to sea. In this manner they continued turning up, till it
was almost high water. At which time his pilot told him he
thought he could now secure him, and the ship, without
running the hazard of passing under the guns of the town;
for that he was come up with a sand which was very narrow,
over which ther was but twelve foot water at the top of the
tyde; and being once got over that, he had depth enough,
and could run on shore where he thought convenient, without
danger of the Parliament ships which drew more water.
Whereupon the Captain took the resolution of passing over his
ship, drawing at eleven foot and a half, and accordingly setting up all his sails, stood boldly over it, and got into the other
channell. The two Parliament ships endeavour'd to follow
him, but having no water enough, stuck fast. The Captain
continued his way down, till he came to a place call'd Paull,
some miles below Hull, on the same side of the Humber, and
there ran his ship a shore, so that she serv'd him for a battery
to defend him in landing the armes and ammunition, which
he immediatly did, and dispatch'd away a messenger to
the King at York to give him notice of his arrivall at that
place.

After which, having severall gentlemen and officers on board,
they fell immediatly to work, and intrenched themselves,

10

while the seamen were unloding, apprehending that their
neighbours of Hull might take them unprovided, and bereave
them of what they had hitherto preserv'd with so much
danger and difficulty; and they us'd such diligence in this,
that they were in a posture of defence before the Enemy
could attempt any thing upon them. For though they of the
town came out, before any releif could be brought from
York, yet seeing how advantageously Straughan was posted,
they return'd without making the least attempt, and left them
quiet till his Majesty sent men to convoy them up to York.

As for the ship his Majesty was moved to have her burnt,
since she must fall of necessity into the Rebell's hands; but
he absolutely refus'd it, saying, She had done him too much
service to be so us'd, and that besides he did not despaire of
having again both her and all the rest in his own possession.
So she was left there after her guns were taken out, which were
carryd to York, and most of her seamen made gunners.

The next day after she was clear'd, they of Hull came out
and took possession of her: however the hope of his Majesty
was in some sort propheticall, for when his Son was restor'd,
that very ship with all the rest came to be in his power.

With this supply of armes and ammunition being enabled
to raise an Army, his Majesty after having secur'd York, and
left those parts in a good condition for his service, went attended
with a considerable number of officers to Nottingham, and
there first set up his Standard. Then it was that the zeal and
affection of those Noblemen and Gentlemen who continued
loyall to him, appear'd in a most exemplary manner, shewing
what might be perform'd, when men well born and rightly prin-
cipled undertake to serve their Prince with diligence; For in a
very litle time, without any fund of mony but what themselves
furnish'd, they rais'd so considerable an Army, that before the
end of October the King was in a condition to fight a battell with

The King sets
up his stand-
ard at Not-
tingham.
Orig. Mem.
Part 1. p.—

the Rebells, thō they had begun to raise forces before him, and wanted neither mony, nor armes, nor ammunition, nor indeed any thing to make themselves as numerous and as well appointed, as they pleas'd; whereas his Majesty, notwithstanding the supply which he had received from Holland, was obliged as he passed along from York to Nottingham, and from thence to Shrewsbery, to disarm the train'd bands in all places, and to furnish his new rais'd forces with their armes; And yet after all those shifts and hardships, many of his men remain'd unarm'd.

His Majesty's Army being thus form'd, he departed from Shrewsbery about the midle of October, with a resolution to incounter the Army of the Rebells; and upon the 22 of the same month he came to Edgecot in Northamptonshire, not far from Bambury, where having notice that the Enemy's forces under the command of the Earle of Essex were within a days march of him, he order'd his whole Army to meet him the next day at Edge hill. He was no sooner arrived there with his first troop, than he saw the van of the Rebell's Army down in the bottom by Keynton, which soon after began to draw up in battell in the plain before that village, but advanced no further.

The Battell of
Edge hill
fought the 23
of October.
Orig. Mem.
Part 1. p. 15.

When all his Majesty's troops were come up to him, he march'd down the hill, and order'd Ruthven (who was then but Feild Marshall thō soon afterwards made Earle of Branford) an experienced officer who had serv'd the King of Sweden in the quality of Major General, to draw up his Army in battell. But the Earle of Lindsay who was Generall, was so much displeas'd at this preference, that he said, Since his Majesty thought him not fitt to perform the office of Commander in Chief, he would serve him as a Collonell, and immediatly went and put himself at the head of his Regimᵗ of foot, which he desir'd might be placed opposite to that of the Earle of Essex, hoping therby that he might ingage him personally. The foot was drawn up that day much differing from the manner now in use, but according to the Swedish Brigade as they then called it, and the horse in two wings; the right commanded by Prince Rupert who was generall of it, and the left by the Lord Wilmott his leiftenant generall. Each wing had a second line or reserve, the one composed of the Lord Digby's and Sir Thomas Aston's regiment, with whom were some dragoons under the command of Collonell Edward Gray, the other of the Lord Biron's regiment, they themselves being at the head of them; and on the right hand of the right wing, were likewise some dragoons commanded by Sr Arthur Aston. According to the best relation of those who were present and could best tell, his Majesty's Army consisted of about eight thousand foot and two thousand five hundred horse, and ten piece of cannon: Or. Mem.
Part 1. p. 16. And the Rebells had between ten and eleven thousand foot, and they somewhat outnumber'd the Royall Army in horse as allso in cannon. As for their order of Battell, they made not their wing so equall as his Majesty's, for knowing Prince Rupert was to command the King's right wing, they put the greatest part of their best cavalry into their left; as having lately felt the effects of his courage and conduct neer Worcester, where being much inferiour in number to them, he routed a body of their best horse: Besides this, to strengthen that wing, they had small plotoons of musquetiers betwixt every squadron, and on their left hand some dragoons: As for their right wing of horse, which were not all come up, they drew that part of them which was present behind their foot, seeing they were not strong enough to encounter with the King's left wing, and lin'd the bushes with some dragoons to make a shew. In this posture they stood, expecting to be be charg'd, without advancing one step to meet the King's Army.

PART
I.
————
1642.
The fight of
Edgehill be-
gun at 3 in the
afternoon,
23 October.
OR. MEM.
Part 1. p. 17.

The King with
the Pce of W,
and the Duke
march'd im-
mediatly af-
ter the foot.
Ibid.

It was almost three of the clock in the afternoon before his Majesty's Army was wholly drawn up in Battell; at which time they march'd on with a slow steady pace, and a very daring resolution. So soon as they were within reach of cannon, the Rebells fir'd at them, and their volly was made before the King's began to play. His Majesty with the Prince of Wales and the Duke of York, march'd immediatly after the foot, attended by several of the Lords whom he had commanded to stay by him, and by the band of pensioners on horseback led on by their leiftenant Sir William Howard; and that it might be known in what part of the Army the person of the King was, he had a scarlet cornet larger than ordinary carryd before him. When the Royall Army was advanced within musket shot of the Enemy, the foot on both sides began to fire, the King's still coming on, and the Rebell's continuing only to keep their ground; so that they came so near to one another that some

The foot so
close to one
another that
they are within
push of pike.

of the batalions were at push of pike, particularly the regiment of Guards commanded by the Lord Willoughby and the Generall's regiment, with some others; in so much that the Lord Willoughby with his pike kill'd an officer of the Earle of Essex his own regiment, and hurt another. The foot being thus ingaged in such warm and close service, it were reasonable to imagine that one side should run and be disorder'd; but it happen'd otherwise, for each as if by mutuall consent retired some few paces, and then stuck

The Foot con-
tinue till night
firing at one
another.
Ibid.

down their coulours, continuing to fire at one another even till night; a thing so very extraordinary, that nothing less then so many witnesses as were there present, could make it credibile; nor can any other reason be given for it, but the naturall courage of English men, which prompted them to maintain their ground, thō the rawnes and unexperience of both partys had not furnished them with skill to make the best use of their advantages. Tis observed that of all nations the

English stick the closest to their Officers, and tis hardly seen that our common Soldiers will turn their backs, if they who commanded them do not first shew them the bad example, or leave them unofficer'd by being kill'd themselves upon the place.

P A R T
I.

1642.

But there was not the same equality of courage in the horse; for the Royalists march'd up with all the gallantry and resolution imaginable, especially the right wing led by Prince Rupert; thō while they advanced, the Enemy's cannon continually playd upon them, as did the small divisions of their Foot which were placed in the intervalls betwixt their squadrons, neither of which did in the least discompose them, or oblige them so much as to mend their pace. Thus they continued moving, till they came up close to the Enemy's Cavalery, which after having spent their first fire, immediatly turu'd their backs, the Royalists pursuing them with great eagernes. One Ramsey who commanded that wing of the Enemys, was it seems so thorowly frighted, that he never left running till he came to London.

The right wing of the King's horse led by Pᶜᵉ Rupert. *Ibid.* p. 18.

The left wing of the Rebell's horse defeated by Pᶜᵉ Rupert. *Ibid.*

While this past, the left wing had not much to do, as having only some dragoons, and two or three regiments of foot before them, of which they made a quick dispatch; and then observing the Enemy's left wing intirely beaten, follow'd the chace of them in stead of falling into the flanck or reere of the Rebell's foot. The same errour was committed by the second lines of each wing; for in stead of staying by their foot, or charging the Enemy's foot, they also follow'd the chace of the routed horse, and continued the pursuit through Keynton, with such eagernes, that notwithstanding all the endeavours which were used by Prince Rupert, they were not to be rallied, till they met with two regiments of the Enemy's foot, who had with them some feild-pieces, and were coming up to joyn the rest of their Army : But the King's horse were then

The King's left wing having routed some foot and dragoons that were before them, follow the chace of the Rebell's left wing and leave their own foot ingaged. *Ibid.*

The same errour committed by the second lines of each wing. *Ibid.*

Pᶜᵉ Rupert endeavours in vain to rally them. Oʀ. Mᴇᴍ. Par: 1. p. 18.

The King's
horse being all
gone off, his
foot is charged
in the flanck
by a part of the
Enemy's horse
wch put them
in disorder.
Ibid. p. 19.

in so much disorder, that it was impossible for Prince Rupert to put them into a condition of doing any further service; it being almost dark before he could bring them back to the assistance of the foot whom he had left ingaged, and who while all this was passing, were reduced to great extremitys; for the Earle of Essex observing that all the King's horse were gone off in pursuit of his left wing, commanded that part of his cavalery which was behind his foot, to charge the King's and the general's regiments in the flanck, just at the time when they were so warmly ingaged at push of pike with his men. Tis true they were not broken with this charge, yet they were put into some disorder, which the Enemy's foot observing, advanced upon them, and drove them back as far as to their cannon; and to highten their success, at the same time they

The King's
Standard
taken and S^r
Edmond
Verney killed
holding it in
his hand.
Ibid. p. 21.

took the King's Standard which was carryd by Sir Edmond Verney, who was killed upon the place holding it in his hand: But the King's cannon playd upon them with such execution that it stopt their further progress, and gave leisure to those regiments on the left hand which had given ground, to put themselves once more in good order, which the Enemy finding, advanced no further. At the same time the remnant of their foot were pressing vigourously on the King's, and had not the right hand Brigade commanded by Coll. Charles Gerard kept their order, and plyd those regiments which advanced upon them, with so great courage that they put the Enemy to a stand, the whole body of the King's foot had run great hazard of an absolute defeat; for had his Majesty's two wings given way, those in the main-battell could have made no long resistance. After this neither party press'd the other, but contented themselves to keep their ground, and continued fireing, till night put an end to the dispute.

And here deserues to be mention'd a gallant action perform'd by the Lord Willoughby, who in the heat of the Action hearing it reported that a blue riban was fallen, and knowing it could be no other then the Earle of Lindsay his father, he hasten'd from the head of the Guards to his assistance, and found him lying in the front of his own regiment with one leg broken by a musket-shott: Now this happening at that point of time when they received the charge of the Enemy's horse, so that it was impossible to carry him off, he stood undauntedly with his pike in his hand bestriding his father, and in that posture wounded one of their Captains in the face, and almost push'd him off of his horse; but his own men at the same time giving back, he was left ingaged in the midst of the Enemies', chusing rather to be taken with his father, that so he might be in a condition of rendering him what service was in his power, then to save himself by leaving him in that distress.

All this while his Majesty was behind the foot; where perceiving the disorder they were in by the charge given them by the horse, and that at the same time the Enemy's foot advanced against them, he resolued to march up to them himself to incourage them by his presence, and therby to prevent their intire defeat; but judging it not fit to expose the Prince and the Duke of York to same danger, he order'd the Duke of Richmond to carry them out of the battell, and conduct them to the top of the hill; who excusing himself from that imployment, the King layd the same command on the Earle of Dorset, who answer'd him with an oath, That he would not be thought a Coward for the sake of any King's Sons in Christendom, and therefore humbly desir'd his Majesty to committ that charge to some other man: Therupon the King layd an absolute command on Sʳ Will. Howard, with his pensioners, which were about fifty, to go off with them. After which his Majesty with those who were remaining with him, pursuing his former resolution, marched directly to the foot, who, according to his expectation took new courage from his presence,

PART I.

1642.

The King perceiving his foot in disorder, marcheth up to them himself to incourage them. Or. Mem. P. 1. p. 20.

The foot take new courage from his Majesty's presence and maintain their ground. Or. Mem. Part 1. p. 22.

16

PART
I.
1642.
The Prince
and the Duke
are carryd out
of the battell
by the King's
order.
Ibid. p. 23.

The Prince
and the Duke
escape nar-
rowly from
being taken
prisoners at
Edge hill.
Ibid. p. 24.

and maintain'd their ground. As he advanced, one of his
footmen was shott in the face just by his horse's side; after
which he continued in the reer of the foot, till the battell was
ended by the night. At the same time when the King was
marching to the foot, S[r] Will. Howard went off with the Prince
and Duke pursuant to his orders, and they had not gone above
musket shott of from the place, when they saw a body of horse
advancing directly towards them from the left hand of the
King's foot; upon which sending to see what they were, and
finding them to be the Enemy, they drew behind a little barn
not far distant from them, which was incompassed by a hedge.
In this barn severall of the King's wounded men were then
dressing, but the Enemy observing the King's men to be within
the inclosure, drew immediatly back without ingaging
them, by which means the Prince and the Duke escaped the
evident danger of being taken; for had they charged that small
party they could not haue fail'd of beating them, considering
the vast advantage of their numbers. Upon their drawing
back to joyn their foot, the small body which attended the
Prince and the Duke, were glad of the occasion to draw off
further to the top of the hill towards the dusk of the evening,
and as the darknes came on both Armys began to draw off,
the Royalists to the broue of the hill, and the Enemy to Keynton: they left six pieces of their cannon behind them in the feild,
and the King's Army some of theirs, without any soldiers to
guard either. The next morning at break of day, his Ma[ty]
seeing the cannon still remaining as they were left, sent five
hundred horse, which brought off both his own and the Enemy's,
in the face of their Army, who saw the action perform'd without once endeavouring to oppose it. It was then proposed to
march down again, and fall upon them; but the King finding
his foot much decreased in number, the greatest part of them
being stragled into the neighbouring villages to get victuals,

thought it not adviseable to undertake that action, and therfore about evening return'd to his former quarters at Edgcott; the Enemy at the same retreating towards Warwick.

And now it remains to give an account of what men were slain, the number of which was not so great as was commonly reported; for according to the best information, there were not above fifteen hundred bodys of both partys remaining on the feild of battell. Of persons of note on the King's side were slayn the Lord Aubigny, brother to the Duke of Richmond and captain of the Duke's troop, Monro a Scotchman, leiftenant collonell to the Generall's Regiment of foot, and some few days afterwards the Earle of Lindsey the Generall dyd of his wounds in Warwick Castle, whither he had been carryd prisoner with his son. There wer wounded the Lord Taff, Colonell Charles Gerard, Colonell Sir Nicholas Biron, Sir George Stroad an officer of the ordinance, Sir Richard Graham one of his Majesty's querryes, and Sir Gervaise Scroop, who was left for dead upon the place and found next morning by his son with three and twenty wounds on him, strip'd of all his cloaths, unable to stirr, and lying amongst the dead bodys. It was the opinion of many chirurgions, that the frost which happen'd that night, occasion'd the saving of his life, by stopping of his blood. On the Rebell's side were slayn the Lord St John, Colonell Charles Essex, and other officers of inferiour quality.

The Royal Standard was once taken by the Enemy, but retaken by Captain John Smith, brother to the Lord Carington; who as he return'd from the pursuite of the Enemy's horse, happily fell upon that body of men which were carrying it away, for which seruice he was by his Majesty made Knight Banneret in the feild.

The day after the Battell, Prince Rupert proposed to his Majesty, that he might be immediatly sent with the greatest part of the horse, and three thousand commanded foot to Lon-

P A R T
I.

1642.

About 1500 men kill'd on both sides at the Battell of Edgehill.
OR. MEM. Part I. p. —

The Royal Standard retaken by a brother of the Lord Carington.
OR. MEM. Part: I. p. 26.

don ; and undertook with them to possess himself of Whitehall and Westminster, and to drive out the rebellious part of the Parliament from thence, and to make good that part of the town 'till his Majesty should come up with the remainder of his Army ; which might easily be effected, before the Earle of Essex with his shatter'd forces cou'd march thither to oppose him : But this so seasonable a proposition was first obstructed, and finally layd aside by the aduice of many in the Councill, who were affraid least his Majesty shou'd return by conquest ; one of them in plain terms telling him, that it was too hazardous for him to send Prince Rupert on that design, who being a young man, and naturally passionate might possibly be urg'd in heat of blood to fire the town. By these and such like cautious remonstrances made and seconded by men of the

The King instead of marching straight to London, is perswaded to take Banbury, and from thence to march to Oxford.
OR. MEM.
Part: 1. p. 26.

same principles, the King was first perswaded to go and take in Banbury, which was commanded by Colonell Fiennes for the Parliament ; and that being perform'd, he was wrought on further, to march from thence to Oxford ; where staying some days, he delayd his opportunity so long that he lost it and the Earle of Essex got before him to the city, which oversight of his Majesty was of fatall consequence to his affaires : For in appearance had he marched directly thither, he had put an end to the warr, and wholy extinguish'd the rebellion. Because the factious party of the Parliament, and all their adherents in the town, were under so great a consternation that they wou'd certainly have gone out at one end of it, whilst his Majesty was entring at the other. But the Earle of Essex being return'd to them, and the King's Army not appearing before they had recover'd from their fright, they took heart again, gave order to recruit their broken forces, and settled the minds of their

The King marcheth at last for London in Nouember, but it

wavering freinds ; as plainly appear'd, when his Majesty afterwards too late advanced towards them.

For leaving Oxford in the begining of Nouember, he marched

at last for London, finding no opposition in his way till he came to Brandford, which was on the twelfth of the foremention'd month: There were quarter'd in that place two or three regiments of the Rebell's foot, with some horse who endeavour'd to make good the bridge; but after a hot dispute which continued for some honres, the pass was forced, and all their foot taken or kill'd upon the place. It has since been confessed by a person of quality, who was then with the Earle of Essex, that had the King's troops marched on without delay, they had infallibly master'd London, the Enemy's forces being so dispersed in severall quarters without the town, and most of the horse on the other side of the water at Kingston; so that when the Earle of Essex came that evening to Hamersmith, he had but a very inconsiderable number of troops with him, and expected every moment to have been driven in to the town. But the next morning most of his forces came up to him, and at the least ten thousand of the train'd bands out of the city; all which he drew up on Turnham Green, so that then it was not adviseable for the King to fight them, they being double his number, nor consequently was it safe for him to stay in their neighbourhood. For which reason the same evening his Majesty drew back to Hampton Court, and the next day passing the river, he marched to Oatlands, from thence to Bagshott, and so to Reading, where the King continued for some days, because the Prince at that time fell sick of the meazell; but so soon as he was recover'd, his Majesty leaving that town garrison'd, march'd on to Oxford.

About the middle of Aprill the Earle of Essex beseiged Reading; of which the King receiuing notice, assembled his Army, and marched up to the releif of it: but failing of his attempt, he return'd to Oxford, and a day or two after his retreat the town was surrender'd to the Parliament: In this expedition he took the Prince along with him, but left the Duke behind.

PART
I.

1642.
was then too late, Essex having got before him.
OR. MEM:
Part 1. p. 27.

His Majesty's forces pass at Brandford in November.
OR. MEM.
Part 1. p. 27.

Earle of Essex' forces being too strong, the King is obliged to draw back to Reading and from thence to Oxford. *Ibid.*

The Prince fell sick of the meazells at Reading.
Ibid. p. 29.

1643.
Reading beseiged and taken by the Rebells, in April.
OR. MEM.
Par: 1. p. 29.

PART
I.

1643.
Prince Rupert
takes Bristol
in July. *Ibid.*

The King go's
thither and
takes the
Prince and
Duke with
him. *Ibid.*

He beseiges
Glocester,
10 August.
Ibid.

The Seige of
Glocester of
fatal conse-
quence to the
King's affaires.
Ibid,

Towards the end of July, Bristoll was taken by Prince Rupert, and about the same time the Queen came to Oxford within a day or two after Bristoll was in the King's possession; he went to that City taking with him both the Prince and the Duke, and about the 10th of August marched to Glocester and beseiged it.

The conduct of that Seige proved fatall to the King's affaires, first in breaking ground at too great a distance, and secondly in preparing gallerys to pass the ditch, which were absolutely unnecessary, the ditch being neither so deep nor so large as to oblige them to that loss of time; To this may be added, that when Sr Jacob Ashlay was ready to spring his Mine, he was hinder'd from it because the Earle of Branford at his attaque was not ready to do the same. All this put togather gave the Earle of Essex leasure to march from London with his Army to the releef of the place; whereas had the Seige been vigourously managed, as it might have been, the town cou'd not have held out aboue four days.

So soon as his Majesty was inform'd that the Rebells were marching towards him, he commanded Prince Rupert with most of the horse, to meet them in their way, to attend their motion, and endeavour all he cou'd to retard their march; which he perform'd with so much conduct, that he hinder'd them at least two days; But it prov'd of no advantage to the King, because he was not far enough advanced in the Seige to master the town in that space of time gain'd by Prince Rupert. And now the Earle of Essex was come so near, that it was necessary for his Majesty to draw off, which he did about the 8th of Sep-

After the
raising of the
seige of Glo-
cester the
Prince and the
Duke are sent
back to Ox-
ford, in Sep-
tember.

tember, and marched towards the Parliament's Army with resolution to engage them. In pursuance of this he arriu'd at Sudely Castle, when the Enemy was at Winchcom; from Sudely the Prince and the Duke were sent back to Oxford: But the Earle of Essex, who having reliev'd Glocester, had no design to fight, gave the King's Army the slip, and retreated with what haste he cou'd to London: So that his Majesty with all his diligence cou'd not overtake him, till they came to Auburn and Newberry where they fought.

Some time before the Seïge of Glocester, the Queen came to Oxford, as has been already mention'd, she continued there till Aprile, 1644, and about that time went to Exceter; where in June following she was deliver'd of the Princesse Henrietta, fifteen days after whose birth, she was forced in that weak condition, for fear of the Parliament's Army, to provide for her own safety by going into France, and to leave the Princesse there.

In the same year about the third of June, his Majesty marched out of Oxford with all his horse and musketiers, to avoid being inclosed in that city by two Armies of the Rebells, the one commanded by the Earle of Essex, and the other by Sʳ Will. Waller, but he left his pikemen and cannon in the Town; he then took the Prince along with him, but thought fitt that the Duke should stay in Oxford. The King passed happily between their Armys, and having got clear of them marched towards Worcester; for which reason the Earle of Essex commanded Sir Will: Waller with his forces to follow the King, and attend his motions, while himself marched into the west as hoping to reduce that part of the country under the power of the Parliament, while Sʳ William by his neighbourhood should find employment for the King's Army: But his Majesty having timely notice of his design, once more gave the slip to Waller and march'd back towards Oxford.

Then sending for his pikemen and cannon to joine him, he turu'd back upon Waller and defeated him at Capredy Bridge on the 29th of June. After which Victory he immediatly follow'd Essex into the west, and drove him up into a nooke of Cornwall to Lestihiel; where that Earle, by the advice of

P A R T
I.

1644.
The Queen is deliver'd of the pᵉˢˢ Henrietta at Exceter in June and 15 days after is forced to retire into France.

The King marches out of Oxford.

The King defeats Waller at Capredy Bridge. 29 June.

He follows Essex into the West and drives him up into a nooke.

Lord Roberts, forsook his Army and went by sea to Pleamouth, (the only garrison remaining to the Parliament in all those parts) After his departure his horse broke through the King's Army, and by the negligence of the Lord Goreing, got to Pleamouth also. The Parliament's foot thus doubly deserted, by their Generall and by their horse, treated for themselves and made conditions to march away leaving behind them their armes, cannon and ammunition.

York beseiged by the Rebells.

While these things passed where his Majesty was in person, his armes in the north were unsuccessfull : For York being besieged by the forces of the Rebells in those parts, Prince Rupert drew together all the troops which he could make in the neighbouring countries, with resolution to releive it ; and the Enemy being advertised of his march towards them, rais'd the Seige, and drew off about four or five miles distance from the town.

The Battell of Marston-moore.

At which time Prince Rupert received a positiue order from his Majesty to fight them. In pursuance of which he sent to the Marquis of Newcastle for all the forces he could spare him out of York. Thus recruited, he follow'd the Enemy, and press'd him so very closse, that he was obliged to turn his face and fight. The day in all probability had been the King's, if the Lord Biron had punctually obeyd his orders, for Prince Rupert had posted him very advantageously behind a warren and a slough, with positiue command not to quitt his ground, but in that posture only to expect and to receive there the charge of the Enemy ; who must of necessity be much disorder'd in passing over to him, as being to receive the fire of seven hundred musketiers in their advance to him, which undoubtedly had been very dangerous if not wholly ruinous to them : But in stead of maintaining his post, as he ought in duty to have done, when the Enemy had only drawn down two or three feild pieces, and with them play'd upon him, he

suffer'd himself to be persuaded by Colonel Hurrey to march
over the morass and charge them, by which inconsiderate action
he gave them the same advantage which he had formerly over
them ; for they charging him in his passage over the ground
already mention'd, he was immediatly routed : Whereupon
thō the left wing commanded by the Lord Goreing had actually
beaten the right wing of the Rebell's Army, yet their left which
was led by Cromwell and David Lesley, after having routed
the Lord Biron, still keeping themselves firme in a body, easily
forced the Lord Goreing out of the feild, and destroyd a considerable number of the King's foot.

Some few days after their Victory, they sate down again
before the town, which was surrender'd to them by the Marquis of Newcastle, who, besides that he now despair'd of
releif, had lost the greatest number of his foot in the late
Battell.

In this manner, that fatall order which was sent to Prince
Rupert, and his obeying it too strictly, occasion'd not only
the loss of the fight, and of the town, but drew after it a more
unhappy consequence, namely the loss of the whole Kingdom.
For after this Battell, which was struck at Marston-moore,
the affaires of his Majesty began visibly to decline, and the
Rebells having reduced that part of the country under their
command (which they easily perform'd and in a short time)
those troops which were under the Earle of Manchester had
leasure and oppertunity to joyn them, and with that reinforce-
ment they were encouraged to fight the second Battell of
Newberry against the King who lost it. And here it will not
be amiss to relate, what has since been averr'd by a person of
quality, who at that time was in the Rebell's Army before
York ; that after they had rais'd their Seige, their Generalls
who were the Earle of Manchester, the Lord Fairfax, and old
Lesley, were under the greatest consternation imaginable, as

Great over-
sights commit-
ted by the
King's ad-
visers, which
occasion'd the
loss of the
Battell of
Newberry.

not knowing how to keep their Army together; so that had they not been pressed by Prince Rupert as they were, and compell'd to come in a battell, they must of necessity have separated within four days at farthest, and consequently have left him in quiet possession of the country.

But this was not the only oversight committed by those who were then in power about the King; for after that series of good successes, which he had first against Waller and after-wards against the Earle of Essex in the west, being return'd to Sherbourn, Prince Rupert came thither to him; where it was resolved in a councill of war that his Majesty should not advance any further then Salisbury, till Prince Rupert first went into Wales to the Lord Gerard, and brought back such forces as could be spared from thence for the reinforce-ment of the King's Army; Till which time it was not thought adviseable for his Majesty to expose himself in fight against the forces of the Enemy, which were now drawing together about Windsor, being recruited by the troops of the Earle of Man-cester which had joyn'd them from the North. But no sooner was Prince Rupert gone for Wales, and the King come to Salisbury, where he had notice had Sir William Waller was at Andover with his forces, but it was resolved to beat up his quarters; which doubtless had been vigourously perform'd, if his Majesty's troops had all come in to the rendezvous at the time appointed.

But while the King was staying for them, Sir William having notice of his intention drew out of his quarters with great dili-gence, So that when his Majestie's Van arrived there; they found the Enemy's already drawn out of the town, and falling upon their rear, they obliged them to a hasty and disorderly retreat: Upon which little success, the Lord Digby ambitious of doing somewhat extraordinary in the absence of Prince Rupert, advised his Majesty to pursue his advantage and follow him to

Newberry: Of which resolution the Enemy having quick
intelligence, drew all their forces into one body, and march'd
to meet him. So that being twice his number, the most seasonable advice his Majesty could have taken, was to haue made
a timely retreat to Oxford, by which means he had given
leasure to Prince Rupert to have joyn'd him with those forces,
which he was bringing from Wales to his Majesty's assistance,
before the Enemy could have forced him to a battell: But
this counsell, which in common prudence had been the only
way of safety, was neglected.

Neither was this the only errour then committed, for when
the resolution was taken to mentain the post they were in, yet
the Army was not intrench (which ought in the first place to
haue been done) thō they had three days leasure to haue perform'd it. But in stead of this, they endeavour'd to make
good the quarter of Spinay, which was too far distant from
their Town; whereas if they had drawn somewhat farther back,
they would have had less ground to maintain, and the advantage of being flanked by Duñington Castle.

I shall omitt the particulars of the ensuing battell, which Battell of Newberry.
was not successfull to the King, and only say, that his Army
drew off in the night, marching first to Wallingford, and then
to Oxford, leaving their cannon in Duñington Castle, which
was presently beseiged by the Enemy, who assur'd themselves
to be masters of it with small expense of time, or labour. But
the event prov'd contrary to their expectation; for before they
could bring their design to pass, Prince Rupert had brought
such recruits to his Majesty from Wales, that he marched
back and releived the Castle, brought off his cannon, and The King re-leeves the Castle of Duñington and offers battell to the Rebells.
offer'd battell to the Rebells, but they not thinking themselves
strong enough to answer the Challenge, kept close within Newberry and refused to fight: wherupon the King's Army drew

PART
I.

1645.

Fairfax be-
seiges Oxford,
where the
King had left
the Duke with
the greatest
part of his
Councill.

The Councill
sends pressing
letters to the
King to come
to the releif of
Oxford.

The Seige is
rais'd.

off next day, as having perform'd the busines for which they came, and this action concluded that Campagne.

About the beginning of March 164⁴⁄₅ his Majesty sent the Prince into the west; And himself marched out of Oxford on the 3ᵈ of May leaving the Duke of York with the greatest part of his Councill in that City: And towards the end of May the Town was beseiged by the new modell'd Army of the Rebells commanded by Sir Thomas Fairfax. There was then in the Town a garrison of about five thousand men experienced Soldiers; and they were so well provided of all things necessary to sustain a Seige, that they were out of all apprehensions of the Town being taken by the Army, which then lay before it. And indeed that Seige was the best thing which could then happen for the King's affaires; for while they were busying themselves in making vain attempts on that Town, they gave him a favourable opportunity and leasure enough to make some considerable progress towards the north, whither he then design'd to go. But whither it was the pannick fear, or (to give it a softer name) the indiscretion of the Councill, they immediatly dispatched letters to his Majesty, pressing him to return to releive them; declaring that in case he did not, they should be forced to surrender up the Town, and they were obstinate to send this message, thō the Governor Collonell William Legg assur'd them positively they were not in the least danger, and that he was furnished with all things necessary for their defence: And soon after he made good his promise; for on the 2ᵈ of June he sallyed out up on the only quarter which was advanced by the Enemy near the Town, on Hadington Hill, from which he beat them, and took and kill'd a considerable number of their men. This Action so startled them, and made them so sensible of the strength within the Town, that they rais'd the Seige immediatly, and, in all appearance, before they had notice of his Majesty's returning to raise it.

The letter sent by the Councill from Oxford, found the King at Leycester, or near that place, which he had newly taken: So that beleeving Oxford to be in danger, he alter'd his resolution of going northward, and march'd back to raise the Seige. But he met with the Army of the Enemy at Naseby, and there fought that unfortunate and fattall Battell, which he lost so absolutely that it was decisive of the quarrell, and the last he ever fought for his Crown and life: for after it, he could never draw together the body of an Army, having there totally lost his old foot. On the other side, the Rebells' Army went on victorious in all places, for having beaten the King's own Army, they lost no time, but march'd directly into the west where they defeated the Lord Goreing, and, before winter, had reduced the most considerable places of that Country under the power of the Parliament. In all other parts of the Kingdom his Majesty's affaires had the same ill success; so that he had now remaining to him no place of tolerable security but only Oxford; to which he retired about the beginning of Nouember, and therein pass'd the whole winter.

About the latter end of Aprill 1646 he went from thence disguis'd, and pass'd undiscover'd through all the quarters of the Enemy, to the Scotch Army, hoping there to have found that safety, which he could no longer expect in a Town which was already block'd up and was immediatly to be beseiged, and not daring to trust his person in the hands of that Army which was coming to beleager it. He had it once in his thoughts to have carryd the Duke along with him, but did not.

On the first of May Oxford was actually beseig'd; and after the Enemy had settled their quarters round the Town, they began to make their approaches to the Est-gate of it from the top of Hedington hill, and ran them down within an hundrd paces of the works of the Town, without coming

P A R T. I.

1645.

TheKing takes Leycester.

The Battell of Naseby. Or: Mem: Part 1. p. 30.

Lord Goreing defeated in the West. Ibid.

The King retires to Oxford the only place of security he had then remaining in England, Nouember. Ibid.

1646.

Oxford block'd up, the King passes disguised thorough the Enemie's quarters to the Scotch Army and leaves the Duke in Oxford. Ibid.

They begin to
treat the 18th.
Or: Mem:
P. 1. p. 30.

nearer; as not judging it necessary to expose their men, or to press the place more vigourously, which they knew in a short time must inevitably fall into their hands. On the 18th of the same month the Councill sent to demand leave of the Enemy, that their Commissioners might come out, and treat concerning the surrender of the Town.

Accordingly the Treaty was begun and carryd on till the 20th of June, before it was brought to a conclusion. During all which time, thō there was no cessation of armes till three days before the Articles were absolutely agreed, yet there happen'd no very considerable action; only cóntinuall skirmishes, which were commonly without the north gate; on which quarter the Enemy had made no approaches, contenting themselves with drawing a line of Countervallation about cañon-shot of the Town, from one River to the other.

In one of these encounters Prince Rupert receiv'd a shot in the right shoulder, of which he soon was well, because it was so favourable that no bone was broke by it.

Oxford sur-
render'd up to
Fairfax the
24th of June.
Ibid.
No article
made for the
Duke, he is
deliver'd into
the hands
of the
Parliament.
Ibid.

On the 24th of June (St John Baptist's day) the Town was surrender'd to Sir Thomas Fairfax: no other Article being made for the Duke then that he was to be deliver'd into the hands of the Parliament, to be disposed of according to their pleasure. And this particular was the more observable, because so exact a care was taken in relation to all others besides the Duke. As for Prince Rupert and Prince Maurice they had liberty to go beyond the Seas; and all other persons had the same freedom in the conditions which were made for them, in case they were so disposed, otherwise they had it at their choice to stay, and the leasure of six months allow'd them to make their peace by compounding for their Estates. Accordingly upon the delivery of the Town, Sr George Ratcliff receiv'd orders from Fairfax to continue with the Duke, till the pleasure of the Parliament should be known in the disposall of his person.

On the same day or the day after they enter'd the Town, the Generall with most of his Officers came to visit his Royall Hyghness, Sir Thomas Fairfax making him a kind of speech which certainly was none of the most eloquent, he being a much better Soldier then he was an Orator. He was the only man of all the Officers who kiss'd not the Duke's hand; for yet they had not banish'd all appearances of respect to the Royall Family. Yet none of them were so ceremonious as to kneel in the performance of that action, excepting only Cromwell who was then Leiftenant Generall.

The Duke remain'd at Oxford till the beginning of July, in which time thō he was not kept a closs prisoner, yet he was never permitted to take the aire without the Town, unless attended with a sufficient guard of horse.

Not long before the Duke went for London, Sir George Ratcliff received letters from the Queen, who was then at Paris, and had heard that his Royall Highnes was yet in Oxford : In those letters he was directed (in case it were yet in his power) either to carry the Duke into Ireland, or to bring him into France to her : But Sir George absolutely refused to comply with either of those commands; alledging for his excuse, that he durst not convey any of the King's Sons out of the Kingdom, without an express order from his Majesty; which nicety, or I may rather call it indiscretion of his, might haue cost his R: Highnes dear, as being the occasion of his being put into the Rebell's hands.

Soon after this, the Duke's Governor received orders from the Parliament to bring him up to London, which was accordingly done; and about three or four miles out of the Town the Duke was mett by the Earle of Northumberland (whom the Parliament had newly appointed for his Governor) and by severall others of the best quality amongst them, who receiv'd him from the hands of Sir George Ratcliff, whom they imme-

PART I.

1646.
Fairfax visits the Duke and makes him a speech. *Ibid.*

Cromwell kneels and kisses the Duke's hand. Or: Mem: P. 1. p. 31.

The Duke carryd to London. Or: Mem: P. 1. p. 32.

E. Northumberland appointed by the Parliamᵗ to be his Governor. *Ibid.*

1646.
Sir George
Ratcliff and
all the rest
of the Duke's
servants dis-
charg'd, and
new ones gi-
ven him by
the Parlia-
ment. *Ibid.*

The Duke
kept at St.
James's with
the Duke of
Glocester
and the
P^se Elizabeth.
Ibid.

Endeavours
made for
the Duke's
Escape. *Ibid.*

He falls sick
of an Ague.
Ibid. p. 33.

1647.
The King de-
livered up by
the governing
party of Scot-
land to the
Parliament of
England.
OR: MEM: '
P. I. p. 33.

Is brought
prisoner to
Holmeby.
Ibid.

Taken from
Holmeby and
brought to the
Army.

The Duke per-
mitted to wait
on his Ma-
jesty at Mai-
den-head.

The City with
a part of the
Parliament
declare against
the Army.
Ibid.

diatly discharg'd from his attendance, togather with all the
rest of the Duke's servants, not so much as excepting a dwarfe
whom his Royall Highness was desirous to have retain'd with
him.

Thus was he carryd to St. James's where the Duke of Glocester and the Princesse Elizabeth already were, having been
left there by his Majesty when he departed out of London:
And in the room of those who were dismissed, the Parliament
put new servants to the Duke of their own chusing. But the
Earle of Northumberland himself and his Lady treated the
King's three children with the same respect and care, as if
they had been intrusted with them immediatly from his
Majesty.

That winter there were endeavours made for the Duke's
escape; Coll. Edward Villars was imployd in it by his Majesty, but by some means or other the design was discover'd to
the Parliament, so that it missed of the effect. The same
winter the Duke was seized with a long ague, which continued
from the end of January till the last of March.

Not long afterwards, the King was deliver'd up by the
governing party in Scotland (of which the Marquis of Argyle
was the cheif) to the Parliament and was brought prisoner
to Holmeby in Northamptonshire, where he remain'd in that
condition till the beginning of the summer, 1647. At which
time he was taken from thence by Cornet Joyce, and brought
to the Army which was then marching towards London. In
their approach to it, as he passed by Maiden-head the Duke
was permitted to go and wait on him, from whence his R.
Highness was carryd back to London.

Immediatly after this, the City with a great part of the Par-
liam^t declared against the Army; Others of them, of which
number was the Earle of Northumberland, left the Town and
went to the Army. The Earle had design'd to have the Duke

privatly conveyd together with his Brother and Sister to Sion house wher he then was, and accordingly sent his brother in law Henry Howard to St. James's to be assisting in their escape. But the City-faction having a jealousy of his intention, caus'd him to be watched so narrowly, that the design was impossible to be effected; for thō they were all prepar'd to go, yet the guards sett about the house were so exceedingly watchfull, that it was impossible to get out of doors without being discover'd. The next day the Parliament searched into this matter with the most exact inquiry they could make, and all the servants were under a strict examination; but that business was soon ended; for the City and that part of the Parliament that joyn'd with them, were forced to submitt, and the Army march'd into the Town.

At the latter end of summer his Majesty was carryd to Hampton-court, and the Duke was permitted severall times to attend him there; going and coming generally twice or thrice a week; till such time as his Majesty made his escape from thence to the Isle of Wight, where he was again made prisoner.

That winter there was another attempt made to have deliver'd the Duke; It was managed by the assistance of Mrs. Kilvert sister to the then Bishop of Salisbury, who waited on the Princesse Elizabeth, and one Hill a barber, who had been placed by the Parliament in the Duke's Service, and whom his R. Highness had gain'd to be serviceable in the design: But when they were almost ready to put it in execution, a letter which the Duke sent concerning that busines, happen'd to be intercepted, by which the whole secret was discover'd; Hill was imprison'd, and, some time after being releas'd, he was discharg'd the Duke's Service. As for Mrs. Kilvert she had better fortune, for it was never found out that she had any part in that design. In the former attempt which had been made, when it came to be discover'd, the Duke hàd resolutely

1647.
Earle of Nor-
thumberland
retires to the
Army and de-
signs to con-
voy the Duke
privately thi-
ther. *Ibid.*

Another at-
tempt made
for the Duke's
escape.
OB: MEM:
P. 1. p. 33.

denyd that he had the least knowledge of it, or that he was any way concern'd in prosecution of it; but the evidence of this last was too clear to be disown'd, for they had the undenyable proof of his letter in their hands, with some Cypher in it, which they knew was of his writing, so that he was forced to acknowledge it.. But upon the first notice he had that the busines was discover'd, he gave the Cypher (which he formerly had received from the King his Father) into the keeping of Mrs. Kilvert, desiring her to hide it in some such part of the house, as was agreed betwixt them, that he might be in his power to recover it again, thō she herself shou'd be sent away.

The Duke
under exami-
nation.
Or: Mem:
Part 1, p. 34.

The Duke had no sooner given this order, then there came to him a Committee of both houses, two Lords and four Commoners, who were sent on purpose to examine him. They began by shewing him the letter which he could not deny to be his own hand writing, they then ask'd him for the Cypher, to which he answer'd, That he had burnt it: After this they examin'd him on severall other particulars, and press'd him exceedingly to discover to them, who had been assisting to him in his intended escape, but found him so very reserued in all which related to that affaire, that he would acknowledge nothing of it; thō they urged so far, as to intimate to him, the danger he run of being sent prisoner to the Tower, in case he would not be ingenuous (so they term'd it) and discover his accomplices. But when they saw that none of their artifices could prevail over his settled resolution, they at last left him: and upon their report made to both houses, the Earle of Northumberland was charged to keep a stricter watch over him, till they had come to a resolution how to dispose of him. It was moved by many amongst them to have sent the Duke to the Tower, and it was once in a probability of being so ordered, but when the first heat was over, by the help of some moderate men in the house of Commons, it was carryd in the negative,

and the charge of the Duke (as above mention'd) committed
to the Earle of Northumberland, which he made difficulty of
accepting, and declared he would not be answerable for him,
or incurr any blame by his escape, if it should so happen. It
was then agreed that nothing should be imputed to him in case
of any miscarriage, and thus taking the Duke in his own terms,
he continued to be his Governor ; only he desir'd them to
appoint some persons who might have a particular eye over his
Royall Highness, to prevent his escape, because he would not
oblige himself to that part of the employment ; This they
granted him, and farther they extorted from the Duke a
promise that he would not receive no letters from any person
whomsoever without imparting them to the Earle of Northumberland ; But nothing they cou'd do or say to him was
capable of hindering him from endeavouring his escape.

And even in the very heat of this affaire while the Duke was
yet under examination, he began to forme a new design for his
liberty, by the assistance of Mr. George Howard brother to
the Earle of Suffolk who at that time was his Master of Horse,
and was placed in his service by the Parliament. Him (*he*)
absolutely gain'd, and sent him to Coll: Joseph Bamfeild, whom
he knew to have been employ'd about the same affaire before
the discovery of the last design, there having been severall
persons intrusted in it, which in all probability was the reason
that it was discover'd ; But Bamfeild's part in it not being
arrived to the knowledge of the Parliament, he had not been
obliged to depart the Town, as many others had been forced
to do. His Royall Highness being therfore sensible of the
hazard he had run by the discovery of his last attempt, was
resolv'd absolutly to committ the management of this to no
hands, but only theirs ; and to reject whatsoever propositions
shou'd be made by any others in order to his escape. By this
means he had the better opportunity of concealing his

The Duke
formes a new
design for his
Liberty. The
success and
various adven-
tures thereof.

intentions : In pursuance of which he refused to receive a letter which was brought him from the Queen his mother, thō it came by one whom he knew to be honest, and might have safely trusted ; which exceedingly surprized the bearer who had long watch'd an opportunity to deliver it ; At last he found, thō they strictly observed all the Duke's actions, the means of offering it, as his R: Highness went into the Tennis-Court at St. James's ; and while he was slipping it into the Duke's hand, he told him softly, It was from the Queen ; to which the Duke only answered, I must keep my promise, and for that reason can not receive it ; saying this, he passed onward so that no notice was taken of the action. When this was afterwards related to the Queen, she was much displeas'd with the Duke, and could not imagine what he meant by refusing a letter from her ; but some time after she was satisfied of the reason. And indeed 'twas necessary for him to be very circumspect, for had he been discover'd in those practices, his former experience sufficiently told him how it was likely to have gone with him.

1648.
All ready for
the Duke's
escape the
20ᵗʰ Aprill.
OR: MEM:
P: 1: p: 37.

But notwithstanding all the diligence which was used by Bamfeild, it was the 20ᵗʰ of Aprill before all things were in readiness for the Duke's escape. During the whole management of this affaire there was no one particular of it committed to paper ; neither was it necessary ; Mr. George Howard every day carrying verball messages betwixt the Duke and Bamfeild, which was all the part he had in the imployment.

The Duke
after supper
go's to play at
hide and seek,
to cover his
designd
e'cape.
OR: MEM:
P. 1: p: 37.

All things being in this readines, on the night of the forementioned day, the Duke went to supper at his usuall hour (which was about seven) in the company of his Brother and Sister ; when supper was ended, they went to play at Hide and Seek, with the rest of the young people in the house : At this childish sport the Duke had accustom'd himself to play for a fortnight together every night, and had us'd to hide himself in places so difficult to find that most commonly they were half

an hour in searching for him; at the end of which time he
usually came out to them of his own accord: This blind he
layd for his design, that they might be accustomated to miss
him, before he really intended his escape; By which means,
when he came to practise it in earnest, he was secure of gaining that half houre, before they could reasonably suspect he
was gone.

His invention had all the effect he could desire: for that
night, so soon as they began their play, he pretended according
to his custom to hide himself, but in stead of so doing, he went
first into his Sister's chamber, and there lock'd up a litle dog
which us'd to follow him, that he might not be discover'd by
him; Then, slipping down by a paire of back stairs which led
into the inmost garden, having found means before hand to
furnish himself with a key of a back door from the said garden
into the park, he there found Bamfeild who was ready to
receive him, and waited there with a footman who brought a
cloke, which he threw over him and put on a perriwig. From
thence they went through the spring-garden, where one
Mr. Tripp was ready with a hackney-coach, which carried
them as far as Salisbury-house. There the Duke went out of
the coach with Bamfeild as if he had intended some visite in
that house, and Tripp went forward with the coach, having
received directions to drive into the City, and keep the coach
as long as he could conveniently at that end of the Town. But
when they were gone, the Duke and Bamfeild went down Ivy-
Lane, wher they took boat, and landed again on the same
side of the River close by the bridge. From thence they went
into the house of one Loe a surgeon where they found Mrs.
Murray, who had women's cloths in a readines to disguise
the Duke. Being immediatly dress'd in them, he departed
thence, attended by Bamfeild and his footman to Lyon-key,
where there waited a barge of four oars, into which they

PART
I.

1647.

1648.

The Duke
disguises him-
self in women's
cloths, and
attended by
Bamfeild go's
down the river
in a Barge of
4 oars.
OR: MEM:
P: 1: p: 38.

36

PART I.

1648.

The Master of
the Barge very
jealous.
OR: MEM:
P: 1: p: 38.

enter'd and so went down the River, the tide serving for the
passage.

They were no sooner in the barge but the master began to
suspect somewhat; for when Bamfeild bespoke his attendance
there with his barge, he had only told him, he was to bring a
freind, but now finding a young woman was brought without
other company, it made him jealous there was something more
in the busines then he had first imagin'd ; The consideration of
which did so much affright him, that his whole discourse in
going down was imployd in telling them, It was impossible to
pass by the Blockhouse at Gravesend without discovery, and
that they had no other way to get on boord the Ship which
waited for them in the Hope, then to land at Gravesend, and
from thence procure a paire of oares to carry them on shipboord. And when Bamfeild debated the matter with him,
shewing the difficulty and hazard of procuring a boat which
shou'd convey them to their ship, he rais'd new objections of
his own danger from the shining of the Moon and other inconveniences ; but while they two were thus reasoning the
matter, the master of the barge became fully satisfied concerning those suspitions which he had, that this woman was some
disguised person of considerable quality ; for peeping through a
cranny of the door into the barge room, where there was a
candle burning befor the Duke, he perceiv'd his Royall Highnes laying his leg upon the table, and plucking up his stocking
in so unwomanish a manner, that he concluded his former sur-
mizes of him were undoubted truths, as he afterwards acknowledg'd to them.

The Duke
discovers him-
self to the
master of the
Barge.
OR: MEM:
P: 1: p: 39.

This Vision so absolutely confounded him, that he hardly
knew what he did or said ; which they perceiving, that (*thought*)
it best for them to confess the truth, and trust him with their
lives, being well assured before hand of his honesty. Therupon the Duke told him who he was, and with all assured him

he would not be unmindfull of this action, but take care of his
fortune, and provide for him ; And that if he thought it hazardous to return to London, he would carry him over with him into
Holland.

    This ingagement confirm'd his mind, and then he assur'd
them, that he would venture to pass by the Blockhouses at
Gravesend, without setting them a shore, which he accordingly
perform'd : For when they approached the Town, he put out
the light, and suffer'd the barge to drive down with the tyde,
by which means they past undiscover'd by the block houses,
and arrived at the Ship, which was a Dutch pinek of seventy
tuns, that lay ready for them at the upper end of the Hope,
and had already been discharged at Gravesend : Sir Nich:
Armorer, Collonell Mayard, and Richard Johnson, with each
of them a servant attending on him, were already before them
on shipboord, in expectation of the Duke's coming which
Bamfeild had intrusted to their knowledge, that by their assistance they might be masters of the Vessell, in case there shou'd
be occasion for it.

He go's aboord
of a Dutch
Pink that
Bamfeild had
prepar'd for
him, to carry
him to
Holland. *Ibid.*

    At break of day, they get their anchors aboord, and setting
sayle with a faire wind, the next morning early came to an
anchor before Flushing : There they stayd, expecting the
benefit of a tyd to carry them up to Middleburg. The master
of the Ship with two of his five hands, went ashore to Flushing
in his boat, intending to be back again by that time the water
was high enough to carry him to Middleburg. But before he
return'd, Owen the master of the barge, who was come along
with the Duke, came down with great amazement into the litle
cabban where His R. Highnes was with the rest of the Company, and told them, That there was a Parliament Frigate just
coming in, which he was confident came in pursuit of them ;
that she wou'd be up with them immediatly, and therfore
they ought to get their anchor on boord as speedily as they

The Duke
comes to an
anchor before
Flushing.
On: Mem:
P: 1: p: 40.

were able, and without loscing time set sayl for Middleburg. One of the company then asking him, whither he were assured it was a Frigate, he, who was a seaman, so positively affirm'd it, that none amongst them having at that time any knowledge of Sea affaires, they were easily perswaded to beleeve him ; where upon they gave orders to the two Seamen, who were remaining still on boord, to get up their anchor, and set sayle, which they refusing to perform till such time as the master shou'd return, they forced them to comply with their orders, by the help of the two servants ; and John Owen charg'd himself with carrying the Ship to Middleburg in safety notwithstand-ing he was told by the Seamen, that there was hardly sufficient water, and that he ran the hazard of loosing the Vessell. But the fear he had of the English Ship, which he took for a man of war that follow'd them, prevail'd above the other of running on ground ; though afterwards it prov'd only to be a merchant man : According as he had been foretold, the Ship struck twice upon the Barr ; yet at length they got over safely, and without any dammage to the Vessell, it being flood ; And they were no sooner over the skole places, then Owen himself acknowledg'd his mistake. And the Master coming on boord at the same time, they arriv'd at Middleburg before the tyde was wholy spent.

The Duke went on shore in his woman's habit and continued there that night; the next day he took boat for Dort; where being arriv'd, he sent away Bamfeild to the Hague to give notice to his Sister and the Prince of Orange of his being there, and to provide him with some cloths, not having brought over any with him, besides the disguise which he then wore. Immediatly (they) sent their Yachts to bring him to Maesland Slyice, whither his sister came to meet him; the Prince of Orange having before mett him, as he pass'd by the Brill, and so

The Duke in danger of Shipwrack. Or: Mem: P: 1: p: 41.

He arrives at Middleburg. *Ibid.*

Sends Bam-feild to the Hague to give notice of his a'rival. *Ib.d.*

Is met by the Prince and P^se of Orange at Maesland Slyice and carryd to Honslardyke. *Ibid.*

soon as he was landed they carryd him to their house of Honslardÿke.

1648.
The allarme at
St. James's
upon notice of
the Duke's
escape.
OB: MEM:
P: 1: p: 42.

Having thus related the Duke's escape, it will not be impertinent to give an account of what pass'd at St James's after his departure. He had not gone an hour from thence, before they began to miss him, and to search for him in every room of the house. Where not finding him, they sent immediate notice of it to Whitehall, and to the Generall Sr Thomas Fairfax. Thereupon there were orders issued out, that all the passages about London should be layd for him, especially the northern road, and those towards Wales, imagining he had either taken that way or towards Scotland. Directions were also given to stop all the Ports; but he was already pass'd by Gravesend before their orders came: And they gave not over their searching for him, till they had news from Holland that he was there.

Soon after this, happen'd the rising in Kent, upon which all the men of war then riding in the Downes declar'd allso for his Majesty, and turn'd all their Officers on shore, making a new choice of Commanders among themselves, whose Loyalty and conduct they might trust; which action was so extraordinary that it deserves a particular relation.

Rainsborough who commanded the Fleet then riding in the Downes, which consisted of one 2^d rate, one 3^d rate, three or four 4th rates, one 5th rate, and three or four 6th rates besides some Ketches, having notice given him, that the three Castles in the Downes were surprized and seized by those of Kent, who had declared for his Majèsty, and being further inform'd that the Town of Deal had been very instrumentall in it, he went on boord of a Ketch, that he might go neerer in to the shore, therby the better to observe what they (were) doing in that Town.

From thence he sent order to his Ships to weigh and get them under sail to stand in as near as they cou'd possibly to

P A R T
I.

1648.
A very extra-
ordinary ac-
tion of one
Lindale a
Bosen, who
with the help
of three com-
mon Seamen
was the means
of bringing off
a whole
Squadron of
Ships to the
King. *Ibid.*
p: 43.

the shore to batter the Town, and do all the mischeif in their power: According to this order they fell to work to get their anchors on boord, which while they were performing in the Constant Reformation (Rainsborough's own Ship) and were heaving at the Capstern, one of the boatswain's Mates by name Rob: Lindale, thought it then the most proper time to execute the resolution which he had formerly taken, and had communicated to three seamen of the same Ship, whom he found to be of his own principles, of doing the King some considerable service in the Fleet; Accordingly he and they, as they were heaving at the Capstern, began to grumble at the orders which they had received, and more at the imployment which was impos'd on them, saying aloud, That they knew no reason they had to batter the Town of Deal, which was full of their wives, children and relations, and to involve them all in that distruction. When they saw this argument began to work on their Companions, they pursued their point, and said, It would be much more honest and more for their intrest to joyn with them who had already risen, and declare likewise for his Majesty : Immediatly the whole Company of the Ship took the word, and cryd one and all, for the King. Lindale then told them, he beleev'd the leiftenant and some other officers of the Ship wou'd be against it, and that therfore they ought speedily to take possession of the gun room, and ther arm themselves ; which being done they might easily secure their officers, and any others which shou'd refuse to joyn with them.

This was immediatly perform'd; and then Lindale went up and seiz'd the officers, telling them plainly their resolution of declaring for the King; and presuming he shou'd not have their concurrence in it, yet he assur'd them that when their work was done, they shou'd be fairely set a shore with all their goods, together with those in their company who shou'd desire it, but that in the mean time, for the common security, they must go into the hold. The Lieutenant and one or two of the other Officers, seeing there was no remedy, submitted without resistance to this order, and glad they were to receive no worse usage. This being done, and all things quietly settled in that Ship, and having secured some others whom he look'd upon as disaffected, he got the Ship under Sail, and went up along the broadside of the Ship that was nearest, declaring what he had already done, and exhorting them to follow his example and secure their disaffected Officers, or otherwise he would sink them : In this manner he went from Ship to Ship, till every one had declar'd for the King. Hereupon Rainsborough seeing his Fleet was under sail, and yet that it came not up to him according to his order, but that they were plying to and again, and speaking to each other, went to them in his Ketch to inquire into the meaning of this odd cariage ; and coming up with his own Ship, ask'd for what reason they had work'd after that manner? and at the same time offer'd to haue gone aboord. But they resolutely told him, that he must not set his foot within the Ship, for they had declar'd for the King, that they wou'd however presently send off to him his goods and servants, together with some Officers whom they had detain'd ; this they immediatly perform'd : but when in the mean time he was entering into farther treating with them, and endeavouring to perswade them to return (as he term'd it) to their obedience, they bad him forbear any discourse of that nature, or otherwise they wou'd fire at him : He seeing it in vain to urge any further arguments, lay by without saying any more, till they had sent him what they promised him ; and then went away in his Ketch up the River, to give notice to the Parliament of what had happen'd. On boord all the other Ships they also turn'd out their Commanders, permitting only some Warrant Officers to stay, of whose Loyalty they were all assur'd.

And now having executed their design, they thought it time to send to the Kentish-men, and let them know what they had done, desiring the gentlemen in that County who were Seamen to come on boord and to command them. In pursuance of which request, Sr William Palmer, Captain Bargrave, Captain Fogg and others, went to them and took the command of their Ships upon them, filling up the vacant places of those Officers whom they had sent away. But before they cou'd put themselves in a readines of sailing out of the Downes, the Earle of Warwick came down to them in a Ketch, being sent thither by the Parliament, to try if he cou'd be more successfull then Rainsborough had been to seduce them from their obedience to his Majesty.

Accordingly the Earle sent to know, If they wou'd suffer him to come on boord, and speak with them? In return to which message, they sent one of the three Seamen who had been so instrumentall in this affaire, to demande what business he had with them; of which they desir'd to be satisfied, before he shou'd have permission to come on boord. To this the Earle replyd, that he was commissioned by the Parliament to come to them and offer them what satisfaction they cou'd desire, with a pardon for what had already pass'd, in case they would receive him on boord of them, and again declare for the Parliament: that farther he was encouraged by a letter from some amongst them to come down, and that they had invited him, with assurance of success in that negociation. The Seaman answer'd, that for the promises made by the Parliament they did not value them; that as they had declar'd for his Majesty, so they were resolved to continue his loyall Subjects; that he knew not who they were who had written to his L̄dsp, and invited him to come down amongst them, but that he was certain his own hand was not to that letter, and thereupon desir'd to see it. The Earle gave it him to read, and when he had perus'd it, he put it into his pocket; and sayd, That thō they could not permitt his Ldꝺp to come on boord, yet he wou'd take order that who ever had written that letter should immediatly wait on him.

Having said this, he return'd on boord the Constant Reformation, with the letter in his hand, and so from Ship to Ship; sending off to the Earle every one of those persons who had subscribed that paper to him.

When the Earle found his perswasions were not prevalent, he sent to desire he might have one of their Ships for his better accommodation in going up the River, ingaging his word to them that it should be return'd. They complyd with this request, and sent him the Nicodemus a sixth rate Fregate, but he broke his promise, and never sent her back.

After this, when they had settled all things in every Ship, they thought the best thing they could do for the intrest of his Majesty, was to sayle for Holland, where they were inform'd the Duke of York was; for there they should be in a readines to receive such commands as either the Prince or the Duke should lay upon them for the service of his Majesty: And accordingly they made the best of their way to Helvoet-sluys, where they arrived about the latter end of May.

The Ships revolted from the Parliament service at Helvoet-sluys in May. Or: Mem: P: 1: p: 48.

Upon their arrivall, they sent to advertise the Duke of what had pass'd, who went immediatly to them, and stayd with them on boord, till the Prince came by Sea from France, and took himself the command of that Fleet; with which some few days after he put out to Sea, and sayl'd into the Downes, leaving the Duke in Holland with his sister; and having before his departure discharg'd Bamfeild from the Duke's service, who being a man of a turbulent intriguing head, had been tampering with the Seamen even while the Duke was on boord with them, and driving on a Presbyterian intrest to the great disturbance of his Majesty's service: for he had push'd the design so far, that he

The Duke takes the command of them till the Prince his brother came. Or: Mem: p: 1: p: 48.

The Prince sayles into the Downes: Leaves the Duke in Holland. *Ibid.*

Bamfeild being a turbulent man and carrying on a Presbyterian intrest, is discharg'd the Duke's service. *Ibid.*

attempted to make use of his credit with the Duke, to have set up that intrest against the Prince; But his propositions being rejected by the Duke and discover'd to the Prince, that unquiet man lost all the advantages that he might have reasonably expected from those Seruices whieh he had lately perform'd. And the Duke was so justly incensed against him, that he would never afterwards readmitt him into his service, thō divers applications were made to him on his behalf: Yet in consideration of what he had perform'd for the Duke, his Royall Highness supplyd his wants; as well as he was able in that low condition to which he was reduced himself, and continued those effects of his charity to him, till some time after his Majesty's Restoration, when he ran himself into such insufferable misdemeanours, that it was no longer fitt for the Duke to supply him.

The Prince
returns to the
Fleet to
Helvoet-sluys.'
On Mem.
P: 1. p: 49.

About the end of the summer, the Prince return'd with the Fleet under his command to Helvoet-sluys, and from thence he went to the Hague. Not long afterwards, the Earle of Warwick with the Parliament Fleet came to Helvoet-sluys; but the Dutch interposing their authority in their own port, hinder'd either side from committing any Act of hostility against each other. When the Earle had stayd till the approache of winter and found he could perform nothing against the King's Fleet, he return'd with the Parliament's from England: and during the same winter, after the Parliament's Ships were

The command
of the King's
Fleet conferr'd
on Prince
Rupert. Ibid.

gone, the command of the remaining part of his Majesty's Ships was conferr'd on Prince Rupert, who together with his brother Prince Maurice went with them first to Ireland, and from thence to Portugal, then to Streights, and lastly to the West

Prince
Maurice with
many of the
Ships lost in
the West
Indies.
Ibid. p: 50.

Indies, where Prince Maurice with many of the Ships were lost, it having never been certainly known where they were cast away, nor any news ever since heard of them: Only it was beleeved, they suffered Ship-wrack amongst the Virginia

Islands; Before this loss happen'd, Prince Rupert's own Ship
the Constant Reformation founder'd under him in a great
tempest, so that he only saved himself, and two or three others,
not without great difficulty and hazard on boord his brother's
Ship; and after having run many adventures, return'd into
Europe in the year 1653, and landed at Nantes.

The Duke stayd about eight months in Holland from his
first arrival thither; having passed all the Christmas at the
Hague with his brother the Prince and his sister the Princesse
of Orange. The day after twelfth day he began his journy
to France in obedience to the commands of the Queen his
mother. He took his way by Brussells, and when he was come
as far as Cambray, he received a letter from the Queen which
gave him to understand what had happen'd at Paris on twelfth
night: The summ of all was this, That the King of France had
been constrain'd by the disorders in that City, to leave it for
his own security; and that he and the Court were removed to
S: Germains: that this was done with so much precipitation,
that he was forced to go away in the night, but that having
thus secur'd himself and drawn his forces together, he had
blocked up Paris with his Army with a resolution of reducing
them to their obedience; her Majesty concluded with her
commands to him to continue where that letter found him,
till he should receive her further orders.

The Arch Duke Leopold, then Governour of the Low Countries, hearing of his R: Highness stay in Flanders, sent one of
his cheif officers to him with a very civill message, and offers
of some more commodious place for his abode then that frontier Town in which he then was, proposing the Abbaye of
St Amand, which was but one day's journy back: which being
accepted by the Duke, he went thither, where he was nobly
entertain'd by the Monks who were of St Bennet's order, and
stayd there till the 8ᵗʰ of February. At which time he receiv'd

P A R T
I.

1648.
Pᶜᵉ Rupert
after four
years absence
lands safe in
France, in
1653.
Oʀ: Mᴇᴍ:
P: 1: p: 50.
The Duke
after eight
months stay
in Holland
begins his
journy to
France the
6. January
164⁸⁄₉.

164⁸⁄₉.
The Duke
stopp'd in his
journy at
Cambray by a
letter from
the Queen.
Ibid.

The Duke
nobly inter-
tain'd at the
Abbey of St
Amand by the
Monks.
Oʀ: Mᴇᴍ:
P: 1: p: 51.

1647.

The Duke
arrives in
Paris the 13ᵗʰ
of Feb. *Ibid.*

letters from the Queen with her commands to come to Paris. In pursuance of which he return'd to Cambray, from thence went to Peronne, and so on to Paris, where he arrived on the 13ᵗʰ of February: For thō the Town continued still to be block'd up by the King's Army, yet he had leave obtain'd for him to go into it, and to be there with the Queen his mother.

Here the
Queen and
the Duke
receive the
news of the
horrid murder
of the King.
Ibid.

A day or two after the Duke's arrivall in Paris, he heard of the most horrid murder of the King his Father; and what impression that made both upon the Queen and the Duke, may be more easily imagin'd, then express'd.

The Duke
waits on the
King and
Queen of
France at Sᵗ
Germains, his
reception
there.
Oɴ: Mᴇᴍ:
P: 1. p: 51.

About the same time the Parisians feeling the smart of their Rebellion, and growing sensible that they could no ways be releeved, came to terms of accommodation, and submitted to the King. When the Peace was made, the Duke went to Sᵗ Germains to wait on the King and Queen of France, where he was received with all the kindnes he could expect, and treated with all the magnificence due to his quality, in the same manner as if the Royall Family had still continued in their former greatnes.

He returns to
Paris, and
stays with the
Queen his
mother.
The King his
brother arrives
from Holland
and both pass
the Summer at
Sᵗ Germains.
Ibid.

After this his Royall Highness return'd to Paris, and there stayd with the Queen his Mother till the King his Brother came out of Holland into France; and then they went together to Sᵗ Germains, the French Court being remov'd from thence to Paris.

1649.

The intention of the King's journy into France was reported to be only in order to take it in his way to Ireland, which had declared for him, and was at that time almost intirely under his obedience, there being litle left in the possession of the Rebells, but Dublin and Londonderry; But in stead of passing only through the Contry, his Majesty stayd allmost all the summer at Sᵗ Germains, and at last was overperswaded to change his resolution of going streight to Ireland and instead.

therof to go to Jersey, whither he set forth on the 19th of September and tooke the Duke along with him.

P A R T
I.

1649.
The King's
and the Duke's
expedition to
Jersey in
September.
Ibid. p: 52.

On the 26th of the same month his Majesty arrived at Coū-tance, and from thence he went down next morning to Conten-ville, where he had appointed to embarke. When he was come thither, most were of opinion that it would be convenient for his Majesty to stay there till next day ; during which time he might inform himself whither the Coast were clear of Parliament Ships, before he adventur'd his person in going over. The Duke and Sir John Berkley were the only two who oppos'd that Counsell, and advised that he should immediatly imbarke, which they carryd, and it may be truely said, that they therby preserv'd his Majesty. The reason which they gave was this, That in all probability there could be no danger if he put to Sea that day, because the wind was but newly come up easterly, and therfore that the Parliament Ships which lay at Guernesy could not take advantage of getting up time enough to hinder him from landing ; but in case he should defer it till the next morning, they might have leasure to put themselves between him and home.

This advice, as is said, prevailing with his Majesty, he sett sayle immediatly, and in the space of three hours he landed safe in Jersey : The next morning (as had been foreseen) by break of day six or seven of the Rebell's Ships appear'd, which gaue chase to the Vessells in which the King's horses were im-barked ; they not setting out till the morning, to avoid being taken, were forced to venture in amongst the Rocks, with all which hazard they had much ado to escape the Enemy ; which makes it evident, that if the King had follow'd the same method, he must have run the Same hazard.

Whilst his Majesty with the Duke stayd in that Island, they received the uncomfortable news of the defeat of the Lord of Ormonde, and the Confederate Loyall Party before Dublin ;

The affairs of
Ireland in a
bad condition.
Or: Mem:
P: 1: pag. 53.

1649.
The King
lays aside the
thoughts of
going into that
Kingdom.
Ibid.

Addresses
made to the
King in Jersey
from Scotland.
Ibid.

1650.

The King go's
to Holland,
the Scots'
Commission-
ers attend him
at Breda, wher
all things
being agreed,
he passes over
into Scotland.
Or: Mem:
P: 1. p: 53.
The Duke
left at Jersey.
Ibid.

Returns to
Paris in Sep:
Ibid:

After which, and the raising of the Seige of Londonderry, his Majesty's affairs in Ireland were in so desperate condition, that the thought of going thither was absolutly layd aside; and therfore the two Dutch men of war which the Prince of Orange had sent to Jersey for the King's transportation into Ireland, were sent back to Holland.

Not long after that, before his Majesty parted from Jersey, some addresses were made to him from Scotland, which were brought him by one Windram a Very loyall gentleman. Vpon which his Majesty took a resolution of returning into Holland, which he judged to be the most proper place of treating with his Subjects of that Kingdom, the best part of which had ever since the murder of the King his Father, protested against and oppos'd the wicked and violent proceedings in England.

In order to this, the spring being now come, his Majesty past over into France, And after having stayd some time at Beauuais with the Queen his Mother, who came thither from Paris purposely to meet him, he pursued his journy into Holland, and having at Breda agreed all things with the Scots' Commissioners he went over into that Kingdom.

In the mean time the Duke was left behind at Jersey, where he stayd till the beginning of September, And then (being so commanded by his Majesty) he return'd into France, arriving at Paris on the 17th of the same month he stayd not long in that City; for in the same letter wherein the King had order'd him to leave Jersey, there were some ambiguous expressions which seem'd to intimate that he desir'd he would go to Holland. These doubtfull words were made use of by some about the Duke, in whom he repos'd the greatest confidence, to make him leave France, particularly by Sir George Ratcliff, Dean Stuart (whom the King had commanded to attend him) and Doctor Killigrew his Chaplain. These having some designs

of their own, were so urgent with him to have him pass into
Holland, that notwithstanding the Queen was wholy averse
from it, yet she could not oblige him to stay at Paris, from
which place he departed on the 4th of October, and arrived at
Brussels on the 13th.

There he continued for some time, receiving first the sad
news of the death of his sister the Princesse Elizabeth, who
dyd in September at Carisbrook Castle in the Isle of Wight;
and afterwards that of the Scots' defeat at Dunbarr, which
happen'd on the 3^d of the same month.

After the Duke had been a while in Brussells, he sent to his
Sister the Princesse of Orange concerning his coming into
Holland ; But the Queen having written to her from Paris, in
what manner the Duke was come from thence, and how unsatisfied she was with him, the Princesse advis'd his Royall
Highness to deferr his journy into Holland, letting him know
how much she was concern'd for the Queen's displeasure to
him, and that it was necessary he should first endeavour to
make his peace with her Majesty, before she could, with respect
to the Queen, invite him to come to her. This letter from his
Sister obliged him to stop at Brussels till these differences could
be composed ; where, not long after, he received the afflicting
news of the death of the Prince of Orange who dyd of the
small pox about the beginning of November. This was indeed
one of the greatest losses which in that juncture of time could
possibly befall the Royall family ; But to allay this Sorrow in
some measure, soon after came the news that his Sister was
deliver'd of a Son (the present P^{ce} of Orange) who was born on
the 14th of the same month, nine days after the decease of his
Father.

The Duke having thus continued at Brussells till the midle of
December, went from thence to Rhenen, a house belonging to
the Queen of Bohemia in the province of Utrecht, which he

Marginal notes:

The Duke at Brussels gets the news of the death of his sister P^{se} Elizabeth, and of the Scots' defeat at Dunbar.
Or: Mem: P: 1: p: 54.

The P^{ce} of Orange dys of the small pox in November. Ibid.

Birth of the present P^{ce} of Orange 14 November. Ibid.

The Duke go's from Brussels to Rhenen in December. Or: Mem: P: 1: p: 54.

P A R T
I.

1650.
Is reduced to
great hardships
for want of
money. *Ibid.*

165?.

The Duke
comes to the
Hague the 12
of January, and
stays there all
the winter.

The Duke go's
to Breda, to
avoid meet-
ing the Par-
liament's
embass".
Or: Mem:
P: 1: p: 54.

had borrowed of her, resolving to live privatly there, till he could perswade his Sister to let him come to the Hague.

During all this while he was reduced to great hardships; for when he left Paris, he was wholy unfurnish'd of mony, and had he not been casually supplyd with the tenths of some Prizes, which were taken by the Jersey Fregats to the northwards, and which by reason of contrary winds had put into Dunkirk, he could not possibly haue subsisted, (*and*) must have been driven to the last extremitys.

So soon he was come to Rhenen, he sent again to his Sister to press his going to her; and not long afterwards she sent him word that he might come, she having now obtain'd the Queen's permission for it. When the Duke had received the wellcom news he immediatly left Rhenen, and came to the Hague on the 12th of January where he continued all that winter, till such time as the Embassadors from the English Rebells were to be received there; and then thinking it no way proper for him to remain in a Town where they were to make their solemn entry, and to avoide the mortification of so disagreeable a sight, when the murderers of his Father were to be received in State, he retired from the Hague to pass some time in the City of Breda.

But when the formalities of that ceremony were over, his Royall Highness return'd and liv'd with so much circumspection at the Hague, that he never met with those Embassadors in the streets. And he had the less difficulty to avoid them, because as on the one side it could not be very pleasing to him to incounter them in a place, where it was not permitted him to take that revenge on them which they well deserved; so on the other, the States had been cautious enough to hinder it, by obliging both him and them to avoid each other, as justly apprehending what might be the consequences of such a meeting; and this warines in the States was no more then

necessary at that time (when it was their intrest to make their
court to England) considering how much those Embassadors
were hated by the common people, who would gladly have
layd hold in the least occasion to have them in pieces. Indeed
the best endeavours and all the authority they could employ,
was but barely sufficient to protect those English from being
assaulted in their house, for which reason they were forced to
assign them a guard of foot, to secure them from receiving
some signall affront; and notwithstanding all this foresight,
both themselves and those of their Traine had many indignities put upon them by the populace.

In the beginning of June the Duke received a letter from
his Majesty then in Scotland, by which he commanded him to
return to Paris, and withall Signifyd his displeasure for his
removall from thence; And by the same letter he was order'd
to dismiss Doctor Killigrew from his service, and no more
to follow the advice of Sir George Ratcliff, but to submitt
himself, and be intirely govern'd by the directions of the Queen
his Mother; all which commands were immediatly obeyd by
his Royall Highness, who accordingly left the Hague, and went
for France and arriv'd at Paris towards the end of June.

The Duke being now of an age capable of enduring fatigue,
the Queen his Mother out of the care she had for him, that he
might improve his knowledge and forme himself, for action,
resolv'd to send him along with the Court of France when they
should leave Paris, of which there was then a probability;
And in pursuance of this design she ask'd leave of the Queen
and Cardinall, that he might follow the King of France. They
readily approv'd of the proposition, with assurances that he
should be particularly in their care: But before the French
Court went out of Paris, there came news, That the affairs of
his Majesty in Scotland went so ill, that he was forced upon a

The Duke
receives a
letter from
the King t⁰
return to Paris.
Or: Mem:
P: 1: p: 55.

He arrives at
Paris in June.
Ibid.

PART
I.

1651.
The Duke
hinder'd from
accompanying
the Court of
France by the
news of the
King's defeat
at Worcester.
Or: Mem:
P: 1: p: 56.
The King
landed at
Feschamp
in Oct': Ibid.

desperate resolution of marching into England; and soon after came the confirmation of his defeat at Worcester, which caus'd the Queen to alter her design of sending the Duke to accompany the Court; and therfore when they left the Town, which was in the latter end of September, and went towards Berry, the Duke remain'd in Paris with her Majesty, where they were all in dreadfull apprehension for the King, and continu'd in that fearfull amazement till the midst of October, when they receiv'd the comfortable news of his Majestys being safely landed at Feschamp in Normandy, being attended only by the Lord Wilmott.

Wee shall not here relate the particular manner of the King's escape, nor all the hazards he ran, or hardships which he endur'd from the time of his being forced to disguise himself, till that of his arrivall in France, Only in generall say, That had not God endued him with much presence of mind and resolution, as well as given him a strong constitution of body, he could never have escaped from England in so almost miraculons a way.

The Duke
go's and meets
the King at
Magny.
Or: Mem:
P: 1: p: 57.

On the news of his arriuall, the Duke thought it his duty to go and meet him: he had the happiness of seeing him at Magny a place between Paris and Rouen, and afterwards attended him to Paris; where he was not only wellcom'd by the Queen his Mother, but received by all the persons of quality then in Town, with all the demonstrations of joy which could possibly be expected. In particular the Cardinal de Retz when he

Cardinal
de Retz
affectionat to
the King, a
particular
instance of it.
Ibid.

came to wait on him, offer'd to lend him a considerable sum of mony, which, being in gold, he for that purpose brought along with him in his coach. But thō he pressed him exceedingly to take it, his Majesty excused himself with many thanks from receiving it. And not only on this, but on all other occasions, that Cardinall allways shew'd himself most affectionate in his interest and service.

His Majesty had not been long in Paris, before some private
overtures, at least intimations, were made to him from some
confidents of Madmoiselle, eldest daughter to the Duke of
Orleans, concerning a marriage to be made betwixt them. Which
proposition was then readily embraced by him, and was likewise approved by the Queen his mother. And he proceeded
so far, that the King was every day to visite her; She at the
same time giving him reason to beleeve that it would succeed.
But on the sudden he found her growing cooler, without
knowing the occasion of it; so that he was obliged in prudence
to forbear his frequent visites, till at length he came to understand the cause of this alteration in her behaviour, which in
effect was this: Some who either were, or at least pretended
to be her friends, put into her head the imagination of a marriage with the King of France, which they made her beleeve
they might compass with great ease, considering the ill condition of his affairs at that time. The Queen and Cardinall (as
they perswaded her) would be forced to consent to it for their
own security, and to draw themselves out of their present
difficulties. This thought as unreasonable as it was, yet was
so strongly imprinted in her mind, that it caus'd her wholy to
break off with the King of England; by which means reaching
at what she could not get, she lost what was in her power to
have had, and miss'd both of them.

About the same time also a marriage was proposed to both
their Majestys for the Duke. The person named was Madmoiselle de Longueville, only daughter to the Duke de Longueville, whom he had by his first wife who was Sister to the
Count of Soissons: This Lady was at that time next to
Madmoiselle the greatest match in France. The King and
Queen of England approving it, proposed it to the Duke, who
for his part being easily induced to it, the Treaty went so far

P A R T
I.

. 1651.
A proposall
of marriage
betwixt the
King and Mlle.
Ibid.

Mlle de Lon-
gueville pro-
pos'd as a
match for the
Duke.
Or: Mem:
P: 1: p: 58.

PART
I.

1652.

that the consent of the Court of France was ask'd, which being denyd it was broken off.

The spring of the year 1652 was now coming, and the Affairs of France were in such a posture, that there remain'd no hopes of an accommodation betwixt the King and the Princes, by the return of the Cardinal Mazarin, but on the other side a probability of great action in that Campagne: This being considered by the Duke, who was very desirous to improve himself that he might one day be fitt * to serve in the French King's Army as a volonteer, And thō when he made this proposition at first, all but Sir John Berkley opposed it, yet by daily urging it, he at length prevail'd, and had the consent both of the King and Queen to go.

When the Duke had obtain'd this, a greater difficulty still remain'd to be overcome, which was want of mony to furnish out an equipage, and to maintain his expences in the Army. Mony was then a scarce commodity in the English Court, which at last the Duke procur'd from a Gascoun call'd Gautier, who had served in England; Of him he borrow'd three hundred pistoles, which with a sett of Poland coach horses, brought out of that country by the Lord Crofts, and given him by the King his Brother, enabled his Royall Highness to fit himselfe out for the Campagne; without this assistance it had been impossible for him to set forth, for at that time mony abounded as litle in the French Court as in the English. Thus accommodated, the Duke set forth with his small equipage, his train consisting only of Sir John Berkley, Collonel Worden, two or three other servants, and as many groomes, without so much as a led-horse in case of necessity; his feild bed

The Duke
obtains the
King and
Queen's con-
sent to go and
serve in the
French King's
Army.
OR: MEM:
P: 1: p: 58.

The streights
the Duke was
in at his
setting out
to his first
Campagne.
Ibid. p: 60.

---

* Here some words appear to have been omitted by the Secretary, who probably intended to have written, " That he might one day be fitt *to command*, *he resolved* to serve," &c. — EDITOR.

and all the equipage of his servants being carryd on two Mules, which were hired only as far as the French Army, where he was promised to be furnish'd with better conveniences for carriage. Yet he chose rather to go this way then not at all. He took care only to manage the busines as privately as he could, for fear of being stop'd, or that some other inconveniency should happen to him, if his intention of going to the King's Army had been divulged : Besides which consideration, it was not thought fitt for his Royall Highnes to take leave of his uncle the Duke of Orleans, against whose party he was going to ingage.

P A R T
I.
1652.

To avoid all which inconveniences, the Duke accompanied the King his Brother to St Germains, under a pretence of hunting; and after he had stayd there only three or four days, he sett out on his intended journy for the Army on the 21th of Aprill ; and passing through the fauxbourg St Antoine, his way lying under the walls of Paris, he could reach no further that night then to Charenton.

The Duke parts from St Germains the 21. of Aprill in order to joyne the Army and begin his first Campagne. Or: Mem: P: 1: p: 60.

The next day he travell'd to Corbeil, where upon his arrivall, he found some companies of the regiment of Guards in the Suburbs ; the Inhabitants having shutt their gates with a resolution not to receive them into the Town : Of which being inform'd by some Officers whom he met there, he was in great apprehension of not being admitted : However he presented himself at the gate, where they made difficulty of receiving him, yet having used some perswasions to them, they at length open'd the wickett, and permitted the Duke to enter on foot, with condition to leave his horses without the gate ; and being once got in himself he wrought upon the Magistrats so far, as not only to take in his horses, but even the guard, by representing to them the danger they ran in case they should refuse them entrance: thō it was most certain, that had they continued to keep their gates shutt, the Court which then lay at Melun,

The Duke perswades the Magistrats of Corbeil to receive the King of France' Guards into the Town, a good piece of seruice at that time. Or: Mem: P: 1: p: 60.

would have found great difficulty in taking it, considering the strength of its scituation, and its nearness to Paris: And had not the King by this unexpected means gott possession of that Town, it had much prejudiced his affairs, as on the contrary it prov'd afterwards a very advantageous post, and was very usefull to him on Severall occasions. So soon as the Court, which (as is above related) lay then at Melun, heard of the admission of those Companies which had been purposely sent before to Corbeil, they came immediatly thither, where the Duke stayd expecting them; and there got a small recruit of mony, another horse and two Mules, all which came very seasonably to him; for he and his poor retenue had not above twenty pistoles left amongst them at their arrivall in that place. And the same evening being the 24th of Aprill, his Royall Higness went to Chätres, severall other volonteirs of the Court accompanying him thither; and there he found the Army, which arriued at that Town but some few hours before him.

The Duke
joyns the
French Court
and the French
Army at
Chätres the 24
Aprill.
Or: Mem.
P: 1: p: 61.

But before we relate the actions of this Campagne and those which succeeded it while the Duke was in the French Army, it will be necessary to take the matter a litle higher, that the Reader may in some measure be inform'd of the State of Affairs, as they then stood in France.

State of the
French Affairs
when the
Duke began
his first Cam-
pagne.
Ibid. pag. 62.

The Crown was reduced to a most deplorable condition in the beginning of this year; Few there were who preserved their loyalty to the King, and even they whose interest as well as duty it was to have maintain'd the Crown, were the chief instruments and causers of those distractions; grounding them-selves on that common and plausible pretence which has occasion'd So many Rebellions in all ages,—namely, The remov-ing evill Counsellors from about the person of the King; to make which Argument the more popular, they farther urged, how great a disreputation it was to France to be govern'd by

a Stranger; when so many Princes of the blood were both
more capable, and more proper to undertake the Ministry then
Cardinal Mazarin.

The heads of this Party were the Duke of Orleans, the King's
unkell, the Princes of Condé and Conty, both Princes of the
blood, who were follow'd by a very considerable part of the
Nobility and cheif Gentry of the Kingdom. To aggravat
which mischeif, almost all the great and populous Towns, and
most of the Parliaments, adhered to them; as in the first
place, Paris, Orleans, and generally all the Citys down the
river of Loire, with Bordeaux and most of the inland Towns.
And thō the Duke of Longueville with the Town and Parliament of Rouen did not positively declare themselves against
the King, yet it was evident that they inclined to the Princes'
Party; To prove which there needs no other argument, then
that in the midst of a Rebellion they sett up for a Neutrality, as
being indeed desirous to be lookers on, and watch their opportunity to take part with the Strongest. For thō many overtures
were made to them from the King, yet they found pretences to
excuse themselves from receiving him into the Town, when his
affaires were in the low condition that he was refused entrance
by all the greatest Cities. In effect the poison was So generally
spread through the whole Kingdom, that even the litle places
took courage from the example of the greater, as has been
already instanced in Corbeil, which had certainly persisted
in excluding the King, if they had not distrusted their own
strength.

To compleat the miserys of that Nation, they were not only
imbroyl'd at home, but had their antient Enemies the Spaniards at their doors, who were ready to add fuell to their fire
by all the means they could imagine, that they might make
their profit of those distractions, by regaining in the space of
some few months, what had been taken from them by the

French with great expence in length of time, and with the loss of
many of their bravest men. Vndoubtedly they had in prospect
far greater designs flattering themselves with the imagination that they shou'd either totally oppress the French, and
ruine their Monarchi, or at least reduce them to so low a
condition that they shou'd not be capable to attacke them of a
long time. Tis reasonable to beleeve they would have effected
one of these, or at least gone farther then they did, had they
taken their measures more justely; but their too cautious
maximes, both then and afterwards, render'd all their undertakings fruitless.

The affaires of France being in this posture, the Spaniards
besides their large promises and making distribution of mony
to severall of the cheif Malcontents, sent some Troopes from
Flanders into France under the conduct of the Duke of Nemours, to strengthen the Army of the Princes; he having been
sent purposly to Brussels to demand their assistance. This
Army of Spaniards which he led, enter'd France in the
beginning of the spring; their numbers were about seven
thousand men in horse and foot, and they pass'd the Seyne at
Mante; of which place the Duke de Sully was then Governour,
who granted them free passage, which had he not done, their
march had been very much retarded, and they could not so
soon have joyn'd the Princes' Army which was assembled
about . . . . . no far from . . . .

After the conjunction of the Princes' Army with the Spaniards, and the taking of Angers by the King, there was nothing
done that was considerable till the action of Blesneau; only
one day as the King's Army was marching up along the
river of Loire, that of the Princes came to Gergeau, and their
Van had already possest themselves of one end of the bridge,
and were preparing to make themselves masters of the Town,
which had nothing of defence but an ordinary gate, and few

or no Soldiers in it; so that had not Monsr. de Turenne come luckely thither upon the first allarme, it had infallibly been taken, and the King's Army therby receiv'd a considerable disadvantage. But more Troopes coming up speedily to Monsr. de Turenne, those of the Princes were forced to abandon their design, and retire with some loss of men ; the most considerable of which was one Monsr. Sirot a Lieutenant Generall accounted one of the best officers they had. After which the Court marched to Gien upon the Loire, where their Army pass'd the River and quarter'd about Blesneau, and the neighbouring Villages either upon or near the Canal de-Briare.

The Princes' Army march'd towards them and camped at Lorris. But some time before this, the Prince of Condé finding his affaires in Guienne to be in a very ill condition, not easily to be remedyd by him, and judging that his person was more necessary at Paris and to be at the head of his Army in those parts, he left Monsr Marsin to command in cheif his forces in Guienne; and he himself attended only by four or five persons slip'd away as privatly as he could, for fear of being taken in his passage which lay through some of the King's quarters ; and very narrowly escaping by the way, he arrived at Paris, whence he immediatly went to their Army, and there having intelligence how the King's forces lay, he resolved to fall into their quarters ; for it was so early in the year, being about the midst of Aprill at furthest, that there was no forage, and consequently the King's Army was constrain'd to take their quarters scatteringly in severall Villages.

Monsieur de Turenne himself lay at Briare and the Mareschal d'Hocquincourt at Blesneau, who having received intelligence that the Princes' Army was upon their march to him, resolv'd on a place d'armes, or rendez-vous, in case of an allarme, betwixt both their quarters, immediatly advancing guards towards the Enemy, and puting some dragoons at a

An account of the busines of Blesneau, wherein the conduct of Monsr de Turenne preserved both the Army and the Crown of France.
Or: Mem:
P: 1: p: 72.

pass, by which in all liklyhood they were to come. Being already in this posture, Monsr. de Turenne who likewise had notice of the Enemie's approache with their resolution of falling into his quarters, went himself to the Mareschall d'Hocquincourt, who lay next the danger, to inform him of it. But he satisfyd himself with depending of his dragoons, who he thought would have given the Enemy a stop at the pass, thō the event prov'd much otherwise; for whither by treachery or cowardise the dragoons were no sooner attacked, then they quitted their posts, and left the pass open to the Enemy, who pursuing their advantage broke in immediatly to Monsr d'Hocquincourts quarters, and beat them up one after another, litle resistance being made: nor was the loss of men considerable on either side, only all the baggage in the quarters were taken, but the beaten troopes got off by favour of the night, yet the terrour was so great that they came not to the Rendez-vous appointed; neither did the Enemy pursue them so far as they might otherwise have done, because of the darknes, and indeed having a greater design in hand; for they well knew that Monsieur de Turenne was not far off, whom they made account infallibly to beat so soon as it was day if he drew not off before.

To confess the truth he ran a great hazard, and with him the Crown of France on that occasion: for had that small Army of his been once routed, in all probability the King had fallen into the Princes' hands, and what the consequence of it would have proved, may be easily imagin'd by the Licentiousness of those times, and the Ambition of some of the great men.

But to return to Monsr. de Turenne, So soon as he had the allarme, he drew out of his quarters, and march'd to the Rendez-vous appointed; at the same time sending out small partys to bring him intelligence of the Enemy, who returning gave him an account that their Army was very near, and had beaten up the other quarter. It was then so very dark that it was impossible for him to consider the post he had taken up ; to march forward was too dangerous, the Enemy being at so near a distance, and to retire might prove ruinous, because he was not with (*without*) a just apprehension of discouraging his men and puting them in a great confusion. Considering those hazards he prudently resolved to stand his ground, and therby give leasure to his partys of coming to him : At the first dawne of the day he found himself close by the Enemy, and had the good fortune to observe an advantageous post where the Princes' Army could not possibly attacke him, but by marching first through a sorte of defilé where only one squadron could come afront, by reason of the wood that was on either side, and the marish grounds and ditches that were in the passage. Behind this passage he drew up his small body of men (for as yet none of the other quarter which was beaten were come up to him, neither indeed did they till the evening) Some of the Officers propos'd to him to line the wood with partys of foot the better to defend the pass ; but he refused it, as he has since told the Duke, on this consideration, That being himself so weak and the Enemy so strong in foot, they would soon have beaten his men out of the wood, which must have obliged him to draw down to their releif, and perhaps so far ingaged him, that he could never have gotten off without indangering his whole Army. In stead of this he took a more prudent resolution, and leaving the wood unguarded drew back above muskett shott from it and the pass ; and there Stood expecting what the Enemy would do. Who seeing him so advantageously posted, thought it too hazardous to attacke him.

Thus they stood both sides in battell, looking on each other without moving, and for some time playing with their great guns ; till Mons'. de Turenne making a shew as if he would have march'd away, began to draw off in very good order; which the Enemy observing thought it now their time of charging him: Wherupon they advanced with their whole Army in battell to the pass, their horse beginning to come over it. There were about six squadrons past the defilé, when Monsieur de Turenne turning back march'd towards them, so that they who already were come over, were forced to retreat in very great confusion, and that to prevent their absolute defeat. And the gross of their Army was then approached so near the pass, that Mareschall de Turenne retaking his former ground, play'd on them with his cannon all the remainder of the day, with great execution, they being so near a distance, and their troopes so closely crowded, that almost every shott took place. At the close of the evening, the troopes of Mareschall d'Hoquincourt came up and joyn'd with Monsr. de Turenne; while they were yet in presence of the Enemy, so that the party was not now so unequall as before. However both of them thought fitt to draw off, and this was the conclusion of that Action, wherein the conduct and resolution of Monsr. de Turenne preserv'd both the Army and the Crown of France; there being no Visible means of maintaining either after a defeat, if not from a totall ruine, at least from suffring such a change as would have produced a long train of discords and disorders in that Kingdom.

After the action of Blesneau, Pⁿ of Condé leaves the Army and go's to Paris.
Oꭆ: Mᴇᴍ:
P. 1: p: 79.

After this action the Prince of Condé left the Army and went to Paris, where he was received with great applause; his party magnifying the advantage he had got, above what really it was. But in the mean time his absence from his Army prov'd very prejudicial to their common intrest; for there was no Commander left in cheif: Monsr. de Tavannes commanding the Princes' troopes, Monsr. de Valon those of the Duke of Orleans, and Monsr. de Clinchamp the Auxiliarys which were sent from Flanders. Therefore, as it allways happens where

there is no supreme authority, nothing was so well order'd as
it might have been. For besides the want of so great a Generall,
as was the Prince, the Lieutenant Generalls, thō each of them
had personall courage, were none of them fitt to head an Army.
And as all great actions have been ever better managed and
with more success by a single person, then by many whose
power is coordinate, So in their particular condition it was
most necessary for them to have had a Supreme Commander
at their head, since, thō their intrest in generall seemed to
be the same, yet all three were jealous of each other. However
it was, Monsieur de Turenne made his advantage of this
equality and independency amongst them ; for notwithstanding
that they lay not far distant from one another, he amus'd them
so, that by taking great and well order'd marches (the Court
moving at the same time) he gave them the slip, and got
betwixt them and Paris ; And though he was to take a great
compass, and as it were to march round them, yet his diligence
was such, that he arrived at Chartres on the 14th of Aprill,
when they were got no farther then Etampes : And hereby
gave an opportunity to the Court of getting to Paris, which
was the resolution taken when he began his march. But what
the reason was, why they went not thither is uncertain ; for
they had been press'd and perswad'd to it both by the Cardinal
de Retz and by the most considerable of the King's party who
resided in the Town; some attributed it to want of resolution
in the Court, who were aw'd and fright'd by intelligence from
such as being no freinds to the Cardinal, desir'd not to see the
King in Paris. However it was, they stop at Melun, and from
thence came to Corbeil about the same time that their Army
arrived at Chartres, at which place the Duke of York joyn'd Or: Mem: P: 1: p: 82.
it (as has been before related) on the very night of their
coming, and from hence forward his Royall Highness was
present and ingaged in all the Actions of this Campagne.

PART
I.

1652.
The famous
action of the
Suburbs of
Etampes. The
first action in
France the
Duke was.
Ibid: p: 83.

There happen'd no considerable action for some litle time after the Duke's arrivall, only small partys were sent out towards Etampes, who brought in daily men and horses which they took at forage; and by those prisoners they understood that the Enemy's whole Army was quarter'd in that Town and Suburbs. But after some few days, Monsr. de Turenne receiv'd a letter from Madmoiselle by a trumpett, in which she desir'd a pass to go to Paris, she having been at Orleans, which Town, by her presence and credit there, she had caus'd to declare for the Princes, and now in her way to Paris she could not avoid passing through both Armys: At first the Mareschall made some difficulty of granting it, without the leave and participation of the Court, and dispatch'd a messenger thither for that purpose; but before his return having consider'd that probably he might make some advantage of her request, and knowing on what day she would be at Etampes, he gratifyd her by the sending of a pass; and having understood by his partys, that the Enemy had not been out at forage for two or three days last past, he conjectur'd that on that day, which was the 3^d of May, Madmoiselle would see the Army, and that on the next she wou'd go away for Paris, so that he reckon'd they would not go out to forage till the 4th; That the forage having been so long deferr'd would be great, and that it was likely enough they would not be very carefull, but that most of the Generall Officers would conduct Madmoiselle part of the way; So that weighing all these Circumstances, he and Monsieur d'Hocquincourt resolv'd to march away all night with the whole Army, leaving only an hundred horse and a small regiment of foot to guard the bagage, which was left at Chãtres.

The King's
Army com-
manded by
M^r.deTurenne
and M^r.d'Hoc-
quincourt
marches to
Etampes.
Or: Mem:
P: 1: p: 85.

This they put in immediate execution, giving but an houres warning for preparation, and that without beat of drum or sound of trumpett, beginning the march about eight of the clock at night. Their design was to have put themselves

between the Enemys Army and their foragers, thinking, as has been already said, that the foragers would be out at the time computed, and they might have swept them all away with them. They march'd all that night in great order and silence, Monsieur d'Hocquincourt having the Van, as it was then his turn; and before Sun-rise they had pass'd all the defilés, having taken a compass to put themselves betwixt stampes and Orleans, which was the way the Enemy used to go a foraging.

They were now getting into order, when some of their small partys, who were sent out for intelligence, brought back word, That instead of the Enemies being at forage; their whole Army was drawn up in battell about a league from them on the plaine above Etampes. Upon which advice the King's forces immediatly drew up in the bottom where they were, and marched directly up the hill with a resolution of ingaging the Enemy; but they, as soon as they perceiv'd this, began to draw back into the Town, which the King's Generalls observing, march'd with their horses at a round trott after them, hoping to have fallen upon their rear before they could all have gotten into shelter, giving direction at the same time to their foot and cañon to make what hast they could after them.

The reason why the Enemy were drawn up in battell before the Town, instead of going out to forage as Mareschall de Turenne imagin'd they would have done, was to entertain Madmoiselle with a vieu of their Army, who that morning was going on her way to Paris without having the least notice of the King's forces being so near; which when they discover'd they ask'd her advice what shou'd be done? to which she answer'd, That they best knew what orders were left with them by her Father and the Prince of Condé; after which she pursu'd her journy, and they drew back into the Town and Suburbs with so much expedition, that before the two Mareschalls Turenne and Hocquincourt had gain'd the heigth above the City, all the troopes of the Enemy were already in security. Upon which sudden retreat of theirs the two Mareschalls took a new resolution, which was to attack the suburbs, for which they sent immediat orders to the foot, that in marching they might prepare for it and get ready their commanded men, which was done accordingly.

Description of
Etampes and
what number
of Troopes
were then in
the Town and
Suburbs.
Or: Mem:
P: 1: p: 88.

Etampes is distant from Paris about fourteen or fifteen leagues, upon the road betwixt Paris and Orleans. Tis situate in a bottom, having a litle river running under the walls on the back part of it, which river falls into the Seyne by Corbeil. All that side of the Town and suburbs, which is on the right hand as you come from Châtres, is commanded by a hill, which yet is not very high; for from the top of an old round tower in the Town which is very high, the plaine which lyes above it or at least a great part of it may be discover'd. The Town-wall (as many are in France) is flank'd with small round towers, not cannon proof, and incompass'd only with a dry ditch on the side towards Châtres. The suburbs on the Orleans side are large and have a river on the one side, and a brooke on the other, which joyn under the wall of the Town towards the Orleans gate; so that there is no communication betwixt the City and the suburbs but through that gate. In this suburb lay part of the Enemys Army which had intrenched themselves, wherunto the brooke had very much contributed, for it cover'd all one side, excepting only a litle space which was near the gate, and which they supplyd with a line. In this quarter lay at that time about nine regiments of foot, as namely those of Condè, Conty and Bourgogne of the Prince's own troopes, with all the auxiliary foot of the Spaniards, as Berlo, Pleur, Vangè la Motte, Pelnitz, and one or two more, and about four or five hundred horses; the reste of their horse and foot was quarter'd in the Town.

As soon as the King's foot came up, they fell on immediatly, scarse staying till their cañon had fir'd two or three shott at the Enemys retrenchments, which was rather done to let them see they had cannon, then for any execution they expected from them. Monsieur d'Hocquincourt's foot had the right hand, so that their attack was made where the brooke was; which prov'd to be deeper then they expected at their coming thither; they not knowing it, march'd down, and came to the very brink of it, the Enemy firing at them all the while, till the officers thrusting in their pikes to fathom the depth found it impassable, wherupon they drew off in good order, and march'd some what higher to a mill.

P A R T
I.

1652.
The King's
Army begin to
attack the
Suburbs of
Etampes.
Or: Mem:
P: 1: p: 91.

In the mean time Monsr. de Turenne's foot, commanded by Monsr. de Gadagne Lieut: Col: of the regiment de la marine, fell in with the Enemy on that part of their line which was in the left hand next to the Town, and without any resistance gain'd it. This was the only part that was ill maintain'd and yet was the place of the greatest consequence, for by losing it they were cutt off from all releif; and to improve this advantage a baricado was made cross the street over against the gate of the Town. At the same time Monsr. de Turenne enter'd at this place all his foot, which instantly made way also for the horse; at the head of which Mareschall d'Hocquincourt came in, but with such eager hast, that he forgott to give order to the rest of his wing what they should next perform, so that they were all following him into the suburb, which being perceiv'd by Monsieur de Turenne, he came up to them, and stopt them all but two or three of the former squadrons, and order'd them to draw off to the top of the hill where all his own horse were posted, because more then enow were already enter'd to second the foot; and besides, the rest of the Enemy's Army, which was in the Town, might have taken a great advantage, if half the horse had been ingaged in the suburbs,

by falling upon the King's forces out of the other gate; their
numbers of horse and foot then in the Town, without reckoning
those who were in the suburbs, equalling all those under the
two Mareschalls.

In the mean time the regiment of Picardy and the rest of
Mons'. de Hocquincourts foot, which march'd upward to the
mill, there passed the brooke, and attacked the Enemy very
vigourously; who all (excepting the regiment de Bourgogne,
which defended the place where Mons'. de Gadagne enter'd)
fought with all imaginable bravery; and even after M'. d'Hocquincourt's foot were enter'd the suburbs, they disputed evry
wall and every place that was possibly to be maintain'd; for
M'. de Turenne's foot so soon as they were enter'd, and had
secured the traverse against the Town, turn'd immediatly to
the right hand, and fell on the flanks of them who defended the
line: Yet notwithstanding they were thus charg'd, and that
at the same time the King's cannon playd furiously upon them
doing great execution, they (as is said) obstinatly disputed every
wall, for the Line ran along the back sides and gardens which
had stone walls, wherin they had made gaps or breaches for
six men to pass a front in their going round the Line: Every
one of these they defended with wonderful resolution, and sometimes forced the King's men from walls they had gain'd; and
once they put them into so great a disorder that they were
driven back a considerable way, and had it not been for the
regiment de Turenne, who made a stand and put a stop to
them, which gave time to the King's men to rally about their
Coulours, it was probable enough that these last had been
beaten out of all they had gain'd; But having repell'd that
effort of the Enemy, they advanced upon them with new vigour,
and drove them before them from wall to wall, till they had
push'd them to the very last.

There the Enemy made a stand, and faceing again upon

their pursuers, beat them back out of the next closs or garden,
and destroy'd many of their men. Tis true that they by
pursuing the Enemy before too hotly had put themselves into
great disorder, some horse of theirs being mix'd with their
foot; but the Enemy did. not pursue their advantage, contenting themselves to have made good their last wall, whilst the
King's men rallyd behind the covert of the next, so that there
was the space of an inclosure between the two partys. And
now the soldiers having sufficiently smarted for their over-
forwardness in pursuite, took breath a while before they would
venture to press on the Enemy again, so that for some considerable time, both parties from behind their walls lay pelting
at each other.

And there the Duke saw an officer of the Enemy (whom he
afterwards found to be Dumont the Major of Condé) perform
an action, which, had it been seconded by his party, might have
put some stop to the current of the Victory on the King's side,
for while both partys were continuing thus to fire at one another, he sallyd out with his pike in his hand, expos'd to all the
shott of the King's party and at the distance only of twenty
paces, the closs being no broder, and advanced half way
towards them; but not being follow'd by any of his men, was
constrain'd to return: this he attempted three severall times,
without any one to second him, and by a miracle of good fortune received no hurt. Which undauntednes of his rais'd so
great an emulation in some of his Maties Officers, that perhaps
it made them adventure more then they would have done at
another time.

A brave action perform'd by one Dumont, and taken notice of by the Duke, who was present in that place where the hottest seruice was. Or: Mem: P: 1: p: 96.

The duty would indeed have been very hard to have directly
attacked the open passage of the Enemys wall, which was
maintain'd by so many resolute men; yet there was an Officer
of the Royalists who ran from the gap of the wall that was on
their side, and in the face of the Enemy came up to their wall,

under which he placed himself as closely as (*he*) could, and was follow'd by as many of the King's men as could stand free from the Enemy's shott, the closs being narrow and nothing but the walls betwixt both partys. There by a new kind of skirmish they heav'd large stones, which lay uppermost on the wall, against each other, so that by litle and litle the wall decreased : At the same time some of the Royall party observing a rising ground, from whence they could see the Enemy behind their wall, and there firing at them with this advantage, it grew too hott for them to keep their ground; especially because while they were thus pelted, they were also pressed by the other Royalists, who were•in front of them; therfore quitting their last wall, they ran for refuge to a neighbouring Church, whither also the regiment of Picardy had driven those whom they attacked, but not being able to maintain it, they were immediatly forced to ask quarter, which was given them. Some few of their horse sav'd themselves over the brooke or river that was behind them, having lost their Commander the Baron de Briole, and the Count de Fursternberg, both kill'd upon the place.

M. de Turenne
advances to
sustain the
baricade.
OB: MEM:
P: I: p: 99.

But while the Royalists were thus hottly ingaged in the suburbs, the Enemy in the Town sallyd out, and attacked the baricade which the Royalists had made a cross the Street before the gate of the Town; and indeed those who defended it were so pressed by the Enemy, that they began to call for the assistance of the horse, and for more pouder : So that had not Monsr. de Turenne himself advanced with a squadron of horse within almost pistoll-shott of the Town, to sustain them and keep off the Enemy, and had he not withall supplyd them with pouder, they had been beaten from that post, which in all probability had been the loss of the whole Enterprise; for all their foot were ingaged in the suburbs to the last man, and had not at that time done their business, the dispute being then at

the hottest; So that had they of the Town recover'd that Baricade, being so strong as they were in foot, they would not only
have releev'd their own men, but have cutt off all the King's
Infantery ; for the Enemy had three thousand of their best foot
still remaining in the Town ; But they were beaten back by
Monsr de Turenne's advancing as he did, and by the vigour of
Gadagne, who defended the baricade and settled the soldiers
well again in that post, which they were almost ready to have
abandon'd : This being done, Monsieur de Turenne drew off
again with the horse. Tis true the Enemy made two sallies
more, but they were both times beat back with loss; after
which the Royalists began to be much more at their ease, and
finished happily their undertaking.

They kill'd above a thousand of the Enemy upon the place,
and took a considerable number of prisoners, so that of the nine
regiments of foot that defended the suburbs, hardly any
escaped. Amongst the prisoners were M^r. de Briol Mareschal
de Camp, M^r. de Montal who commanded the Prince of Condé's
regiment of foot, M^r. Dumont Major of the same regiment,
whom, when the Duke saw prisoner, he recolected to be the
same whom he had seen do so bravely at the defence of the
last wall, where he sallyd thrice out (as has been already related)
but was not follow'd by any of his men. Besides these above
named, there were also taken all the officers and soldiers of
the three French Regiments of Condé, Conty and Bourgogne;
and of the auxiliaries, the Baron de Berlo Mareschall de
bataille, Vange, Pleur and la Motte, all three Colonells with
their men and officers. The Royalists lost at least five hundred who were either kill'd or dyd afterwards of their wounds,
but not one of note. Some Captains they had kill'd. The
young Comte de Quincé was shott through the body, and Count
Carlo de Broglio throw the arm, but both recover'd.

By the exact account which the Duke gives in his Memoires

P A R T
I.

1652

An account of
the slain and
prisoners at
the attack of
the Suburbs of
Etempes.
OB: MEM:
P: 1: p: 101.

written in his own hand of every particular circumstance of this great Action, it may be observed that his Royall Highness (thō he never mentions his own danger) was present in the places where the Service was hottest, which demonstrably appears by his remembring Monsr. Dumont when he was taken prisoner, to be the same person whom he had seen performing that bold action above mention'd at the last wall in the suburbs of Etampes.

This Action as it was very daring, so it was also very fortunate; and, perhaps, had the two Generalls known the weakness of their foot, before they ingaged, they had not attempted it, for they had not there present above two thousand. Tis true the whole number was to have been five thousand, but their march was so suddain, and in the night, that many of the foot who were gone out in small partys, came not up before the Action was quite over, wheras on the other side the Enemy in the suburbs were near three thousand foot, besides four or five hundred horse, and in the Town was the same number of foot, and the rest of their horse was equall to the King's; But the raison which made the two Generalls undertake it, was, in the first place, the great disorder in which they observ'd the Enemy to be when the King's forces first appear'd on the top of the hill which overlooks the suburbs; and secondly the knowledge they had of the officers with whom they had to deal, who thō sufficiently brave in their own persons, yet (as has been formerly hinted) * as the affairs required; And besides, being equall in command, what one directed, another might contradict, or at least give out orders to one part of the soldiers which might prove destructive to the other. And of this the Royall Army it self found the inconveniency in this

---

* The words omitted seem to have been, *were not so subordinate*, &c. (see page 63.)

very enterprise; for when they drew off in the evening from the suburbs, Mons'. d'Hocquincourt who had the Van march'd away directly for Etrechy without halting, or having the least consideration how he left Mons'. de Turenne, who had the rearguard, and was to draw off the soldiers from the baricade before the gate, and out of the suburbs, where many of the men were yet plundering; so that had the Enemy taken the advantage then offer'd, they might easily have beaten the King's whole Army: for the Van was almost at their quarters, before the Reer was wholy drawn off from their posts. And had those of the Town sallyd out from the Paris-gate, they might have got betwixt the two bodies of the Royalists, and taken their choice of first defeating which they pleas'd, and both successiuely. But in stead of this they bent all their forces on Mons'. de Turenne's men as they were drawing off, and indeed press'd them so hard, that Mons'. de Turenne in person, the Duke being with him, was forced to advance with som horse to disingage and bring off the foot. When they had gain'd the top of the hill, My Lord Berkley who attended the Duke, told Mons'. de Turenne, that the Van was march'd away; to which he reply'd, shrugging up his shoulders, that it was now too late to remedy it. They therfore retreated as fast as they were able, incumber'd as they were with all the prisoners which they were to bring off, and were not a litle glad when they got to their quarters at Etrechy, which is two leagues from Etampes in the road to Paris. And the next day they march'd back to their bagage which they had left at Châtres.

This succes was of great reputation and advange to the King's affaires, and gave such encouragement to the Court, that the Cardinall resolv'd that Mons'. de Turenne should block up the Enemys Army in Etampes, where it was known their forage began already to grow very scarce. And accordingly he dispatch'd his orders to Mons'. de Turenne, and at the same

PART I.

1652.
The Royalists draw off in the Evening from the suburbs of Etampes. OR: MEM: P: 1. p. 103. Mr. Hocquincourt marches away directly to Etrechy with the Van, leaving Mons'. de Turenne alone, incumber'd with all the prisoners to bring off the rear guard. Ibid. p: 104.

The Court encourag'd by the succes of the attack of the suburbs, resolves the Seige of the Town of Etampes. OR: MEM: P: 1: p: 105.

time was making provision of what Artillery he could, especially of great Cañon and all other necessarys, as well for the
attack, as the blockade.   But before these preparations were
in a readines, the Army was forced to march to Palaiseau,
having consum'd all the forage in the neighbourhood of Châtres;
from whence they marched on the 6th of May, and stayd at
Palaiseau till the 26th.   That day they marched to Etrechy,
and the next they incamped very near Etampes, on the same
hight which is so near it.

There they began to make a line of Contravallation against
the Town upon the ridge of the hill, and within muskett
shott of Etampes.   As they began this work, those in the Town
made frequent sallys out upon them to hinder their proceeding.
At one of which attempts they cutt off above a hundred of the
King's workmen, before the guard could get a horseback, but
then they were very vigourously repulsed by the Marquis de
Richelieu who commanded the guard and preserved the rest of
the workmen.   The next day the Lines were finish'd, which
were but very mean, for besides the hardnes of that stony
ground, the Royall Army was in great want of tooles; nor was
there a stick of wood in the whole Country to make fascines ;
and some of the foot were lodged in the ruines of the suburbs,
where they had beaten the Enemy before, and which those of
the Town had burnt down upon the notice of Mr. de Turenne
marching towards them.   Notwithstanding that the Royall
Army lay within less than Cañon shott of the Town, yet the
scituation of it is so exceeding low, that they could not trouble
the beseigers with their great guns; thō from the great Tower
which is exceeding high, the Enemy could discern with
ease all that was doing in the Camp, which was of great
advantage to them.   The beseigers made also a bridge over
the River which is below the Town, to hinder the beseiged
from foraging, and were also preparing to make bridges over
the brook and River above it; by which they would haue so

straitned them, that in all probability they had either starv'd
them out, or forced them to come forth and fight with them at
great disadvantage. But while the King's Army was in the
midst of these preparations and designs, the Duke of Lorraine
came suddenly and broke all their measures.

This Prince had given the Cardinall such assurances of his
being in his interests, that he had sent orders to the Mareschall
de la Ferté then Governour of Lorraine to permitt the Duke to
joyn togather his divided troopes; which he had no sooner
got into a body, but he march'd immediatly into France, and
declared for the Prince^{s,} having had an underhand correspondence with them during all the time that he was treating
with the Cardinall. This intelligence being brought to M^r.
de Turenne, caus'd him to alter the methods he had taken; for
instead of making it his only business to starve Etampes, he
now resolvd to try his fortune against it by plaine force, knowing that if he could not carry it soon, the Duke of Lorraine would
suddenly be up with him, and relieve it.

On this consideration, therfore, he fell vigourously to work,
and rais'd his batteries; some upon the Line, and others
in the bottom, close to the Orleans-Gate, and began to
play upon that gate, and the wall betwixt it, and the great
Tower, with resolution to storm an outwork which the Enemy
had made betwixt the foremention'd places, but some what
nearer to the gate then to the Tower; And to that purpose
Monsr. Gadagne with a thousand commanded men was order'd to attack it, which he so well perform'd, that after some
dipute he master'd it and lodged upon it without any considerable loss, thō it was distant from the wall of the Town but
pistoll-shott: During this attack severall bodies of horse were
drawn out and placed betwixt the Town and the line on the
side of the hill, to hinder the Enemy from sallying out on the
back of the commanded men who made the attack; but the

On the news
of the Duke of
Lorraine's
marching into
France, M. de
Turenne
presses the
Seige of
Etampes.
OR: MEM:
P: 1: p: 109.
Mr Gadagne
storms an
outwork and
masters it, but
is beat out
again.
OR: MEM:
P: 1. p: 110.

horse, who were placed within half musket-shott of the Town, were drawen off again just at break of day. The Sun was no sooner risen, then the Enemy made a sally, some of them coming along without the Town-ditch, to fall on Gadague's men in the reer, while others attack'd them in front; And thō Gadagne did all that a good Officer could perform, yet he was beaten from the outwork with the loss of many of his men, and with much difficulty got off himself by making his retreat along the ditch of the Town to a baricade which the beseigers had made before the Orleans-Gate. He was already given for lost, because he came not off with the rest, and indeed his escape was very strange, for he was amongst the Enemys horse; but two or three Sergeants, and as many Musketeers standing resolutly by him, he disingaged himself (*with*) much ado, and came off unhurt, thō he had above twenty thrusts of swords, and some of pikes in his buff coat, which being an extraordinary good one was no peirced.

When this happen'd, Móns^r. de Turenne was newly gone to his quarter, having been all night upon the line; and had no sooner the alarm, but he went immediatly and commanded all the foot of his quarter to march down towards the work. His own regiment was the first that march'd, and he commanded them to regain the outwork. They presently went on in the face of both Armys, all of which were either spectators of that

A daring action performed by the Reg^t of Turenne in regaining the outwork.
OR: MEM:
p: 1: p: 112.

action, or ingaged in it; and without any manner of diversion, or so much as one Cañon shott to favour them, they came up to the attack, having only before them some commanded men of their number, who had been beaten out, led by a Captain of Picardy; but he being kill'd in marching up, his men ran away and carryd along with them some part of the right wing of Musketeers of M^r. de Turenne's regiment: Notwithstanding which discouragments, and the continuall fire which was made at them both from the work and the wall of the Town, they march'd on without firing one single shott; the Captains them-

selves taking the Colours in their hands, and marching with
them at the head of their Soldiers till they were advanced to the
work; which was crowded with men as thick as they could
stand by one another ; and then at one instant pour'd in their
shott, and came up to push of pike with so much gallantry
and resolution, that they beat out the Enemy, and lodg'd themselves upon the work. All this they perform'd with the loss of
only one Captain of the regiment, and one or two more inferior
Officers, not many of the private Soldiers falling. And indeed
it was a wonder to observe that so small a number drop'd as
they were marching up, considering that there was not one
shott made on the beseigers' side to oblige the Enemy to keep
down their heads one moment; so that they had their full
leasure to take aime, and it being then dry weather, from the
line one could easily discerne their shott beating up the dust,
as thick almost as hail, amongst the commanded men as they
went on: It was universally confess'd by all who were then
present that they never saw so daring an Action. Mons‌ʳ. de
Turenne himself, and the most experienced officers of the Army,
were all of opinion, That it had been impossible for them to have
done so much, if their Colours had not been always in their
view. And this Action was partly the occasion that the
regiments afterwards made them new Colours; for both the
old regiments, and others, had taken an ill kind of pride in
having their Colours tatter'd out, and worn so bare, that there
was almost nothing to be seen but the Ensigne staff: the
regiment of Turenne being the only one which had any visible
Colours, not excepting the French Guards themselves.

One would have reasonably (*thought*) that after this, both
partys shou'd have been quiet for the remaining part of the
day, but it prov'd otherwise; for the Enemy remembring how
easily they had beaten the Royalists out of the work in the
morning, and withall being sensible of what importance it was

PART
I.

1652.
The beseiged
sally out and
attack the
lines.
Or: Mem:
P: 1: p: 116.

to them, resolv'd on making an attempt to regain it: To which
end, about two or three of the clock in the afternoon, they sallyd
out with twenty squadrons of horse, and five battaillons of
foot, resolving at the same time to attack the line, and dislodge
the Royalists who were in the outwork. Mr de Turenne, who
happen'd to be upon the line at that instant, seeing them come
out both with horse and foot, sent to command all the troopes
to their severall posts, and order'd all the foot which was
remaining in the quarter to come immediatly to the place
where he was in person; and farther, to gain time, commanded
one of the three squadrons, which were then upon the guard,
to go out of the line, and charge the first body of the Enemy
which was coming up. These orders were with great bravery
executed by the Count de Renel who commanded that squadron;
but the men being overpower'd, were beaten into their lines;
Some of them and of their horses were kill'd in the ditch of the
line; others even within the line itself, which (as we have
hinted) was so inconsiderable, that they who could no enter by
the avenue (for it cou'd not be well call'd a bariere, because
the Country affoorded not wood enough to make one) leap'd
over the line, and very few of them fell into the ditch by leaping
short. The Count de Schomberg who was then but a volonteer
with the Duke of York, was shott through the right arm by an
officer of the Enemys, as he was standing in the avenue.

Schomberg
wounded.
Or: Mem:
P: 1: p: 118.

The Duke
advances up
with M^r de
Turenne to
the avenue.
Ibid.

At the same time when Mareschall de Turenne sent out this
body of horse to charge, he advanced up to the avenue with
the two remaining squadrons and the Duke with him, beleeving
the Enemy would endeavour to press in there. The Mareschall
and those who were with him were now in a very uneasy
posture, the body of horse which had been commanded out
being beaten in; no troopes coming up to their releif; the
Enemy advancing against them with three battalions of foot
and severall squadrons of their horse, some of which were

already within pistoll-shott of the line,.and expecting only the coming up of their foot, which were within half muskett shott of them, and were still advancing. To resist all these Monsr. de Turenne at that instant had only two squadrons of horse, and here and there a foot Country (*centry*) on the line ; which rather shew'd the Enemy the weaknes of those they had to deal with, then to do them any considerable harm ; not one of the Cañoniers was on the battery which was upon the line, so that the Enemy receiv'd not a shott from the great guns: and besides all this, M. de Turennes party had no hope of any considerable body of foot, which could be with them soon enough for their releif ; for the action of the morning had drawn most of them to the Orleans' suburbs : In the mean time the Enemy advancing still, was come so near, that the Duke had not time so much as to a light and put on his armour, but was forced to get it put on as he sat a horseback on a pad, which he had not time to change thō his charging horse stood ready by him.

In this condition they were, when there came to their assistance about two hundred Musketeers of the regiment of Guards, which was the whole number that could be pick'd up from all the quarter. These coming to the line, receiv'd command from Monsr. de Turenne not to mind so much the firing alltogather, as to be sure to take good aime, which accordingly they did, and to so good purpose that it was beleev'd never so small a body of men did so great execution ; for at their first Volly they so clear'd the first three squadrons of the Enemy, and there fell so many of their officers as well as troopers, that the second firing oblig'd them to draw farther off, they being at that time within the distance of pistoll-shott of the line ; and then M^r. de Turenne's musketeers plyd the Enemys foot who were still advancing towards the line ; but (very fortunatly for the Royalists) as they were coming up, they found a bank which cover'd them all but their heads from shott ; and when they

had once receiv'd the benefit of this shelter, it was no longer
in the power of their officers to make them stirr, or to advance
one foot forward; thō they were seen from the line using their
uttmost endeavours both by cutting them, and advancing themselves to encourage them by their own example; but it was
all to no purpose: So they stop'd there, and only fir'd on the
Royalists at that distance; had they not happen'd on that
shelter, in all probability they had gone fair to beat Monsʳ de
Turenne's small party from the line; but by this time the
horse of the other quarter were coming up to their releif, so
that now the Enemy began to think of making their retreat.

While this Action continued, where M. de Turenne was in
person, the other body of the Enemy which went towards the
outwork, had no better success then their companions; for
having farther to march then those who attacked the line, the
Royalists on that side had more leisure to put themselves in a
posture of receiving them; and Monsᵗ. de Tracy, who com-
mánded the German horse which were in the seruice of the
King of France, having the alarm at his quarter, and hearing
that the Enemy attaqued Mʳ. de Turenne's, in stead of coming
within the line, thought it better to go between the line and
the Town; which succeeded very happily, for by that means
he met those of the Enemy who were going to attack the outwork: And thō he had but four squadrons with him, and
consequently was much outnumber'd by them, yet he charg'd
them so vigourously that he put them to a stand, which gave
time to more troopes to come up to his assistance, commanded
by the Marquis de Richelieu; Thus reinforced, they gave another
charge, and constrain'd the Enemy to retire in great disorder;
but this second push being under the shott of the Town, the
Royalists thought it too hazardous to pursue them.

That party of the Enemy which was ingag'd with Mʳ. de
Turenne, being stop'd (as is above related) they began to retire,

and, now seeing that other party beaten, drew off more speedily then they had come on. By this time the greatest part of the beseiger's forces were come to the line, and severall of the officers were very urgent with M^r. de Turenne to fall out and pursue them; but he thought it not convenient, telling them, if he should do it the success could be of no great importance, the Enemy being so near the place of their retreat; so that it would only expose their men to the shott of the Enemy from the Town, and to be forced back in disorder. Thus the Enemy drew in again, having receiv'd a very considerable loss especially of officers, wher of about sixty fell upon the place.

After this unsuccessfull attempt, the beseiged were contented to live more quietly by the beseigers, and troubled them no more with any great sallies. But the beseigers for their parts press'd hard upon them at the Orleans-gate, and from the outwork which they had taken from them; and they had at last made such progress, that they had log'd their Miner in the wall of the Town, when they receiv'd advice that Monsieur de Lorraine was marching with all imaginable expedition towards Paris, and that they were preparing for him a bridge of boats to pass over the Seyne a litle above Charenton; which oblig'd M^r. de Turenne to think of raising the Seige, to prevent his being inclosed between the Enemys two Armys.

And to that purpose the Royall Army began to draw off their great guns from the nearest batterys; but they were so ill provided with teames to draw their cañon and amunition, that the Court was necessitated to send them all their coach-horses, those even of the King and Queen not excepted; and with all this shifting, they were yet so ill furnish'd, that they were forced to send off one half, the day before they left the Town, and to bring back the horses on the next day to draw off the remaining part of their Artillery.

PART I.

1652.

The Miner log'd in the wall of the Town. Or: Mem: P: 1: p: 126. The Duke of Lorraine's march obliges M. de Turenne to raise the Seige of Etampes. *Ibid.*

PART
I.

1652.
They raise the
Seige in great
order, June 7.
Ibid. p: 127.

On the 7th of June early in the morning, the Royall Army being then in battell, they began to withdraw their men from the outwork which they had taken; which was perform'd in great order by M^r. de Navailles, who commanded in that post, thō the Enemy press'd hard upon him; and so soon as he was come up, the Army began to march, at the same time setting fire on their hutts: And indeed it was perform'd with so much regularity, that it afforded a pleasing kind of object; for while the first line stood their ground, the second march'd off about twice twelve score, and then drew up again, facing towards the Town; After which the first line went also off with a slow motion, the Enemy in great numbers coming out to skirmish and firing on them, till they pass'd betwixt the intervalls of the second line; and when they had march'd off the same distance, which the other line had done before, they halted again, and fac'd about, at which time the other line began to move. After this slow but orderly manner, they retreated about a league, and then seeing no considerable attempt was made on them, they march'd away directly to Etrechy, where they continued but two or three days, and then drew off farther from Etampes to a village call'd Ytterville towards Corbeil, and from thence to Balancourt; where having notice that the Duke of Lorraine was come to Villeneuve St Georges with his Army, M^r. de Turenne resolv'd to make a sudden march and fall on him before he could joyn the Army that was left behind at Etampes; nor was this impracticable, for besides that he had the conveniency of passing the Seyne at Corbeil where there was a garrison of the King's, and where his Army could leave their bagage with security.

M. de Turenne
marches to
Villeneuve S^t
Georges, where
he surprises
the Duke of
Lorraine.
Or: Mem:
P: 1: p: 131.

Accordingly he march'd early in the morning on the 14th, passing over the River as he had design'd at Corbeil, from whence he march'd directly towards Villeneuve St Georges; and his march was so well order'd and perform'd with so much

diligence, that the first intelligence the Enemy had of him,
was the unexpected appearance of his whole Army before
them.

It was in the beginning of the afternoon when the two Armys came in sight of one another; but M[r]. de Turenne found he could not possibly attack the Enemy on that side, they being cover'd by a brook, which coming from Brie falls at that place into the Seyne; So that without losing any time, he march'd up along the brook till he found a passage over it, continuing his march all night and leaving great woods on his left hand. About break of day the Van of his Army was arrived at Grosbois which is within litle more then a league of Villeneuve S[t] Georges.

At that time he had a message sent him from the Duke of Lorraine, which was brought by Mons[r]. Beaujeu, who had been imployd to that Duke from the Cardinall, they two having all along kept the negociation on foot betwixt them; M[r]. Dagecourt Captain of the Guards to the Duke of Lorraine, accompagn'd the messenger of the Cardinall; and brought propositions from him; the first of which was to desire Mons[r]. de Turenne not to advance neerer him; after which, he gave the Duke of York and M[r]. de Turenne an account of the King of England's being with the Duke of Lorraine, and that his Majesty was come to that Duke's quarter the night before, upon the same business of an accommodation. M[r]. de Turenne having weigh'd the matter, desir'd his Royall Highness to go immediatly to Villeneuve S[t] Georges, to which he was easily dispos'd, because the King his Brother had sent him word that he desir'd to speak with him; The Duke therfore went, and had Monsieur de Lorraine's honour ingag'd for his return: But notwithstanding this beginning of a Treaty, M[r]. de Turenne's Army continued still to march, and would not be hinder'd by the artificiall delays of the Duke of Lorraine.

He receives at Grosbois a message from the Duke of Lorraine. *Ibid.* p: 132.

The Duke sent to Villeneuve S[t] Georges with proposalls to the Duke of Lorraine. On Mem: P: 1: p: 133.

1652.
The King of
England at
theConference
with the Duke
of Lorraine,
and the
motives
thereof.
Ibid. p: 134.

But that it may not be wonder'd at, on what occasion the King of England took upon him this mediation, and came concerning it to that Duke, the Reader is to know, That his Majesty being at Paris receiv'd a letter from Monsieur de Lorraine, in which he gave him an account of his being in treaty with the Court of France, and that the business was drawing so neer an amicable conclusion, that he accounted it as good as done; That therfore he desir'd his Ma^ty to give himself the trouble of coming to him, to finish all, and become his guar-rantee, as also to carry him to the Court which was then at Melun. The King upon the receipt of this letter, went imme-diatly to Chaillot, where the Queen his Mother then was, to acquaint her with the affaire, and advise with her what was fitt for him to do on that occasion. Her Ma^ty was of opinion that the King should not go, saying, she knew the Duke was unsincere, and intended only to act over again some of his old deceits; in which case it was not adviseable for the King to be security for him, who was not much accustom'd to keep his word. But the inclination his Ma^ty had to be instrumentall in an affaire which would be of so great advantage to the Court, prevail'd upon him beyond all other considerations: Having taken this resolution, to lose no time, he took coach immediatly, not so much as staying to change his cloths, and went to Villeneuve St Georges, taking with him the Lord Rochester, Lord Jermyn, and Lord Crofts; when he was got as far as Charen-ton, he met the news of the two Armys being in presence of each other, as also a farther request from the Duke of Lorraine that he would hasten to him. Being arrived at Villeneuve St Georges, he found M^r. de Beaujeau with that Duke, who was imployd from the Court to negociate the Treaty. He also observ'd, that Monsieur de Lorraine was extreamly discompos'd and apprehensive of the neighbourhood of Monsr. de Turenne's Army.

Presently after the King's coming, the foremention'd Enuoyé and the Captain of the Guards, were dispatch'd away with the Duke's propositions to M^r. de Turenne, which found him near Grosbois as has been already said. But it not being yet certain what might be the issue of the Treaty, the Duke prepar'd to receive the Royall Army in case they should attack him, posting himself with all the advantages which the ground affoorded him; and working very hard all night on five redouts with which he cover'd his front, he had finished them in the morning.

PART
I.

1652.

The Duke of
Lorraine
posted at
Villeneuve S^t
Georges with
all the advan-
tages the
ground could
affoord.
OR: MEM:
P: 1: p: 137.

His Army consisted of about five thousand horse, and three thousand foot, with a small train of Artillery, and he drew up his forces in this following manner ; he placed the greatest part of his foot in those redouts above mention'd, keeping one great battalion 'for a reserve behind the midlemost redout, having most of his cañon placed upon a height by the gallows just above the Town ; his horse was drawen up in two lines behind the redouts, his right hand was cover'd by a great wood, and his left by the Town and the ascent from it ; which was so extreamly steep that it was impossible to approach him that way, or to do him any prejudice, so that they could only attack him on his Front.

He drew up
his forces in
excellent
order. Ibid.

Being drawn up in this excellent order, by which (to do him no more then common right) he shew'd himself a great and experienced Commander, he stood prepar'd for what might follow, either an attack of the Royall Army or an accommodation by way of Treaty.

When the Duke came to Villeneuve St Georges, he went directly to wait on the King his Brother, who told his Royall Highness the occasion of his being there, and then desir'd him to use his best endeavours that the Treaty might succeed, by which his Ma^{ty} might be disingaged from so perplexing an affaire ; for supposing that no effect should follow from these

The Duke
arrives at
Villeneuve S^t
Georges.
OR: MEM:
P: 1: p: 139.

overtures, but that the two Armys should come to an ingagement, the King was very much put to it how he should behave
himself: It was not consisting with his reputation, when there
was a suddain prospect of a battell, to withdraw without having
his share in the honour of it; but which side he was to take,
was a matter of no slight consideration: He had been sent for
by the Duke of Lorraine to assist him in his Treaty with the
Court; he had particular obligations to him, and was then in
his quarter where he had lodg'd all night: On the other side,
he was at that very time under the protection of the King of
France, and, by his permission, in his Country; besides which,
he had a pension from him, which in that juncture was the only
visible support he had: But the consideration which press'd
him most was, that in fighting for the Duke of Lorraine, he
manifestly appear'd in the quarrell of Rebells against their
Lawfull Soveraign, and even to continue long in his quarters
for that very reason look'd not well, and yet he knew not
handsomly how to leave him.

His Majesty therfore ask'd the Duke, what were the propositions which he brought from Monsr. de Turenne? to which
his R. Highness answer'd, that in short they were these following: That the Duke of Lorraine should immediatly cease
working at the bridge of boats over the Seyne; that he should
ingage himself to march out of France within the space of
fifteen days, and at the same time oblige his word that he
would never more assist the Princes; And as to the first article
concerning the bridge, that he had brought an officer Monsr.
Varenne by name, who was commission'd to go and see it put
in execution; without which preliminary Monsr. de Turenne
was resolv'd not to proceed upon any of the rest. When the
Duke had given this account to the King, his Ma^{ty} told him,
that he fear'd the Duke of Lorraine wou'd never be brought to
sign any such proposalls, knowing what he had promis'd to the

M. de Tu-
renne's pro-
posalls to the
Duke of
Lorraine
brought by
the Duke.
On: Mem:
P: 1: p: 141.

Princes at Paris; To which the Duke replyd, That it must then
be decided by the sword; for he was well assur'd that M^r. de
Turenne wou'd not chang his mind. Immediatly after this,
Monsieur de Lorraine came in to the room, to whom the Duke
deliver'd what he had in charge; he receiv'd the message in his
ordinary way of raillery, but his Royall Highness cou'd easily
perceive that what was naturall to him at another time, was now
extreamly forced. As to the first proposall of laying aside his
working at the bridge, he answer'd that he was content, and
immediatly sent an officer of his own in company of M^r. de
Varenne, to forbid the farther prosecution of it; but as to the
others, he protested that he could never be induced to make so
dishonourable conditions. Whereupon his Royall Highness
ask'd him, if he shou'd carry back that answer? to which the
Duke of Lorraine replyd, that he could give him no other. But
because Monsieur de Lorraine thought that the Duke was more
inclin'd to see the two Armys ingaged, then that the business
shou'd end peaceably, he desir'd the King to send the Lord
Jermyn back along with his R. Highness, to try if he cou'd
perswade M^r. de Turenne to more reasonable termes.

While this negociation was carrying on, Monsr. de Turenne
lost no time, but advanced with all imaginable speed; so that
when the Duke and Lord Jermyn were come to him, the Army
was all in battell within less then a league of the Enemys posts,
and marching on as fast as their present posture would allow.
The Duke deliver'd Monsieur de Lorraine's answer, and the The Duke returns to M^r. de Turenne and delivers the Duke of Lorraine's answer. Or: Mem: P: 1: p: 145.
Lord Jermyn urg'd all the arguments, and us'd all the per-
swasions he could invent, to incline M^r. de Turenne not to insist
so rigourously on his propositions; but he was not able to
prevaile for any part of them to be released: wherupon he
return'd to let the Duke of Lorraine know the result of the
affaire.

Lord Jermyn was very desirous that the Duke would have

PART
I.

1652.

The Duke
refuses to
return back
with Lord
Jermyn to the
Duke of
Lorraine's
Army.
Ibid. p: 146.

return'd with him, as hoping by that means to have gain'd some longer time, and supposing that M^r. de Turenne would not begin his attack till the Duke was come back with a finall answer; But his R. Highness absolutly refus'd to go, assuring him, that M^r. de Turenne could never be capable of committing so great an oversight as the loss of so much time, because he well knew, that the Army of Etampes must be already on their march, and would infallibly appear very suddenly on the other side of the River; that upon this consideration the Duke was almost certain that the Armys would be ingag'd before he could come back. His Royall Highness further added, that his presence would be no inducement to the Duke of Lorraine to finish the agreement, but that the advance of the Royall Army might be a more prevailing motiue to hasten the conclusion of the Treaty. With this reply Lord Jermyn went his way, and the Army continu'd to march forward; so that they were already

The King of
England
comes to M^r.
Turenne's
Army, and
makes a last
attempt for an
accomodation.
Or: Mem:
P: 1: p: 147.

come within canon-shott of the Enemy, when the King himself came to Monsieur de Turenne to make the last attempt on his resolution but M. de Turenne begg'd his pardon for insisting still on the same conditions which he had sent, and added, that he knew his Ma^{ty} had so much concernment for his King, as not to press him on any change of his proposalls.

The Armys were then so very near that every moment of time was precious, and therfore the King desired Monsr. de Turenne that he would send for the last time to the Duke of Lorraine; to which he consented, and Monsr. de Gadagne was commission'd to him with the former termes in writing, and order to tell Monsieur de Lorraine, that he must immediatly signe them, or he would give the signall for the fight. When M^r. de Gadagne came up to the Duke of Lorraine, he found him by the gallows, where some of his cañon were placed; and having read the paper, he call'd out to the canoneers to fire, for by that time the Army was advanced very near them; but it seems

the canoneers were privatly better instructed then to obey, for
they did not do it; and Monsr. de Gadagne plainly told the
Duke of Lorraine, that they durst not; once more assuring him,
that he must either sign, or expect instantly to be attack'd.
Wherupon Monsr. de Lorraine sign'd the Treaty, and M^r. de The Duke of Lorraine signs the Treaty. Or: Mem. P: 1: p: 149.
Gadagne brought it back: The effect of which was what
has been already mention'd, That the Duke of Lorraine should
march immediatly away, and be out of the French Dominions
within the space of fifteen days, with a solemn ingagement
never afterwards to assist the Princes.

So soon as Monsr. de Turenne receiv'd it, he commanded
his Army to make a halt, and sent to demand hostages for the
performance of the Treaty; with all requiring that the Duke of
Lorraine should immediatly begin his march. All was done
accordingly: The Count de Ligneville Lieu^t. Generall of his
horse, and Monsr. Dagecourt Captain of guards, were sent as
pledges, who were to be return'd so soon as Monsr. de Vaubecourt
(who was order'd to march along with Monsieur de Lorraine on
Monsr. de Turenne's party) should send word that he was out
of the French Dominions. The King of England after the The King of England returns to Paris. Ibid. p: 150.
paper had been brought back and ratifyd, came to see M^r. de
Turenne's Army, after which he return'd to the Duke of
Lorraine, and taking his leave of him went back to Paris.

Whilst this Treaty was transacting, Monsr. de Beaufort the
great favorite of the populace at Paris, was in the Duke of
Lorraine's Camp, having with him five hundred horse, which he
had brought out of that City. These his troopes were by the
Articles permitted to return to Paris, but no mention was made
of him their Commander: when he saw the paper of agreement
in this manner sign'd, he doubted of his own security, and being
unwilling to trust to the courtesy of Monsr. de Turenne, he
took a trumpetter along with him, and passing the River at
Villeneuve St Georges, he posted away to Paris; where, at his

PART
I.

1652.
The Duke of
Beaufort
inflames the
people of Paris
against the
King of
England.
Or: Mem:
P. 1: p. 151.

arrivall, he inflam'd the people against the King of England, by suggesting to them with much malice, that it was by the per-swasions of his Ma.^ty, that Monsr. de Lorraine had made the Treaty; whereas in truth if he was instrumentall in it, it was at the desire of the Duke of Lorraine, who pressed him for his assistance in bringing matters to an accommodation: But these insinuations wrought so farr upon the multitude, that it might haue being of dangerous consequence to the King; In so much that both he and the Queen his Mother, were obliged for their security to leave the Town in as privat a manner as they could, and go to St Germain's, till the rage of the Rabble was in some sorte abated.

The Duke of
Lorraine in
execution of
the Treaty
begins his
march home-
wards.
Or: Mem:
P: 1. p. 154.

After the King of England was departed from Villeneuve St Georges the two Generalls met, and some few cold compliments having pass'd between them, each returned to his own Army; Monsr. de Lorraine began to march away, Monsr de Turenne's Army in the mean time standing still as they were drawn up in battell. Monsr. de Lorraine, with his forces on their way homewards, pass'd through a long and narrow défilé in view of the Royalists, and very near them, so that they were all abso-lutly at Monsr. de Turenne's mercy, if he had not been a more faithful obseruer of his word then Monsr. de Lorraine. His troopes had no sooner enter'd that narrow passage or défilé, when the Army of the Princes, marching from Etampes, began to appear on the other side of the Seyne; which, upon notice of what had pass'd, in stead of coming towards Monsr. de Turenne's Army (*continued*) their march to Paris.

M.^r. de Turenne
leaves Ville-
neuve S.^t
Georges and
marches to
la Cheurette
near St Denis
where the
Court then
lay the 1.st of
July.
Ibid. p. 152.

Monsr. de Turenne remain'd for some few days at Villeneuve St Georges, and departing thence the 21 of June, by small marches he came to Lagny, and there past the Marne on the 1.st of July, camping at a Village by the Seyne called la Chen-rette, about a league from St Denis where the Court then lay. In one of these mention'd marches at a place called Gorges,

Monsr. de Turenne was joyn'd by the Mareschall de la Ferté, who reinforced the King's Army with the troopes he had brought from his government of Lorraine, consisting of three or four Regiments of horse and two regiments of foot.

In the mean time the Princes' Army which came out of Etampes in hope of joyning with Monsr. de Lorraine, being frustrate of that expectation and not in a condition of keeping the feild against Monsr. de Turenne, lay near St Cloud behind the Seyne; so that now M^r. de Turenne having no other Enemy upon his hands, was resolv'd to ingage with them upon almost any terms, and accordingly the same day that he arrived with the King's Army at la Cheurette, he began to make bridges over the Seyne, which could not suddenly be perform'd, the River being very broad in that place; and least the Enemy should interrupt the work, the two regiments of la Ferté's foot were commanded over into an Island, at the point of which it was intended to pass the Army over the bridge; and the situation of the place was so favorable to the Royalists and so disadvantageous to the Enemy, whose side of the River was the lower ground, that they durst not adventure to dispute the passage, or to hinder the progress of the bridge.

Tis true, they made a shew of disturbing the Royalists at first, and with that intention had lodg'd about a hundred foot behind a bank on the other side of the River, having also drawen up severall squadrons of horse at some distance behind their foot; but their horse were soon dislodg'd by the King's Cannon, which playing furiously upon them, they were forced to withdraw beyond reach of gun-shott; their foot still remaining upon their post, as judging themselves to be in security; but the event shew'd they were mistaken, for one la Fuitte, (*Fitte*) Major to M^r. de la Ferté's regiment of horse, a Very daring man and an active Officer, having found a place in the River, where the going in had good footing at the bottom, and

PART
I.

1652.
M^r. de la Ferté joyns M^r. de Turenne at Gorges.
Ibid. p. 153.
The Princes' Army which came from Etampes lay near St Cloud behind the Seyne.
OB: MEM:
P. 1. p. 157.
M^r. de Turenne begins to make bridges over the Seyne in order to attack the Princes' Army.
Ibid. p. 153, and 158.

where he could see the going out at the other side was as secure,
propos'd to swimm over with fifty horse, and cutt off those foot
of the Enemy, which lay pelting at the workmen. His proposition was accepted, and his attempt succeeded: for before the
Enemys horse (which were with drawn to a distance) could
come up with him to the rescue of their fellows, he cutt off
the hundred foot; and such of them as were not slain, he brought
over in boat, and swamm back in safety with his horse, not
having lost one man in the action. After this, the workmen
carryd on the bridge without any further interruption: but
least the Enemy might make a more vigourous attempt the
next morning to hinder the passage of the Army, severall of
the smallest feild-pieces, with more men, were Sent into the
Island, where the two regiments of la Ferté's foot were allready
lodg'd, with orders to make a work for their better security.

The P^{ce} of
Condédecamps
from St Cloud
and marches
towards
Charenton.
O$_R$: M$_{EM}$:
P. 1. p. 155
and 160.

In the mean time the Prince of Condé who was then incamp'd
at St Cloud with the main body of his Army, considering that
it would be very difficult for his men, who were on the lower
side of the River, to hinder the passage of the King's Army who
were on the higher ground, and that probably their bridge
would be finished next day, thought it best for him no longer
to remain in that post, but leave them a free passage. And
being very doubtfull whither the Town of Paris would receive him
with his troopes, in case he should be driven to a necessity, he
marched away in the dusk of the evening towards Charenton,
and pass'd his troopes over the bridge of St Cloud, with design
to place himself behind the River of Marne, where it would have
been very difficult for the Royall Army to have perform'd any
thing against him. To expedite his passage at St Cloud, he
had likeways prepar'd a bridge of boats, over which he past his
foot, at the same time that his horse were marching over the
bridge of the Town, so that in a short space his whole Army,
togather with his cañon, baggage and ammunition, were in

safety on the other side. Then he march'd through the Bois de Boulogne, and came to the gate of Paris called De la Conférence, where entrance being refused him by the Parisians, he took his march quite round the City, according to the resolution he had taken, in case he were not admitted; his design now being to get to Charenton, and pass over the Marne there, where being betwixt the Seyne and the Marne, he could better defend himself, then where he was before incamp'd.

Intelligence of all this was immediatly brought to Mon^r. de Turenne, by a Messenger sent on purpose to him from some favourers of the King's Party in the Town, who because the gates were shutt, were forced to let him down in a basket over the wall. At the first notice of the news, the King's troopes were order'd to begin their march; and the Mareschall himself gallop'd before to St Denis (by which place the Army was to pass) that he might conferr with the Cardinal on what was next to be put in execution. It was concluded betwixt them, to use all possible diligence to attack the Prince of Condé before he could secure his troopes in Charenton. This being resolved, the Mareschall rejoyn'd his Van, just as they were come up to St Denis, and hasten'd their march, without making any stay either for ye cañon, or for the Mareschall de la Ferté's foot, which were all past over that night into the Island in two ferry boats; so that if the Army had halted till these had joyn'd them, they had undoubtedly lost the opportunity.

Marching therfore with all expedition possible, as they came to la Chapelle they perceived the Rear Guard of the Enemy, wherupon Monsr. de Turenne himself advanced a litle before his troopes to observe their posture; and finding that to favour their retreat, they had put some musketeers into certain wind mills, and other litle houses which were at the entry of the fauxbourg St Denis, he caus'd some of his own commanded

PART I.

1652.

Intelligence sent to M^r. de Turenne from the favourers of the King's Perty in Paris. OR; MEM: P. 1. p. 161.

Tis resolved to attack the Prince of Condé before he reach'd Charenton. Ibid. p. 162.

M^r. de Turenne marching with all expedition discovers the Enemys Rear and attacks them at the entry of the fauxbourg St Denis. OR: MEM: P. 1. p. 162.

foot to advance against them, who in a moment beat out the
Enemys foot from those places, and made way for the King's
horse to charge their Rear-guard in the very street of the
fauxbourg. The Enemy receiv'd the charge with resolution
enough, but at length were routed, many of their officers being
either kill'd or taken, of which latter sort was one M^r. Des-
marais a Mareschall de Camp who commanded them, and who
after having receiv'd some wounds was made prisonner, as also
the Count de Choiseüil a Captain of horse. On the King's
side not any officer of quality was wounded, excepting Monsr.
Lisbourg Lieutenant Collonel of Streff, which was the regiment
that charg'd, who was shott through the body.

After this Encounter which succeeded so happily, the
Royalists advanced and press'd the Princes men so hard, that
they got up to charge them again close by the hopital of S^t
Louis; where they also routed the remaining part of the
Enemys Rear-guard which consisted of betwixt two and three
hundred horse, and had for a good while the execution of them,
taking or killing most of their officers and soldiers before they
could reach the body of their Army, which was then retiring

The P^{ce} of
Condé not
able to reach
Charenton is
forced to draw
in the faux-
bourg S^t
Antoine.
Or: Mem:
P. 1. p. 165.

into the fauxbourg St Antoine: For M^r. le Prince of Condé
finding how hard M^r. de Turenne press'd upon him, and that
it was imposible for him to reach Charenton, was resolv'd on
playing the best of a bad game; and to that purpose drew into
the fauxbourg afore mention'd, where there were very strong
retrenchments already made by the inhabitants for their own
security, during the Civill War: Without this casuall remedy
the Prince and all his Army had infallibly been lost; for it was
all he cou'd perform, to distribute his men to their severall
posts before they were attacked; So that if the barricades in
the street had not been ready made, he had been surprised in
a defenceless posture. So soon as M^r. de Turenne came up to
the main body of the Enemy, which (as has been said) was

drawing into the great street of the fauxbourg St Antoine, he was forced to a sudden stop, for his Van only was there, and he could not make another charge upon the Enemy without his foot, which was not yet come up to him; so that he saw them draw in before him without being able to hinder it, for want of Infantry.

By this time, the King, Cardinal and all the Court were come to Charonne (where there is a hill which overlookes all those fauxbourgs) to be Spectators of the remaining Action.

So soon therefore as the foot was come up, they dispatch'd a messenger to Mr de Turenne, with orders for him to fall on; thō neither the Cañon was come nor M^r. de la Ferté's foot, neither had his men any tooles but their hands to help them in breaking or pulling down the garden-walls and barricades; and thō M^r. de Turenne desired them by the messenger to haue patience for a litle time, since it was impossible for the Enemy to escape, unless the Parisians open'd their gates to them (which the Court beleeved they would not do, having assurance from the well-affected in the City to the contrary) and withall told them, that the Prince of Condé could neither add any new retrenchments to those which he had found already made, nor any way better his condition, by the King's Army stayin for their cañon, and tooles, without which it would be difficult to force the Enemy, or indeed to perform any thing against him, considering the strength of the barricades, and garden-walls; adding also that in case he should receive a check, it might be the loss of the whole enterprise, which could not possibly miscarry, when his troopes should be provided of what they wanted, and had the assistance of their Cañon; yet such was the eagernes or rather blind precipitation of the Court, that by new Messages they still press'd the Mareschall to an attack; and even Monsr. de Boüillon himself, who was but newly reconciled in the beginning of that Campagne to Cardinal

The Court at Charone spectators of the action of the fauxbourg St Antoine. OR: MEM: P. 1. p. 166.

Precipitation of the Court pressing M^r. de Turenne to fall on. OR: MEM: P. 1. p. 168.

PART
I.
1652.

Mazarin, was more urgent then any man with his Brother the Mareschall de Turenne; being of opinion, that it was better to follow that rash advice, then to expose himself to the censure of some about the King, who might be apt to say, That he deferr'd the attack in favour of the Prince of Condé : thō if former passages between the Prince and the Mareschall had been well consider'd, it would have been found, that the Prince had disobliged him beyond any possibility of reconciliation : But Mons'. de Turenne was not yet so well establish'd in the opinion of the Court, nor his Integrity so thorowly known, that he durst hazard it by refusing to act against their orders, thō they were contrary to his own judgment; neither durst he assume so much to his own Conduct and Experience, as afterwards he did on severall occasions.

Account of
the famous
Action of the
barricades of
the fauxbourg
S' Antoine.
Ibid. p. 169.
The first bar-
ricade attack'd
and carryd
w'ᵗʰ great
bravery by the
french Guards
and the
Marine
Regim'. *Ibid.*

Being therefore thus overswayd, he prepared to attack the barricades: the French Guards, and the Marine Regiment, seconded by the King's own Gens d'armes and Chenaux-legers, on the right hand of all the rest, attacked the first barricade of a narrow street which opens into the great street of the fauxbourg S' Antoine, just where it joynes upon the market place. The success was answerable to the bravery of the undertaking, for notwithstanding that the houses and walls on both sides of the street were crowded with defendants, yet they beat the Enemy from the barricade, and drove them from before them from house to house. But this prosperous beginning was ren-

M. de S'
Maigrin
advancing
the horse with
too much heat
and precipita-
tion, rashly
pursues the
Enemy to the
market place
where the
Prince of
Condé was.
Oʀ: Mᴇᴍ: |
P. 1. p. 169.

der'd ineffectuall by the heat and rash ambition of the Marquis de S' Maigrin, who commanded the Gens d'armes and the Chenaux-legers; for he, seeing the good success of the foot whom he was to second, and desirous of his share in the honour of the action, press'd on with great precipitation through the midst of the foot, in that strait passage of the street, not haning the patience to suffer them to finish their work of dislodging the Enemy from all the houses as they went along, but still pur-

suing those who fled even almost to the market place, he came
up at last to the place where the Prince of Condé was in person;
The Prince, observing the fault committed by the King's horse,
and resolving not to lose his opportunity, went himself at the
head of five and twenty officers and volonteers, who were next
him, and vigourously charg'd them in the narrow street, whilst
at the same time those of his foot, who were not yet driven out
of houses next him, fir'd upon them from the windows on both
sides of the street ; so that the foremost of those led on by
Maigrin, being thus furiously charg'd in the front, and pelted
in the flancks, were in a moment either kill'd or wounded :
wherupon the rest of that body of horse immediatly ran, and
were not only routed themselves, but carryd along with them
the foot who were in the street; and those of them who were
in the houses on either side, observing what had happen'd to
their fellows in the street, got out of doors as fast as they were
able, every man shifting for himself by flying : The Enemys
foot at the sight of this, recovering courage, pursu'd them
eargerly, and regain'd not only all the street, but all the ground
to the very last barricade; which was made good by Monsieur
de Turenne himself, who was come thither, and without whose
presence even that also had been lost.

In this unfortunat attempt, the King's Party did not only
lose many officers and persons of quality, as S‍ᵗ Maigrin, the
Marquis de Nantoüillet, and severall other kill'd upon the
place, but many also who dyd of their wounds afterwards,
amongst whom was Monsʳ. de Manchini the Cardinal's nephew,
a gallant youth of great hope and expectation, and Fouillou
ensigne of the Queen's guards, with many others. And which
was of worse consequence, the two Regimᵗˢ of root imploy'd in
this attack were so ill handled, that they were not in a condition
of doing any farther seruice for some hours after ; and all that

P A R T
I.

1652.
The Prince of
Condé at yᵉ
head of 25
Officers and
Volonteers,
charges Sᵗ
Maigrin, and
recovers all
the ground
the Royalists
had gain'd.
Ibid. p. 170.

Mʳ.deTurenne
in person
makes good
the last barri-
cade.
Oʀ: Mᴇᴍ:
P. 1. p. 171.

Sᵗ Maigrin,
Nantouillet,
Manchini and
Fouilloukill'd.
Ibid.

could be epected from them, was only to maintain the barricade which they had wonn, and which was now their post.

At the same time when this attack began, the foot Regiment of Turenne made another upon some houses and gardens possessed by the Enemy more on the left hand ; and on their left hand again, two other Regiments of foot, Vxelle (*d'Uxelles*) and Carignan, now form'd into one battaillion, storm'd a guarden wall next adjoining to the great street of the fauxbourg. When the Regim^t of Turenne fell on, they had warm seruice, and gain'd severall gardens and houses from the Enemy ; but they, seeing what had befallen their next neighbours on the right hand, adventur'd not to make any further impression, but only maintain'd what they had taken.

The Regim^t of Turenne gain severall houses and gardens.
Or: Mem:
P. 1. p. 172.

And here must not be ommitted a passage, which appear'd to be very extraordinary ; There was a squadron of horse compos'd out of the Regim^ts of Clare and Richelieu which was order'd to second the battallion of Turenne ; As these men were marching up behind the battallion of foot, they receiv'd a smart volley of shott in their flanck, which was powr'd on them from a neighbouring wall; they had a considerable loss of men by it, and were put into such a disorder, that they absolutly ran ; which their Officers seeing, did their duty with great resolution, and coming up to the foremost, stop'd them ; and in a moment put them in order again, and march'd up to the post appointed: After which it was observ'd, that never men acted with more bravery then they did, and continued so to do for the remainder of the day. This particular deserues the rather to be remarked, because 'tis very seldom known, when Soldiers have been once frighten'd so as to run, that they have ever perform'd any good action the same day. The seruice was so hott, that no one Captain of the whole squadron escap'd from being either kill'd, or dangerously hurt. Of the Regiment of Richelieu there remain'd not one alive, saving only the Captain Lieu-

A squadron of horse appointed to sustain the Regim^t of Turenne, first run, but then recovering their fright, no men after that did better.
Ibid. p. 173.

Very hott Seruice at this attack.
Or: Mem:
P. 1. p. 174.

tenant who was call'd la Loge, a very gallant man ; and he also was shott with a muskett through the body, of which he afterwards recover'd.

PART
I.
1652.

About the same time when these began their attack, Vxelles and Carignan began theirs also in the wall above mention'd : While they were marching up, the Lieutenant Collonels of both regiments were kill'd, which yet occasion'd no stop in the battallion ; for they went on directly to the wall, the Enemy all the while plying them with their shott as thick as haile, neither stayd they till they had placed themselves under it betwixt the holes which the Enemy had made in it. Being lodged there, a new mañer of fight began, there being only the wall between the two Partys, for not being able on either side to do any great execution with their musketts, they heav'd massy stonnes against each other over the wall, shott their pistolls through the holes, and thrust their swords through the cranies; one party endeavouring to maintain possession, and the other to make them quitt it.

The Battaillion of Vxelles and Carig'an storme a garden wall near the barricade of the great Street. *Ibid.*

This unusuall way of Combat lasted long, because the Royalists wanted tooles and iron-cro's to break down the wall. The horse which were appointed to second those foot, were drawn up over against the great street, just out of reach of muskett shott, to prevent the Enemy from sallying out from the Barricade, and from falling on the foot who were imployd in attacking the wall. As for the Barricade itself, it was not thought expedient to attack it, for they judg'd it impossible to carry it, because it was so commanded by the houses of which the Enemy were possest in front of it, that it was not to be attempted without first mastering them.

And now the remaining part of the foot commanded by Monsr. de Navailles, and consisting of the Regiments of Picardy, Plessis-Praslin, Douglas, and Bellecense, attacked another Barricade which was more down ward to the River,

M.deNavailles with the rest of the King's foot attack a Barricade, cross the Street near the garden of Rambouillet, and gain it. OR MEM: P. 1. p: 176.

PART
I.

1652.

and a cross the street of that fauxbourg, which is in the way
to Charenton near the garden of Ramboüillet; and after some
resistance gain'd it, dislodging the Enemy from the houses
round about it: When they were masters of it, they contented
themselves with maintaining their possession, and thought it
not expedient to press the Enemy any further, because they
had found that behind this Barricade there was a large open
place where the Enemy had drawn up a party of their horse,
and behind that also were garden walls and houses filled with
foot, so that nothing was to be undertaken rashly against such
a strength. But as it had not been prudence in them to attempt
farther, so on the other side the Enemy thought it not convenient to expose that body of horse to no purpose, and therefore
began to draw them off behind those houses and gardens that

Mr. de Clin-
villiers passing
through the
Barricade to
charge the
Enemy with
his horse, is
routed and
taken pri-
soner.
OR: MEM:
P. I. p. 177.

were in their possession: Which being observ'd by Mons'. de
Clinvilliers a Mareschall de Camp who commanded the King's
horse upon that post, and he mistaking that retreat for a plain
flight, march'd hastily through the Barricade which he had
gain'd to charge them with his horse, but the Enemy perceiving
that he could not pass but with two a brest, a party of their
horse weeld immediatly about, and charg'd him before he cou'd
draw up in order, half his men being yet unpass'd; making use
of this advantage they routed his men, and took him prisoner,
severall of his Officers and Soldiers were slain, and the rest were
driuen headlong by the Enemy through the Barricade; having
clear'd their place they retir'd on a round trott, the King's foot
in the mean time playing hard upon him.

The King's
cannon being
come up, are
planted at the
wind-mills,
from whence
playing down
the great
Street they
do terrible
execution.

By this time some of the cannon was come up with Mr. de
la Ferté's two Regiments of foot; The foot was immediatly
order'd to releeve the Guards and the Marine Regimt which had
been so cruelly shatter'd, and to make good the posts which had
there been taken; And the cannon (which were but six pieces)
were carryd to the wind mills, which were within less then
muskett-shott of the mouth of the great Street; down which

passage they began to play very furiously, and did terrible execution as could be plainly seen, the Street being full of men and baggage; but it was clear'd almost in an instant, and then they began to batter the houses which commanded the passage to the Barricade: They were only of slight materialls, and such as we call paper-buildings, so that every shott went through and through; and yet they were maintain'd with so much resolution by the defendents, that the Royalists were not able to dislodge them with their great guns, For they continued firing out of the windows and through the very holes which the Cannon had bor'd.

WHILE this Seruice lasted in that place, peales of thick and furious shooting were heard down at the Barricade where Mons'. de Navailles commanded. Whereupon Mons'. de Turenne gallop'd where the noise call'd him, but before his arriuall, the engagement was at an end; thō for the time it lasted it was exceeding eager. The occasion of it, as the *M. de Beaufort who had* Duke was since inform'd by some who were then in the Seruice *not been yet ingag'd, en-* of the Princes, and ingaged in that very action, was this; Mons'. *deavours to regain the* de Beaufort having been almost all the morning in harangueing *Barricade gain'd by M.* of the people of Paris, and endeavouring to perswad them to *de Navailles.* open their gates to the Prince of Condé and his troopes, when *OR: MEM:* *P. 1. p. 179.* he found that he was not able to prevaile, came out of the Citty, and having been informed what hot Seruice there had been, and how bravely the Prince and those persons of quality who were about him had behav'd themselves (for they came not out till after S' Maigrin was kill'd) was all on fire with emulation and resolv'd on doing something as remarkable. He *M'. de Beaufort's pro-* therfore propos'd to Mons'. de Nemours (with whom he had a *posall accept-* *ed by M'. de* quarrell then depending) that they shou'd endeavour to regain *Nemours, and* *all the other* the Barricade gain'd by M'. de Navailles, as an action of the *persons of* *quality in the* greatest importance to their party. The proposition bein as *P⁰ᵉ of Condé's* *party. Ibid.*

PART
I.

1652.

The Barricade
is attacked
with great
bravery and
resolution,and
as vigourously
defended.
Ibid. p. 180.

M*. de Ne-
mours has one
of his fingers
shott, as he
had his hand
upon the Bar-
ricade, and
M*. de Roche-
foucault is
shott throw
both the eyes.
OR: MEM:
P. 1. p. 180.

A remarkable
accident con-
cerning M*. de
Flamarin who
was kill'd at
this attack.
Ibid. p. 181.

readily embraced as it was offer'd, they put it in immediat execution, and were follow'd by all the persons of quality who
were in a condition of Seruice, for many of the bravest amongst
them had in the former part of the action been kill'd or disabled.

These two then putting themselves at the head of a good
body of foot march'd on with great resolution and bravery to
attack the Barricade, which was very strongly guarded; for
behind it was the Regiment of Picardy, and on each hand of
it, in the passage of the Enemy. was a house, in one of which
was Plessis-Praslin and in the other Douglas, so that they must
march betwixt those houses before they cou'd come to the
Barricade; which they perform'd, notwithstanding all the shott
which was made as thick as the Royalists could fire at them
as they pass'd over the open place without stopping till they
came up to the Barricade itself, but there they found so
vigourous a resistance, that it was impossible for them to master
it ; they were beaten off with considerable loss, many persons
of quality hurt and killed, Mons*. de Nemours was wounded
in severall places, and one of his fingers shott from his hand as
it was upon the Barricade, Mons*. de la Rochefoucault was
shott in at the corner of one eye, the bullet coming out under
the other, so that he was in danger of loosing both, Mons* de
Guitaud (*was*) shott into the body, and severall others.

Amongst many who were kill'd was Mons* de Flamarin, whom
we cannot but mention particularly for this remarkable accident : He had been foretold by some of those cantin fellows who
gott their living by fortune telling, That he shou'd be hang'd,
the phrase in french is, That he should dy, *la corde au col*, that
is with a halter about his neck ; a kind of death which no gentleman ever suffers in that Country, the ordinary way of executing any of the Noblesse, or persons of quality, being by
beheading. Yet this unfortunate gentleman ended his days

exactly according to the prediction: for falling by a shott, and being left for dead, close by one of the two houses formerly mention'd that were before the Barricade, one of the men that were in these houses seeing him ly so near them, and observing that he was richly cloth'd, withall beleeving according to appearance that his pockets were as richly lin'd, had a great longing to strip and search him; but some of the Enemys being lodged in the neighbouring houses, and behind the walls of that open place which commanded the ground where this dying gentleman lay amongst many other bodys, for which reason they durst not venture out to rifle them; at length they bethought themselves of an invention to draw him to them; for having gotten a rope they made a nooze at one end of it, put it over his head with their pikes, and so drag'd him into the house then just expiring; thus the prophecy was literally full--fill'd.

But to return to our relation: Monsr. de Turenne coming to the place and finding the Enemy repuls'd, seeing also that the post was in a good condition, return'd to the wind mills where his cañon were planted at the upper head of the great street; and observing that the Enemy still maintain'd their houses before the Barricade on the left hand, as well as the garden walls on the right, commanded some of the horsemen to alight (all the foot being already employd in the attack) and to assault the houses by a back way, which one had discover'd, and which was left unguarded. This was perform'd with that extraordinary valour, that not one of the Enemies escaped who were lodged in those houses, all of them being either kill'd or taken, their number was above a hundred persons.

Just when the King's horsemen began this attack, the two Regiments of foot which had been so long against the garden wall on the right hand of the Barricade, began to get the mastery of some of those holes which the Enemy had defended

PART
I.

1652.

The houses before the great Barricade holding out still, M^r. de Turenne commands some horsemen to alight and assault them by a back way; they gain the houses and kill above 100 persons. Or: Mem: P. 1. p. 183.

The garden wall in the right hand of ye Barricade, after having held out so long, is at last master'd by the Royalists, who make here a terrible execution on the Enemy. Or: Mem: P. 1. p. 183.

P A R T
I.

1652.

with so much obstinacy, they had now made them wider with their hands for want of other tooles ; which the Enemy perceiving, and well knowing that the intention of the Royalists was to force their passage into the garden through the gap which they were endeavouring to make, they immediatly abandon'd the whole wall, thō they had a·squadron of horse to second them in the garden ; which the Royalists perceiving; plyd them so hard, that the horse following the example of the foot began to run.   In that place they receiv'd a considerable losse, for there being but one outlet from the garden for their escape, and every man striving tó be formost in that fearfull hurry of horse and foot, they so crowded each other, that they chock'd the breach and stuck together in a lump; while the Royalists pouring their shott upon their backs made a terrible execution of them, and presently breaking down the wall, forced their passage into the garden : which being beheld with great amazement by their fellows who were posted at the great Barricade, and the Royalists begiñing to fire at them at the same time from the houses on the other side, they were seiz'd with such fear, that they drew off, and abandon'd it.

The Enemy
abandon the
great Barricade.
OR: MEM:
P. I. p. 185.

The Royalists tooke immediate possession of it, but pursued not the Enemy ; for it was then resolved to make a generall attack on all sides.   In order to which all necessary preparations were making, and a breathing time given to the men, who indeed had need of it, for they had undergone intollerable toyle, and fought with great earnestness all the fore part of the day ; which, besides the heat of the action, was one of the most soulty (that) was ever felt.   All things being now ready for the generall attack, and so disposed that in all probability the King's party should have gain'd an intire Victory, the signall being given, which was the firing of three cannon, the Royalists began their attack.   Monsʳ. de la Ferté was posted on the right hand of the great street, and Monsieur de Turenne

A generall
attack
resolved.
Ibid. 184.

The signall
given and the
attack begun.
Ibid. 185.

on the left, who advancing with a strong party both of horse and foot, resolved to fall on at a new place, more inclining to the left hand, where he hop'd he should not meet with such good Barricades, it being near the Bastille: But when he approached the place, and was just ready to attack it, the Bastille began to fire their cannon at the Royalists, which surpriz'd them not a litle, having flatter'd themselves with other hopes, and having had assurances from within, that Paris would only stand neuter and not permitt the Army of the Princes to save themselves within their walls. This made Monsr. de Turenne instantly suspect what he found immediatly after to be true, which was, That they had open'd their gates to the Princes, and receiv'd their forces; for when their Barricades were attacked, they made no countenance of defending them, but only retreated in good order from their Severall posts, leaving only some few men at each of them, all the rest of their troopes being alredy drawn in to the Town; and those small partys which were left, as the Royalists aduanced upon them, drew off also, and were pursued by them to the very gate of the Town. The King's Generalls seeing how the Enemy had sav'd themselves, were of opinion that there was nothing remaining for the Army to do but to march back to their baggage, which was left behind at la Chevrette just by St Denis, and there to refresh their men.

This was accordingly perform'd, carrying with them their wounded men, which were in great numbers, as it must needs have happen'd where the seruice was so long and so very hott. There were kill'd upon the place as near as cou'd be computed about eight or nine hundred of the Royalists, amongst whom (*were*) many officers of note and persons of condition; as the Marquis de St Maigrin, who was a Mareschall de Camp, if not Lieutenant Generall, thō at thattime he only acted as Lieu-tenant of the Cheuaux-legers, three or four Lieutenant Collonels

PART I.

1652.

The Bastille fire their cannon at the Royalists and Paris opens its gates to the Prince of Condé'sArmy, which is hereby sav'd from an entire defeat.
Ibid.

The King's Army march back to la Chevrette.
Or: Mem: P. I. p. 186.

8 or 900 of the Royalists kill'd in this action.
Ibid.

PART
I.

1652.

of foot and many Captains, besides other inferiour Officers and Volonteers: They had also many Officers and people of quality wounded, as Mons'. Mancini the Cardinall's nephew, whom wee have already mention'd, who was shott through the thigh, Fouilleaux ensigne of the Queen's guards shott through the body, and Mons'. de Mespas an old Mareschall de Camp hurt in the foot, all which besides many others dyd afterwards of their wowns; the Count d'Estrées Mareschall de Camp, Pertuixt Lieutenant of the guards to Monsieur de Turenne, Lisbourg Lieutenant Collonel to Stres (*Streff*) and the Cheualier de Neuville; this and divers others were likewise wounded, but they recover'd of their hurts. Monsieur de Turenne himself was very much expos'd that day, and so was consequently his R. Highness the Duke who accompanied this great Generall all along, and hazarded his person where ever he was; but thō it was his R. Highness good fortune to receive no hurt himself in this days' warm action, yet Collonel Worden one of the Grooms of his bedchamber who was obliged still to be near him, got a considerable wound.

Of the Enemy were kill'd upwards of a thousand, amongst whom were great numbers of Officers and men of quality, there being scarce one of their considerable Officers that was not either kill'd or wounded, except the Prince of Condé, the Prince of Tarante, and the Duke of Beaufort: It has been affirm'd by many who were well acquainted with the Prince of Condé, that he never perform'd the part of a Generall or a Soldier better then in that action, nor ever expos'd his person to greater hazards then that day, And truely it was his only vigour which preserv'd his Army from utter ruine in the very beginning of it. And the Prince himself has since confess'd to his R. Highness the Duke, that he was never so long expos'd to danger as he then was. And that which added the greatest lustre to the Prince's reputation was that he was attacked by

M'. deTurenne
exposes him-
self very much.
The Duke
accompanys
him all along.
Coll. Worden
one of y'
Duke's grooms
of his bed
chamber and
obliged still
to be near him,
is wounded.
OR: MEM.
P. 1. p: 187.
Above 1000
men kill'd on
the P'' of
Condé's side.
Ibid. 188.

The P'' of
Condé never
so much
expos'd nor so
long as he was
this day.
OR: MEM:
P. 1. p: 188.

Monsr. de Turenne, whom all men must acknowledge to haue been the greatest Captain of the Age, and equall to the greatest of any former times: It been (*being*) most evident that in all this War, he not only perform'd the part of a great Commander, but that he sav'd the Crown of France by his Counsell as well as by his Conduct, as will yet more manifestly apper hereafter in the following Relation.

P A R T I.
1652.

In the mean time it will be expected, that an Account should be given in what manner and by whose means the Army of the Princes was admitted into Paris, and what was the managin in the Town, while the two Armys were fighting in the faux-bourg. It has been already said, that the City had refus'd the Princes' Army leave to march through it, when they came to the porte de la Conférence, thō the Prince himself and all his freinds within had endeavour'd it to the utmost of their power: for those of the Loyall Party in the Town made use of this maine Argument, That thō they were indeed against the Car-dinal, and wish'd his ruine, yet it was unworthy of the Parisians, as they were good Frenchmen, to suffer an Army, partly compos'd of Spanis troopes, and the greatest number of whose Officers were either Subjects to that King, or in his pay, to enter within their walls; That they knew not what disorders might arise from so unwarrantable an Action, or what com-motions it might cause in the people, when they beheld so unusuall a sight, as the Cross of Burgundy flying up and down their streets, which they were only accustomed to see hanging in their Churches; That it would look as if they had already submitted to the Spanish Yoke, to see so many red Scarfes strutting in the midst of Paris, where they were never seen in that provoking number since the Rebellion of the Holy League; In fine, that it was the intrest of Paris, as well as of all other great Cities, not to admitt an Army under whatsoever specious pretext. These and many other reasons so prevail'd, that the

How the Princes' Army came to be admitted into Paris.
Ibid. p. 189.

Town continued firme in the resolution of shutting their gates against the Princes' Army. But when the fight already was begun, the Prince sent Mons'. de Beaufort thither to press them once more; since there could be no other retreat for him, and that he must infallibly be lost, if they persisted to refuse him entrance. But all that Mons'. de Beaufort could urge was to no purpose; the Royalists who were within so vigourously opposing it. As for the Duke of Orleans he was so far from attempting to harangue the people in his behalf, that he stood ashtonish'd at the danger, and was so throughly frighted, that he commanded the gates of his pallace to be shutt, and his Coaches in a readiness at a back door of the gard (*gardens*) to carry him to Orleans, as giving all for lost at Paris: But his daughter Madmoiselle shew'd herself of a more masculine temper; she consider'd, that if the gates were not open'd to the Prince, and that with speed, both himself and his troopes must be cutt in pieces, and consequently their whole party ruin'd: She therfor went to the Hotel de Ville, where they were gather'd together, and spoke to the Magistracy of the Town, being attended to the place by a great Rabble; so that with her arguments and their clamours, which were mix'd with threatnings, she oblig'd the Mareschall de l'Hôpital and the Prevôt of the Marchands, to give order to the Captains of the Burgers who commanded at the Porte St Antoine, to let in the Princes' Army: She herself carryd this order to the gate and saw it executed, which when she had done, she went immediatly into the Bastille and commanded them to discharge their cañon against the King's troopes just as they were beginning their generall attack. In this manner the Prince of Condé and all his Army were preserv'd by the courage and dexterity of that Princesse.

Mademoiselle
obliges the
Mareschall de
l'Hopital and
Provost des
Marchands to
give order to
open the
Porte S^t
Antoine and
let in the
Princes'Army.
Or: Mem:
P. 1. p. 192.
She sees her-
self the order
executed, and
the Cañon of
the Bastille
discharg'd.
Or: Mem:
P. 1. p. 193.

This business of the faùxbourg was scarce over, when there happen'd a very great disorder in the Town: It was on the

4ᵗʰ of July two days after the attack, when a Councill was assembled at the Hotel de Ville, with an intention of procuring the Duke of Orleans to be declar'd Lieutenant Generall of France, and of uniting themselves inseparably to obtain the removall and banishment of Cardinal Mazarin out of the French Territories, of chusing the Duke of Beaufort Governour of Paris in the place of the Mareschall de l'Hôpital, and of removing le Tabure from being Prevôt des Marchands, whose room was to be supplyd by Broussel ; and this Assembly, by which they hop'd to have establish'd their party, prov'd to be one of their cheif causes of their ruine, by so violent a combustion, as was likely to have been fatal to all the Members of that Councill, and to have made the Prince of Condé losse all the benefitt of what had pass'd at the fauxbourg Sᵗ Antoine. Wee cannot say that he was author of so pernicious a design, which every one who has been tax'd with it has equally denyd and shifted it from himself upon some other ; but whosoever was the promotter of it, this is certain, that while the Councill was thus sitting, there came a confused multitude compos'd of men of all sorts and conditions, with weapons in their hands, crying out, That they would not only have all things settled according to the direction and pleasure of the Prince of Condé, but demanded also to have instantly delivered to them such as were either Vulgary accounted, or but suspected to be friends to Cardinal Mazarin, and seeing their clamour did not prevaile they began with great violence to force the Town house ; and because the Mareschall de l'Hôpital with some other resolute men endeavour'd to maintain it against them, they set fire on the gates, and shott in at the windows, so that many were slain within the house, and severall who chose rather to trust the Rabble with their lives, then to run the hazard of the flames, venturing out amongst that furious multitude, were barbarously murder'd; and the blindness of their rage was such, that they

P A R T
I.

1652.
A great commotion in Paris, wherof the Pᶜᵉ of Condé was suspected to be the author.
Ibid. p. 194.

made no manner of distinction betwixt those who held for the Royall party, and those who were of their own, but dispatch'd them in a general massacre. It has been since observ'd that more of the popular faction fell, then of the Loyall. The whole weight of this commotion and all that ensued of it, fell upon the Prince of Condé; no body looking on the Duke of Orleans, as to haue had least hand in it. And this disorder was follow'd by an accident, which thō not altogether so considerable, yet was greatly prejudiciall to their party. It was the death of the Duke of Nemours who was kill'd in duell by the Duke of Beaufort, they having for a long time born a mortall hatred to each other, thō they wer Brothers in law.

The Duke of Nemours kill'd by the Duke of Beaufort in a duell. OR: MEM: P. 1. p. 197.

While these things pass'd about Paris, the Spaniards made good use of their opportunity; for having taken the feild early, that Campagne they regain'd many of those places which they had lost in former years, and that without much difficulty, both in Flanders and els where, there being no Army to oppose their progress.

The Spaniards prepare to march into France with 25000 men. Ibid. p. 197.

And it was thought that at the solicitation of the Princes, the Arch Duke prepar'd to march into France in the beginning of July with his whole Army, which consisted of five and twenty thousand men or upwards of that number. On the intimation of this news the Court of France which still continu'd at Sᵗ Denis was exceedingly alarm'd, and enter'd into consultation what was expedient for the King to do having so small an Army.

Upon this news it is resolved that both Court and Army should march within two days to Lyons. Ibid.

At length it was resolved that both Court and Army should march away for Lyons within two days, and it was then about the middle of July.

The same evening that this resolution had been taken in Councill, Monsieur de Turenne went to Sᵗ Denis and the Duke was with him; they went straight to Monsʳ. de Bouillons lodging, to learn from him what the result of that debate had been, before they went to Court. Monsʳ. de Bouillon told the

Mareschall what had been resolved concerning the Court, and
the Armys march to Lyons, and added, that he thought they
could not in prudence fix on any other resolution. Withall he
related to him the arguments which had been us'd on that Sub-
jcct; and which had determin'd the Councill on that course.
They were these following, That there was no other place but
Lyons where the King's person could be in safety, that being
the only great Town which would receive him ; That the Spanish Army was actually marching into France which the King's
Army was no ways able to resist; That the Court and Army
remaining where they were, shou'd be inclos'd betwixt the
Spaniards and Paris; That so long as the person of the King
was safe, their condition was not desperate, but if he shou'd
once fall into the hands of the Spaniards, or the Princes, there
was no further hope remaining for the Loyall Party ; That
Lyons was a place from whence they might make head against
any Enemy, all the adjoining Country being intirely at the
King's devotion; for which and other reasons he thought it y°
best and only advice which could be taken.

To which Mons.ᵣ de Turenne answer'd his Brother, If this be
done, we are absolutely ruin'd without any prospect of recovery ;
for if once the King marches as far as Lyons, he may take it
for granted that all the frontier Townes, with those of Picardy,
Champagne and Lorraine, and others on that side of the
Country, which now hold for him, seeing themselves abandon'd
by him, will make their conditions either with the Spaniard or
with the Princes, after which both will be at leisure to deal
with him ; and who knows what thoughts such a posture of
affaires will put into the heads of people, even to canton or
divide the whole, at least that part of the Kingdom which they
haue in their possession ; and when they haue once settled all
behind them, they will undoubtedly march after us, and increasing in strength as we decrease both in that and in reputation,

PART
I.

1652.
Mons.ʳ de
Turenne go's
to the Court
at Sᵗ Denis
and the Duke
with him.
Oʀ: Mᴇᴍ:
p. 1. p: 198.

M. de
Turenne's
reasons
against the
journy to
Lyons.
Oʀ: Mᴇᴍ:
P: 1. p: 199.

will never suffer us to live in quiet, but drive us perhaps as far
as Italy. Besides these he gave many other convincing reasons
against that resolution, and at length concluded, it was his own
opinion, that the Court in stead of retiring to Lyons, shou'd go
to Pontoise (it being a strong post) with the guards that ordi-
narily attended them ; neither was there any probability that
such attempts wou'd be made from the Parisians, who still
seem'd to preserve a kind of reverence for their King : In the
mean time he with the Army wou'd advance towards Compiegne to observe the motion of the Spaniard, and hop'd by the
favour of that Town and the Rivers which were near it, to secure
himself against them, and if not to frustrate their designs, at
least to render them more difficult ; and besides he was confident
that the Spaniards who are jealous and overcautious people,
seeing him advance towards them, wou'd be apt to refine upon
his proceeding, and imagine he wou'd never venture it without
good grounds for such a daring ; that is, unless some private
Treaty were on foot betwixt the Princes and the Court, which
their former experience of the French genius had taught them
to expect, and wou'd be no new thing if it shou'd now
happen.

Having convinced his Brother by these reasons, they went
together to the Cardinal, and argued the design with him ; who
weighing the strength of what they urg'd, on second thoughts
enter'd at length into their reasons, and was brought over to
their opinion. In this manner the journy to Lyons which had
been fixed to a day, was on the suddain wholly layd aside. And
on the 17th of July the Court mov'd to Pontoise, and the Army
march'd towards Compiegne, camping under the walls of it on
the third day after they sett out. In the mean time the Spanish
Army was still advancing towards them, and was as far on their
way as Chaunay. Into which place the Duke d'Elbeuf had
very inconsideratly put himself with seven or eight hundred

Cardinal
Mazarin con-
vinced by Mr.
de Turenne's
reasons, and
the journy to
Lyons is
alter'd. The
Court moves
to Pontoise
and the Army
marches to
Compiegne.
OR MEM:
P. I. p. 201.

horse, which he gather'd out of his government of Picardy; and order'd his affaires so very ill, that when he thought to haue march'd out upon sight of the body of the Spanish Army, he found a party of theirs had possess'd themselves of a pass at a small distance from the Town, which cutt off his retreat, so that he was forced to continue where he was, and take his fortune. In short, having no foot but only of the Burgers, and the Town it self being too weak to be maintain'd, he was driven to capitulate after two days Seige, with conditions to yeeld up the place, and his troopes to march out on foot, leaving their horses behind them to the Enemy.

After this accident, it is not certainly known for what reason, whither for that which Monsr. de Turenne had guessed, or for some other, the Spanish Army advanced no further into the Country ; After they had taken Chauny, they did not so much as put a garrison into it, nor lay Seige to any other Town in those quarters, where no opposition could haue been made, but contented themselves with staying for some time in France, and eating up the Country; only it was conjectur'd, that they thought it more their business to recover what they had lost in Flanders, then to push for any thing so far in France, looking on the Princes and their Party as strong enough to resist the King, especially with such troopes as they could send to their assistance: But if they should have made the Rebells an over match for the King's Army, then by consequence the King must have absolutly submitted to the Princes, or fallen into their hands; by which means the whole force of France being then united, they should soon have been forced to quitt their hold, and lose what so ever they had gain'd within the body of the Country, which was too far from Flanders to be succour'd. And besides they fear'd that grasping at the shaddow there, they might forfeyt the opportunity of regaining what they had lost at home.

The Duke d'Elbeuf wth 800 horse in Chauny, forced to surrender the place to the Spaniards, leaving his horses behind him.
OR. MEM.
P. I. p. 202.

PART
I.

1652.
The Spanish
Army returns
into Flanders,
leaving y^e
Duke of
Lorraine on
the frontiers
to assist the
Princes.
Or: Mem:
P. 1. p. 203.
The King's
Army returns
towards Paris,
The Duke
still moving
with it. Ibid.
The Princes'
Army keeps
under the
walls of Paris.
Or: Mem:
P. 1. p. 203.

Whither these were their reasons can not be positively said, but certain it is, that they acted as if they were; for having devour'd the product of the Country where they lay, not long afterwards they return'd into Flanders, and recover'd many of their Towns in those Provinces, leaving the Duke of Lorraine with his own troopes on the frontiers to be ready to assist the Princes, if occasion were, with a detachment out of their own Army commanded by the Duke of Wirtemberg.

When the body of the Spanish Army was out of France, the King's Army return'd towards Paris, the Duke still moving with it, as he did during all this long, fatiguing and dangerous Campagne. All this time the Army of the Princes lay under the walls of Paris, not being strong enough to ingage with the Royall Army; and besides they were apprehensive in case they should leave the Town, the King's party which were within it and were now increasing every day, would at length prevaile; the fury of the people beginning already to decline, and their eyes being somewhat open, so that in spight of their seducers they began to See how much they had been deluded, and had thoughts of returning to their duty. To which they were the more encouraged, because Cardinal Mazarin about that time

Cardinal
Mazarin
withdraws.
Ibid. p. 204.

withdrew out of the French Territorys; for so soon as the Court was come to Pontoise, he prepar'd for his retreat as a thing most necessary for his own concernments, and very much conducing to the King's intrest: Since by his departure, the maine pretence of the Rebellion was taken away, and the eye sore of the people removed out of their sight; neither by thus absenting himself, was he the farther from being restor'd in case the affaires of his Ma^ty went better, being assured that he might

The Queen
of France a
Princesse of
great firmness
and constancy.
Ibid.

rely on the Queen's inviolable firmness to him: for not only the Cardinal but all the world was satisfied, that when she had once given her word, her constancy was never to be shaken, she being certainly a Princesse of so firme a Soul; and so unal-

terable in her resolution, as hardly any age has shewn her equal,
none her superiour; of which she has given innumerable
proofs.

Some indeed were of opinion, that the Cardinal had run a
great hazard of not being recall'd, if Mons'. de Bouillon had
liv'd longer; beleeving that he, who was a man so knowing and
of so great capacity, having his Brother Monsieur de Turenne
at the head of the King's Army, might have playd his game so
dexterously as to haue made himself first Minister: But whither
he or the Mareschall had any such designs can not well be
determin'd. This is undoubted, that only they two in all the
Court were capable of undertaking and menaging an affaire of
so high a nature. However it were, the death of the Duke of
Bouillon put an end both to those discourses, and to the apprehension of any such alterations.

But to returne to the affaires of the Army: After the Spaniards'
returne into Flanders, Mons'. de Turenne (as had been said)
march'd back towards Paris. It was about the beginning of
August, when the Army were as far on their way as Tillay,
within a league of Gonesse where they continued till about the
end of the same month; it being a proper post for the Mareschall, as well to observe from thence the motion of the Princes'
Army which remain'd still on the other side of Paris, as to ly
betwixt them and any succours which might be sent them from
the Spaniards. During his residence in those quarters, he had
notice that the Duke of Lorraine was once more advancing The Duke of
Lorraine
with all his forces, which were reinforced with divers of the enters once
more into
Spanish troopes under the command of the Duke of Wirtem- France.
Or: Mem:
berg, by the way of Champagne and Brie, with an intention P. 1. p. 205.
to joyn the Princes' Army. This intelligence caus'd Mons'. de
Turenne to march towards the Marne, and in his way having
further notice of their approache, he pass'd that River at
Lagny, and advanced as far as St Germain a small Village

PART
I.

1652.

about three leagues distant from that Town, and near Cressy en Brie.

Being come thither, he receiv'd orders from the Court not to attempt any thing upon the Duke of Lorraine, nor to stirr from that place till farther orders, unless the Duke of Lorraine should march on towards Paris from the quarters where he then lay: In which case he should use his best endeavours to hinder him from joining with the Princes. This command from Court was grounded on a Treaty which Monsr. de Lorraine was then concluding with them, and had sent his Secretary for that purpose; promising in the mean time to keep his station without advancing any further, till either all things were adjusted or the Treaty broken off. But according to his wonted manner of proceeding, he enter'd into it only to amuse the Court, hoping by those dilatory artifices to gain the opportunity of slipping by Monsr. de Turenne, and either to get into Paris, or to meet the Princes in his way to it, without hazarding a battell. And had not Monsr. de Turenne trusted him less, and known him better then the Court, he had then certainly compass'd his design. For the Court being deluded by his faire pretences of an accommodation, had given leave to his Secretary at his return from Pontoise, to enjoyne Monsr. de Turenne not to stirr from his post, and to acquaint him with the progress of the Treaty; which he had no sooner done, and passing on to his master had given him notice of it, then that Prince; quite contrary to his ingagment, began to march, hoping to pass by the King's Army and come to Villeneuve St Georges, before they could have intelligence of his moving, or be in a condition of hindering him. And here can not (*be*) ommitted a particular answer, which Monsr. de Turenne made to that Secretary, which was, That the promises of Monsieur de Lorraine, and just nothing, were the same thing to him. In pursuance of what he had said, and to justify his own opinion

The Duke of Lorraine amuses the Court with a Treaty, while he endeavours to slipp by M^r.deTurenne and get to Paris, or joyne the Princes' Army.
Ibid. p. 206.

The Court deluded by M^r. de Lorraine's artifices, enjoyns M^r.deTurenne not to stirr from his post.
OR: MEM: P: 1. p: 206.

of Monsr. de Lorraine's sincerity, he resolved to march the
very next day, which was the 5th of September, to Brie-Comte
Robert, that he might be more in the way of opposing M. de
Lorraine's designs, in case he should march as he beleev'd he
wou'd, and, according to his custome, break his word. Upon
which occasion Monsr. de Turenne was heard say, That thō
his orders from Court were positive not to leave his post, yet
being morally certain that the Duke of Lorraine intended to
deceive them, and knowing that it was for his Master's intrests
that he shou'd march, he thought it better to venture his head
by disobeying those orders, then by following them to let
Monsieur de Lorraine gaine his post and pass by him.

Monsr. de
Turenne
chuses rather
to venture
his head by
disobeying the
Court's orders,
then by fol-
lowing them
to let M^r. de
Lorraine
gaine his
point.
OR: MEM:
P. 1. p. 209.

Accordingly he began his march next morning, and Sent his
quartermasters away before him to marke out the quarters at
the foremention'd place, where they mett with M^r. de Lorraine's quartermasters, who were come to the same Town on
the same errand ; he being himself on his march already, and
intending to lodge there that night ; The Mareschall's quartermasters immediatly return'd to bring him the news of it, and
found him with the Van of the Army which had newly pass'd
a défilé. Monsr. de Turenne without loosing a moment's
time, sent presently notice of it to the Mareschall de la Ferté,
whose turn it was that day to have the Reer, and desir'd him
withall to come and speak with him, that they might resolve
betwixt themselves what was instantly to be put in execution ;
And because M^r. de la Ferté came not so soon as he expected,
he went back leaving his troopes drawn up where they were,
and met him at the défilé : wherupon having conferred together a litle time, they alter'd their resolutions of going to
Brie-Comte Robert, and resolved to march directly to Villeneuve
St Georges, which was a post of great importance : And M^r.
de Turenne, to delay no time, march'd thitherwards with his
horse at a round rate, ordering his foot and Cañon to come

M. de Turenne
and M. de
Lorraine's
quarter-
masters meet
at Brie Comte
Robert.
Ibid. p. 208.

Mr de Turenne
resolves with
M^r. de la
Ferté to march
to Villeneuve
St Georges.
OR: MEM:
P. 1. p: 208.

P A R T
I.

1652.

after him with all possible expedition; and desiring M^r. de la
Ferté to use the like, being very apprehensive least the Duke
of Lorraine, who knew as well as himself the advantages of that
post, shou'd get there before him : for he was confident that
upon the Intelligence which his quartermasters brought him,
he would also change his resolution of lodging at Brie, and
endeavour to possess himself of Villeneuve St Georges.

Neither was the Mareschall de Turenne deceived in his conjecture, for the Duke so soon as he had notice of the Royalists'
march, continu'd his own to Villeneuve St Georges, so that both
Armys march'd with all imaginable speed, to prevent each other
in the first possession of that place, having the brook or River
of Yerre betwixt them; And thō the Royalists us'd their utmost
diligence, yet the Van of the Enemy were already in the Town
before they came up to it, and Monsr. de Lorraine thought himself so secure of that post, that he wrott a letter to the Prince of
Condé, and dated it from thence to give him assurance of his
being there. Which particular his R. Highness the Duke happen'd afterwards to know, from the very Officer that carryd the
letter, and who in his return from Paris was taken by some of
M^r. de Turenne's men. The news of the Royall Army being
there, was so surprising to this Messenger, that he could scarcely
beleeve himself to be in their hands, till he was brought to M^r.
de Turenne, to whom he confessed in presence of his R. Highness
what is here related.

M^r. de
Lorraine's
Van gets
before them
to Villeneuve
St Georges,
but is driven
out of that
post by M^r.
de Turenne.
Or: Mem:
P. 1. p. 210.

Had not the advantage of the ground been on Monsr. de
Turenne's Side, the Duke of Lorraine had undoubtedly maintain'd that post : But thō he had just gotten the start, and was
enter'd into the Town with his Van, and that some of his
troopes had already pass'd the Yerre, which at that place falls
into the Seyne, yet M^r. de Turenne coming with his Van upon
the hill, which both overlooks and commands the Town and
Rivers, drove the Enemy out of the place, and possest himself

òf the bridge over the Yerre which is adjoining to the Town's
end ; the Duke of Lorraine's Army being at the same time so
near, that they fir'd with their cañon at the first squadrons of
the King's horse, which appear'd on the top of the hill. So
that in effect the Royalists gain'd that post, not only by the
diligence of their march, but allso by the advantage which they
received from the higher ground. As for the foot and cañon
they came not up till the very close of the Evening.

The Enemy, seeing that the Royalists were possess'd of that
post which they had intended for themselves, went and incamped about half a league from them, over against a litle
Castle call'd Ablon which stands on the Seyne, about half a
league from the Town up the River ; and within a day or two
afterwards, the Prince of Condé march'd from Paris with all his
troopes, and joyn'd him there, having pass'd over both his horse
and foot in two or three large boats which he found accidentally
on the River.

When the Enemys two Armys wer thus in conjunction,
they thought themselves secure of Victory, having thrust the
King's Army into a narrow nooke, as it might be call'd, betwixt
the Yerre and the Seyne, and being double their number ; for
they took it for granted, that the bread which the Royalists had
in their quessons being once spent, which cou'd not last them
above four or five days at farthest, they shou'd not be able to
provide themselves with more, so that without striking so much
as a single stroke they should conclude the warr. And they
had reason for this beleef, for the King's foot found nothing in
the Town for their Subsistance, to help out that small proportion
of their bread, the Armys having been so lately there ; And
besides there was such a scarcity of forrage, that from the very
first night of their coming to Town, many of their troopers were
forc'd to feed their horses with vine leaves. This melancholy
welcom they found at their entrance into Villeneuve St Georges,

PART
I.

1652.

Mr. de Lorraine
camps at
Ablon.
Or: Mem:
P. 1. p: 211.

Pce of Condé
marches from
Paris and joyns
the Duke of
Lorraine at
Ablon. *Ibid.*

The two
Armys being
joyn'd, they
block up Mr.
de Turenne
and reckon to
starve him in
Villeneuve
St Georges.
Ibid.

The King's
Army in great
Straits at
Villeneuve
St Georges.
Or: Mem:
P. 1. p: 212.

P A R T
I.

1652.

and had it not been for four or five great boats, which they had the good fortune to find and secure for their uses the first night of their coming thither, their ruine had been inevitable; for without them it had been impossible for them to have made their bridges over the Seyne, and consequently they could never have been able to subsist as they did during the space of a whole month: It concern'd them therefore to lose no time in making them, so that they fell immediatly to work, and in two or three days they had finish'd one of them, and made a work on the other side of the Seyne, to cover and secure both that and the other bridge which was compleated in some few days after it. And to finish both these bridges, nay one may say to begin

Industry to
make two
bridges over
the Seyne.
Or: Mem:
P. 1. p. 213.

them, there was neither mony, nor timber, nor so much as planck; but the great industry of the Officers of the Ordnance supplyd all those defects, and overcame the difficulties of the undertaking, with the help of three hundred pistoles which they were forc'd to borrow from the Gamsters, there no being so poor a sum as that in the hands of the King's Intendants of the Army, and by plucking down some houses for the timber work, together with all the gates of the Innes of which there were many in that Town, and of the other houses which had any large enough for that purpose, which serv'd in stead of plancks; with these and the like shifts both the bridges over the Seyne were finish'd; and the effect of them was, that during some time the King's Army had that side of the River free for forrage.

Then to put themselves into a condition of maintaining the

The Royalists
intrench
themselves
towardsLimay
to secure their
post at
Villeneuve.
Ibid.

post in which they were, they began to intrench themselves on the only side where they could be attacked, which was towards Limay; for as they lay incamped, they were cover'd with a wood on their right hand, by the Town and the River of Seyne on their left, and their back was defended by the Yerre; so that they had no other work but to secure their front, which look'd towards Limay and Gros-bois, and to perform that they had no more to do, but to continue the Lines betwixt the (*five*) redouts, which were yet entire since the Duke of Lorraine's incampment in that place: And they work'd both at the intrenchment and the bridges at the same time.

While the Royalists were thus imployd, the Army of the Enemy decamp'd from the River's side, leaving first a garrison in Ablon, and march'd towards Brie, intending to pass the Yerre about that place, so that they might the better be able to inclose Monsieur de Turenne on every side : While they were taking this compass, the Royalists' bridges over the Seyne being now finish'd, it was thought necessary to take in the Castle of Ablon, wherein, as has been said, (*the Enemy*) had left some Soldiers ; because it being just upon the River, gave much hindrance to the communication with Corbeil by water, from whence the King's Army had their dependance to be furnish'd with all manner of provisions.

In order to this design, Monsr. de Renneville was commanded out with a party of horse and foot, and two pieces of ordinance, to take that Castle ; and accordingly he march'd over the bridge of Boats, where M^r. de Turenne was in person to view them as they went, and to forward the finishing of the other bridge : But before Renneville could approach the Castle, intelligence was brought to Monsr. de Turenne at the bridge, that some Squadrons of the Enemys horse began to appear betwixt the wood and Limay ; upon which he immediatly sent a contermand to Renneville, ordering him to return with his party into the Camp, and himself went up the hill to discover the Enemy at a nearer distance; beleeving from the first notice that their whole Army was marching towards him : Neither was he deceived in his conjecture ; for by that time he had gain'd the length of that eminence, he saw their foot beginning to appear ; and that he might be inabled to make a true judg-

PART I.

1652.

The Enemy decamp from Ablon and Pass the Yerre at Brie, in order to inclose M. de Turenne on all sides.

Or: Mem: P. 1. p. 214.

PART
I.

1652.
Mr. de Turenne
puts himself
amongst the
Skirmishers to
discover the
Enemys
intention.
The Duke
accompanys
him.
Or: Mem:
P. 1. p: 216.

The Duke is
the first that
observes that
the Enemy was
retrenching
and informes
Mr. de Turenne
therof. *Ibid.*

The Royalists
palissade their
Lines and
open'd their
redouts
behind.
Or: Mem:
P. 1. p. 217.

ment, whither or no they intended immediatly to attack him, and (*or*) only to post themselves where they then were, he put himself amongst the Skirmishers; all those who were about him being well mounted, amongst whom was his R. Highness the Duke, and they went so near the Enemy who gave ground in skirmishing, that they were able to make their observations: But Mr. de Turenne who saw not clearly at a distance, would not trust his own eyesight, he therefore desired the Duke to observe as exactly as he could, and inform him what the Enemy was doing; And his Royall Highness was the first person who assured him, that he saw plainly they were intrenching, which was presently confirm'd by some others of the Company: Being assur'd of this, he drew back into his Camp, not a litle satisfied that they had no intention of storming his Lines, which then were in no good condition of defence, as not being yet finish'd.

To strengthen them therfore he commanded that they should be pallissaded, which was executed in the space of six houres, Every Regiment both of horse and foot working incessantly at that part of the Line behind which they were drawn up. This being once perform'd, the Army now thought themselves moderatly secure, and their next imployment was to open those redouts behind, which they had found ready made by the Duke of Lorraine at his last being in that place; judging it more expedient to haue them open, then that they should be wholy clos'd up behind: because in case the Enemy should gaine any of them, it would be difficult to recover them if they were not open.

At the same time that the Prince of Condé came and lay before the Royall Army at Limay, the Duke of Lorraine with his Army lodg'd themselves about a league from the Royalists, up the brook betwixt them and Brie; so that they were so closly block'd up, that the Enemy thought themselves secure

of them, and that in the compass of a litle time they should
either starve them out, or force them upon some desperate
undertaking. The Prince of Condé where he lay, which was
at no greater a distance from Mons'. de Turenne's Lines then
cañon-shott, had intrenched himself very strongly; and when
that was done, his next imployment was to make a bridge of
boats over the Seyne about a league from the Royall Army
down yᵉ River, by that means to hinder all foraging on that side
of the River, and to leave the Royalists no secure place of
foraging, or any way of bringing of Convoys with safety from
Corbeil : for the Duke of Lorraine's troopes were continually
out in partys, and obstructed as much as in them lay the
Royalists' communication with that Town, on the Brie side of
the Seyne; and the Prince of Condé's troopes, when their
bridge was once finish'd, obstructed it on the other side. But
before the Prince had compleated his bridge, Mons'. de
Turenne sent out a party of horse and foot with two pieces of
cañon, and tooke the Castle of Ablon, which absolutly secur'd
the communication with Corbeil by water, and he order'd such
diligence in foraging, that his Army had made tollerable provision for themselves, having eaten up the whole Country
within a reasonable distance from their Camp betwixt Paris
and Juvisy. But when one (once) the Prince's Bridge was
finish'd, they were put to hardships to secure their foragers;
And had any one of those partys miscarryd, the condition of
the King's Army had been desperate, being then reduced to
such extremities, that they were constrain'd to send out the
greatest part of their horse and some foot to secure them ; and
that which render'd it yet more difficult was that they were
oblig'd to go out so far to find provisions, that their foragers
could not return on the same day.

But at length the King's Generalls found an expedient
which prevented the danger, and made the foraging as secure

PART
I.

1652.
The Pᶜᵉ of
Condé in-
trenches
himself aᵗ
Limay within
Canon-shott
of Mʳ. de
Turenne's
Lines, and
makes a bridge
over the Seyne
to hinder the
Royalists
from foraging.
Or: Mem:
P. 1. p. 218.

Mʳ. de Turenne
takes the
Castle of .
Ablon which
secur'd the
communica-
tion with
Corbeil by
water.
Ibid.

Great hard-
ships to secure
the foragers of
the King's
Army.
Ibid. p. 219

Expedient
found by the
Generalls to
make it more
easy.
Or: Mem:
P. 1. p. 219.

as the nature of the thing could bear. The way was this: Before the foragers went out, they sent partys of horse on both sides of the River towards Corbeil, to discover whither or no the Coast was clear, and at the same time others from that Town; for they had order'd 300 horse which came from the taking of Montrond, to continue at Corbeil for that purpose. These came out from thence and met the foragers half way, and after they had inform'd each other of what they had seen in their scowring about the Country, return'd on both sides from whence they came, and according to the intelligence which they brought, the foragers either proceeded or were stop'd. When they went out, they forag'd beyond Corbeil passing over the River of Essoñe, which falls there into the Seyne: When they were once on the farther side of it they were secure, and had leasure quietly to gather their provisions; where staying to rest their horses for one night, they return'd to Corbeil, and, the former precaution of double partys from Corbeil and from the Camp being us'd, the foragers came back safe, some times on one and some times on the other side of the River, according as they had observ'd that the Coast was clear, And by following this method they never had the least accident in all the Convoys of their forage; so that it may be truly said, the whole fortune of the French Monarchy depended on each of those Convoys, for had any one of them miscarryd, the Army had been lost, and after that the ruine of the Crown must have succeeded.

But while the Royall Army continu'd to be bloock'd up in this manner, their small partys were not idle, ranging over all the Country on that side of the River which is towards Orleans, even to the gates of Paris, which was no small inconveniency and vexation to that City, interrupting all their Commerce on that side of the Country; and on the other side of the River they were no less molested by troopes of their own Party; So

The Country about Paris molested by the troopes of both Partys.
OR: MEM:
P. I. p. 221.

that it was not long, before they were sensible of the mischeifs which are inseparable from the neighbourood of two Armies : And this was the more greivous to them, because they had been positively assured from the P^{ce} of Condé, that within ten days after he had continu'd at Villeneuve St Georges, the warr shou'd be determin'd by the King's Army's surrendring itself for want of all manner of provisions, and that consequently they should be eas'd from the burden of so many troopes. And truly they pleas'd themselves with that vaine imagination for some time, being fed with promises from day to day, that all things were drawing to a conclusion ; But when they saw at length that they were deluded of their expectations, and that nothing happen'd of all that had been promis'd, it made them much more inclinable to the Court then they had been formerly, and inspir'd them with more becoming thoughts of returning to their duty: for they (*now*) began in good earnest to consider, what a folly and madness it was in them to suffer themselves to be devoured by Strangers, with no prospect of benefit accruing to their City or of advantage to the French Nation, but that they were only to be made the stalking horses of some ambitious spirits, to further them in their pernicious design of ingrossing and usurping the Supreme power ; and all this to be perform'd at their own expence. When once these reasonable thoughts were enter'd into their minds, it was no hard matter for the Loyall party in the Town to make their advantage of the good impressions, and to foment the misunderstandings which began to kindle betwixt the Parisians and the Princes. In these honest endeavours the Cardinal de Retz was never wanting to perform his part; and the divisions amongst them increasing daly, there happen'd severall great disorders in the Town, which added to the courage of the King's Party, and lessen'd the credit of those popular Bouttefeux, who till then had a great intrest with the common people.:

The P^{ce} of Condé assures the Parisians that in ten days the King's Army at Villeneuve will be forced to surrender. *Ibid.*

The Parisians disappointed in the hopes the P^{ce} of Condé had given them, begin to be weary of the warr and to think of returning to their duty. OR: MEM: P. I. p:222.

These things refreshing the remembrance of what had past at the Hotel de Ville, quite ruin'd the reputation of the Princes, and gave the Parisians plainly to discern what they ambitiously design'd.

But to return to what past in the Army during all the time of the Blockade: there never happen'd any action of great moment, the circumspection of the Generalls being such in the Convoys of the forage, that the Enemy were never able to give them the least disturbance; and the Retrenchments withall being so strong, that no attempt durst be made upon them where they lay. Yet ther happen'd frequent Skirmishes, which were not to be avoided on either side by reason of the nearness of the Lines, and that every day some partys of the Royalists went out to forage. One day above all the rest there was a considerable Skirmish, which was occasion'd by the coming of the Duke of Orleans to see the Rebells' Army. For when he came to the Prince of Condé's quarter, many of the young men of quality who had attended him from Paris, had a desire to shew their bravery, and went off their Lines to pickeere with the King's Soldiers, who seeing them advance in such numbers, came out of their Lines to ingage them. And this was like to have produced a generall Combat even against the inclination of their Commanders; for not only the horse were pickeering on the plain, but severall of the loose foot were at the same work amongst the vinyards, which were planted on the side and all along to the top of the hill. The Royalists' Volonteers who were but few, and other Skirmishers on horseback, ingaged themselves so far, that Monsr. de Turenne was forced to send out M^r. le Marquis de Richelieu with severall small bodies of horse, about twenty men in each, to disingage them; which the Prince observing, did the like on his side, for fear his men might allso run themselves into some inconveniences. Thus either party drew off into their Lines, it being hazardous for

A considerable
Skirmish
occasion'd by
the Duke of
Orleans
coming to see
the Rebells'
Army, which
was like to
produce a
generall
Combat.
OR: MEM:
P: 1. p: 224.

horse to be long without the Retrenchments, because the Lines were so close to each other, that being furnish'd as they were with cañon, the shott which was levell'd at the horse, most commonly fell into either Camp; In this Skirmish there were severall men kill'd and wounded, as well as ye Royalists as well as of the Enemy. Of the first was the Marquis de ——, who was slaine, and a Captain of Douglas call'd Tivy was taken prisoner; who within few days after made his escape and brought to Monsr. de Turenne the news, that the Prince of Condé was retir'd from the Army, being sick, and gone to Paris, where the leaders of the Faction were still endeavouring to keep up the hearts of their declining party, with false hopes of seeing the Royall Army perish for want of victualls and provisions. Whither their cheif heads beleev'd it or not, I cannot say, but certain it is that, if they did, they tooke false measures: for the longer the Army stayd at Villeneuve St Georges, the better they were supplyd, being furnish'd very plentifully with all they wanted down the River from Corbeil.

During this time there happen'd one memorable Action which we cannot but relate. It was perform'd by one Seguin a Captain of horse of Beauveau's Regiment, who frequently went out on partys. This Seguin being abroad with a hundred horse, and having put himself in ambush to fall on the foragers of the Enemy, when they were come and settled at their work, broke out upon them; but in stead of charging them, having discover'd a squadron of horse which was posted at a litle distance from him on a heigth, and which he imagin'd was their only Convoy, he took a resolution of fighting them: So he march'd towards them on a round trott; but when he was just approaching them, he perceived four Squadrons more appearing, and immediatly turning to his men, told them, It was now too late to think of a retreat, and that they must instantly resolve to work out their safety with their swords; That their only way

PART
I.

1652.

The P^ce of Condé retires from the Army sick, and go's to Paris.
O^r: Mem:
P. 1. p: 228.

A memorable action of one Seguin a Partisan, who with 100 horse attacks five Squadrons of the Enemy, kills 60 on the place and takes 50 prisoners.
O^r: Mem:
P. 1. p. 225.

1652.

was to divide themselves into five bodies, and each of them to charge one of the Enemys : This was done according to his orders, drawing up but two deep; and they attack'd the Enemy so vigourously that they routed them, killing sixty on the place, of which number some were Officers, and taking fifty prisoners with a Major and one or two Captains : Those whom they defeated were the old Regiment of Wirtemberg.

The Court was all this while either at Pontoise, or at St Germain's, and maintain'd their intelligence at Paris ; being very well inform'd how affaires were managed in that place, and how unsatisfied the Parisians were with the proceedings of the Princes, and the continuance of the Warr at their very gates. Seeing therfore that the inclinations of the people were now more favourable to them, and their condition receiving dayly

The Court orders the two Mareschalls to endeavour to bring off the Army from Villeneuve St Georges. OR: MEM: P. 1. p. 228.

some amendment, they sent to the two Mareschalls de Turenne and la Ferté, to know whither they thought it possible for them to bring off the Army from their post, without suffering some affront from the Enemy ; and that in case they cou'd perform it, they shou'd draw off and endeavour to joine the Court, in favour of the designs and practices which they had then on foot in Paris : The Generalls having received these orders, began to provide for the departure of the Army ; and in pursuite of their Instructions, order'd twelve bridges to be made over the small River, under pretence that they were for the conveniency of the foragers ; and at the same time they

The Royall Army begins to draw off from Villeneuve St Georges the 4th of October in theEvening, and they arrive next morning at Corbeill without the least hinderance. OR: MEM: P. 1. p. 229.

sent directions to those troopes who were lying (*near*) to Corbeil, to make some redouts upon a higth before that Town, under the same pretence of securing the retreat of the Foragers, in case they shou'd be attacked on that side of the Country.

When both these commands were executed on the 4th of October, an hourt before Sun sett, order was given to prepare for marching, and that all things shou'd be carryd with great silence. By that time it began to be dark, the baggage had orders to sett forward. to Corbeil on the lower way, along by the River side; some horse and dragoons were commanded to march at the head of them, and to draw up under the redouts by Corbeil. So soon as the baggage had past the bridges over the brook, the troopes in their order began to march; but neither the Guards or Centrys were drawn from the Line, till the whole Army was past over the bridges, and then they came off and broke them, that the Enemy might not be able to follow them in case their retreat shou'd be discover'd: But they were so far from suspecting any thing of that nature, that they had design'd that very night to have storm'd the Regiment of Nettencour, which was posted, on the other side of the Seyne, in a work which the Royalists had made to secure their two bridges over that River, in which there was also a guard of fourty horse; and that the Enemy might carry it the more easily and hinder the King's troopes that were within it from succour, they caus'd severall great Floats of wood, of such as usually come down that River for the consumption of Paris, to be let loose and sett adrift, the weight of which if they came to bear upon the bridges, would infallibly break them: And these Floats, which came driving down the stream for the space of a league above the bridges, had the effect which the Enemy desir'd; for just before the men who lay there intrenched had orders to draw off, the Major, who waited on Mons'. de Turenne to know when it shou'd be time for them to come over to joyne the rest of the Army, going to carry them their orders, found the bridge broken, and brought an account of it to the Generall; who immediatly order'd them to march to Corbeil on that side of the River where they were, as not thinking it convenient to forestow his march by staying till he could pass these men and their baggage over, most of the troopes having already pass'd the other bridges. Yet these men were so fortunate as not to meet any obstacle in their way, so that the next morning they joyn'd the Army at Corbeil.

A litle before day, the party that was commanded to storm that work which the Royalists had left, approached the place, and not only found that it was deserted, but that the whole Army was dislodged and gone, which was the first notice the Enemy had of their departure: They made their Commanders acquainted with it, but it was already too late for them to fall upon the Royalists' rear; And had they been sooner advertis'd of it, though they had follow'd the King's Army, in all probability they cou'd have done them litle harm : for by that time the Army had march'd a league or somewhat more, the ground was so very favourable for them, that they had no apprehension of the Enemys force. For on one hand they had the River, and the forest of Sennard on the other, so that the Emy could not fall into their flanques, and then the distance from the one to the other was not so great, but that they could easily fill the whole extent of the ground ; so that they could not be outwing'd, and still the nearer they approached to Corbeil, it grew the narrower.

In this manner, without the least hindrance or molestation, the Royall Army arrived at Corbeil, the hindermost troopes thereof being enter'd before Sun rising. They rested all that day in those quarters; and not being certain whither or no the Enemy might march after them to attack them in that place, they immediatly fell to work and intrenched their Camp, thō they were to continue in it but for one night. And the next morning being the 6th, they march'd away, and went that evening as far as Chaumes with intention to pas the Marne at Meaux, and from thence to joyn the Court.

That first day's march to Chaumes was very long, especially considering that it was in the power of the Enemy to have

The Royall
Army march
the 6th to
Chaumes.
OR: MEM:
P. 1. p: 231.

fought the Royalists, if they had so resolv'd ; for which reason
during the whole day the Army march'd so orderly, that in a
quarter of an hour they might all haue been drawn up in battell:
For that wing which was formost march'd two squadrons a front,
which were the two first squadrons of each line of that wing
according to the order of battell, that of the first line marching
on the left hand, and the other of the second line on the right ;
keeping the same distance as they were accustomed to be from
one another, after the manner of the two first: The foot in like
order follow'd the horse, the first line of foot marching after the
first of horse, and the second after the same manner ; the Gens
d'armes marching in their usuall place in time of battell betwixt
the two lines of foot, and the other wing of horse follow'd the
foot in the same method : so that whensoever the Enemy had
come to charge them, they needed only to have faced to the left,
and they had been in battell, as may be easily discern'd by the
following Draught.

₊ *Although a space is left in the M.S. no Plan was inserted.*—EDITOR.

The Train of Artillery, with the quessons, march'd on the right
hand of the foot, and the baggage on the right hand of them.
In this order march'd the Royall Army during the whole day,
expecting the Enemy who came not to disturbe them ; and
that day being once over, they no longer beleev'd they would
be attacked ; and so the following days the march was continued with more ease and conveniency, and less circumspection.
Having march'd by Presle, Tournam, and Quincé, on the 1|ᵗʰ

P A R T
I.
1652.
Order of the
march of the
King's Army
to Chaumes.
Ibid.

The Royall
Army pass the
Marne near
Meaux the
1|ᵗʰof October.
OR: MEM.
P. 1. p. 233.

they pass'd the Marne neer Meaux, and incamped the same night at Boretz; from whence they march'd to Mont l'Eueque, then to Courteuil, where they had the River which runs by that place to cover them.

While they made this march, the Enemy was in great perplexity and amazment that the Royalists were so unexpectedly gott clear of them, which absolutly ruin'd the Enemys credit with the Parisians; for having given them dayly assurances, that they would suddently conclude the warr by famishing the King's Army, and that hope being now vanish'd, the eyes of that people were fully open'd, and they saw clearly into the rest of their delusions; and at the same time feeling the intollerable burden of the warr, and of so many Armys even at their doors, their desires were increas'd of freeing themselves at once from all their grievances by the return of their King, which good inclinations of theirs were not neglected by the Cardinal de Retz, and others of the King's Party ; which now visibly increasing every day, the Prince of Condé, and Duke of Lorraine, found it was not their intrest to stay any longer with their Armys thereabouts, for they saw by experience that the longer they stayd the fewer friends they had, and that no other means was left to preserve those few they had yet remaining in that Town, then by marching their Armys away from the neighbourhood of it, and carrying the warr to a greater distance : And besides the weight of these consider_ ations, the winter was now drawing on apace, and the Country about Paris quite devour'd, so that it would have prov'd very difficult to have made an Army subsist in those quarters : For these and perhaps some other unknown reasons, they were forced to a resolution of leaving Paris, and found there was no other expedient but to winter their Armys in Champagne and Lor_ raine; the Spanish Army being to joine them at Rhetel, and to assist them in taking such places in those Countries, as wou'd

The King's
Party in Paris
increasing
dayly, the P.
of Condé and
Duke of
Lorraine
resolve to
march from its
neighbour-
hood and
carry the warr
to a distance.
OR: MEM:
P. I. p. 233.

secure them in their quarters. As for the Duke of Orleans and his daughter Madmoiselle, it was thought necessary that they shou'd remain still at Paris, to use their intrest and endeavours to hinder that Town from receiving the King.

Those resolutions being once taken by them, they were speedily put in execution; for by that time the King's Army was come to Courteuil near Senlis, which was about the 14th of October, theirs pass'd by them on their march towards Champagne.

When it was known at Court that the Enemy had left Paris, they judg'd it their intrest to get into it: And Monsr de Turenne, who had once before propos'd it to the Councill that they should march directly to that Town, went on purpose to the Court which then lay at St Germains, to perswad them to it a second time; Letting them see the necessity of such a resolution, that this was the most proper time to adventure it, and not to suffer the disgust which the Parisians had to the Princes, to wear off by their absence: To strengthen this advice, he made it manifest, That if the King possessed not himself of Paris, there was no possibility of procuring winter-quarters for their troopes, and consequently he cou'd have no Army in readiness against the next spring, to oppose so powerfull an Army as he shou'd then have upon his hands; for shou'd Paris refuse to admitt the King, the rest of the great places wou'd undoubtedly follow their example; To conclude, he affirm'd that all depended on the good or ill Success of that affaire. These reasons, which are but lightly touch'd here, were set forth so fully and so convincingly by M^r. de Turenne to the Councill, that the resolution of going to Paris was approv'd as absolutly necessary, and in pursuance of it the Court sett out from St Germains. And being now as far on their way as the bois de Boulogne (for they were obliged to go by St Cloud, the other bridges being broken down) they were mett by some who came out of

PART
I.

1652.

They march their troopes towards Champagne, passing by the King's Army at Courteuil the 14th of October.
Ibid. p. 234.

Monsr. de Turenne go's on purpose to Court to perswadethem to go to Paris.
Or: Mem: P. 1. p: 234.

Convinc'd by M^r. de Turenne's Arguments, the Court sets forth from St Germains to go to Paris.
Ibid. p. 235.

PART
I.

1652.
Some Trim-
mers from
Paris meet the
Court at bois
de Boulogne,
and disswade
coming to
Paris.
Or: MEM:
P. 1. p. 235.

Paris, true trimmers, who addressed themselves to certain
members of the Councill, to whom they represented the hazard
of their present undertaking, and how dangerous a consequence
it might be, to adventure the person of the King and his only
Brother in Paris; and they so fill'd their heads with these
suspitions, that they went immediatly to the Queen's Coach in
which the King was, to informe of it and to diswade him from
so desperate an attempt: Wherupon the Queen stop'd her Coach,
and call'd for the rest of the Councill and M^r. de Turenne to
advise what was fitting to be done.

All the
Councill of
opinion, that
the Court
should return
toS'Germains,
excepting M'.
de Turenne.
Ibid.

After they had debated the Affaire some time, they were all
of opinion, That their M^{aties} shou'd return to St Germains,
excepting only Monsr. de Turenne, who persisted in the former
resolution, urging all the arguments which had perswaded that
opinion, to continue in it, and to go through with what they had
undertaken; Adding, that it would now be both prejudiciall to
the King's affaires, and withall dishonorable, as shewing a
manifest want of resolution, to return when they were so far
advanced on their way to Paris; That it would bring a Contempt on the Court, dishearten their Freinds, and encourage
their Enemys; In short, that they must expect from this
timerous change in their resolution, all the ill consequences
which had been formerly represented to them; That he look'd
on those persons who brought this advice, either as covert
Enemies to the King by endeavouring to hinder his coming
into Paris, or at least as men of weak judgments, on whose

The Queen of
an undaunted
courage, pre-
fering M'.
de Turenne's
opinion to
that of the
whole body of
the Councill,
resolves to go
on to Paris.
Or: MEM:
P. 1. p. 236.

opinions his Majesty ought not to rely. His arguments were
so prevalent on the Queen, who was certainly a Princesse of
a most undaunted courage, and consequently not easily to be
frighted, that notwithstanding all the reasons which were offer'd
to her by the whole body of the Councill, She resolv'd on going
forward; Saying, that she thought it better to expose herself
and her Sons to all those dangers, on so considerable an occasion,

then to ruine the honour of both by so mean an action as their return: Besides that it wou'd be the certain way to render their condition desperate, and that they must never hope to come into Paris if they lost the present opportunity.

Thus the Affaire was settled, and his Majesty at the head of his Guards march'd on, entering into the Town at the Porte St Honoré: So far from meeting the least opposition, that he was saluted every where as he past along, with great acclamations of joy, and follow'd by a Vast concourse of people to the Louure. The Duke of Orleans, as the King enter'd at one end of the City, went out at the other; And as for his daughter, Madmoiselle, she stayd in her lodgins at the Tuilleries, till she receiv'd a Command from his Ma^ty immediatly after he was in the Louure, to depart from Paris, which accordingly she obeyd.

The King of France enters in at the Porte St Honoré at the head of his Guards without the least opposition. *Ibid.*

The Duke of Orleans retires out of the Town. *Ibid.*

Orders sent to Madmoiselle to retire also from Paris. *Ibid.*

This was no sooner done, then Monsr. de Turenne return'd to the Army, and about the end of the month began his march after the Enemy, who had taken theirs through Champagne, and in passing had possest themselves of Château-Porcien, and Rhetel upon the Aysne, which they took without much resistance. From thence they went to St Menehou which was very well defended, thō forced at last to surrender on composition, for besides the ordinary garrison that was in it, there were but four Companies of the Duke's Regiment, which got into it before it was invested; for when the Enemy left Paris, the two foot Regiments of la Ferté and York, with some horse of la Ferté's troopes, were sent away in all hast, with orders to put themselves into St Menehou, and the places of Barois; and Monsieur de la Ferté himself went also to Nancy, to secure his government of Lorraine in the best manner he was able, suspecting that the Enemy's design would be to take up their winter-quarter in those parts, as accordingly it came to pass.

M^r. de Turenne returns to the Army and with it marches after the Enemy. OB: MEM: P. 1. p: 237. The P^ce of Condé takes Château-Porcien and Rhetel. *Ibid.*

M^r. de la Ferté marches to Nancy to secure his governm^t of Lorraine. *Ibid.*

PART
I.

1652.
The Duke
marches with
M. de Tu-
renne's Army
toChampagne,
they quarter at
Balieux the
2ᵈ of Novem-
ber. *Ibid.*
The Soldiers
so drunk with
new win,
that there
are not enough
of them for
the ordinary
for the Duke
and Mʳ. de
Turenne.
Ibid.

Count
Fuensaldagne
joyns the
Princes' Army.
OR: MEM:
P. 1. p. 237.

The Pᶜᵉ of
Condé takes
Sᵗ Menehou
the 13 Nov.
Ibid. p. 238.

. The Duke went along with Mʳ. de Turenne, who march'd his Army directly for Champagne. In their march to Epernay they quarter'd on the 2ᵈ of Nouembre at Balieux, where they were oblig'd to stop a whole day; because the Soldiers in coming thether found so great a quantity of new win, after the Vintage in a Country which was plentifully stor'd with that liquour, that of all the foot there came not enough up to the quarter, to make the ordinary guard for the Duke and Mʳ. de Turenne; so that they stirr'd not till the 4ᵗʰ. When they got their men together, they continu'd their march to Dizi neer Epernay, where they passed the Marne on the 5ᵗʰ of November, to keep that River betwixt them and the Enemy, who were then about Rhetel; the Royall Army not being of sufficient strength to adventure neer them in that open Country. For besides the forces which the Prince of Condé and Duke of Lorraine had brought with them from Paris, the Count de Fuenseldagne had joyn'd them with a considerable part of the Spanish Army; it was therfore thought best to follow them at a convenient distance, still keeping some River, or some great défilé betwixt the Royall Army and them, or keeping such a distance from them, that they ran no hazard of being surpriz'd or engag'd before they were aware.

On the 6ᵗʰ they came to Chaype (*Cheppes*) which is a litle short of Vitry le François; and after they had stayd there three or four days, they pass'd the Marne and quarter'd at Vitry le Bruslé, thence came to the fauxbourg of Vitry le François on the 16ᵗʰ, still governing their motion according to that of the Enemy. During the time that they were about these places, the Enemy took Sᵗ Menehou on the 13ᵗʰ. From that Town they licens'd the troopes of the Duke of Orleans (which were with him) to return into France, on condition they shou'd not serve during the rest of the Campagne, or any where in that side of the Country. Wherupon they went immediatly to quarters

137

appointed for them in Picardy, and were the next year sent to serve in the Armys on the other fronteers of France. After this the Enemy went and beseiged Barleduc, in which Town Monsr. de la Ferté had plass'd one Roussillon to command, with such a garrison as was sufficient to haue defended it a longer time then he did. And such was his folly, that he refus'd to be strengthen'd with more men; for while the Enemy was yet at St Menehou, M. de Turenne sent a recruit of 500 foot to St Dizier, with orders to march for Barleduc, in case the Governour should haue occasion for them: But his answer was, that he had men enough, and thanking Monsr. de Turenne for his care of him, assur'd him with all, that he was well prepar'd to receive the Enemy whensoever they shou'd dare to approach him. After this, when he was ready to be invested, he sent Monsr. de Turenne word of it, with new promises that he wou'd give a good account of the place.

PART I.

1652.
Barleduc beseiged by the P^{ce} of Condé.
Or: Mem: .
P: 1: p. 238.

It was on the 18th, when this news came to M^r. de Turenne, when he was at Vitry le François, whereupon he march'd away to releeve it with all possible expedition; and that the Enemy might have no intelligence of his approache, he repassed the Marne at Vitry, and leaving the River on his left hand, march'd up along by it, and by break of day came to St Dizier. At that place he made a halt to refresh his Army for some few houres; but just as he was preparing to march again, he received intelligence that both the Town and Castle were surrender'd to the Enemy; for which reason he advanced no further but quarter'd there. This uncomfortable news exceedingly surpris'd the Royalists; and they were the more sensible of it, because it disappointed the design, not only of succuring the place, but also of defeating the Enemy, at least of puting them to so hasty a retreat, that they must of necessity haue lost their baggage and their cañon; and certainly never Enterprise was better design'd, or more

M.deTurenne marches from Vitry le François the 18 November to releeve Barleduc.
Ibid. p. 239.

M.deTurenne is Stopp'd at St Dizier with the news of Barleduc's being Surrender'd.
Or: Mem: P: 1: p. 239.

M. de Turenne's great conduct in the Enterprise of releeving Barleduc.
Ibid.

P A R T
I.

1652.

judiciously conducted: for thō the Royall Army was much inferiour to the Enemys in number, yet the ground was such, that the Royalists ran no hazard in marching to them; it being a woodland Country on that side of Barr, and Monsʳ. de Turenne having then six thousand well disciplin'd foot, his Army having been reinforced both with horse and infantry by the occasion of severall troopes from the garrisons of Artois and Picardy and other places, which could well spare them when the Enemy was departed out of France, and consequently distant from those parts.

By the favour of these foremention'd woods and suddainness of the march, M. de Turenne might reasonably expect to haue been upon the Enemy, before they shou'd have been advertis'd of it; they cou'd haue received no considerable benefit by their

Description of the Enemys post before Barleduc where Mʳ. de Turrene propos'd to attack them. Or: Mem: P. 1: p. 240.

intelligence: for such is the Situation of the place, and such the disadvantage of the post for those who attack the Town, against the Enemy who comes to releive it on that side, that their retrenchments are not to be maintain'd; for the woods extend in length within a league of the Town, and from the woods to the Castle lyes a spacious plaine: The Castle and the upper Town are placed upon that levell, and upon the brink of a descent which leads to the lower Town; a brooke or litle River runs at the bottome. The bottome itself is narrow and the ascent on each side steep and troublesome. So that he could haue been ingaged only by those of the Enemy who were on his side of the River, and they would haue past their time but litle at their ease between his Army and the Castle; neither could they haue been able to maintain that post betwixt the wood and the Castle, nor in their drawing off cou'd they haue kept their order; so that in all probability he shou'd have pressed them till they had tumbled upon one another: And this Mʳ. de Turenne undertook, when it was beleev'd that the Enemys whole Army was together in a body, thō in all liklyhood the ——— shou'd haue found a much easier task P A R T
I. of it; because the Count Fuensaldagne was already march'd away from their Army, having drawn along with him the greatest part of his forces, as not beleeving Monsr. de Turenne to be so strong as he was, and imagining that those troopes which the Prince of Condé and Duke of Lorraine had with them, were sufficient to take in all the Barois, and there to make good their winter quarters.

1652.
The indis-
cretion of the
Governour of
Barleduc
occasions the
loss of the
Town.
Or: Mem:
P. 1: p. 241.

Thus by the rashness and indiscretion of Monsr. de Roussillon who commanded in Barleduc, what M^r. de Turenne had so well design'd was render'd ineffectuall. And certainly never any man playd a more inconsiderate part then that addle headed Governour; for thō he had sent word to M. de Turenne that he expected to be invested, and saw the Enemy marching towards him, yet he was so stupidly negligent as to suffer the four best Companies of his garrison to be surprised in the lower Town, which was defended with a wall sufficiently strong and incompass'd with a wett ditch, so that it might haue been maintain'd with ease till a breach had been made: But the Enemy having master'd it the first night they came, yet thought it not convenient to make their attack upon that side, but the next day rais'd a battery upon the plaine against the Castle; and their guns no sooner playd, that the Governour sent out to parley before any thing like a breach was made in the wall, agreeing to march out the next morning. At the taking of this Town the Duke of Lorraine lost Mr Fouge (*Fauge*) a Lieutenant Generall, and the best Officer in his Army; he was kill'd the neight after they had taken the lower Town, and procur'd his own death by strange caprice of folly: for being at supper with the Prince of Condé and severall others, in one of the next houses to the upper Town, and making a debauch, he grew so drunk, that he ran out in a foolish bravery at a back door with a napekin on his head, to be discern'd the

The best
officer of the
Duke of
Lorraine's
Army kill'd by
his own folly.
Ibid.

P A R T
I.

1652.

The sudden
surrender of
Barleduc
breaking
M. de
Turenne's
measures, is
the occasion
also of the loss
of Ligny, Voy,
and Com-
mercy.
Or: Mem.
P. 1. p. 242.

The Duke of
Longueville
brings a
recruit to M.
de Turenne
from Nor-
mandy. Ibid.

better in the night, and to provoke the Enemy to shoot at him.
The Cheualier de Guise and the Prince of Condé himself ran
out after him to bring him back; but before they could hale
him in, he receiv'd a shott which kill'd him.

The sudden surrender of this Town not only broke the measures for releeving it and defeating the Enemy, but had a worse
consequence, for it gave time to the Enemy to make themselves
masters of Ligny, Voy, and Commercy, because M^r. de Turenne being ignorant of M^r. de Fuensaldagne's departure durst
not come too near them, for which reason he stayd two or
three days at St Dizier; they in the mean time taking in the
places abovemention'd, which were but slightly man'd with
inconsiderable garrisons, and made litle or no defence.

From St Dizier the Royall Army advanced after the Enemy,
and came to Stinville, where there came up to them a considerable recruit out of Normandy composed of the Duke of Longueville's Regiment of horse, which consisted of three hundred,
and that of his foot which were about twelve hundred, with
them came also the Earle of Bristol's Regiment of horse and
Company of ordinance; and thõ they were all but new rais'd
souldiers, excepting the company of ordinance, so that no great
service cou'd be expected from them, yet their number did
good, because they gave reputation. At this Town of Stinville,
Monsr. de Turenne had the first intelligence that the Count of
Fuensaldagne was gone from the Prince's Army with his
troopes; and upon this notice which was given on the 25th,
he march'd the next day to give battell to the Prince of Condé
and the Duke of Lorraine, or in case they avoided it, to drive
them out of those quarters, where they had propos'd to themselves to winter: and indeed they were So secure of it in their
own opinion, that they had issu'd out their orders accordingly,
but it appear'd by the event that they had taken wrong measures; for upon M. de Turenne's advancing to them the next

day, they were so far from being able to compass their designs, that they durst not stand, but found that it was their safest course to march away with all possible expedition, passing the Maze near Voy, in which place the Prince of Cónde was, when he had notice of Monsr. de Turenne's advancing towards him: After which leaving the River on their left hand, they made what hast they could towards Luxembourg, and M^r. de Turenne follow'd them so close, that for the most part he came about noon to the place where they had quarter'd the night before, and from whence they had march'd the same morning. After this manner he pursu'd them, till he came to St Michel on the 30th on the forenoon, where finding it was to no purpose to follow them any further, they being so near the shelter of their own Country that they were out of danger, he gave over following them; his thoughts being intent only on finding out means to refresh his Army, especially the foot, which were exceedingly harrass'd with the great and painfull marches they had taken, and were now starving for want of bread: for the Enemy as they march'd before them had eaten up the Country, and the quessons were quite empty, it being actually impossible for the Commissary of the Victualls to provide bread for them.

Upon the Army's arrival at St Michel, M^r. de Turenne sent into the Town that they shou'd bring out some bread for the releif of the foot; but they making a difficulting of obeying him, and pretending they could not furnish so great a quantity in one day, he found there was no other way of preserving those distressed soldiers but by quartering them all upon the Town; for which reason he march'd into it with the foot, Gendarmes and cannon, quartering the horse in the neighbouring Villages. The Army's stay in this was very short, however it serv'd to refresh the soldiers; for so soon as the Mareschall la Ferté, in whose Government it was, had notice of their being there, he came in great hast from Nancy, which is about ten or twelve

PART I.

1652.
The P^{ce} of Condé marches away with all expedition.
OR: MEM: P: 1: p: 243.

M^r.deTurenne pursues him close till he came to St Michel on the 30th November. *Ibid.*

M.deTurenne obliged for preservation of his wearyed Soldiers, to quarter them upon the Town of St Michel. OR: MEM: P: 1. p. 243.
Mareschall de la Ferté so offended at this quartering, that in a long time after he cou'd not be reconcil'd to M. de Turenne. *Ibid.* p. 244.

---

leagues distant from St Michel, to desire Monsr. de Turenne to leave the Town, being very much offended at his quartering there; in so much that he was (*not*) throwly reconcil'd to him in a long time afterwards, which prov'd exceedingly prejudiciall to the King's Seruice, as by the sequell will be seen. Upon his summonds the next day after his arrivall which was the 2^d of December, the Army drew out; but M^r. de la Ferté was so much enraged by seeing that some of the men had been bolder then became them in their quarters, taking more then meat and drink, that as they were marching out, he himself attended by his guards fell upon such of them as stragled or were loytering behind, hacking and hewing them as if they had been Enemys. In so much that coming near the quarters of the Gendarmes who were not yet march'd out, nor wholly drawn together, one

M. de la Ferté escapes narrowly being kill'd by one of the Earl of Bristol's troopers. Or: Mem: P: 1. p: 244.

of the Earle of Bristol's troope whose name was Manwaring, seeing how furiously he dealt his blows, and not knowing the person of the Mareschall, took him and his guards to be the Enemy, and in that opinion made up to him, and sett his pistoll to his brest which fortunatly for both miss'd firing. Thus the Mareschall escap'd from being kill'd, and the horseman was knock'd down and wounded by the guards in six or seven places, of which he afterwards recover'd. And C. Berkley, who was then Cornett to the same Company of Gendarmes, miss'd but narrowly of the same usage; for hearing the noise which was made by the Mareschall and his Guards, and taking it for granted, as Manwaring had done before him, that the Enemy was in the Town, he went up to the corner of the street along which they were coming, with his pistoll in his hand, and at their approach discovering the Mareschall, made but one motion of puting up his pistoll and taking off his hatt; by which means he escap'd better cheap then his Trooper, because he was known to him.

The Army quarter'd that night at a Village call'd Villotte,

and the next day march'd to Trouville which lyes betwixt Barr and Ligny : And that evening M. de Turenne sent a party of horse and foot with cañon and all things necessary to attack Ligny. They immediatly fell to work, and without more ceremony made a battery within less then half muskett shott of the Town, a trench on each hand of the battery to secure the foot, and behind that an epaulement or blind for the horse, cañon proof, about muskett shott from the place : All this was perfected before Sun-rise the next morning, and then the battery began to play ; at evening somewhat before the Sun went down, a large assaultable breach was made : The only difficulty which remain'd was to get over the ditch which was wett, and somewhat deep, and withall so brode that the ruines of the wall had not fill'd it up ; but by the help of plancks and ladders and long poles which the Soldiers carryd along with them when they storm'd it, they passed the ditch without much difficulty, and came up to the breach, where the Enemy making but a faint resistance immediatly abandon'd it, and retire into the Castle which was a place of greater Strength.

These things being thus executed, the next day M. de Turenne march'd with his Troopes to the Suburbs of Barleduc, Monsr. de la Ferté continuing with his at Ligny against the Castle, and the Duke going with Monsieur de Turenne to Bar ; where the very first night of their approach, they began to raise a battery against the lower Town, which was perform'd with exceeding ease under the shelter of some houses which were almost upon the edge of the ditch, there being but a narrow way betwixt them and it. By morning their guns began to play, and though they were but few, and very small for battering pieces, two of them being twelve pounders, one eight, and the other two but Six ; yet all of them being home bor'd and well fortified, they serv'd sufficiently for the work ; for they gave them their double charge of pouder, and Monsr. de Champ-

PART
I.

1652.
The King's
Army beseige
Ligny.
Or: Mem:
P: 1. p: 245.

M. de Turenne
beseiges
Barleduc.
Or: Mem:
P: 1. p. 246.
M. de Ferté
continues the
Seige of the
Castle of
Lagny, and
the Duke go's
with M. de
Turenne to
Bar. Ibid..

PART I.

1652.
A breach
made in the
lower Town
of Barleduc
and M^r. de
Tott with the
regim^t of
Picardy
appointed to
storme it.
Ibid.

fort lieutenant of the ordnance, playd them so warmly, that by
Sun-set they had open'd a faire breach; The Regiment of
Picardy as being eldest was to storme it, and Monsr. de Tott
the eldest and indeed the only Lieutenant Generall then serving
in that Army was to lead them on. The place where they had
made the breach was adjoining to the gate, on the right hand
of the entry into the Town, and had no considerable fianke,
but one of the round towers of the gate. That place was chosen
for the battery, because at any other they must haue been at the
trouble to haue fill'd the ditch, as well as to haue* been a breach
(*to have made a greater breach elsewhere*) which would haue
taken up more time then they were willing to spare before they
storm'd the place; but here they had the convenience of passing
the ditch over the bridge of the Town, and of leaping down-
ward where the draw-bridge was drawn up, from whence they
went under covert of the wall to mount the breach, which was
not far distant. All things being thus prepar'd for the assault,
M^r. de Turenne caus'd the battery to give two or three rounds
upon the Tower, or Gate house, which was the only considerable
flancker that commanded the breach; that by shattering it, the
men might haue the easier work, after which he gave the word
to Monsr. du Tott for the assault, which indeed he obeyd; but
in stead of ordering the Commanded men to fall on first, and
staying himself with the body, he (who was the only officer
whom his R. Highness ever saw drunk in the French Army
during all the time he continued in it) having drunk more then
ever Comander ought to do, went on with the Sergeant; and, as
he step'd out of a litle door which was in the false gate, which
is just at the entrance of the bridge before the passage to the

M. du Tott
(the only
Officer whom
his R. H. ever
saw drunk in
the French
Army) going
on further
then he ought
in the assault,
is shott dead.
O_R: M_{EM}:
P: I. p: 247.

---

* This, with some few other omissions, have been corrected by a reference to
the Extract from these Memoirs, as far as related to the Wars of M^r. Turenne,
which King James sent to the Cardinal de Bouillon. — E_{DITOR}.

10

drawbridge, was shott dead: But that misfortune stop'd not
the men, who all pass'd throw the narrow gate one by one, and
so went forward to the breach by the way already described;
and thō the Enemy made a very brave defence, so that the
cannon could not drive them from the Gate-house, yet M. de
Turenne's Soldiers enter'd throw the breach, and not only
Master'd it, but drove the Enemy from the Barricades which
they had made behind it, and the streets, forcing them backward into the upper Town.

There happen'd an accident to the Governour was name
was Despiller, which very much facilitated the taking of the
lower Town. It seems that seeing it so late, he thought he
would not be storm'd that evening and for that reason was
remaining in the upper Town, when the noise of the attack
summoning him to his duty, he came down at the head of two
hundred men to reinforce those whom he had left to maintain
the breach; But in riding down, his horse fell with him, and so
bruis'd his leg that he was forced to be carryd back into the
upper Town. Had not this misfortune arrived to him, it was
beleeved the place had not (*been*) carryd so easily; The
beseigers receiv'd no considerable loss of men in this attack, for
besides Mʳ. Tu Tott no man of quality was kill'd, excepting only
the Marquis d'Angeau a Volonteer. Of the wounded there was
Monsʳ. Poliac the first Captain of Picardy, who commanded
that Regiment the Major Officers being absent, and another
Captain of the same Regiment called Godonviller. The first
was shott into the shoulder, and the latter into the belly, of
which both recover'd.

Having thus master'd the lower Town, the forces were employd against the upper Town and the Castle. The day on
which the lower Town was taken, the Cardinal Mazarin came
to the Army, and brought severall troopes along with him to
reinforce it; The recruits had been drawn together from divers

PART
I.

1652.

The lower
Town of
Barleduc
taken by
assault.
Or: Mem:
P: 1: p. 247.

Cardinal
Mazarin
comes to the
Army before
Barleduc.
Ibid. p: 248.

P A R T
I.

1652.

places, and were commanded by the Duke d'Elbeuf, and the Mareschall d'Aumont. The Cardinal was present when the lower-Town was taken, and thō when the King's troopes were Masters of it they well knew nothing could be done on the upper Town that way, yet they were obliged to take it, that the foot might be lodged in it, the season of the year being past for camping, and there happening at that time a very hard frost; so that they could never haue carried on the Seige without quartering in the lower Town, where the Soldiers found not only shelter for themselves, but Cellars well stor'd with wine and Granaries with corne, which was a wellcome refreshment to them in that hard and bitter season. As for the horse they were conveniently quarter'd at the adjacent Villages, as near to the Town as they could be lodged.

The Pᶜᵉ of
Condé endea-
vours to
relieve Bar.
Oʀ: Mᴇᴍ:
P. 1: p. 249.

But this Wether hinder'd not the Prince of Condé, who was rather encourag'd by it to endeavour the releif of the place; of whose march the Royalists being timely advertis'd, it was resolved by the Cardinal and the Generalls, that Monsʳ. de Turenne and the Mareschall de la Ferté should take the greatest of the horse, and betwixt the number of two or three

The two
Mareschalls
leaving the
Duc d'Elbeuf
and Mˢˡˡ
d'Aumont to
continue the
Seige, go to
meet the
Prince of
Condé.
Ibid.

thousand foot, with six feild pieces, and march towards the Enemy to meet them on the way, leaving the Duke d'Elbeuf and the Mareschall d'Aumont with the remainder of the foot, and some few horse to continue the Seige. The Duke went along (with) Mʳ. de Turenne. As for the Cardinal he went along also, but did not quarter at the same Village with the Army, but in some one behind them. Having then intelli-gence that the Enemy was coming by the way of Vaubecourt a bourg, about five leagues from Barleduc, the Army march'd towards them, Monsieur de Turenne having the Van, and advanced as far as Condit intending to quarter in that place, which is but a league and a half short of Vaubecourt; where just as the formost troopes were come into their quarter, they had notice by a party of theirs which came into them, and brought prisoners along with them, that the Prince of Condé was newly march'd into Vaubecourt, intending to quarter there that night, and having no intelligence of the Royalists being so near him.

P A R T
I.
1652.

Monsieur Turenne sent immediatly to the Mareschall de la Ferté to give him notice of this, and withall to signify his opinion; which was, That they ought presently to march and fall upon the Prince of Condé, whom they should certainly find in great disorder, the quarter being plentifully stor'd with wine and all manner of provision, which would render it more difficult for their Commander to draw his men together, and cause them afterwards to stand to their armes, and get to horse; for their surprise would be so great to find the King's Army there, whom they imagin'd to be so far from them, that in all probability it would secure the Royalists an easy victory: But the Mareschall de la Ferté instead of consenting to this proposition, came himself to Monsieur de Turenne, and told him, He thought it no ways proper for them to attempt any thing of so great concernment, without the participation of the Cardinal who was so near; and therfore advis'd that he shou'd first be made acquainted with it, and his directions receiv'd, before they undertook the Enterprize. Mons'. de Turenne, tho very unwillingly, was constrain'd to yeeld to this opinion; upon which they dispatch'd a Messenger to inform the Cardinal by word of mouth, of the great advantage which was given as it were into their hands; who no sooner heard of it, but he return'd the bearer in all hast to give his approbation: But tho the Cardinal was only distant about a league or two at most, yet before his approbation could be had, the opportunity was overslip'd; for just as the Army was setting forward, another party of the Royalists brought word, that the Prince of Condé already was dislodg'd, as they beleev'd, because the Bourg was all on fire, and the horse guard which they had seen on the other side of it was drawn off.

M. de Turenne
proposes to
march and fall
upon the P^{ce}
of Condé at
Vaubecourt,
where un-
doubtedly
they had
surprised him.
O<small>R:</small> M<small>EM:</small>
p. 1. p. 250.

M. de la Ferté
opposes the
proposall,
under pretence
that the Car-
dinal ought
first to be
advertis'd,
but in effect
out of spleen
to M. de
Turenne.
O<small>R:</small> M<small>EM:</small>
P. 2. p: 250.

By staying to
haue the
Cardinal's
approbation,
they lose the
opportunity
of defeating
the P^{ce} of
Condé, who
never escap'd
a defeat more
narrowly.
O<small>R:</small> M<small>EM:</small>
P. 1: p. 251.

148

PART
I.

1652.

On the Armys advancing a litle further, they perceiv'd the first part of this intelligence to be true, by the rising flames which were easily discern'd by night, and they were inform'd by another small party that the Prince was march'd away with extraordinary hast; wherupon the King's troopes drew back into their quarters, not thinking it expedient to go further from Barleduc then they were. The next day they were inform'd by some inhabitants of Vaubecourt, that the occasion of the fire which was seen in their Bourg proceeded from the Prince of Condé, who having notice of the Royalists' coming, commanded his Trumpetts immediatly to sound to horse; and seeing his men not over hasty to leave their quarters which were so well provided, caus'd some houses to be fir'd at each corner of the Bourg, therby to constraine his men to come forth, and make ready for their march.

Tis most certain that the Prince never escap'd a defeat more narrowly then this; and he took such warning by it, that he thought it not convenient for him to stay any longer in those parts, Seeing the Royalists were so strong as to continue two Seiges with half of their Army, and come out with the other to meet him in the way. He therfore march'd out of the Country, and left the King's Army in quiet to finish their design of reducing those and other places in the Dukedom of Bar. And he had reason to think himself oblig'd to M^r. de la Ferté for escaping as he did, for had not he oppos'd the Counsell of the Mareschall de Turenne, the Prince had certainly been surprised. Neither did Monsr. de la Ferté want either judgment or Souldiership to discern the advantage, but his spleen was such against M^r. de Turenne for having lodg'd in St Michel, that he regarded not what prejudice he did to his Masters seruice, if he could hinder the other from performing so considerable an action, and from the honour which he shou'd obtain by doing it. Vndoubtedly it was for this, and no other reason that he propos'd the

The P^{ce} of Condé marches out of the Country. O_R: M_{EM}: P. 1: p. 252.

sending to the Cardinal, that at least if the Cardinal came not himself, it might be sayd that the Mareschall de Turenne was order'd by him to undertake it. And 'tis very credible, that had any other man but himself committed such a fault which was visible to all the world, he had payd deerly for his mismanagement; but he was so considerable by his commands and dependencies, that the Cardinal never took the least notice of it.

P A R T
I.

1652.

The Royall Army continued at Condit till the 1|th, and then having notice that the Prince was gone quite away, M. de la Ferté with the greatest part of the foot and some of the horse return'd to Bar, and Mr. de Turenne with the rest went and quarter'd at Contrisson, (*Contrusson*) and the Villages about it, as Revigny aux Vaches and other places which were not distant from above four leagues from Bar, where they had covert for themselves, and forage for their horses, and were in a readiness for any seruice requir'd from them. As for the Cardinal, he was quarter'd at a Village call'd Faine (*Fains*) a league on this side of the Town, where he continued during all the Seige, which lasted not long after the Prince of Condé was retreated; yet they suffered two breaches to be made before they thought of surrender. The first of which being in such a place as in all appearance was assaultable, yet prov'd otherwise upon the King's troopes storming of it; for when the men had mounted it, they found the depth too dangerous for leaping, it being a full pike's length from top to bottom by reason of the hollownes of the ground which was not discernable from without; so that the Soldiers were forced to retire, and came not off without some loss. Wherupon a new battery was rais'd against the Castle, where when they had made a considerable breach, the Enemy began to capitulate, and were finally constrain'd to surrender both the upper Town and the Castle, and to yeeld them-

M. de la Ferté returns to the Seige of Bar, and M. de Turenne quarters with the horse in the adjacent Villages. OR. MEM. P. 2. p. 252.

The Cardinal quarters at Faine. *Ibid.*

After two breaches made, the upper Town and Castle of Barleduc surrender'd about the middle of December. OR: MEM: P. 1. p: 253.

selves prisoners of warr, which was done about the midst of the month.

And here wee cannot forbear to mention a remarke which the Duke made upon this occasion, That the accident which made the first of the above mention'd breaches useless, and the place unasaultable, may teach a Governour who defends a Town to do that by art which here was done by nature: for if a wall be but reasonably strong and has a sound foundation, the Governour may haue time to dig a pitt behind the place where the Enemy begins to batter, so as to render the breach as fruitless to the Assailants, as the first of these prov'd unprofitable to the Royalists.

An Irish
Regiment of
foot made
prisoners of
warr at the
Seige of Bar,
offer their
seruice to the
Duke, and are
incorporated
in his Regiment
and sent to
Ligny. *Ibid.*

In this Town of Barleduc amongst the other troopes which were left in it by M. de Lorraine, there was an Irish Regiment of foot, who seeing themselves prisoners of warr, and like to continne long in that condition, their Collonel dying the same day on which the Town was deliver'd up, and Lieutenant Collonel having made his escape, sent to offer their seruice to the Duke, in case his R. Highness could obtain their liberty from the Cardinal; which being easily granted by him, that Regiment consisting in ten Companies with all their Officers were incorporated in the Duke's, and sent to Ligny, before which place the others were.

M. de la Ferté
presses the
Castle of
Ligny.
Or: Mem:
P. 1. p. 254.

And now that Bar was taken, the Mareschall de la Ferté's men were likewise order'd to go thither and hasten the taking of the Castle, where no considerable attempt had yet been made while the other Seige continued ; Then the Mareschall began to batter the Castle, but before the breach was made assaultable, he could not perfect it for want of cannon bullets, which gave opportunity to the Defendents to fortify the top of it with a very strong pallisade : This being observ'd by the Mareschall, he fasten'd a Miner on to the same place, which was easily fix'd

in the ruines of the Wall, so that in a litle space of time, the Mine
was made, charg'd and filled, and in a condition to be fired.
Wherupon the Mareschall commanded the Regiment of York
and Douglas to prepare for the attack at the springing of the
mine; and order'd his own Regiment whose turn it was to go on,
to be in a readiness to second them : All things being prepar'd
in this manner, fire was given to the Mine; and in the midst
of the smoke before it could be discern'd what effect the Mine
had produced, the Count d'Estrées, who commanded in the
attack, order'd it instantly to be made. Accordingly they fell
on, passing over the ditch which was very brode upon the yee
(ice); But when they came to the breach they perceived the
Mine had fail'd their expectation : for in stead of inlarging
the breach, it had only carryd away the outward part of the
Wall as far as where the Enemy had plac'd their pallisade, so
that there was no possibility of mounting to it. Upon this
miscarriage of the Mine, there was a necessity of making a
retreat, which while they were performing (the) yce broke under
them, and most of them fell into the (ditch); which second accident gave more leasure to the Enemy to do more execution on
them. Thus for want of a litle patience to see what effect the
Mine had wrought, the Regiment of York lost four Captains,
some Lieutenants and Enseigns, and about a hundred men
slain outright; and the Regim^t of Douglas two Captains and
neer fifty private Soldiers, besides many Officers and Soldiers
hurt. That night the Miner was once more set on work, and
the next day being the twenty second of December, they
in the Castle began to parly, capitulating for the same conditions
which those of Bar had received before them.

These two places being thus surrendered, the Cardinal was
still desirous that the Army shou'd go forward and take S^t
Menehou; and in order to that design having left those places,
which they had newly master'd, well garrison'd, and the breaches

The Regim^u of
York and
Douglas lose
a great many
officers and
Soldiers by the
miscarriage of
a Mine, in the
last attack of
the Castle of
Ligny.
Or: Mem:
P. I. p. 255.
The Castle
of Ligny
capitulates
the 22 of
December.
Ibid.

as well repair'd as the shortness of the time, and the Season of the year permitted, the troopes march'd away from Contrusson to Doucet on the 27th, and the next day came to Sommyeur, where the continu'd till the 30th. During this whole march all the Army was quarter'd in Villages, the severity of the winter not suffering them to incamp; for the Wether at that time was so excessiue cold, that there was no possibility either for men or horse to be abroad. The day they came to Sommyeur which was the 28th, the frost was so very sharp, that all the horsemen were forced to dismount and march on foot, leading their horses, to keep warmth in their bodies by their motion; and about thirty or forty soldiers the same day miserably perish'd throw the extreamity of cold; for so soon as any of them who were not warmly cloth'd, grew weary, and sat down for ease, the frost pierced them, and they were never able to raise again, severall of which poor people the Duke himself saw frozen to death, and more had been, if the care of their Officers had not prevented it: For they, seeing the poor creatures almost ready to sink, caus'd them to be taken up and carryd on horseback to the next quarter, where by giving them strong waters and other comfortable remedies, they sav'd many of them. That which made the troopes the more sensible of this hardship, was that there was not the least shelter, for they were then marching over the large and open plaines of Champagne, which levell Country with a peircing north East wind blowing directly in their faces augmented the inclemency of the Wether; And indeed the whole Army suffered so extreamly by that days march, that it was one of the causes they did not attack St Menehou: For on occasion of this cruell Wether Monsr. de Turenne went to the Cardinal, and once more represented to him the difficulties of laying Seige to such a Town in so hard a season; That the troopes could not be there furnish'd with those conveniences, which they found at Bar and Lagny, neither covert for their foot, nor forage for their horse

In the march of the Royall Army to Sommieure, all the horsemen are forced to dismount and many Soldiers perish for cold, severall of which the Duke himself saw frozen to death 28 Xber. Or: Mem: P. 1. p: 255.

in the neighbouring Villages, here being no lower Town to be taken without making Trenches, nor Suburbs for the shelter of the men ; That this was a place, which would require a formall Seige, both for its strength and the great number of its defendents, and then the Country round about it, which was lately devour'd by the Army of the Enemy when they took it, could supply no forage for the horses, So that in stead of taking turne of fortune, and making a happy end of the Campagne, they should hazard the ruine óf the Army and be forced to raise the Seige dishonorably.

These Considerations were so strong and so manifestly true, that they convinced the Cardinal, who suffer'd himself to be perswaded by them to lay aside the thought of taking in St Menehou : So that the Army march'd on towards Rhetel by Menecour (*Miocour*) and Grivy, and on the first of January, 1653, quarter'd at Attigny, which is scituate on the River Aisne, about three or four leagues above Rhetel, where the next (*day*) they pass'd the River and lodg'd that night at Saux aux Bois. But finding that Rhetel would prove too hard a work for them to undertake at that time of the year as well as St Menehou, for the same reasons they pass'd by that place also, and went to attack Château-Porcien, a place about two leagues below Rhetel upon the same River, having there the same conveniences of attacking it, as they had before at Barleduc ; being certain to Master the Town the first night, where there was room sufficient to quarter the greatest part of their foot, at least as many as was necessary to carry on the Seige, the Castle only being tenable.

This being so resolved, M^r. de Turenne (whom the Duke allways accompagn'd) quarter'd with most of his horse, and some few foot, at Soin (*Son*) (where they arriv'd on the 6th of January) and the neighbouring Villages, a league and a half from Château-Porcien, as the more proper place for hindering

PART I.

1652.

The Cardinal perswaded by M. de Turenne's reasons, lays aside the design of beseiging St Menehou. OR: MEM: P. 1: p. 257.

The Army marcheth towards Rhetel, 1. January, 1653.

During this Seige the Duke is quarter'd with M. de Turenne at Soin, to hinder succours.

PART
I.

1653.
The Seige is
carryd on by
M. d'Elbeuf
and M.
d'Aumont.
Ibid.
any succours from being put into that Town: The Care of advancing the Seige was repos'd on Monsieur d'Elbeuf and M. d'Aumont. The Mareshall de la Ferté quartering at * * * * * * * with his horse, for the same purpose that Monsieur de Turenne lay at Soin, and the Cardinal lodging at Balhan..

Very hard
duty in the
out quarters,
where the
Duke was
during the
Seige. *Ibid.*
The Prince
Condé himself
approaches to
try if he could
releeve the
Town.
Or: Mem:
P. 2. p. 257.
Wee shall not relate the particulars of this Seige where the Duke was not constantly present, only what pass'd in the out quarters where his Royall Highness was, which were upon hard duty during all the time that the Seige continu'd; which happen'd from the approache of somme troopes of the Enemy and of the Prince Condé himself, who came to try if he could possibly releeve it. Therfore Mons'. de Turenne to prevent being surpris'd in his quarters, and to keep himself in a readiness to hinder the Prince from passing by him and putting succours into the Town by night, order'd all the horse that were quarter'd in the Villages about Soin, to march thither every evening, and continue there all night, returning after Sun rise to their own quarters: The same method was duly observ'd by all the Mareshall de la Ferté's horse which were distributed in the Villages about him; And on this hard duty the troopes continu'd during the Seige, which lasted not long. For the beseigers being possessed as they were of the Town, it was no hard matter to fasten the Miner to the Castle, and so as it was charg'd, and ready to spring, the Governour who was call'd Dubuisson capitulated to yeld in four days, if during that time he was not releeved.

The Enemy having notice of this Treaty came as far as Chaumont to try if it were practicable to succour it; and before the Terme was quite expir'd, on the very last day of it, the

---

* * * The same blank occurs in King James' condensed and less confidential Narrative of these Wars, which was drawn up for the Cardinal de Bouillon. — EDITOR.

Royalists verily beleeved it would have come to an engagement, their partys bringing them word that the Enemy was advancing towards them : Upon which intelligence they were drawn up in battell in the plain above the Castle, just in the passage of the Enemy, if they should endeavour to releeve the place. Thus the Royall Army stood expecting them till noon and then they had the news of their return: Within an hour afterwards the Castle was deliver'd up according to the agreement, upon the ordinary Articles of being conveyd to their next garrison with their armes and baggage; it being not worth the labour to haue had them prisoners of warr like those of Barleduc and Ligny, considering the sharpnes of the Season, which yet continued in extreamity, and that the Royall Army both horse and foot had endur'd so much that they were glad to possess the Castle on any termes. The foot especially were reduced to cruell hardships, the Country being wholy ruin'd, and no possibility of furnishing them regularly with bread, the Commissary of Victuals having none, and no stores of Corne were in any of the neighbouring Towns ; so that many of the Soldiers were forced to eat horse flesh, and all sorts of unwholsome miserable food for the bare sustenance of life. Amongst the rest they were driven to feed on the Stalks of Cabbages, which they call'd the Cardinal's bread.

Château-Porcien being thus taken, not only the Soldiers, but even the Officers themselves had hopes of going immediatly into winter-quarters, and in that beleif they march'd away on the 13th January and, passing the Aisne, quarter'd that night at Poilcour and the adjoining Villages . From thence they continned their march as far as Proüilly which lyes betwixt Rheims and Fismes, very neer the Veste : There they quarter'd two or three days, but in stead of going forward to winter-quarters, the Cardinal order'd them to march back over the Aisne, which they pass'd on the 20th at Pont-à-Vere, to retake

PART I.

1653.

Château-Porcien deliver'd up to the King's Army.
Or: Mem: P. I. p. 258.

The Soldiers in the King's Army forced to eat horse flesh and Stalks of Cabbage, which they call'd the Cardinal's bread.
Ibid. p. 259.

The Army in their way to winter-quarters are ordered by the Cardinal to march back again and retake Vervins.
Or: Mem: P. 1: p. 259.

PART
I.

1653.

Vervins a Town of considerable strength, which was only incompass'd with a wall, and had been master'd and garrison'd by the Spaniards in the foregoing summer. Thō this place was incapable of maintaining a Seige against an Army, yet it was a good quarter, and would haue given much trouble to the neighbouring Countries; for which reason the Cardinal was desirous that the King's troopes should not end the Campagne before they had master'd it. Never was march more grudgingly undertaken by the common Souldiers, or even by the Officers, who wer all of them worn out and sinking

A very uneasy
march for an
Army sinking
under the
fatigue of
So long a
Campagne.
Ibid. p. 260.

under the fatigue of this long Seruice. And indeed it prov'd very uncomfortable march to them, for the frost (*being*) newly broken, the ways were deep and almost impassable for baggage throughout that mountainous and deep claye Country, which lyes betwixt Pont-à-Vere and Laon; and thō after they had pass'd thus far, they march'd in a more open and plainer Country, yet the ways continued deep and rotten. In this march the Army lost the greatest part of their baggage and many horses, meerely by the badnes of the rodes, no Enemy being neer to trouble them; and on the 25th they came to Vaupe distant about a league from Vervins.

The Duke
viewing
Vervins with
M.deTurenne
and going near
to make his
observations,
is like to be
made prisoner
by a party of
the Enemy
who fir'd at
him.
OR: MEM:
P. I: p. 260.

At this place the Duke escap'd narrowly from being taken by the Enemy; for as he rode a long with Monsieur de Turenne to view the Town, his R. Highness and another Gentleman going somewhat near, the better to make their observations, were mett by a small party of horse belonging to Vervins, which they mistook for their own Souldiers, and were within pistoll shott of them before they were sensible of their errour; and had not the Enemy then fir'd at them, they had undoubtedly ridd in amongst them, and it would haue been very hard for them to gett off.

They begin to
attack Vervins
the 26. Jan⁷.
Ibid.

The next day about a thousand foot, and two hundred horse, were commanded out of the severall quarters to begin the attack of the Town, the garrison of which consisted in six hundred foot and three hundred horse commanded by Mons'. de Bassecourt, Collonell, and a very brave Gentleman. The first night the Souldiers lodg'd themselves under the Shelter of some outhouses and gardens close by the Town wall, and the next night made a battery; which the Enemy seeing, began to Capitulate, and march'd out on the 28ᵗʰ of January with their armes and bagge.

PART I.

1653.

The Town is surrender'd the 28ᵗʰ. Or: Mem: P. 1: p. 260.

The Army receiv'd litle or no loss at this short Seige, yet tho it cost so litle time, the Souldiers repin'd sufficiently against the Cardinal, for not sending them directly from Château-Porcien into winter-quarters; in so much that when the Enemy from the walls of Vervins, according to the usuall custome, began to raile at him, the Souldiers in stead of replying in his defence, only Said, *Amen*, to all their curses, that word serving for a burden to every imprecation of the Spaniards.

M. de Turenne after having taken possession of Vervins, march'd back his Army to Laon, where all the troopes are sent to their severall winter-quarters. Or: Mem: P. 1: p. 261.

The 28ᵗʰ January in the morning Mʳ. de Turenne went and saw Bassecourt march out with his Souldiers, and having taken possession of the place, he march'd back with his Army to Fessy sur Saare, and from thence to Laon, where all the troopes were sent into their severall winter-quarters; And the Duke, the Cardinal, and all the Generalls and persons of quality went for Paris, where they arrived on the 3ᵈ of February.

In this manner ended that long Campagne, (*during*) which Monsieur de Turenne severall times by his conduct and Counsell preserved the Monarchy of France, to his immortall fame and glory.

The Duke the Cardinal and all the Generalls return to Paris the 3ᵈ of feb: Ibid.

When his R. Highness arrived at Paris, he had the Satisfaction not only of paying his duty to the Queen his Mother, but also of meeting there his Brother the Duke of Glocester, and his Cosen Prince Rupert. The first of them, after a long detention in the hands of his bloody Enemies, who had murder'd his

The Duke returning from his first and long Campagne, meets at Paris his Brother the Duke of Glocester and his Cosen the Pᶜᵉ Rupert.

158

PART I.

1653.

Father, was at last lett loos by them, not out of any principle of humanity, but meerly to save the charges of maintaining him any longer; And the other who was given over for lost, after having escap'd a thousand dangers at Sea for the espace of four years, happen'd also to come thither at the same time. But of all this which occur'd whilst his Royall Highness remain'd at Paris, he makes no mention in his Memoires; for it seems, that his thoughts where then so full of the Warr, that he reckon'd the time lost and not worth the remembring which was not imployd in the feild.

THE SECOND PART.

IN this year, 1653, his Royall Highness made his Second Campagne, in the company and under the conduct of Monsieur de Turenne, the greatest Captain of this and perhaps of any age, who was not a litle delighted in having so illustrious a person for his Schollar in the discipline of warr. Of this Campagne his R. Highness gives the following Account in the Memoires written in his own hand.

P A R T
II.

1653.

THE CAMPAGNE of this year began but late on either side, which could not be otherwise considering how long it was before the last ended. Yet thō wee went last out of the feild, and many of our troopes had taken up their winter-quarters in Poitou, Anjou, la Marche, and other remote Provinces, Our Army was notwithstanding in Champagne by the latter end of June; with so much dilligence, that wee beseiged Rhetel before the Spanish Army was gott together out of their winter-quarters. This place was of great consequence, being situated upon the River Aisne, and being an inlet into Champagne, of which it is a member; so that partys from thence might make incursions almost to the gates of Paris, and raise contributions even in its neighbourhood. It was taken about nine months before by the Prince of Condé, and put into the hands of the Spaniards upon his conjunction with them.

It seems a litle strange that a place of this consequence, and which in all probability would be the first attempt of the French

The Duke's
Second
Campagne
under M. de
Turenne.
OR: MEM:
P. 2: p. 1.

The French
beseige Rhetel.
OR: MEM:
P. 2. p: 1.

PART
II.

1653.

to retake, should be no better provided with sufficient numbers of men for its defence; for thō the Marquis of Persan a very good officer was Governour of it, yet Monsʳ. de Turenne without staying to make a Line of Circumvalation, storm'd the outworks the first night, and carryd them without any extraordinary loss of men. One cheif reason why the outworks were so easily gain'd was, that thō they had a good ditch and were high enough, yet being only of earth, and having no palissades, but upon the parapett, the French were the more encouraged to venture on them ; for when the Soldiers had once got up to them, their advantage was equall to that of the Enemys within, so that the greatest number must consequently carry it.

This Success did so hearten our men, and discourage theirs, that the Town itself whose best strength consisted in the outworks, was quickly forced to capitulate ; for wee brought our battery so near by the advantage of the outworks, that wee made in a short time two sufficient breaches, at each attack

Rhetel sur-
render'd up to
the French the
9ᵗʰ of July.
Oʀ: Mᴇᴍ:
P. 2. p. 6.

one, in the wall which was none of the strongest. This oblig'd the beseiged to parly on the 8ᵗʰ of July, and the next day to surrender the Town upon termes of marching away with their armes and baggage to their nearest garrison. The Articles being perform'd, our Army stayd a day or two to repair the breaches ; and having provided the place with all things neces-sary, and left in it a sufficient garrison, wee march'd away towards Guise, having been inform'd that the Enemy had appointed their generall Rendezvous near that place.

But in our march thither, when wee lay incamped by a Vil-lage call'd Noircour, Intelligence came from the Governour of Rocroy, that part of their Army, which was marching to the

The French
march from
Noircour in
hopes to
surprise the
Enemy, but
are disap-
pointed.
Ibid. p. 8.

Rendezvous, was quarter'd in severall Villages about Chimay, Trelon, and Glajon, on the other side of the great woods of the forest of Ardennes, which were extended down that way ; upon which information, our Generalls resolv'd to march with all their

troopes and some few feild pieces, leaving only five or six
hundred men to guard the baggage, and to pass these large woods
in hopes of surprising the Enemy in their quarters before they
could haue notice of our march. It happen'd to be Mons'. de
Turenne's turn to lead the Van, who us'd all possible expedition,
but after having pass'd by a certain Abbey call'd Bussilly, and
got with the Van as far as Anort, (*Nost*) which is almost on the
farthest side of the woods, wee had intelligence by a small party
which brought in some prisoners, that they had been advertis'd
of our coming ; so that seeing our design to be discover'd, wee
march'd back by the same way wee came, and joyn'd our
baggage on the 14th where wee had left it at Noircour, after wee
had been three days abroad in this expedition ; and from thence
we march'd to Haris on the 17th, and so to S. Algis, where the
King of France, and Cardinal Mazarin came to us.

On the 25th wee went and camp'd at Ribemont, and in the
mean time the Spanish Army consisting at least of thirty thousand men, assembled on the fronteers near l'arbre de Guise,
and with proportionable train of Artillery and provisions of
Victualls, began their march to enter France ; of which the
King being informed, it was debated in Councill before him
and the Cardinal what was fittest for him to do, having so
strong an Enemy to encounter, and our Army in the whole not
amounting to above six thousand foot, and being scarce ten
thousand horse. Some were of opinion that all our foot, excepting only a thousand commanded musketeers, should be cast
into the fronteer Towns, with some few horse to accompany
them ; and that with this small proportion of Infantry and the
body of our horse, wee should keep near the Enemy's Army to
incommode and harass them, as much as wee were able, by
falling on their foragers and cutting off their Convoy's, in order
to hinder them from attacking any of our Towns.

Others were of opinion that wee should not separate our

Side notes:

PART II.
1653.

The Spanish Army on the fronteers 30000 strong. Or: Mem: P: 2: p. 10.

The French being not above 16000 men, it is debated in Councill before the King and Card¹ Mazarin what is fittest to be done in this conjuncture. *Ibid.* p. 11.

The opinions were divided. Or: Mem: P. 2: p. 11.

P A R T
II.

1653.

M.deTurenne
refutes the
two former
opinions and
gives his own,
with the
reasons therof.
Ibid. p. 12.

Army, but endeavour with the whole body of it to defend the
passages of the Rivers in case they should advance into the
Country, thinking it to be of dangerous consequence (since
Bourdeaux still held out) if wee should permitt them a free
inrode towards Paris, which was so lately reduced to the
King's obedience.

But Monsieur de Turenne was of a quite different opinion
from the two former; For, said he, should wee divide our Army,
and put most of our foot and some horse into the Garrisons,
wee should leave ourselves so inconsiderable, that the Enemy
would easily drive the remaining small body of our forces into
what part of the Country they should please; after which they
would haue their choice of beseiging any of our Towns, by
falling back upon them, and haue leisure enough to entrench
themselves before wee could joyu together our Separated forces:
besides which they would then be so far advanced in their
work, that it would not be adviseable for us to sitt down before
any of their places, for before wee could haue made any considerable progress in a Seige, they would haue taken a Town,
and been upon us; So that wee should be sure, according to
that method, to haue lost one of our places, without Mastering
one of theirs, thō of less importance. On the other side, thō
wee kept our whole Army in a body, and lay behind our
Rivers, with an intention of hindering the Enemys from passing
over and advancing into our Country, wee should faile of
what wee proposed to ourselves by that undertaking; for knowing them to outnumber us very much in foot, it would be
very difficult for us to maintain any pass against them;
and besides it would not only be a very great discouragement to our Soldiers to be forced from their posts, but
the consequence would also be very dangerous 'from the
effects it might haue at Paris and in the Countries: So that
considering the whole matter, he was of opinion, That wee should

keep our Army intire and with it observe the motion of the
Enemys, keeping as closs to them as conveniently wee could,
either behind or on one side of them, without exposing ourselves so far as to be forced to an Ingagement when wee found
it not for our advantage; by observing which method he hoped
to (be) able to hinder them from beseiging any place of consequence, in doing of which they must be obliged to separate
their Army, which they would hardly adventure to do, whilst
wee were attending them so near, that before they could haue
intrenched themselves and made their bridges of communication, wee should haue the opportunity of falling on which
part of them wee pleas'd; And besides he beleev'd not, that
they would advance farr into the Country, seeing that if they
did, wee should be able to hinder any Convoys from coming
to them, without which they could not possibly subsist, or continue long in the heart of the French Dominions.

These and other reasons offered by Monsr. de Turenne prevail'd upon the Cardinal, and consequently upon the King and
Councill; so that orders being given, and measures accordingly
taken for carrying on the Campagne, the Court retired from
the Army.

In the mean time the Enemy having drawn all their forces
into a body, began their march into the French Dominions
betwixt the Rivers of Somme and Oyse; and incamped at
Fonsomme and Fervaques; from whence they marched onwards
on the first of August, and pass'd within sight of us the same
day, continuing their march towards Ham, having the Somme
on their right hand, and camp'd about St Simon and Clastres;
where they imployd a whole day in passing the défilés: In the
mean time upon their approche, wee put ourselves on battell,
and seeing they came not to us, but continued their march, wee
march'd the same day down along the River by which wee
lay to a Village call'd Chery-Maiot, not farr from la Fere;

The opinion
of M. de
Turenne
prevailes, and
his Counsell
is followed.
OR: MEM:
P. 2: p. 16.

The Spaniards
march into
the French
Dominions
August 1st.
Ibid.

The two
Armys in
Sight of one
another.
Ibid.

The French
put themSelves
in battell.
Ibid. p: 17.

where wee imployd all the next day in making bridges for our
foot, and passages for our horse, intending to pass that River
in case the Enemy pursued their march any further into the
Country, of which wee had notice the next morning by our
partys: But yet Monsieur de Turenne, unwilling to expose
himself by marching over till he were more certain of the way
they took, went over himself at break of day with about a
thousand horse, and finding that the intelligence which his
partys had brought him was altogether true, he sent back his
orders for the Army to come over to him, which being perform'd
wee march'd down the River, and camp'd on the third of August
at Fargnier, having the woods to cover us from the Enemy,
which were of as great security to us as a River; and receiving
intelligence that they were advanced as far as Roye, which they
took and plunder'd (it being only defended by the Townsmen,
who thō they had no troopes amongst them yet suffer'd batteries to be rais'd which playd upon them before they would
surrender) wee came on the 5th to Noyon, and hearing there
that Roye was taken, wee advanced on the 9th to Magny; which
thō on the other side of the woods was yet so fast a Country,
that wee were in no manner of danger, and besides it was not
our design to keep too far distance from the Enemy.

From thence Monsr. de Schomberg was sent with the Gendarmes, which consisted of about two hundred and fifty horse
and a hundred foot, to cast himself into Corbie; and at the
same time about three hundred foot were sent into Peroñe,
which were the only troopes wee ever put into any place from
the Army, and having notice that they were drawing down
towards the Somme, not far from Corbie, wee posted ourselves
at Epperville closs by Ham on the 10th of August.

Wee were no sooner arriv'd there, but wee received intelligence
that the Count of Megen, with about three thousand men, was
to march out of Cambray the next day, to convoy great store

of provisions and all things necessary for a Seige, with great
numbers of Pioneers, and all sorts of ammunition, and that he
was to march with them to the River of Somme betwixt Peronne
and Corbie, where, after they had mett him, new measures
were to be taken : On this advertissement wee took our march
passing over the Somme at Ham, and setting out a litle before
Sun sett, with an intention to fall on that Convoy, which wee
hop'd to find on the plaine about Bapaume; And to make the
greater Expedition, wee march'd away with all our horse,
leaving only some few behind, to come along with the foot,
artillery and baggage, which had order to follow with all
imaginable diligence. Being come to Peronne by break of
day, with our horse, wee took out from thence all the foot which
had been sent thither from the Army, and all the garrison could
spare beside, and continued our march towards Bapaume:
Being come within two or three leagues of that place, wee
halted to refresh our horses, and sent our partys towards
Cambray, to give us notice of the motion of the Convoy: By
noon they brought us intelligence, that the Enemy had begun
their march out of Cambray, but being advertiz'd of our coming
were return'd into the Town: having received this information,
and withall, that the Enemy's Army was come to the Somme
near Bray, wee march'd back and met our foot, Artillery and
baggage on the 1[th that night at Manancourt, a Village which
ly's at the head of a litle brook, that runs from thence by Mont
St Quentin and so into the Somme, not far from Peronne.

There wee camp'd that night, and having notice the next
morning, that the Enemy was making bridges over the River
where they lay, it was thought expedient for us to retire, the
same day, a litle back to Allayne another Village on the same
brook, near Mont St Quentin; having notwithstanding resolved
in case they should pass the Somme, that wee should post
ourselves some what above Manancourt, in a place which both

1653.

The French endeavour to Surprise a Convoy of the Enemys, but are discover'd. On: Mem: P: 2. p. 20.

The French campe at Manancourt the 1]th August. Or: Mem: P. 2: p. 22.

11

our Mareshalls had view'd and determin'd there to draw up our Army in battell, upon the first notice wee should haue of their approche to us. But thō this was resolved by both our Generalls together, it was alter'd by one, without staying to hear from the other, on the next morning being the 13th : For M^r. de Turenne according to his usuall custome going out of his quarters by Sun rise, with some few in his Company, first went to visite our horse guard, which was on the other side of the brook ; And from thence seeing nothing, nor hearing any news of any of our partys, which he had sent out the night before to bring him notice of the Enemys motion, he went to Peronne to send partys along the Somme, on the other side, to try if they cou'd discover any thing of the Spaniards' march; Not beleeving it possible that they cou'd be coming to us, but that either from Bapaume or by some of our own partys wee

The Spaniards coming up unexpectedly to the french Army, Surprise them.
Or: Mem: P. 2: p. 24.

should haue been advertized : Yet it happen'd otherwise, for the Enemy march'd with so much diligence, that their Van was past Bapaume before break of day ; so that neither our partys which were driven in there, nor any from the Town cou'd give us notice, the Spaniards being gotten betwixt us and

M. de la Ferté takes the allarme and marches back to Mont St Quentin with the left wing.
Ibid.

them ; and the first intelligence wee had of them was by M^r. de la Ferté's horse guards, which were at the head of the litle brook : And he took the allarm so hott, that in stead of marching up to possess the ground, which was resolved on the day before, he having the left wing and being nearest it, march'd back towards Peronne, passing through our right wing; which following the orders they had received the day before, was beginning

M. de Turenne returning from Peronne, finds the Army in disorder and is forced to joyn his troopes with M^r. de la Ferté's.
Or: Mem: P. 2: p. 25:

to march towards the fore appointed place where they were to be drawn up in battell.

In this disorder wee were when Mareshall de Turenne came back from Peronne, and finding that already M. de la Ferté with the left wing was beginning to draw up on Mont St Quentin, he went to his own troopes, which were to compose the right wing and joyn'd them with the left; it being then too late to possess ourSelves of the former ground, because the Enemys Van was already very near it.

There he resolv'd to expect the Enemy, who came on with great joy, as knowing the advantage they had over us, both in numbers and by getting us into a plaine feild, where wee could neither retreat from them, nor avoid fighting, if they pleas'd to ingage us; And indeed I beleeve that if wee had not chang'd our ground wee should certainly haue been beaten: for, besides that they were much Superiour to us in number, as wee were then drawn up, the ground was such, that wee shou'd not haue been able to haue done any thing; because thō our order of battell was very good according to the new method, and that our second Line was placed at a convenient distance behind the first, and a reserve of twelve Squadrons of horse, with two battailons of foot behind that again, and our left wing placed upon Mont St Quentin, yet our right was in evident danger of being routed, for our utmost Squadron on that hand reached within pistoll shott to the bottome of a litle hill, to which the Enemy were marching, and from thence they could haue gall'd us in the flanck, and playd upon us both with their cannon and Musketeers, before they came down to charg us: so that, as I

The right wing of the French in evident danger of being routed, if M^r. de Turenne had not provided against it by changing the ground.
Ibid. p. 26.

sayd, wee had manifestly been beaten, without being able to haue fought, it being then too late to haue chang'd our posture: And indeed not only M. de Turenne, but all of us who were on the right wing plainely saw it; neither can I say that ever in my life I perceiv'd so much confusion, and such signs of being beaten, as were visible in the face of the Soldiers. Monsieur de Turenne no sooner had observ'd it, but he gallop'd away to M^r. de la Ferté on the left wing to give him notice; and withall to assure him, That if wee continued in that posture wee should infallibly be routed; that therfore he was resolved to march up the hill, towards the Enemy, seeing wee could not be

in a more disadvantageous position than now wee were; neither
was there any other way remaining to encourage our Soldiers:
Having told him this, and desired him to follow us, he return'd
speedily to our wing, and march'd up the hill immediatly at
our head.

He was no sooner arriv'd there with the first Squadrons, but he
sent Monsr. de Varennes (an old experienced Officer) who had
been Captain of his guards in all his German warrs, and in whom
he had great confidence, to go before and view the ground over
which wee were to pass: Wee had not march'd above a mile,
when he came back to his Generall, and let him know, that if
he would come along with him, he would shew him such a post
as he was sure would be of great advantage, and that it was not
farr distant. M^r. de Turenne accordingly went before to
observe it, and found it to his great satisfaction such a one as
would wholy secure us from the Enemy: for in our right hand
wee had the brook, which comes from Roiset, and afterwards
falls into the Somme a litle above Peronne; and on our left a
hill so inaccessible and steep, that neither horse nor man cou'd
climb it; and the distance betwixt both was no more, then that
twenty or thirty Squadrons cou'd possibly be drawn up in it.
Before us there was a litle Valley, and on that part of it which
lay nearest to the brook was a Ravine or small Gully, which
wou'd haue been very difficult for any to haue pass'd, and horse
especially.

The French
being now
advantage-
ously posted,
they expect
the Enemy
with cheer-
fulness.
Or: Mem:
P. 2: p. 29.

This was the post where wee drew up, and where wee were
no sooner posted, but the whole countenance of the Army was
changed, and our men had their accustom'd cheerfulness in
their faces, so that I am confident, had the Enemy attack'd us
in that place, wee shou'd haue beaten them: For thō their
numbers almost doubled ours, yet our troopes being very good,
and well posted, wee had a great advantage; And that wee might

make it yet more secure for us and more difficult for them, when they shou'd endeavour to approche us, wee immediatly fell on making five Redans, open behind, and each of them capable of containing an hundred musketteers ; between which wee placed our cañon which were about thirty, so that the Enemy must haue endured the fire of all these, before he cou'd so much as see our troopes which stood behind, and then received a charge either of horse or foot, which was in our choice : After all this, the ground was so very narrow, that the Army under Monsr. de Turenne's command (being the right wing and half the foot) was constraint to be drawn up in four or five lines, behind each other. As for M^r. de la Ferté, he drew up with his troopes, which consisted of the left wing and the other half of the foot, all along the top of the Steep hill I haue already mention'd, which cover'd our left hand and fronted that way. So that in case wee had been attacked by the front, he cou'd easily haue drawn his men to haue seconded us of the right wing.

It was, as I remember, betwixt two and three of the clock in the afternoon when wee drew up with our first Squadron in this post, when wee saw the whole Spanish Army march in battell to us, and coming about the end of the wood directly in our faces. This wood ran from within muskett shott of our Redans, all along upon the very height and browes of the steep hill which wee had on our left hand, which also happen'd to straighten the ground by which they were to approche us : In this manner they came on, thinking to haue fallen on us immediatly ; but being come within a mile and a half of us, or near that distance, they made a halt, wherupon most of their foot went down to the River to quench their thirst, being sufficiently tir'd with their long march, and almost chock'd for want of water, having met with none since they

The whole SpanishArmy march up in battell against them. Aug: 13. O R: MEM: P. 2. p. 19.

parted from the Somme, till they arrived at this place; So that it was absolutly necessary for their Officers to give way, that they should drink and refresh themselves.

The Prince of Condé, as I haue been since inform'd, would haue fallen upon us that evening, the 13th of August, but the Count de Fuenseldagne oppos'd it, representing to him the weariness of their men, especially their foot, who after so tedious a march through a dry Country, and in so hott a Season, were not reasonably to be put on further duty till the next morning; besides which, it would be very difficult and almost impracticable to draw them from the River-side that evening; that so small a delay could not prejudice the Enterprise because they had us in their power, so that wee could not possibly get from them; but in the mean time their Soldiers would recover their Spirits and Strength by a good night's rest, and then they had the day before them: As for us, at so short a warning wee could not do much for the further securing of ourselves; but that they might haue the remainder of the evening to view the posture in which wee lay, and to observe the ground over which they were to pass to us.

These arguments so prevail'd with the Prince, that the thought of doing any thing farther that day was layd aside; and they camped in battaill where they lay. Next morning when he and the rest of their Generall Officers had view'd and consider'd the ground, finding the great advantages wee had by reason of our post, they gave over the intention of attacking us in that place; and so the two Armys continued in presence of each other, during three or four days: in all which time there happen'd no considerable action, but almost perpetuall skirmishes. Yet there fell out one thing, which tho of no great concernment might deserve to be mention'd.

The two Armys remain three days in presence of each other.
On: Mem:
P: 2. p: 31.
Frequent Skirmishes happen'd.
Ibid.
A remarkable action of one Bellechassaigne.
Ibid.

There was a Lieutenant of horse in the Regiment Royall whose name was Bellechassaigne, a great goer out on partys,

who was desirous to try if he could take some considerable
Officer from the very Camp of the Enemy; having this in his
head, he askt leave of Mons'. de Turenne to go out with a small
party, which being granted him, he chose about fifteen good
men to follow him, and with them put himself into the wood
which I haue mention'd, which reach'd from our Redans to the
Enemy's Camp. Being there he order'd his Soldiers to disperse
themselves, and, under covert of the wood and favour of the
night, one by one to get into the Camp, where they were to
rejoyne again about midnight, at such a place as was a very
remarkable (*one*) in their Camp, and was seen from ours; where
being met, they should receiue Instructions what to do: having
given them this order, they all separated from each other, got
safely amongst the Enemies, and assembled at the time and
place appointed; from thence they went in a body to the Tent
of one of the Prince of Condé's Major Generalls, or Mareshalls
de Camp. This Officer's name was Mons'. de Ravenel,
whom they intended to take out of his bed, and carry away
with them; his Tent standing most conveniently for their business, and having no guard before it, which was the reason why
they chose him out; all those of a Superiour quality having foot
guards at the entrance of their Tents. Some of them therfore
alighting from their horses went directly in, and had already
seiz'd on two or three of his Servants without noise; when just
as they were going to haue taken him, one of the prisoners
slipp'd out of their hands, and gave the alarm, which forced
Bellechassaigne to leave Ravenel and make what hast he could
possibly to Save himself, which he did and brought along with
him a horse or two, and as many of those whom he had first
secur'd. He might haue kill'd Ravenel himself, but in those
Countries they make not Warr so brutally, for I never knew
any unhuman act committed either by French or Spaniards all
the time I serv'd amongst them.

PART
II.

<u>1653.</u>
The Spaniards
decamp the
16 Aug:
Or: Mem:
P. 2. p. 33.

But to proceed : After the Enemy had stayd three or four days facing us, on the 16ᵗʰ of August about break of day wee heard them sound to horse and beat the march for the foot; and by that time it was break of day, wee saw them begin to march : Vpon which wee stood immediatly to our armes, and Monsʳ. de Turenne himself with two Squadrons of our horse guards went up towards their Camp, the better to observe which way they bent their march, that therby he might make some kind of conjecture what place they intended to beseige. When he was come about half way distance betwixt our Camp and theirs, he left behind him one of the Squadrons and advanced with the other, yet somewhat farther and then stayd with it;

The Duke
and Mʳ. de
Castelnau are
sent by M. de
Turenne to
follow the
Enemy and
view their
Camp.
Or: Mem:
P. 2: p: 33.

sending me, with Monsʳ. de Castelnau and about twelve more, all Officers or Volonteers who were excellently hors'd, to go on as far as conveniently wee cou'd, with order not to engage, but to come off in case wee should be push'd. Accordingly wee went up into the very Camp of the Enemys, and as far as the hutts of the foot, when the Reer of their Cavalry were not yet gotten out of the Camp. There wee made a stand and had a perfect view of their whole Army, after which wee went within pistoll shott of their last Squadrons, not offering to disturb them, nor they us : Thus when wee had satisfyd ourselves with looking, and saw plainly they bent towards Sᵗ Quentin, wee return'd to Mʳ. de Turenne, who straight going back to his own Camp, dis-

M. de Beaujeu
is sent to
secure Guise.
Or: Mem.
P. 2. p. 34.

patch'd away Mʳ. de Beaujeu one of our Lieutenant Generalls, with twelve hundred horse and six hundred foot, to cast himself either into Guise, which place he beleeved the Enemy intended to beseige, or into any other place before which they should offer to ly down. And Beaujeu made such expedition, that he got into Guise just as their first horse appear'd to invest that Town : which when the Enemy perceived, and withall the great diligence which our whole Army had us'd for the same intent, they layd aside the thoughts of that Enterprise;

and after having stayd some few days in that neighbourhood, march'd back, and incamped at Caulaincourt, within a league of the Abbey of Vermand, upon the same brook, about two leagues from St Quentin, it being so far on the way from thence to Peronne.

PART II.

1653.
The Spaniards incamped at Caulincourt.
Ibid.

As for our Army, so soon as M^r. de Beaujeu was detach'd, wee march'd also, causing our baggage to pass the River before us through Péronne, which was the only Pass therabouts. When they were gott over, wee began to march through the Town with the whole Army; when wee saw the Enemy at such a distance from us, that there was no farther danger of their marching back to fall upon our Reer, before wee cou'd get on the other side of the River. And thō that Town be very long, and that there is one bridge only over the Somme; yet by that time it grew dark, M^r. de Turenne with the Van got as far as Golancourt, which is within a league wide of Ham. 'Tis true the Reer cam not up till the next morning, but however it had the same effect with the Enemy as if they had been there in a body, for their partys who saw us cross the River gave them an account of our being there; So that as I observ'd, not only the march of Beaujeu, but also our diligence, hinder'd the Enemy from beseiging Guise: And, as I remember, M^r. de Turenne answer'd some about him, who were representing to him that it was impossible for half our Army to come up that night, considering the length of his intended march and the expedition he used in marching, That what they objected was very true; notwithstanding which if he could but reach his quarter with the Van that night it would produce the Same effect, as if the whole Army were in presence; because that wee being cover'd by the Somme, their partys could give no other account of us, but by the fires which they observed; and seeing them in great numbers they would return with a false intelligence, that wee were advanced so far. And certainly

M.deTurenne by his diligent march prevents the beseiging of Guise.
Or MEM: P. 2. p. 35.

P A R T
II.

1653.

not only in this particular, but generally in all others, never did any Generall take better measures in his marches, or guess'd more probably at the designs of the Enemy then he.

The next morning when the troopes were all come up, and that he was advertis'd from Guise that the Spaniards were at a loss, having miss'd their purpose, wee thought it expedient to continue where wee were without advancing any farther, as being well warn'd by our late Escape; So that the Enemy coming to Caulincourt, wee remained at Golancourt to observe their motions.

The French
quarter at
Golancourt
to observe the
Enemys
motions.
Ibid. p. 36.

While wee lay in that quarter M^r. de Turenne having notice from our partys, the Enemys foragers were accustom'd to pass the brook behind which they lay and come up towards Ham, having with them only a small Convoy, orderd M^r. de Castelnau to take a thousand horse, and to try his fortune on them, in case they came abroad to forage next day: In the evening the ten Squadrons were commanded out, and as soon as it was dark M^r. de Castelnau march'd with them to Ham; where having drawn them up, in stead of passing through the Town, as he ought to have done while the darknes continu'd, he stayd on the outside till break of day; then going through the Town himself, he sent out two partys, to see if those foragers were abroad, leaving still his body on the other side of Ham; and when at last his partys had brought him intelligence that the Enemys were at forage, he sent for all his horse to come over to him, which indeed they did, but by that time wee had travers'd the length of the Town, and were beginning to march towards the Enemy, wee saw they were almost all gone back into their Camp, having taken the alarm at the partys which were sent out to discover them, So that wee tooke not above twenty or thirty at most of all their men, thō wee detach'd some after them, who glean'd up to the number I haue mention'd.

M. de Cas-
telnau is sent
to attack a
Convoy of the
Enemys
foragers.
Or: Mem:
P: 2: p. 36.

Thus what M^r. de Turenne had so well design'd, was wholy
frustrated by the unskillfulness of him who commanded us :
for thō he was perfectly stout, and was besides a good foot
Officer, who understood very well how to carry on a breach,
yet he was very ignorant in commanding horse, which he not
only shew'd on this occasion, but by what he did afterwards ;
so that many men were of opinion, that what he knew was rather
gain'd from the experience of a long practice amongst the foot,
then by any naturall talents beyond other men : But the whole
management of this Action was only a chaine of the greatest
faults in conduct ; for after that which he had already committed, in stead of returning back immediatly into onr Camp
(which was his duty (*when*) he had fayl'd of his Enterprise) he
march'd on directly towards that of the Enemy, over a bare
plaine, till wee came within half a league of it, and there halted,
staying there I am certain above an hour, which was the greatest
madness imaginable; for by it wee were expos'd, and that
unavoidably, to be routed in case they had come out upon us,
as in reason they ought to haue done, and there was scarcely
an Officer, or even privat Soldier there, who did not plainly see
it and apprehend the consequence; for the Enemy could see
at least a league and a half behind us, the Country being very
bare and open, and that wee had none to second us, and cou'd
count our numbers to a man ; and alltho they were to pass
the brook, behind which they lay, yet that was so just under
the command of their whole Camp, that wee cou'd not haue
hinder'd their coming to us. Having stood thus, as long a time
as I haue mention'd, looking on them to no manner of purpose,
he drew us off, and then left an ambuscade for the Enemy of
about a hundred horse in a small Village, as wee march'd away,
which was as foolish as all the rest ; for the Enemy were too
cautious to permitt any of their men to pass the brook
afterwards.

PART
II.

1653.
Great faults
comĩtted
by M. de
Castelnau in
the conduct
of this affaire.
Ibid. p: 37.

In the mean time Monsr. de Turenne being concern'd for us, because wee had Stayd out so long, and fearing wee might be prest in coming off, came himself from the Camp with four or five Squadrons of horse, and three or four hundred foot, passing over the River through the Town and advancing a litle way from thence; placing his men So, that they might make a retreat for us, in case wee had been pushed or forced to a hasty retreat. He had not long been there when to his great comfort he saw us coming back, and not in that manner which he apprehended.

The Spaniards
decamp from
Caulincourt,
1st Sep.
OR: MEM:
P. 2: p. 39.
They beseige
Rocroy. *Ibid.*

After this wee continu'd in the same quarters till the first of September, and then the Enemie first decamping from Caulin-court, began their march towards Rocroy in order to beseige it. Into which place it was impossible for us to cast any man, thō wee knew the garrison was weak, and that we had notice of the Enemies march that way. For the Enemy when they went from Caulincourt, immediatly sent off a considerable body of horse to invest it, and to hinder any succours from being put into it; and the Situation of the Town is such, that standing in a litle plain environ'd with woods, whoever is first posted there can easily forbid any passage to it. Therfore thō wee endeavour'd to reinforce that place, wee were never able to effect it.

The French
march to
Mousson and
beseig it the
10 Sep:
OR: MEM:
P. 2: p. 39.

So soon as wee had information of their march that way, wee began ours, and passing the Oyse by la Fere continued in our march straight to Mousson, Leaving Laon on our right hand, and quarter'd at Espe; from thence to Condé sur Aysne, which is not far from Château-Porcien, and so to la Chesne, and to Remilly which is within a league or two of Mousson: And the next day being the 10th of September wee passed the River below that place, and took up our severall quarters, M^r. de Turenne below the Town and M^r. de la Ferté above it. M^r. de Turenne's horse were upon one Line stretching from the neighbourhood of the River to the top of the hill, somewhat more then cañon shott from the Town ; As for himself, he with his foot and Gendarmes, camp'd in a litle Valley about half cañon shott from the place ; and finding yet another valley, which was narrower, and somewhat nearer the Town, he there quarter'd the Regiment of York, and that of Guyenne: and the same night, without farther delay, fell to opening the Trenches from the place where these two Regiments were quarter'd. At this time also Monsieur de la Ferté began his approches, but quarter'd not so near, himself or his Soldiers, as wee had done. But before I proceed further, it will be necessary for me to give a short description of the place.

Mousson stands upon the Meuse, about midway betwixt Description of Stenay and Sedan; over the River it has a bridge which was Mousson. cover'd by a hornwork : The Town is fortifyd with a good old Or: Mem: P. 2: p. 40. wall, well flanck'd with round towers, some of which especially one towards the hill was very large; it had also a very good dry ditch with a strong pallisade in the midst of it and in most parts of it. The out parts of the ditch are faced with stone, which is no small strengthning to a place ; and because that side of the Town which is farthest from the River is somewhat commanded by a hill at the foot of which it stands, they had made an Envelope of an half bastion, and three or four whole bastions to cover it: And on both sides down to the River, severall half moons with other outworks. As for the garrison of Mousson, it consisted as near as I can guess in fifteen hundred foot and betwixt two and three hundred horse ; the Governour was call'd Wolfe, an old German Collonell. That which occasion'd this garrison to be made So strong, was, that the Enemy when they design'd to beseige Rocroy, had sent away the Count de Briol with a body of men, with which he was order'd to secure this place, Stenay, Clermont, and St Menehou; not doubting but wee should sit down before one of them, so soon as they began

PART
II.

1653.

Relation of
the Seige of
Mousson.
Or: Mem:
P. 2: p. 41.

with Rocroy. Briol upon our marching that way, Satisfied himself with putting into Mousson so many men as made up the number I haue mention'd, keeping the rest in reserve, to provide for the other places, which belong'd to the Prince of Condé whose officer he was.

Having given this account of the place and the strength within it, I proceed to the Relation of the Seige. The first night of our being before the Town, as I sayd, wee began our approches, and carryd them on a considerable way : Wee also rais'd a battery of five or six guns, which was perform'd with litle loss by the Regiment of Picardy the first of the old Regiments, it being the custome of the French Army that the first Regiment has allways the honour to break ground first in all Seiges, how many soever are made in the Campagne, The next night the Regiments of La Feuillade and Guyenne had the guard of the Trenches, and made a very good advance without any considerable loss. At the same time a Regiment of foot, which was quarter'd in some houses near the bridge, had orders to storme the horn-work before it, which they perform'd and carryd it with litle or no loss, the Enemy not thinking convenient to dispute it, but drawing off into the Town as our men advanced. The third night the Regiment of Turenne took their turn, and carryd on the Trench so near, that the next night the Regiments of York and Palleau brought it to the very edge of the ditch belonging to the outworks ; and the same night fasten'd a Miner in the face of the half bastion of the Envelope I haue already mention'd, having broken the pallisades which were in the ditch, to make his passage thither. He continued working till the afternoon ; about the beginning of which he call'd out to our Soldiers which were in the head of the Trench, That he wanted drink and candles, and till he were supplyd with them he must cease from working : Upon which a Sergeant of York was order'd to carry him what he wanted, and that his passage

might be more secure, all the men in the Trench were commanded to stand to their Armes, and those who were at the
head of it, to give a Voly, when the Sergeant was ready to take
his run to the Miner; and they and the rest to continue firing
till they were sure he was in safety : This was accordingly perform'd, and he pass'd through the ditch to the Miner without
having one shott made at him.

That night the Regiment of Picardy had again the guard of
the Trenches; and the next day as I was going to the head of
the approches, accompanyd by Monsr. d'Humieres, Monsr. de
Crequi and somme others, while wee stayd a litle time in the first
battery a great shott came from the Town, which pass'd through The Duke iu
three barrells of powder, without firing them, which had it done, danger of
being blown
all who were in the battery had inevitably been blown up: But up.,
O$_R$: M$_{EM}$:
the danger came so suddainly and was so soon over, that none P: 2. p. 42.
of us had time to be concern'd for it.

The next day came up a battallion of the Regiment of Guardes,
consisting of above six hundred men in ten Companies, and commanded by Monsr. de Vautourneu; and according to their privilege had the guard of the Trenches the same night, relieving the
Regiment of Picardy: And when Monsr. de Castelnau, the only
Lieu^t Generall then in the Army, came according to his usuall cus- The Regim^t
of Guardes
tom into the Trenches, to command there, they absolutely refus'd refuses to
obey any man
obedience to him, pretending they were not to obey any man but the Generall himself,
but the Generall himself: of which Monsr. de Turenne being O$_B$: M$_{EM}$:
inform'd, he went thether to accommodate the business, but P: 2. p. 44.
finding Vautourneu very obstinat and positiue in that point, he
desir'd M^r. de Castelnau to retire into his tent, and repose himself that night, because he had taken so much paines and so
litle rest the night before ; adding, That he himself would do his
office for him, and watch in the Trenches : Castelnau obeyd
and went away, and Monsr. de Turenne did, as he had Sayd,

P A R T
II.

1653.
The Dispute
is decided by
an order from
the Court.
Ibid.

there being indeed a necessity incumbent on him So to do, for avoiding any farther dispute in that matter which he was also unwilling to decide: But he immediatly dispatched a Messenger to Court, to informe them of it, who sent a positiue order to the Guardes, That they should obey the Lieu^t Generall. This command came back before it was their turn to mount the Trenches the second time, after which the dispute was no more revived. But yet it prov'd of advantage to the seruice, for the Guardes thought themselves obliged in honour to make a very great advance that night; which they perform'd, being both encouraged by the presence of the Generall and by the prudence of his directions; for they did not only make a blind all along the bottom of the ditch of the Envelope, by the help of the pallisado's which were in it, which went directly upon the great Tower, but also made a lodgement along from the place where the ditch of the Envelope joyn'd with that of the Town to a half moon, which was on our right hand and which also was abandon'd by the Enemy, from whence wee design'd to get down into the Town ditch and there to lodge our Miner.

Thus far wee had advanced very speedily, but when wee came to make our descent into the ditch of the Town, wee found more difficulty then were expected; for the next night endeavouring to continue at the same rate wee had begun, by making a lodgement against the pallisado's which were in the midst of the ditch, thō wee carryd on that work with great vigour, yet when it was almost perfected, the Enemy beat our men out of it, by throwing down great store of hand granades, fireworkes, and fire it self, so that it was impossible to continue longer there, and make good our undertaking: yet (*we*) were not discouraged by the unsuccessfulness of this first attempt, but for two nights following very obstinatly pursued the design of lodging ourselves, but all to no purpose: for thō wee finish'd our work, yet the Enemy burnt us out, by throwing down

The French
make a lodge-
ment in the
ditch of the
Town, but are
beat out again.
Or: Mem:
P: 2. p: 45.

upon us such vast quantities of fireworks, and combustible matter, that they ruin'd our work.

This made us cast about to go on some other way with more security ; and therefore the next day, wee endeavour'd to make our descent into the ditch, by cutting a trench from the top of it, where wee lodged, and so sloping along the side : but wee also fail'd of effecting this ; for, besides that the Enemy had a low flanck, in which was only one small piece of ordnance, which lay so much under our battery that wee could not bear upon it, or dismount it, and that when wee descended into the ditch, it playd levell on us, wee also found (when wee had got down half way) the wall I formerly mention'd, which of itself would haue stopt us ; thō the great gun had not gaull'd us from the flancker. So soon as it was day that single peice destroyd all the blinds wee had been making ; After which wee were constrain'd to haue recours to the old method of sinking a well, out of the lodgement wee had in the ditch of the half moon, and so that way to go in to the bottom of the ditch : Wee fell in hand with it as fast as possibly wee cou'd, and also endeavour'd to fasten our Miner to the Town-wall by the means of Madriers, which are planckes nine inches thick at least, cover'd with tinn or raw hides, or both, the better to resiste the force of fire ; Those they carryd, and set up against the wall under which the Miner fell to work ; having barrells fill'd with earth on each side of him for his security from the small shott of the flancker, as the Madriers were to preserve him from the hand granado's, stones, and fire, which they threw incessantly upon him with great violence, thō without effect : So that they were convinced that unless they cou'd invent some other means of dislodging him, he would soon haue gott so far into the Wall, that there would be no farther hope for them ; finding also that thō it was a dry ditch, wee had made so great lodgements all along the edge of it, that they could

PART
II.

1653.
They attempt
the descent
into the ditch
by another
method, which
proves as
ineffectuall as
the former.
OR: MEM:
P. 2: p. 45.

Recours is
had at last
to the old
method of
sinking a well.
Ibid. p. 46.

The Miner is
fasten'd to the
Town wall by
the means of
madriers.
Ibid.

PART
II.

1653.
A Bomb hung
down by a
chaine and
firing closs by
the Madriers
destroys them,
and the Miner
is burnt in
his hole.
OR: MEM:
P. 2: p. 47.

do nothing by a sally, they invented another way that was more secure, which was by hanging a bomb or great granado down by a chaine and closs to the side of the Madriers, which firing blew them all away, and then they threw over so much combustible matter, as burnt the Miner in his hole. The Miner at the other attacke had no better success, for Mons'. de la Ferté having the same desire to make a quick dispatch, fasten'd a Miner to the body of the place before he had made a lodgment under the Wall, so that the Enemy having found him, immediatly smother'd him with smoke, he being already so far enter'd that the fire cou'd not reach him, but as I sayd, the smoke stiffled him.

Perpetuall
Raines during
the whole
Seige.
OR: MEM:
P. 2: p. 47.

During the time of this whole Seige, wee were much troubled and hindered by perpetuall raines and stormes so violent, that they very often blew away our blinds, and wash'd down some parts of our Trenches which for the most part were fill'd with water, the Sky being seldom clear for above three hours togather: and that which makes me remember this the more particularly, was, that one morning very early, going down with some others to the approches, when wee came into the ditch of the Envelope, which went straight upon the great Tower, and was our only way to the lodgement, where wee were working att the well I have already mention'd, wee kept close to the pallissado, where the blind should have been, and thō nothing but the very beginning of it was left standing, all the rest being blown down, yet all of us were so busily imployd in piking out our way (the ditch being full of dirt and water) that not one single man tooke notice that the blind was ruin'd, and consequently wee in open view, till wee were gotten half our way, and then, one of the company who observ'd it first, propos'd that wee shou'd return; to which I well remember I would not consent, urging, That since wee were now so far onward, the danger was equall in going forward or in returning: so wee

The Duke
going down to
the approches
is in eminent
danger, but
rejects the
proposall of
returning
back; his Starr
saves him.
Ibid. p. 48.

continu'd going on to the head of the attacke as wee first
intended; but in all the way while wee were thus exposed,
there was not one shott made at us, at which wee wonder'd;
but afterwards when the Town was surrender'd, the Governour
inform'd us of the reason, That he himself happening to be upon
the wall at that very time, and knowing me by my Starr, had
forbid his men to fire upon the Company, which is a respect
very usuall beyond Sea. But he had not the same consideration
for those afterwards, who were commanded to repair the blind;
for I hauing given notice to the Officer who was in the Trenches,
of its condition, he gave order to haue it mended, and severall
of those who were employd in that work were slayn, and others
hurt.

About the same time, when wee began to sink our Well in
the ditch of the half moon, wee also lodged a Miner at the foot
of the great Tower, under shelter of the Madriers, who had
better fortune then the former, and work'd into the wall; when
he was gott within as far as he design'd, but had not yet begun
to make his chambers, he sent out word to M^r. de Turenne,
that he heard the Enemy at work in a Countermine, and that
as near as he could guess, they would be upon him in some few
hours, long before he could finish his undertaking; Upon which,
he gave immediat orders to put some barrells of powder in the
hole he had already made, and then to stop it as firmly as they
could, intending by this only to ruine the Enemies Countermine and Miners, well knowing it could not bring down the
Tower: his orders were speedily put in execution, and because
the powder must needs blow backwards, he withdrew his men
from such parts of the approches as were neighbouring to it,
or in danger of any hurt from it, and himself and severall others
went and stood in the first battery, which was distant from the
Tower about half muskett Shott; under this shelter he expected
the effect: when fire was given, it produced all that wee design'd,

A Miner
lodged at the
foot of the
great Tower.
O^r: Mem:
P. 2: p. 48.

A Counter-
mine of the
beseieged is
discover'd, and
blew up.
Ibid. p: 49.

for it only enlarged the hole which our Miner had made, and as wee learn'd afterwards kill'd those of the Enemy, throwing to a far distance severall great stones with a much violence as if they had been shott out of a cañon, some of which hitt the battery behind which wee stood, and others wee saw fly much farther. So soon as the blow was over, Monsr. de Turenne, having seen what it perform'd, sent back the Miner into the hole, which was now widen'd, and sent along with him a Sergeant, and six men to guard him who might easily be lodged in it, with all Security from the Shott of the Enemy.

This which concern'd the firing of the Mine pass'd all in the day time; when it was night wee thought it convenient to open the Well which wee had sunk, and which was now as low as the bottom of the Town ditch, for it would haue taken a longer time, then we cou'd spare, to go all the way under ground as far as to the wall, and being already sunck so low were secur'd both from great and small shott, and had nothing farther to apprehende in our opinions but hand granado's, fire works, and fire it self: But wee had no sooner open'd it, then the Enemy discovering it, by the light of the fires which they had made, roull'd from off the walls a Bomb, or Mortar-Granado, by the means of two strong pieces of timber fasten'd together; the Bomb lighted full into the mouth of the Well, and kill'd four or five of our men who were working within it, and withall, so terribly shook the lodgment just above it, where M^r. de Turenne, myself, some Officers, and many volonteers were then standing, that wee all beleev'd at that moment it would haue been shatter'd to peices: yet it stood; but it was above a quarter of an hour before any could go down to work again by reason of the smoke and dust; And then, thõ the Enemy continually plyd that place with hand-granado's, fire, and fire works, and now and then a Bomb (none of which last happen'd to be So justly directed as the first) yet wee carryd on our Trench as

far as the palisado's which were in the midst of the ditch; but
by reason of that storme of fire works which the Enemy without
ceasing powr'd upon us, wee were obliged to cover it again
with planks, fascines and earth upon them, for the security of
our men. When wee were advanced as far as the palisado's,
wee were forced again to drive under ground, the Enemy still
heaving over vast quantities of wood and combustible matter,
and wee being then so very near the wall, that it was impossible
to go forward any other way.

Advancing in this manner wee fasten'd our Miner at length
to the body of the place; wee lost that night a considerable
number of our men. La Feuillade had his head broken with a
hand-granado, M^r. d'Humieres had likewise a blow on the side
of his, with a small shott, which first came through the lodgment, and then after glancing from his head, pass'd through
the leg of a pioneer, and lastly strook the toe of my boot,
without doing me any harm. M^r. de Turenne continu'd on the
place all night, with out whose presence I am confident the
work had not been done.

At the same time M^r. de la Ferté was so far advanced in his
attacke, that his Mine was ready to spring next day, it was
accordingly sprung after dinner: M. de Turenne with
severall of his Officers and Volonteers went to see what effect
it would produce, but went not down into those Trenches, his
coming being only out of curiosity. The Mine was made in
the angle of a Tower and the wall, and was so order'd as to
blow up not only the Angle, but also that part of the Tower
and Wall which was nearest to it: when it was fired and the
smoke gone off, wee saw it had only done its intended work
upon the Wall, and very angle, but that the Tower was yet
standing; only there was a great crack quite through it: but
immediatly after the firing of the six guns upon the edge of

The Miner
fasten'd at
length to the
body of the
place.
Or: Mem:
P. 2: p. 51.

The Duke in
danger of a
bullet which
Struck only
the toe of his
boot. Ibid.

the ditch, all togather, that part of the Tower came also down to our great satisfaction.

I haue been told by some who were then in the battery with Mons:· de la Ferté, when this happen'd, that when he perceiv'd that part of the Tower next the Angle came not down with the other, he was in great rage against the Cheualier de Clerville, an Engeneer, who had the care of carryng on the Mine, threatning him furiously for his negligence and ignorance:· At which the poor man much frighten'd, and fearing som severe usage from the Mareshall, but withall observing that the part which was yet standing shook, desir'd that the six guns which were in the battery might all be levell'd at that part of the Tower and fir'd at it all togather, which he said would probably bring it down : This being immediatly done had its desired effect, and he escap'd a cudgelling.

The breach that was made by it was very faire, so that our men the same night made a lodgment on it, which being perform'd and our two Mines on the other side of the Town in readiness to spring, the Governour thought it now high time to begin a Treaty for the surrendring up of the place; and the next morning beat a parlee, at the same time sending out Officers to treat. The articles were soon adjusted, which were, that he should march out next day with armes and baggage, and be conveyd as far as Montmedy a neighbouring garrison of the Spaniards.

Thus wee master'd the Town of Mousson in the space of seventeen days from the opening of the Trenches, without the loss of many men, or of any considerable Officer, or Volonteer of quality, excepting the Vidame de Laon, a nephew of Mons:· de Turenne, and second Son to the Count de Roussy, who was shott dead in the Trenches, as one evening he was going down to the head of them betwixt Mʳ. d'Humieres, and Mʳ. de

Mousson is
surrender'd
the 27ᵗʰ of
Sept.
Oʀ: Mᴇᴍ:
P. 2: p: 52.

Schomberg. ·The greatest loss wee had was in our horses, of P A R T
II. which very many dyd by reason of the ill weather ·and‚clay ground on which they were camp'd. 1653.

But here I think it will not be amiss if· I make a short An account of the methods digression to ·give account of some of their methods in France of carryin on Seiges in g for the carrying on a Seige, and of the extraordinary care and France. Or. Mem. pains which the Generall Officers usually take on such occasions, P. 2: p. 53. to which I cheifly attribute their speedy taking in of Townes : They trust to no body but themselves to view, and make their observations ; Mʳ. de Turenne. went in person to view all the ground about Mousson, taking with him Mʳ. de. Castelnau, ‚when, as in another Army, I have seen the Generalls· trust a Sergent de bataille or some inferior Officer to do it, so that they were wholy guided, and in a manner govern'd by their (*the*) eyes and· advice of other men : but Monſʳ. de Turenne made use of his own judgment, where he thought it most proper to break ground, and· which way to run the Trenches ; when, night came, he himself was present at the opening of them, and continued there allmost till break of day : Besides it was ·his· constant method, during this whole Seige to go into the Trenches both morning and evening, In the morning to see if the work ·was well perform'd, at evening to resolve what would be the work that night, having in his company the Lieuᵗ Genˡ: and some of the cheif Officers who that night were to command in the Trenches, to instruct them himself what he expected to be done. Again after supper he went to see them begin their work, and would continue with them more or less, as he found it necessary for the carrying on of the present design.

While he was once in the Trenches, during this Seige, I Or: Mem: P. 2: p. 54. remember an odd accident, which happen'd when I was present and which I will relate, thō besides my present purpose : A Captain of the Regiment of Guyenne, being newly come to the Army, and that Regiment being then on duty on the Trenches, he approch'd Mons'. de Turenne to salute him; It happen'd, that, at the same time he was bowing down his head, a small shott from the Town struck him in the skull, and layd him dead at the Generall's feet: at which unhappy chance, some who were present made this unseasonable raillery, That if the Captain had been better bred, he had escap'd the bullett, which only hitt him there, for not bowing low enough to his Generall.

But to proceed·: the Commander in cheif, is not only thus diligent, but all the inferiour Officers are obliged to be as carefull in their severall stations: particularly in all the time of this present Seige, in our side of the attack wee had not so much as one single Ingeneer, nor did I ever observe them to be made use of at any other place, but only as overseers of the work, most of the Officers understanding very well how to carry on a Trench, and to make a lodgement. As for the Mines, they haue a Captain of Miners who has a care of carrying them on, when the Generall has resolved where they shall be.

And not only from my own observations, but by what I haue learn'd from others who haue had more experience and seen more seruice then myself, I find and am settled in my opinion, That no Generall ought wholly to confide in any Ingeneer for the carrying on of a Trench, it being not reasonable to beleeve, that one who is to be allways there, will hazard or expose himself as far as Officers, who are to take their turns, and who are push'd on by emulation of each other to make dispatch, and carry on the seruice with all diligence: And besides it gives more opportunity to Officers to understand that work, then otherwise they would haue; which appears most plainly by the Army of the Hollanders, for there, where all was resolv'd on by their Generall upon consultation with the Ingeneers and the overseers, few Officers ever arrived at any knowledge in carrying on the Trenches, their imployment being only to guard them, and the workmen, and command their Soldiers to fire, they not·

being answerable for the advancing of the work : so that unless an Officer were naturaly' industrious to learn and applyd himself to it, he receiv'd but small improvement. But what I haue said concerning the carrying on of their approches in Holland, I confess I haue not spoken of my own knowledge, but only from hear-say of persons, whose judgment and integrity I suppose I may reasonably trust: yet this I can affirm, that I haue known very few of whatsoever Nation who were much the better for what they had learn'd in that Country ; thō I haue known many good Officers who haue serv'd there, yet they gain'd their experience els where.

At this Seige was made no line of Circumvallation ; for besides that wee were affraid in case wee had gone about it, so much time would haue been taken up, that the Enemy would haue compass'd their business, and gain'd Rocroy, before wee could haue taken Mousson (and then our Lines would haue signified litle to us) the Situation of the place was such by reason of the River Chiers, which cover'd us on the Luxembourg side, and then runs into the Meuse betwixt us and Sedan, that it was in stead of a line to us to hinder smaller succours from being put into the Town; wee having small advanced guards upon all the passes of that River, so that nothing could come that way without being discover'd, and that time enough to be prevented. On the other side the Enemy was so thorowly imployd at their Seige of Rocroy, that they could not think of endeavouring to releeve Mousson.

On the same day when the Town was surrender'd, which was the 27th of September, wee march'd to Amblemont in our way towards Rocroy with intention to try what could be done in order to the releif of it ; but when wee were come as far as Varnicour, wee heard of its being deliver'd up.

After these two Seiges, there happen'd litle of Action betwixt either Armys during the remainder of the Campagne; for besides that the Season of the year was too far spent to undertake any considerable Seige, the Spanish Army had suffer'd much more at Rocroy, then wee at Mousson, and their numbers were so diminish'd, that out of that consideration, and our keeping so closs to them, therby to prevent our frustating any new undertaking, they durst attempt no more that year; but imployd their time in marches and countermarches, on the other side of the Somme, eating up all the forage of their fronteers, as wee did on this side of the same River in observing all their motions.

But while wee thus continued to hold them in play on that Side of the Country, the Court having got together some troopes, besides the guards of horse and foot, which are constantly attending on it, and some which were detach'd to them from

the Army, undertook the Seige of S⁺ Menehou, which at first was carryd on by three Lieut⁺ Genˡˡˢ; Monsʳ. de Navaille commanding the troopes belonging to the Court, Mʳ. de Castelnau those which were sent from Monsʳ. de Turenne, and Monsʳ. d'Vxelles such as had been spar'd out of Monsʳ. de la Ferté's troopes. And thō two of these three above nam'd were as able Officers for all Sorts of duty as any others in the Kingdom of France, and thō Mʳ. de Castelnau thō not so proper for feil Seruice understood the business of a Seige as well as any man, yet these three being all in equall command, manag'd the main affaire so ill, and went so slowly on with it, that the Cardinal was forced to send the Mareshall de Plessis-Praslin to take the supreme command upon him, after which the Seige advanced with more Success.

Some days after the begining of this Seige, M. de la Ferté with the greatest part of his horse came and quarter'd about   to hinder any releif from coming into the place, because the Duke of Lorraine was marching down that way with his Army. In the mean time M. de Turenne was

quarter'd with his forces behind the Somme betwixt Roye and
Corbie; from which place seeing litle probability of action
there, I ask'd leave of M^r. de Turenne to go to the Seige of
St Menehou; and being obliged to take Châlons sur Marne in
my way thither, at which place the Court then resided, I was
stayd so long on one pretence or other in that Town, some times
for want of Convoy, another while, upon the news of the King's
removal within a day or two, so that they could not spare any;
that notwithstanding my continuall pressing to be gone, the Town
of St Menehou sent out to treat of a surrender the same day I
waited on the King of France to the Castle of Ham, which is
within two leagues of St Menehou : so that I miss'd the seeing
of that Seige, and went the next day with his Ma^ty to view the
approches, and the breach which had been made in the body
of the place, before they came to Articles of Capitulation.

: Thus ends the Relation given of this Campagne by his
Royall Highness, who upon the removall of the French Court,
return'd likewise to Paris where he arrived the beginning
of X^ber, and there spent the ensuing winter : towards the end
of which, the King his Brother took his resolution of leaving
France by reason of the Treaty of Amity then on foot between
that Crown and Oliver Cromwell newly made Protector ; For
Cardinal Mazarin thought it, at that time necessary for the
preservation of the French Monarchy, to keep fair with that
Vsurper. The Duke attended his Brother on his way towards
Germany as far as Chantilly, where they took leave of each
other, in hopes of a more happy meeting thereafter.

P A R T
II.

1653.

The Duke is
disappointed
in his desire to
see the Seige of
St Menehou.
Or: Mem:
P. 2: p. 57.

PART
II.

1654.

The Duke's
Third
Campagne
in France.
Or: Mem:
P. 2: p. 59.

The Seige
of Arras.

The Spaniards
sitt down
before it the
3ᵈ of July.
Ibid.

Chev. Crequi,
Sᵗ Lieu and
d'Equancourt
sent from the
French Army
with succours
to the Town,
they force
their passage.
Or: Mem:
P. 2. p. 59.

OF the CAMPAGNE here ensuing his Royall Highness gives the following account in his Memoires.

THIS YEAR the French Army under the Command of Monsʳ. de Turenne, and the Mareshall de la Ferté, was not assembled soon enough to prevent the Spaniards from beseiging Arras. On the third of July they satt down before it, with an Army consisting of thirty thousand men well furnish'd with all things necessary for so great an Enterprise. One thing which induced them to undertake that Seige, was their being advertis'd of the weaknes of the Garrison, which was not So strong as it ought to haue been, thõ not so weak as to oblige the Governour to quit any of his outworkes which were very great. Our Generalls being sensible of this defect, sent away about a thousand horse in three bodies, one commanded by the Chevalier of Crequi, another by Monsʳ. de Sᵗ Lieu, and the third by the Baron of Equancourt. Sᵗ Lieu got into the Town with about two hundred horse, the first or second night after the Town was invested, through the Prince Condé's quarter; The Baron d'Equancourt two nights after him with three hundred horse through the Lorraine's quarter, and the Chevalier de Crequi forced his passage into the Town some days after both, through the Spanish quarter before the Line was finish'd. This was all the succour could be spar'd from the French Army. As for foot, wee durst not venture to send any, it being so plaine a Country about the Town, that they might haue been easily discover'd and defeated when once the Enemy had taken up their quarters before the Place.

Another reason why they lay down before Arras was, that wee had beseiged Stenay; which place they hop'd would haue endur'd so long, and taken up so many Troopes, that they might have compass'd their design before wee could haue endéd our Seige, or at least as soon; and that, during this, our Army would not be of strength enough to undertake any thing upon them, which indeed was not ill conjectur'd : for wee were (*so*) very weak that wee stirr'd not from about Peronne to approche their Lines till about the 16th of July, when wee heard they were near finish'd, for fear of ingaging ourselves so near a great Army, in a Country so bare and open.

I joyn'd the Army by Peronne before they march'd, being to Serve that year in quality of one of the Lieutenant Generalls, under Monsr de Turenne, and tooke my day according to the date of my Commission as the youngest who serv'd in that Army. About the 16th, as I haue sayd, wee began our march towards Arras, and camp'd at a Village call'd Sains, near Sauchy-Cauchy which lys betwixt Cambray and Arras about five leagues distant from the last of these places ; The next day, wee continued our march to Mouchy-le-Preux, Mr de Turenne taking that compass about the Country to cover himself by some brookes, that in case the Enemy should draw out upon him, he might be able to avoide fighting, And he was so cautious the day before he came to Mouchy-le-Preux, that when he arrived at a brooke which was half a league short of the foremention'd place, he there drew up his Army in battell, and afterwards pass'd over himself with some horse and dragoons to view the ground where he intended to incampe, and gave not orders for the Army to come over to him till the evening, but stayd upon the place to see if the Enemy had any intentions of drawing out against him ; resolving that in case they should that day

Stenay 54. beseiged by the French, is one of the reasons why the Spaniards beseiged Arras. *Ibid.* p. 60.

The Duke joyns the Army by Peronne, and serves in quality of Lt Gen^{ll} under M. de Turenne. OR: MEM: P. 2. p. 60.

The French Army march towards Arras, the 16 of July. *Ibid.*

PART II.

1654.

haue attempted any thing, our Army should not haue gone over: When evening came, and the Enemy appear'd not, wee pass'd the brooke, but it was then so late that nothing could be attempted by them in all lykelyhood for that night.

The French camp at Mouchy-le-Preux. OR: MEM: P. 2. p. 61.

Our Troopes no sooner were camp'd, but they fell to work about our Line, every Regiment both of horse and foot labouring at it on that part which lay before them; and this they perform'd with So much diligence, that next day they were in some tollerable posture of defence; but when once it was finish'd wee thought ourselves absolutely secure, it being a very advantageous post, and not of too great a front, for the Army wee had then; The brooke which I haue already mention'd covering our left wing, as the Scarpe did our right: so that if the Enemy had drawn out to engage us there, when we first put ourselves in battell in that post of Mouchy-le-Preux, or before our Lines were finish'd, wee should haue had faire play for it, notwithstanding they were so much stronger, because they could not outfront us, nor fall into our flankes; And wee had so good an opinion of our own courage, as never to be unwilling to venture an Engagement with them where they could not outwing us.

I haue heard since when I was in Flanders and elswhere, many taxing the Spaniards for not coming out against us the first day of our being in that post, or as wee came to possess ourselves thereof; and some report that the Prince of Condé propos'd it to the Spaniards: But I can not affirme this, neither will I take upon me to censure them for not doing it, because I haue not heard their reasons for this omission, though they may be easily conjectur'd. But whither they had it under their consideration or not, wee took our precautions in coming thither, as if wee believ'd they would make some attempt on us; and, being once posted, wee lost no time to intrench our-selves: for certainly that post of Mouchy was very strong,

Description of the post of Mouchy. OR: MEM: P. 1. p: 62.

because that not only both our flancks were cover'd, as I haue P A R T already said, but also our Line ran along upon a heigth from II. Mouchy which was in the midst, and both overlook'd and commanded on either side down to the brooke and River of Scarpe ; So that had the Enemy advanced upon us in the day time, our cañon, which for the most part were planted on that height of Mouchy, would haue gall'd them terribly, after which wee had still the advantage of the ground.

Monsieur de Turenne's own quarter was at this place of Mouchy, having with him the greatest number of his foot, his horse were incamp'd on two Lines, which reached to the brooke, together with the rest of his foot; Monsr de la Ferté had his quarter at the right hand of all our Line down by the side of the River Scarpe, at a Village called Peule, One part of his foot were incamped by him, the other part at Mouchy, and his horse also upon two Lines betwixt Mouchy and his quarter : Our reserue was in its proper place just behind Mr de Turenne's quarter, which was in the midst.   Thus our Incampment was in order of battell, only wee had some foot at each extremity of our Lines, and in the midst of our wings of horse, that our Line might be the better defended.

When wee were thus posted, and our Line finish'd, wee sent out considerable partys of horse, almost every night, to hinder any Convoys from coming into the Enemie's Camp; and notwithstanding that they sate down before Arras as well appointed with all things necessary, as was usuall for Armys at that time, yet so great a body of men as they were within their Lines was of necessity to haue some communication with their own Country ; and whether it was, that they were really in want of powder, or that it was only out of precaution, from almost the first days of our being in their neighbourhood, they sent out partys of horse to supply them with it, which went to Douay, Cambray, and other places of theirs, and some of their

1654.

The order of the Incampment. *Ibid.* p. 63.

The French sent out every night considerable partys of horse to intercept Convoys. OR: MEM: P. 2. p: 65.

P A R T
II.

1654.

Garrisons sent to them, each trooper carrying a bag of fifty pound weight of powder behind his horse: These partys they kept continually going, scarsely intermitting any night, and thō wee liad partys very often abroad to intercept them, it was never our fortune to surprise any of them, the Country being so very open, that unless by accident they should fall into the midst of our partys, they could not be intercepted: Yet wee seldom sent out less then a thousand or twelve hundred horse under the command of some Lieutenant Generall, who march'd out of the Camp in the evening. They who were sent abroad out (of) Mons' de Turenne's Army, posting themselves betwixt the Camp and Bapaume in some Valley or other place where they could not be easily discover'd, till they came out against the Enemy, having small outguards round about them to give notice of any thing that pass'd and, besides them, Centry's every way that they might not be surpriz'd; and M' de la Ferté did the like on his Side, his party's advancing betwixt the Camp and Lens.

A Convoy of
the Enemy's
powder
Carriers
blown up by
an odd acci-
dent.
Or: Mem:
P: 2: p. 65.

But though neither ours, nor his could meet with any of these powder-carriers, yet by an accident hapening amongst themselves, one of their Convoyes chanced to miscarry; For one night as wee were with M' de Turenne, visiting the guards, wee perceived a great blaze of fire, quick and violent like that of the blowing up of gunpowder; and it seem'd to us, as if it had been at the quarter of Mons' de la Ferté: But as (we) went down that way to inquire of it, our Sentinels who were upon the heigth of Mouchy, inform'd us, that they had likewise seen it, and that it was not where wee had imagined, but on the plaine farr beyond those quarters towards Lens, which caus'd us to wonder the more what it might be. The next morning wee were fully Satisfied concerning it, that an entire Regiment of horse, consisting of Six score, going from Douay to the Enemie's Camp, all of them Officers as well as Souldiers having

behind them a bagg of powder, besided about fourscore horses
laden with hand grenades, which were led by Countrymen on
foot, had been all blown up, but by what accident, none of
those who were brought prisoners into the Camp could tell.
Indeed it was a very dismall object, to behold a great number
of poor men, who were brought into our Camp with their faces
disfigur'd and their bodies burnt by powder, so that few of them
recover'd, their Companions having been all kill'd outright.
These prisoners were brought in by some of our partys who
were out on that side of the Country, who seeing the flash at a
great distance, rode up to the place to gaine a more clear
knowledge of the matter; they also brought along with them
some few scorch'd horses, and a paire of kittle drums which
belong'd to that Regiment, and all the men who had any life
remaining in them. I happen'd since, when I was in Flanders,
to talke with a Lieutenant of horse who was the only man
that could give an account, how that accident befell them; for
seeing his face had been burnt, I casually ask'd him how he
came by that misfortune? He answer'd me, that it was by the
blowing up of powder at such a time near Arras; and upon
my examining him concerning the particulars of it, he told me,
That happening to be in the Rear of the whole Regiment, he
saw one of the Troopers with a pipe of tobacco lighted in his
mouth; wherupon he rode up to him, and taking it gently
from him, threw it away after which he beat him with his
sword: The Soldier being drunke, pull'd out his pistol, and
presented it to his breast; upon which the Lieutenant threw
himself from his horse apprehending what might happen, and
the Trooper at the same instant firing at him, it lighted on the
bag behind the s^d Lieutenant's horse, which taking fire, blew it
up, and so, from one successiuely to the other who was next, it
spred through the whole Regiment: he being on the ground

PART
II.

1654.

A party of the
Spaniards
beat a French
party com-
manded by
the Marq. de
Richelieu.
Or: Mem:
P. 2. p: 67.

In another
rencountre of
partys M^r. de
Beaujeu a
French Lieu^t.
Gen^{ll} is kill'd.
Ibid.

escap'd best cheape, having only his face, his hands, and some
parts of his bod scorched.

This accident was So very remarkable, that I could not but
mention it, especially because it was the only party of the Enemy
which miscarryd, or which indeed wee mett with excepting
twice; one which was rencountred by the Marquess de
Richelieu commanded by the Comte de Lorge, but there the
advantage was not on our side, for the Comte resolutely
forc'd his way through the Marquess's men, beat them, and
took three or four of his Captains, loosing only twelve horses
laden with powder, and getting safe with the rest into the Lines
of their own Camp. The other was yet of worse consequence
to us, by the considerable loss wee Sustain'd in the person of
Monsr.de Beaujeu, the Lieu^t Gen^{ll} who commanded our party;
he being sent out by M^r. de Turenne with a body of eight
hunderd horse, and having notice of a Convoy which was to
come into the Enemy's Lines by the way of . . . .
. . . * immediatly taking that way about break of day he
mett a party of the Enemy commanded by M^r. Druot (Droot)
a Colonell coming from the Enemies Camp; the numbers of
both sides were in a manner equall, but the Enemy had no
advertisement of our being there; yet it so happen'd that most
of our men were at that time dismounted from their horses,
expecting intelligence of the Supposed party which came the
other way, which made it easy for Droots men to overrun as
they did the two first Squadrons, before they could mount;
And as for Beaujeu, his misfortune was such, that as he was
going to put the next Squadron in order, he was slayn, and
that body also beaten: So that if the Regiment of Beauuau

---

* The same space is left in the abridged Narrative of Marshall Turenne's
Campaigns, which James the Second sent to Cardinal de Bouillon. — EDITOR.

(*Beauveau*) had not made a stand, and put a stop to the Violence
of the Enemy, by beating their first Squadron which had done
all this execution, our whole party had been absolutly defeated.
But this advantage gave leasure to the rest of our men to put
themselves in order, and to receive a charge from the Enemy,
which was not very vigourous, Droot having been hurt in the
former by the Regiment de Beauveau; so that there was no
great mischeif done at that bout on either side, they only
disordering each other: wherupon the Enemy, not knowing
the certain number of our men, and fearing they might be
stronger then indeed they were, judg'd it convenient for them
to march away, and our Soldiers having lost their Commander
were enough content to escape as they did, and thought not
of following them; so that in this action, it might be said that
both were beaten: As for the number of the Slayn and prisoners
on either side, it was very inconsiderable excepting the loss of
our Lieu^t. Generall.

. For my own particular I was once a broad in my turn, with The Duke go's out in his turn with a party of 1000 horse.
On: Mem: P: 2. p. 68.
about a thousand horse, and being posted in a litle Valley with
my party, my Centryes being out every side, a party of the
Enemy consisting of an hundrd horse coming from their
Camp to go for Cambray, surprised a Corporall and two
Centryes, just as he was about to releive them; who being ask'd
by those who had made them prisoners, what our numbers were?
The Corporall answer'd, About a hunderd, and that most of
us were dismounted, feeding our horses: which they beleeving
came furiously down upon us at a great gallop their trumpett
sounding the charge before them; but when they were with in
pistoll-shott of us, perceiving their mistake, and that in stead of
a small party, and those off their horses, they were to deal with
severall Squadrons all on horseback, they retired faster then
they had come on: Which I observing, was a moment in doubt
what I should do, imagining at first they would never haue

P A R T
II.

1654.

The Duke
pursues a
party of the
Enemy, but
could not
overtake
them.
OR: MEM:
P. 2: p. 69.
He takes
another party
of the Enemy
of a 100 horse
all prisoners.
Ibid.

advanced with so much fury, if they had not been well seconded; but immediatly weighing with how much precipitation they ran off, I concluded their number to be no more then what I saw, wherupon I order'd the Squadron upon the head of which I was, to disband after them, myself with the rest riding softly after: but they made such hast, that our Soldiers could not overtake them; yet they escap'd not, for they fell into the hands of another party of ours, which took them every man. The same morning also, another party of theirs was taken by me; for as I was marching back towards the Camp, a small detachment of mine brought me word, that they had discover'd about a hunderd horse of the Enemy, putting themselves in ambuscade a litle before day in a neighbouring Village: upon which intelligence I march'd with my whole party as near the Village as I could, without being seen by them, sending a small number of my men to draw them out of their ambuscade; with order, that when the Enemy came out to charge them, they shou'd retire to the main body. This they perform'd so dexterously, that the Enemy were closse upon us before they perceived us, So that none of them escap'd from being taken.

While these things pass'd without the Camps, the Enemy before Arras having finished their Line on the 14th August open'd their Trenches the same night, following the Seige with all manner of diligence, and pressing the Town so very hard, that thō Monsr. de Mondejeu who was Governour, perform'd all the parts of an expert Commander, and was assisted by Monsr. de St Lieu, the Cheualier de Crequi and the Baron d'Equancourt, with all imaginable gallantry; yet the Spaniard gain'd ground upon him every day, and by the *   of August had made themselves masters of the corne de Guiche;

---

* The date is equally omitted in the Narrative that was sent to the Cardinal.

and not only of the outward but of the inward also, as may be
seen by the plan of it; continuing to push on their work with
vigour, notwithstanding the resistance which they found. This
obliged the Governour to send out severall Messengers to our
Generalls, some of which came safely into our Camp to inform
us of the condition of the place.

One of these Messengers having swallow'd the Note he
brought, wrapt up in lead (that in case he had been taken and
searched it might not haue been found about him) and coming
at a time when the Generalls were very impatient to hear from
the Town, the Messenger was not able to voyd the paper in
above 24 houres, though severall purges were given him to
bring it out of his body: This gave them great anxiety, and
particularly Monsr de la Ferté cryd out with a great passion,
Il faut éventrer le coquin! " the rascall must haue his belly ript
up," since he will not voyd it: This put the fellow into such a
fright, that being then just at the door of the Tente, the peice
of lead came immediatly from him; and by the account it
brought, made us defer attacking the Lines of the Enemy
before the Stenay troopes were come up to us, the Town not
being so prest as wee had reason to beleeve it was by some
letters wee had intercepted from the Enemy's Camp to some
in Flanders, wherin they confidently affirm'd they should be
masters of the Town by St Laurence's day at furthest; which
with the news wee had from the Army before Stenay, that the
Seige there did not advance so fast as wee expected, and so no
liklyhood of having those troopes before that day, had made
our Generalls resolve not to stay for them, and forthwith to
attacke the Lines, ordering every Squadron of horse and
battalion of foot to provide themselves with such a number of
fascines and hurdles within two days. The reason of this provision was, because the Enemy had made without the utmost
ditch of their Line, about six rowes of holes, of a foot and a

P A R T
II.

1654.

The Gover-
nour sends
Severall
Messages to
inform of the
condition of
the place.
Ibid.

remarkable
Story of one
of those
Messengers.
Ibid.

PART
II.

1654.

half, or two foot diameter, and three foot in depth, that our
horse might not be able to pass to the edge of the out ditch,
and with the help of these hurdles wee hop'd to get over them:
But, as I haue already Said, those apprehensions were all blown
over by the Note which the Messenger had brought them, and
by the good news which arriv'd the next day from before
Stenay, which imported that it would soon be taken; They
thought it reasonable therfore to attend the coming of those
troopes, and in the mean time wee continued our preparations
for attacking the Lines when it should be judg'd fitt.

After the
taking of
Stenay M^r.
d'Hocquin-
court joyns
the two Mare-
shalls Turenne
and la Ferté,
with the
troopes y^t
cam from
that Seige.
OR: MEM:
P. 2: p. 71.

About the   of August wee had notice from M^r. d'Hocquincourt, to whom the Court had newly given the Command
of the troopes that had been before Stenay (for it was not he
but Mr. Faber Governour of Sedan who had commanded them
before when they took Stenay) that he was within   days
march of us, and desir'd to know whither he should come up
and joine us, or incampe at some other place; to which they
return'd this answer, That Monsr de Turenne wou'd meet him
with fifteen squadrons of horse at   and that if M^r.
d'Hocquincourt would come thither before and bring with him
all his horse, they too would go together, and view a post upon
the brook (*de Crinchon*) near Riuiere ; where they beleeved
would be found a convenient place for him to campe, and where
by intrenching himself a litle, he might be secure from any
attempt which the Enemy could make on him.

M. de Turenne
and M^r. d'
Hocquincourt
meet to view a
post for the
latter to camp
in.
OR: MEM:
P. 2: p. 72.

Accordingly Monsr. de Turenne and the other, mett at the
place appointed on the 17th of August: But instead of going
as they had resolved, to view that post, having immediatly
received notice of a great Convoy coming to the Enemy from
St Omer and Aire, by the way of St Paul, under the command
of Mr de Boutteville, they march'd away on the instant with

They march
to intercept a
Convoy of the
Enemy. *Ibid.*

their horse, and left word for M^r. d'Hocquincourt's foot, cañon,
and baggage which was then about Bapaume, to make what

expedition they could after them to St Paul; taking their way by Buquoy, and so along by the woods, to cover them as much as they could possibly, because they had no horse to guard them. In the mean time wee with the Cavalry were come as far as St Paul, where wee had intelligence that the Convoy having had notice of our coming that way, was return'd to Ayre, for which reason wee went no farther after them: But finding the enemy had possessed themselves of that Town, and had left four or five hunderd dismounted troopes in it for its defence, it was thought fitt by our two Generalls to stay where wee were till our foot came up, and then to attack it, it being a very considerable post which had been of great seruice to the Enemy; for most of their Convoys had come Safely to them by that way, and it was their usuall resting place betwixt their garrisons on that side of the Country and their Camp, so that it was necessary for us to take it from them. It cost us litle time and labour, for as soon as our foot and cannon were come up which was on the 18th when our Batterys were made, they capitulated, and, as I remember, were made prisoners of warr.

This being perform'd, the next day wee marched back towards the Lines and quarter'd at Aubigny, where, coming early to our quarters, Monsr. de Turenne according to his custome took with him a Squadron or two of horse and went on towards the Enemies Lines; and when he was come near an old Roman Camp, which was call'd by the Country-men Coesars's Camp, where the Scarpe and a litle brook joyne together, he found the Enemy had there an advanced guard of horse, which upon our coming towards them retir'd to the other side of the brook; by which means Monsr de Turenne had the leisure to view that post which was not distant from the Line of the Enemy above twice cannon shott.

And he found it so proper for his turn, that he propos'd it to Monsr d' Hocquincourt, as a much securer and better post

P A R T
II.
1654.
Missing y^e
Convoy they
attack St.
Paul, and take
the 500 men
y^t were in it
prisoners of
warr.
Ibid.

M^r.deTurenne
views Coesar's
Camp and
proposes it
to M^r. d'Hoc-
quincourt.
O$_R$: M$_{EM}$:
P. 2: p. 73.

P A R T
II.

1654.

to all intents, then that of Riuiere : Wherupon the next day being the 20th wee march'd thether, and to render it yet more secure, Monsr. d'Hocquincourt ordered his men to make a Line from the River to the brook; and finding that the Enemy had put five hunderd men into the Abbey of Mount St Eloy, which was but just on the other side of the River, he resolved to attack it the next day notwithstanding its neighbourhood to the Enemies Lines ; that by possessing it he might the better keep them in.

To secure
this post,
Hocquincourt
attacks the
Abbey of
Mount S^t
Eloy.
Or: Mem:
P. 2: p. 73.

Being thus resolved, the next morning early he pass'd the River, which is there but very small, and drew up all those troopes in battell betwixt the Abbey and the Line, excepting such of the foot as were commanded to attack the place : At first the Enemy made shew as if they intended to mentain the Outwall, but upon the advancing of our foot they quitted it, and retir'd into the Abbey it self which had a good old wall about it, flancked with round Towers. So soon as wee were masters of the Outwall, wee made Embraseurs through it for our cañon ; and began to batter the wall of the Abbey ; But finding that our cañon could not do much at so great a distance, wee rais'd a slight battery, which was indeed no more then a blind within the Outwall, and brought thether our great guns, where in four hours they began to make a breach, and while the cañon perform'd their part, the foot did theirs also : for having got by the shelter of some walks, and litle garden-walls within pistoll-shott of the foot of the main-wall, they fasten'd a Miner to it by the help of Madriers, and just as the Miner was ready to go on with those who were to carry the plancks to secure him, our foot which were cover'd by the garden-walls drew out from behind them, and stood firing as fast as they were able, for half a quarter of an hour together, at the Enemys loop-holes, that the Miner might lodge himself with more safety ; which being done they drew back behind the walls again. They were the French and Suisse Guards who perform'd this, and notwithstanding they approched so very near, and were seen from head to foot when they drew out, yet they lost very few men in the Action. At the same time the Regiment de la Marine found the means of lodging themselves, by the favour of a litle banck close to the Tower which wee were battering: so that those within the Abbey thought it was now high time for them to capitulate, which they did, yeelding up the Abbey and themselves prisoners of warr.

This being done, Monsieur d'Hocquincourt drew back over the brook to Coesar's Camp, and Monsr. de Turenne march'd away from thence, with his fifteen Squadrons of horse and two Troopes of Dragoons, to his own Camp. In his way thether he resolved to take a view of the Enemies Line on that Side, and in order to it, march'd down from Mont St Eloy, straight upon them, till he came within half cañon shott of them, and so keeping still the same distance from their Line, continued his march round that part of it which was on that side of the River Scarpe, till he had fully view'd it. During all this time the cannon shott from the Line playd hard upon us, and not without doing execution, there being not any of the Squadrons that escap'd without the loss of two or three men at least, and many of them lost more, besides horses, which caus'd some of the old horse Officers to murmure that they should be expos'd in that manner, as they then thought, to no purpose, And this was the only time while I serv'd in the French Army, that I ever knew Monsr. de Turenne blam'd for hazarding his men unnecessarily. But the same Officers acknowledge they were in the wrong for thus taxing their Generall, after wee had forced those Lines which wee came then to obserue; for then the reason was evident why he expos'd not only his men, but his own person to that danger, it being at that very time, that he chose the place where he resolved to attack the Line. And indeed had he not gone so near with his whole body, the Enemy's horse guards

PART II.

1654.

The Abbey of Mont St Eloy surrender'd up to the French.
On: Mem:
P. 2. p. 75.

M. d'Hocquin-court draws back to Coesar's Camp, and M^r.deTurenne returns to his own Camp. In his way he vews the Enemies Lines,together with the Duke.
Ibid.

They are very much expos'd.
On: Mem:
P. 2. p. 75.

This the only time the Duke ever heard M.deTurenne blam'd for hazarding unnecessarily his men.
Ibid. p. 76.

The reason why he expos'd himself in this manner and the great utility thereof.
Ibid.

would not haue retired as they did within their Line; and then he could not haue view'd it so exactly, for wee approched so near with some few .loose horse, that Mr. Jermyn's (*Lord Germain*) horse was kill'd under him with a small shott from the Line, which peirced him through and gave his master a terrible blow on the leg afterwards.

Thus Mons'. de Turenne by passing so near them, had the opportunity of viewing most exactly the strength of each quarter of the Enemy, all their troopes standing to their armes as wee marched along by them. He observed the quarter of Don Fernando de Solis to be the weakest, not only in men, but in the fortification of it; for which reason he resolv'd to make his strongest impression there. Some of our Officers as wee were marching down towards the Lines from Mont St Eloy, were bold enough to represent to Mons'. de Turenne, the extreme hazard which he ran by going so near the Enemy in so open a Country, who (*where*) they could tell every man wee had, and therby knowing our force, might draw out and defeat us without any danger to themselves; which he freely acknowledg'd they might do, and that were it on the Prince Condé's side as it was on the Spaniards, he would not haue made the Venture: but having serv'd amongst the Spaniards, he well knew their methods of proceeding, And he was certain, that upon our first approche towards their Lines, Don Fernando de Solis would not dare to do any thing of himself, without sending first to the Count of Fuensaldagne who was Governador de las Armas; and the Count would either go himself or send to advertise the Archduke of it: after which they would send to the Prince of Condé, whose quarter was quite on the other side, and give him notice, at the same time desiring him to come to the Archduke's quarter where they were, to haue a Junto to consider what must be done on that occasion; And while this consultation which must pass through so many formes was making, wee should haue

M.deTurenne foretells exactly what ye Spaniards' proceedings would be, upon his approching their Lines. Or: Mem: P. 2. p. 77.

leisure to view their Lines, and afterwards to pass by them without running any other hazard then that of their cañon from their Lines. It happen'd just as he had foretold it would, and all those very Formalities were actually observ'd by the Spaniards, as the Prince of Condé himself told me afterwards in Flanders; but by that time they had resolved at their Junto to fall upon us, wee were wholly out of their danger and gotten in to our Camp.

Monsieur de Turenne having taken this view, it was now time for us to put some thing in execution in order to releeve the Town; for by a letter from the Governour, our Generalls had notice that he had very litle pouder left, so that unless he were speedily succour'd he must be forced to capitulate. This hasten'd our resolution of attacking their Lines; which had never been attempted but by the means of Mons'. de Turenne, who consider'd nothing but the public good, and the carrying of the King's Seruice; most of the other Generall Officers having by-ends and interests of their own, which made them declare openly against the taking of such a resolution, and oppose it with all the arguments they could invent. For M'. de la Ferté, he was unwilling to run the hazard of losing so many of his Soldiers, as in all probability must be kill'd in the attempt; for being of so much consideration at Court by reason of his troopes, he was unwilling they should be lessen'd. Mons'. d'Hocquincourt was Governour of Peroñe, which if Arras was once taken, would then more frontéer then it was before, and a considerable part of the contributions belonging to that place, would fall to him: The same reason prevail'd with M'. de Navailles Governour of Bapaume, and with Mons'. de Bar Governour of Dourlans, both of the Lieutenant Generalls; and most of the rest, excepting only myself and the Count de Broglio looking on it as a desperate peice of seruice, gave their opinions against the attack; for by weaving the attempt they

PART II.

1654.

The Governour of Arras presses for speedy Sucour. On: Mem: P. 2: p. 78.

The releif of Arras had never been attempted but by the means of M'. Turenne. Ibid.

The other Generall Officers oppose the undertaking for their own by-ends. Ibid.

Most of all the L' Gen'ls excepting the Duke and y' Counte de Broglio gave their opinions against the attack of the Lines. Ibid. p. 79.

PART
II.
1654.

secur'd their persons, and if the attempt were made and
succeeded not, they might be able to say, it was undertaken
contrary to their judgment: And this is not sayd as my bare
conjecture, but was very apparent; for Mons'. d'Hocquincourt
and his Officers propos'd to make a tentative, as they call'd
it, or an offer, without pushing for the Saving of our honours,
judging it impossible to effect the Enterprise. M. de la
Ferté even after it was resolved on, a day or two before
the attack, sent his Trumpett to Mons'. de Turenne, hoping
by the Relation he should give, to fright him from attempting
it, which appear'd by the manner of his coming; for he
came in to Mons'. de Turenne's Tent as he sat at Supper with
severall Officers, and told him, he was sent by his Master to
give him an account of what he had seen in the Enemies
Lines, he being newly come from thence, and adding, that he
was bound in conscience to give him a true relation of it. He
then told him, That they had made their Lines extraordinarly
strong, having inlarged their ditch and rais'd their Line; that
their out ditch was very difficult to pass, and that without it
there were severall ranks of holes, with stakes betwixt every
hole, and that their Lines were well furnish'd with Souldiers to
defend them. Upon this Mons'. de Turenne grew angry, and
commanded him to be gone, telling him withall, That were it not
for the respect he bore his Master, he would haue layd him by
the heels for talking in that manner: For indeed this discourse
being made in a publick place, might haue been of ill consequence to discourage all who heard it, had they not guessed
he had been order'd by Mons'. de la Ferté to give this tragicall
account.

M. de
Turenne's
reasons against
the proposall
of making only
a faint attempt.
Or: Mem:
P: 2: p. 81.

But Mons'. de Turenne's judgment was too well settled, to
give way of his artifices, So that in stead of suffering his own
reason to be shaken by them, he made the falsness of their
arguments appear. As for the tentative, he convinced those

who upheld it, that they (*were*) under a manifest mistake, for
in stead of saving their reputation it would haue a quite contrary
effèct; because by making a faint (*feint*) attempt, without
pursuing it, every one would see they intended nothing more,
so that they should haue the disrepute of Sacrifising two or three
hundred men to no purpose: And then as to the probability of
our succez in attacking the Line, he said, Wee should fall on
with no less then fifteen battallions upon one front, that some
of these would find none to oppose them or at worst only some
scatter'd men ; That those who found no form'd body to make
resistance, would doubtless fix themselves on the Line where
they fell on, and that consequently all the rest of our foot coming
to that place, if they could not force their way where they
attack'd, must by being masters of the fire, beat off the Enemy
and make an entrance for the horse ; That by attacking them
in the night, one quarter durst not come to the assistance of the
other, for that by reason of the false attacks, each fearing for
himself, would not dare to forsake his Station, and help his
Neighbour till break of day, and before that time wee should
haue forced our passage through their Lines ; That what he
most apprehended was some disorder or accident in our march
thether, for he was very confident, that were wee once ready
drawn up, where wee intended our attack, wee should be able to
force our way : And to strengthen these his reasons, the Court
was absolutely for the attempt, so that infine it was resolv'd on,
notwithstanding all the trickes and reluctance of those who
oppos'd it.

The time appointed was the Eve of St Lewis his day, being
the night of the 24th of August; and thō none in the Army
besides the three Generalls knew the certain time, yet the whole
Army had orders to prepare for it, and to provide themselves
of fascines and hurdles and all other necessaries for such an
undertaking ; neither were they obliged only to make these

he Shews a
probability
of Success
according to
the method
propos'd to
attack the
Lines.
On: Mem:
P: 2. p. 82.

The Court
being abso-
lutely for the
attempt, it
is at last
resolv'd on.
Ibid. p: 83.

All the pre-
parations
made, and
publick prayers
order'd at the
head of each
Battalion and
Squadron.
On: Mem:
P. 2. p. 83.

PART
II.

1654.

M.deTurenne
instructs the
Officers how
to beahave.
Ibid. p. 84.

preparations, but those which were full as necessary, which were publick prayers at the head of each Battalion and Squadron for severall days before, and as many as could, confessed, and received the blessed Sacrament: So that I am confident no Army ever show'd more markes of true deuotion then ours at that time. And now that the night for the attack drew near, Monsr. de Turenne did on all occasions discourse with the Officers concerning the mañere of it, and what resistance wee were like to find, instructing them how to behave themselves according to the Severall occasions which might arise, and accidents which might happen : But above all things he recommended to them the care of keeping their Men in perfect order when they were once with in the Lines, and to be very cautious that they advanced not too fast, after they were gotten in ; for then was the criticall time of care and discipline, there being more danger of being beaten out, then there was hazard in entring, for it was to be expected that all the forces of the other quarters would come powring in upon us: and that wee shou'd not think of going straight forward to the Town, but shou'd march along the Line and clear that before us, and beat the Enemy before wee thought of marching to our freinds. These kind of discourses he had every day with his Officers, as occasion was presented, in common talk, and more especially with the Generall Officers. And I am apt to beleeve that from this manner of conversation, historians haue made speeches for many Generalls who never made any to their Armys when they were upon the point of giving battell ; for such ordinary discourses as I haue mentioned, appear to me to be much more usefull then set formall speeches, which can not be heard but by very few, in an open field, where they are commonly feign'd by writers to haue been spoken : whereas by familiar conversation with Several Officers, the Generall do's not only instruct them much better, and at more leisure, but is ready at the same time to answer any of their objections, and to clear any doubt which may arase. I know not whither any of the two other Generalls did the same, but I am a witness that it was done by Monsieur de Turenne.

P A R T
II.

1654.

And now all things being fully prepar'd for the attack, all the men of quality at Court, who were of age to draw a sword, came from thence into our Army to haue their share both of the honour and the danger of so great an undertaking. And some of them happening to dine with Monsr. de Turenne, and myself, at the Marquess d'Humieres his tent, about two days before the attack, after diner had a desire to see the Enemie's Lines. Monsr. de Turenne therfore gott on horseback with all those who had din'd together, and went out of our Line towards one of our out horse-guards. Just as wee came out wee saw a small party of ours pursuing a party of the Enemies, which had fallen on our foragers, who were then returning to our Camp. Monsr. de Turenne observing this, commanded us who were with him, to try if wee could get betwixt them and their Line, and cutt off their way, at the same time ordering the horse guards to second us. But tho wee were well hors'd, they got to their guard before wee could joine them, and upon our advancing up towards them, they drew into their Line, and left some few foot, which were making fascines in a litle wood which was about half cannon shott from their Line, to our mercy ; and these wee made prisoners : And here Monsr. de Turenne took this opportunity of Viewing that part of their Lines, which he had not seen before.

All the men of quality at Court came to the Army to haue a share in the action. Or: Mem: P. 2. p. 85. M.deTurenne with the Duke and severall other persons of quality, get on horseback to view the Lines. Or: Mem: P. 2. p. 86.

The Duke with some others order'd to pursue a party of the Enemy. *Ibid.*

They pursue the party into their Lines and take some foot prisoners. *Ibid.*

But he continu'd not long there, for they plyd us very hard with their cañon, and wee saw them getting in horse back as fast as they could. So that it was evident they would come out upon us, it being the P^{ce} of Condé's quarter : Therfore wee drew off and went towards a Castle call'd Neufville S. Vât which was not above a league distant, in which wee had foot,

PART
II.

1654.

The Enemys
horse draw
out and the
P^{ce} of Condé
himself at the
head of them.
OR: MEM:
P. 2. p. 87.
M.deTurenne
orders M. de
l'Islebonne to
come up to
him with all
speed. *Ibid.*

and as wee were descending from the high ground on which
wee were, wee saw about a league from us the Convoy of our
foragers, consisting of twelve Squadrons of horse commanded
by Monsr. de l'Islebonne, a Lieu^t Genl, marching home to our
Camp.

At the same time Seeing the Enemys horse beginning to draw
out of their Lines, Monsr. de Turenne alter'd his course a litle,
and march'd towards Monsr. de l'Islebonne, sending before
and ordering him to come up to us with all speed : Having
hopes that in case the Enemy should follow us, wee should be
able to do somewhat on them. By this time our number was
increased, so that besides the Squadron of guards, which was
with us, wee were about sixty or seventy officers and volonteers : But they Enemy follow'd us no further then the top of
the hill which was within cañon shott of their Lines, and
thether came the P^{ce} of Condé himself with about fourteen

TheEnemy not
pursuing, he
countermands
M. de l'Isle-
bonne. *Ibid.*

Squadrons of horse. When Monsr. de Turenne saw they
follow'd us no farther, he sent word again to Monsr. l'Islebonne that he should continue on his march to our Camp ; and
sent back the Squadron of the guards to their post, himself
going with the Officers towards the Castle I haue already
mention'd.

But he had not gone farr, when some few scatter'd men came
from the heigth, where the P^{ce} of Condé was in person, and
endeavour'd to gain the top of another rising ground up which
wee were marching, to discover what strength there was behind
us ; which being observ'd by Monsr. de Turenne, he was not
willing they should get above us, and by that means discern
that wee had none to second us, and for that reason commanded out half a score volonteers to hinder their design ; of
which number were M^r. Jermyn, Mr. Charles Berkley, Briscara,
Trigomar, and others, whose names I do not now remember.
At the same time wee drew up in a body upon the top of the

hill, and faced towards the Enemy: But our young Volonteers were not Satisfied with performing only what was order'd them, but followed these loose men farther then in reason they ought to haue done, that is, even to (*the*) bottome, which was betwixt us and the Enemys bodys of horse; which the P^{ce} of Condé seeing, commanded one of his Squadrons of horse, namely the Regiment d'Estrées with the Duke of Wirtemberg at their head, to come down at full speed upon our young men, and endeavour to cutt off the way of their return. This obliged Monsr. de Turenne to order us with our small body to meet and charge them, thereby, to disingage our friends; And then again he sent for Monsr. de l'Islebonne and the Squadron of guards to Second us.

It was all wee could do to save our Volonteers, but in preserving them wee ingaged ourselves by charging the Duke of Wirtemberg, and thoug our body was not neer so strong as his, wee routed him, and pursued him down into a litle meadow, which lay in the bottom; from thence wee follow'd him up a litle balk, where his men turn'd upon us, and gave us a volley of their Carabins, which gave a litle Stop to us by their knocking down severall of our men and horses. This being observed by the Enemy renew'd their courage, and they charg'd down upon us the Second time with so much vigour, that they forced us back, press'd upon us, and made us begin to turn our backs. But at the same time the Squadron of guards, who as they were going to their post had seen the beginning of the skirmish, came into our releif, and just as they came up to us, myself and Monsr. de Joyeuse turn'd and put ourselves at their head, leading them up to charge the Enemy in the flanck:· but at the instand when wee were puting this in execution, the whole Squadron ran and left us two ingaged, non staying with us but two or three of our Servants.

P A R T II.

1654.
Some Volonteers of M. de Turenne's, pursuing farther then they ought, are in danger to be cutt off. OR: MEM: P. 2: p. 88.

The Duke and others order'd to charge the Enemy and disingage the Volonteers. *Ibid.*

Tho fewer in number they charge ye Duke of Wirtemberg and route him, but are afterwards forced back. *Ibid.*

The Duke and M. de Joyeuse put themselves at the head of a Squadron of the guards, and lead them to charge, but the whole Squadron running, leave them expos'd to the Enemy with 2 or 3 Servants only. OR: MEM: P. 2. p. 89.

The Duke and
M. de Joyeuse
endeavouring
to Save M.
d'Arcy, escape
themselves
with much ado.
OR: MEM:
P. 2: p. 89.

M. de Joyeuse
receives
here a shott, of
which he dyd
afterwards.
Ibid.

Almost at the same point of time Monsr. d'Arcy a gentleman of quality had his horse kill'd under him, and wee endeavour'd to get him off; I call'd to him to get off, but he seeing a loose horse which had lost his rider, would needs catch him, and stayd so long in endeavouring it, that though I and Monsr. de Joyeuse did all wee could to lay hold of him and gett him off, wee were not able to performe it: and indeed wee endeavour'd it So long, and ingaged ourselves so far, that wee were both in danger of being taken, and had much ado to escape ourselves. As for Monsr. de Joyeuse he had the misfortune to receive a shott through the Arme, of which afterwards he dy'd, but I got off without any harme. M^r. Jermyn was like to haue been taken in endeavouring to save one Beauregard, whose horse being also kill'd, he help'd him up behind him, but the horse would not carry double, and bounding threw him off; Therupon Jermyn advis'd him to lay hold on his stirrup, by which means he brought him a litle way from the Enemy, till at length being press'd by them, he was forced to quit him, and then Beauregard was made prisoner. M^r. Berkley help'd to get off Monsr. de Castelneau, whose horse was shott in five places, so that he was hardly able to bear him from the Enemy; which Berkley seeing, dismounted, and lent the other his own horse, after which he gott upon another on which (*one of*) Monsr. de Castelneau's pages was mounted, and with much difficulty escaped.

The Enemy had the chase of us for almost a mile, and had pursued us farther, had not Monsr. de l'Islebonne with his twelve Squadrons come to our relief; but seeing him they retir'd time enough for their own safety, without being oblidg'd to run for it. Besides d'Arcy and Beauregard, there were some others taken, and almost all the pages who were there with their Master's cloakes. Very few were kill'd and not many hurt;

yet it vex'd Mons'. de Turenne to haue received that litle affront
in person, and made him desirous to haue some kind of revenge,
and he hop'd to haue had it that very night; for having receiv'd
intelligence that the Enemy were accustom'd to come out of
their Lines and forage in the night, he resolved to fall upon
them.

And to that purpose so soon as it was dark, he march'd out
of his Camp in person with all his horse then in his Camp with
him, which were about fourty Squadrons, and took along with
him three or four Lieu^t Generalls, amongst whom he divided
them, himself marching at the head of all: But whither the
intelligence were false, or that they, having notice of our design,
were gone off before wee could reach the place where wee were
inform'd they us'd to forage when wee came thether wee found
no body; so that having miss'd of our expectations, Mons'.
de Turenne made the Van of that which was the Rear, and
march'd back, as he thought, towards his Camp. The night
happen'd to be exceeding dark, and our guides mistaking their
way, in stead of leading us to our Camp brought us to the Lines
of the Enemy.

It was the Prince of Condé's quarter which they mistook
for ours; and upon the Centry's asking who went there? they
were answer'd Turenne; he repeated the question, and
demanded farther if it was not Lorraine they meant? but they
answer'd again that it was Turenne, upon which he fir'd at
them; Then some of our men who continued still in their
errour, cryd out to him not to fire, for M^r. de Turenne was there
in person: This obliged the Enemy to fire some few small shott
at us, and one great gun, which absolutely undeceived us, but
withall put us into the greatest disorder imaginable, causing
such a panique fear in our common men, that I am confident,
if that moment fourty horse had come out upon us, wee had
been defeated. The cheif, or rather the only cause of the first

P A R T
II.

1654.

M.deTurenne
marches out
in the night
time with 40
Squadrons,
thinking to
surprise y^e
Enemys
foragers; the
Duke with
him.
On: Mem:
P. 2: p. 90.

The Guides
mistaking the
way, M. de
Turenne in
stead of being
led back to his
own Camp, is
brought to the
Enemys Lines.
Ibid.

The Army is
in great dis-
order by this
mistake.
On: Mem:
P. 2. p. 91.

disorder was the darkness of the night, our Squadrons being
therby obliged to march so 'close to one another, for fear of
loosing the File, that upon the sudden stop which was made
by the first Squadron when the Centry fir'd, those behind came
shouldring one upon another and broke their order; But upon
their firing afterwards from the Line, the formost giving a litle
back and altering their course immediatly to wheel about
towards their own Camp, the confusion was so great, that of ten
Squadrons which ought to haue been behind mine, there was not
one at our marching back, So that I happen'd to haue the Reer
in coming off; but the hurry was soon over, for wee all gott safe
into our Lines, as also those Squadrons which had lost their
way.

The Duke
herebyexpos'd
to bring off –
the Reer, tho
it was not his
turn. *Ibid.*

This happen'd, as I said, about a day or two before wee
attack'd the Lines, And now our fascines and hurdles and
other necessarys for such an attempt, being fully provided, our
Generalls resolv'd to attack the quarter of Don Fernando Solis
with their whole forces, as being the weakest in all respects, and
farthest distant from the Prince of Condé: This quarter began
on the north side of the River above the Town, and joyn'd to
that of the Count of Fuensaldagne. To favour this undertaking,
three false attacks were order'd to be made on the other parts
of the Line; the time appointed, an houre before day on the
25th of August.

All things
provided for
the attack of
the Lines.

The Quarter
to be attack'd
resolv'd upon.
Or: Mem:
P. 2: p. 93.

In performance of this resolution, Mons'. de Turenne and
Mons'. de la Ferté with their two Armys began with the Van
of their troopes to pass over the Scarpe out of Mons'. de la
Ferté's quarters, about Sun sett. It was Mons'. de Turenne's
turn that day to lead, and they had a great march to come to
the place appointed for the attack; but it was so well order'd
that there happen'd no confusion in the way, there being very
many bridges over the Scarpe made, and such care taken, that
no ill accident arrived to them in their march. Every man

The time
appointed the
25th August
Eve of St
Lewis' day.
Ibid.
Order of ye
march. *Ibid.*

knew his own business. The first line of the foot pass'd over
the bridge, which was on the left hand of all the others, and
nearest to the Enemies Line. On the next bridge to that on
the right hand of them, the horse pass'd over which were to
second them. On the third, the Reserve of horse and foot :
On the next to it, the Traine of Artillery, with all that belong
to it; so that with only faceing to the left wee were in battalia,
and in a readiness to falle on; every battalion having their
Pioneers, and commanded men, ready at the head of them, and
each Trooper carrying two fascines a horseback before him,
to deliver to the Foot when they should haue occasion. for
them. As for our baggage it was order'd to be in a readiness,
but not to stirr out of the Camp till it was broad day-light,
because no guard was left with it; but afterwards to come to
us as they could.

This was the order of our march, which was perform'd with
such conduct and exactness, that wee came just at the houre
appointed, to the place where wee were to meet M. d'Hocquincourt with his troopes. In all this way wee halted but once,
and that but for a very litle time, without haning given the least
allarme to the Enemy in the march; though for the greatest
part of the way, had not our musketeers observ'd their orders
very carefully in hiding their metches, the Enemy from their
Lines must needs haue discover'd them. I remember that once
that night, out of curiosity to see how they observ'd their orders,
I went without our Foot at a litle distance from them, and could
not so much as perceive one lighted match.

And here it will not be amiss to mention our order of battell,
and how our Generall Officers were disposed, but I shall only
be very particular in those who belong'd to Monsr. de Turenne:
He divided his eight Lieu^t Generalls equally betwixt the horse
and foot, four to each. To the first Line of foot compos'd of
five battalions he appointed three, The Count de Broglio

PART II.

1654.

The Soldiers' great care in hiding their metches. Or: Mem: P. 2: p. 94.

Order of Battell with the Severall posts of the Gen^t Officers. Or: Mem. P. 2. p. 94.

P A R T
II.

1654.

commanded Picardy and the Suisse which were the two right hand battalions; Monsr. de Castelneau, those of Plessis and Turenne which were on the left hand, and M. du Passage that of la Feuillade which was in the midst. To command the horse which seconded these; consisting of about twenty-four Squadrons, he appointed also three : M^r. de Barr had the charge of those on the right hand behind M^r. de Broglio, Myself on the left hand behind Monsr. de Castelneau, and Monsr. d'Eclinvillers in the midst. The reserue of foot consisting of three battalions was commanded by Monsr. de Roncherolles, and that of horse by Monsr. de l'Islebonne who had under him eight Squadrons : This was Monsr. de Turenne's order of battell for that occasion.

The Duke's
post at the
head of the
left wing of M.
de Turenne's
horse.
Ibid. p. 95.

M. de la Ferté
draws up on
the left hand
of M^r. de
Turenne, and
M^r. d'Hoc-
quincourt on
his right.
Ibid.

Monsieur de la Ferté who drew up on his left hand, had one only line of foot consisting of six battalions, two lines of horse behind them, and a reserue of horse; Monsr. d'Hocquincourt who was placed on the right hand, had first four battalions of foot, then a line of horse, and behind them a second line of foot of four battalions more, with some horse on their wings, and a small reserue of horse not exceeding three or four Squadrons. Wee also had three false attacks; the first, of Monsr. de Turenne's troopes compos'd of two battalions of foot, being York and Dillon, and six Squadrons of horse, all commanded by Monsr. de Tracy who had orders to get as neer as he cou'd without being discover'd to the Prince of Condé's quarters; but not to fall on, till he heard the attack begun on the other side by us, and then to march directly to the Barrier of that quarter which he had been shewn some days before, and through it to endeavour to force his passage into the Town. The false attack from Monsr. de la Ferté's troopes was commanded by M^r. de la Guillottiere, who was to fall upon the Count de Fuensaldagne's quarter with two battalions, six Squadrons, two troopes of Dragoons, and two great guns. The false attack of

Three false
attacks.
Or: Mem:
P. 2. p. 95.

Monsieur d'Hocquincourt was not considerable, being only of
four Squadrons, and some ropes with metches ty'd to them,
commanded by Mr. de St Jean, who was to make his on
Prince Francis of Lorraine's quarter. These were the orders
of the Severall Armies for the attack of the whole Line.

· And now Monsr. de Turenne being come to the place
appointed, found Mr. d'Hocquincourt already there in person,
but without his troopes which were not yet come up, tho they
had but a very litle march to make. Hocquincourt said, his
men were just coming, and would immediatly be upon the
place, till which time he desir'd the attack might be deferred.
But Monsr. de Turenne answer'd, That he could not possibly
delay it, being now so neer the Line, that the Enemy would
soon discover him, that therfore he desir'd him to make what
hast he could to fall on after him: And his own troopes being
by this time in order, he led them on himself (*on*) horseback to
attack the Line.

Wee had in our march thether a very still faire night, besides
the benefit of the moon, which sett as favorably for us as wee
could desire, that is, just as wee came to the place appointed.
As the moon went down, it began to blow very fresh and grew
exceeding dark, in so much that the Enemy could neither see
nor hear us, as otherwise they might; and they were the more
surprised when the first news they had of us, was to find us
within half cañon shott of them. I remember not to haue seen
a finer sight of the nature, then was that of our foot when they
were once in battell, and began to march towards the Lines;
for then discovering at once their lighted metches, they made a
glorious shew, which appear'd the more by reason of the wind,
which kindled them and made them blaze throw the darkness
of the night; for the breeze keeping the coal of their metches
very clear, whensoever any of the Musketeers (*happened*) to shog

F F 2

P A R T
II.
1654.

M.deTurenne
leads on his
troopes to
attack the
Line without
waiting for
Mr. d'Hocquin-
court's men
that were not
come up.
OR: MEM:
P. 2: p. 96.

In approching
the Lines
the Soldiers
lighted their
metches;
d'scover'd all
at once, make
a glorious
shew, the
night being
very dark and
windy.
OR: MEM:
P. 2: p. 97.

P A R T
II.

1654.

against each other, the metches struck fire, so that the sparkles were carryd about by the wind to increase the light.

Wee were no sooner discover'd by the Enemy then they fir'd three cannon at us, and either made fires or sett up lights along the Line: Our foot then lost no time in falling on; but had

M. de
Turenne's foot
fall on, the
horse keeping
close to their
rear oblige the
men to do
their duty.
Or: Mem:
P: 2. p. 97.

not the vigour of the Officers who led them, and the horse by keeping so close to their rear, obliged the common men to do their duty, they had not perform'd it as they ought, nor as I allways till that time had observ'd them to do, for I never knew them to go on so unwillingly as then; which notwithstanding, they stopt not till they came to the Line it self, where the resistance they found was not So great as they suspected;

They master
that part of
the Line
which they
attack'd.
Or: Mem:
P. 2: p. 98.

for in a very litle time all our five battalions made themselves masters of that part of it which they attacked; and then they

The horse
march up to
the holes
before the
Lines, and
there throw
down their
fascines and
wheel off again
till passage
was made.
Ibid.

who were appointed for that worke, began to make passages for the horse to enter, and every Squadron of horse went up to the very holes which I haue mention'd and then threw down their fascines, which the foot immediatly took up and help'd to fill up both the ditches. This being perform'd the horse wheel'd off, and drew up about thirty yards behind, expecting till passage should be made for them.

It is whisper'd
to the Duke
that M. de
Turenne was
hurt, and that
matters went
ill on the right
hand.
Or: Mem:
P. 2: p. 98.

While this was doing, one came to the left hand of the attack where I was at the head of the horse, and whisper'd to me that M. de Turenne was hurt, and that matters went no well on the right hand: Upon which intelligence to incourage the foot, and to let them understand how near wee were to them, I

The great
conduct and
courage of his
Highness on
this occasion.
Ibid.

commanded the kettle drums to beat, and the trumpets of the Squadron of horse at the head of which I was to sound, which being heard by all our other horse, they did the like. This incouraged our foot sufficiently, but was of some prejudice to my own Squadron, and to that which was next it, for from a Redan on my left hand, the Enemy by the beat of the kettle

drums and sound of the trumpetts found where wee were, and
plyd us with their shott. The Kettle drum was soon silenced,
he being the first man who was kill'd of that Squadron where
I was.

This happen'd just as Monsr. de la Ferté was beginning his
attack, he having not put his men so soon in order as M^r. de
Turenne had : But he either had not so good fortune, or found
more resistance then our foot ; for thō his Officers led up their
men with good resolution into the very ditch, yet they were not
able to master the Line, but were beaten off, and came running
away to shelter themselves amongst the horse which I commanded. The disorder was very great, the Officers complaining
aloud, that they had been abandon'd by their Soldiers, and
the Soldiers crying out, that they had follow'd their Officers,
who had not behav'd themselves as became them : which part
had justice on their side I know not, but beaten off they were,
and the horse far'd the worse for their ill success ; for the
Enemy seeing their lighted metches, plac'd their small shott
amongst us with much more certainty then they could before.

By this time the* Foot of our attack had made passages for
our horse to enter, and Monsr. de Turenne's Regiment of Foot
had found a Barriere which they open'd, and therby sav'd
themselves the farther trouble of making a passage : Upon
notice of which, Monsr. de Turenne order'd M^r. d' Eclinvillers
to enter the first with four Squadrons of horse, and to be
seconded by me ; accordingly he enter'd the Lines with his
three first Squadrons, but as the fourth was going in, they who
had beaten off la Fertés Foot came along the Line to this
Barriere, and finding only this Squadron of horse entring there,
(the foot which had first master'd this Barriere having drawen

PART
II.

1654.
The Duke's
Squadron
much expos'd
and his kettle
drum kill'd
hard by him.
Ibid. p. 99.
M. de la Ferté
begins, his
men are
beaten off.
Ibid.

they shelter
themselves
amongst the
horse com-
manded by the
Duke, and do
therby con-,
siderably
augment the
danger that
Squadron was
expos'd to.
Ibid.

M.d'Eclin-
villers is
order'd to
enter the
first with 4
Squadrons of
horse and the
Duke to
seconde him.
OR MEM:
P. 2. p. 99.

---

* In the Cardinal de Bouillon's abridged Narrative, the King used the expression,
Cependant l'Infanterie de l'attaque. — EDITOR.

PART
II.

1654.

off from thence, and advanced farther within the Line somewhat more on the right hand, as not thinking it necessary for
them to stay and maintain that post when once the horse was
enterd) powr'd into them a volly of small-shott, and threw

Eclinvillers'
4 Squadrons
beat off and
the Barriere
shutt upon
them.
OR: MEM:
P. 2. p. 100.

severall hand granàdos in amongst them; with which the
Collonel who commanded that Squadron, one Bodervitz a
German, being shott from his horse thō not slaine, and his
Major also much wounded, they were beaten off and the
Enemy shutt that Barriere upon us.

The Duke
being repuls'd
here, seeks an
other passage
where he
enters at the
head of
Turenne's
Regiment.
Ibid.

Seeing therfore I could not enter there, I went along the
Line on the right hand till I found another passage, by which
I enter'd at the head of M^r. de Turenne's own Regiment of
horse, which on that occasion made but two Squadrons; and
finding the Enemys hutts on fire, which prov'd of great
advantage to us (and As I heard afterwards was first thought
upon by one Bout-de-bois Lieu^t. Coll^l. to la Feuillade) I
avanced farther to see if any of the Enemy were yet drawn up
behind them, and notwithstanding that some of their horse
were still continuing there, it was so dark, that with the two

The third
Squadron
which follow'd
the Duke,
defeat a Reg^t
of the Enemy
and take the
Commander
prisoner.
Ibid. p. 101.
The Duke
advancing
still, comes to
ye counterval-
lation. Ibid.

first Squadrons I pass'd betwixt them without either seeing
them, or being discover'd by them; But the third, which was
the Regiment d'Espence (de Beauveau) lighted on them, beat
them, and took the Marquis de Conflans prisoner, who commanded the Regiment wch they defeated. By this time the
day began to break, and I still advancing, came to the Countervallation, where finding no passage in it —*; yet I found none,
till I came to the River above the Town which divided the

---

* Here is another omission, which may be supplied from the Narrative sent to
the Cardinal de Bouillon : — "Où ne trouvant point de passage vers la ville, il la
cotoya, l'ayant toujours à sa gauche, et n'en rencontrà point qu'en arrivant à la riviere
au-dessus de la ville que séparoit le quartier de Lorraine de celui de Fernand Solis,"
&c. — EDITOR.

Lorraine quarter from that of Don Fernando de Solis. And
seeing that none of ours had yet pass'd over into the Lorraine
quarter, I alter'd my resolution and thought it proper for me
to go over the bridges into it.

This I undertook with the Reg^t. of Turenne only, which
made but two Squadrons, the rest of the horse which should
haue follow'd me having lost their way, and advanced as far as
Prince Francis of Lorraine's Tent without finding any opposition.
But being there, I saw four or five Squadrons of the Enemy
drawn up, about the distance of muskett-shott from me upon
another litle heigth. Wherupon I thought it best to halt a litle,
till more horse came up to me, and drew up both my Squadrons
upon one front, which just fill'd up the distance betwixt the
Line and the Tents; after which I sent away three or four
persons severally to bring the horse I wanted. While I was
there expecting them, the Duke of Buckingham came up to
me, and ask'd me, Why I would not pursue the Victory, and
charge those horse which were before me? To which I answer,
That I had no mind to receive an affront, and expose my self
to a certain defeat, what I saw of the Enemy already being
twice our number, besides what part of them might be behind
the heigth on which they were; That should wee advance and
be beaten, the Enemy might make himself master of the bridges
which wee had pass'd, and break them down, by which means
they wou'd both save themselves and the baggage of that
quarter; That if they came up and charg'd me where I then
was, I should at least ingage them on equall termes, because
they could not outflanck me; besides which I had here the
advantage of the ground; In short, that I expected more horse
every moment, which being come I would then go and charge
them. Thus resolved I continued there, and would not give
way to his importunitys.

The Enemy and wee stood looking on each other for some

Finding no passage in the countervallation, he enters into the Lorraine quarter wth two Squadrons only, the rest having lost their way. Or: Mem: P. 2. p. 101.

He draws up within muskett shott of 4 or 5 Squadrons of the Enemy, and halting sends for more horse. Ibid.

The D. of Buckingham's imprudent proposall of charging the Enemy, with his R. H. reasons for rejecting it. Ibid.

PART
II.

1654.

The horsemen
quitt their
ranks in spite
of y⁰ Officers
and fall to
plunder P⁰⁰ of
Lorraine's
Tent.
Oⁿ: Mᴇᴍ:
P. 2: p. 103.
Non left with
the Duke but
Officers
and the 12
Cornetts.
Ibid.
Yᵉ Duke is
forced to ride
back himself
to fetch more
horse.
Oⁿ: Mᴇᴍ:
P. 2: p. 103.

He brings up
the Squadron
of Villequier,
which he had
hardly drawn
up in order
when they ran
and left him.
Ibid.
The Duke
intending to
return again
with 4
Squadrons
into the
Lorraine
quarter, is
prevented by
d'Hocquin-
court. *Ibid.*

time, no horse coming to me ; but, in mean time, some scatter'd men of ours fell to plunder Prince Francis his Tent, where besides his plate, there was a month's pay for his Army in ready mony, which had like to haue occasion'd our paying dear for it; for our horsemen hearing the noise which those plunderers made in taking it, in spight of their Officer's commands and threatnings, quitted their ranks one after another, and fell to ransack the Tent for their share of the booty ; so that at last there were none left with me but Officers, and the twelve Cornetts; which being in full sight of the Enemy, I expected every moment to be charg'd and beaten : Being in this perplexity and hearing no news of those severall persons whom I had sent for horse, I thought it expedient to go myself and fetch them, and recommending to Mousʳ. de Montaulieu the Lieuᵗ Collˡ to make good that heigth till my return, I rode back, and found the Second Squadron of Villequier on the other side of the bridge going towards the Town, which I stop'd, and putting myself at their head, march'd over again : But scarce had the rear of the Squadron past the bridge, and the head being gott off from a small causwey begun to draw up into order again, when those horse which I had left to face the Enemy came running down the hill upon me in great disorder ; At this the Squadron which I brought with me took such a fright, that they also ran and left me, it being impossible to stop them. Wherupon I repassed the bridge, having seen four Squadrons on the other side of it, intending with them to come over again into the Lorraine quarter : But before I could bring them to the bridge, the Mareshall d'Hocquincourt with all his horse, and severall Squadrons of the other two Armies were come thether, and began to pass.

Seeing this, I thought there were horse enough that way, and so in stead of following them, I march'd directly the other way, betwixt the Countervallation and the Town, towards the Count the Count de Fuensaldagne's quarter with my four Squadrons, two of which were Gendarmes commanded by Monsr. de Schomberg, the other two the Regiment de Gesvres, under Monsr. de Querneux. Being come with these upon a heigth from whence I could take a large view of all about me, I saw upon another heigth before me, betwixt the two Lines, severall Squadrons of horse drawn up facing towards the place wee enter'd. At first thought they were the Enemy; but seeing one of the Squadrons in red coats, I alter'd my opinion, and beleeved them to be our horse, taking that particular Squadron to be either the King's Chevaux-Legers, or his Gendarmes, their coats being of that coulour: Upon which conjecture I marched towards them to joyn my Body to theirs, because by observing their posture I knew they were facing an Enemy; but what that Enemy was I could not discern, a higher ground being interpos'd on my left hand which hinder'd my sight.

But by that time I was gott to the bottom of the hill and was beginning to march up, an Officer came to me from Monsr. de Turenne, with orders to come immediatly to him, and told me, that those whom I had taken for friends were enemys, and that Monsr. de Turenne was on the heigth over against them, who was in great want of troopes: Being thus inform'd I march'd back to joyu him, and came very opportunely with my four Squadrons, he having at that time about him only three Squadrons, and one Battalion which was rather for shew then of any use, it being compos'd of men and Officers rallyd together, who had been broken either by the Enemy, or by plundring.

And here it will be proper to give an account how Monsr. de Turenne came thether, and how he happen'd to be in the posture in which I found him. The Reader is then to understand, that Monsr. de la Ferté being repulsed at his own attack, enter'd the Line where wee had gone in before him: Being once there, he was desirous of doing something extraordinary; and putting

PART II.
1654.

M.deTurenne sends for the Duke to come immediatly to him.
OR: MEM: P. 2. p. 104.

The Duke comes very opportunly to M. de Turenne's Succour, who was in great want of troopes.
OR: MEM. P. 2. p. 105.

P A R T
II.

1654.

himself at the head of ten or twelve Squadrons of horse, some
of which were his own and some belonging to M^r. de Turenne,
it being now brode day light, he advanced along betwixt the
two Lines towards the Count de Fuensaldagne's quarter; and at
the same time, some of the Foot of both their Armies advanced
also, amongst whom was the Battalion of the French Guards
belonging to M. de la Ferté's Army, but these last came up in
a disorderly manner along the line of Countervallation. Some
horse of the Enemy were drawn up, and yet standing on a heigth:
These being seen by Monsr. de la Ferté, he march'd down the
hill where he then was to charge them. But just before he
ingag'd them, Monsieur de Turenne came up to the place from
whence la Ferté was newly gone, and was much troubled to see

M. de
Turenne's
great foresight
and conduct.
OR: MEM:
P. 2: p: 106.

him go on in that manner; he would willingly haue stopt him,
but he came too late: so that all he could do was to stay two
Squadrons which were following him, to draw them up upon
the heigth, and to rally the battalion I haue already mention'd;
telling those that were about him, That he fear'd they should
presently see la Ferté rowted; after which he himself should
be hard put to it, to maintain that hill on which he was. As he

M. de la Ferté
is beaten as
M^r. de Turenne
had foretold.
Ibid.

said, so it happen'd, for M. de la Ferté was sufficiently beaten;
and at the same time when they charg'd him, they sent some
horse to fall upon our foot which were without the Countervallation, and cutt most of them in pieces, taking, as I remember, severall Officers of the Guards, but not offering to follow
their advantage, or to advance up the hill where M^r. de Turenne
was drawn up; but, in stead of doing so, withdrew to the
heigth from whence they came when they charg'd Monsr. de la

The Duke
draws up his
Squadrons
within the two
Lines on the
left hand
of M. de
Turenne's.
OR: MEM:
P. 2. p. 107.

Ferté.

In this posture I found affaires when I joyn'd M^r. de Turenne,
who immediatly commanded me to draw within the two Lines,
and draw up my Squadrons on the left hand of those who were
already there: He then inform'd me of what had happen'd

there, and that he apprehended, if the Enemy could gett toge- **P A R T**
ther any foot, they would advance upon us and give us work **II.**
enough to defend ourselves, there being no relying on those
whom wee had there with us. After this, he enquired of me
where I had been, and what was become of his Regiment of
horse, and I gave him an account of all that had happen'd to
me, and others, where I had been.

1654.
The Duke and
M. deTurenne
give account
to each other
of what had
happen'd
them. *Ibid.*

By this time some of our cañon, I think seaven, were got
into the Line, and came to us, to our great Satisfaction, with
some few other Squadrons of horse; and our cañon began to play
upon the Enemys horse, doing great execution amongst them.
But notwithstanding this, Mous^r. de Turenne was not without
some apprehentions of what might happen, as doubting that
the Enemy might advance upon us with foot; for seeing how
ill our horse maintain'd their order, and that almost all our four
(*foot*) were in confusion by their plundring; so that no body of
our men was left in order, but that which was about himself, it
was with no small reason that he fear'd some ill revolution in our
success, in case he should be worsted where he was : But he
continued not long in this apprehension, after our great guns
began to play; for whether it was that they made the Enemies
post too hott for them, or that for other reason they thought it
not expedient for them to stay any longer there, about half an
hour after the first gun was fir'd against them, they began to
draw off. Once wee perceived some of their foot appearing,
but immediatly they drew out of sight again; and this happen'd
some what before their horse drew off.

The Cañon
having begun
to play, the
Enemy drew
off.
Or: Mem:
P. 2. p. 106.

I haue since been informed by some who were then with the
Prince of Condé (for it was he who was there and perform'd
all that was considerable on the Enemys side) That he intended,
if he could haue got two battàlions of foot up to him, to haue
come and charg'd as M. de Turenne beleeved he would ; and
that once he had gather'd that number, which were those whom

The P^{ce} of
Condé was at
the head of
this party of
the Enemy
that had
beaten M. de
la Ferté, and
'twas he that
did all that
was consider-
able in that
side.
Ibid. p: 108.

PART
II.

1654.

Condé and
Turenne, these
two great men,
without being
advertis'd of
each others
being there,
find it out on
both sides by
their mutuall
conduct.
Ibid.

M. de Belle-
fonds pressing
on the Pᶜᵉ of
Condé's rear
as he retir'd,
is beaten.
Oʀ: Mᴇᴍ:
P. 2. p. 109.

The Prince
rallys his men
and marches
to Cambray,
and the
Archduke and
the Count
Fuensaldagne
retire to
Douay.
Ibid.

Account of
what was done
by Mʳ. d'Hoc-
quincourt.
Oʀ: Mᴇᴍ:
P. 2. p. 109.

wee saw appear, yet so soon as they came within rach of our cannon, they wou'd not be perswaded to advance one foot farther, but shog'd off.

And here 'tis admirable to consider, that these two great men, without being any other way advertis'd of each others being there, yet found it out on both sides by their mutuall conduct; Monsʳ. de Turenne positively affirming that the Pᶜᵉ of Condé was on the other hill, and that otherwise he would haue press'd those troopes more then now he would adventure to do; and the Prince of Condé saying the like of Monsʳ. de Turenne, adding farther, That if any one besides him had been there, he would certainly haue charg'd him.

This very consideration made Monsʳ. de Turenne, when the Prince drew off, not to follow him or endeavour to press upon his Rear; being satisfied with what already was perform'd, and unwilling to trust fortune with any thing farther, when the main of his design was already accomplish'd.

But Monsʳ. de Bellefonds, with some of the horse belonging to the Town, was not so cautious; for endeavouring to do some-what on the Prince's Rear as he passed the River into the Archduke's quarter, he was received so warmly that he was beaten off with loss: After which the Prince went over at his ease, for the rest of our troopes took warning by the success of their fellows, and ventur'd not again to charge him; and when he had pass'd through our old Camp, he began to rally his scatter'd men beyond the brook, and march'd away for Cambray. As for the Archduke (*and*) the Count de Fuensaldagne, they went to Douay with not above a Squadron or two in their company, and pass'd through our baggage, where the Archduke was known by some of Monsʳ. de Turenne's Servants; and had one Squadron of our horse been there, they might probably haue taken him.

'Tis now reasonable I should give some account of what was

done by M^r. d'Hocquincourt. I haue already mention'd in
the beginning of this Relation, that, when Monsr. de Turenne
fell on, he was not in a rediness with his troopes, and as I haue
been since informed by some of his Officers, it was break of day
before he began his attack. He storm'd the Line on the right
hand of the place where wee enter'd, and found litle or no
resistance; So that the greatest Imployment of his foot was to
make a passage for his horse, at the head of which enter'd the
Mareshall himself, and came directly to the bridge, over which
he pass'd into the Lorraine quarter, after I had been there and
was gone out of it. And along with him went most of the
horse belonging to the other two Armys. He met no opposition
till he came to the brook which divided the Lorraine from the
P^{ce} of Condés quarter, where he found M^r. de Marsin drawn up
on the other side with severall Squadrons of horse, which stopt
him there a considerable time ; the Army having some few
foot, or some Troopers with their Carabins who maintain'd that
passage so long, that most of the foot in that quarter had leisure
to get off : and when some of our horse coming out of the
Town upon him, oblig'd him to draw off, he made his retreat
in so orderly a manner, that he march'd out of the Line without
being broken, making use of his foot or Troopers who stood in
stead of them, as he had done formerly at the brook : For as he
drew out of the Line he placed them behind it, from whence
they fir'd upon our horse, who not being so well order'd nor
led on as they ought to haue been, were kept at a distance by
the fire they made ; so that under their favour M^r. de Marsin
gott out of the Line, and So march'd off in excellent order, till
he joyn'd the Prince of Condé at the same time when he was
rallying his men as I haue related.

Much about this time, when Monsr. de Marsin was making
his retreat out of the Line, M^r. de Mondejeu Governour of
Arras being come out of the Town, some (*of*) the old horse

PART
II.

1654.

He storms the
Line with litle
or no resist-
ance.
Ibid.

Passes after
the Duke into
the Lorraine
quarter.
Ibid.

M. de Marsin
maintains the
passage of a
brook against
him for a long
time and then
retreats in
good order.
Ibid. p. 110.

PART
II.

1654.
M. de Mon-
dejeu is desir'd
by some
Officers to put
Mʳ. d'Hoc-
quincourt's
men in better
order then
they were.
His generous
answer.
Oʀ: Mᴇᴍ:
P. 2: p. 110.

Officers seeing him, desir'd he would put them into better order, because neither M. d'Hocquincourt nor any of the Generall Officers there present, had perform'd that part of their duty as they ought: But he absolutely refused it, saying, he came only there as a Volonteer, and thought it very unreasonable for him to pretend to share in any part of the honour of that day with them; that the ordering of their men belong wholly to them : and as for himself, that he had gain'd sufficient reputation in the defence he had made, and was now come out with no other intention then to serue those who had so bravely releeved him.

Account of the
false attacks
and what
happen'd.
Oʀ: Mᴇᴍ:
P. 2: p: 110.

It remains now that I relate what happen'd in our false attacks. As for those of M. de la Ferté, and M. d'Hocquincourt, they follow'd their orders punctually, and no considerable accident befell them, but that the first had the best part of the plunder belonging to the Count of Fuensáldagnes quarter, which was the place appointed them for their false attack: But Monsʳ. de Turenne's had not so good fortune, M. de Tracy who commanded them, and who follow'd also very punctually his orders, having had a much different adventure : For being commanded to march without the least noise into a bottom which was within canon-shott of the Enemies line, and there to ly closs, without falling on, till some time after wee had begun our attack, which wee supposd that of necessity he must haue heard, it happend quite otherwise; because the wind proving contrary, and with all blowing fresh when wee began to storme the Line, he heard nothing of it. At last the day breaking, and no noise coming to him, he and all his men were verily perswaded that some accident had hinder'd our attack : however he resolved to stay in his post somewhat longer, and there he continued till he saw some horse coming out of the Line, which he conjectur'd to be such as were sent abroad to make discoverys ; and presently after them a Squadron or two which he took to be the

horse-guard coming to their accustom'd post, but seeing more
still coming out, he concluded it was to fall on him as having
discover'd where he lay. Vpon which he orderd his two
Battalions of foot, to Save themselves by marching to the Castle
of Neufville vitas, which was close by them; and himself with
the horse took their way towards Bapaume. He had march'd
a good part of his way thether, before he was sensible of his
mistake, but the foot whom he left at the Castle were sooner
undeceived, for most of the Lorraine horse and many out of
the P^{ce} of Conde's quarter drew off that way, it being their
nearest passage to Cambray; which our foot seeing, they
commanded out the Aide-Majors of each Regim^t with fifty
men apeece, to skirmish with them as they past by. This they
perform'd, but at length they advanc'd so far, that some of the
Enemies horse gott in amongst them, and kill'd every man of
that party.

PART
II.

1654.

, I will not take upon me to give an exact account of what
numbers were slain on either side in this memorable action;
But by what I saw myself of the bodies lying on the place, as
well freinds as foes, I could not guesse them to be above four
hundred. Wee had never a Generall Officer amongst that
number, and I remember but one Collonell, M. de Puymarais,
Coll^l of horse, a brave young gentleman, Son to Monsr. de
Barr, one of our Lieu^t Gen^{ls}, but very few Captains. It fell so
heavy upon none as upon that Squadron of Eclinvilliers who
had behav'd themselves so ill a day or two before, where Monsr.
de la Ferté led up to charge when he was beaten: They were
it seemes desirous to recover the reputation they had lost, and
therfore charg'd so home, that the rest giving ground sooner
then they, they were worse beaten, and I was inform'd most of
their Officers kill'd upon the place.

Account of
the Slain.
OR. MEM.
P. 2: p. 113.

The number of our wounded men was not considerable:
Monsr. de Turenne had a bruise, besides a shott upon his armes,

And wounded.
OR: MEM:
P. 2. p: 113.

and his horse shott under him. Monsr. de la Ferté had his horse kill'd. But of all our Genl Officers I remember not any hurt, excepting the Count de Broglio who was shott through the thigh; and of inferiour Officers the number was not great. The Volonteers all escap'd well, excepting those who were with M^r. d'Humieres, who received so home a charge from one of the Enemies Squadrons, that the Marquis de Breuauté et la Clotte, two of them, were so desperatly wounded that they dyd afterwards. Biscara and others of them were much hurt, as also the Cheualier de S^t Gé and severall Officers of his Regiment.

On the Enemies' side the General Officers escap'd well, for I remember not to haue heard that any of them were hurt or taken, excepting the Baron de Briolle, one of the P^{ce} of Condé's Mareshalls de Camp, who was a very brave old gentleman; and who, thō he had the misfortune to be taken and wounded in fighting against his King, yet some days before he dyd of his hurts which he then received, show'd he was no Rebell in his heart, however accidentally he had been one: for Sending for his Son who had been made prisoner with him, he told him some honres before his death, by what inducements and in what manner he had been drawn into rebellion; after which he commanded him on his blessing, never to be seduced again, on what pretence soever, to take up armes against his Soveraign. Vpon which admonition of a dying Father the young man so heartily repented, that he prov'd himself both a loyall Subject, and a dutifull Son : Vpon which account he was sett free.

I can not be exact in the number of the prisoners : but it was comonly reported that they were about three thousand, And I am apt to beleeve the account was true, for fifteen hundred of the Lorraine foot were all taken together in an envelope which was in their quarter. Wee found about sixty

On the Enemies' Side the Baron de Briolle wounded and taken with his Son.
Ob: Mem: P. 2: p. 114.

his dying admonitiᵒⁿ to his Son, never to take up armes againsty^eKing.
Ibid.

Prisoners taken by the French about 3000.
Ibid. p. 115.

three brass cannon of all sorts within the Line, and all things
proportionable for so great a Train. As for their baggage, they
lost it all, amongst which our Soldiers found good plunder, the
General Officers in those Countrys being all serv'd in plate, and
every one obliged to haue a considerable quantity of baggage,
because it was impossible to subsist without it in such Armies:
And to shew in what Vast proportion they use to be furnished,
some few days after this, when our Army passed over the
Escaut below Cambray, it was commonly reported by some
who pretended to haue reckon'd the number, that wee had
above seaven thousand waggons and carts attending us, our
Army at that time not consisting of many more then twenty
thousand men ; thō when wee were all together at forceing of
the Lines, wee were about fourteen thousand foot, eleven
thousand horse, and four hundred Dragoons.

The day after wee had thus releeved our Town, I was sent
with two thousand horse to Peroñe where the Court then was,
to convoy it to Arras, where they continued for some few days;
During which time our Army camp'd within the Lines of the
Enemy, our men making use of their hutts, and finding their
quarters so well furnish'd with forage, that wee never sent out
for any, while wee stayd upon the place.

On the last of August wee march'd towards Cambray and
camp'd at Sauchy-Cauchy, and at the same time the Court
return'd to Peronne. On the 3ᵈ of September wee march'd to
Thun Sᵗ Martin, which stands on the Escaut, and there pass'd it on
bridges which wee made, advancing the next day as far as Saulsoy,
which is the midway betwixt Cambray and Valenciennes : And
the next day wee came to Kircurayn, (*Kievrain*) which is two
good leagues short of Sᵗ Guilain. The 6ᵗʰ wee fell back upon
Quesnoy, a Town situate between Valenciennes and Landrecies ;
in which place thō there was a Governour, yet he had no cousi-
derable garrison. The Town of itself was not Strong, the outworks

Sidenotes:
1654.
63 brass cañon and all the Enemies baggage.
Oʀ Mᴇᴍ: P. 2. p. 115.

Above 7000 waggons attending the Army to carry their baggage when they march'd away from Arras, being then but 20,000 men. *Ibid.*

They were about 25000 strong when they forced the Lines. *Ibid.*

The Duke Sent with 2000 horse to Peroñe to convoy the Court to Arras. *Ibid.*

The Army marches towards Cambray the 31 August. Oʀ Mᴇᴍ: P. 2: p. 116.

having been demolish'd after the Spanish fashion, which is only
enough to hinder them from being defended, but with all so litle
slighted, that they may be repair'd with ease, and put into as
good a condition as before. This place was surrender'd to us,
the day after wee came before it. It was no sooner in our hands
but wee employd ourselves in repairing the old out-works, and
raising new where they were wanting.

Some few days after, leaving a strong garrison in Quesnoy
wee march'd to Bavay, and so to Binche on the 11ᵗʰ. The Town
last mention'd lyes two or three leagues wide of Mons, and is
of equall distance with Mons from Brussels. Binche was
deliver'd to us on the same day wee came before it. Here wee
stayd till the 22, only to eat up the Enemies' Country, and give
leisure to our men in Quesnoy to fortify themselves.

During this march Monsʳ. de Turenne, who was then our
Sole Generall, the other two Mareshalls having left the Army
when wee left Arras, gave more employment to the Lieut.
Generalls, then they were used to haue; for before this time
none but he whose turn it was, had any thing in particular to
do, more then to attend the Generall; but he now order'd, that
as he whose day it was, march'd at the head of the horse which
had the Van, so also he who had been releeved, should march
at the head of the Foot, and he who went out before him, at the
head of the other wing of horse which had the Reer; so that
every day there were three Lieutenant Generalls on duty. And
he found so great ease and benefit by this new order, that
during all the time I continued afterwards in the French Seruice,
he kept it up. And he further directed them, that whensoever
they came to any brook or défilé, they should not stay till
those before them were passed over, but make a passage for
themselves, on the one hand, or on the other, keeping still the
Van betwixt them, and that side on which the Enemy might
come: by which means he was inabled to make greater

marches; for generally after this, observing the method above
mention'd, wee pass'd over the défilés at once in three places. ·

In the time of this march the Enemys Cravats were very
busy about us, so that it was not safe for any man to straggle,
thō never so litle, from the body of the Army. And sometimes
they would get up by two or three in a Company into our
Army, and when they found their opportunity, take some or
other, and carry him away : One of them was once so bold, as
to put himself into the rancks of the first Squadron of the Reer
of horse, at the head of which I march'd. I remember that
immediatly after I had pass'd a défilé, and through some bushes,
which were on the other side of it, hearing a noise in the
Squadron behind me, I turn'd about to ask the reason of it;
when some of my Soldiers brought before me a Cravat, who had
placed himself in the midmost ranck of that Squadron, as if he
had been a Trooper belonging to the Regiment, and was so
unfortunate to put himself the very next man to one, whom he
had taken some few days before, being also at that very time
mounted on the horse which he had then taken from him :·But
he was soon discover'd by the Trooper, who therupon calld out
aloud, This is he who tooke me prisoner some days since,
and this is my horse on which he rides. He layd hold on him
immediatly and brought him to me. The fellow confessed, that
himself and some others of his Camarades, the Cravats, had
put themselves in ambuscade behind those bushes which I had
newly pass'd, and had resolved to disperse and mingle with
the Army : That had it not been his misfortune so to haue
placed himself as to be discover'd, he was confident that before
night he had taken a prisoner, instead of being one himself.

A bold action
of one of the
Enemies
Cravats : he is
discover'd and
brought before
the Duke.
OR: MEM:
P. 2. p. 119.

In this our march I know it was wonder'd at by some, that
so considerable and victorious an Army as ours then was, should
undertake no Seige of consequence that Year; But if they had
consider'd, how far the season of a Campagne was then declin'd,

1654.
The taking of
Quesnoy of
great impor-
tance for facili-
tating the
designs of
next year's
Campagne,
already con-
trived by M.
de Turenne.
Or: Mem:
P. 2: p. 117.

and that wee were not furnish'd with provisions of any sorte for
a great undertaking, they could not haue thought it strange,
that wee contented ourselves with taking of Quesnoy ; for thō
that Town of itself was not very considerable, yet it was of
great advantage to us for the carrying on of our designs in the
next Campagne: for Monsr. de Turenne, even thus early, had
contrived the business of the next year. And thō it was a bold
undertaking to make good that place, seated as it was in the
very midst of the Spanish garrisons, yet our fortifying it,
renderd his designs for the ensuing year more easy to be compass'd, and in particular the taking of Landrecies, of which I
shall say more in its proper place : So that in reality the taking
and making good this Town, was of more consequence to us,
then any other Town which wee could haue master'd at that
Season of the year.

The Enemy
draw together
their baffled
Army about
Mons.
Or: Mem:
P. 2. p: 117.

While wee stay'd at Binche, the Enemy drew together their
baffled Army at Mons, sheltering themselves under favour of
the Town, and endeavouring by their partys to molest our
foragers. But such was the vigilance and conduct of our
Generall, that they did us litle harm ; thō their Cravats were
still plying about us, and laying many ambuscades with small
success : Yet one day I remember, they miss'd but narrowly of
taking an advanced horse-guard which was on that side of the

They miss
narrowly
taking an
advanced
guard of the
French, who
were running
rashly into
one of their
ambuscades,
if his R. H.
who chanced
to be there,
had not pru-
dently forseen
the danger and
prevented it.
Or: Mem:
P. 2. p. 120.

Camp, and consisted of four Squadrons posted behind a brook,
having also an advanced guard of about thirty horse upon a
heigth on the other side of it ; I happen'd to come just as they were
releeving it by four other Squadrons, and I pass'd a brook at
the head of the party who went to releeve the advanced guard,
with M^r. d'Humieres, and severall Officers of the guard in my
company. Being come up to that post, wee saw a party of
the Enemys horse about our own number, coming out from a
wood, which was on our left hand, towards us ; but when they
were at the distance of half cañon-shott, they turn'd off again

as if they were affraid of being follow'd : wherupon some of the
Officers propos'd to me, that I should pursue, and push them ;
Monsr. d'Humieres and some few with him, who were somewhat
advanced before the rest, began immediatly to gallop after
them ; which been (*being*) seen by those about me, they spurr'd
on eagerly, and left me, without receiving my answer whether
or not I would approve it. At this I put on my horse to his
full speed, and got to the head of the formost; It was all
I could do to stop their rashness, and they grumbled sufficiently,
that I had hinder'd them from taking the whole party, But I
told them, I was as morally certain as I could be of any thing,
that by stopping them I had preserv'd them from some
ambuscade, and that I could not beleeve the Enemy would
haue come so near us, but out of design to decoy us into some
inconveniency. My opinion prov'd true, for no sooner had I
stop'd my men, but the Enemy turn'd about and fac'd us,
offering to draw us on by skirmishing ; But when they saw
that they could inveigle us no farther, they march'd away
towards Mons : Immediatly after which I saw two hundred
horse go off, which had hidd themselves in a litle bottom behind
a wood not far distant, and thether it was that the first party
had design'd to haue drawn us. Upon which discovery both
Mous^r. d'Humieres, and the rest of the Officers thank'd me for
preventing their pursuite : for had, they gone forward, in all
probability most of them must haue been taken, because our
main-guard, which was posted on the other side of the brook,
could not haue releeved them time enough ; the défilé over the
brook and afterwards through the Village, on the other side of
which the advanced guard was placed, being so great, that the
Action had been past, before their friends could haue come up
to their assistance.

After wee had stayd at Binche about ten days, and eaten up
all the forage of the neighbouring Country, Monsr. de Turenne

PART
II.

1654.
M. de Turenne
marches back
his Army
towards Ques-
noy, by the
way of Mau-
beuge.
Or: Mem:
P. 2. p. 122.

His great
caution in
this march,
because he
had so great
an Enemy as
the Pᶜᵉ of
Condé in his
way. *Ibid.*

Description
of M. de Tu-
renne's order
of march.
Or: Mem:
P. 2. p: 122.

thought it was now high time for him, to draw back towards Quesnoy, before the falling of the rains which would haue made the ways troublesome for our cañon, and so vast a quantity of baggage as wee had then in our Army.

Having taken this resolution he chose to return by the way of Maubeuge, because the Country betwixt that place and Binche was more open and had fewer défilés then the direct way to Bavay. And besides this consideration he had another full as prevalent, which was, that the Spanish Army lay then at Mons; so that in case he should haue taken his march by them, he must haue bad no less an Enemy then the Prince of Condé in his way, before whom there was no making a false step; and wee could not but expect to haue him on our wings, in our drawing off, and watching all opportunitys of the least advantage which should be offer'd to him.

Mons'. de Turenne therfore to avoid an affront on his first days march, which was the 22ᵈ of September, sent off all the baggage at break of day, with about six or eight Squadrons of horse, and M. de la Ferté's Dragoons, which march'd at their head, or on their flancks, as occasion offer'd.... They were no sooner in their way, but he follow'd the Reer of them with his Van, and that he might be the less expos'd to any attempt, he march'd in a closer order then he formerly had used, as by the draught of it may more easily be seen.

Here the * draught - - - - - - - - - - - .

- - - - - - - - - - - - - -

Yet he so managed it, that he could suddainly put himself into his ordinary forme of battell, and that without the least confusion; for upon the right hand of all march'd the first Line of that wing which had the Van that day, upon their left hand half of the first Line of foot; Again on their left hand the

---

* None was inserted either in the original M.S. or in the Narrative of Monsʳ. de Turenne's Campaigns sent to the Cardinal de Bouillon. — Editor.

second Line of horse of that wing which had the Van; and on
their left hand, the other half of the first Line of foot: And so
after the same manner on their left hand, the other wing of horse,
and the second Line of foot; and on the left hand of all, the
reserue of horse; so that wee march'd with four Battalions and
five Squadrons of horse afront, Each file consisting of - - -
- - Battalions and - - - - - Squadrons. In this
order wee march'd with our greatest cannon in the Van, and
some few small pieces in the Reer, and as wee came to any pass
or défilé, the Reer faced about with their feild pieces, while the
Van past over; which when they had done, then they drew up
on the other side, and faced about also, leaving sufficient space
for the rest of those who were to follow them, to draw up after
they had pass'd : In this maner they continued, till all were
come over to them, and then the whole body began to march
again.

By that time wee had march'd above a league, wee discover'd
about fourty Squadrons of the Enemies horse coming towards
us on our right hand: The main-body of them came not within
cannon-shott of us, keeping still a narow brook betwixt us and
them, and only sending over it their Cravats, with a Squadron
or two of horse to second them. The Cravats came so very
near us, that severall of our Foot just stepping out of their rancks,
fir'd on them betwixt the Intervals of the horse, which having
done, they return'd into their order. Thus they march'd along
by us, skirmishing, and wee never making any stop for them.
They follow'd us till they came to a pass not far distant from
Maubeuge, expecting still to find an opportunity of doing some
execution on us. But our Generall was so carefull, and order'd
his march with so much caution, that thō the Prince of Condé
himself was at the head of those Squadrons, he was never able
to fasten one charge upon us, or to put any of our horse into
the least disorder; neither indeed were they in any liklyhood

The Enemies'
Cravats skir-
mish with the
French.
On: Mem:
P. 2. p: 124.

M. de Tu-
renne's march
so well or-
der'd, that the
P. of Condé
himself, at
the head of 40
Squadrons, is
not able to
fasten one
charge upon
him. *Ibid.*

PART
II.

1654.
of doing it, unless it were once, and that was at the pass I mention'd near Maubeuge. Att that place they press'd a litle on our last troopes in their going over; but seeing our men turn'd so readily upon them, and in so good order, they thought it not expedient to charge them, but after having thus tasted them, suffer'd them to draw off quietly: By this time they found it was to no purpose to follow us any farther, for they durst not adventure to pass the défilé after us, for fear of exposing themselves too much, and therfore march'd back towards their own Camp, while wee continued our way to Maubeuge.

It was dark night before wee got thether, and thō our Camp was mark'd out to us betwixt the woods and the Town, yet what through the darknes, and what by confusion in which wee found our baggage, and more them (*than*) both by the straightness of the ground betwixt the Town and woods, none of our troopes could find out their appointed quarters; so that they fell into a very great disorder, aud were so intangled amongst the baggage, that Monsr. de Turenne could not possibly disengage them, or bring them into order. At last finding there was no remedy for the confusion, he got together two or three battalions of foot, and plac'd them without all our baggage, in that side on which the Enemy might possibly haue come. He stayd with them all night in person, and so soon as it was broad day light drew up the Army again into good order, and that day being the 23^d of September wee march'd to Bavay.

In our going thether, the whole Regiment of the Enemies Cravats pursu'd a small party of ours to the very Van of the Army, and came so near us, before they were aware of it, that all of them were in danger of being taken: for our two first Squadrons disbanded after them, and follow'd them so close, that they had no other way for their Escape then to gain the shelter of the woods; many of them being forced to quitt their

M. de Tu-
renne's Army
at Maubeuge
so intangl'd
with the bag-
gage, that he's
forc'd himself
to watch all
night to guard
the Camp.
Oʀ: Mᴇᴍ:
P: 2. p. 125.

A Regiment of
the Enemies'
Cravats pur-
suing a party
of the French,
is defeated.
Oʀ: Mᴇᴍ:
P. 2: p. 125.

horses for their own preseruàtion : And truly, I beleeve, they lost more men and horses on that occasion, then ever at any time before or since.

P A R T II.

1654.

At our arrivall at Bavay wee demolisht the walls of that litle Town, the inhabitants wherof had abandon'd it the first time wee camp'd by it. It had four Roman ways mett in it, and being not above three or four leagues from Quesnoy, it might haue been very troublesome to that garrison, and disturb'd them in raising their contributions, if the Enemy had put any troopes in it during the winter.

M deTurenne demolishes Bavay. *Ibid.* p. 117.

From Bavay wee march'd the next day to Baudignies, and camp'd close by the Quesnoy. There wee stayd till the 28th, and then march'd to Château Cambresis, after wee had consum'd the forage therabouts. During the time of our abode there, the workes of the Quesnoy were so far advanced, and the place so well furnish'd with all kinds of stores and other necessaries, that the winter now coming on apace, it would haue prov'd too difficult a peice of work for the Enemy to undertake, after wee were drawn off into our winter quarters.

Marches to the Quesnoy and campes there till the 28th Sep : and then marches to Chauteau en Cambresis. *Ibid.* p. 126.

While wee continued at Château en Cambresïs, one of our Convoys of forage was like to haue been defeated, and was so near it, that the Count de Renel, a Collonel who commanded it, was made prisoner at the first charge, in leading up the foremost Squadrons which were broken by the Enemy ; and had not the remaining horse, which were of the old Regiments, as namely, la Valette, Grammont, and others, after that, done their part with great bravery, they had been cutt off intirely and all our foragers expos'd : But notwithstanding that they saw their Commander taken, and their first Squadrons routed, they advanced upon the Enemy and forced them to draw off, without any further attempt ; after which they march'd away with the

One of the French Convoys of forage like to be defeated, Count de Renel who commanded it being taken prisoner. On: Mem: P: 2: p. 126.

P A R T
II.

—————

1654.

M. de Turenne go's abroad himself to forage with a Convoy of 20 Squadrons and two battalions.
Or: Mem:
P. 2: p. 127.

M. de Schomberg in danger of being routed, escapes by doing a bold action.
Or: Mem:
P. 2: p. 127.

foragers to our Camp, without having lost any of them. The Party of the Enemy which made this onsett, came from Cambray, and, as I was inform'd, consisted of eight Squadrons of horse, ours were about the same number; and had the Enemy improv'd their first advantage, they must certainly haue beaten the whole party, and taken as many of our foragers as they could haue driven away with them.

This adventure obliged M^r. de Turenne to be more cautious afterwards in his forages, and to send out Stronger Convoys with them. Two or three days after this accident, when they went abroad again, he himself went along with them to the same place where the Count de Renel had been taken, but with a much stronger Convoy; for he took with him above twenty Squadrons of horse, two Battalions of foot, and about four feild peices, supposing the Enemy would now come Stronger out upon our foragers then formerly, and he was not deceived in his conjecture: for some time after he had posted his troopes for the best security of his foragers, wee saw about six Squadrons of the Enemy coming out of a wood which was close by us, and where they had been in ambuscade. They cam on at a round gallop, as if they would haue fallen on two or three Squadrons of our Gendarmes, who were drawn up in a litle bottom betwixt the wood, and a Village where many of our foragers were at that time loading their horses: On one side of this Village was Monsr. de Turenne himself with the greatest part of the horse, and one battalion of foot; but, there being a small pass betwixt us and the place where the Gendarmes were posted, which were commanded by Monsr. de Schomberg, had the Enemy push'd on vigourously, they might haue routed him, before wee could haue come to his releif: he therefore, cousidering the danger in which he was, found there was no way of saving himself, but only by a bold action; and accordingly

advanced towards the Enemy, who seeing him come up to
charge them, and not being able to discern what was in the
bottom from whence he came, in all probability imagin'd he
had more behind to second him, for immediatly they withdrew
into the wood again: he was very glad of their retreat, as he
had reason, and stopt short upon the litle higth where he then
was, without offering to follow them, because he was not strong
enough, besides he knew not what other troopes they might
haue, either within the wood or behind it. There he stayd,
more horse being sent from us to strengthen him, till our
foragers were all loaded, and that wee began to draw off; which
wee did without seeing any other Enemy appear.

Ever after this wee sent such strong Convoys with our
Foragers, that for the rest of the Campagne the Enemy made
not any attempt upon them : And wee were full as carefull
of the Convoys which wee sent to the Quesñoy with provisions, for all of them were so well guarded, that the
Spaniards thought it not for their advantage to sett upon
them.

The last that went thether while wee stayd at Château en
Cambresis, was commanded by me, after which wee march'd
into forage-quarters, and spent some weeks upon the fronteers.
There wee took two Castles, one call'd d'Anvillers, and the other
Girondelle not far from Rocroy, which wee demolish'd : And
then it was time for us to march into our winter quarters,
the cold season being so far advanced, that it was become
too late that year for the Enemy to attempt any thing upon
the Quesnoy.

PART II. 1654.

The Duke commands the last Convoy sent to Quesnoy, after which the Army having spent some weeks in forrage-quarters and taken two Castles, they march'd to their winter quarters. On: Mem: P. 2: p. 128.

The Campagne of 1654 being thus ended, his Royall Highness
repair'd as formerly to the French Court at Paris, where he
arrived about the midle of December, and there spent the

PART
II.

1654.

remaining part of the winter: Towards the end of which his brother the Duke of Glocester took his leave of him, the King his brother having .sent My Lord of Ormonde on purpose to bring him to him at Colen.

The summer following his Royall Highness went to make his fourth and last Campagne in France, of which he gives the following account in his Memoires.

THE DUKE'S FOURTH AND LAST CAMPAGNE
IN FRANCE.

T HIS CAMPAGNE of 1655 began with putting in execution what was design'd the year before, when wee took and fortified Quesnoy; for wee open'd it with the Siege of Landrecies, and then our Army found the benefit of having that place to freind. For immediatly after they sat down before Landrecies, the Enemy came and posted themselves betwixt that Town and Guise, therby to hinder all communication betwixt our Army and our own Country; so that had not this been timely foreseen, and their design frustrated by our laying up a magazine of all necessarys in Quesnoy, sufficient for the carrying on of that Seige, Mons'. de Turenne must haue been put to great extremities; Wheras he was now so much before hand with the Spaniards, that the post which they had taken up, was of small advantage to them, and no manner of hindrance to the French in pursuance of their Seige, Convoys passing every day with great ease and security from Quesnoy to the Camp: So that no other inconvenience follow'd from the Enemies being posted near Guise, then that it hinder'd some Officers and Volonteers from getting into the Army, while the Seige lasted, whose affaires had hinder'd them from marching with it, when it came before the Town.

Of this number I was one; for which reason I shall not give a particular description of that Seige: Most of us who came short, and could not joyn our Army time enough, were either at Guise or la Fere while this Seige continued; I was myself at the last of these places, expecting the opportunity of some

PART
II.

1655.

Is open'd with the Seige of Landrecies.
ORIG: MEM:
Par. 2. p. 130.

The Duke absent from this Seige, and why. *Ibid.*

The Duke waits at la Fere an opportunity to joyne the Army.
OR: MEM:
P. 2: p. 131.

PART
II.
___
1655.

Convoy to favour my desire of being present at the Seige; but the Spanish Army was so posted in our neighbourhood, that the passage was render'd too difficult for any of us to attempt. Monsr. de la Feuillade, with two or three officers and a small party of horse, ventur'd to haue pass'd, but they were mett by the Enemy and beaten, la Feuillade himself being taken and desperatly wounded. This ill success of his, so far discourag'd all of us, that wee layd aside the thought of it; so that till the Enemy drew off, which was a day or two before the surrender of the Town, wee came not to our Army.

M. de la Feuillade endeavouring to pass is wounded and takenprisoner. *Ibid.*
The Duke joyns ye Army a day or two before the surrender of Landrecy. *Ibid.*

This Seige was a very favorable one to our Soldiers; those of the Town contenting themselves with a bare defence, according to the ordinary formes, and not making any vigourous Sallys during the whole time it lasted; so that wee lost as few men, as could possibly be expected, in the mastering of such a place, and no officer of note but Monsr. de Tracy, who had the Command of all the German horse, as being the eldest Collonel of them. The Garrison held out only, till a breach was made by a Mine in the face of one of their Bastions, and a lodgment made upon it, after which they capitulated and Surrender'd.

Landrecies surrender'd up to the French. *Ibid.* p. 132.

After the Town was deliver'd up to us, Our Army stayd by it some days to repair the breaches and outworks, and to slight our Line of Circumvallation; and the Enemy drew back into their own Country betwixt Mons and Valenciennes behind the Rivers, not thinking themselves strong enough, as indeed they were not, to hazard a battell with us on equall termes; So that their business was to attend our motions, and endeavour to hinder our undertaking any other considerable Seige.

The Spaniards draw back into their Country. Or: Mem: P. 2. p. 132.

And now by that time wee were in a readiness to march, the King and the Cardinal came to the Army, and wee march'd down along by the Sambre, as far as la Bussiere, which is within a league of Thuyn, a small Town belonging to the Pays

The King of France and Cardinal Mazarin joyn the Army. *Ibid.*

de Liege. Having spent some time in this march, and stayd a day or two at la Bussiere, wee march'd back, and passing by Avênes invested la Capelle; and thō wee camp'd within a league or two of it with our whole Army, yet on better consideration wee did not beseige it, as not judging it a place of so great importance, that our Army should lose so much time as was necessary to reduce it. And therfore leaving it, wee pass'd the Sambre, advancing into Haynault as far as Bavay on the 1[of August. The Town I last mention'd is betwixt Quesnoy and Mons; and our intentions were to advance yet farther into the Enemie's Country, and to pass the Haisne, a litle River which coming from Mons, takes its course by St Guislain, and falls into the Schald at Condé: But sending to view the passages upon it, wee found that the Enemy had fortifyd the River from St Guislain as far as Condé, with a very strong Brestwork and Redouts, with platformes ready made in them at the distance of every three or four hundred paces; which together with the difficulty of approaching the River itself, by reason of the lowness of the Country, which was full of ditches, and there being no way to come to the River but along narrow dikes, made the passage very hard to be forced. Which notwithstanding, in a consultation that was held in the King's presence, where were assisting the Cardinal and the two Generalls, M^r. de Turenne and M^r. de la Ferté, together with the Mareshalls de Villeroy, de Grammont, du Plessis, and myself, it was once upon the point of being resolved, that wee should attempt to force our passage au Pont de Haisne; And had it not been for M^r. de Turenne, that opinion had taken place: for the Cardinal hauing propos'd it as an undertaking which would be of high reputation in the world, if wee could make a way over a River in the face of a formidable Army, he was seconded and his advice confirm'd by most who were there

PART II.

1655.
The French invest la Capelle.
Ibid.

They Leave la Capelle, passing the Sambre they advance to Bavay, Aug^{r}1[.
Ibid.

The Spaniards fortify the Haine from St Guislain to Condé.
OR: MEM: P. 2: p. 133.

A Councill held in the King's presence, the Duke assisting there with the Card^l. and M.deTurenne.
Ibid.

The Cardinal proposes to force the passage at Pont de Haisne, and his advice is seconded by most of the Genl Officers.
Ibid.

PART
II.

1655.

M.deTurenne
opposes it.
Ibid. p. 134.

Gives his
reasons.
OR: MEM:
P. 2. p. 134.

present, whither out of complaisance, or by the force of his reasons, I shall not pretend to judge; but resolv'd on, it had been, had not M^r. de Turenne oppos'd it, by representing the great difficulties which would be found in that attempt.

For, said he, Besides that the whole River is strongly fortifyed all along, there is no approaching it but by the side of a Dike, by reason that all the ground on our side is full of ditches, so that the Enemy would haue a double advantage over us; and thō at last, I beleeve, wee may force our passage, wee should unavoidably loose many men in compassing our design: he added, That it was not this consideration alone, which mov'd him to disuade that undertaking, but the beleef he had, that the thing we aim'd at, might be effected without running So great a hazard, or venturing the lives of so many Soldiers; That instead of our endeavouring to force a passage there, wee should rather march, and pass the Escaut somewhat below Bouchain, and then passing by Valenciennes and leaving it on our right hand, should march to Condé, and there pass the Escaut again; That in so doing, wee should take the Enemy on the flanck, and therby render that great intrenchment of no effect to them.

M. de
Turenne's
opinion pre-
vailes in
Councill and
his proposal
being approv'd
of, the French
Army marches
towards Bou-
chain. *Ibid.*

The Spaniards
post them-
selves advan-
tageously by
Valenciennes.
Ibid.

The French
pass the Schald
the 14th of Aug:

With these and other arguments he convinced the Cardinal, and all those of the Councill who had abetted his opinion: And in pursuance of M. de Turenne's proposall, wee march'd immediatly from Bavay towards Bouchain, upon notice of which the Enemy march'd also toward Valenciennes, and posted themselves very advantageously, having their Right cover'd by the woods of S^t. Amand, and their left by the Town, and the old Line ready made to their hands, upon Mont Azin, from the woods to the Town; and instead of endeavouring to hinder our passing the River, they fell on repairing the old Line, which by the next morning was put into very good defence; which whilst they were a doing, wee past the River on our bridges of

boates, and by eight next morning, being the 14th, pass'd over
our whole Army, leaving some few troopes behind to secure our
baggage from the garrison of Bouchain.

I haue been since inform'd by some of the Enemys own
Officers, who were then upon the place, that they came thither
with an intention of making good that post, for upon the
proposall of that march, the Prince of Condé oppos'd it, unless
they would absolutely resolve to maintain it when they were
once there ; telling them plainly, That he would not stirr a step,
unless the Spaniards would ingage their promise to do this ·
They gave him all the assurances he could desire: Yet he
foretold them, that in that post, wee should certainly come
upon them, and then it would be too late to think of retiring,
by which they would expose their whole Army to be beaten.
But whatever arguments he urg'd were not sufficient to divert
them, for march they would ; but at the same time they
confirm'd their promise to him, of making good that Post: So
wee found them there.

And now our Partys having brought us word how they were
posted, so soon as wee could put our troopes in battell, wee
march'd towards them ; and being come within a league of
them, seeing they were well intrenched on that advantageous
post, wee halted till our cañon and ammunition, which were
somewhat behind, could come up to us. During this our stay,
Monsieur de Turenne went with a Squadron or two, to view
their Line, advancing till he came within cannon shott, and
then they fir'd at him with their great guns; which confirmed him
in the beleef, that they would maintain their post: upon which
he commanded M^r. de Castelnau with his Camp-Volant, which
consisted (*of*) about twelve Squadrons and two or three
Battalions, to march, and post himself on the Enemys right
hand on the high way which comes from St Amand ; that at

PART.
II.

1655.
and march'd
to the Enemy.
OR: MEM:
P. 2. p. 135.

The P^{ce} of
Condé was
against the
Spaniards of
taking that
post unlesse
they would
resolve to
maintain it.
Ibid.

M.deTurenne
go's to view
the Enemies
Line.
OR: MEM:
P. 2: p. 136.

He detaches
M. de Castel-
nau to attack
them on the
flanck design-
ing himself to
attack their
front. *Ibid.*

P A R T
II.

1655.
The Enemy
draw off
towards
Condé. Ibid.
Castelnau is
order'd to
press upon
their reer, and
endeavour to
retard their
march till
M.deTurenne
could come up
with the body
of the Army.
Ibid. p: 137.

the same time wee should attack their front, he might see what could be done upon their flank.

No sooner was Castlenan gott thether, but he perceived the Enemy was drawing off towards Condé, of which (he) immediatly advertis'd M. de Turenne; who order'd him to press upon their Reer, and by that means retard, if possibly he could, their march, till he could come up himself with the body of the Army: and till wee receiv'd that advice which wee had from Mr. de Castelnau, wee perceived nothing of the Enemys retreat; neither indeed could wee by reason of the ground; their Line being, as I haue said before, upon a heigth, so that wee could only discover such troopes as they would shew us.

It seems that so soon as the Arch Duke, and the Count de Fuensaldagne were inform'd that our whole Army was past the River, and that they saw us marching up towards them, they repented themselves of being So far ingaged; and, as the Prince of Condé had foretold them, resolv'd to march back to Condé, and there to pass the River. This resolution they took without consulting him, so that the first notice he had of it, was by an Adjutant, who brought him word, that the Arch Duke was marching away, and desir'd him to bring up the Reer, and make good the retreat, thō it was the turn of the Spaniards to haue done it: And that they might haue as litle disorder as they could, they sent their great cañon into Valenciennes, and only carryed off with them their small feild peeces.

The Pce of
Condé hard
put to it, if
Castelnau had
done his part.
Ibid.

Had Mons'. de Castelnau done his part as he ought according to his orders, and also as he might, the Prince of Condé would haue been reduced to great extremitys: Tis true he fail'd not in point of courage, but meerly in conduct, for he was so hasty that coming to the Pont de Beuerage (where runs a brook which coming from the woods falls into the Escaut on the other side of Valenciennes, where Mons'. de Marsin was posted with

severall Squadrons and some Dragoons) he would not stay for
his foot, but endeavour'd with his horse alone to haue forced
the pass upon him, and charg'd over the bridge twice or thrice,
thō he was still beaten with some losse, and at last was forced
to Stay till his foot were advanced to him; who were longer
in coming up then they needed to haue been, by reason that
all his horse were gott before them into the way.   But so soon
as the Enemy discover'd his foot advancing, they immediatly
drew off, and left the bridge free for him to pass over, which
he did.   And by this time, Monsr. de Turenne was come up
with his Van, to the Reer of M^r. de Castelnau's troopes, and
sent severall Messengers to him with orders, that he should press
the Enemy as much as possibly he could, therby to hinder their
march, that he might come up with them in their retreat: But
Castelnau perform'd not what was expected of him, suffering
himself to be overreach'd by some of the Prince his Officers,
who bringing up the Reer of their Army and seeing M. de
Castelnau advance before his troopes, ask'd to speak with him
upon parole; To which he consenting, because they were of
old acquaintance, he order'd his men at the same time to halt
a litle, while they were passing their compliments: Mean while
the Prince of Condé commanded his men to make what hast they
could, to secure themselves by getting off; and so amused our
Lieu^t Gen^ll, till a man whom they had left on the top of a rising
ground, which was behind them, made a signe to them, and then
they took their leave immediatly of Castelnau, and gallop'd
after their troopes : By this means they gain'd so much time,
that they pass'd the River, before our men could come up with
them again.

Soon after this, Monsr. de Turenne arriv'd at the place where
Castelnau had drawn up his men within cañon-shott of the
River, and saw the Enemys Army drawn up on the other Side
of the River by Condé: And then Monsr. de Castelnau gave

Great over-
sight of Cas-
telnau in
letting himself
be overreach'd
by Some of the
P^ces. officers.
Or: Mem:
P. 2. p. 138.

Castelnau's
mistake is the
occasion of a

K K 2

PART
II.

1655.

Sharpness
afterwards
between the
Pᶜᵉ of Condé
and M. de
Turenne.
Oʀ: Mᴇᴍ:
P. 2: p. 146.

Monsʳ. de Turenne an account of what had past, and added, That the last Squadron of the Enemys horse were forced to swimm the River to Save themselves: This mistake of his caused some Sharpnesse more then ordinary between the Prince and Monsʳ. de Turenne, by an accident which happen'd some days after as the Reader will find in the following account.

The Enemy had no Sooner past over the River, but they broke the bridges, so that they were in a further danger, and, as I remember, march'd the same afternoon for Tournay. Wee quarter'd that night at Frane, closs by Condé, and the next morning fell to making our bridges over the River, about a

The French
beseige Condé.
Oʀ: Mᴇᴍ:
P. 2. p. 139.

league below the Town; intending so soon as they should be finish'd to attack that place. At first it was resolved that only Mʳ. de Castelnau and Mʳ. d'Vxelles, with the troopes which they commanded, should be employd to take the Town, while the two Mareshalls, with the rest of the Army, should cover them from any attempt from the Army of the Spaniards. And so they began to make their approaches to the Town; But the very first night they found so vigourous a resistance from the Defendants, whose workes indeed were very slight, but lin'd with great numbers of men within them, that it was found too hard a taske for them alone to undertake.

Two attacks,
the one carryd
on by the 2
Mareshalls,
the other by
Castelnau and
Vxelles. Ibid.

Of this the two Mareshalls being advertis'd, they came them selves, and carryd on one of the attaques, leaving the other to the conduct of the two foremention'd Lieutenant Generalls. And here wee found a very favourable shelter, from the houses of a small fauxbourg which was before the gate: for thō the Enemy had burnt it, yet not hauing time to pluck down the walls, it prov'd beneficial to us; for from thence wee began our Trenches, which was but litle above half musket shott from the Town. The first night of their being open'd at our attack, they were mounted by a Battalion of the Guards commanded by

Vautourneux, the eldest Captain of these ten Companies;
and at the Lieutenant Generall's attack was the Regiment
of ————.

That night wee made a very good (*attack*) at both places; yet
wee lost betwixt three or four hundred men at those two attacks,
of which number were Severall Officers. At our approche wee
lost Monsr. de Vautourneux, who seeing one Captain LLloyd (a
Welshman and an Engeneer, who had been bred up under the
Prince of Orange and was a stout colerick man) coming back
from the Trenches after he had perform'd his duty, traced out
the work, and sett the workmen upon their imployment, ask'd
him, why he returned so soon? Saying withall, That he was
certain he could haue not perform'd all he had to do in so short
a time; after which he let fall some words, as if he doubted of
his courage: At which the Engeneer was so incensed, that it
made his Welsh blood boyle with him; So that he told Vautourneux, That if he pleas'd to go and look upon what he had
trae'd out, he should find he had not been wanting in any part
of his duty. Vpon this they both went together to view it, and
the shott from the Enemy flew so fast, that Vautourneux was
kill'd before he could get to the head of the workmen, and
Captain LLloyd shott through the head.

The next night a Battalion of Suisses had the guard of the
Trenches at one attack, and the Regiment de - - - - -
at the other, both which attacks carryd on their Trenches
within pistoll shott of the Town: that night wee lost at
least as many men as the former. The third night, an other
Battalion of the frech Guards releeved the Suisses at our
attack, and the regiment de - - - - - - - at the Lieu^t
Generall's. That night at our attack, there happen'd a very
great mistake, which caus'd the loss of many men: It was the
turn of Monsr. de la Ferté to be in the Trenches, who coming
in the Evening to take a view of what had been perform'd there,

PART
II.

1655.
The 3ᵈ night
a mistake, in
taking the
pallisades to
be without the
ditch, whereas
they were
within it,
occasions the
loss of many
men. *Ibid.*

and to resolve what was to be farther done, suppos'd that he was now neer enough to endeavour to make a lodgment against the pallisades, which both he and all the Officers concluded to be without the ditch on the very edge of it; And accordingly, he order'd his men to lodge themselves at the foot of them, which so soon as it was dark, they attempted to haue done: but when they came to the ditch, they found the pallisades were not before it, but upon the barme, which, notwithstanding, they pass'd the ditch which was but shallow, and not broad, in obedience to their orders, and endeavour'd to haue lodged themselves at the foot of the pallisades upon the barme, which they disputed so long, that they lost a considerable number both of Soldiers and Officers; and at last were constrain'd to draw off, and content themselves only with carrying on their Trench to the edge of the ditch. And here it is not to be wonder'd at, that this mistake was made; for the ditch, as I said, being narrow, and it being generally the Custom, that the pallisades were placed without it, they took it for granted, that so they were: to which I might add, that it was exceeding difficult to the eye to distinguish att a distance, where they were sett.

Condé sur-
render'd up
to the French
the 19 of Aug.
Oʀ: Mᴇᴍ:
P. 2. p. 142.

The next day the Count de Henning Governour of the place sent out to treat, and made his conditions to march forth with his armes and baggage on the day following, which was the 19th of August. He accordingly perform'd his Articles, and came out with upwards of two thousand foot, and some few horse.

M. de Bussy-
Rabutin sent
out with 7 or
8 Squadrons
to guard the
foragers, falls
into an ambus-
cade of the
Enemy.
Oʀ: Mᴇᴍ:
P. 2. p. 143.

While wee lay before this place, Monsʳ. de Bussy-Rabutin, Mestre de Camp de la Caualerie, being sent out with seven or eight Squadrons of horse to convoy and guard our foragers, while they were about their work on the other side of the Escaut, betwixt Sᵗ Crepin and Valenciennes, having plac'd his troopes before the Villages in which our men were foraging, and towards the Evening, when our foragers had almost ended

their work, and were most of them gone home loaden, seeing two
Squadrons of the Enemies horse appear in the plaine betwixt
him and Valenciennes, he was desirous to fall upon them; being
also prest to it by Severall Volonteers and persons of quality
who happen'd to be with him, amongst which were the Prince
de Marsillac and the Count de Guiche: He therfore march'd to
them with all his horse; Vpon which they drew off at a round
rate, and he follow'd them: But when he was almost got up
to them, they faced about on the suddain, and at the same time
twelve or fourteen Squadrons came out of a litle bottom, where
they had been all that time in Ambuscade, which so much
surpris'd both him and all his company, that at first they
knew not what resolution they should take; and at length when
he was going to haue charg'd them, he hauing then no other
choice to make, as he had order'd matters, but either to charge
there, or to retire back and make good a défilé that was behind
them, he was determin'd by the men themselves; who without
waiting for his command, chose the latter, which they had
reason enough to do, seeing themselves so far outnómber'd by   His men outnumber'd by
the Enemy, so they faced about, and made the best of their   the Enemy
  break and run,
way to the défilé, crying out, as they broke and ran, *Au défilé!*   but rally afterwards at the
meaning they would rally at the pass, and they were as good as   pass and make
  it good.
their words; for so soon as they were come thether, they rallyd   Or: Mem:
  P. 2: p. 144.
very well, and the Enemy being Satisfied with what they had
taken in the poursuit, press'd them no farther. These Regiments
that did this, were of the best of our Army, and most of them
old Troopers as well as Officers, and had they not done that
they did, the loss had been much more considerable.

In this rencounter wee lost above a hundred horsemen, and   Above 100
  horsemen
a Cornett or two of the Regiment Royall, who happening to be   lost in this
  rencounter
taken by some of the Prince of Condé's troopes, he sent them   and a Cornett
  or two of the
back to the King by one of his own Trumpeters; but his   Reg^t Royall.
  Ibid.

PART
II.

· 1655.

The P^{ce} of
Condé Sends
back the Cor-
netts to the
King of
France, who
refuses to
accept of
them. *Ibid.*
A Letter from
M.deTurenne
to the Car-
dinal, inter-
cepted by the
P^{ce} of Condé.
Or: Mem:
P. 2: p. 145.
The Prince
upon this oc-
casion writes a
sharp letter to
M.deTurenne
and sends it
byaTrumpeter
Substance of
the Letter.
Ibid.

M. de Tu-
renne's answer
to the Trum-
peter threat-
ning him.
Ibid.

Ma^{ty} refused to accept of them, and so those troopes of the
Regiment which had lost them, march'd without any during
the rest of the Campagne.

There happen'd also about that time an accident, which
caus'd a worse understanding betwixt the Prince of Condé and
Monsr. de Turenne, then is usuall betwixt persons of their
quality commanding against one another : For a letter which
the Mareshall had written to the Cardinal being intercepted,
wherein he gave his Eminence an account of what had past in
the retreat, when the Spaniards quitted their post neer Valenciennes; The Prince, into whose hands it fell, after hauing read
it, sent a Trumpeter, with a letter to Monsr. de Turenne, which
was full of very Sharp and ressenting expressions, some of which
were to this purpose, That had he not known M. de Turenne's
own handwriting, he should haue thought, that the account
which was given to the Cardinal in that paper, had rather
been written by some Gazettier, then a Generall; and clos'd
his letter with these words, That had Monsr. de Turenne been
at the head of his Army, as himself was at the Reer of his, he
would haue seen the contrary of what he writt, none of his
horse being forced to swim the River to Save themselves in their
Retreat. Monsr. de Turenne grew very angry at the reading
of this letter, and told the Trumpeter, That it concern'd him to
haue a care, how he brought any papers of that nature; and
warn'd him of it, That if he committed the same fault again,
neither his character nor his Livery should protect him; but
that for this time he was contented to let him go, though he had
well deserv'd to be punish'd for bringing so injurious a paper.
The Prince was not long ignorant, that Monsr. de Turenne had
written nothing but what had been told him by Monsr. de
Castelnau, and therfore was sorry that he had written so angry.
and offensive a letter; yet, till the conclusion of the Warr,

they were never heartily reconciled ; I mean, they liv'd not with
that Civility towards each other, as men of their quality and
posts are accustom'd to do in those parts.

And now Condé being taken, and wee hauing left a sufficient
garrison within it, our Army march'd on the next day which
was the 20th of August to St Guislain, and beseig'd it, Monsr.
de Turenne having his quarter at a Village called Hornu, and
M^r. de la Ferté his, on the other side of the River. At this place
the King of France and the Cardinal came to the Army, and
were quarter'd at the Castle of Bossut, a litle below the Town,
on the same River. This Town is very strongly situated,
standing very low, and the River of Haisne running through it ;
so that they can drown at their pleasure most of the ground
about it, as now they had, for which reason wee found difficulty
enough in the carrying on our Trenches : 'twas also very hard to
make a line of Circumvallation, because bridges of communication could not be made without great trouble : So that at
the best, notwithstanding all our endeavours, our Trenches were
full of water, especially when wee came neer, and our approches
might more reasonably be call'd blinds of fascines, then any
thing else ; because the water being even with the ground, wee
could neither sink ourselves, nor make use of that earth to cover
us. Yet surmounting all these difficulties, wee carry'd the Town
in the space of three days, after wee had broken ground.

When wee came first to our quarters at Hornu, (*Horn*) it
was exceeding dark ; so that, thō severall of our Generall Officers
had houses mark'd out for their reception which were within
lesse then cañon-shott of the Town, they knew it not, till next
morning, when they were waken'd with the thundering of the
great Guns from the Town ; and the houses being all paper
buildings, they were soon dislodged, as in particular Monsr. de
Passage, with others, who were all obliged to seek their quarters
out of gune shott. I onely made bold to stay in mine, which

P A R T
II.
_____
1655.

The French
beseige S^t
Guislain the
20th of Aug.
O_R: M_{EM}:
P: 2: p. 146.

Great diffi-
culty of carry-
ing on the
Trenches,
most of the
ground about
the Town
being drown'd.
O_R: M_{EM}:
P. 2. p. 146.

The Duke
is the only
Generall
Officer that
venturs to stay
in his quarters,
which were
within litle
more then
muskett shott,
of the Town,
during all tho
time of the
Seige of S^t
Guislain.
O_R: M_{EM}:
P. 2: p. 147,

indeed being litle more then muskett-shott from the Town, they neglected it so much as not to shoot at it, as supposing that nobody would stay in it; so that I remain'd there in great security during the time the Seige lasted.

At this place the French Guards, according to custome, had the guard of the Trenches the first night; it being an indisputed right in those Countrys, that how many Seiges soever, thō of very short continuance shall happen in a Campagne, the eldest Regiment has allways the honour of first breaking ground.

A dispute
betwixt M. de
Montpezat
and the Grand
maitre d'Artil-
lerie, decided
in favour of
the Lieu⁰.
Generalls.
Oʀ: Mᴇᴍ.
P. 2. p. 147.

There happen'd a dispute that night betwixt M^r. de Montpezat the eldest Lieu^t Generall, and the Grand Maistre de l'Artillerie, occasion'd by the first mention'd sending his orders to the latter, to furnish him with some necessarys which he wanted for carrying on the Trenches, the first night they were open'd ; which the other refus'd to obey, pretending he ought to receive no orders but from the Generall himself: Of which M^r. de Montpezat complaining the next day, the dispute was decided in favour of the Lieu^t Generalls, that the Grand Maistre was obliged to receive orders from any of them: Upon which result, for so long time as he continued in the Army, he officiated no more as Grand Maistre, but had a Comission, granted him for Lieu^t Generall and served only in that capacity.

Wee lost no many Soldiers at this Seige, nor do I remember that any Officer of note was kill'd; only the Cheualier de Crequi and Monsr. de Varennes were wounded, besides some other Officers, as Monsr. de Chavigny Aide Major to the Regiment of Guards, and since Pere de l'Oratoire; The Cheualier de Crequi was wounded at Monsr. de la Fertés attack, and dangerously

M. de Varennes
shot in the
thigh as he
was talking
with the Duke.
Oʀ: Mᴇᴍ:
P. 2: p. 148.

hurt in the head, of which notwithstanding he afterwards recover'd, and Monsr. de Varenne was shott in the thigh at our attack as he was talking with me.

In three nights wee carryd on our approches to the edge of

the ditch, and the next day, the Governour Don Pedro Savali sent out to capitulate, and march'd out of the Town the next day following which was the 25th. .

While wee were busied at this Seige, the Enemy divided their Army ; the Arch Duke and Count de Fuensaldagne with most of the Spanish foot and some horse, were at Notre-Dame-de-Halle, The P^{ce} of Condé with the greatest part of his at Tournay, the Lorrainers at Ath, and the Prince of Ligny with about four or five thousand men at Mons.

And now the year was so far spent, that it was not thought expedient for us to undertake any other Seige, So that wee spent severall days in the same quarters where wee were when wee Satt down before St Guislain, from which place the Court departed, some few days after it was taken. During the time of our abode there, wee work hard both at that Town and Condé, adding new fortifications to them, but our cheifest care was to secure our Foragers, and to eat up the Country round about those garrisons ; that by so doing wee might make it impracticable for the Enemy to beseige them in the winter. And to that intent wee continued in our Camp by St Guislain, till our men had quite made an end of the Forage thereabout, and wee took care allways to send out strong Convoys with our foragers, to prevent their being beaten or taken by the Spaniards. Sometimes Monsr. de Turenne himself went out with them ; and when he did not, there was allways a Lieu^t Generall at the head of those partys, which had never less during our abode in that place then two thousand men to guard them.

Having taken these precautions, wee never received any affront or considerable loss in our Forage : yet notwithstanding all the care which could be taken, some small partys of the Enemys would be still abroad, and glean up here and there a man or two ; it being impossible to restrain our Vedettes from running out beyond our Guards, where commonly they were

1655.
St Guislain surrender'd to the French 25 Aug.
Ibid.

The Spaniards divide their Army.
Ibid. p. 149.

The French Army remains about St Guislain in order to fortify that Town and Condé, and eat up the Country.
OR: MEM: P. 2: p. 149.

P A R T
II.
1655.
The Enemies'
Cravats very
troublesome to
the Foragers.
OR: MEM:
P. 2. p. 150.
M. de Tu-
renne's care
to prevent
their designs.
Ibid.

surpriz'd ; And of all the Enemies' horse, none did us so much
mischeif as their Cravats, who in litle partys would be perpetually upon our Foragers : but to prevent their designs as
much as possibly wee could, Monsr. de Turenne order'd, That
every Squadron of horse should send along with their Foragers,
three or four Officers well mounted, so that when any of these
Cravats fell upon their fellows, they might joyn twenty or thirty
of them together, which were enough to beat off one of those
straggling partys : By this means our Foragers were better
protected then before, and many of the Cravats taken.

The Duke
commands the
last Forage
that was made
in that quarter,
and which was
the greatest
and the most
dangerous.
Ibid. p. 151.

The last Forage wee made while wee stayd in that quarter,
was the greatest of any, and of the most danger, being to go
as far as Chievres and the Abbey of Cambron ; the first of which
places is but the distance of a large league from Ath. This
Convoy was commanded by men (*me*), and being to march so
great a distance from our Camp into the midst of those places
where the Enemies troopes were quarter'd, I had five Battalions
and fourty Squadrons with two pieces of cañon along with me.
And as I gave a particular account of one considerable Forage
which was made in the foregoing year, I shall do the same
of this.

A particular
account of the
great Forage
at St Guislain,
which was
commanded
by the Duke.
Ibid.

Having consider'd that I was to be ingaged so far in the
Enemys Country, I thought it necessary to take what precautions
I could, and to that purpose before day I sent a party of horse
to a great wood, through which I was of necessity to pass, to
stopp all the Foragers there, and to permitt none of them to go
on beyond those limits, till I came thither myself with the
Troopes I commanded. This being perform'd according to
my order, I march'd through the wood, and drew out upon the
plaine before any one Forager was there. In the wood I left
a Battalion, that from Mons, partys of foot might not intercept
them when they return'd loaden. Then I gaue my orders, that
the Foragers should not presume to disband, or march faster.

,then the Convoy ; but go along with me upon the same front on each hand of the Squadrons. In this manner I march'd till I came almost within a league of Chievres ; and it was an extraordinary sight to see about ten thousand Foragers, most of them with scythes in their hands, with the Officers before them marching as they did, the front of them being almost half a mile in breadth : But when they came within sight of that part of the Country, which had not been already forag'd, it was altogether impossible either for me or their particular Officers to keep them in order any longer, or to hinder them from disbanding, and making what hast they could to forage. Which when I observ'd, I left the remainder of my foot, and some horse together with the cañon, upon the heigth where I then was, near a Village; and myself with the greatest part of the remaining horse, march'd at a round trott after the Foragers, and when they were fallen to their work, I placed myself before them betwixt Chievres and Brugelet, by that means to cover them from those in Ath. At the same time sending the Count de Grandpré with the rest of the horse the other way, ordering him to draw up by a Village call'd Leuse, therby to Secure our Foragers from any partys which might come out from Mons.

And upon this occasion I cannot forbear to mention the great order and justice which was observ'd amongst Foragers ; for he who first enters into a Feild of Corne or Meadow, keepes possession, and none will offer to come within such a distance of him, and not to leave him sufficient forage to load his horse : And whosoever gets first into a Barne, or on a Hay-mowe, no man offers to disturb him, or to size on any thing, till he has provided for himself ; so that First come first serv'd.

About noon I had an alarme, but it prov'd to be only Mons'. de Rochepair, who had been abroad with a party of about a thousand horse, and was returning to the Camp, without having

P A R T
II.

1655.

The Prince de
Ligne intend-
ing to fall on
the Duke's
Foragers, is
hinder'd by a
false intelli-
gence and the
Forage by
this means
escapes a great
danger.
OR: MEM:
P. 2: p. 153.

done any thing: I desir'd him to stay with me, not knowing
what use wee might haue of more men: And now hauing
continued there till all the Foragers had loaden, and were gone,
I march'd back to the Camp after them, loosing only half a
score, who had past over the brook by Cambron contrary to
order, and were taken by a small party of the Enemy. I haue
since been told by the Prince de Ligne, and other Officers of
the Spanish Army, That they had intended that day to haue
fallen on our Foragers, and had appointed a Rendezvous for
most of their horse from Tournay, Mons, and Ath, (and) haue
met for that design; but that when I march'd out with our
Foragers, there was so great a noise in our Camp, that some
of the Prince de Ligne's small partys brought him intelligence
to Mons, that our whole Army was on its march: wherupon he
sent immediate notice of it to the Rendezvous, and they all
march'd back into their severall quarters, apprehending to meet
with the Van (of) our Army: Thus in all appearance by this
mistake, that Forage escap'd a great danger; for it would haue
been very difficult to haue gott off in safety, when so great a
body of horse should haue fallen on them.

The French
Army marche
to Leuse the
19th Sep. and
rests there to
eat up the
forage.
Ibid. p: 154.

Some days after this, all the Country about us being now
quite eaten up, wee past the River, and Camp at Outrage on
the 14th of September, and on the 19th wee march'd to Leuse
a Bourg in the midway betwixt Tournay and Ath; where wee
rested for some days, till wee had also eaten up most of the

They take the
Castle of
Briffeil.
OR: MEM:
P. 2: p. 154.

Forage in those parts. During our stay there, wee took in the
Castle of Briffeil, in which the Enemy had a garrison, who
would not deliver it up till they saw our cañon in battery against
them.

They quitte
the Enemies
Country and
march to ..
Pommereüil
the 26 Sep-
tember and
thence to
Angre. Ibid.

Having stayd as long as it was convenient in that quarter,
wee began to think it necessary for us to go out of the Enemys
Country; and on the 26th of September, wee march'd to
Pommereüil near Pont de Haisne. The next day wee past over

that River, and camped at Angre upon the Hosneau (*Anirt sur l'Haisneau*) about a league from Keuvrain up that brook. This quarter and all adjoining to it, had been so consum'd, that the very first night of our coming thether, our Foragers were forc'd to go out two leagues for nothing but for straw. So that had any one proposed to haue stayd there, about three or four days, it would haue been judged impracticable. Notwithstanding which Mons'. de Turenne maintain'd us there without want above a fortnight; which was impossible to haue done, had he not order'd us to provide ourselves with corn when wee went from Leuse: at which time our waggons were not only as full as they could hold, but every Trooper carryd a sack of corn behind him, the day wee came thether, which enabled us to subsist so long as wee did in that leane quarter; where there was so litle Forage in the neighbourhood, that I do not remember wee sent out above thrice while we continued there.

At this place also I commanded the last Forage which wee made, and was forced to go almost as far as Bouchain before any thing could be found, most of our men coming loaden only with Straw. The occasion of our long stay in that place, was to furnish the two Towns which wee had newly taken with all manner of Stores and necessary provisions, and for finishing of some works which were absolutely needfull for their Safety.

When this was done, about the 11ᵗʰ of October wee march'd to Barlaimont, and on the 22ᵈ to the Abbey of Marolles; where wee thought wee should haue continued for some time: but having received intelligence that some troopes of the Enemy were drawing down that way, wee thought it expedient for us to remove from thence to a place called Vandegies-au-bois, where our Generall received orders to march towards la Fere; the Court being then just advertis'd, that the Mareshall d'Hocquincourt was making a Treaty with the Prince of Condé, to deliver up to him Ham and Peronne, of both which places he

PART II.

1655. •
The Country about Angre so consum'd that they are forced to go two leagues for Straw.
Ibid. p. 155.

Yet M. de Turenne maintaine the French Army ther above a fortnight.
Ibid.

Here at Angre the Duke likewise commands the last Forage which was made on that quarter.
Or: Mem: P: 2. p. 156.

PART
II.

1655.
The 4ᵗʰ No-
uembʳ M. de
Turenne
comes with
the Army to
Mouy hard by
la Fere, where
he is order'd
to leave it and
come to Com-
piegne (where
the Court then
was) to con-
sult concern-
ing M. d'Hoc-
quincourt.
Oʀ: Mᴇᴍ:
P. 2: p. 158.

M.deTurenne
goingtoCourt,
leaves the
Army under
the Duke's
command at
Mouy, at the
very time the
peace was con-
cluded be-
tween France
andCromwell.
Ibid.

The Duke
marches the
Army to Mon-
decour, the
10 of Nov:
Ibid.

The affaire of
M. d'Hoc-
quincourt
being accom-
modated, M.
de Turenne
returns to the
Army the 14ᵗʰ
Nov: and soon
after that the
Duke go's to
Court when
the Army was
just preparing
to go to winter
quarters.
Oʀ: Mᴇᴍ:
P, 2. p. 159.

was Governour. In pursuance of which order Monsʳ. de Turenne came with the Army on the 4ᵗʰ of Nouember to Mouy, a Village upon the River of Oyse, about two leagues above la Fere ; where so soon as he arriued, he received a letter from the Cardinal to leave the Army there, and come himself to Compiegne where the Court then was, that they might consult together, what resolution was to be taken, in case the Mareshall d'Hocquincourt should not hearken to the offers which were made him from the King, and receive the Enemy into those two so considerable places, upon the River of Somme.

Accordingly he went thether leaving the Army under my command, who was then the only Lieuᵗ Generall remaining with it, all the others having had leave given them before to go away, when they askt it, there being no probability of Action. By this accident I came to haue the command of the Army committed to me, at the very time when the Peace betwixt France and Cromwell was concluded and actually publish'd, and by which Treaty, I was by name to be banish'd France. The Army stayd at Mouy during some days, and there I received orders to march with it to Mondêcour on the 10ᵗʰ of Nouember. That Town is betwixt Noyon and Chauny, and there I stayd till Monsʳ. de Turenne return'd to the Army, which was about the 14ᵗʰ, when the affaire concerning Mʳ. d'Hocquincourt was wholy accommodated, and the Court was secur'd not to lose those two places. After which I obtain'd leave from Monsʳ. de Turenne to go to the Court, the Army being at that time just ready to go into their winter-quarters, and no likelyhood of any more action that Year ; for as long as there was any, I thought myself obliged in honour not to quitt the Army, tho I knew the Treaty betwixt the Crown of France and Cromwell, by Vertue of which I was presently to leave the Country, was already sign'd on both sides.

The French Court was then at Compiegne, where I was

received as kindly as ever, both the Queen Mother of France and the Cardinal making their apologies to me for the Treaty which they had concluded, and telling me they were Sorry the condition in which they were, had forced them to make an Alliance so contrary to their inclinations; but withall they assured me, I should not find the least alteration in their kindness, and they would still continue the same care which they ever had of me. The Cardinal acquainted me with the reasons which had induced him to this Peace, excusing it to me as a thing which he had been obliged to do, out of meer necessity for the seruice and safety of the Crown : for that, had he not then closed with Cromwell, the Spaniards had prevented him, by strikeing up an alliance with that Vsurper, having offer'd to assist him in taking Calais, which they would haue put into his hands. That therfore foreseeing the dangerous consequence of such a Treaty, he had upon the Same grounds concluded a Peace with Cromwell; and, that notwithstanding any proviso that might be made in it against me, I should still find the Same markes of his Master's esteem and kindness for me : And truely upon this occasion, I cannot but do the Memory of the Cardinal that Right to affirm, that he had been a very ill Minister, if he had not made that Treaty with Cromwell in such a juncture of affaires ; and the King of France would haue had just reason to be ill satisfied with him, if he had missed that opportunity.

I stayd at Compiegne some few days, and then went to Paris, where I arrived the 23ᵈ of November, and soon after the Court likewise return'd thether. And now thō, by the Treaty which they had newly made, I was not to stay in France, yet the Cardinal being willing (*unwilling*) to put that hardship upon me, who was so nearly related to the King of France, and Grandson to Henry the 4ᵗʰ, and apprehending likewise in case I should leave the Country, that he should not long retaine the

PART II.

1655.
The Duke is received very kindly at Court and great apologies made to him for the Treaty with Cromwell.
Ibid.
The Cardinall's reasons for striking up a Peace with Cromwell.
Ibid.

The Duke justifys the Cardinal for the good Services done to the King his Master upon this occasion.
Or: Mem: P. 2. p. 160.

The Duke returns from his 4ᵗʰ and last Campagne in France to Paris the 23 Nov. *Ibid.*

Irish who were in the French Armys, propos'd to me, That, if I pleas'd, he would use his endeavours to perswade Cromwell to give his consent for me to remain in France, and to serue again in the Armys; assuring me at the same time, that in case he could not prevaile with him, my pension at least should be secur'd to me and punctually payd to whatsoever Country I went, provided I enter'd not into actuall seruice against France.

At the Cardinal's request Cromwell consents that the Duke should stay and serve in any of the French Armys except that of Flanders.
OR: MEM: P. 2: p. 160.
It was not long before the Cardinal received an answer from Cromwell to this effect, That he consented to my Stay in France, and to my Serning in any of their Armys, excepting only that of Flanders; as not thinking it his interest that I should continue in that Army whither he was obliged by the Treaty to send a considerable body of men for the assistance of that Crown. Vpon which the Cardinal offer'd me to serue as Captain Generall under the Duke of Modena, who was

Vpon which it is offer'd to his R.H. to serve in Italy as Captⁿ Genˡˡ under the Duke of Modena.
Ibid.
The Duke accepts of the offer, and the thing was accordingly agreed upon to be put in execution the following Campagne, but was afterwards alter'd.
Ibid.
generalissime of all the forces of France, Savoy, and Modena, in Piemont; which offer I willingly accepted of, because I was still desirous to be in the Armys, and there to improve my knowledge. And I was also the more inclin'd to Serue in that Country, because my Aunt the Duchess of Savoy desir'd to haue me neer her, and had written to the Queen her Sister concerning it, having on all occasions shewn a particular concern for me; And for these reasons it was so resolved at that time, but alter'd again before the next Campagne, of the reasons mention'd in the ensuing Part of these Memoires.

Thus ends the Relation given by his R. H. of the Campagne of 1655, which was the last he made in the French Seruice.

THE THIRD PART.

IN THIS year, 1656, about the beginning of February, the Princesse of Orange came to Paris to see the Queen her Mother, and his Royal Highness the Duke of York went to meet her betwixt Peronne and Cambray, and came along with her to Paris; where she was received with great civility by the Court, which came to meet her out of Town, and carryd her to the Palais Royal, where they left her with the Queen her Mother.

Some few days after this, it being reported, that the King of England was to go from Colen into Flanders, all the Irish Colonells who had serv'd in the French Armys, under Monsr. de Turenne and Monsr. de la Ferté, hearing of it, writt to the Duke to offer him their Seruice and receive his directions what they should do; as being ready to obey his orders in any thing, that became men of honour and good Subjects. To which offers of theirs his Royall Highness return'd them his acknowledgments, recommending to them the care of keeping their Soldiers together, and by no means to permitt them to go into Flanders by piece meale, or in scattering partys, thō they might be invited So to do by Some from the Spaniards, upon the occasion of his M^{aties} being there; which would be of no advantage to them, but put them out of a capacity of serving their King with their whole Regiments, when any opportunity should present itself: besides, that their going off in such a

PART III.

1656.
The P^{sse} of Orange comes to Paris to See the Queen.
OR: MEM.
P. 3. p. 2.

The Irish Colonells offer their seruice to the Duke.
OR: MEM:
P. 3. p. 4.

M M 2

P A R T
III.

1656.

manner might be of prejudice to his affaires, while he continued in that Country, and that when it should be a proper time for him to make use of their offer, they should be sure to hear from him, in case they hearken to his Councell to keep their Regiments entire and full.

A particular
account of
the handsome
carriage of
Col: Rich:
Grace, when
he quitte the
Spanish
Seruice.
Ibid. p. 5.

And here his R. H. takes particular notice in his Memoires of the handsome carriage of one of those Colonells, when he quitted the Seruice of the Spaniards. This gentleman by name Col: Richard Grace, after having seru'd the late King Charles the 1st till the surrender of Oxford, then going into Ireland, had there seru'd the King Charles the 2d, so long as any part of that Island held out for him; when that Warr was ended, he obtain'd leave from the English Rebels to carry over a Regiment into Spain of his own Countrymen: The Regiment he brought over with him, consisting of above twelve hundred men; he procur'd a very favourable and honourable Capitulation for them: but as Soon as they arrived there, the Spaniards wholly broke the Capitulation they had made with him, and us'd his men so very ill, that before he could march them into Catalonia he had lost halfe his number. Notwithstanding which bad treatment, he serv'd in the Spanish Army with good reputation, till the end of the Campagne: At which time being left in garrison in a Castle upon the fronteers, which was a considerable post, and considering that by the ill usage he had received, and was like to receive for the future, he should in all probability lose the remainder of his Regiment; at the same time also, hearing that the King his Master was in France where he was honourably treated, and that his Royall Highness was also in the French Seruice, he resolv'd to Stay no longer with the Spaniards. Yet, notwithstanding that they had broken their Articles with him, he would not for his own sake do any thing unbecoming a gentleman, but would leave them fairly.

To which purpose he sent to the Mareshall d'Hocquincourt,

10

who at that time commanded the French Army in Catalonia, to let him him know, that on such a day, which was mention'd by him, he would march off with his Regiment on these conditions, that his Regiment might be upon the same foot with the Irish Regiments then in the French Seruice, and that they might be permitted to go and serue their own King, when-soever his affaires requir'd their Seruice: These conditions were easily accepted, and great offers made him in case he would deliver up the Castle; But that he absolutly refused, and only desir'd the Mareshall to send some horse on the day appointed to bring him off. When that time was come, he sent to the neighbouring garrison of the Spaniards to give them notice of his intention, that they might give order to some of their men to come and take possession of the Castle, as he march'd out of it, and that by his giving them this notice, they might perceive he intended only to march away with his Regiment, and not to deliver up the Castle to their Enemies; he also waru'd them, that they should not send above two hundred men till he was march'd out of it: for in case they gave him any reason to suspect, that they intended to betray him, he would give up the Castle to the French. This pre-caution of his secur'd him from their Sending any more troopes then he had desir'd, and as soon as they approched the place, he permitted them to enter at one gate, while he march'd out at the other, and went off to the French horse that waited for him.

But to returne where wee left. After this address, which was made to the Duke from the Irish Collonels, there came certain news, That the King was in Flanders, and that he had concluded a Treaty with the Spaniards; which made most people beleeve that his R. H. was also to go over to them: Upon which occasion, as he was one day talking with Mons'. de Turenne (with whom he was used to speak very freely of his

M. de Turenne advises the Duke to write to the King

PART
III.
_____
1656.
his Brother,
for leave to
Stay and Serve
in France.
OR: MEM:
P. 3: p. 7.

concerns) he advis'd him to write to the King his Brother, and
to offer to his consideration, That having serv'd so long in
France, and having received the greatest part of his education
there, since his departure from England, it might be of great
advantage to his Maties. Seruice, if his Royall Highness were
permitted to continue there, that so he might keep up the intrest
he had made, and the freindship he had contracted with many
considerable persons both in the Court and Army ; with whose
assistance when a proper time should offer it self, he might be
in a condition of doing his Ma^{ty} some seruice : wheras he
should run great hazard of losing that intrest with his friends,
and quite incapacitate him to make them usefull, either to the
King or to himself, if he should go into Flanders where he
could do his Ma^{ty} no great Seruice ; That his Brother the Duke
of Glocester was there already, which ought to be enough to
satisfy the Spaniards, especially since they had not desir'd the
Duke's coming thither, nor so much as mention'd him or taken
the least notice of him, in what had pass'd betwixt them and
his Ma^{ty} ; and in case they should desire the King to send for
the Duke into Flanders, his Ma^{ty} might consent privatly to his
R. H. stay in France, and seem publickly to be very much
displeas'd with him, for not obeying those pretended commands,
therby to keep faire with the Spaniards ; and that this coñivence
should be kept so secret, that no one person shou'd be privy to it,
but only who should be sent with the proposition.

The Duke
comunicats M.
de Turenne's
advice to the
Queen, and
both approv-
ing of it,
Charles Bar-
clay is pitch'd
upon to carry
the proposall
to the King.
OR: MEM:
P. 3. p. 8.
The Duke's
appoint^t in
France 6000
pistoles a year,

This advice of Monsr. de Turenne was so much approv'd by
the Duke, having first communicated it to the Queen his
Mother, who was also pleas'd with it, that he resolv'd to send
Charles Berclay (*Berkley*) with all speed to make this proposition
to his Ma^{ty}, charging him also to inform the King particularly
of his present condition as to his subsistance ; which considering
all things was reasonably good, his Royall Highness having at
that time an appointment of six thousand pistoles a year, well

payd, besides the helps he had by his Regiment of foot, and Troop of Scots Gendarmes, which together with what should be farther settled upon him when he should go into Piemont, would inable him to live at ease and with decency, till his Ma^ry should haue some occasion for his seruice in relation to England.

When the Duke had writt his letters and fully instructed Charles Barkly, in all he had to say in that affaire, just as he was ready to take his journy, he unfortunatly broke his leg; which obliged his R. H. to make use of Doctor Fraiser (who was then going to wait on his Ma^ty) to be the bearer of his letters, he having at that time none about him, whom he could spare, who was so fitt to be imployed in that business, or who was more in his confidence then the Doctor; who indeed perform'd his part with all exactness, in representing to his Ma^ry who was then at Bruges, the reasons which mov'd his R. H. to make that propositiou. But neither what the Doctor said, nor what the Duke had written, had the desired effect: for his Majesty, and his Ministers, would not be induced by any means to hear of his R. H. continuing either in any part of France or in the French Seruice; and the King was so far from being willing to connive at it, that he presently layd his absolute commands upon the Duke, to come away to him into Flanders with all hast imaginable, thō (as has been already said) the Spaniards had not then desir'd it, or made any the least mention of the Duke to his Majesty.

Sir Henry Bennett, who was at that time the Duke's Secretary, and very inward with those that were in favour with the King, was the person sent to the Duke with his command; which so soon as his R. H. had received, he writt back word immediatly, That he was ready to obey his Majesties orders without delay: and in pursuance of them, he sent to the French Court then at Compiegne, to inform them of the commands which he had

PART III.

1656.
besides his Reg^t of foot and his troop of Scots Gendarmes. *Ibid.* p. 9.

Charles Barclay, fully instructed and ready to part with the Duke's letters, breakes his leg. *Ibid.*
The letters are Sent by DoctorFraiser. *Ibid.*

The King refuses to consent to the Duke's Stay in France, and lays his absolutecommands on him to come away to him into Flanders with all hast. O^r: Mem: P. 3. p. 9.

Sir Henry Bennett is sent with this command to the Duke,who immediatly complying with his Ma: orders, sends for leave from the French Court,andprepares himself for his journy. *Ibid.* p. 11.

received from the King his Brother, and to desire their leave that he might go to him : which the Court readily consenting to, his R. H. began to set himself in order for his journy.

That which urg'd the Duke to make the greater speed, was the great desire he had to clear himself to his Majesty from some reports which had been made of him, and which had gain'd so much beleif both with him and his Ministers, that they were the principal occasion of sending Sir Henry Bennett to hasten his journy ; one of whose Instructions by word of mouth was to inquire of the Duke, Whither it was true, as his Maᵗʸ had been inform'd, that his R. H. intended to send Tuke into England to treat with Some persons there, and whither his Sister, the Princesse Royall, was not to furnish Tuke with mony for his journy. When Sir Henry Bennett deliver'd this message, he told the Duke also, That had not he hinder'd it, his Maᵗʸ had put this Article into his written Instructions, so much he was perswaded of the truth of that report : By which it may be easily concluded, what Strange Stories were then both raised and credited concerning the Duke, and what groundless jealousies they had of him ; he never having had the least thought of Sending either Tuke or any other man into England, or ever endeavouring to haue any correspondence there with any one, not judging it to be his business : nor did he so much as try to procure mony out of England from the well affected there, who us'd from thence to supply his Maᵗʸ ; of which supply's the Duke never had any part, excepting two hundred and fifty pounds which was brought over to the King by R. Nicholas from the Countess of Devonshire, with a desire that his R. H. might haue a share of it.

Yet how groundless soever these suspitions were, most certain it is, that they were credited, and therfore it will be necessary to shew, what the Duke had reason to beleeve was the occasion of them : In order to which wee must look backward with his

Some false reports of the Duke credited by the King and his Ministers, are the occasion of pressing his journy.
Or: Mem:
P. 3: p: 11.

His R. H. declares he never had the least thought of sending Tuke into England.
Ibid. p: 12.
No ever so much as tryd to procure mony from thence. Ibid.

The Factions at Court are the occasion of these reproche as the Duke plainly Shews by the following account.
Or: Mem:
P. 3: p: 13.

R. H. as far as his Maties coming into France, after his miracu-lous escape from the battail of Worcester.

At the King's first coming to Paris, his Ma^{ty} made use of the Lord Jermyn, in most of his affaires, trusting him as far as any one in the management of his most Secret busines; which trust he continued to him, for some time after the coming over of the Chancellor of the Exchecquer, Sr Edward Hyde, who by degrees gott the favour and entire confidence of his Ma^{ty}; which was also much farther'd by the King's freinds and Servants in England, who desir'd that their addresses might rather pass by him, then through the hands of any other person. This consideration principally together with the concurrence of some other accidents, increas'd his favour with the King so far, that by degrees he began to withdraw his confidence from the Lord Jermyn, and at last only to let him participate of such affaires, the knowledge of which was common to him, and all the Councill ; which by litle and litle caus'd no very good understanding betwixt him and Sr Edward Hyde.

The King withdrawing his confidence from L^d. Jermyn, and Chancellor Hyde getting by degrees the entire favour of his Ma^{ty}, these two favorites become jealous of one another. Ibid.

There happen'd also about the same time another accident, to make the breach yet wider; which was the advice given by the Chancellor to the Countess of Morton (then Governess to the Princess Henriette) not to marry Sir John Berkley, because he judg'd it both improper and very inconvenient for either of them on severall reasons, which counsell he thought himself obliged to give as being very much a freind to both. But it was not so looked on by Sir John Berkley, who fell out with him upon it, and heighten'd the breach between him and the Lord Jermyn, hardly ever forgetting it, but being ever after-wards on all occasions his bitter Enemy.

Sir John Berkley falling out with the Chancellor sides with Lord Jermyn and widens the breach be-tween them. Or Mem: P. 3: p. 14.

And now this animosity betwixt the Chancellor and the Lord Jermyn, encreasing every day, caus'd at length some coldness to grow betwixt the King and the Queen his Mother,

The animosity of these two Factions oc-casion'd at last a coldness between the

PART
III.
———
1656.
King, and
Queen Mo-
ther, the first
supporting the
Chancellor
and the latter
countenancing
L⁴ Jermyn.
Ibid.

his Ma^ty looking on himself as obliged not to let the Chancellor suffer for the confidence which he had reposed in him; and her Ma^ty not thinking herself in the wrong to countenance the Lord Jermyn, who had so long serv'd her, and had her entire confidence, and the sole management of all her affaires. By this means there arose two factions in that unfortunate Court, which were not fully reconciled till some time after his Maties happy restoration.

The Duke by
being in the
Army avoids
happily enter-
ing into these
Factions.
Or: Mem:
P. 3. p. 14.

In the mean time it was very very difficult for the Duke so to fashion his behaviour, that he might equally perform his duty both to the King and to his Mother; and his taske had been much harder, had he not had good fortune, as he calls it, to be in the Army in the year, 1652, when most of this happen'd, So that when his R. H. came back, things had already taken their bent, and no hopes were left of a better understanding.

Attempts
made to re-
move the
Chancellor.
Ibid. p. 15.
The accusa-
tions against
him being only
the effects of
malice, they
strengthen the
King's kind-
ness to him.
Ibid. p: 16.

In the following year some attempts were made to remove the Chancellor, by accusing him of betraying his Maties Counsells, and holding correspondence with Cromwell: but these allegations were so triviall and frivolous, that they manifestly appear'd to be nothing but the effects of malice against him, and therefore produced the contrary effects to those which some desired, and strengthen'd the King's kindness to him; as giving him just occasion to beleeve, that these suggestions against him, proceeded all from one and the same cause, namely, from the ambition which some people had, to enter in his room into the first trust of his Maties affaires, if once they could remove him from that Station.

The Duke
keeps himself
still free from
these In-
trigues, but
some of his
Servants are
led into them.
Or: Mem:
P. 3. p. 16.
Sʳ Henry
Bennett the
Duke's Secrʸ
sides wᵗʰ the

In the year 1654, his Ma^ty left France and went to Colen. During all this time the Duke kept himself out of these troublesome Intrigues, as much as possibily he could, and his being so frequently and so long together in the Armys was of great advantage and ease to him in that particular; but his domestick Servants were not altogether so free as himself, from entering into prejudices and partialitys, as being led into them,

either by some Relations or intrest of some kind or other : For
S' Henry Bennett his Secretary, having had the same Imployment under the Earle of Bristoll who was a great freind to the
Chancellor, went along with him, in which resolution he was
also confirm'd by some litle quarrells which had happen'd
betwixt him and Sir John Berkley; and as for Mr. Charles
Berkley and Mr. Henry Jermyn, they took part with Lord
Jermyn, by which means, thō really the Duke was not ingag'd
himself in these Intrigues, yet his having more kindness for
Charles Berkley and Henry Jermyn then for any others, caus'd
some to report and to look upon him as an Enemy to the
Chancellor ; which together with his living so kindly with the
Lord Jermyn (which he first began to do in obedience to his
Maties Commands) gave more occasion for those reports, and
had made such an impression with those who had most credit
with the King, that by that time the Duke came to Bruges,
they gave beleef to severall malicious. Storys which were
forg'd, and were of the same nature with the Story already
mention'd relating to Tuke. And 'twas this that put them
upon a design of removing from about his R. H. all those
Servants who were not entirely in their intrests, so Soon as he
should arriue at Bruges.

AND now to return where wee broke off. His R. H. having,
in pursuit of his Maties order, gott himself in readiness to begin
his journy about the beginning of September, he resolved in the
first place to go to Compiegne and take his leave of the Court :
At which time there happen'd an accident, which in any other
Country might (*haue*) occasion'd great trouble to his R. H. which
was, that the Marquess of Ormonde, at the request of the
Spaniards, was sent by the King of England to the Town of Condé,
then block'd up by them, and to be deliver'd up to them in a
few days. The Marquess, when the garrison capitulated, sent in

N N 2

PART
III.

1656.
Chancellor
and L'Bristoll,
in opposition
to Sir John
Berkley, who
with Charles
Berkley and
Henry Jermyn
was on Lord
Jermyn's side.
Ibid.

The Duke
having more
kindness for
Charl Berkley
and Hen:
Jermyn, then
others, and
living freindly
with Lord
Jermyn, was
what gave
occasion to
the reports
above men-
tion'd, and
make him be
look'd upon
as an Enemy
to the Chan-
cellor.
Ibid. p: 17.

'Tis also the
occasion of
the design
which was
taken of re-
moving those
Servants the
Duke had a
kindness for,
as soon as he
should arrive
at Bruges.
OR: MEM:
P. 3. p: 17.

The King
Sends the
Marq. of Or-
mondetoCondé
to command
the Duke's
Regim'. and
L' Muskerry,
to quitt the
FrenchSeruice
and repair
immediatly to

PART
III.

1656.
his Ma^{ty}. This
happening
whiletheDuke
was preparing
for his depar-
ture might
haue occa-
sion'd trouble
to him. *Ibid.*
Lord Mus-
kerry's answer.
Or: MEM:
P. 3. p. 18.

The Duke
taking his
leave of the
Court at
Compiegne, is
promis'd the
continuation
of his pension
in case he did
not ingage in
actuall Seruice
againstFrance.
Ibid. p. 19.

The Duke
perceives by
the King's
letters, that
his Ma^{ty} de-
sir'd he should
leave Sir John
Berkleybehind
him. *Ibid.*

to his Nephew Muskerry, who had a Regiment of Irish there,
and to Sr John Darcy the Duke's Lieu^t Collonel, to command
them, in the name of his Ma^{ty}, upon their marching out,
immediatly to quitt the Seruice of the French and to repaire
to him. To which Muskerry answer'd, That thō he had all the
duty for his Ma^{ty}, which a good Subject was obliged to haue,
yet being already ingag'd in the French Seruice, he look'd on
himself as bound in honour, before he left it, to ask his pass ;
which he would immediatly, so soon as he should joyn the
French Army : This message, as reasonably might be expected,
made a great noise at the Court ; yet it hinder'd not the Duke's
being very well treated there, when he came to take his leave :
for they assured him, notwithstanding what the King of England
had done in sending the Marquess of Ormonde on such an
account to Condé, that he should still haue his pension
constantly paid him, in case he did not ingage in actuall
seruice against them.

After this, his R. H. returning to Paris, prepar'd himself in
three or four days to sett forwards on his journy to Flanders.
But before he left Paris, he found by severall letters which he
receiv'd from the King his Brother, that his Ma^{ty} desir'd he
should leave Sr John Berkley behind him in that Town.
Which thō not directly mention'd, his R. H. could not but take
notice of, by the King's pressing him to make hast to him,
saying particularly in one of his letters, That it concern'd his
seruice very much that he should come immediatly to him,
and that in case his mony busines or any other affaire he had,
were not yet settled, he might however come away himself, and
leave Sir John Berkley behind him to dispatch it. By this
and many other expressions, the Duke plainly perceiv'd the
design which was carryd on by some, to remove Sir John
Berkley from his Seruice, and to bring in again Sir George
Ratcliffe, an absolute creature of those who were most inward

with his Majesty. But this their project did not take, for the
Duke's affaires were so soon settled, that he obeyd his M^{aties}
Commands by making all possible speed in coming to him,
and yet he carryd Sir John Berkley along with him ; as being
certain that in case he should haue (*left*) him behind, it would
haue prov'd very difficult for him to haue had him again, as he
found by what happen'd after his arrivall at Bruges.

On the 10th of September the Duke set out from Paris, all
his equipage and servants, excepting two or three, having begun
their journy two days before. That night his R. H. lodged at
Verneuil with Monsieur de Metz ; and the next day went in
his coach to Clermont, intending there to take post, and to be
that night at Abbeville where he should meet with his equipage
and Servants. But as he came to the gate of Clermont, he met
one whom he had sent before to provide post horses for him,
who told him, that Lockart Cromwell's Ambassador was there,
and lodg'd at the post house, it being the best Inne of the
Town : upon which the Duke sent the same person again before
him, with order, that the horses should be ready brought to the
door of the post house. When he came thither, he commanded
the Coach to stop, and got on horseback where he was, in the
open street, continuing on his way without making the least stay
in that place, but only to gett on his boots which he had in the
Coach. And as he was much surpriz'd to find Lockart there,
so was Lockart no less at his R. H. coming thither, as apprehending what might happen to him on the Duke's account,
and being sensible how kind the generallity of the common
people, as well as those of better quality, were to him, and what
hatred and aversion they had to the English of Lockart's party.
The allarm which Lockart took from this consideration, caus'd
him to assemble all his Servants in the Inne where he was, with
their swords and pistols, and all their horses were order'd to be
ready Saddled, and bridled : As for himself, he stood at the

PART III.

1656.
The Duke obeys the King's commands in going to him wth all speed, but he thought fitt to carry Sr John Berkley along with him.
O_R: M_{EM}: P. 3: p. 20.
The Duke sets out from Paris y^e 10th X^{ber}. *Ibid.*

He meets Lockart Cromwell's Ambass^r at the Post House at Clermont, his R. H. prudent behaviour and conduct on this occasion. O_R: M_{EM}: P. 3. p. 21.

PART
III.

1656.

window in the inner part of the Inne which look'd just upon the gate, with the cheif of his Retinue about him. His hatt was off, and, for that reason, all the rest of them stood uncover'd ; 'tis probable he chuse to haue it so, therby to avoid the putting it off on the one hand, and to shun censure on the other, in case he should not uncover. His footmen, and a good Company of sturdy fellows, stood within the Court at the bottom of the Stairs. And it so happen'd, that the Coach wherein the Duke was, stopping just before the gate towards which the window fronted where Lockart stood, his R. H. saw him there : And it was not without reason, that he was apprehensive of what might happen to him, for before the Duke could get on horseback, almost all the people of the Town were gather'd together about him ; so that upon the least word or intimation that his R. H. had given, he verily beleeved they would haue fallen upon the Ambassador.

The Duke
arrives at
Abbeville.
Or: Mem:
P. 3. p. 22.

But that fright was of no long continuance, for the Duke made no stay when once he was on horseback ; and the Same night, as he had purpos'd, he joyn'd his equipage at Abbeville. And in this it happen'd, as it do's in many other things, that what was done by the Court in civility to his R. H. and to avoid any ill accident, had like to haue prov'd the occasion of one : for Lockart being at Compiegne was sent away to Clermont, which was not far distant from Court, meerly that he should not be

His R. H.
civilly entertain'd in all
the places he
passes, at
Montreuil,
Boulogne, and
Calais.
Or: Mem:
P: 3: p. 23.
He is met at
Gravelines by
the Marq' of
Ormonde,
which wellcoms him into
that Country.
Ibid.

present there at the Duke's arrivall ; and his R. H. staying in Paris a shorter time then the Court beleeved he would, after he had taken his leave of them, was the occasion of his finding Lockart in that place.

From Abbeville his R. H. went to Montreuil, thence to Boulogne, and so to Calais, at all which places he was very civilly entertain'd. From Calais he went to diner at Gravelines, the first place upon that Coast, then belonging to the King of Spaine. There he was mett by the Marquess of Ormonde,

according to the appointment of the King his Brother, and
wellcom'd by him into that Country. The same night he went
to Dunkerque, and the next day he arriv'd at Bruges, his Ma^{ty}
and the Duke of Glocester coming out as far as Furnes to meet
him.

And now it was not many days after the Duke's being at
Bruges, that he was satisfied he was in the right to bring Sir John
Berkley along with him ; For thō, as to his own particular, he
was us'd with great Civility, yet even his Ma^{ty} himself, as well
as those about him, look'd very coldly on Sr John and treated
him accordingly. So that it was evidently seen that those who
had most credit with the King, were at watch for any pretence
of sending him away: and this Storme did not only threaten
him, but his Nephew and Henry Jermyn also, against whom
there was no occasion to be found, but only their being neerly
related to Sir John and the Lord Jermyn, and their being faithfull to the Duke and intirely trusted by him ; so that if their
design against these three Servants of his had taken effect, his
R. H. had suffer'd more then would haue fallen to their share :
for in what a miserable condition must he haue been, if he had
permitted those in whom he had the most confidence, and for
whom he had the greatest kindness, to be torne from him ? and
to haue had none remaining about his person, but such as he
could not reasonably trust, and whom he knew to be the great
promoters of these designs? who were so blinded, and carry'd
away by their private passions, interests, and animositys, that
they consider'd not in the least the interests of their Master, if
they were put in ballance with their own, to the compassing of
which they were wholly bent; of which number were Sir Henry
Bennett, and Henry Killigrew, who besides the malice which
they had against their former fellow-servants, hop'd together
with Sir George Ratcliffe to haue the management of the Duke's

PART
III.

1656.
He arriues at
Bruges ; the
King and the
Duke of Glo-
cester come as
far as Furnes
to meet him.
Ibid.

Sir John
Berkley is
treated very
coldly at
Court, and all
the pretences
watch'd for to
send him away.
Ibid.

What a hard-
ship it was
upon the Duke
to haue his
best Servants
torn from him.
OR: MEM:
P. 3. p: 24.

mony, and in time his favour also, when the others were once removed.

1656.
To mortify
the Duke they
talk of an old
English Cus-
tome, that it
was not in his
power to chuse
his own Ser-
vants, which
was a mistake.
Or: Mem:
P. 3: p. 25.

And to shew that this was not the only design on foot to mortify the Duke, severall of the King's Servants and Ministers, began to talk of an old English Custome (as they pretended) that it was not in the Duke's power to make choice of his own Servants, but that it belong'd to the King to do it, which was a very great mistake in matter of fact; the case being very different betwixt a father and a brother, and betwixt a child, and one arriv'd at man's Estate.

The King
presses the
Duke to write
to Sʳ Ja:Darcey
to come with
his Regimᵗ to
Flanders, tho
his R. H. as-
sured his Maᵗʸ
that it would
haue no good
effect, but be
only a pretext
to the Cardˡ
to take away
his R. Hˢˢˢ
pension.
Ibid.

But that no way might be left untryd to do his R. H. a prejudice, they prevail'd with his Maᵗʸ to press and command him, to write to Sir James Darcey to come into Flanders with his Regiment, notwithstanding that the Duke told his Majesty, he was certain his letter would be of no effect, because he knew very well that Sir James would not do it, thō Muskerry and the other Irish Collonels would obey; That without producing any good effect, such proposition would only make a noise in France, and serue the Cardinal for a pretence to take away the Duke's pension, which would not be very convenient for him, before he knew what would be done for him in the Country where he was; That as yet he had no assurance of seruing there, the Spaniards not having yet hearken'd to any overture which had been made concerning it.

But all his R. H. reasons signified nothing, write he must: and that there was some other end in it, then meerely to procure that Regiment to come over into the seruice of the Spaniards, appear'd plainly enough from the litle care they took of conveying this letter to Sir James Darcey; for he had it not in six weeks after it was written, and had not then receiv'd it, had it not been for Charles Berkley who lay still at Paris, not being quite recovered of his broken leg, so that the

Cardinal got notice of such a letter being written, and had time enough to confirm Sir James Darcy in his resolution of staying in France: So that when at length he receiv'd the letter, he not only excus'd himself, but hinder'd severall Officers from coming over, thō the rest obeyd and came away, when Muskerry with the other Collonels left the French Seruice.

PART
III.

1656.
Sᵣ Ja: Darcy receiving the Dukes letter excuses himself, but Muskerry and the other Collonelsobey and came away
Oᴙ: Mᴇᴍ:
P. 3: p. 26.

And as the Duke was press'd at Bruges to many things of this nature which were of no advantage to the King, and yet might be of great prejudice to himself; so on the other hand, he receiv'd letters from Paris written to him from the Lord Jermyn, and others, disswading him from entring into the Spanish Seruice, as a thing no way proper for him to undertake, having liv'd so long a time in France, and been treated there with so much kindness, and receiving at that time a pension from thence; These and other arguments they us'd to hinder him from ingaging with the Spaniards: But their reasons were so weak, that it was easy to find they were only plausible allurements suggested to them by the Cardinal, who hop'd that if his R. H. could be so managed as not to enter into the Seruice of the Spaniard, he should be able to retain the Irish still in France.

Letters are written from Paris to the Duke, disswading him from entering into the Spanish Seruice. *Ibid.*

In short they prevail'd not with the Duke, for he answer'd them, That he look'd not on his obligations to France as such which could hinder him in honour from serning Spain, or any other Crown, in case he should design so to do for his own interest; and that thō he should not find his account in taking armes for Spain, yet if the King his Brother should command him, it was his duty to obey him; So that whither he consider'd himself as a Soldier of fortune, or as a Subject, in either case he could not conceive why it should be ill relish'd in France, whom Soever he Seru'd.

The Duke's Answer.
Oᴙ: Mᴇᴍ:
P. 3: p. 26.

Not long after this, his R. H. accepted of the offers which were made him by the King his Brother, and the Spaniards, and enter'd into their seruice.

The Duke accepts of the offers of the Spaniards, and enters into their Seruice. *Ibid.* p. 27.

PART
III.
———
1656.
The P^{ssc} of
Orange comes
from Paris to
Bruges in Nov:
Or: Mem:
P. 3: p. 27.
Troubled to
See the Duke
ill us'd, she
takes his part.
Ibid.

This affaire was but newly settled, when his Sister the
Princesse Royall came to Bruges from Paris, about the end of
November. She was not a litle troubled to see the Duke us'd
in the manner above related, so that she took his part, and us'd
all the credit she had for his assistance; which being observ'd
by those in favour, and they also perceiving, that they could
not prevaile with him by perswasions to part with Sir John
Berkley, or any other, went now another way to work,
resolving to lay hold on the first occasion, right or wrong, to
find fault with Sr John, and then send him away : And what
triuiall exceptions they were forced to lay hold on against him,
and what just reason the Duke had to be scandaliz'd at their
procceeding, will appear in the following instance.

Not many days before Christmas, his Ma^{ty} went to Bruxelles,
to settle his affaires of the greatest concernment with the
Spaniard, leaving the Duke in the mean time at Bruges, to bear
his Sister company.

The Spaniards
resolve to put
an oath of
fidelity to all
the King's
Subjects, to be
true to them.
Ibid. p. 28.

On Christmass eve the King return'd, and the same night the
Duke being inform'd by the Lord Muskerry, that the Spaniards
had resolved to administer an oath of fidelity to all such as came
over to the Kings Seruice, by which they should be obliged to
be faithfull to the Spaniards, his R. H. was much scandaliz'd
at it, as a hardship which was never impos'd upon the Prince
of Condé's troopes, or those of Lorraine, and which might
prove prejudiciall even to the King; because it might in reason
startle those who were now upon quitting the French Seruice,
meerly out of duty to him, if they saw they were to be ingaged
in oath to the Spaniards preferably to him, on which termes it
was likely they would not come over.

The Duke
scandaliz'd at
this hardship
put on the
King's Subjects
contrary to his
Ma^{ty} Seruice,

When this was first told to the Duke, he could hardly beleeve
it ; but meeting in the presence Chamber with the Earle of
Bristoll, who was the person by whom the King had been

perswaded to consent to it, the Duke told him of the report
and inquir'd of him, what truth there might be in it? Vpon
which question, the Earle of Bristoll flew out into a very high
passion, saying, That whoever had inform'd the Duke of it,
was a Traitor to his Ma^ty and a Villain, and that it could be
told him of no other end, then to set him against it, which
would be ruinous to the King's affaires. He us'd many other
passionate expressions, which can scarse (be) call'd arguments,
to make it appear a monstrous crime in him who had thus
inform'd the Duke; thinking, as he had reason to beleeve, that
this had come from Sir John Berkley, and that he had not
only given his R. H. notice of it, but had also given him bad
impressions concerning it.

The Earle of Bristoll spoke So loud, that his Ma^ty, who was
in the same room, and at not great distance, heard all he said;
and coming to the Duke, he took part with the Earle of Bristoll,
further telling his R. H. that now he might plainly see how
ill affected they were to the Spaniards, and to himself, who
had inform'd him of that Oath, which must needs haue been
represented to him out of an ill intent. After which the King
press'd him to name the person who told it him: from which
the Duke excused himself, and sayd, He hop'd his Ma^ty would
pardon him, if he did not name him, after what had been said
by My Lord Bristoll, it being now almost as much as to accuse
him of high treason; That his R. H. very well saw who was
pointed out by the Earle, but it was not the first time he had
been mistaken, for that upon his word it was not Sir John
Berkley; and that, if the matter were well consider'd, it would
be found almost impossible for him to haue had so speedy a
knowledge of it; That he was about to haue nam'd the person
to the Earle, at the very beginning of his discourse, but that he
grew into so great a heat, and flew out into such disrespectfull
expressions, that afterwards his R. H. thought fitt to say no

o o 2

PART
III.

1656.
asks Ld Bristoll
what truth
was in it?
On: Mem:
P: 3. p. 28.
The E. of
Bristoll Pas-
sionat and
disrespectfull
answer to the
Duke in the
King's pre-
senceChamber.
Ibid. p. 29.

The King
joyns with the
E. of Bristoll
in his opinion
and presses the
Duke to name
the person who
told him of the
Oath.
On: Mem:
P. 3: p. 29.

The Duke
assures ye King
on his word,
that it was
not Sr John
Berkley, but
excuses him-
self from
naming the
person.
Ibid.

PART
III.

1656.

Lord Bristoll
finding himself
mistaken in
the man he
aim'd at, grew
calme and askd
his R. H.
pardon.
Or: Mem:
P. 3. p. 30.

more, but withall he was certain, if he had nam'd the man, no
farther noise had been made of it; That for what concern'd
the thing it self, it was certainly no crime for any man to tell
it him, for that his Ma^{ty} having once resolv'd on it, his R. H.
thō his own opinion was against it, did nothing to hinder the
thing from being done.

When My Lord Bristoll had heard the Duke's answer, and
saw he was mistaken in the man at whom he aim'd, he grew
calme, and, before the King, ask'd his R. H. pardon, if the Zeal
he had for the Kings seruice had made him forgett himself so
far, as to say any thing which was unbecoming the respect he
ow'd him: Thus that Conversation ended.

And now as to (*the*) Oath itself, the Duke verily beleev'd
that had it been never so litle opposed, the Spaniards would
not haue insisted on it, as they did. And farther, had not my
Lord Bristoll (without any such intention) put a jealousy into
their heads, as if the King design'd to haue had an Army
according to the present example of the Prince of Condé, and
the Duke of Lorraine; by proposing first to them the making
up of a body of ten thousand men, to be commanded by the
Duke with cañon and all other necessary provisions, the
consequences of which the Spaniards had already felt to their
cost; they had never imposed such an Oath upon all his Maties
troopes, nor afterwards given them so small encouragement,
notwithstanding their promises to the contrary: all which
proceeded from their apprehensions, least that body of foot
should grow too considerable, and by that means become
formidable to them.

Lord Bristoll
after a long
preamble of
protestations
of freindship,
advises the
Duke to order

And now the day after what had pass'd betwixt the Duke
and the Earle of Bristoll, that Lord came to him in his chamber,
and desir'd to speak alone with him: After which, he began
with a long preamble of the great duty and esteem he had
for his R. H. and, if he might presume to Say it, a great

kindness for his person, besides what he ow'd him on other
accounts; and then he assur'd him, that not only himself, but
his two freinds, the Marquess of Ormonde and the Chancellor,
would put him at the head of all affaires, if he would please
but to follow their aduice, and be kind to them. After much
inlarging upon that Subject, he turn'd his discourse, and began
to speak to his R. H. concerning Sir John Berkley, proffering
to be very much his freind, and that he would be ready to
Serve him in all things which lay within his power ; for which
reason he desir'd his R. H. if he had any kindness for Sir John,
that he would be pleas'd to order him to withdraw himself for
some time, the King being so much incensed against him,
that his longer stay would but increase his displeasure, and
make his reconciliation the harder ; whereas a litle absence,
and his making thos acknowledgments which he ought, might
in a short time restore him to his Maties favour and good opinion.
But when by the Duke's answer, he perceiv'd his Rhetorique
could not prevaile with his R. H. to consent to that proposition,
he then told him in another kind of tone, That it was the
King's absolute pleasure Sir John Berkley should withdraw,
and that his Ma^ty was so firmly resolv'd on that point, that
there was no remedy, but go he must : and besides, That the
King had said so much to Don John of his being dissaffected
to the Spaniards, and had made such impressions in him by
those discourses, that it was now no longer in his Maties power,
thō he should desire it, to retain him any longer in the Country.
At last he concluded with Saying, That he would repeat all
this to Sir John Berkley, and advise him as his freind to
submitt patiently to it, and use his best endeavours to gain his
consent.

To this long discourse, the Duke only answer'd, That he was
sorry that such ill offices had been done to Sir John Berkley;
both in relation to his Ma^ty and to Don John ; That it was a

P A R T
III.

1656.
Sir Jo: Berkley
to withdraw.
Or: Mem:
P. 3. p. 31.

Finding the
Duke was not
to be prevail'd
upon by his
Rhetorique, he
then told his
R. H. plainly,
it was the
King's absolute
pleasure.
Or: Mem:
P. 3. p. 33.

The Duke's
modest answer
to th'eParle of
Bristoll.
Ibid.

II

PART
III.

1656.

busines of such a nature, that should he give his consent to it, it would lessen him very much in the esteem of the world; for how should he be look'd on in case he abandon'd his innocent Servants, at least so reputed by him, to the malice of their Enemies? And how could he ever expect for the future, that any one would haue any manner of dependance on him, when they should haue such an example of his R. H. weakness before their eyes.

E. Bristoll delivers the same Message to Sir Jo. Berkley.
OR: MEM:
P. 3: P. 33.
The P. Royall troubled at this affaire, for the sake of both her Brothers, yet advises the Duke to stick firm to his old Servant.
Ibid.

The same Counsell given him by all his freinds and by everybody but Lord Bristoll and his faction.
Ibid.

In this difficult juncture, to avoid coming to heats with the King, his R. H. resolves to withdraw privatly into Holland.
OR: MEM:
P. 3. p. 3

With this answer, the Earle went from the Duke and deliver'd his message to Sir John Berkley: And now the matter was no longer a Secret, for it had taken wind, and was the common discourse of the Family; so that before night the Princesse Royall tooke notice of it to the Duke, as being very much troubled at it for the sake of both her Brothers, and very apprehensive of what might be the issue: However she advis'd him upon the whole to stick firm to his old Servant, and not to consent to his departure. The same Counsell his R. H. had given him from all his freinds; there was the old Lord Balcarras, and others, and indeed every body, excepting my Lord Bristoll and his freinds, sayd the same thing to him.

Wherupon seeing that it was not in his power to keep Sir John any longer with him, and that if he should dispute the matter any further, it might occasion some heats betwixt his Maty and him, which for his own part he was resolved by all manner of ways to avoid, he thought the best thing he could propose to himself in so difficult a juncture, was to withdraw privatly to Holland, hoping to obtain while he was absent, what he was certain would be denyd him, remaining there. Having then consulted with Sir John Berkley, Harry Jermyn, and Charles Berkley, concerning the manner of doing it, it was resolv'd, that in order to facilitate the Duke's design, his R. H. should consent to the absence of Sir John Berkley, and that two days after he had withdrawn himself, the Duke should follow as privatly as he could.

After this resolution was once taken, the Duke declared his consent that Sir John Berkley should go; which surprized all his freinds exceedingly, they not knowing his private intentions: and particularly he was much reproched by his Sister for it, and blam'd by all the rest, which he bore as patiently as he could, not telling them the true reason why he gave his consent to the departure of his Servant. And that which help'd the better to disguise his intention of leaving the Country, was the trouble which was apparent in his countenance; which every one interpreted to be caus'd by his being forced to part with Sr John Berkley, when indeed it was for being constrain'd in a manner to withdraw himself, as having no other way remaining, to preserve to himself the right he had to be master of his own family, and to keep his reputation.

There was also another consideration which fortifyd very much the resolution his R. H. had taken, which proceeded from the Stories the Earle of Bristoll had told him, concerning the ill opinion which Don John had conceived of Sir John Berkley, and how far he was unsatisfied with him for being so much a Frenchman, which caus'd the Duke to apprehend, that he might haue the same opinion concerning himself; which if so, he was certainly to expect no extraordinary good usage in that Country. And therfore all things consider'd, his R. H. was fully determin'd to persist in the resolution he had taken to withdraw; and accordingly every thing was prepar'd in order to the putting his design in execution, in the manner following, as it is related by the Duke himself in his Originall Memoires of the ensuing year.

PART III.

1656.
Having concerted his retreat wth S^r Jo: Berkley, Char: Berkley and Harry Jermyn, the better to cover his design, he declares his consent to let the first go. *Ibid.* p. 34.

He bears patiently the reproches of his Sister and blame of all his freinds, for abandonning his Servant. *Ibid.*

E. of Bristoll's Stories of the ill opinion Don John had of S^r Jo: Berkley, and the apprehension that Don John might haue the same opinion of himself, confirm'd his R. H. in his resolution of withdrawing. O$_R$: M$_{EM}$: P. 3. p. 35.

PART
III.

1657.
Sir Jo: Berkley
parts from
Bruges the 2 or
3 of January,
and 2 or 3 days
after, the Duke
follows him.
OR: MEM:
P. 3. p. 35.
He is allarm'd
by a message
from his Sister,
the morning of
his departure.
Ibid.

ON THE two or three of January 1657, Sir John Berkley
went from Bruges, with order to stay for the Duke at
Flushing, and within two or three days after, his R. H. follow'd
him. On the morning of his departure, rising somewhat earlyer
then his ordinary houre, he call'd up his Brother the Duke of
Glocester, as if he had intended to go out a shooting: But before
he was ready, his Sister sent up to him to desire, that ere he
went abroad, he would come and speak with her; which
alarm'd him not a litle, and caus'd him to imagine, that she had
some suspition of what he intended to do, and would endeavour
to disswade him from it. With this beleef he went to see her,
and had not the room been somewhat dark (she being in bed)
she could not but haue taken notice of the disorder in which
he was, when he first enter'd into her chamber, and by it haue
suspected his design. But so soon as she began to speak to him,
he was freed from his apprehensions; her busines being only
to advertize him of a quarrell which she beleev'd was betwixt
two of their Servants, that so his R. H. having notice of it, might
prevent their fighting. After this he went out from her, not

The Duke im-
parts nothing
of his design
to his Sister,
and why.
OR: MEM:
P. 3 p: 36.

having said any thing to make her suspect the least part of his
intention; for thō he was assured that she was too much his
freind to haue hinder'd his departure, in case she could not
haue prevail'd upon him with her arguments to stay; yet even
for her own sake, he would not acquaint her with his design, as
being apt to beleeve that she would haue had her share in the
advising part of it; so that if she should now happen to be
question'd concerning it, she might be able to affirme with
truth, that she was wholly ignorant of his purpose to go
away.

He waits on
the King
before he go's.
Ibid.

Before the Duke gott on horseback, he went and waited on
his Ma.^{ty}, and from thence after a short stay, he and his Brother

tĥe Duke of Glocester went out of the Town, taking their way
towards Sluyce, for his R. H. pretended to shoot in that side of
the Country. He took along with him Harry Jermyn and
Charles Berkley, with two or three of his under servants, in
whom he had the greatest confidence, leaving behind him Sir
Henry Bennett and Harry Killigrew, whom he durst not trust,
with all the rest of his family. And being come to a Village
near Sluyce, he pretended to his Brother, that (*he*) was to meet
some body who was come out of England about affaires of
great importance, and had appointed to speak privatly
with him at Sluyce ; That if he would go to the Downes,
and shoot for an hour or two, he would return and find him out;
but that in case he came not according to the time he nam'd,
he desir'd he would stay no longer for him, but return to
Bruges, where he intended to be also before the shutting of the
Gates.

His R. H. having thus parted with his Brother, he went to
Sluyce, where he made no stay ; but passing directly through
the Town, went over into the Isle of Cassant, where leaving his
horses, with orders to follow him, he reached Flushing before
night. There he found Sir John Berkley, and went on the same
night to Middlebourg. Being in that Town he resolved to
make· what hast he could to Vtrecht, having at that time a
purpose of going into France by the way of Germany, to
avoid passing through any of the Spanish Dominions. But
it then happening to freeze very hard, he was forced to take his
way by Tervere, Ziriczee, Bommene, Sommerdyke, Helvoet
Sluys, the Briel and Maesland Sluys ; the ordinary (*way*) being
all shutt up with ycé.

To Tervere therfore the Duke came next morning, where
finding a lusty French Ship which was ready to· set sayle for
France, Sir John Berkley propos'd their embarking upon her,
that by venturing that way they might save so great a journy

VOL. I.   P P

PART
III.

1657.
He pretends to
go a shooting
and carrys the
Duke of Glo-
cester abroad
with him.

Having parted
with his
Brother near
Sluyce, he
went that night
to Flushing wᵗʰ
Harry Jermyn
and Ch: Berk-
ley, where he
joyn'd Sʳ John
Berkley and
went on to
Middlebourg.
Ibid. p. 37.

Next Morning
to Tervere,
where he's
advis'd to
profite of a
French Ship
that was there

PART
III.
——————
1657.
ready to Sayle
to France, but
is dissaaded
by Charles
Berkley.
Or: Mem:
P. 3: p. 37.

as they had to take by land. But Charles Berkley oppos'd
this Counsell, by representing the danger of the Sea at that time
of the year, and the hazard his R. H. should run, in case they
mett with any English man of Warr; *whose custome it was to*
search any stranger's Ships, to see if they had any English Seamen
on board of them, and if they found any such, to take them out:
and thō it might so happen, that they should not know the
Duke, yet they might carry them all away, as being their
Countrymen.

The Duke
continues his
journy to
Holland.
Ibid. p. 38.

These reasons prevail'd with his Royall Highness, and so he
continu'd on his journy; and imbarking there on an ordinary
passage-boat, he got that night to Ziricksee, and from thence
by waggon to Bommene: And the same night going on board
again of a small passage-boat, he landed next morning on the
Island of Sommerdyke, and crossing it in waggons, embark'd

In crossing in
an open boat
to Helvoet
Sluys, he is in
great danger,
and like to be
driven out to
Sea with the
yce. *Ibid.*

once more at the Town it self for Helvoet Sluys. He went in
an open boat which was the last that ventur'd over, the water
being then almost chock'd up with yce; and the hazard was
thought to be so great, that all the people of the Town came
out and stood upon the shore to see them go: And indeed there
was so much yce, that they had great difficulty in getting over,
and they once fear'd they should be driven out to Sea; But at
length after much struggling, they landed about a league below
Helvoet Sluys, and the same day reach'd the Brill. The next

Sir Jo: Berkley
is sent from
Maesland
Sluys to the
Hague, to
know if his
R. H. might
Stay privatly
in the Country
for some few
days.
Or: Mem:
P. 3: p. 39.
The Duke
continues his
journy to
Vtrecht. *Ibid.*

day they pass'd over to Maesland Sluys, from whence his R. H.
sent Sir John Berkley to the Hague, to know if he might haue
the liberty of staying privatly in the Country for some few
days, without having any notice taken of him. Sir John, when
he was sent on this busines, had directions to follow the
Duke to Vtrecht, whither his Royall Highness continued on
his way; and they (*then*) after his arriuall there, Sir John
Berkley came thither to him, and inform'd him, that he might
stay in safety according to his desire.

The Duke continued in that Town a day or two ; during which time, considering again what resolution it were best for him to take, .at length he concluded on writing to his· Ma[ty], to inform him of his reasons for absenting himself, and to continue therabout, till the Messenger he sent with his letter should return ;· and not to pursue his intended journy into France, in case he should receive a good answer. · In the mean time that he might ·be more privat, he went to Zuleystein, where he was very kindly entertain'd by the master of it ; who was a very honest Gentleman of the Duke's acquaintance, and a natural Son to Henry Prince of Orange, who ·had marryd Mrs. Killegrew a maid of honour to the Princesse Royall, some years before.   Having stayd with him a week, he was invited by another acquaintance Mr. Vandernatt to Dieren, where he was housekeeper to the Prince of Orange.

While the Duke was there, Mr. Vandernatt was invited to a wedding ·at Amsterdam; and his R. H. taking only Harry Jermyn along with him, went thither in his company, being sure that nobody there would know him, and having a desire to see that Town again, and to haue the divertissement of seeing the ceremonys of a wedding in it, which are very formall, and continue for severall days : But having seen enough to satisfy his curiosity in two days space, he return'd to Dieren, and from thence to Zuleystein, where he had the first account of what had pass'd at Bruges, on the occasion of his departure thence.

So soon as they saw the Duke of Glocester return'd, and that his R. H. came not back by the shutting of the ports, they presently suspected the truth of the whole matter. Vpon which his Ma[ty] the next day dispatch'd away the Marquess of Ormonde after him into Zealand ; who, upon his arriuall there, finding the Duke was gone forward into Holland, return'd and gave his Ma[ty] an account of it. Some days after, the King

PART III.

1657.
From Vtrecht he writes to the King, and resolves to wait his Ma[ty] answer, before he pursu'd his intended journy into France. *Ibid.*

He is invited to Dieren by Mr. Vandernatt. Or: Mem: P: 3. p. 39.

From Dieren he go's with M[r]. Vandernatt to see a wedding at Amsterdam. *Ibid.*

PART
III.

1657.

hearing that his R. H. had thoughts of going into France by the
way of Colen (*Cologne*) sent Coll. Blague to meet him there, and
perswade him to return, with offers of giving him all sort of
Satisfaction. But afterwards, finding by the Duke's letters
that he had then no such intentions, but was still in Holland,
his Ma^{ty} again dispatched the Marquess of Ormonde to him, to
offer severall things in order to his return ; but not with proposals altogether so satisfactory, as those which had been sent
before by Collonell Blague.

The Duke
receives the
King's letters
by My Lord of
Ormonde at
Zuleystein,
and is so well
Satisfied with
them, that he
presently took
his resolution
to return to
Bruges.
Or: Mem:
P. 3. p. 41.

My Lord of Ormonde found the Duke at Zuleystein newly
return'd from Dieren ; and, delivering his Maties letters to him,
gave his R. H. so much satisfaction, that he told him he resolv'd
next day to go so far in his way to Bruges, as Breda. The
substance of the message was, That his Ma^{ty} assur'd him, if he
would return, not only himself but all his Servants should be
treated with all kindness, so that he should haue no further
occasion to complain ; That as to Sir John Berkley, for the
present he should stay in Holland, but that within a month, he
might haue free leave to come and wait upon his R. H. again,
and that things past should be forgotten.

His R. H.
returns to
Bruges, and is
receiv'd very
kindly by the
King.
Or: Mem:
P. 3: p. 41.
He dismisses
Harry Kille-
grew and S^r
Hen: Bennett
from his
Seruice. Ibid.

Being come to Breda, his R. H. made no stay in that Citty,
but the next day continued on his journy for Bruges, where he
was received very kindly by the King. And now immediatly
after his return, being inform'd how disrespectfully Harry
Killegrew had spoken of him, and how ill he had behav'd
himself during his absence, he dismissed him from his seruice ;
and also Sir Henry Bennett, who soon after was sent Enuoye
into Spain by his Ma^{ty}, to make him amends for the place of
Secretary, which he had lost with the Duke : so that now his
R. H. had none left in his family, but such as were absolutly
his own.

Sir Jo: Berkley
returns to

About a month after this Sir John Berkley return'd to

Bruges, according to what had been agreed, and not long after-
wards, at the Duke's request he was made a Lord. About the
same time the Princesse Royall left Bruges, and went for
Holland, and at the beginning of the Spring, his Ma^{ty} and all his
Court remov'd to Bruxelles. Where when the Duke arriv'd, he
found that to be true which had been told him before by Father
Peter Talbott a Jesuite, who was then very intimate with Don
Alfonso de Cardennas, which was, That Don John had never
said any such things to the Earle of Bristoll, concerning his
R. H. and the Lord Berkley, as the said Earle had reported to
him ; That it was true, ill offices had been endeavour'd to be
done to both, which at first had made some impression ; but
that Don John, and more especially the Marquis of Caracena,
and Don Alfonzo de Cardennas, were soon satisfied of the
untruth of those suggestions, which consequently had prov'd
of advantage both to his R. H. and to the Lord Berkley, and
had done no good to the Earle of Bristoll.

This with other indiscretions of his, caus'd the two Spanish
Ministers not only to loose the opinion they had formerly conceived of him, but also to be very much unsatisfied wth him,
and that not without occasion. For at his first coming into the
Country, being very perfect in the Spanish tongue, and
exceeding dextrous in all the arts of insinuation, and gaining
the favour of great men (thō not of keeping them) and being
also employd by his Ma^{ty} about most of his affaires, he wrought
himself very far into the good opinion and favour of Don John,
and into the esteem of the other two. Which he finding, was
not yet satisfyd ; but by flattering Don John, and feeding
his humour, (who was somewhat curious in Astrology) by casting
his nativity, and talking perpetually to him of Crowns and
Scepters, by which pleasing kind of discourses, he suppos'd
his credit to increase with him, and his interest to be greater

1657.
Court, and at
the Duke's
request is made
a Lord. *Ibid.*
The P^{ss} of
Orange returns
to Holland, and
the King and
Court remove
to Bruxelles.
Ibid.
The Duke at
Bruxelles finds
out the false-
hood of some
of the E. of
Bristoll's
stories. *Ibid.*

E. Bristoll
by his indis-
cretions loses
himself with
the Spanish
Ministers, and
how.

then really it was, So that he endeavour'd to advance himself
to the management of the affaires of that Country, even to
the other Ministers; which, they perceiving, soon put an end
to those his vain imaginations, and made so true a picture
of him to Don John, that he also, either out of prudence,
seeing the jealousy which the other two had of him, or that he
was really convinced of the character which they had given of
him, gave over his conversation, and would haue no more to
do with him.

Thus the Earle of Bristoll fell again, as he had done before
in other Countries, from the hopes he had conceived of being
at the head of affaires, into his first circumstances. And now
since wee haue mention'd this particular, wee shall also relate
here, how the Earle lost himself in France according to the
account the Duke had thereof at the first bound.

A particular
account of the
E. of Bristoll's
behaviour in
France, and
how he lost
himself there
also by his im-
prudence, and
ingratitude to
the Cardinal.
Or: Mem:
P. 3: p. 43.

At his coming into France, which was about the first warr of
Paris, or somewhat before it, in the year 1649; he, as became
one who was obliged to quitt his Country for the sake of his
Loyalty, follow'd the Court, and in a skirmish against the
Parisians, where the P^ce of Condé was present, neer the Bois de
Vincennes, very fortunatly for himself, receiv'd a shott through
the thigh, upon which accident more notice and care was taken
of him, then otherwise had been: and being a man of quality,
and recommended by the Queen of England, he had an Imployment given him in the Army; about the year 1651 he was made
a Lieu^t Generall, and somewhat before the breaking out of
the Second Warr of Paris in 1652, when the Duke of Nemours
had brought some troopes out of Flanders to joyne the Princes
Army, passing the Seyne at Mante, the Duke of Sully for
giving passage to them, was turn'd out of that Government, and
the Earle of Bristoll put into his place: which sufficiently
shew'd the great trust and confidence which the Cardinal

repos'd in him, by giving him so considerable and so profitable
a Command.

That summer, in July, the Court went to Pontoise, and continued there, and at Mante, for the most part, till their returne to Paris. And soon after their arrivall to Pontoise, the Cardinal went from thence out of France: Not long after this, some of the Court who were desirous of keeping him away, endeavour'd to set up a third party, the better to satisfy themselves in that design, and gave themselves the name of True Frenchmen; pretending they were against the returne of the Cardinal for no other reason, then that they were sensible that whenever it happen'd, it would be of exceeding prejudice to the King's affaires. This pretence being very plausible, many considerable persons of the Court, and more particularly those of the long robe, were concern'd in it; and amongst the rest, the Earle of Bristoll, forgetting not only that he was a Stranger, but also the obligations which he had to the Cardinal, ran along with those people, and was so indiscreet as one day to give the Queen this very advice, Of not permitting the Cardinal ever to return : Upon which he wholly lost himself both with the Queen and Cardinal; wheras had he continued steady in their interests, as he ought in reason to haue done, and only obeyd, without taking upon him to advise, he had certainly in a short time been made Mareshall of France: in stead of which, upon the Cardinal's return, at the end of that long Campagne, his Government was taken from him, both his Regiments (for the raising of which he had received mony in the summer) were reformed, and no recompence given to him, as was to others. And upon occasion of an indiscreet action done by him, either out of the love which he had, or thought he had, for the Duchess of Chatillon, he retir'd soon after into the South of France; but whither of his own free motion, or by order of the

PART
III.

1657.

Court, is uncertain. There he liv'd privatly till the Campagne of the Seige of Pavie in the Milanoise, at which Seige he seru'd as Lieu^t Generall under the Duke of Modena, Generall of the French troopes in that Country, and the next year went to his Ma^ty in Flanders.

But to returne where wee left. The Time was now drawing on for the next Campagne, which was his R. H. first Campagne in the Spanish Seruice, wherof he himself gives the following Account.

THE DUKE'S FIFTH CAMPAGNE,

AND THE FIRST HE SERV'D IN THE SPANISH ARMY.

======

AMONGST the preparations for this CAMPAGNE, that which the King my Brother and I did cheifly labour for, was the making up of his Maties six Regiments of foot ; wherof one was English, one Scotch, and the rest Irish, which were compleated to above two thousand men, all of them drawn out of France, which was a double seruice to the Spaniards. And if they had thought fitt to perform what they had promis'd, which was but a pistole a head, and armes for every man that came over, with good usage afterwards, these troopes would certainly haue increased to twice that number at their going into the feild. But notwithstanding this pcice of Seruice in bringing them from France, and the facilitating the Spaniards retaking St Guilain at the latter end of winter, while the King was yet at Bruges, by the intelligence which his Ma^ty had there with the Irish Regiments garrison'd in that Town, without which, it had been impossible to haue taken it at that Season of the year; yet they had conceiv'd such jealousy that the King's troopes were too numerous, that they gave them all manner of discouragment : for which reason their numbers could not be increased, and indeed it was all could be done, to keep them as strong as when I march'd them into the feild at first, to joyne the Spanish Army.

PART
III.
_____
1757.
Two thousand
of the King's
Subjects Serve
under the
Duke in
Flanders this
Campagne.
OR: MEM:
P. 3. p. 45.
They had been
double that
number, if the
Spaniards had
not given them
all manner of
discourag-
ment. *Ibid.*

PART
III.

1657.
The jealousy
of the Spa-
niards foment-
ed by the P^ce
of Condé.
On. Mem.
P. 3. p. 46.

This jealousy of theirs was fomented by the Prince of Condé, who had so lately gott the better of Monsr. de Lorraine, and procur'd him to receive the usage which was known to every one, therby to make himself more necessary to the Spaniards: so he apprehended, that if the King's troopes should become too considerable (foot being what the Spaniards wanted most) he himself might in his turne receive the same usage; and therfore thō he liv'd in all appearance well with the King, yet he endeavour'd all he could to increase the jealousy of the Spaniards, and to hinder by all óther means the growing of our troopes.

These jealou-
sies occasion'd
in part by the
unreasonable
proposalls of
the E. of
Bristoll.
On: Mem:
P. 3. p. 47.

There was also another motive to their jealousies, which was, that the Earle of Bristoll had made unreasonable propositions to them, when he was first imployd by his Majesty to negociate with Don John, concerning the forming of a body of men for him in Flanders: For he, being sent from the King who was then at Bruges to treat of that affaire, talk'd of nothing less then an Army of ten thousand horse and foot, with a train of Artillery proportionable; which so allárm'd the Spanish Ministers, as would haue render'd it altogether impossible to be effected if design'd, And by this extravagant proposall, he was so far from advancing his M^{aties} affaires, that he gave the Spaniards occasion to be jealous of our grouth.

The Duke
disabuses the
Spanish
Minister, con-
cerning all the
Stories rais'd
of him. *Ibid.*

While I stayd at Bruxelles, I satisfied them so well, concerning all the Stories which had been rais'd of me, that Don John and the Ministers had no ill opinion of me, and the Prince of Condé liv'd with me very civilly. And now before my going to the Army, the Earle of Bristoll procur'd his Ma^{ty} to do a thing, which in itself was plausible enough, but the intention of it was to do me a displeasure: It was the ingaging

E. Bristoll
procures of the
King, to make
M^r. de Marsin
Lieu^t Gen^{all} of
all his Maties
forces, and

Monsr. de Marsin into his seruice, and making him Lieu^t Generall of all his forces, which either were or should be rais'd; with an intention, that he should be immediatly under me both

in Flanders and in England, in case any opportunity should
call us thither : So that the King being above me, and Monsr.
de Marsin the next under me, I might haue the less power and
authority, or rather be made a meer Cypher. And to make
him the more absolutly his, the Lord Bristoll prevail'd also
with his Ma^{ty} about the end of that year, to recompence him
before hand for seruices to be done in England, by making
him Knight of the Garter: And had not the Chancellor hinder'd
it, he had also obtain'd for him (*himself*) the quality of an
English Earle, which had yet been more extraordinary then
the first. Thō truely the man of himself was a very good
Officer as any I knew, and had the reputation of being so
bȯth in France and Flanders, and in all places where he had
serv'd ; yet rewarding him before hand with such extraordinary
marks of honour, was a thing unusuall.

P A R T
III.

1657.
Knight of the
Garter, in view
of future
seruices. *Ibid.*

The season of the year now call'd us into the feild; and the
beginning of this Campagne prov'd very glorious to the Prince
of Condé, For as he was at la Bussiere upon the Sambre,
which is distant about sixteen or eighteen leagues from
Cambray, being the place appointed by him for the Rendezvous
of all his horse, where he was to view them before their coming
to the generall Rendezvous ; he had word brought to him, that
the French Army under the command of Monsr. de Turenne
and Monsr. de la Ferté, had beseiged Cambray, which place
he knew was very ill provided of a garrison ; wherupon he
immediatly marched away, to endeavour the releeving it
before the French could haue intelligence of his coming, or
haue So perfected their Lines, as to hinder him from entering
into the place and releeving it. And he order'd his march So
exactly, that he came thither in the night, and found very
litle opposition : For thō the French were on horseback, and
ready to receive him, yet he charg'd vigourously throw' the
two Lines of horse which he encounter'd in his way, who were

A braue
action of the
P^{ce} of Condé
in releeving
Cambray, be-
seig'd by M^r.de
Turenne, and
la Ferté.
Or: Mem.
P. 3. p. 48.

not able to resist so great a body as he had with him; especially considering that it was his busines only to break through them, and force his passage into the Town. Which he soon perform'd, and with very litle loss gott to the Counterscarpe, and so was received into the Town with great joy by the Count de Salazar the Governour; who so litle expected such a releif, and was so much surpris'd at it, that the Prince stood waiting at the Palisade for a long time before he was admitted. And indeed the Governour had reason to be overjoyd at this succour, for besides that he was no great Soldier, his garrison, as I said, was very weak; in so much that if it had not been releived in so criticall a juncture, he had abandon'd the Town and only maintain'd the Citadell.

Reason why
Cambray was
so ill provided.
OR: MEM:
P. 3. p. 49.

I beleeve this was the only time, when that place was so ill provided of men; and the reason of it was, That the Spaniards having had notice, that Cromwell was to send six thousand foot that year to the Seruice of the French, they expected that some maritime Town of theirs would be attacked in that Campagne; which caus'd them to fill such places with their men, and consequently to leave their more inland Townes but thinly man'd : of which the Cardinal being advertis'd, he thought it now a proper time to attack Cambray, which he had more desire to take then any other, having, as I haue been inform'd, a kind of longing to be made Prince and Bishop of it; and therfore order'd the two Mareshalls to undertake that Seige, well hoping they would haue better fortune in that attempt, then the Count d'Harcourt had some years before. And they had certainly carryd it, but for this accident : For had not the Prince of Condé been at the Rendezvous before mention'd, but continued at Bruxelles, none of his Officers durst haue undertaken it without him; and the Spaniards would haue consum'd so much time in considering, and debating the methods of releeving it, that the French would haue leasure to haue finish'd their Lines, and then the place had certainly been lost.

PART
III.
1657.

And as the Count Salazar was surpriz'd to find himself thus unexpectedly releived, so were both the French Generalls, especially Monsr de Turenne; who depending on the usuall delays of the Spaniards, and their slow execution of what they so leysurly resolve, thought it not possible to haue had any of their troopes upon him So Suddainly : But having learn'd from the confession of some prisoners then taken, both the number and quality of their troopes, and who commanded them, he thought it not convenient to make any longer Stay ; but rais'd the Seige the next morning, and sent to the Court to give them notice of what had happen'd, and to receive their directions for what was next to be attempted.

M.deTurenne
raises theSeige
of Cambray.
Ob: Mem:
P. 3. p. 50.

So soon as Monsr de Turenne was drawn off from Cambray, the Prince reinforced it with such a number of men as was sufficient to secure it from running the like hazard that year, and then return'd himself to Bruxelles ; sending the rest of his troopes to the generall Rendezvous, which was near Mons in Haynault.

The P^{ce} of
Condé having
reinforced
Cambray, re-
turns himself
to Bruxelles,
and sends his
troopes to the
generall Ren-
dezvous near
Mons.
Ibid. p: 51.

This action of his obliged the French to alter their measures, and caus'd them to divide their Army, and lay aside the thought of undertaking any considerable Seige in that Campagne. They sent the Mareshall de la Ferté to take in Montmedy in Luxembourg, which thō it was but a litle place, yet was strong and of great importance: And for Monsr de Turenne, he with the other part of the Army drew down towards the Sea side, that the English foot might joyn him the more easily ; which when they had done, he march'd back again to obserue the motion of our Army.

M^r. de la
Ferté beseiges
Montmedy.
Ob: Mem:
P. 3. p. 51.
M.deTurenne
observes the
motion of the
Spaniards'
Army. Ibid.

Wee were by this time drawn to our generall Rendezvous near Mons ; and on the 19th of June wee march'd with all our Army to Mierpottry upon the Sambre, somewhat above Thuin.

The Spanish
Army marches
from their
general ren-
dezvous the
19th of June.
Ibid.

PART
III.

1657.
They order
their marches
as to make
beleeve they
intend to
releeve Mont-
medy. *Ibid.*

But their
intention was
to fall back
and Surprise
Calais.
Ibid. p: 52.

On the 22ᵈ wee pass'd that River, and the next day wee camp'd
by Philippeville ; and marching that way through our own
Country, as if our design was to releeve Montmedy, Monsʳ.
de Turenne with his Army made great hast to get thither
before us : but wee had no such intention, our design being
only to amuse him and beget in him that opinion ; and by
that means to get the Start of him, and marching backward
suddainly to fall on Calais, which he (we) hop'd to carry in few
houres, having knowledge of a weak part of it by which wee
thought wee should easily be masters of it.

It was not only at this time that the Spaniards had taken
that Enterprize into their consideration ; for they had being long
designing it even before the Arch Duke left Flanders, who in
his time had sent Engeneers disguis'd thither, and they had
discover'd this weak part of it ; but at this time they had layd
their project so well, that nothing could be better design'd, So

The project of
Surprising
Calais, carryd
on with great
Secrecy and
conduct and
all probability
of Success.
Oꜱ: Mᴇᴍ:
P. 3. p: 52.

that they had all the probability imaginable of effecting their
purpose ; for it was manag'd and carryd with so much secresy
and conduct, that the Enemy had not the least suspicion of it.
When wee march'd from Mons wee had left such a body of
horse behind, that with drawing out some foot from the
neighbouring garrisons, they were sufficient to perform the first
part of the undertaking : And now being advanc'd so far on
our way towards Montmedy as Philippeville, and seeing by
Mʳ. de Turenne's march, that he beleev'd wee would endeavour
to releeve that place, Wee alter'd our Course, and on the 26ᵗʰ

Don John, Pᶜᵉ
of Condé, and
Caracena,
march before
with the horse;
the Duke
and M. de
Marsin follow
with the foot.
Oꜱ: Mᴇᴍ:
P. 3. p. 53.
The Pᶜᵉ de
Ligny pitch'd

began our march directly towards Calais.

Don John, the Prince of Condé and Caracena, march'd
away with the horse the nearest way, and left me and Monsʳ
de Marsin with the foot to follow after as fast as wee were able,
the baggage and cannon being order'd to march more within
our own Country. The Prince de Ligny was the man pitch'd
upon for the execution of this Enterprise, and to haue the first

and maine part of it. In order to which, he was sent away the day before to those troopes weé had left behind for that seruice.

P A R T
III.

1657.
upon to
execute the
Enterprize.
Ibid.
The Duke's
severall
marches with
ye foot.
Or. Mem.
P. 3. p. 53.

The first night of my march, I reach'd Tilly with the foot, the next day being the 27th the Suburbs of Mons; the* 28th Briffeuil, the 29th, passing the Sehald at Tournay, I came to Pont a Tresin, from whence on the 31st wee march'd by the walls of Lisle, and passing the Lys at Armentieres, wee quarter'd at Niepkerk. The next day being the first of July, wee went to Hasebrouck, and the 2^d to Arques, which is within a league of St Omer; where when I arriv'd early in the morning, thinking yet befóre night to haue reach'd Calais, I receiv'd a letter from Don John which gave me notice of the miscarriage of the Enterprise, with orders for me to stay at Arques till I should hear farther from him: The account of which ill Success in short is this.

Account of the
manner how
Calais was to
have been
Surpris'd; and
how it came
to miscarry.
Ibid. p: 54.

The Prince de Ligny march'd from Gravelines as soon as it was night, to put in execution the design which had been so well contriv'd for the surprise of Calais; which he was to attempt at low water, by seizing first that part of the Town without the walls, adjoyning to the Key: for had he been once master of it, the place could not haue held out above twelve hours, the garrison being weak, as well as the Town on that side of it. But he coming half an hour too late, the water was then so high that it was impossible for him to pass, so that he was constrain'd to draw back; having done nothing, but only given the Town a hott alarm, and by his coming along by the Sea Side to the very place where he should haue enter'd,

---

* It is extremely difficult to follow his Royall Highness, and the Secretary in their orthography of the Names of Places, so as to preserve any thing like correctness. The Duke's line of March is thus described in the French Memoir which James the Second sent to the Cardinal de Bouillon: *Le vingt-huit à Bruxelles, le vingt-neuf ayant passé l'Escaut à Tournai, il vint camper à Pont-à-Bouvines: le trent-un il marcha le long des murailles de Lille, passa la Lys à Armentieres et campa à Nieukerke.* — EDITOR.

therby discover'd to the Governour the weakness of that part; who being sensible how narrowly he had escap'd, immediatly put that side into such a condition as never to be surpriz'd again : And thus wee fail'd of our design, having made so great a march to so litle purpose.

About the 4ᵗʰ of July, our horse and foot came together at Quiernes (*Querne*) within a league of Ayre, and within a day or two after, our cannon and baggage came also up to us. On the 6ᵗʰ wee march'd to Bouré close to Lillers, where wee continned for some days. About the 12ᵗʰ wee went to Broüay, the next day to Lens, and the day following to Roeux (*Reu*) upon the Scarpe, a litle below Arras. On the 15ᵗʰ to Sauchy-Cauchy betwixt that and Cambray. At this quarter wee stayd till the 21ˢᵗ, and then march'd to Marcoin.

All this while that wee were marching up and down to no manner of. purpose, Monsʳ de la Ferté continued his Seige at Montmedy; which being a place of strength, and having good men in it, made a brave defence, and held out longer then was expected by the French. In the mean time, Monsʳ de Turenne was either obseruing our motions, or not far from Montmedy, to hinder any releif from being put into it : So that wee had no action during the forepart of this Campagne, but wee had marching enough; for from Marcoin, wee march'd to le Catelet on the 27ᵗʰ, the next day to Feruaques, and the 29ᵗʰ to Origny upon the Oyse; where staying but one day wee march'd to Wadencour (*Eglancourt*) near Guise, and there wee camp'd till the 8ᵗʰ of August, when wee march'd to Feron, the next day to Macon near Chimay, and the 10ᵗʰ to Amblain (*Aublin*) about a league short of Marienbourg.

At that place wee had notice of the taking of Montmedy (which had been so well defended that they began not to parley, till the Enemy had lodg'd themselves in the Bastion and rais'd a battery of six guns to batter the cutting off) and that Monsʳ.

de Turenne was march'd towards Flanders, there to undertake
some Seige. Vpon which intelligence, wee began our march
that way on the 14th, and never stop'd till wee came on the 20th
of the same month to Calonne upon the Lys, which is within a
league of St Venant, before which place Monsr. de Turenne was
sat down, ere wee could arriue thither ; and had so advanced
his Lines, that both in consideration of their strength, and our
own weakness, it was not expedient for us to attempt the
releeving of that Town, by attacking their Lines, but to try what
wee could do by cutting off their provisions, and endeavouring
to hinder four or five hundred waggons, which were at
Bethune, from bringing them bread and ammunition for the
carrying on of the Seige; of which waggons wee had notice,
that they were to march with their Convoy the next day from
Bethune to their Camp, which were distant from each other
about three leagues.

Vpon this intelligence, it was resolv'd that wee should march
the next morning with our whole Army, and post ourselves at
Montbernenson, (by which Village the Convoy was of necessity
to pass) that thereby wee might hinder its passage to the Enemys
Camp: And because the place where wee then lay, as well as
the formost part of the ground, over which wee were to march
the following day, was an inclos'd Country, wee had commanded
men appointed to march with tooles at the head of each
Regiment, to make passages for them ; so that when wee came
out upon the plaine, which was within cannon shott of the
Enemies Line, wee might soon be put in battell. The next
Morning, being the 22d, wee were in a readiness to march
presently after Sun rise, in pursuance of what had been deter-.
min'd the day before; yet wee sett not forwards till almost
noon : What was the reason of this delay I cannot imagine, it
being a thing easy enough to be foreseen, that by our Stay wee
might run the hazard of losing our opportunity, and give leisure

Order of the
march of the
Spanish Army.
Or; Mem:
P. 3: p: 58.

The Duke
marches at the
head of the
foot, per-
forming that
day the office
of Mestre de
Camp Gene-
rall. Ibid.

The Duke
perceiving the
Convoy draws
up his foot in
battell. Ibid.

The Duke
advertises the
Pᶜᵉ of Ligny
that he had
but to march
up with his
horse,and take
all the Convoy.
Or; Mem:
P. 3. P. 58.
The Pᶜᵉ of
Ligny answers,
that he durst
not fall on
without Don
Joᵗ: order.
Ibid.

The Duke
gallops up to
him and urges
him not to lose
So faire an
opportunity,

to the Convoy to get into the Line. I am sure, some were not
wanting to put Don John in mind of it, and myself for one;
but wee began our march never the sooner for that advice.

At length somewhat before noon, wee began to march, and in
battalia; The Prince de Ligny (*Ligne*) Genˡˡ of the horse at the
head of the right wing, the Prince of Condé at the left, and
myself (whom Don John had desir'd that day to perform the
office of Mestre de Camp Generall) at the head of the foot.
As for Don John and the Marquis of Caracena, they march'd
before with their three troopes of guards, till they came within one
Closs of the plaine, and there according to their usuall custom
took their Siesta (or afternoon's Sleep). In this order wee
march'd on slowly, by reason of the inclosed Country: And when
I, who was at the head of the foot, had but one Inclosure more
to pass, before I came out into the open plaine, I perceived the
Enemies Convoy beginning to come down from Montberñenson,
and making what hast they could to get toward their Camp.
Having therfore pass'd the last hedge, I began to draw up my
foot in order of battell, as fast as they came out of the Inclo-
sures; And seeing that the Prince de Ligne was also gott into
the plaine (on my right hand which was neerest to the Enemies
Line) with four or fiue Squadrons, I sent to him to advertise
him of the approche of the Convoy, and that it was absolutly
in his hands; he having nothing more to do, then to march up
to them, and take them all, before they could get to the Line,
they having only three Squadrons of horse to guard them : To
which he return'd this answer, That he had observ'd all this,
as well as myself, and was not ignorant how easy it was to
intercept that Convoy, but he durst not fall upon it, without
order from Don John or the Marquis of Caracena.

Vpon this I gallop up to him, and urg'd him as earnestly as
I could, not to lose so faire an opportunity, by being so scrupulous : but he replyd, That I knew not how punctuall the

Spaniards were; for should he attacque the Enemy without
order, it might cost him his head; especially if he should not
succeed in his attempt, or should receiue any litle affront. To
which I answer'd, That he had no reason to apprehend any
ill success : for thō Mʳ. de Turenne should happen to draw out
some horse, yet he would nev.er venture his foot from the Line;
and that in case he should be question'd by the Spaniard for
this action, I consented to take all the blame upon myself, and
he might justly excuse himself by saying, He did it in obedience
to me, who acted that day in the quality of their Mestre de
Camp Generall. But notwithstanding all the Arguments I
could use, I could not prevaile with him to charge them. Thus
that opportunity was lost; for, while this dispute lasted, the
Convoy made what diligence they could, as perceiving the
greatness of their danger, and past by us.

At length when the busines was past retriving, and that the
foremost of the waggons were already enter'd within the Lines of
the Enemy, the three Troopes of Guards came up to the Prince
de Ligny, with orders to him to fall upon the Convoy, which
immediatly he did; adding to them only his own Troop of
Guards, and I likewise sent mine along with them. The four
first went on so fast and so disorderly (having at their head
the Count de Colmanar, a young unexperienced man, nephew
to the Marquis de Caracena) that had the Enemies three
Squadrons which brought up the reer of their waggons stood
their ground, they must haue beaten them. But Berkley the
Captain of my Guards with his Troop, seeing their errour,
follow'd them in good order, which sav'd them from receiving
an affront: for when our men had charg'd and beaten those
Squadrons, they pursued them as disorderly and with as much
heat as they had before done, when first they advanced against
them ; so that some of them were enter'd into the Enemies
Line, and ingaged pell mell amongst them, they having not had

PART
III.

1657.
offring to take
the blame on
himself: but
could not pre-
vaile on him to
charge. Ibid.

Orders are
brought at last
to the Pᶜᵉ de
Ligny, to fall
on when it was
too late.
Oⁿ MEM:
P. 3. p. 61.

The Duke
sends his
Troop of
Guards along,
who by their
good order
save the other
4 Troopes from
receiving an
affront. Ibid.

P A R T
III.

1657.

time to shutt their barriere; But they came off as fast again as they came on, and stop'd not till they were gott behind my Troop of Guards, which by that time were advanced within muskett shott of the Line, and there they rallyd. After they had put themselves in order, they were grown cool enough to let my men bring up the Reer, without offering to take the post of honour from them, as they might haue done.

In this manner they all drew off and joyn'd our Army, which by that time was all gott out upon the plaine, and drawn up in battell, within cañon shott of the Enemies Line; where having stayd some time, wee drew a litle back, and camp'd upon Montbernenson. And so escap'd the Convoy, getting into their Camp, without the loss of one single Cart or Waggon, only losing some few men, who were kill'd or taken by the Guards; of which number was the Marquis de Renty, a man of quality, who dyd of his wounds some few days after, and one Tiernen or Quirnen (*Quiernèux*) who commanded the Regiment de Gesures.

The Conuoy
scapes and
gets into the
Enemies Camp
without the
loss of a single
waggon.
ORIG: MEM:
P. 3. p. 61.

The same evening after the Convoy had escap'd, and that wee were drawing off to Montbernenson, I talk upon parole with the Marquis d'Humieres, and some other Officers of the French Army, who came out of their Lines on purpose to find an occasion of speaking with me. There happen'd to be with me one Tourville, who commanded a Regiment of horse in the Prince of Condé's troopes, who was to haue the guard next morning with a Spanish Regiment of horse, at the foot of the hill which I haue mention'd, and which was within cannon shott of the Lines; who having been shewn where his post was to be, and beleeving the cannon would begin to play at them as soon as day should break, ask'd an acquaintance of his what Officers of the Artillery were in the French Army? Who having nam'd them to him, Tourville desir'd that Gentleman to remember him to one of those Officers, who was his particular

The Duke
talks w^th.
the Marq.
d'Humieres
and others
with the
French Offi-
cers upon
parolle.
OR: MEM.
P. 3. p. 66.

freind, and to intreat him that next morning, when he should see two Squadrons at the bottom of the hill, he would levell his guns at that which should be on the right hand of the highway, (which was a Spanish Regiment) and not at the other on the left, that being his Regiment. And accordingly when the morning came, they playd their cannon altogether at the Spanish Regiment, killing several men and horses, before they were order'd to draw off, and plac'd not so much as one single shott into his Squadron.

I haue been since inform'd by one who knew it very well, that upon our coming to Calonne, Reynolds who commanded the English, which were sent by Cromwell, offer'd to M^r. de Turenne, that in case he would let him haue only two thousand horse, he would with them and his own six thousand foot fall upon our Army where they then lay; thinking that number of horse sufficient in that inclos'd Country, and relying on the bravery of his English foot, who had been accustom'd to hedge fighting, to supply their want of numbers: But Monsr. de Turenne refus'd to give him his consent, as not judging it practicable to hazard so great a body as they were, on so desperate an undertaking.

And now having fail'd of intercepting the Convoy, and not thinking ourselves strong enough to force their Lines, wee consider'd what course wee should take to oblige the Enemy to raise their Seige, or what place wee should attempt our selves, which wee might probably take before they could make themselves masters of St Venant: And at length it was resolv'd, That wee should immediatly march and fall upon Ardres. This was concluded at a Council of Warr the next morning, after wee came to Montbernenson; but the putting it in execution was delayd till the 25th, upon very weak reasons, at least such in my opinion: For it seems they fear'd least the Enemy not having yet begun their approches, might raise their Seige, and

P A R T
III.
1657.

Reynolds offers to M. de Turenne to fall upon the Spanish Army with his 6000 English foot, letting haue but 2000 horse, but his offer is rejected.
Or: Mem: P. 3. p. 62.

The Spaniards failing of their Enterprise upon the Convoy resolve to attack Ardres.
Ibid. p. 67.

The march to Ardres delayd till the 25th of Aug:upon very weak reasons.
Or: Mem; P. 3. p. 6^7

The Espanish
Army arriues
before Ardres
the 27ᵗʰ
August. *Ibid.*

coming after us ingage us to fight against our will. Tis certain that this deferring our design, prov'd very prejudiciable to us; for Monsr. de Turenne lost no time, but open'd the Trenches the same· night that wee came to Montbernenson, from whence wee mov'd not till the 25ᵗʰ in the morning, and on the 27ᵗʰ wee came before Ardres.

Had they
begun their
attack that
night, they had
carried the
place, but they
lost time with
an useless Line
of Circum-
vallation.
Ibid.

Coming thither in the forenoone wee made hast to secure our severall quarters, so as to hinder any releif from being put into the place, there being then in the Town not above three hundred Soldiers. Wee immediatly fell to work on our Line of Circumvallation, in making which wee spent that day and night, which in the opinion of most men was only losing so much time, as in effect wee found it; for had wee begun our attack the first night, in all probability wee had carryd the place.

The Spaniards
apt to flatter
themselves
with assurance
of Success, a
particular
instance
hereof. *Ibid.*

And here I cannot forbear to mention one particular passage, to shew how apt the Spaniards are to flatter themselves with assurance of success; for the Marquis de Caracena's Trumpetter being come from the French Army before St Venant, had given account to his Master, that the Town was not really so press'd by the Enemy as wee had thought, and as indeed it was, which the Said Marquis us'd as an argument, against our making so much hast in our Seige of Ardres: And thō I gave them an account from a footman of mine, who had been in their Camp for severall days, and who came from thence with the same Trumpetter, having also been in the Trenches, That the French were already so far advanced, that on that very day, or at farthest on the next, they would be Masters of the place, yet neither Don John nor the Marquis de Caracena, would beleeve it, but said it was impossible. This passage is So perfectly of a pcice with their former negligence, in letting the convoy pass by them at St Venant, which they might with so much ease haue taken, that I could not chuse but be very much scandaliz'd at the conduct of the Spaniards on both the occasions, as not being yet accustom'd to their methods, that being the first year I serv'd amongst them: And I remember, that complaining to the Prince of Condé of the first of these errours, the night after the Convoy was gotten into the Enemys Line, I was answer'd by him, That he well saw that I was Stranger to the proceedings of that Spanish Army, but that I was to prepare myself to see more and grosser faults committed by them, before the end of that Campagne; And so it prov'd, as the Reader will haue occasion to observe.

P A R T
III.

1657.
The Duke
very much
Scandalis'd at
these methods
of the
Spaniards,
complains of
them to the
Prince of
Condé.
Or: Mem:
P. 3. p. 63.

But that the reason of all these miscarriages may be more evident, it will not be amiss to take some View of their way of living. As for Don John, he observ'd the same formes of gravity and retirdness in the feild, as he us'd when he was at Bruxelles; as it was full as difficult to get access to him abroad, as at home: for as I observ'd before, at that very time when the Convoy above mention'd was passing by, he and the Marquis de Caracena were taking their Siesta within a feild or two of the Plaine; and thō they who were about them saw the Convoy coming down the hill, yet they durst not awake them to give them intelligence of it, which had it been done, the Convoy must of necessity haue been taken: And it appears yet more strange to me, that men of so much bravery and good sence as both Don John and the Marquis de Caracena were, should let themselves fall into those formes, which they could not but understand must occasion the loss of many opportunitys, and prove very prejudiciall to their Master's seruice, as well as to their own particular reputation.

A View of the
Spanish way
of living with
the Caracter
of Don John
and Marq. de
Caracena.
Or: Mem:
P. 3. p. 63.

The Marquis was certainly a very good Officer, had serv'd long, and pass'd through all the degrees, in so much that by his own merite he had advanced himself to the post which he then enjoyd. And had not Don John had the misfortune (as I may call it) to be educated as a Son of Spain, he had undoubtedly

PART
III.

1657.

prov'd an extraordinary man, being endued with very good naturall parts, as well as courage: But, as I sayd, neither he nor the Marquis alter'd their way of living in the feild, from what they had practis'd when they were at Bruxelles. When the Army march'd, they were never at the head of it, unless perhaps in presence of the Enemy; But by that time half the Army was march'd out of the Camp, they gott on horseback, and went at the head of their three troopes of Guards straight forward to their quarters; never so much as once minding the Army, nor going before to see wher the Camp was mark'd out for them, nor to view the place which was chosen by the Generall Officer: so that in case of an allarme or approche of an Enemy, they knew nothing of the ground, nor so much as where the main or the advanced guard were. As for Don John, he for the most part went directly to bed, how early so ever it were, when he came to his quarter; he likewise sup'd in bed, and rose not till next morning; and those days when the Army did not march, he seldom stirr'd abroad, or gott on horseback: so that the Major Generalls, in effect, did all the office of the Generalls.

But to return to our Seige of Ardres. On the 28th of August, a Councill of Warr was assembled at the Marquis de Caracena's quarter, where the resolution was to be taken where wee should begin our attackes: When wee were all mett, wee were conducted up to the top of a Tower which was there, from whence with perspective glasses wee view'd the Town, and without any other help, or information, the Councill resolv'd there of the attacks; and order'd, That the Spaniards should make theirs upon the half moon betwixt the two bastions; That I should make mine upon the bastion of the right hand, and the Prince of Condé his on the left: And no time being to be lost, it was also resolved, That, if it were possible, they should fasten their Miners to the body of the place that night.

These things being thus order'd, I, and the Prince of Condé,

The Spaniards view Ardres from a Tower wth perspective glasses, and therupon resolve their attacks.
OR: MEM:
P. 3: p. 67.
The Spaniards to attack the half moon between the 2 bastions, the Duke ye bastion of the right, and the P^ce of Condé that of the left. *Ibid.*

not thinking what wee had seen from the Tower a sufficient measure for our undertaking, went ourselves, and took a neerer view of our severall attacks. Don John, and the Marquis de Caracena went not in person, but only sent a Major de Battaille, to bring them a farther information of their own attack; it not being the custom of the Spanish Generalls to expose themselves on Such occasions. '

And now all things being in a readiness, so soon as it began to be duskish, wee fell on with our attacks, all of us at the Same time, upon a Signall, given from Dom John's quarter, never stopping till wee came to the very edge of the ditch, and indeed finding no resistance in their works, they not having men enough to man them. When wee had thus far proceeded, our 'men were set immediatly to work, to make them secure lodgments before wee adventur'd to fasten our Miners.

At my attack, it was my own Regiment commanded by the Lord Muskerry that fell on, having a Captain with some commanded men out of each of his other battallions, to strengthen them. I went not on with them to this attack, but stayd behind to see them furnish'd with fascines and what ells they wanted. And when that was done, I went down to them, having the Duke of Glocester in my Company. I found there to my satisfaction, that the Lord Muskerry had order'd all things in the best manner, and had almost finish'd a lodgement just upon the edge of the ditch, over against the point of the bastion, which commanded into the ditch on both sides of it, and had already lodged the body of the battallion in the ditch of the Raveline, which cover'd the point of the bastion.

Finding all things in so good a posture, I now thought it time to endeavour to fasten my Miner to the wall: but perceiving by moon light, that there was some water in the bottom of the ditch, I sent a Sergeant to sound the depth of it; who brought me an account, that it was very shallow, and would be of no

PART
III.

1657.
The Duke and ye P^ce of Condé go in person to take a neer view of the Severall attacks. *Ibid.*

In the Duke's attack Lord Muskerry went on first with his R. H. Regiment. O^r: Mem: P. 3. p. 68.

After having order'd all things, the Duke himself go's down to ye attacke with his brother the Duke of Glocester. *Ibid.*

PART
III.

1657.
The Miner
being fasten'd
to the wall,
the Duke and
his brother
return to their
quarter.
OR: MEM:
P. 3. p. 69.

hindrance to the Miners. Vpon which I sent them down with a Sergeant, and some Soldiers, to carry the Madriers, under the shelter of which they lodg'd themselves. This being done, I and my Brother came out from the attacks, and went back to our quarter.

As for what past in the other attacks, I shall not give so particular a Relation, because I saw them not : only this in generall, that both of them had the same good Success in theirs, and that they also had fasten'd their Miners to the place ; so that wee doubted not, but that wee should be master of it in 24

Don John dis-
approves the
Duke's and ye
Pce of Condé's
exposing their
persons in
going down to
their attacks.
Ibid. p: 70.

honres. I cannot here omit relating a Saying of Don John's, who, as he and the Marquis de Caracena were sitting in their Coaches at a good distance behind their attack, out of shott from the Enemy, being told that the Pce of Condé and myself were gone down into ours, answer'd, *No hazen ben*, 'tis not well done of them.

Vpon intelli-
gence of St
Venant's being
surrender'd to
the French,
the Spaniards
immediatly
resolve to raise
the Seige of
Ardres.
OR: MEM:
P. 3. p. 70.

In the morning presently after sun rise, Don John had intelligence that St Venant was surrender'd to the French, and that Monsieur de Turenne was marching to us ; Vpon which he assembled the junto, where it was immediatly resolv'd that wee should raise our Seige. Our great concernment then, was to get our men out of the attacks ; wee not having had time to work backwards to make a Trench and haue communication

Great danger
in drawing off
the men from
the attacks.
Ibid.

with them. So that when they drew off from their severall attacks, they must of necessity be expos'd to all the great and small shott of the Town. And now, they having receiv'd their orders for it, their first work was to bring off their Miners,

My Lord
Muskerry's
conduct in
bringing off the
Duke's Miners.
OR: MEM:
P. 3. p. 71.

which was done at my attack by the care of Lord Muskerry, who before he acquainted any of the Officers with the orders which he had receiv'd, sent one done to his Miners, to let them know, they must endeavour to come off as well as they could ; and that to favour their retreat, he would command his men to fire as fast as they were able, which he perform'd, telling his

Soldiers, that he was advertis'd how that part of the wall was contermin'd, and for that reason he withdrew them: And indeed they gave so good fire, that under the protection of it, the Miners gott up to the lodgment to him, without receiving any hurt.

This being perform'd, he told his Officers what orders he had; and commanded them, that when he gave the word, they should draw off as speedily as they could, and rally at the place which he shew'd them, a litle above muskett shott from the Town. While this was doing, I sent a party of horse consisting of about thirty with a Lieutenant, ordering him to get as neer the Town as was possible without exposing his men, till he saw our foot begin to come out f$_{ro}$m the attack, and then to gallop in amongst them, and if they saw any Officer or Soldier fall, to bring him off; and, having given this order, I follow'd myself to see it put in execution. Where observing, that as my men were coming out of their attack, the Lieutenant had only drawn his party under covert of a hedge, within muskett shott of the Town, but had not follow'd my orders, I gallop'd up to him, and again commanded him to do it; which he obeyd, and went with his men scattering to the very edge of the ditch, by which he made amends for his not performing his first orders. And notwithstanding that (they) fir'd thick and warmly from the Town, there was only Captain Kinf, (Keith) amongst all the Officers who received any hurt, and but very few Soldiers; not one dying of his wounds; which as it was very lucky, so it was also very strange, they having no shelter till they got (out) of reach. Whither they had the same good luck at the other attacks, I know not, only I was inform'd, that some of their Miners were kill'd by the Enemy.

After wee had thus drawn off our Soldiers from the attacks, where our loss was very inconsiderable, it was time for us to send away our baggage for Gravelines; and as soon as that

PART III. 1657.

The Duke sends a party of horse to gallop in amongst the foot as they retir'd, and bring off such of them as shou'd drop. OR MEM: P. 3. p. 71. And he follows himself to see this executed. Ibid.

The Lieu⸍. not following the orders, the Duke himself gallops up to him and obliges him to perform it. Ibid. p. 72.

In drawing off from Ardres the Spaniards haue a very uncomfortable march. OR MEM: P. 3. p. 72.

was dispatch'd, wee follow'd ourselves with the whole Army, and had a very uncomfortable march : for when wee were come to the skirts of the lowlands, wee were oblig'd to make a halt there, 'till our baggage and cañon were gotten on the dyke, the only one which led to Gravelines from Polincour, (*Polincove*) and which was almost unpassable by reason of the extraordinary rains that fell. This heavy way, together with the continuation of the rains, and stormy winds, and the darkness of the night (it being almost sun sett before the Van of the Army enter'd upon the dyke) and the frequent Stops wee were forc'd to make, by reason of our baggage which was before us, put our troopes into so much disorder, that the Officers had no command over their men, but every one made what hast he could to gain some shelter for himself; so that ten men were not left together of any one Regiment by the morning, and it was all wee could perform, to get them into a body the next day.

Severall
marches and
quarters of
ye Spanish
Army.
Or: Mem:
P. 3. p. 73.

On the 30th at night wee quarter'd at Broukerke; And in the mean time, the French Army was not without their share of those hardships and ill weather, for they were marching towards us all the same night over the plaine of S[t] Omer, in almost as great disorder as wee were. On the 31 wee pass'd the Colme, and quarter'd at Drinkam (*Dringam*) and the Villages about it; the Country being so much inclosed, that it had been very difficult for us to haue camp'd in battalia; and besides there was no necessity of it, the Enemy being then at - - - - - - but wee judg'd it necessary for our weary troopes, to give them that refretchment af the fatigue of such intollerable marches, as they had suffer'd during that Campagne.

The French
take la Motte
au bois, and

Wee continu'd but two days at that quarter, and the 2[d] of September wee quarter'd in the Villages under Mont Cassell, where wee remain'd till the 7th. At which time having receiv'd

intelligence that Monsr. de Turenne was about la Motte-aux- **P A R T**
Bois, wee drew back the same day to Wormhout; where, so **III.**

soon as wee had notice that the French had taken la Motte-
aux-Bois, the news of which was brought us on the 12th, and
that they were again marching towards us, wee repass'd the
Colme the next day with resolution to defend that Riuer, and
quarter'd all along it. The Spaniards were to maintain that
part of it from the Fort of Link, which reaches almost to
Spikere; I was quarter'd next them, and had under my
defence from the place where they ended towards Bergue, S^t.
Vinox; and the Prince of Condé from my quarter to the Town
of Bergue.

In this posture wee lay (having broken all the briges and
cast up works behind the foords) till the 17th, when wee were
advertis'd that Monsr. de Turenne was marching about, to take
us on the fianek, having pass'd the Colme above Link: Upon
which information most of the Spanish Regiments (I mean such
as were Natives from Spaine) were sent with some horse to
put themselves into Gravelines. The three Italian Reg^ts
commanded by Don Tito de Toratto (*del Prats*) were order'd
to the fort of Mardyke; and the rest of the Army drew off,
and incamp'd behind the Canal which go's from Bergue to
Dunkirk; The Prince of Condé having his quarter in Bergue,
Don John his in Dunkirk, and I mine at Coukerke (*Oudekerke*)
a Village in the mid-way betwixt both, planting all our cañon
upon batteries, which wee found ready made all along upon the
Canal.

A day or two after wee were drawn off from the Colme and
posted, as I haue already said, the French Army came before
Mardyke and beseiged it; That being the only maritime place,
which at that Season of the year they could undertake: And
this they did in some measure to comply with the Treaty they
had made with Cromwell; for by it they had obliged themselves

1657:
march towards
the Spaniards.
Ibid. p: 74.

The Spaniards
repass the
Colme, and
quartering
along it resolve
to defend it.
Ibid.

Their Severall
posts.
On: Mem:
P. 3. p: 74.

Upon notice
that M. Tu-
renne was
marching
about to take
them on the
flanck, t^he
Army divides,
and most of
ye Spanish
Regiments
were put into
Gravelines.
Ibid.

Three Italian
Reg^ts. are sent
to the fort of
Mardyke, and
the rest
incamp'd
behind the
Canal of
Dunkirk. *Ibid.*

The Duke
quarters in
Coukerk, P^ce
of Condé in
Bergue, and
Don John in
Dunkirk. *Ibid.*

The French
beseige
Mardyke.
Ibid. p: 75.

to put some Sea Town into his hands before the end of that Campagne. And as for Dunkirk, and Gravelines, they had been so well provided for, all the year, and the last of them had so strong a recruit just then put into it, that it was impossible for them to hope they could succeed against it, especially considering where the remainder of our Army was then posted; so that the fort of Mardyke was the only place they could attack.

They sat down before it in the evening, and just as they came to post themselves about it, I took our horse Guard, which was without the gate of Dunkirk, to attend me while I went to view their Army, as they were marching up to it. When I was about cañon shott from Dunkirk, I left them behind me to secure my retreat, in case I should be push'd by the Enemy, and went on myself with about fifteen Officers and others in my company, all of them well hors'd, till I came so near the French Army, that, as they march'd, some of their

Officers who were at the head of the Reg^t de Picardy, came out at a small distance from the rest, and fir'd at me with their fusils, which they carryd on horseback before them; they being just coming to that ground, and that being the very place on which they were to camp. So soon as their Soldiers had layd down their armes, and those who were appointed, were fallen to work to hutt themselves on the place which was mark'd out

for their quarter, severall Officers, both of that Regiment and others, came out again to drive me back; which I seeing, went off towards my horse guard. And as they press'd me, being now come closs with me, some of them took notice of a great greyhound, which they had seen with me while I was in the French Army. Upon which they call'd out, and enquir'd, If the Duke of York were there? and being answer'd, that he was, and I turning about at the same time, they immediatly cryd out, *Sur parole*, desiring they might speak with me.

Here upon I stop'd, and they coming forward, lighted off their horses to Salute me; and there being amongst them severall persons of the best quality, all of my old acquaintance, I also alighted, and wee continued talking together for almost an houre, 'till Monsr. de Turenne sent to them to come away. There wer at least two or three hundred of the French Officers, amongst whom was the Marquis d'Humieres, the Count de Guiche, Castelnau, and, in a word, almost all the persons of quality. As for my self, I had not above twenty in my company, amongst whom was a Spanish Officer of horse; who seeing me turn about, when I was nam'd and call'd to by the French, ask'd me what I intended to do? I commanded him to keep closs to me, and he should see; assuring him withall, that there was no danger for either of us. I haue related this passage thus particularly, that it may be obseru'd what civilitys pass'd betwixt Enemies in that Country; and that I had as many freinds in the French Army at that time, when I was actually in seruice against them, as I had when I seru'd under them. And this their civility had such effect upon some of the English who were with them, that it oblig'd them to perform the like, which cost them deer, as hereafter will be Seen.

Whither this conversation of mine with the Enemy gave any umbrage to the Spaniards, I cannot positively say; but after the end of the Campagne, Móus^r de Marsin, as of himself, advis'd me not to practise it so often as I had us'd that year, for the Spaniards were a jealous kind of people, and perhaps were not much Satisfyd with it, though they had taken no notice of it to me. To which I answer'd, That if they harbour'd any suspitions concerning me, or lik'd not those proceedings, they were very much in the wrong: since they could not but see how faithfully I had Serv'd them in that Campagne, and would still continue so to do, as became a man of honour, and that when any occasion of action offered itself, I would as freely

PART
III.

1657.
The Duke Stops and has an houre of conversation with these French Officers who were all persons of quality and of his old acquaintance.
Ibid.

The Duke had not above 20 in his Company, and the French were 2 or 300, which allarm'd a Spanish Officer that was wth y^e Duke of York 'till his R. H. assures him ther was no danger.
Ibid. p: 77.

M. de Marsin advises the Duke not to converse So frequently wth the French, the Spaniards being jealous of it.
O_R: M_{EM}: P. 3. p. 77.
The Duke's answer to this advertisment.
Ibid.

charge upon any of my acquaintance in the French Army, as any Spaniard of them all : But that for conversing with them, on a favourable opportunity, I must not refuse so small a thing to my own particular Satisfaction, it being of no prejudice to the Spaniards, for me to preserve the acquaintance which I had in the French Army, with whom I had serv'd so many years. And to let them see, that I intended it for no other purpose, I would not suffer any of the Prince of Condés Officers to go along with me upon such occasions ; which I acknowledg'd they had no reason to like, but might justly be jealous of it : And this method I observ'd the year following with great exactness, whenever I spoke with any Officers of the French Army.

But to return where I left. The same night that the French Army came before Mardyke, they began to work at their Line which was towards us, and at their attacks to the Fort also.

The French before Mardyke come and forage with in half cannon shott of the Spaniard's lines.
Or: Mem: P. 3. p. 79.

The next morning, having great want of forage (wee having eaten it all up while wee lay along the Colme) they came and began to forage in two or three great farmes, which were within half cannon-shott of our Line; that being the only place where they could hope for any, within a reasonnable distance of their Camp, because it had hitherto been preserved by Guards, which wee had sett on purpose to hinder our own men from foraging it, by reason that it belong'd to the Relations of some Officers in our Army. Wee had there also at that time a horse guard of about a hundred men (it being the only avenue to our Camp on that side) who seeing the Enemy come up with horse and foot before their foragers, were forced to draw off. And the Officer who commanded them, thō he saw with what intention the Enemy came thither, yet according to the laudable custome of the Spaniards durst not fire the farme, as he might easily haue done, because he had no orders for it.

When the Van of the Enemys Convoy of foragers came within shott of our Line, our cañon began to play upon them.

I was quarter'd within less then half a mile from thence, and hearing our cannon, I went immediatly that way, to inform myself of what was doing. Just at my coming, I found their Van beginning to lodge themselves at the farme houses, and preparing for their own security, as well as they were able, against any attempt which might be made against them, in case wee should endeavour to force them out At this place I mett the Prince de Ligny (*Ligne*) who at that time executed the Office of Mestre de Camp Generall. Immediatly I demanded of him, what his intentions were, and whither he would permitt the Enemy to forage quietly before our faces? But he answer'd, as he had done formerly, that without orders from the Marquis or Don John, he durst attempt nothing. To which I replyd, That if he stayd till he could hear from Dunkirk, the French would haue secur'd themselves, so that then it would not be in our power to dislodge them, and burn the forage. To which he again answer'd, That he well saw the reasonableness of the thing, but would not venture upon any thing without express orders. At last I told him, That since he durst not undertake it, I would run the hazard of it with my own men, desiring no other help from him, then only to draw all his foot to the Line: But to this he answer'd, That the bridge being in the Spanish quarters, he could not permitt me to go, because if any thing were to be undertaken, it must be by Spaniards.

After this discourse which produc'd nothing, the Enemy foraged without the least disturbance from us (while wee were expecting orders from Dunkirk) only our great guns continually playd upon them: Soon after this, the Prince of Condé came thither also from Bergue, whom I inform'd of what had pass'd betwixt me and the Prince de Ligny, and he confess'd, That what I had offer'd to do, was faisable, and fitt to be undertaken; but that he did not at all wonder, that the Prince de Ligny refus'd his consent to it, and by that time I had serv'd the

1657.
The Duke hearing the Cañon, go's to see what was a doing.
Or: Mem: P. 3. p. 79.

Meeting the Pᶜᵉ of Ligny, he asks him, if he would suffer the Enemy to forage quietly before their faces?
Pᶜᵉ Ligny's answer. *Ibid.*

The Duke offers to run the hazard wᵗʰ his own men, desiring only of Pᶜᵉ de Ligny to draw all his foot to the Line: but is not permitted.
Or: Mem: P. 3. p. 79.

The Pᶜᵉ of Condé confesses that what the Duke offer'd was faisable and fitt to be undertaken. *Ibid.*

Spaniards as long as he had done, I should be us'd to their
customs of committing many faults of this nature. And now
the Enemy having forag'd there, as long as they themselves
thought fitt, drew back to their   , leaving behind them
about a hundred horses which had been kill'd by our cannon :
what men they lost wee knew not, so that they must haue
carryd them away with them, or buried them where they could
not be found, for our men who went thither afterwards found
no bodys.

The fort of
Mardyke,
Surrender'd to
the French, is
put into the
hands of Rey-
nolds pursuant
to the Treaty
withCromwell.
Or: Mem:
P. 3. p. 80.

Two or three days after this, the Fort of Mardyke was
deliver'd to the French ; who the next day, pursuant to their
Treaty with Cromwell, put it into the hands of Reynolds, who
commanded the English troopes. And as soon as they had repair'd
the Fort, and slighted the Trenches, which took them up but a
very litle time, the French Army march'd away, drawing back
into their own Country and into forage quarters. As for us,
wee continued camped where wee were, giving out still that
wee woult attempt the recovery of Mardyke.

The Spaniards
continue still
in their
quarter w^ch
proves a very
unwholsome
one, hardly
one Officer
escaping an
ague excepting
the Duke him-
self. Ibid.

This quarter prov'd a very unhealthfull sickly place to us,
for few of the Officers or Soldiers, excepting only the naturall
Spaniards escap'd agues ; in so much that wee had never half
our men together, in a condition of doing duty. It fell the most
Severly on those troopes which I commanded ; for excepting
myself, there was scarsly an Officer or Volonteer of quality, or
any of my servants, who was free from an ague. My Brother

The Duke of
Glocester
forced to quitt
the Army Sick,
and the P^ce of
Condé so ill,
that he was
given over by
the Phisitians.
Or: Mem:
P. 3. p. 80.

the Duke of Glocester went out of the Army sick of that distemper ; and the P^ce of Condé was seiz'd with it to that degree,
that he was once given over by the Phisitians, hardly escaping
with life. Soon after this his Ma^ty came to the Army at
Dunkirk, to solicite Don John concerning his own private

affaires, and also to remind him of some promises which he
had made him in relation to England.

By this time also, the English who were in Mardyke began

to repaire the old fortifications about that Fort, which was the easier for them to do, because the ditches had been left entire, and only a small part of the parapet thrown down. Don John having receiv'd intelligence of this, resolv'd one night to march thither with the whole Army, to destroy in the space of a night, the workes at wch they had been labouring for a month; which he undertook rather out of ostentation, and to make the people imagine that he had still a design upon that Fort, then out of any reall opinion he had, that so inconsiderable a busines was worth the exposing the lives of so many men.

The evening being now come which was appointed for this undertaking, he march'd out of Dunkirk at the head of the Troopes, the King of England being with him: It was then so very dark, that wee were forced to make use of lights to conduct us in our way thither; which being perceiv'd by the Enemy, they prepar'd themselves to receive a storme, as beleeving that wee came thither with that intention, or at least that wee design'd to sitt down before the place, and they presently set up great lights round the compass of the Fort. When wee were arriv'd within less then cañon-shott, wee extinguish ours; and then his Ma^ty, Don John, and the Marquis de Caracena, stayd with the horse, and let the foot march before them: The Spanish Infantry commanded by Mareshall de battaille, march'd on towards that part of the outworkes which look'd towards Dunkirk; the Count de Marsin with the Prince of Condé's foot, to the side which regards Gravelines; and I, at the head of my foot, betwixt both. While wee were marching up towards them, they plyd us very hard both with great and small shott from the Fort; and the small Fregatts which lay in the Splinter, playd fiercely upon us with their Artillery. All which did very litle execution on our foot, who, being once gott under shelter of the old out works, lay very safe from all their shott: some of the Squadrons that were behind

PART III.

1657.
repair the old Fortifications at Mardyke. *Ibid.*

Don John marches out of Dunkirk wth the whole Army to destroy the fortifications of Mardyke. The King of England go's with him. An Account of this Expedition. On Mem: P. 3. p: 81. The King, Don John, and Caracena stay with the horse. *Ibid.*

The Duke, the P^ce of Condé's foot and Marsin march before with the foot. *Ibid.*

The cañon from the Fort and from the Fregats playd hard upon them. *Ibid.*

T T 2

P A R T
III.

1657.
My L⁴ of
Ormonde has
his horse kill'd
under him, as
he was coming
down with the
King to See
the foot.
Oʀ: Mᴇᴍ:
P. 3. p. 82.

us, scap'd not altogether so good cheap; for the shott which flew over the foot fell in amongst them, killing severall men and horses: And as his Maᵗʸ once came down to see what the foot were doing, My Lord of Ormonde, who was with him, had his horse kill'd under him with a cañon bullet.

So soon as wee had posted ourselves with our foot, every one of the bodys sent over their workmen, with commanded men to secure them; and because the ditch where I was happen'd to be so very deep, that I could not possibly send over my men in that place, I was forced to send them about by the Spanish attack, that they might come to the post assign'd them. And that I might haue a communication with them while they were throwing down their workes, I fill'd up the ditch with fascines, and made a passage over to them, that in case the Enemy had sallyd out I might haue been in a readiness to releeve them. So soon as our workmen were placed, the commanded men, who were with them, began to fire upon the Fort, and continued so to do during all the time wee stayd, which was till almost break of day: Then wee drew off in very good order, having slighted those outworkes, and by that time it was brode day light, wee were all come back to Dunkirk.

The Spaniards
after having
slighted the
outworkes of
Mardyke draw
off in good
order by break
of day. Ibid.

I am confident the Enemy was muche more surprised at our going off, then they were at our coming on: for they so litle beleev'd that wee were retir'd, that thō our men ceas'd firing when they began to draw off, yet they within continued to shoot for at least half an hour after wee were gone, as beleeving wee had still been there. I cannot certainly say what loss wee had amongst the horse, but I could never hear of above twenty; and amongst the foot, but one Officer, who was a Captain in the Duke of Glocester's Regiment: of private Soldiers not above three or four were kill'd outright, and about eight or ten wounded. The English in the Fort (as I haue been since inform'd) had but one man kill'd; and they so much beleev'd that wee came

But one man
of the English
in the Fort
kill'd in this
expedition, wᶜʰ
was under-
taken by Don
John out of
ostentation.
Oʀ: Mᴇᴍ:
P. 3. p. 83.

10

with intention to attack them, that upon our first approche they dispatch'd away a Messenger to Monsr. de Turenne (who was in his forage quarters) to advertise him, they were beseiged; who upon this information began his march, and was coming to releeve them; but upon other notice given him that wee were gone off, he return'd into his quarters.

Some few days after this, wee made an attempt upon the Small English Fregats, which rode within the Splinter. The first design wee had upon them, was to haue endeavour'd to haue burnt some of them with two fire Ships, which for that purpose were made in Dunkirk: But so soon as they were fitted and ready to go out, the Seamen of the place found difficulties in the executing of that Enterprise; it not being practicable, but with an easterly wind, during the spring tide, by reason of the Sands; for which consideration they propos'd in stead of burning, to surprise the two headmost Fregats which lay there, being the Rose and Truelove of six or eight guns each of them: to perform this they were to man out twelve Shallops; and accordingly one night when the tide serv'd them, it being very calme, and somewhat misty, they went out, and at the same time Don John call'd his Ma^{ty}, who with the persons of quality and Officers, walk'd along upon the Strand to behold the issue of this attempt: And being come over the place where the Fregats rode, wee heard an English Seaman from on boord one of them, ask aloud, What Ship's boat that was? Upon their not answering, the Seaman at the same time seeing another Shallop coming up to lay him on boord, he gave the allarm, and fir'd a gun into one of the Shallops, which took place in her, and shott one of the Rower's legs; upon which accident, and firing a few small shott more at them, all our Shallops ran away most shamefully without any farther attempt, and so this expedition ended; after which there was nothing more endeavour'd against either the Fort or Ships.

P A R T III.

1657.

An attempt made by the Spaniards upon the small English Fregats in the Splinter. *Ibid.* 2 fire Ships prepar'd to burn them, but the execution found to be impracticable. *Ibid.*

12 Shallops man'd out to Surprise 2 of the English Fregats.

The King, Don John, and all the persons of quality upon the Strand, to behold the issue of the attempt. OR: MEM: P. 3. p. 93.

The Shallops run Shamfully. *Ibid.*

PART
III.
.1657.
Reynolds, in
imitation of
the French, is
desirous to
convers. wᵗʰ yᵉ
Duke.
Oʀ: Mᴇᴍ:
P. 3. p. 83.

But Reynolds, who commanded the English, seeing how the French Officers were us'd to converse with me, and with what civility they treated me upon all occasions, was very desirous to follow their example; and in order to it, sought all opportunitys of speaking with me, or some of my Servants as they rode abrode towards Mardyke, which was their custom almost every day. And once happening to see some of our people therabout, he sent to speak with them. The Lord Newbourgh and Coll: Richard Talbott fortun'd to be the men, to whom he sent; the first of which had received great civilities from Reynolds upon some occasions in England, and the latter had his life Sav'd by him in Ireland: so that both of them, being willing to hear what he had to say to them, came up, and enter'd into parlee with him.

After some discourse, he ask'd them, If I did not some times walk that way? And upon their answering, That I did; he inquir'd whither they thought I would be willing, to let him haue the honour of speaking with me, as he did with them, because he was very ambitious of it. They told him, they beleev'd I would not refuse it him: and as soon as they came back to Dunkirk, they inform'd the King and me of what had past.

The King and
the Duke
being inform'd
by Lᵈ New-
bourgh and
Coll: Talbott,
of Reynold's
desire, rid
frequently out
that way to
give him
opportunity of
Satisfying his
desire.
Oʀ: Mᴇᴍ:
P. 3. p. 84.

Vpon this notice wee went out more frequently on that side, then wee had accustom'd to do, therby to give him the opportunity he desir'd: And about two or three days after, My Lord Newbourgh ask'd his Mᵗʸˢ permission to go and speak with Reynolds; which being granted, he took Mr. George Hamilton along with him, and went up to the Enemies horse-Centry, desiring him to tell his Generall, that he was there, and requested to speak with him. Reynolds came out immediatly, taking with him only one gentleman Mr. Crew; Being come up to my Lord Newbourgh, he enquir'd of My Lord, who were those whom he Saw at a litle distance from him, under the Sandhills?

He only nam'd me to him ; Upon which Reynolds ask'd, If he might not then go and speak to me? Hereupon My Lord Newbourgh sent Mr. Hamilton to the King and me, to let us know what Reynolds desir'd ; and his M^{ty} bad me go.

I took along with me Mr. Hamilton, and Berkley the Captain of my Guards: As soon as Reynolds saw me coming, he came on to meet me, and was going to alight from his horse, and salute me on foot: But Mr. Crew dissuaded him from it ; yet in all other things he behav'd himself with great civility and respect to me.

He began his discourse with great compliments, desiring me (to whom he us'd the Title of Highness) not to look on him as one sent over by Cromwell, but as one serving the King of France ; and that he should be as ready, as any of the French, to pay that respect which was due to me : To which I answer'd as obligingly as I could, considering him as a man of whom good use might be made, when occasion should serve. And truly by the whole manner of his discourse, it was easily to be seen, that he had somewhat to say which he was not willing Mr. Crew should hear : But he keeping very close to him, he only let fall some dark expressions, implying that he hop'd a time might come wherin he might be seruiceable to me ; and thus after wee had been about half an hour together, wee parted very well Satisfied of each other.

But, however, this Enterview and some other Civilities which he shew'd the King and me, cost him dear : for besides the order he gave to the Ships in the Splinter, not to shoot when either of us were abroad on that side (which was punctually observ'd) he sent severall presents of win to My Lord Newbourgh, desiring him to dispose of them to those, for whom My Lord knew he had a great respect : All which proceedings gave such jealousies to some of the English Officers who serv'd under him, that they writt to Cromwell to give him notice of what had pass'd. And one Coll. White hir'd a small Vessell, on purpose to go over into England and accuse him; of which he being advertis'd, imbark'd himself on the same Vessell with White, with intention to justify himself: But both of them mett a futall disappointment of their purpose; for by the carelesness of the Master, notwithstanding that by a Fregatt which he mett, as he was standing over for England, he was advertis'd, that by the course he took he must be stranded on the Goodwins, and that severall guns were accordingly fir'd from the fregatt to warn him of his danger; yet he either not heeding, or not understanding those signs, kept on his course, by which means both the Vessell and every man in her, were lost upon those Sands.

I haue sinee been inform'd, that Cromwell had so much ressented what had past at Mardyke, that he was resolv'd to haue sent for Reynolds; and, if he could not haue satisfied his jealoussy concerning him, to haue depriv'd him of his Command, but his unfortunate accident put an end to all.

Soon after this was sent over Collonell Lockart a Scotsman, who had maried one of Cromwell's Relations, to Command in stead of Reynolds. And not long after the enterview, his Ma[ty] return'd to Bruxelles, having perform'd all he had to do at Dunkirk. Don John also and the Marquis de Caracena went for Bruges, and from thence to Ghent, leaving me behind at Dunkirk to command the Army. The Country was still cousen'd by them into a beleef, that so soon as the French Army were gone into their winter quarters, they intended to beseige Mardyke, for by spreading this report, they hop'd to get some mony from the Province of Flanders; and the more to keep them in this opinion, great magazins of fascines and

gabions were made, with all other things necessary for a
Seige.

In this expectation they kept the Army together at Dunkirk, till new year's day : At which time I receiv'd orders for sending all the troopes into their severall winter quarters ; Which having distributed to them, I went to Bruxelles, where Don John and the Marquis were arrived some days before me.

1657.
The Duke
having dis-
tributed the
troopes into
their winter-
quarters,
return'd to
Bruxelles the
1ˢᵗ Jan. 1658,
and So put an
end to this
Campagne.
Ibid. p: 87.

1658.

BEING now come to Bruxelles in the begining of January, 1658, I made no long stay in that City; for so soon as I had dispatched my small affaires, I went to my Sister who was at Breda, where my Brother the Duke of Glocester had been already for some time to recover of his ague, which at my arriuall had just left him. After I had remain'd there till the midle of February, wee went all three together to Antwerp there to meet his Majesty.

While we resided in that place, there were strong reports of something to be undertaken in England; and that all things were in such a readiness, that at the breaking of the frost, when the Six flutes which were brought in Holland could come to Ostend, Soldiers should be put immediatly on boord them, who together with some men of war, which lay ready there and at Dunkirk, were to be landed in some part of England, where it was also said wee had intelligence of forces which would joyn ours at their arrivall: But at the same time there were others who were so far from giving credit to those rumours, that they were of opinion nothing could be done: for looking more deeply into the matter, they saw that both the King and the Spaniards, by these reports, aim'd on either side to excuse themselves for non performance of the Treaty made betwixt them; thō 'tis true the Spaniards by not performing their part, render'd it impossible for the King to comply with his engagements, at least to do what otherwise he might haue done.

And now while this discourse was at the hottest, the Earle of
Bristoll having almost quite lost himself with the Spanish
Ministers, was endeavouring his uttmost to ingratiate himself
with the Prince of Condé; who at that time also, had neither
any great esteem nor kindness for him. Being full of his design,
he came one day to me in the Princesse's chamber, and began
a discourse with me concerning the busines of England: After
a long conversation with me upon that subject, he sayd, That
thō he doubted not but our designs there would meet with the
desired success, yet he (*it*) would not be amiss to think before
hand, what wee should do in case of a miscarriage; and that one
of the things which he thought most necessary to be look'd after
(which also more immediatly concern'd me) was to consider
of some meanes to preserve the troopes which wee had already,
and to increase their numbers by all the meanes wee could
imagine; which if done, would render me more considerable
with the Spaniard, besides the common advantage which would
redound to the Royall party; That for the present he had
nothing to propose towards the compassing of this design, but
desir'd me to take it seriously into my thoughts, and he would
also do the like; and that in case I would permitt him, he will
speak with me again, when he had any thing in a readiness to
offer: Thus wee parted, and he spoke no more to me upon that
Subject during two or three days.

In the mean time this discourse had given me a very hott
allarm, not doubting that I should haue some extraordinary
proposition made to me, which would not be to my advantage:
and that consideration put me upon ghessing of what nature it
might be: It happen'd as I was rowling over these things in
my imagination, one of my Servants told me of a discourse,
which an Officer belonging to the Prince of Condé had held
with him some days before; by the relation of which, I immediatly ghess'd what would be propos'd to me, and accordingly

P A R T
III.

1658.
The E. of
Bristoll lost
with the Spa-
nish Ministers,
endeavours to
ingratiat him-
self with the
Pᵒᵉ of Condé.
Oᴙ: Mᴇᴍ:
P. 3. p. 89.
his discourse
with the Duke.
Ibid.

The Duke is
allarm'd at
what Lᵈ Bris-
toll had Said to
him, and
guessing at his
design, he
advises with
his Sister.
Oᴙ: Mᴇᴍ:
P: 3. p. 89.

gave my Sister the knowledge of it; advising with her, what answer I should make when it should be offer'd to me.

A day or two after this, the Earle of Bristoll came again to me, and after another eloquent preambule, and a protestation that what he was going to propose to me was not only for his Maties Service, but for my particular advantage; in short his proposition was, That his Ma^ty should joyn his troopes to those of the Prince of Condé, by which means they would be So considerable, that the Spaniards must be forced by necessity to comply with the promises, which they had made to the King for the recruiting of his forces, which it was apparent they had no inclination to do, having no great care or consideration of those which he already had; That as to what concern'd the command which I should haue, there might be care taken to accommodate it, the Prince of Condé being very easy to live withall, and having a great esteem of me.

Lord Bristoll's proposall, that the Kings troopes under the Duke's command should joyn to those of the P^ce of Condé. Or: Mem: P. 3. p. 90.

He us'd these and many other arguments to perswade me to be of his opinion: To which I answer'd, That it was a busines of great importance, and ought to be Seriously weigh'd, before any resolution could be taken in it; that accordingly I would consider of it, and speak with him again. I say no more to him at that time, that he might not perceive the dislike I had of it. When he was gone, I not a litle troubled how to govern myself in this affaire; for I saw very well it was a snare layd for me: If I should haue approv'd the proposition, I had certainly lost my self with the Spaniards, who would haue taken it very ill, that I should haue put them upon the hardship of refusing any thing to the Prince of Condé, who was then So Strong, and So necessary to them; And I my self could not but be unwilling to consent to a thing, which would haue been prejudiciable to my reputation : for thō I had serv'd in Severall capacities under Monsr. de Turenne, I did not think that after

E. of Bristoll endeavours to perswad the Duke to be of his opinion. The Duke's answer. Ibid. p: 91.

The Duke Sees the Snare layd for him in this affaire by Ld Bristoll, and is troubled how to govern himself in it. Or: Mem: P. 3. p. 91.

having served so long, and commanded the King my Brother's
forces the year before, it became me to come under any other
person. On the other side, if I had openly discover'd any
aversion to it, I should haue expos'd my self to the ill offices,
which might haue been done me with his Ma^ty upon that
account; by their representing to him, that for a punctilio of
my own, I was willing to obstruct what was intended for his
Seruice, and also I should haue had the Prince of Condé my
Enemy: all which considerations, together with the confidence
I had that the Spaniards would never consent to such a proposition, whensoever it should be made to them, strengthen'd me
in the resolution of appearing wholly passive in the matter, so
as neither to put it forward nor obstruct it.

Some time after this his Ma^ty went to Bruxelles, and I with
my Sister return'd to Breda, where having stayd with her three
or four   , I went back to Bruxelles to waite on the King:
So Soon as I was return'd, they began again to talk with me
concerning that affaire; And one day particularly, the King
call'd me and My Lord Bristoll into the Chancellor's closett,
where the matter was debated; And I who since my return
thither, was more then ever confirm'd in my opinion, that the
Spaniards wou'd never be induced to suffer it: Accordingly I
spoke but litle, and at length it was concluded amongst them,
that the Earle of Bristoll should conferr with the Lord Barklay,
(*Berkley*), how to propose it to the Spaniards, and after what
manner the whole affaire was to be conducted. In order to this,
they two had a meeting once about it, and no more; for by this
time My Lord Bristoll began to see, that it was a matter not
to be effected: because the Prince of Condé, having consider'd
that it woulg give great umbrage to the Spaniards, and withall
finding that it could not possibly be compass'd, went himself to
Don John, and acquainted him with the proposition which
the Earle of Bristoll had made to him, at the same time shewing

P A R T
III.

1658.

The Duke
resolves to be
passive in the
matter.
Or: Mem:
P. 3. p. 92.

The King calls
the Duke and
Ld Bristoll,
and the
proposall is
debated in the
Chancellor's
closett. *Ibid.*

The P^ce of
Condé ac-
quaints Don
John with L^d
Bristoll's pro-
possall, which
puts an end to
this whole
affaire.
Or: Mem:
P. 3. p. 93.

The affaire
proves of
advantage to
the Duke with
the Spaniards,
but do's him
harm with the
Pᶜᵉ of Condé.
Ibid.

The Six flutes
prepar'd in
Holland, for
an attempt to
be made in
England, are
taken by yᵉ
English. *Ibid.*

Preparations
at Bruxelles
for *the
Campagne
of* 1658,
wᶜʰ is the
Duke's last
Campagne.
Ibid.

The King
having intelli-
gence from
England that
Dunkirk
would be
beseiged,
acquaints the
Spaniards and
presses them
to recruit it.
Oʀ: Mᴇᴍ:
P. 3. p. 94.

his own dislike to it. That Conversation made an end of the whole affaire, and of the Small remaining credit of My Lord Bristoll with Don John and the Spanish Ministers: But on the other side, gave them a very good impression of me; for inquiring into the bottom of it, they easily found the great aversion I had to it: But as it prov'd of advantage to me in relation to the Spaniards, so he (*it*) did me harm with the Prince of Condé, who ever afterwards quite alter'd his way of living with me; and on the contrary liv'd much better then he had done the year before with all those, whom he knew to be no freinds to me and to my concernments.

In the begining of the spring, as soon as the frost was broken, the Six flutes above mention'd were taken by the English, betwixt Holland and Ostend; and so a conclusion was put to all the discourse of attempting any thing in England for that year.

All our thoughts at Bruxelles were now taken up with our preparations for the ensuing Campagne; and, as the time of action was approching, the Spaniards applyd their greatest care in providing for those places, which they judg'd were in greatest danger of being beseiged by the French Army: for all our Intelligence agreed, that this year the Enemy would undertake some considerable Seige. The thought of this gave great perplexity to the Spaniards; for not having a body of foot sufficient to man their important fronteer towns, as they ought to haue been furnish'd, they were forced to leave some of them very slightly guarded.

His Mᵗʸ press'd them very much to recruit Dunkirk with a strong garrison, letting them know, that he was assur'd by his letters from England, and by others which he had found means to intercept from thence, That the first thing the French would undertake would be to beseige that Town, they being press'd to it by Cromwell; and that accordingly both in France and England all things were preparing for it: And this was not only once said to them, but repeated every week, as the letters which were sent from England still confirm'd it: But all these advertisements wrought no effect upon the Spanish Councells; they giving litle credit to them, as being perswaded that the intelligence was false, and that such reports were contrived artificially by the Enemy, to oblige them to leave Cambray, or some other of their inland Towns, unprovided of defence; what had happen'd the year before, at the place last mention'd, had rais'd such apprehensions in them as outweigh'd all the reasons which had been given them by the King: And besides, they beleev'd, the Cardinal had still a longing to that Town, so that neither his Treaty with Cromwell, or any other consideration, would hinder him from undertaking that Seige, unless it were so well provided for, and secur'd against him, as to render it too difficult a peice of work: With these and other reasons, rather plausible then strong, they flatter'd themselves into a beleef, that Dunkirk was not in any danger of being attacked that year. Wherupon they did not only leave it very slenderly guarded, but also without furnishing it with such a proportion of ammunition as was requisit; at the same time disposing most of their foot into the Towns of Artois, as Ayre and St Omer, and into the fronteer places of Haynault, and reinforcing the garrison of Cambray with a considerable body of horse and foot; but as for Dunkirk, they added nothing to the ordinary garrison. Neither was this all, for they neglected the finishing of two Forts of four bastions each, which they had begun upon the Canal betwixt that and Bergue, which if they had once perfected and man'd, would haue render'd the Seige of Dunkirk a much more difficult peice of work; for the Enemy must of necessity haue master'd one of those two Forts, before they could haue begun a formall Seige.

PART III.

1658.

They neglect the advertisement given them, and why. *Ibid.*

The Spaniards reinforce Cambray and other Towns, but neglect Dunkirk, and leave two forts upon the Canal unfinish'd. Oᴖ: Mᴇᵐ: P. 3. p. 95.

I cannot forbear upon this occasion, to make this remarque, araising from what I haue observ'd when I was either in the French or Spanish Army ; That of all the Fortifications of this nature, or Intrenchments for the defence of Rivers, I never Saw any which the Spaniards made, that were of great advantage to them ; for either they were not finish'd time enough to defend them, or were render'd useless by the French marching about, and falling into their flanque, as I haue already mention'd in the year 1655, when Mons'. de Turenne endeavour'd not to force the great retrenchment which they had made all along the River betwixt Condé and S' Guislain, but fetching a compass about, went to Condé and tooke it, therby making frustrate all the great labour they had taken. And indeed 'tis very difficult in such Countrys to make any works which will prove of use; for an Army which is once Master of the feild, will with a litle time and patience find the means, either of forceing their passage over such a work or river, or, by marching about, get into the Enemies Country some other way : So that in my opinion, thō it may be necessary on some occasions to make them, yet a Generall never ought to rely upon them.

The French, according to their custom, drew first into the feild this year ; and in their way to Dunkirk, at Cassel, took prisoners of warr the Duke of Glocester's Regiment of foot, which consisted of four hundred men ; they having been very unadvisably sent thither by Mons'. de Bascourt a Mareshall de battaille, under whose command were all the Troopes which acted on that side of the Country, it being a place not possibly to be defended : And at the same time he sent my Regiment of about five hundred men, with some other small foot Regiments which were quarter'd at Hondescote, with some few horse, into S' Omer, thinking the French would haue sate down before it. But when, by their passing by him, he saw their design was

upon Dunkirk, he endeavour'd, thō too late, to haue cast some
men into it; and only made a shift to get in himself with some
few horse. Much about the same time the Marquis de Leyde
(*Léede*) Governour of that Town, gott in also with great difficulty,
he being at Bruxelles soliciting for supplys of men and ammu‐
nition, when the first intelligence arrived, that the French were
marching thither: At which time, and no sooner, they order'd
all the troopes, which were in Nieuport, Dixmuyde, and Furnes;
(of which they were jealous thō without reason, because they were
all English, Scots, and Irish) to march for Dunkirk, (*reserving*) only
the King's Regiment of foot, which was upwards of four hundred,
and then lay at Dixmuyde; but these also came too late, the
Town being block'd up already. So that the Marquis de Leyde
found himself beseiged in a place, the main strength of which
consisted in the outworks, which were very large, all of earth,
and very easy to be approched. To all this great extent of
ground which was to defend, his garrison was no ways answer‐
able, for it consisted but of a thousand foot, and eight hundred
horse, and his provisions of pouder and other necessarys were
very scanty, even with reference to the Small number of his
men.

The certain intelligence of this Seige being come to Bruxelles
about the end of May, gave no small trouble to the Spaniards,
especially when they saw all hopes of putting succours into
the place by Sea were wholly vanish'd, by reason that the
English Navy under the command of Generall Montague was
now come before it; So that the only prospect which they had
of releeving it, was by the Army: And therfore it was imme‐
diatly resolved in a Councell of Warr, (where were present all
the Generall Officers) that the Army should draw together at
Ypres with all imaginable hast; pursuant to which, the orders
were immediatly dispatch'd for all their troopes to meet at the
Rendezvous appointed.

PART
III.

1658.
Dunkirk
beseigd by the
French, the
Governour
with much ado
gets into it.
Ibid.

Troopes
orderd at last
to reinforce
Dunkirk but
too late, the
Town being
block'd up by
the French so
that they could
not gett in.
Or: Mem:
P. 3. p. 97.

The garrison
of Dunkirk
only 1000 foot
and 800 horse
strong.
Ibid. p. 98.

About the end
of May.

No prospect
left of Suc‐
couring Dun‐
kirk but by the
Army.
Or: Mem:
P. 3. p. 98.

The Rendez‐
vous of the
Spanish Army
at Ypres. *Ibid.*

PART
III.

1658.
They meet y^e
7th of June and
march Strait
to Furnes.
Ibid.

M. d'Hocquin-
court, lately
come from
France, joyns
the Spanish
Army near
Furnes. *Ibid.*

Accordingly on the 7th of June all the Army and the Generall Officers were there. At their first meeting they resolv'd to march to Furnes, and on the 9th they camp by Nieuport; On the next day betwixt Odekerk and Furnes, whither came to us the Mareshall d'Hocquincourt, who was lately come out from France by the way of Hêdin a Town in Artois, of great importance, upon the River of Canclie; which upon the death of the Governour, by means of the Lieutenant du Roy and his Brother in law, revolted from the obedience of the King their Master, and call'd the Spaniards to their assistance, with whom they finally agreed to deliver the Town up to them, in consideration of a Summ of mony; and accordingly having receiv'd it, the Spaniards were put into possession of the place.

As for the said Mareshall, he had all along maintain'd a secret correspondence with the Lieu^t du Roy, as having designs at the same time of flying out into Rebellion, and of alluring most of the Noblesse, and Commonalty of the Vexin, and lower parts of Normandy, to haue joyn'd with him : But his contrivance being discover'd before he was fully in a readiness to put it in execution (a fate which for the most part attends such undertakings) he was forced to consult his own safety, by flying as speedily as he could. Notwithstanding which it was beleeved by many, that had not this instant Campagne prov'd So very unsuccessfull to the Spaniards, some disturbance would haue follow'd in those parts.

Resolv'd in a
Councell of
warr, that y^e
Army should
march the 13th
and camp
amongst y^e
Sand-hills, as
near the
Enemies Lines
before Dun-
kirk as they
could, and that
on the 12th y^e

To return again to our main business. On the 11th it was resolved in a Councell of Warr, at which were present Don John, the Prince of Condé, the Marquis de Caracena, the Mareshall d'Hocquincourt and the P^{ce} de Ligny (Don Estevan Gamarra and myself being accidently not there) That on the 13th, wee should march with the whole Army as near as wee could conveniently to the lines of the Enemy, amongst the

II

Sand-hills, and there incamp; that by placing our selves so
closs to them, wee might be in a readiness to attack them,
when wee saw our proper time; and that on the 12th, the day
before our appointed march, all the Generall Officers should
go with two thousand commanded foot and four thousand
horse, to view the place where they would camp, and themselves pitch upon it.

But before I proceed any further, I shall give a more parti-
cnlar account of what pass'd at this Councell; because that
most of those who were present at it, haue since endeavour'd
to clear themselves, either from giving that advice which I
haue mention'd, or even of consenting to the resolution which
was then taken. And this Relation which I am now giving,
I had from one of those who was assisting in it, and was
desirous amongst the rest to clear himself from the imputation
of giving that advice, or consenting to it.

So Soon as the persons whom I haue already nam'd were
sett in Councell, Don John inform'd them of the cause of their
meeting, That it was to consult on the most proper method
of releeving Dunkirk: He let them know the present condition
of the place, which was such as requir'd a speedy succour; and
after having inlarg'd upon these heads, he propos'd to them
that the Army should march to Zudcote, and camping there
amongst the Sand-hills, as near as they could to the Enemies
Lines, should watch their opportunity of attacking them.
After this proposition there was a long silence, and no one
arising to oppose it, he said, Since I see you all approve of
what I haue proposed, let us now consider after what mañer,
and what time, wee shall march thither: Vpon which it was
resolv'd, that they should all go the day following to view
the ground for incampment, and observe the Line of the
beseigers.

I shall not take upon me to accuse or excuse any who were

x x 2

PART
III.

1658.
Gen^{ll} Officers
should go and
view the place
and pitch the
Camp.
On: Mem:
P. 3. p. 99.
The Duke was
not present at
this Councell
of Warr. Ibid.

Most of the
persons that
were present
at this Councell
endeavourd to
clear them-
selves for hav-
ing advis'd the
resolution that
was taken in it.
On: Mem:
P. 3. p. 100.

A particular
account of
what past in
this Councell
of Warr. Ibid.

PART
III.
━━━━━━
1658.

then present at this hasty resolution; thō I haue read a
Relation which was printed and published by a freind of the
Marquis de Caracena, wherein the Author endeavour'd to lay
the whole weight of that resolution on Don John; And I haue
also read the answer to it, where-in Don John was justified,
and it was made to appear, that in case the Marquis had so
been pleas'd, he might easily haue inder'd that march, by only
declaring himself against it, he having practis'd that very way
in things of far less consequence then this; for his power was
such, that he had but to Say he thought it not for the King's
seruice to put in execution such a resolution, and Don John
must acquiesce in it: in Spanish it is more strongly exprest,
No sera de servicio del Rey; and this power he made use of
the year before at la Cappelle.

In pursuance
of the Reso-
lution of the
Counsell of
Warr,theGen⁰.
Officers go to
view the Ene-
mies Lines and
the place of in-
campment.
Oʀ. Mᴇᴍ.
P. 3. p. 101.
The Duke and
yᵉ Marq: de
Caracena and
Gamarra
chuse the
ground to
lodge the
Army.
Oʀ: Mᴇᴍ:
P. 3. p. 102.
Mʳ. de Boutte-
ville viewing
the Lines of
the Enemy
begins a Skir-
mish wᵗʰ their
horse guards.
Ibid.

But resolv'd it was; and in pursuance of it, wee went on the
12ᵗʰ, with our four thousand horse, and the commanded foot,
with intent to view the Enemies Line, and chuse the place for
our incampment. Being advanced as far as Zudcote, wee halted
there, and first made choice of our ground to lodge the Army,
before wee went nearer to discover the Enemy: This was done
by the Marquis of Caracena, Don Estevan de Gamarra, and
my Self, who taking some horse along with us, went a cross the
Sand-hills, till wee came to the Strand. In the mean time
Mons'. de Boutteville was gone with our Cravatts along the
hight way betwixt the Sand-hills, and the meadow ground,
advancing towards the Enemies horse guard so far, that he began
to Skirmish with them, and forced them to give back a litle; by
which means he had the opportunity of coming within a convenient distance of their Lines, and viewing them.

As he was returning to give the Generalls an account of what
he had observ'd, he met the Mareshall d'Hocquincourt, who
earnestly desir'd him to turn once more, Saying, he would charge
the Enemies horse guards; and notwithstanding that Mons'.

de Boutteville us'd many arguments to disswade him (as having already done what he intended, and brought back a prisoner or two with him, which he had taken amongst the Sand-hills) yet the Mareshall continued obstinate, and over-perswaded him to go back, by which he did not only ingage himself, but almost all the reste of the Generall Officers at a great distance from their troopes: for the Prince of Condé Seeing him go that way, walk'd after him, and Don John, hearing the Prince was gone on towards the Line, did the like: and last of all, I, having observ'd all that could be Seen where the Marquis and I had been together, and coming that way, where I heard that those whom I haue already mention'd were gone before, put on at a large gallop after them, and came up to them just as Monsr. d'Hocquincourt had forced the Enemies horse guards to retire. In performing which, Henry Jermyn on our side, and the Marquis de Blanquefort, at present Earle of Feversham nephew to Monsr. de Turenne, on the other, were both of them shott through the thigh.

The Mareshall d'Hocquincourt was now come within muskett shott of a redoubt, which the Enemy had advanced upon a heigth, somewhat before their Lines; when at the very moment that I came up to him, he received a shott in the belly from the S^d. Redoubt, of which presently after he dyd: Vpon this wee drew off, the Enemy at the same time beginning to advance upon us; and the Prince of Condé with his people, being very busy in taking the papers out of the Mareshall's pockets, not knowing whither they shoull be able to bring off his body, a Gentleman who belong'd to the s^d Mareshall came to me, and desir'd me to face about, to give them the leysure of bearing off his Master's corps; which at his request I did, and so with some difficulty the body was brought away. But had the Enemy press'd hard upon us, wee had not only been forced to haue left it behind, but all the Generall Officers there present had

PART III.

1658.
M. d'Hocquincourt obstinate obliges Bouteville to return with him and charge the Enemy a Second time. *Ibid.*

The Duke coming that way and hearing Don John and the P^ce of Condé were gone towards the line, he did the like. Or: Mem: P. 3. p. 103.

E. Feversham and Henry Jermyn both shott throw the thigh. *Ibid,*

M. d'Hocquincourt at the moment the Duke came up to him, receives a shott in the belly, of which he dys. Vpon this the Spaniards drew off, and the Enemy advance upon them. *Ibid.*

The Duke faces about, to give time to carry of M^r. d'Hocquincourt's corps. Or: Mem. P. 3. p. 103. All the Generall Officers in

P A R T
III.

1658.
danger of
being made
prisoners.
Ibid. p. 104.
Marq. de
Caracena
chides them,
for having so
rashly exposed
themselves
with a few
Cravatts, at so
great distance
from their
troopes. *Ibid.*

June, 13, the
Spaniard's
Army removes
to the ap-
pointed Camp
amongst the
Sand hills.
Ibid.
Posture of yᵉ
incampment of
the Spanish
troopes. *Ibid.*

M. de Turenne
without con-
sulting with
any person,
resolves to
march next
morning and
attaque the
Span: in their
Camp.
OR: MEM:
P. 3. p. 105.

run the hazard of being made prisoners, they having no other horse with them besides Cravatts, who were not capable of sustaining a vigourous charge, and being distant from their own troopes above a mile. But at length when all was over, up came the Marquis de Caracena with three troopes of Guards to our assistance, who chid us all for having expos'd ourselves as wee had done.

After this wee return'd to the body of our Army, but so disorder'd by the fatall accident which had happen'd to the Mareshall d'Hocquincourt, that wee march'd back to our Camp by Furnes, without viewing any part of the Enemies Line or taking any other consultation about our going thither. The day following wee remov'd to the place which wee had chosen for our incampment; having our right to the Sea, and our left to the Canal of Furnes. Wee lay with our foot upon one Line before our horse, which reach'd from the Sand-hills next the Sea, as far as the ditches, which are nearest to the foremention'd Canal: our horse were on two Lines behind our foot, and as for our baggage, wee left it behind at Furnes; for our traine of artillery, by good fortune, it was not yet come to the Army: so that wee had neither cannon nor tooles, nor hardly powder enough for our foot; without all which necessarys wee came and camp'd within less then twice cannon shott of the Enemies Line.

Wee came thither with the Van of our Army about eleven of the clock in the forenoon. And, as I haue been since inform'd, it was evening before Monsʳ. de Turenne could be drawn to beleeve, that wee were there with our whole Army, or that wee came with a design of camping in that place: But about that time a prisonner was brought, who assured him of both. Wherupon, without consulting one moment with any person, he immediatly took the resolution of marching to us the next morning, and fighting us.

Accordingly he gave out orders for all his troopes to be in a readiness at that time : And sent for the English, that were quarter'd at Mardyke, to march up to him; which they immediatly obeyd, and march'd all night, having a great compass to take, and were by day-break at his quarter : But while the French were preparing to come out upon us, the next morning, wee took no measures in our Army as if any Enemy were to be expected ; for when the orders were given in our Camp at night, there was no prohibition made to our horse of going out to forage, till the pleasure of the Generall should be further known, as is usuall in the like cases : But they were permitted to go abroad, as if no Enemy had been near us. And that it may be seen, how litle some of our Generall Officers beleev'd the French had any such intention (or at least would haue it thought that they so beleev'd) happening myself to be at supper that night with the Marquis de Caracena, and the Company falling into discourse on the Subject of our coming thither, and what the French might probably attempt against us, I said, That for my own particular I lik'd not our being there upon such termes as wee were then, having no Lines nor any thing to cover us from the Enemy ; and that it was my opinion, if they fell not upon us that very night, I was very confident they would give us battaill the next morning: To which both the Marquis and Don Estevan de Gamarra answered; that it was what they desir'd : To which I reply'd, That I knew Monsr. de Turenne So well, as to assure them they should haue that Satisfaction.

The next morning about five of the clock, our horse guard brought us intelligence, that they saw some horse drawing out of the Enemies Lines, which they suppos'd came with design to beat them in; upon which our whole Army tooke the alarme, and stood to their armes, and the Generalls went out to discover what the Enemy was doing. I was the first who came to our horse guard, and going as far as the outmost Sentrys, I

PART
III.

1658.
outmost
Sentrys, where
he discovers
the Enemies
whole Army
comin up to
them. g
Or: Mem:
P. 3. p. 106.
Returning
back to ye
Camp, he
meets Don
John, who
would not
beleeve that
ye French in-
tended to give
battell.
Ibid. p: 107.

plainly saw that their whole Army was coming out of their Lines; Their horse, with four small feild peices, advancing along the high way betwixt the Sand-hills, and the meadow grounds, and the French foot drawing out on their left hand, having thrown down some peices of their Line that they might march out at least a Battailion a front; and farther on their left hand, which was nearer to the Sea, the English were drawing out, whom I easily knew by their redcoats: Of all which having taken a distant view, I went back to give an account of it, and before I reach'd our Camp, I mett with Don John, who asking me, what were the intentions of the French? I answer'd him, That they were drawing out to give us battell; which he seeming not to beleeve, said, their design was only to drive in our horse guards. I replyd, That it was not the custom of the French to march out with such a body of foot, as I had seen, compos'd of the French and Suisse Guards, the Regiments of Picardy and Turenne, all which I knew by their coulours, as well as the English by their redcoats, and with so great a body of horse as those I had observ'd with their cañon before them, with a bare intention of forcing in our horse guards.

The Pce of
Condé give
the same
account of the
Enemy that ye
Duke had
given. Ibid.
The Pce of
Condé assures
the Duke of
Glocester, that
within half an
hour he should
See a battell.
Or: Mem:
P. 3. p. 107.
The Genll.
Officers go
each to their
respective
posts, and
attend the
coming of the
Enemy. Ibid.

Before I could add any other arguments for the confirmation of my opinion, or Don John had the leysure of replying, the Prince of Condé came up to us, who had also been at one of our horse guards, and gave the same account which I had done; and seeing the Duke of Glocester there, ask'd him, If he had ever seen a Battell? who telling him, he had not; the Prince assured him, that within half an houre he should behold one: And now, there being no farther room to doubt of the Enemies intention, all the Generall Officers parted from each other, and went to their respective posts; with resolution to attend the coming of the French, and to fight them where wee were, having the advantage of the ground, which wee must haue lost, had wee advanced towards them.

Our Army was drawn up after this following manner: Our
Foot, which were about six thousand, were divided into fifteen
Battalions, and were all upon one Line, excepting two of them;
They reach'd from a high Sand hill into the meedows adjoyning
the Canal of Furnes: The naturall Spaniards had the right hand
of all, who consisted of four Regiments; Don Gaspar Boniface
his Regiment was plac'd upon the high Sand hill, nearest to the
Strand; Behind which was that of Francisco de Meneses, facing
towards the Sea, to be in a posture of opposing any which
should offer to fall into their flanck: On the left hand of the
first which I haue mentiond, was that of Don Diego de Goni,
commanded by Don Antonio de Cordoua, on whose left hand
was placed the Marquis de Seralvo at the head of his Regiment;
next to whom were the King's and the Lord Bristoll's Regiments,
both which made up one Battalion alone, and was commanded
by the Lord Muskerry; And for a reserve behind those two
Battalions, Coll: Richard Grace with the Lord Newbourgh's
Regiment, making likewise one Battalion. On the left hand
of the Regiment of York, were three Walloon Battalions, after
them one of Germans, composed of four Regiments; Next to
which upon the last Sand hill, towards the Canal of Furnes,
was plac'd Guitaud's Regiment of Germans, being the first of
the Prince of Condé's foot: The rest of them, which were three
Battalions, were drawn up betwixt the Sand-hills and the Canal,
by the high-way side and in the meedows.

On the Sand hills, where our Foot was drawn up in this order,
wee had a great advantage of the Enemy, there running a ridge
from one side to the other, upon which they were posted; so
that the Enemy must be constrain'd to charge us up the hill,
which every one knows is a greater disadvantage on the Sand,
where the footing is loose, then on firm ordinary ground. As
for our Horse (which should haue been eight thousand thō at
that time they were scarcely half so strong, the greatest part of

1658.
The Spanish
Army how
drawn up in
Battell.
Ibid. p. 108.

P A R T
III.

1658.

The order of
Battell of the
French Army.
Or: Mem:
P. 3. p. 109.

them being gone out to forrage and not returning till after wee
were beaten) the Spanish Horse were drawn up in two Lines
behind our Foot, amongst the Sand hills; The Prince of Condé's
in more Lines behind his Foot, betwixt the Sand hills and the
meadow-grounds; in many places there being not room for
above three or four Squadrons a front: so that I am not
absolutly certain, in what number of Lines they were drawn up.
In this order wee stood expecting the Enemy, whose Army,
according to my best remembrance, were marshall'd in the
manner following. Their Foot were drawn up in two Lines of
seven Battalions each: The first Line was commanded by a
Lieu't Generall Mons'. de Guadagne, and compos'd of one
Battalion of the French Guards which had the right hand, and
march'd along under the Sand hills by the high way side;
Next to which was one Battalion of the Suisse Guards, which
went along by the top of the Sand hills, next the high way; On
whose left hand was the Regiment de Picardy makin one
Battalion; and then on the same front that of Turenne, which
was the last of the French Battalions on the first Line; on
whose left hand were three of the English Regiments, each of
which made a Battalion, the last of them reaching as far as
the Sand hills next the Sea: And before each Battalion of this
first Line, they had commanded Musketeers (which was the only
time that ever I knew forlorne hopes us'd beyond the Seas in
any battell) But as Monsieur de Turenne advanced, seeing wee
had some foot in the meadows, he took the right hand Battalion
of the second Line; and made it march on the right hand of
his Horse in the meadows; this Battalion was commanded by
Mons'. de Montgomery one of his Nephews. As for their
second Line of Foot, it consisted of the same number of
Battalions, three of which were English, and the rest French.
For their Horse, they had about five or six Squadrons betwixt
their two Lines of Foot; and their right wing came along the

high way, just beneath the Sand hills, commanded by the
Marquis de Crequi, a Lieu^t Generall, having as many Squadrons
a front as the ground would bear, which in divers places was
not above three or four; before whom march'd four feild peices:
Their left wing commanded by Monsr. de Castelnau a Lieu^t.
Generall, came along the Strand, with feild peices attending
them ; and severall of the English small Fregatts having the
advantage of the tyde of flood, stood in as near the shore as
possibly they could see amongst the Sand hills. This was the
order of the French Army : And in this manner they advanced
upon us, while wee only stood our ground, and expected them.

The first who engaged us were the English led up by Major
Generall Morgan ; their Generall Lockart (for what reason I
know not) being with Monsr. de Castelneau at the head of
their left wing. But immediatly before their falling on, Don
John sent me, and desired me to go to our right hand, and
take a particular care of that part, where he saw the Englis
were advancing ; Which I did, taking no troopes along with
me from the middle of the Line, where I then was, excepting
only my own Troope of Guards, and a hundred commanded
men, with two Captains, and Officers proportionable out of my
next Battalion, to reinforce the naturall Spaniards. Which Foot
I joyn'd to Boniface, where I judged they would make their
greatest effort, and which was (of) the greatest importance to
be maintain'd, it being the highest of the Sand hills on that
side, and advanced somewhat farther then any of the rest which
were thereabout, commanding also those which were nearest
to it.

This was all I had leisure to do, before the English attack'd
us ; who came on with great eagerness and courage : But their
heat was such, that they outmarch'd the French, so that had
the opportunity been taken, they might haue paid deer for
their rash bravery, But they, whose busines it was to haue

PART
III.

1658.

The Crom-
welian English
are the first
that fall on.
OR: MEM:
P. 3. p. 110.
The Duke is
desired by Don
John, to go to
the right wing
to take care of
that part
where the
English are
advancing.
OR: MEM:
P. 3. p. 110.
He carrys only
his own
Troope of
Guards and
100 com-
manded men
with him, and
joyns Boni-
face's post
where the
greatest effort
was like to be
made.
Ibid. p. 111.
The English
come on with
great heat and
courage. Ibid.

PART
III.

1658.

taken that advantage, either tooke no notice of it, or had some other reason, unknown to me, why they sent not some Horse to fall into their flanques; Whatsoever the occasion was, the opportunity was let slipp, and the English came up without the least disturbance to make their charge.

Boniface, as I haue already said, was posted on the highest Sand hill, which was somewhat advanced before any of the others, so that the battell began there. It was Lockart's own Regiment which charged those Spaniards, and was commanded by Lieu^t. Coll. Fenwick; who so soon as he came to the bottom of the hill, seeing that it was exceeding steep, and difficult to ascend, commanded his men to halt and take breath for two or three minutes, that they might be more able to climb and do their duty.

While they were thus preparing themselves, their commanded men opening to the right and left, to give way to their main body which was to mount the higth, were continually firing at Boniface; and as soon as the body were in a condition to climb, they began their ascent with a great shout, which was generall from all their foot. But while they were scrambling up in the best manner they were able, the Lieu^t. Coll: fell in the middle way, being shott through the body; which yet hinder'd not the Major, who was called Hinton (since a Captain in the Duke of Albemarle's Regiment) from leading on his men together with the rest of their Officers, who Stopt not till they came to push of pyke; where notwithstanding the great resistance which was made by the Spaniards, and the advantage they had of the higher ground, as well as, that of being well in breath, when their Enemies were almost spent with climbing, the English gain'd the hill and drove them from off it: The Spaniards leaving dead upon the spott, seven of eleven Captains which commanded in the Regiment, together with Slaughter and Farrell, two Captains whom I had joyn'd to that Regiment

Lockart's Regim^t. is the first that charge.
OR: MEM:
P. 3. p: 111.

Fenwick, L^t. Coll: of Lockart's Reg^t, Kill'd. *Ibid.*
The Major leads on the Regiment.
OR: MEM:
P. 3. p. 111.
They come to push of pyke with the Spaniards, and drive them from the hill.
Ibid.

of 11 Spanish Captains, 7 left dead upon the spott.
Ibid. p. 112.

just before; besides many of their reform'd Officers (their stands of Pykes being for the most part made of such) Yet this ground had been so well disputed, that the English, besides their Lieu^t. Coll: lost Severall Officers and Soldiers.

And now, having thus far carryd on their busines successfully, so soon as they had put themselves again in order, and recover'd breath, they came down the Sand hill, which I observing, went to charge them with my own Guards and those of Don John ; but being come up almost within reach of their pykes, I found the ground to be such, as render'd it almost impossible for me to break into them: notwithstanding which I was resolv'd to endeavour it, and accordingly charg'd them thō to no purpose : for what with the advantage of the ground, and with the stout resistance they made in that first charge, I was beaten off, and all who were at the head of my own Troope, were either killed or wounded ; of which number I had been one, had not the goodness of my armes preserv'd me. The cheife Officers of my Troope escap'd better then those belonging to Don John ; for of mine, only Charles Berkley the Capitaine of my Guards was hurt, and of the other, only the Count de Colmenar who was Captain of it, came off unwounded, amongst all the Officers : neither did their common men fare better, the loss falling so heavily amongst them, that thō I endeavour'd all I could to rally them, it was not possible for me to perform it. But I had better fortune with those of my own Guards, for I gott all of them together who were yet in a condition of doing duty, which were not above forty.

The Duke at the head of his own Guards andDonJohn's charges Lockart's Regim^t. but with the advantage of their ground and theirStout resistance, he is beaten off. *Ibid.*

All those that were at ye head of ye Dukes Troop either kill'd or wounded. And the Duke himself receives a shott in his Armour. OR: MEM: P. 3. p. 112. Charles Berkley Captain of the Duke's Guards wounded. *Ibid.*

When I had rallyd this small party, I went to Boniface, where first Don John, and after him the Marquis de Caracena had been endeavouring to rally them, but not being able to do it, were gone off. When I came up to that Regiment, I was not able at first to make them stand ; but while I was trying my authority amongst them, I saw there one Elvige a Lieutenant

The Duke having rallyd the remainder of his own Guards,endeavours also to rally Boniface Reg: which neither Don John nor Caracena had been able to do. *Ibid.*

11

PART
III.

1658.

An Officer of
the King's
Regiment
crying out,that
yᵉ Duke was
there, all the
English of that
part face about
and joyn his
R. H.
On: Mᴇᴍ:
P. 3. p. 113.
The Spaniards
follow the ex-
ample of the
English, and
draw up in
good order.
Ibid.

The Duke's
answer to
Caracena,who
ask'd him why
he did not
charge again.
Ibid.

Lockart's
Regimᵗ. ad-
vancing to-
wards the left
hand, comes
even upon a
line wᵗʰ the
Duke's rallied
party. Ibid.

of the King's Regiment, who had been commanded along with the hundred men whom I had sent to strengthen that Battalion; and asking him, what, was become of his Captains? he answer'd me, they were both slaine with most of their Soldiers; and that he was the only Officer of that party that had escap'd unhurt. Upon which I commanded him to stay with me, and call his men together, which he did, and crying out aloud to them, That the Duke was there, those who heard him faced about immediatly, and came up to us. At the same time seeing the Major of that Spanish Regiment, I call'd to him, That he should make his men follow the example of those few English, it not being the custome of Spaniards to run when any others stood; and upon the Major's reproching them with that, they stopt, and drew up in good order. And now the Marquis of Caracena coming back once more, demanded of me, Why I charg'd not the Enemy with my Horse? I answer'd him, I had already done it, and (been) worsted for my paines; farther telling him, That considering the present posture of the Enemy, it was impossible to be done, and at the Same time shewing him, what I had affirmed, from behind the next Sand hill.

Presently after this (the Marquis being gone again) Lockart's Regiment, which, as I haue already said, had beaten off our Horse, advanced not directly forward, but bent a litle towards their left hand; and wee lost sight of each other, by reason of the unevenesse of the ground (a Sand hill being interpos'd betwixt us) so that by that time I had got the Regiment of Boniface in order, and those few Horse which I had with me, this English Battalion was come even upon a line with us, just upon my right hand, a Sand hill only being betwixt us: Wherupon I faced touards the Sea, and marching at the head of my Foot, as I came up to the top of the Sand hill, I perceiv'd the English coming up on the other side to me: upon which I gott from betwixt them, commanding the Major who was with me at the head of Boniface, to charge them in the front, whilst I with my Horse would fall into their flanque.

When I had given this order, I put myself immediatly at the head of my forty Guards, and charg'd that Battalion So home, that I broke into them, doing great execution upon them, and driving them to the edge of the Sand hill next the Strand. As for the Battalion of Boniface they did not charge, seeing I had already broken the English; but discovering from the top of the Sand hill, where they were, that our whole Army was in route, they scatter'd, and every man endeavour'd to gett off, which few of them were so lucky as to perform.

Tis very observable that when wee had broken into this Battalion, and were gott amongst them, not so much as one single man of them ask'd quarter, or threw down his armes; but every one defended himself to the last : so that wee ran as great danger by the butt end of their musketts, as by the volley which they had given us. And one of them had infallibly knock'd me off from my horse, if I had not prevented him when he was just ready to haue discharg'd his blow, by a stroke I gave him with my sword over the face, which layd him along upon the ground.

The Duke of Glocester, who during the action of all that day had seconded me, and behav'd himself as bravely as any of his Ancestors had ever done, had his sword either struck out of his hand by one of the Enemy, or it flew out of his hand by a blow which he had given ; but which of the two I remember not : It happen'd that a gentleman, one Villeneuue, Ecnier to the Prince de Ligny, who was next him, saw this accident ; wherupon he leap'd down immediatly from his horse, took up the sword and delivered it to my Brother, who with his pistoll in his hand, stood ready to secure him till he was remounted. But immediatly after, the same gentleman was shott through

P A R T
III.

1658.
The Duke charges them with his 40 Guards, breaks into them, drives them before him and do's great execution upon them. Or: Mem: P. 3. p. 113.

The Battalion of Boniface Seeing y⁰ whole Spanish Army routed, they scatter and leave the Duke. *Ibid.* p. 114.

Lockart's Battalion, tho broke, not one single man of them ask'd quarter. Or: Mem: P. 3. p. 114.

One of them going to knock the Duke from his horse, with y⁰ butt end of his muskett, is prevented by y⁰ Duke with a Stroke of his Sword over the face which layd him on the ground. *Ibid.*

The Duke of Glocester's brav behaviour, he has his sword struck out of his hand, w⁰ʰ is taken up and given back to him by a querry of y⁰ Pᶜᵉ de Ligny. *Ibid.*

1658.
a French
Squadron,
falling into the
Duke's flanck,
he and his
small party had
undoubted-
ly been cutt off,
if the French
had not been
at the same
time charg'd
by the P^ce de
Ligny.
OR: MEM:
P. 3. p. 114.
The Duke
takes this
opportunity,
and getts off,
and the P^ce de
Ligny escapes
another way.
OR: MEM:
P. 3. p. 114.
The Regiment
of Boniface is
all cutt in
pieces, and the
rest of the
Spanish
Regiments
taken in their
posts.
Ibid. p. 115.
Account of
what had past
in the left
wing.
OR: MEM:
P. 3. p. 115.

the body; notwithstanding which it was his fortune to gett off, and to recover of his wound.

I had no sooner made this charge, but I was obliged to make what hast I could to get away; for a Squadron of the French Army from the Strand, had gott up amongst the Sand hills, just as I was charging, and had into my flanque; So that they had undoubtedly cutt me off with my small party, had they not been charg'd themselves, at the same time, by the Prince de Ligny, who thō he did not defeat them, yet he gaue them a litle stop; which opportunity I took to get off, and the Prince, after he had made his charge, escap'd another way.

By this time not only all the Regiment of Boniface was cutt in peices, but the rest of the naturall Spanish Regiments were all taken in their Severall posts by the Horse; for they were not charg'd by the English as they ought to haue been, had our Countrymen march'd directly onwards: but so it happen'd, that when the other two Regiments of them, saw the resistance which was made by Boniface, they all bent that way, marching by the flanque, only firing at the other naturall Spaniards as they pass'd along, and marching up the Sand-hill after Lockart's Regiment.

While these things were passing on our right hand next the Sea, our left wing received as hard measure from the Enemy as wee had done; for the four feild peices, which, as I sayd, advanced along the high way, under the Sand-hills, terribly gaul'd both our Horse and Foot which were before them: So that the Foot Guards and the Regiment de la Couronne (the last of which was commanded by Monsr. de Montgomery, and having been taken out of the Second Line by Monsr. de Turenne, as I haue said, was placed on the right hand of the Guards in the meadow grounds) seeing that wee had three small Battalions betwixt the Sand-hills and the Canal, they advanced against

them, but our Battalions making a very fainte resistance ran
away. Upon which the French horse advanced before their
foot, as many Squadrons a front as they could march, commanded by the Marquis de Crequi, a Lieu^t Generall, and
were charg'd so vigourously by the Prince of Condé's horse, that
they were beaten back behind their foot: yet at length, notwithstanding all he could do, they having horse and foot against
horse alone, they forced him from his ground, and oblig'd him
to run for it, as fast as his neighbours had done before him;
thō he did what was possible to be done, in both capacities, both
as a Generall, and as a Soldier; in so much that at the last of
the three charges, which he made with his horse, he was in
great hazard of being taken.

As to what pass'd on the right wing of the Prince of Condé,
upon the Sand-hills betwixt him and the place where the naturall
Spaniards were drawn up; The Regiment de Guitault (*de Guis-
card*) (which was posted upon the Sand hill next to the high way
along which came the right wing of the French Cavalery) did
not Stay for a charge from the Suisses, but fir'd at too great a
distance and presently ran away: The four next Battalions did
the like, none of them Staying to be throughly charg'd; which
cowardise of theirs, and the defeat of Boniface his Regiment,
who were beaten from their ground, strook such a terrour into
our horse, which were drawn up behind our foot on the Sand-
hills, that the greatest part of them, especially those of the
Second line, ran away without being charg'd, or even without
seeing an Enemy, thō most of their Officers were not wanting
to their duty, in endeavouring to stop them: Those few who
had courage enough to Stay, perform'd their parts like men of
honour, as shall be mention'd in its proper place.

The next to these three Regiments, of which I haue spoken,
was my own, which stood a litle longer then their neighbours
on the left hand; But a voice coming behind them, that the

PART
III.

1658.
M. de Crequi
advancing the
French horse
against the
Spanish foot
that were
running away,
the P^ce of
Condé charges
him with his
horse and
beats him back
behind his
foot. *Ibid.*

On the P^ce of
Condé's right
wing the Reg^t
de Guitault,
with the 4 next
Battalions, fire
at a distance
and run im-
mediatly away.
Ibid.

which the
horse behind
this foot See-
ing, the most
part of them
run without
seeing an
Enemy. *Ibid.*

The Duke's
Regim^t. stand
their ground,
till a voice
from behind
advertising
the foot to

1658.
Save them-
selves, made
them also
break and run
with their
neighbours.
OR: MEM:
P. 3, p. 116.
Coll: Grace
marches off his
Reg'. in good
order, without
losing one
man.
Ibid. p: 117.

foot should save themselves, that Battalion broke also, the
Soldiers leaving their Officers, and running away; which Coll:
Grace seen (*seeing*) who was drawn up behind them, thought
it was high time for him to endeavour to save his Regiment,
and march off in good order at a round rate in three divisions ;
by observing of which discipline, and keeping them together,
he had the good fortune to gett off a cross the high way; to the
Canal of Furnes, along which he made his retreat without losing
a man.   But my Regiment was attended with worse luck; for
thō Mons'. de Roc with his Regiment of horse went up and
charg'd the Cardinal's Gensdarmes, killing with his own hand
Mons'. du Bourg who commanded them, and beating that

The French
horse over-
taking the
Dukes Regim'.
not one of it
Soldier or Offi-
cer escap'd,
but My lord
Muskerry.
OR: MEM:
P. 3. p. 117.

Squadron; yet they who should haue seconded him being gone,
and more horse coming on to charge him, he was forced also
to make the best of his way, and shift for one.   Those horse
which he had beaten soon overtook my Regiment, so that
excepting My Lord Muskerry, who was fortunate enough to
get a horse accidentally, not a Soldier or Officer escap'd.

Much about the Same time, one Michel an old German
Collonel, with his Regiment of horse, charg'd the Battalion of
Turenne after they were march'd down from the hill, on which
our Foot had been drawn up; but he was not able to break
them, they receiving his charge in so good order, that they
kill'd him with the greatest part of his Officers, and beat off his
Regiment of horse without any loss but of the Lieu' Collonel

Michel and
Roc, the only
two Coll: of
the Spanish
Horse that
behav'd well
in this battell.
Ibid. p. 118.

Betbesé, who was slain at the head of the pikes with a pistoll
shott.   Besides these two Collonels, I know not of any Spanish
horse that behav'd themselves well in this battell, or if they did,
it never arriv'd to my knowledge.

The Duke
incompass'd
on every side
w'ᵗʰ the French
horse, and
none of his
own men
standing,

I must go now a litle back to give a further account of my
own fortune : As soon as I came off from charging and breaking
that Regiment of English, I thought it but reasonable to endeavour my own escape, the French horse having already incompass'd

me on, every side, and none of our men standing.: But
not knowing what success wee, might haue had in our left wing,
where the Prince of Condé was, I resolved in the first place to
go thither, and see in what posture our affaires were there. I
had not now above twenty horse remaining with me; the rest
of my Guards which were with my Lieutenant, being parted
from me as I came from amongst the English : The Smalness of
my number prov'd my best security ; for with those who still
continued about me, I was strong enough to deal with any
loose men, and yet was not so considerable as to provoke any
bodys to disband after me : And by Some of the Enemys wee
were taken for one of their own partys ; for as I was coming
off, I saw four or five of their Troopers falling upon an Officer
of mine, on Lieu^t Victor, since a Captain at Tangier : I went
up to them, taking them indeed for some of our own horse, and
call'd out to them in french, That they should let him alone, for
he was one of our own Englishmen : Accordingly they dismiss'd him, giving him his sword which they had taken from
him, and went off themselves, mistaking me for one of their own
Officers: Thus both I and they were in an errour, and I knew
not my own mistake till Victor told me of it afterwards.

I continu'd my way forward, and made a shift to pass through
the French, trotting in good order, 'till I overtook Coll: Grace
and his Regiment before they gott out from amongst the Sand
hills; going by the Regiments of Picardy and Turenne, which
were then as far advanced as where our men had been
incamped the night before; and coming down into the high
way, under the Sand hills, I found all the Prince of Condé's
Troopes already beaten, he having then made his last
charge; So that he was constrain'd to run with them, and as I
sayd, with great difficulty escap'd. The throng being very
great in the Village of Zudcote, through which the high way
went, and the Enemy pursuing us with great eagerness, I had

P A R T
III.

1658.
escapes with
20 horse and
go's to see how
matters stood
on the left
wing. *Ibid.*

The Smalness
of the Duke's
number prov'd
his best
Security.
Or: Mem:
P. 3. p. 118.

The French
mistaking the
Duke for one
of their own
Officers, at his
desire they dis-
miss an Officer
of his whom
they had
taken.
Or: Mem:
P. 3. p. 119.

P A R T III.

1658.
The Duke escapes narrowly being taken at the village of Zudcote.
Or: Mem: P. 3. p. 119.

He overtakes Don John, the Pce of Condé and Caracena, on the other side of Zudcote, wher all make a litle stand and face about to give Don John time to change his horse, and then all sett spur again till the Enemy left pursuing.
Ibid. p. 120.

All the Genll. Officers except Don Stevande Gamarra behav'd well, and exposed their persons very much.
Or: Mem: P. 3. p. 120.
Don John and Caracena very near being taken. Ibid.

Pce de Ligny charg'd very handsomly.
Ibid. p. 121.

no other meanes to avoid being taken, then to disingage myself from the crowd, and to take another way, which was round about the Village leaving it on my right hand. And to shew how near I was to be made prisoner, a Collonel under the Prince, one (de) Morieul, meeting me just as I came down the Sandhills, and not following my example of taking round the Village, but mingling with the crowd, immediatly after he was parted from me fell'd into the hands of the pursuers, and was made a prisoner. As for me I gott safe into the way again on the other side of the Village, where Don John, the Prince of Condé, the Marquis de Caracena, and others, were already gott before me. Soon after which, wee were obliged to make a litle stand, and face about, to give Don John de leisure to change his horse, his own by some accident being fallen lame; which being done, wee sett spurrs again to our horses, and did not stop, 'till the Enemy had left pursuing us.

I shall not take upon me to give a particular account of what was done in this engagement by our Generall Officers, because I haue received no particular information of it: Only this I know in grosse, that all of them behav'd themselves very bravely, excepting Don Estevan de Gamarra; the rest of them so far exposing their persons, that they escap'd not without great hazard. For the Prince of Condé, and myself, I haue already given a Relation of our fortunes: And concerning Don John, I haue been inform'd, that he stayd so long, that he was in danger of being taken: And the Marquis de Caracena was so near it, that before he gott out from amongst the Sand hills, a horseman of the Enemys had layd hold on his bridle; but the Marquis at the same time striking him over the face with his cane, (having nothing els in his hand) so stun'd him, that he let go his hold, and so the Marquis had leisure to escape. To what concerns the Prince de Ligny, I haue already mention'd how handsomly he behavd himself when he charg'd; but how he gott off, I am not certain : But for Don Estevan de Gamarra who commanded as Mestre de Camp Generall, and was at the head of the foot, he went away at first, and never stopt till he came to Nieuport.

I haue not yet given an account of the Battalion, which was compos'd of the King's Regiment and the Earle of Bristoll's, and I should be very injurious to the first of these two, if I should pass them by in silence. They were posted, as I haue said, next the naturall Spaniards ; and notwithstanding that they saw all on the right and left hand of them already routed and gone off, yet they continued firm (I mean that part of the Battalion which was compos'd of the King's Regiment) for they were all English ; As for the other part of it, which was form'd of My lord Bristoll's men who were Irish, they indeed went away, when they saw all their freinds about them beaten ; neither was it in the power of their Officers to hinder them, thō they endeavour'd it ; but seeing their paines were to no effect, they ran for company, excepting Captain Stroad (*Stroud*) an English Gentleman, who was Captain Lieu^t. of that Regiment ; for he came and put himself at the head of the remaining part of the Battalion, with his own Countrymen : But this was not the only discouragement which these English had, for both the Lieu^t. Collonell and Major had forsaken them before the Irish, the first upon pretence of going for orders, and the other upon an account which was not a jot more honorable. The Lieu^t. Coll: was rewarded for his paines as he deserved ; for being mett by some of the lose French horse, who were then gott behind them, he was shott into the face, somewhat below the eye, and the bullet came out behind his neck ; of which wound he narrowly escap'd with life : he was also unhors'd, and being in this condition, one of my Guards, the only man amongst them who behav'd himself ill and who was not an Englishman, accidentally found him, and help'd him off.

PART III.

1658.
Don Estevan de Gamarra ran away at first, and never stopt till he came to Nieuport.
OR: MEM: P. 3. p. 121.
An account of the gallant behaviour of the King's Regim^t. all of them English. *Ibid.*
These see all on their right and left hand routed. *Ibid.*
Lord Bristoll's men, who were Irish, run likewise and forsake them. *Ibid.*

And their Lieu^t. Coll: and their Major abandon them.
OR: MEM: P. 3. p. 121.

PART
III.
1658.
Notwithstand-
ing all which
discourag-
ments, they
stand firm and
maintain their
ground in the
midle of the
Enemy.
Ibid. p: 122.

When offer'd
quarter by the
Enemy, they
answer, That
they had been
posted where
they were by
ye Duke, and
would main-
tain their post
as long as they
could. *Ibid.*

They are told
that ye whole
Army is
routed, but
they refuse to
believe an
Enemy,
hearken to no
capitulation
till they are
assured by two
of their own
Officers, that
none of their
Army was left
standing but
themselves;
upon which
they at last
Surrender
upon very
honourable
termes.
Or: Mem:
P. 3. p. 122.

But none of these misadventures did at all daunt the King's
Regiment : They continued to stand firm, and maintain'd their
ground, thō they beheld the first Line of the French passing by
them on their left hand, and the Cromwellian English on their
right, till the second Line came up to them. It was the
Regiment of Rambures which advancèd to charge them (their
Collonel commanding that Line, and being at their head.) This
Officer seeing not a man standing of all our Troopes, excepting
this small body which was before him, went up to them himself,
a litle before his men, to offer them quarter; To whom they
return'd this answer, That they had been posted there by the
Duke, and therfore were resolved to maintain that ground as
long as they were able : He replyd, That it would be to no purpose for them to stand out, their whole Army being already
routed, and having left the feild. They answer'd again, That
it was not their part to beleeve an Enemy: Upon which he
offer'd them, that if they would send out an Officer or two, he
would himself carry them up to a Sand-hill which was behind
them, and then they should perceive, that what he affirm'd
was true: Accordingly they sent out two Officers, Captain
Thom: Cooke and Aston, whom he conducted as he had
promis'd to the Sand-hill which he had nam'd; from whence
they could easily discover, that none of our Army was left
standing excepting only themselves, after which, he brought
them down again to their own men. Wherupon they told him,
That in case he would promise they should not be deliver'd
up to the English, nor be stripp'd, nor haue their pockets
search'd, they would lay down their armes and yeeld themselves his prisoners; to which he immediatly agreeing, and
giving his word for the performance of those Articles, they
accordingly yeelded, and his promise was exactly kept to them:
by which their honorable carriage, they far'd much better then

the other Regiment which deserted them ; some of whom were slaine, and the rest taken and stripp'd afterwards.

I haue now given the best account I am able of the whole Action, and it remains, that I should say something of the number of the Slaine on both sides and of the Prisoners. As for the Slaine, they amounted not in all to above four hundred ; amongst which on our side there fell the Count de la Motterie and of the Spanish troopes, Collonel Michel, with most of the Captains of Boniface, one of Seralvo, and another of Goni, (*Gomez*) as also Don Francisco Romero Governour of the two Troopes of Guards, with two or three more of his Officers : Of those whom I commanded, there were kill'd three Captains, Slaughter of the King's Regiment, ———— of my own, and Farrell of the Lord Bristoll's, besides some Lieutenants and Ensignes, and two Brigadeers of my Troope of Guards. Of the P^ce of Condé's Troopes, I remember none of quality but the Count de Meille a Lieu^t. Generall, with some few Captains. Of the Spanish Officers, were taken the Marquis de Seralvo, Risbourg, Conflans, Belleveder, the Prince de Robec, Don Antonio de Cordoua, Don J. de Toledo y Portugal, Don Joseph Manriques, Don Luis de Zuniga, Le Baron de Limbeck, Darchem, Baynes, all Collonels of horse or foot, and M^r. de Montmorency, Captain of the Guards to the Prince de Ligny. Most of these were abandon'd by their men, and were taken, because they would not make such hast away as their Soldiers had done : I cannot say what Captains and other inferiour Officers were made Prisoners, only, that of the naturall Spanish Regiments of foot, few or none escap'd, because they behav'd themselves very honorably ; But of the horse, the number of Captains and Officers under them, was no way proportionable to the number of Officers in my Troopes. Of my own Regiment, not an Officer escap'd taking, excepting My Lord Muskerry who commanded it ; and of the private Soldiers, not twenty. As

1658.
The number of the Slaine on both sides at the Battell of Dunkerque not above 400 men.
Or: Mem:
P. 3. p. 123.
Name of Severall of the chief Officers that were killd on the Spanish Side. *Ibid.*

Names of those that were taken Prisoners.
Ibid. p. 124.

for the King's Regiment, it was intirely broken. The Earle of Bristoll's Regiment had the same fate with mine, few or none getting away; but of his Guards not above five or six were · taken. As for the cheif Officers under the Prince of Condé, Mons'. de Coligny et Boutteville, both Lieu' Generalls, were made Prisoners with Meille (who dyd of his wounds) and Mons'. des Roches Captain of his Guards: He lost no many of his foot, for they not doing their duty as became Soldiers, and being near the Canal, had an easy opportunity of escaping; his horse, thō they fought bravely, yet lost fewer then the Spaniards, and amongst them all not one Collonel.

The loss on y*
French side
very inconsi-
derable, names
of some of
their Officer's
thatwerekilld.
OR: MEM:
P. 3. p. 125.

How many of the Enemy were slain, I know not certainly, only in generall, that their loss was very inconsiderable both as to the number and the quality; for I haue not heard of any other Officers who were kill'd on their side, then Mons'. de la Berge (who had been Captain of M'. de Turenne's Guards, and was then Major Generall of the Foot, which is less then either a Lieu' Generall or a Mareshall de Camp) Mons'. de Bebsey Lieu' Collonel of Mons'. de Turenne's Regiment of Foot, and Du Bourg Lieu' of the Cardinal's Gensdarmes: Of the English sent by Cromwell, Fenwick Lockart's Lieu' Collonel, with two Captains, four Lieutenants, and four Ensignes; Of the English common men about a hundred; and the Major of the Same Regiment, with two Captains, and some Lieutenants and Enseigne's hurt.

The Spaniards
had no cañon
nor baggage to
lose.
They rally
their beaten
Army at
Furnes. Ibid.

As for baggage and cannon, wee had none to lose, our traine by good fortune not being come up to us; and our baggage being left behind at Furnes, at which place wee rally'd our beaten Army.

A generous
action done in
behalf of y*
Duke, by
Mons'. de
Gadagne a
French Lieu'.
Generall. Ibid.

And here I must not forgett to mention, what Mons'. de Gadagne a Lieu' Generall in the French Army, and who commanded the French Foot that day, did on my behalf, when our Army was intirely routed, and none left standing on the feild, hearing that I was taken prisoner by the English, he took two or three Squadrons of the French horse along with him, whose Commanders were his particular freinds, and went with them across the feild to the place where the English then were; fully resolv'd, in case my fortune had been such, to haue rescued me by force out of their hands: But coming amongst them, and after a diligent inquiry finding there was no truth in that report, he return'd back with that satisfaction to his own command.

At our first coming to Furnes, and for some days after the Battell, wee thought our loss had been more considerable, then afterwards it prov'd; for most of our foot Officers, as well as our common Soldiers, gott off, some by making their escape from the Enemy, others, and especially the Officers, by giving small summs of mony to those who (had) taken them; of which number was Don Antonio de Cordoua, with many other Collonels and persons of note: So that by that time wee came to Nieuport, which was about the 26ᵗʰ of the same month, all our Regiments of foot, excepting the King's and the naturall Spaniards, were almost as strong as when they came into the feild.

As for Monsʳ. de Turenne, so Soon as he had beaten us, he march'd back into his Lines, and continued his Seige, So that within   days afterwards, Dunkirk was surrender'd to him; which had not been so soon given up, if the Marquis de Leyde the Governour, had not been wounded, of which hurt he dyd with in few days.

After yᵉ Battell, M. de Turenne marches back into his Lines and continues the Seige of Dunkirk, which in a few days after is Surrender'd. Oʀ: Mᴇᴍ: P. 3. p: 126.

Wee remain'd at Furnes till the 26ᵗʰ, about which time the news was brought us, that the Town was to be deliver'd up, and then wee drew back to Nieuport. So soon as wee came thither, wee had another Junto, to consult what wee should do when the Enemy were masters of Dunkirk. Vpon which it was proposed by Don John, that wee should put our Selves all along

Juin 26. The Spanish Army draws back to Nieuport, where a Junto is held to consult what was to be done after yᵉ loss of Dunkirk. Oʀ: Mᴇᴍ: P. 3. p. 126.

PART
III.

1658.
Don John
proposes to
defend the
Canal betwixt
Nieuport and
Dixmude.
Ibid. p. 127.
The Duke
declares his
opinion against
this proposall,
and gives his
reasons. *Ibid.*

the Canal betwixt Nieuport and Dixmude, and endeavour
to ,defend it. Some who spoke after him, agreed to this, and
others did not directly oppose it. But when it came to my
turn to speak, I declar'd my opinion against it, and gave my
reasons, because wee had not a sufficient strength of foot to
maintain that post against a Victorious Army, ours being also
dishearten'd by their late defeat : I also desir'd them to consider
into what miserable condition wee should be reduced, in case
that passe should be forced upon us ; for then it would be too
late, and perhaps impossible to think of securing our great
Towns, since the Enemy would haue their choice of attacking,
and also of mastering which of them they pleas'd ; besides
what other unknown mischeifs might arise from so hazardous
an undertaking.

The Duke pro-
poses dividing
the Army, and
Securing the
chief Towns.
OR: MEM:
P. 3. p. 127.

Having us'd these and other arguments against it, I propos'd
that wee should divide our Army, and disperse it, as wee should
judge most convenient, amongst our great places on that side of
the Country where wee were, a particular regard being had to
those Towns, which in probability wee might expect to be next
beseiged ; That this provision being made for their Security,
what place soever should be attack'd, might be in a condition
of making a vigourous resistance, or at least defend itself so
long, that when it should be taken it would be too late for the
Enemy to sitt down before another ; That during this Seige, wee
might haue leasure to draw the rest of our Troopes together,

The Duke's
motion is ap-
prov'd of, and
tis resolv'd the
Army Should
divide.
Ibid. p: 128.
The Duke and
Caracena are
left wth 4000
horse and foot
in Nieuport,
which was the
place most
likely to be
attack'd. *Ibid.*

and withall might watch our opportunity of attempting somewhat against the Enemy.

Vpon this motion of mine the whole affaire was again
brought under a debate, and it was resolved at last, to divide
our Army. Myself and the Marquis de Caracena were left in
Nieuport, which place wee beleev'd would be next attempted :
Wee had with us about two thousand foot, and as many horse.
The Prince of Condé went to Ostend, with a sufficient body of

men for the defense of that strong place; Don John with some
foot and a considerable body of horse put himself into Bruges;
and the Prince de Ligny with the remainder went to Ypres.
At our coming out from this Junto, the Prince of Condé ask'd
me, Why I would venture to contradict Don John, as I had
done? To which I answer'd him, Because I had no desire
to be forced to run again, as wee had done so lately at
Dunkirk.

This resolution being thus taken, the troopes began their
march the same day to the severall posts which were assign'd
them: And within   days after, Monsr. de Turenne with
the body of the French Army came to Dixmude, and the
Marquis de Crequi with the Van came and camp'd within
litle more then canon-shott of Nieuport, betwixt that place
and Dixmude, intending the next morning to haue pass'd the
Canal which runs from Nieuport to Ostend, and to cutt off all
our communication with that place; at the same time also the
whole Army was to haue come up to him, with intention to
beseige us. But the next morning as they were ready to haue
march'd, Monsr. de Turenne receiv'd orders from the Cardinal,
not to attack till further directions from him, nor to undertake
any other action, the King his master being fallen desperatly
ill of a fever at Calais: By which accident wee escap'd a
Seige, and a most evident danger of being taken; for so careless had the Spaniards been, that when the Marquis de Crequi
was come, and camp'd within our neighbourhood, wee had
not amunition sufficient for fifteen days; So that notwithstanding the great strength of our garrison, wee could not
haue defended the Town long.

But within a day or two after, wee were plentifully furnish'd
with powder and shott from Ostend: So that if wee had been
attacked, wee should haue been able to haue made a good
defence. And to inable ourselves the better to sustain a Seige,

PART III.

1658.
The P^{ce} of Condé go's to Ostend.
Or: Mem: P. 3. p. 128.
DonJohn go's to Bruges, and P^{ce} de Ligny to Ypres. Ibid.

The King of France desperatly Sick at Calais, is y^e occasion that Nieuport escapes a Seige.
Or: Mem: P. 3. p. 129.

PART
III.
_____
1658.
The Duke and
Caracena
make some
new outworks
at Nieuport,
and prepare to
Sustain a
Seige. *Ibid.*

They open the
Sluces. *Ibid.*

M.deTurenne
wth the body
of y^e French
Army at Dix-
mude. *Ibid.*

A new meeting
of the Spanis
Generalls at
Planquendal.
O^R: M^{EM}:
P. 3. p. 129.

Resolv'd that
Don John,
P^{ce} of Condé,
and Caracena,
should draw a
body together
to observe y^e
motions of
M.deTurenne.
Ibid. p. 130.

And that the
Duke wth
another body
shou'd remain
at Nieuport,
and Secure it,
Ostend, and
Bruges. *Ibid.*

The Duke
and Caracena
going back
from the
meeting to
Nieuport,
haue a hott
alarm for fear
of being inter-
cepted. *Ibid.*

Caracena
go's to the

wee began a new Conterscarpe, and five half moons, with a *langue de Serpent* without the Canal, which incompass'd the old outworkes, which wee finish'd in the space of eight days, and then open'd our sluces to drown the Country round about us; but it had not the effect which wee expected, the ground about the Town being higher then it was suppos'd to haue been, however it did us some Seruice.

As for the French Army, the body of it continued about Dixmude, and Monsr. de Crequi lay within cannon shott of us, during all the time that the King of France was in danger by his fever. In this intervall our Generalls had a meeting at Planquendal, a Village which lys upon the Canal betwixt Bruges and Nieuport; where it was resolv'd that so soon as the French Army should march from Dixmude, Don John, the Prince of Condé, and the Marquis de Caracena, should draw together to Bruges as many men as could be spar'd out of the other Towns, into which they had put their Army, with which body they should observe the motions of Monsr. de Turenne; and that I should still remain at Nieuport, with another body of horse and foot, thō of a less proportion then the former, to secure and take care, as well as I was able, of that place, Ostend, and Bruges.

This was the summ of their resolutions at that meeting; and as myself and the Marquis were going back to Nieuport, wee had a hott alarm, and were obliged to trott for two or three miles riding, for fear of being intercepted, before wee could reach that Town; Monsr. de Varennes a Lieu^t. Generall of the French, being come down to the Side of the Canal to view it, and having pass'd some of his Hórse over it, which gave us that allarm. Soon after this, the body of the French Army remov'd from Dixmude, but Monsr. de Crequi was left with the Troopes under his command, at the place where he then was incamp'd: Vpon notice of which, the Marquis de Cara-

cena, in pursuance of what had been concluded at the last
meeting, went from Nieuport, taking with him some Squadrons
of Horse, and such Foot of the naturall Spaniards, as having
been taken in the late Battell, and had made their escape
out of the French Army, or bought themselves off, and with
them march'd to the Rendezvous appointed, to joyn with Don
John, and the Prince of Condé.

1658.
Rendezvous
appointed,and
the Duke
remains Sole
Chief Com-
mander in
Nieuport.
Or. Mem.
P. 3. p. 130.

I think it not materiall enough, in this place, to make a
relation of all the petty skirmishes, and driving in of each
others Guards, which pass'd betwixt us and Monsr. de Crequi ;
nor of the litle stratagems and denices which were used, to take
or beat the advanc'd Guards on either side, both of Horse and
Foot, which wee were obliged to keep within muskett-shott of
one another; So that there hardly pass'd a day without action,
thõ not considerable enough to be related.

Dayly Skir-
mishes betwixt
the Duke's
advanced
Guards a..
Nieuport and
those of Monsr.
de Crequi.
Ibid, p. 131

Not many days after the Marquis de Caracena had left
Nieuport, Monsr. de Crequi drew off from his post in our
neighbourhood, to go and joine Monsr. de Turenne who lay
neer - - - - ; And had not an accident interveen'd, in
all probability he had not march'd away so quietly : for about
noon, I had intelligence from my out guards, that the Enemy
was preparing to remove, and that already their baggage was
going out of their Camp: Wherupon I went immediatly to see
whither that report was true, and at the same time gave order,
for six hundred commanded Foot to be drawn out of all the
Regiments, and to come to me with what expedition they
could make : As also, that all my horse should get ready with
the same diligence, and draw into the Conterscarpe, on that
side of the Town which was next to the Enemy ; my intentions
being to try what could be done upon their reere, in their
going off.

M. de Crequi
drawing from
Nieuport, the
Duke resolv'd
to fall upon his
reer. Ibid.

Being come to my outworkes, I found the intelligence to be
true, and that not only their baggage was gone out, but that

the troopes already were beginning to march: I therfore. sent again for the Comanded Foot, as also for my own Troop of Guards, and two or three Squadrons more, to come immediatly to me: The Horse came accordingly, but not the Foot; for they linger'd so long, that before they were with me, the Enemy was drawn off at so great a distance from the Town, that I thought it not safe to attempt any thing upon them. So that there pass'd nothing betwixt us, but only a slight Skirmish of Some loose Foot on either side, and one charge of Horse which was given by Some of our Volunteers, without order, to a small party of the Enemies Horse who brought up their Reer upon the dyke, in which a mettled page of mine, one Litleton, charg'd so home, that he was taken.

But the Foot coming too late, nothing could be attempted, only Some light Skirmishes past, in one of which a page of the Duke's was taken prisonner.
OR: MEM: P. 3. p. 132.

The slowness of the Foot, which ruin'd this design, was occasion'd by the loss of a small Vessell, which happend to be cast away that morning closs by the Town, having run on ground before day at high water, so that when the tyde went off, she was left dry upon the Sands; which being seen by our men, they went to plunder her, and the Ship being laden with wine and brandy, most of our foot Soldiers had made themselves so drunk, that when they were commanded to their armes, it was not in the power of their Officers to take them from their liquour, et gett them together time enough to come to the place where I expected them.

What was the occasion of the Dukes Foot coming up too late, which ruin'd this design.
OR: MEM: P. 3. p: 133.

As for the remainder of this Campagne, I shall not give a particular account of it, because I was not present in the feild; Only this in short: The Prince de Ligny, with the body which he commanded about Ypres, was defeated by Mons'. de Turenne, who accidentally lighted upon him with the Van of his Army near - - -, where he expected not to find him; And having cutt off all his Foot, followed him to Ypres, and beseig'd that place which he took within few days, and then march'd to Oudenarde, which he also master'd, it being a place

M. de Turenne defeats the Pce de Ligny; cutts off all his Foot, and follows him to Ypres, wch he beseiges and takes in a few days. Ibid.
M. de Turenne takes Oudenarde, and

of great importance, thō at that time of litle strength, Scituated
upon the Scalde. In this Town he left a strong garrison, as
also in Dinse, and most of the places on the Lys: So that.this
blow given to the Prince de Ligny, prov'd to be of worse couse-
quence to the Spaniards, then the defeat which wee receiv'd
near Dunkirk; for had it not been for this last misfortune, in
all probability the French had done litle during the rest of the
Campagne, besides the taking of Gravelines, after the time
which they were obliged to loose, while their King lay so
disperatly sick at Calais: But the defeat thus given to the
Prince de Ligny, put into their hands the opportunity of taking
in so many Towns, as otherwise they durst not haue attempted.

This I speak knowingly, having been inform'd of.the whole
matter since that time, by one who could give .me the best
relation of it. But to return to my own affaires at Nieuport:
Not long after the Marquis de Crequi had left his quarters near
that Town, Monsr. de Turenne being marchd toward - - -,
I drew out the troopes which remain'd with me, and march'd
with them to the Suburbs of Bruges, governing my motions by
the intelligence I had of those which were made by the Enemy,
and still keeping behind one of the Canals, that I might avoid
the hazard of engaging upon unequall termes, or of receiving
the least affront: by this means also taking care, that the Enemy
might not get betwixt me and any of the Towns which were
intrusted to my particular inspection.

‥About the 16th of September, I march'd back to Nieuport,
where I received the wellcome news of Cromwell's death; which
I sent immediatly to Don John, at the same time desiring him
to send Some other who might take upon him my command;
it being of absolute necessity for me to go to Bruxelles, and
attend the King my Brother upon this new alteration of affaires
in England.

PART
III.

1658.
leaves a strong
garrison in it,
as also in Dinse
and in most of
the places on
the Lys.
On: Mem.
P. 3. p. 133.

Upon M. de
Turenne's
marche, The
Duke draws
his Troopes out
of Nieuport,
and marches
to Burges,
governing his
motions by
those of y^e
Enemy. Ibid.
Sept. 16. The
Duke marches
back to Nieu-
port, where
upon the news
of Cromwell's
death, he sent
immediatly to
Don John,. to
desire him to
send Some
body to take
his command
upon him, that
he might go
and attend the
King his
Brother upon
this new
alteration.
On: Mem:
P. 3. p. 135.

P A R T
III.

1658.
Sept: 21.
Monsr.deMar-
sin is Sent to
Nieuport to
releeve the
Duke, who
go's to Brux-
elles to the
King, and
returns no
more to the
Army; the
Season being
too far spent
before he
could leave
his Majesty.
Ibid.

Monsieur de Marsin was he that was order'd to releeve me; who arriving at Nieuport on the 21st of September, I immediatly made what hast I could to Bruxelles, and return'd no more to the Army, the Season of the year being too far spent before I could leave the King; so that there was not any need of my presence at the place of my Command: And when the French Army was march'd back into their own Country, and our Troopes dispos'd into their winter-quarters, I went to Breda to the Princesse my Sister, where I continued for some time.

Thus ends the account given by his R. H. of the year 1658; which was the last Campagne he made in the Spanish Seruice.

1659.

P A R T
III.

1659.

THE Death of Cromwell, and the disturbances which most men foresaw would ensue upon it (his Son Richard having neither the parts nor vigour of his Father to govern and keep in order the Army) had rais'd the spirits of the Royall Party, which before were very low, by having so often attempted and so often miscarryed in their endeavours to restore the King: So that now forgetting all the hazards which they had already run, and dispising those to which they were again to expose their lives and fortunes, they fell to work afresh; and by the Severall changes which happen'd afterwards in a litle space of time amongst their Enemies, had the opportunity of carrying on their design with a greater liklyhood of success then ever: for they had not only provided themselves with armes and mony for a rising, but had engaged in severall parts of the Kingdom many considerable men of the Presbyterian Party; and besides them, divers other persons whom either their interest, or their misled judgment, had hurryd into actuall Rebellion either against the then present King, or his Father: In the West of England, Collonel Popham, In Wales, Mansfield, In Chesshyre, Sir George Booth, In Lincolnshyre, Collonel Rossiter, In Norfolk, Sir Horatio Townshend; besides Sir William Waller, and many other men of great interest in the Countries where they liv'd: Of the Army, Coll: Charles Houard, Coll: Ingolsby, and others who by the death of Cromwell, and the laying aside

The Death of Cromwell raiseth the Spirits of the Loyall Party.
On: Mem: P. 3. p. 136.

They provide armes and mony for a rising, and ingage many considerable men in the King's interest.
On: Mem: P. 3. p. 136.

Names of Severall of the cheif persons ingaged in the Royall Party.
On: Mem: P. 3. p. 137.

PART
III.

1659.

Names of the
persons in
England who
were particu-
larly Intrusted
with the
managment
of his Ma:
affaires called
The Select
Knott.
OR: MEM:
P. 3.ͬ p. 137.
The 1ˢᵗ of
August ap-
pointed for a
generall rising,
and the King
and yᵉ Duke
to be there in
person to head
them. Ibid.
This great
affaire upon
the point of
being exe-
cuted, is
brought to
nothing by the
treachery of
one man, Sʳ.
RichardWillis.
Ibid. p. 138.

of his Son, had either lost their commands or were in fear of losing them ; such especially as had been of that Party which advised Cromwell to take the Crown upon him : In the City, Major Generall Brown, and in the Navy, Generall Montague. As for Genˡˡ Monk, who commanded in Scotland, it is doubtfull whither at that time he had it in his thought to perform, what afterwards he brought So well to pass.

Most of these whom I haue nam'd, were so far ingaged by those whom his Majesty intrusted with the managment of his affaires in England (who were these following Lord Bellasise, Col: John Russell, Sir William Compton, Coll: Edward Villars, Lord Loughbourow, and Sir Richard Willis) that the first of August was appointed for a generall rising through all England : And his Maᵗʸ had resolv'd to be there in person to head them, together with the Duke, at their first appearing in the feild. Every thing was accordingly prepar'd, and the King had already taken his measures, how and at what place he should land, and from thence to go where the risings were to be : But being in this readiness, and the time almost come for the embarquement to put this great affaire in execution, it was all dash'd and brought to nothing by the treachery of one man.

This person was Sir Richard Willis, as it was afterwards discover'd to his Majesty by the means of Mʳ Moreland, he being one of those who was intirely trusted by the King in the managment of this design, and of THE SELECT KNOTT (as they call'd them) and having been so all along, was corrupted by Cromwell for some   before he dyd ; and constantly betrayd to him during his life, and after his death to those who succeeded him, our whole affaire, thō not the persons of any of his freinds (for such was the agreement he had made with that Party) undertaking either to frustrate any of the King's designs, or at least to advertise them so early, that they might secure themselves from any such attempt : And he never fail'd them in any

Willis dis-
covers the
affaire but not
the persons.
Ibid.

thing he promis'd; nor was ever press'd by Cromwell or others
after him, to discover any particular persons who were carrying
on his Majesty's Seruice; neither did he betray any of them
in this present juncture, thō he had it in his power to haue put
the Duke of Ormonde into their hands, when he was privatly
in England.

P A R T
III.
1659.

And now, according to his former practises, he set upon it
to break this whole design: which he compass'd, by perswading
THE SELECT KNOTT, when all things were in a readiness and
the day appointed just at hand, to deferr the rising for ten days
longer; using such arguments to work them into his opinion,
as indeed were plausible enough, thō not convincing, if they had
been throwly consider'd. But there was no room left for suspicion of such a man, whom they look'd upon as one firm to his
Master's seruice, and to be as forward as the best of them for
such an undertaking; So that his advice prevailing, orders
were accordingly dispatch'd to all who were ingag'd, that they
should not take up armes till farther directions were sent them:
Only Sir George Booth had no notice given him of this countermand, of whose intentions to rise, Willis accidentaly knew
nothing; But at the same time he sent over to Bruxelles, and
advertis'd the King that the busines was put off, when both the
King and Duke were just ready to haue come for England.

Willis per-
swads
The Select
Knott.
to defer the
rising for ten
days.
OR: MEM.
P. 3. p. 138.

This journy being thus deferr'd, his R. H. thought he had
time enough before him to make a visit to his Sister, who was
then at Honslarcdyke near the Hague, and to be back again
with his Ma[ty] before he should sett out from Bruxelles: But it
prov'd otherwise; for the day after his R. H. departure from
that place, the news was brought thither, that Sir George Booth
was up in Chesshyre, with a considerable body of men. Vpon
which intelligence, his Ma[ty] beleeving his freinds might also rise
in other parts, as encouraged by this example, thō the last day
appointed was not yet come, thought it proper for him to go

The rising in
England being
deferr'd, the
Duke go's to
visit his Sister
at Honslarc-
dyke.
OR: MEM:
P. 3. p. 139.

PART
III.

1659.
Upon the news
of Sr George
Booth's rising
up in Ches-
shyre, the King
parts privatly
from Bruxelles
and Sends
notice to the
Duke to follow
him. *Ibid.*

over into England by the way of Calais; at the same time
sending the Duke notice of it, that he might follow him: And
the next day he sett out privatly from Brúxelles, taking along
with him of his Servants only the Duke of Ormonde, Lord
Bristoll, Daniel O'Neale, and Titus.

As for the Duke, so soon as he had received the King's letter,
he came away for Bruxelles without stopping any where: He
enter'd privatly into the Town and went immediatly to Mr.
Secretary Nicholas' lodgings, from whence he sent word to the
Chancellour, that he should come thither to him, that he might
know from him what farther directions his Maty had left for
him; which were only these, that he should make hast after
him to Calais, where he should know more, and that the Duke
of Glocester should still remain at Bruxelles till farther orders.
Having received this short account, he made no longer stay
then just to put on his disguise, in which he was resolved to go
to England; and taking with him only Charles Berkley and a
Trumpetter, he travell'd day and night till he had overtaken

The Duke
overtakes the
King neer
St. Omers.
ORIG: MEM:
P. 3. p. 139.
'tis resolv'd ye
King should
go to Calais,
and the Duke
to Boulogne
to provide a
Vessell. *Ibid.*

his Majesty at Hazburck, short of St. Omers, where it was
concluded that the King should go to Calais, and the Duke to
Boulogne; where he was to provide a Vessell which might be in
a readyness to transport him into England, but not to stirr till
the King sent his commands from Calais. Thus they parted,
and his Maty arrived that night at his journys end, as he had
design'd; but his R. H. got not to Boulogne till the next
morning.

The Duke has been since inform'd, that from the very time
his Maty left Bruxelles, the resolution was taken of his going to
Fontarabie, he not having any opinion that Sir George Booth's
business would succeed, But that however he thought it not
amiss to go by Calais, that in case some others of his freinds
should rise, and new hopes be given him, he should be in a
readiness to go over: if not, then to continue on his journey to

Fontarabie. Whither this was true or not, is uncertain; but if it was true, the Duke was not made acquainted with it: for he did so firmly beleeve that he should pass over into England, that the same day he arriv'd at Boulogne, he sent Charles Berkley to the Lieu^t. Governour, to desire his assistance in procuring a boat for his passage into England, pretending that he had obtain'd leave from the Duke to go over privatly about some concerns of his own; and that the Lieu^t. Governour might haue no suspicion of the Duke's being there, his R. H. writt a letter to him, dating it from Bruxelles, which letter M^r. Berkley deliver'd to him, and according to his desire he was immediatly furnish'd with a small Vessell; and now the Duke stayd only for his M^{aties} further orders for Calais, beleeving he should receive commands for his passage.

Within a day or two, the King came himself to Boulogne, in his way to Abbeville, and told the Duke, That by the last letters which he had received at Calais, he had heard of no other rising, then only that of Sir George Booth; for which reason he thought it not convenient for either of them, as yet to adventure over the Seas; That, for himself, his intentions were to go along the Coast towards Dieppe and Rouen, and if he heard any better news, then to pass over into the West to Popham, or into Wales to Mansfield: But for the Duke, he was order'd to hover about those quarters where he then was, and had permission given him to receive and open all letters which should be directed to the King; and, for the rest, it was left wholly to him to govern himself as he thought fitt, according to the intelligence which he should receive: Notwithstanding which, some few days after, Doctor Allestree refus'd to give him a letter, which he brought out of England with him, for the King.

After these directions, the King left his R. H. and went on to Rouen, from thence to St. Malo, and so by Rochelle to

P A R T III.

1659. The Duke knows nothing of the King's intention of going to Fontarabie. OR: MEM: P. 3. p: 140.

He gets a Vessell ready. Ibid.

The King comes to Boulogne, tells the Duke it was not convenient yet for either of them to venture over. Ibid. p: 141. his Ma^{ty} go's along the Coast, and orders the Duke to hover about where he was, and open all letters from England to the King OR: MEM: P. 3. p: 141.

PART
III.

1659.
The King go's
to Fontarabie.
Ibid.
The Duke go's
with Titus to
Calais to get
news from
England.
Ibid. p: 142.

The Duke is
inform'd
there by one
Dawson, that
a Troop of
Horse was
waiting to
sease the King
and the Duke,
at the place
they were to
land at, Line-
court.
Or: Mem:
P. 3. p. 142.
Willis the
person that
discover'd this
secret landing
place to the
Rebells. *Ibid.*

A Huguenot
Captain in-
formes ye L^t.
governour of
Calais that y^e
Duke was
there in dis-
guise, and that
he had seen
him.
Or: Mem:
P. 3. p: 14.
The Gates are
shutt and the
Duke sought
after, but y^e
Informer
found to be
mistaken.
Ibid.

Thoulouse; from thence to Sarragossa, and then back again to Fontarabie, hearing the conference at that place was not yet ended betwixt the French, and the Spaniard. His Ma^ty at his departure from Boulogne had left M^r. Titus with the Duke, and within few days after they went together to Calais, there to informe themselves more particularly of the news from England; where Titus mett with M^r. Dawson newly arriv'd out of Kent, who told them, that the very day wheron he expected the King and the Duke at Linecourt, a Troop of Horse came thither, thinking to haue found them there, and that it was not without great difficulty he escap'd from them, and gott over into France: This accident being related to the Duke, surpris'd him very much, knowing how few were intrusted with the secret of their designing to go to that house; But afterwards when the practises of Sir Richard Willis came to light, he was known to be the person who had discovered that design to the Rebells.

There happen'd likewise another accident, while the Duke was then at Calais, which had like to haue given him some trouble, and might also haue been of bad consequence to others. It happen'd that an over-officious Captain, a Huguenot, who was in the Garrison of that Town, advertis'd the Lieu^t. Governour, Monsr. de Courtebonne, that the Duke was there in a disguise, and that he himself had seen him, knowing him very well, as having been in the French Army while the Duke serv'd there, and withall he gave notice where his R. H. was lodg'd: Upon which the Lieu^t. Governour commanded the gates to be shutt, and taking a Guard along with him went to the place, conducted by the Huguenot Captain. It was a blind ale-house in a by-part of the Town, where he was led with an opinion of finding the Duke: But coming thither, he found the Informer was mistaken, for the person prov'd to be Mr. Edward Stanley, Brother to the Earle of Darby, who was

newly come to Calais, as were also many English gentlemen;
who hearing of the rising in England, came from all parts
with intention to go over and serve their King.

But the Lieu^t. Governour not content with this, and being
told by the same person, or some other, that the Duke was in
Town, went on with his inquiry, and search'd the house of one
M^n. Booth an English-woman, where commonly her Countrymen us'd to lodge, leaving no part or corner of the house
unsearch'd; but thō the Duke lay not there, yet by accident
he had like to haue been found there: for he was going to that
very place, when Titus met him in the street, and told him
that the gates were commanded to be shutt, and that a search
was actually making for him; for which reason he refrain'd
from going thither, and gott into a house where the Lord
Berkley and the Lord Langdale were, and there he continued
till night, and then return'd to the Inne where he had taken
up his lodging.

The Lieu^t. Governour after this, made no further inquiry,
but caus'd the gates to be open'd again an hour before night.
Of all this the Duke was soon advertis'd; and some advis'd
him to go out of Town the same night before the gates were
shutt, that he might be so much taker (*farther*) on, in his way
to Boulogne; but he refus'd that Counsell, because perhaps
there might be a trap layd for him, and the gates on purpose
left open to apprehend him as he returned out. He therfore
judg'd it not secure for him to give them such a mark of knowing him, as they would haue, if he went out so hastily at so
undue an hour. But betwixt twelve and one he had a hott
alarm at his lodging, and verily beleev'd they were come to
take him; for he was waken'd with great knocking and
bouncing at the door of the Inne, and going to the window,
he heard, as he thought, the noise of Soldiers; neither was he
mistaken in that opinion, for so they were: But their busines

The Duke advis'd to go out of the Town in the night, but thinks is not fitt. *Ibid.*

The Duke had another hott allarm in his lodging at midnight. On: Mem: P. 3. p: 144.

The Duke
returns to
Boulogne next
morning.
OR: MEM:
P. 3. p: 144.

He receives
letters from
the Queen w^{ch}
commands to
find out his
Ma^{ty} whom
M.deTurenne
desired to
Speak with.
Ibid.

The Duke go's
Abbeville, and
sends Cap:
Cook in
further quest
of the King to
Dieppe and
Rouen.
OR: MEM:
P. 3. p: 145.

Having no
account of the
King, his R.H.
go's himself
privatly to
M.deTurenne
at Amiens.
Ibid.

Monsr. de Tu-
renne gener-
ously offers to
ye Duke, of
furnishing him
with troopes,
armes, pro-
visions, trans-
ports, ships,
&c. to pass
over into
England. *Ibid.*

was not to search for the Duke, it was only to bring home the
master of the house, who was dead drunk and brought home
betwixt four of them.

The next morning his R. H. in pursuance of what he had
resolv'd, went away for Boulogne, and return'd no more to
Calais during all the time of his residence in those parts. Some
time after, Captain Thomas Cook came thither from Paris,
with letters to the Duke from the Queen his Mother, and
commands to find out his Ma^{ty}. These letters likewise inform'd
him, that Monsr. de Turenne who was then about Amiens
desir'd to speak with the King in reference to his affaires in
England. Upon which the Duke went immediatly to Abbeville,
hoping there to haue found the King; But his Ma^{ty} was
departed from thence, and all his R. H. could hear of him,
was that he was gone towards Dieppe, and thither he sent
Captain Cook after him; who missing of him there also, went
in quest of him as farr as Rouen, but his Ma^{ty} was gone from
thence also on his way to St Malo: Wherupon Cook return'd
to the Duke, and gave him account of his fruitless diligence.

The busines was of too great importance to be neglected,
and therfore his R. H. resolv'd on going himself privatly to
Monsr. de Turenne: when he was come to him at Amiens,
Monsr. de Turenne told him, He had desired to speak to the King
his Brother, but since his Ma^{ty} was not to be found, he would
do him the same seruice in the Duke's person: Therupon he
offer'd him his own Regiment of foot, which he would make up
twelve hundred men, and the Scots-Gendarmes, to carry over
into England with him; That besides this, he would furnish
him with three or four thousand spare armes, six feild peices
with ammunition proportionable, and tooles, and as much meale
as would serve for the Sustenance of five thousand men for the
space of six weeks, or two months; and farther, would furnish
him with Vessels for the conveyance of all this into England,

and permitt the Troopes that his Ma^{ty} had in Flanders, to march
to Boulogne and there imbarke, with orders to follow the Duke
as fast as Vessells could be provided for them; advising his
R. H. to send directions to them, that they should march
immediatly to St Omers where a pass should meet them.

And that all these preparations might be compass'd with
more ease and certainty, he offer'd the Duke to pawne his plate
and make use besides of all his interest and credit, to make up
such a sum of mony as should be thought necessary for the
carrying on of the business: Concluding all with this expression,
That his R. H. might easily beleeve he had no orders from the
Cardinal, who was then at the Conference, to perform all this;
but what he did was freely of himself, out of no other motive
then kindness to the Duke, and to his family.

· Tis not hard to imagine, that his R. H. accepted of this noble
Offer with great joy, and that he lost no time in designing where
to land with these forces. The place resolv'd on was Rye, and
that in case the Country should come in to him, he should
march on to Maydstone and Rochester; if not, then to fortify
that Town, which by reason of its situation might be made
so strong within few days, that Lambert should not easily haue
forced him out of it; and he would haue found him work enough
in that Seige, to haue divided the forces of the Rebells, and
disorder'd all their methods.

·These things being thus resolv'd, and order'd, the affaire was
put into a forwardness; and Monsr. de Turenne gave the Duke
a letter to (the) Lieu^t Governour of Boulogne, wherein he was
commanded to furnish his R. H. with all the Vessells, and Fisher-
boats which he could get together in all his Government of the
Boulonois. The Duke gave this letter himself to the Lieutenant
du Roy, with another from the Mareshal d'Aumont his
Governour, which the Queen had procur'd and sent to the

M.deTurenne offers also to pawne his plate, and use all his credit, to make up a sum of mony for carrying on this enterprise. OR: MEM: P. 3. p: 146. An all this freely of himself out of Kindness to the Duke and to his Royal family. Ibid.
The Duke accepts the offer wth joy, and Rye is the landing place resolved upon. Ibid.
The Duke getts letters from M^r. de Turenne, and from the Mareshall d'Aumont, to the Lieu^t. du Roy of Calais, ordering him to assist his R. H. wth Ships and all he could desire. OR: MEM: P. 3. p: 146.

1659.

The Duke of
Bouillon, and
otherNephews
of M. de Tu-
renne, were to
go Volonteers
with his R. H.
Ibid. p: 147.
The Duke
ready to im-
barke the next
day, is stop'd
by the news of
Sr George
Booth's defeat.
Ibid.

M.deTurenne
advises the
Duke to haue
patience and
wait a better
opportunity.
OR: MEM:
P. 3. p: 147.

The Duke
fearing the
King might be
landed in the
West and in
difficulties,
presses M. de
Turenne to let
him go over to
his Maties
assistance, but
could not pre-
vaile. *Ibid.*

Duke from Paris, by which the Lieu^t was likewise order'd to assist his R. H. with Vessels, and all things he could desire.

The busines was now so far advanced, and in such a readiness, that the Duke of Bouillon, and others of M. de Turenne's Nephews, were to haue gone Volonteers with the Duke; and the next day was appointed for his R. H. and his Soldiers to imbarke at Estape, to which place the Troopes were already upon their march, when letters from England brought the unwelcome news of Sir George Booth's defeat by Lambert. Upon which the Duke, being then at Boulogne, went to M^r. de Turenne who was at Montreuil to informe him of it; who in that juncture thought it not advisable for his R. H. to adventure into England, but counsell'd him to haue patience and expect a better opportunity, which could not be long wanting to him, by reason of the disorders and distractions which must of neces-sity happen amongst them in England: Notwithstanding which reasons, the Duke press'd him to consent that he might go, telling him that he beleev'd the King might be landed in the West, or somewhere in Wales, and be there ingag'd in difficulties and dangers; and that if his conjecture should prove true, there was no other way of saving his Ma^ty and gaining time for him to attempt any thing considerable, but the Duke's going over, and making a diversion: But these arguments could not prevaile on Monsr. de Turenne to give his R. H. the leave which he So earnestly desir'd; for he replyd, That he was very confident his Ma^ty was not gone for England, and that thō he were, it was not reasonable for the Duke to hazard himself, when there was no probability of Success: He therfore counsell'd his R. H. to return to Flanders, and there to expect some news from the King his Brother, and fresh intelligence from England. And when he had concluded with this advice, knowing the Duke wanted mony; he lent him three hundred pistoles, and gave him a Pass. And thus an end was put to this * design; and the Duke return'd to Bruxelles.

· In this way he pass'd through Peronne; where he privatly visited the Governour of that place, the Marquis d'Hocquincourt, an old acquaintance of his, whom he had known in the French Army, who us'd him with all imaginable civility and kindness. The 11th of September he reached Cambray, and from thence went straight to Bruxelles: where he found, that notwithstanding the Duke of Glocester had deliver'd to the Marquis de Caracena the letters which his R. H. had written from Boulogne for the marching of his Troopes to St Omer, yet the Marquis would not permitt them to stirr out of their quarters; thō he was sufficiently press'd to it by the Duke of Glocester: But he still answer'd, he did not beleeve Mr. de Turenne durst let them pass through any part of his King's Dominions, without order, which he knew he could not haue. Nor would he suffer them to draw down to the Sea-side, to which he was also urged by the Duke of Glocester, when he found he could not obtain his first point. What his reasons were for refusing these two requests, the Duke could not learn; but as it happen'd, the denyall prov'd to be of no prejudice to his Majesties affaires; Only it gaue opportunity to See what was to be expected from the Marquis, if things were left to his management.

This design being thus blasted, and no hopes left of attempting any thing in England at that time, the Duke past the remaining part of this year at Bruxelles, expecting the King his Brother, who arrived thither from the Conference at Fontarabie a litle before Christmas.

PART
III.

1659.
M.deTurenne lends the Duke 300 pistoles, and gives him a pass to return to Flanders.
Or: MEM: P. 3. p: 148.

The Duke arrives at Bruxelles, where he finds that Caracena tho press'd by the Duke of Glocester, would not lett the English Troopes march as the Duke had orderd.
Ibid. p: 149.

---

* Here ends the condensed Military Narrative, which was given to Mareshall Turenne's Nephew, the Cardinal de Bouillon, by James the Second.

And to shew here, what litle expectation even the most
intelligent Strangers had at that time, of those Changes which
happen'd so soon afterwards in England ; his Ma.ty as he came
back from Fontarabie through France, press'd the Cardinal very
earnestly for leave to Stay, thō never so privatly, with the Queen
his Mother, which small favour he was not able to obtain ;
and therupon was forced to return to Bruxelles much against
his inclination, having only Stay'd some few days with the
Queen at Colombe (which he tooke in his way) a civility which
could not well be refus'd him.

1660.

THE hopes concerning England being now reduced to the lowest ebb, in the beginning of the year, 1660, an offer was made to the Duke, of commanding in Spain against Portugal, and also to be their High Admiral with the Title of Principe de la Mare; which office, the Duke has been told, was never given to any but the King's Sons or near Relations, and whoever enjoys it commands the Galleys as well as Ships, and wherever he lands he commands as Vice Roy of that Country whilst he stays in it; he has also the fifts of all Prises, and a great Salary, besides other considerable perquisits: So that this was not only a very honorable post, but also a very advantageous one even as to profit, which was what the Duke then wanted. He therefore readily consented to the offer which was made to him, the King his Brother ratifying it with his free permission.

And now his R. H. was preparing to go for Spain in the ensuing spring, when that Voyage was happily prevented by the wonderfull Changes, which were almost daily produced in England: And when the motion was once begun, it went on so fast, that his Majesty was almost in his own Country, before those abroad, especially the Spaniards, would beleeve there was any Revolution towards it; for even after Sir John Greenfeild was come over to the King from Gen^ll. Monk, they yet beleev'd him as far as ever from his Restoration, and were so possest of that opinion, that they let him go into Holland. And at last when his Ma^ty was at Breda not many days before he embarked for England, the Marquis de Caracena endeavour'd to perswad him to return to Flanders.

1660.
The Duke is offer'd to command in Spain against Portugal, and to be made high Admiral of Spain, with the Title of Principe de la Mare.
Or: Mem: P. 3. p: 150.

The Duke preparing to go for Spain, in the Spring, is happily prevented by the wonderfull sudden Changes in England. Ibid.
The King is almost in his own Country, before the Spaniards would beleeve there was a Revolution towards it.
Or: Mem: P. 3. p: 150.
The King at Breda, the Marq^s. de Caracena endeavours to perswad him to return into Flanders. Ibid.

PART
III.
───────
1660.

He pretended he had busines of importance to acquaint his Ma^ty with from England, some persons being come over from thence to Bruxelles, who had great offers to make to him : And he sent the Count de Grammont with letters to him on that occasion, desiring his Ma^ty would be pleas'd to give himself the trouble of coming but as far as Antwerp, or at least to West-Wesel, he not being able to wait on him (as he knew he ought) any where out of his Master's Dominions. But his Majesty had no inclination to venture his person in the hands of the Spaniards, not knowing what the consequences might be ; And besides he could easily judge, that it must either be a pretence to draw him thither, or indeed a thing not worth his journy, his return to England being then ascertain'd.

His Ma^ty
has no inclin-
ation to trust
his person into
the hands of
ye Spaniards.
Ibid.

Yet not to
disoblige Cara-
cena, he sends
ye Duke to him
to Bruxelles to
hear what he
had to impart,
which was only
an ayry project
from Scott.
Or: Mem:
P. 3. p. 151.

But because he would give the Marquis no reason of complaint, he sent the Duke to Bruxelles, and desir'd the Marquis to impart the busines to him ; When his R. H. came thither, he found it was only Coll: Bampfeild who was come over with some ayry proposition from Scott, and some of that Party : From whence the Duke concluded, that his Ma^ty had done wisely not to stirr from Breda.

The Duke
returns to y^e
King who soon
after go's to the
Hague. Ibid.
His Ma^ty em-
barkes for
England at
Schevelin in
May. Ibid.

When his R. H. had stayd a day or two with the Marquis, he returned to the King his Brother, who some few days after went to the Hague, where he was very well received ; and embarking himself at Schevelin about the latter end of May, (23^d) on boord the English Navy, commanded then by Generall

And arrives
with the Duke
of York, and
ye Duke of
Glocester, in
London, the
29. May 1660.
Ibid. p. 152.

Montague, he landed with his two Brothers, The Duke of York and the Duke of Glocester, at Dover, the - - (25th) of the same month, and made his entry into London on the 29th, which happen'd to be his Birth-day.

HERE ENDS THE FIRST VOLUME OF THE MANUSCRIPT.

THE LIFE

OF

H. R. H. JAMES DUKE OF YORK,

LORD HIGH ADMIRAL OF ENGLAND,

LORD WARDEN OF THE CINQUE PORTS,

&c. &c. &c.

COLLECTED OUT OF MEMOIRS WRITTEN BY HIMSELF.

THE SECOND PART.

** By this SECOND PART his Majesty's Private Secretary,
who collected the various circumstances of his Royal
Master's Life out of his Private Memoirs, does not appear
to have intended any reference to those Divisions of
the Stuart MSS. which had been referred to by him
throughout the preceding Volume, but to mark the
respective Volumes, or Tomes, of his Biography of J A M E S,
of which this is lettered at the back as Tome 2ᵈ. and
carries on The Life of H. R. H. The Duke of York from
the Restoration of Charles the Second to his death. —
EDITOR.

THE LIFE

OF

JAMES THE SECOND,

KING OF GREAT BRITAIN,

COLLECTED OUT OF MEMOIRES WRITT IN HIS OWN HAND.

THE SECOND PART.

1660.

NEVER was greater joy known in England then upon the reception of the King, and never was any people so happy as those of our three Kingdoms were upon the Restoration of his Majesty: To be sensible of it, we need but reflect on their past miserys, and what their sufferings were by a Rebellion which lasted from the year, 1641, to 1660, without intermission. In which the whole frame of the Government

The joy and happines of Eng^d, upon the King's Restoration.

was overturn'd, Monarchy destroyd, the King murder'd, and
to make it yet more horrid by a pretended Court of Justice;
the Nobility and Gentry brought low, many of which had
the same fate with their King; the Church Government quite
destroyd; and a Commonwealth, or rather Anarchy, set up by
the force and influence of an Army, whose Officers for the
most part were of the meanest sort of men, even brewers,
Coblers, and other Mechanicks. After this, Cromwell their
Generall usurped the supreme authority, and under the name
of Protector govern'd more arbitrary, then ever any King of
England had done before him. After his death, his Son Richard
stept in to the Government; and was immediatly turn'd out by
the Army, who took the Supreme power into their hands, and
knew not how to dispose of it. But after severall changes
and convulsions of State, God out of his great mercy to these
Nations, and the more to shew his Omnipotent hand, made
use of Generall Monk, as an Instrument (thō a weak one) to
restore the King without one drop of blood shed, to the
astonishment of all the Christian World.

The deaths of
the Duke of
Glocester, and
the Pᵐ of
Orange.

Nor did ther happen any thing in this first year of the
Restoration, to interrupt the publick joy of the Court, and of
the Nation, but the untimely deaths of the Duke of Glocester,
and the Princesse of Orange; the first in September, and the
other the Christmas following, and both of the small pox: That
Duke had all the naturall qualitys requisit to make a great
Prince, which made his loss the more sensibly felt by all the
Royall Family: Which greif was renned and augmented, by
the death of his Sister the Princesse of Orange so suddenly
following, whose personall merits, and particular love of all
her Relations, which she manifested in the time of their distress,
caus'd a sorrow for her death, as great as was their esteem
of her.

We must not forget to mention in this year, so important
and so extraordinary a passage of the Duke's life, as was his
first marriage with the Lord Chancellor's daughter. Extraordinary indeed both in it self, and in the consequences both
good and bad which in process of time followed from it. When
the Princesse of Orange came to Paris to see the Queen her
Mother, the Duke being (*there*) at that time, as has been before
mention'd, M^{rs}. Anne Hide was one of her Maids of Honour,
who ther attended her : It happen'd that after some conversation
together, the Duke fell in love with her, she having witt, and
other qualitys capable of surprising a heart less inclinable to
the Sexe, then was that of his Royall Highness in the first
warmth of his youth. She indeed shew'd both her witt and her
vertue in managing the affaire so dexterously, that the Duke
overmaster'd by his passion, at last gave her a promise of
marriage some time before the Restoration : Not long after
which, the Lord Chancellor, her Father, being then uppermost
in the Kings favour, the Duke chose that time to beg his
Majesty's leave, to perform what he had promis'd ; which at first
his Majesty positively refused, and used many arguments to
dissuad the Duke from that resolution ; and not only his Ma^{ty},
but many of the Duke's freinds, and most especially some of
his meniall Servants, with a violent Zeal opposed the match.
However (the Duke still continuing constant in his resolution
to be true in his word, and chusing rather to undergo the
censure of being fraile in promising, then of being unjust in
breaking his promise) the King at last, after much importunity,
consented to the marriage ; and it may well be suppos'd that
My Lord Chancellor did his part, but with great caution and
circumspection, to soften the King in that matter, which in
every respect seem'd So much for his own advantage. The
King's leave being thus obtain'd, the Duke without loss of time

1660.
The Duke of
York's 1st
mariage with
Ld Chancellor
Hide's daugh
ter.

privatly married the young Lady, and soon after own'd the marriage. It must be confessed, that what she wanted in birth, was so well made up by other endowments, that her cariage afterwards did not misbecome her acquired dignity.

Soon after this in the beginning of January 1661, one Venner a fifth Monarchy man, and a holder forth amongst them, after having preached to his Congregation and fasted all the day with them; being full of the Spirit of Rebellion, march'd out of their meeting house with thirty in his Company all arm'd; between eleven and twelve at night, and ran about the Streets crying, Live King Jesus, and that all should follow him that were for King Jesus, and those that did not should keep their houses. Some of the Constables hearing this, went to suppress them, but thō three or four of the Watches joyn'd together, they durst not venture upon them; so that Venner march'd throw the Town without any opposition, and none of his party being mad enough to come and joyu with him, he and his Company betook themselves to the woods near High gate.

The King at
Portsmouth,
to see the
Queen mother
and P⁻ Hen-
riette imbarke
for France, at
the time of
Venners insur-
rection.
The Duke
indispos'd
Stays behind
at Whitehall.

At this time it happen'd that his Majesty was at Portsmouth, having gone thither with the Queen his Mother, and his Sister Princesse Henriette, to see them imbarke ther for France; but the Duke being somewhat indispos'd stayd behind at Whitehall: The Generall who was at the Cockpit, had soon the allarme, and came and waked the Duke to give him an account of it; wherupon they sent out some of the few horse which were yet left not payd off, and the Generall's own Troop commanded by Sir Philip Howard, to look after them: But Venner keeping the woods, and the Horse not knowing the Country, did not light on them.

After two or three days lurking, Venner and his men leaving the woods before day marched into London; and came through

Allgate about seven in the morning, crying as before, Live King Jesus, and that such as were for him should joyu them. There they found no resistance, and so passing by Leaden-hall, and driving before them such loose men of the Militia as offer'd to appear upon the noise, they pass'd on by the old Exchange, and advanced as far as Woodstreet, where a party of about twenty horse commanded by one Corbet came up to them, but the Street was so narrow, that the horse could not break in upon them; By this time the Trainebands were up, and came so thick upon them, who had only two men that joyn'd them in all their march throw the City, that they were forced to get into a house where they defended themselves.

Whilst this pass'd in the City, news of it was brought to the Duke and the Generall at Whitehall by a Messenger; who told them that when he came away, Venner and his Company were come up as far as Leaden-hall, beating all before them: Wherupon the Duke and the Generall immediatly took horse, there being no more left on the guard. But as they went on, so many of the Nobility and Gentry with their attendants came and joyn'd them, that when they were got as far as St Paul's, they were no less in number then fifteen hundred horse.

There they met the Lord Maior, Sir Richard Brown, who told them, that Venner and all his party were either taken or kill'd; That the Militia which beseiged them, and (*had been order'd to*) drive them out of the house which they so obstinatly defended, (*could not do it*) without firing it, which for good reasons they durst not do; till at last one Lambert a Seaman (who afterwards for his good Service was made Commander of the Duke's Yacht, and in the end of the year 1665 was slain on board the ANNE a Third rate) perswaded some of them to follow him and get up on the top of the house, which they did and forced their entry that way.

The Duke and the Generall march towards Venner with about 20 horse.

TOME
II.

1661.
All Venner's
men killed or
wounded,
before they
could be
mnsterd.

These desperate men were almost all killed or wounded before they could be master'd, and one only of them ask'd for quarter; at which a Camarad of his, that layd wounded in the room, endeavour'd with his Sword to kill him, reviling him for being so mean as to ask quarter. Venner had no less then nineteen wounds on him, and it was with great difficulty that the Surgeons kept him alive, till he could be condemn'd and hang'd; as he, and the rest of his fanatick Crew that were left alive, soon were, except two who were made use of as witnesses against the rest.

And so ended this mad attempt of a furious Zeal, which seem'd in a manner design'd by Providence to convince the King and his Ministers, of the necessity of providing better for the safety of his person, and the Security of the Government, then hitherto they had done, by letting them See what dangerous spirits lay still scatter'd about in the body of the Kingdom; Nor indeed could it well be otherwise, since so very lately the Government of the Nation was in the hands of phanaticks, and that men of the same temper were still in being, thō not in power.

The Duke
upon the
occasion of
Venner's busi-
nes, proposes
in a Councill
the keeping
up some
and raising
more Troops
for the Secu-
rity of the
Government.
The Duke's
advice is fol-
low'd.

For this reason it was, that the Duke proposed to the Councill, which was called in the time of the Insurrection, That they should write to his Majesty, and desire him to Stop the disbanding of the Generall's Troop of horse Guards and the Regiment of foot, which were to have been payd off that day, and that he would rather think of raising more men for the security of his person and Government; Which advice his Majesty follow'd, and immediatly gave order for the raising a new Regiment of Guards, of twelve Companies, to be commanded by Collonel John Russell, and a Regiment of horse of eight Troops, of which the Earle of Oxford was to be Collonel, and also a Troop of horse Guards to be Commanded by the

Lord Gerard: he likewise sent for the Duke's Troop of Guards
which were then at Dunkirk. Morover he gave out Commissions to the Earle of · - - , and the Earle of - - - ,
for Regiments of horse, and that they should name their under
Officers, who likewise had Commissions, and should list men
in their Severall Counties, who were not to be in present pay,
but in a readiness in case there should be any occasion for their
seruice.

It may be wonder'd at, that the Lord Chancellor and the
Earle of Southampton, the King's Cheif Councellors, who had
been eye-witnesses of the Insurrections and Rebellions in the
time of King Charles the first, and what he suffer'd for want of
good Guards, should now be so careless of the King's·safety,
as not to have advised him to secure himself from such dangers
for the future: And in this I can not but think My good Lord
Hawly a wiser States-man then they ; for upon this occasion
he told the King, That the better he was guarded, the more his
Enemies would fear him, and his Friends love him.

Now this is the more to be wounder'd at in these two Lords,
because they together with the Bishops, were the great opposers
in the House of Lords of the King's inclination and intention
to grant, according to his promise given at Breda, a Toleration
to Dissenters so limited, as not to disturb the publick peace
of the Kingdom : So that all this being put together, it plainly
appears, that the consequence unavoidable of their Counsels,
was to irritate an Enemy, and not to arm against him, which
shews that a misguided Zeal of Religion often turns the brains
of the wisest heads ; for it was that only which made the
Chancellor (who in all other matters was true to the interest and
honour of the Crown) oppose here in both, the King's and the
Duke's Sentiments; and in some Sorte cause a breach of publick
faith, or at least of the King's word, which ought to have been
Sacred and inviolate.

1661.
Caracter of
some of his
Matie cheif
Ministers.

Now in reguard of the influence which Ministers of State have upon all proceedings of the Government, in which his R. H. had so great a share, as to the executive part, in being High Admirall, It will not be improper to give here a short account of their persons and qualifications, who were then imployd and taken into trust by his Majesty. We have already observed that for some time before the Restoration,

L^dChancellor,
Duke of
Ormonde and
the E. of Bris-
tol in no good
understanding
together.

there was no very good understanding between the Duke and the Kings Ministers, which were then the Lord Chancellor Hide, the Duke of Ormonde, and the Earle of Bristol: The last of these, having declar'd himself a Catholick some months before the Restoration, took no longer his place in the Privy Councill, but nevertheless was as much trusted in the secret affaires as formerly. But this Triumvirat held not long together; for the Earle of Bristol endeavour'd to ingross, by some by ways, more of the Kings favour to himself, then the Chancellor was willing to allow him; This after some time broke out into an open war between the two pretenders, In which Bristoll was at first worsted, the Chancellor having on

his side the Earle of Southampton, a person much esteem'd by the King and the Kingdom, and who had no good opinion of the Earle of Bristol; who being of a haughty temper could not bear this preference of his Enemy, but fell therupon into violent courses and expostulations even with his Majesty himself: And thō at first he did not succeed therein, yet afterwards (as it will appear) in conjunction with other Enemies of the Chancellor, he gained his point in dismounting his adversary, but without any other advantage to himself, except the guilty pleasure of revenge.

Now whereas the King had layd his commands upon the Duke, to live well with all those that were trusted by his Majesty, this was now the more easily obey'd, in relation to the Chancellor, upon the consideration of his daughter; and

from that time forwards his R. H. was a fast freind to the
Lord Chancellor, as far as consisted with his duty to the
King.

That Minister, in generall, was very loyall and true to the
interest of the Crown ; but I can not excuse him from having
been very faulty in not procuring (or at least endeavouring it)
in the first Parliament, after the Kings return, a Repeal of all
those Statuts so injurious to the Crown, that past in the long
Rebellious Parliament; which, if well sollicited, might easily
have been obtain'd at that time, the Parliament being then in
so loyall a temper and so hearty for the King. With the like
facility, he also might have obtain'd such a Revenue settled
upon the Crown, as might have secured it for the futur from
the attempts of factious Spirits, and such terrible calamitys as
lately it had sustain'd. The Chancellor wanted not skill and
foresight to make him sensible of all this : and therfore some
have thought, not improbably, that this remisnes of his proceeded from a jealousy, that the King was inwardly inclin'd to
Popery : wherfore he, himself being a zealous Protestant,
thought it not expedient to have his Majesty too much at ease,
and be trusted with too large a power.

It was by the advice and negociation of this Minister, that
in the year, 1662, the marriage between the King and the
Infanta of Portugal, was concluded ; which in appearance was
advantageous to the Crown of England, and would have really
been so, if the Town of Tanger which was given in part of the
portion, could have been made (as then it was beleeved it could
be) a safe harbour for our Ships, and if the Queen had proved
fruitfull, as it was likewise hoped she would : One would have
thought that My Lord Chancellor's fortune and greatnes was so

L⁴ Chancellor
Loyal, but
faulty in not
getting the
Acts of the
long Parl⁺.
repeal'd, and
a competent
Revenue
Settled upon
the Crown in
his Ma: first
Parl⁺.

1662.
The King's
Marriage with
the Infanta of
Portugal,
negociated by
theChancellor.

firmly establish'd, as never to be moved by bringing a Queen into England of his own chusing, and by having his daughter married to the next Heir, then in being, to the Crown. But to let us see how short sighted, as to future events, and how apt to misreckon even the wisest men are, those very things which seem'd at first the props of his greatnes, proved at last to be the occasion of his fall, and a load and charge upon him, under which he sunk : for his Enemies afterwards made the barrennes of the Queen (especially his own Daughter proving fruitfull) a crime in him, pretending he either did, or might have known it, considering the Age and Nation of the Queen; And how far this jealousy may have enter'd into the King himself, to make him the more easily part with his Minister, I leave it for others to guess.

The King, and the Duke meet the Queen at Portsmouth, where she landed the 24th May.

Vpon the news of the Queen's arriuall in Portsmouth road, under the conduct of the Earle of Sandwich, The Duke attended by many of the Nobility went by the King's order, to wait on her Majesty on board some leagues off at Sea, and bring her to land : Where she arrived the 24th of May, and was received by the King, and led by him to her lodging ; where, after she had reposed for some litle time, their Majestys were marryd by My Lord Aubigny Almoner to the Queen, but So privatly (not to offend the Protestants) that none were present but some few Portugaises, as witnesses : Soon after this, the King and Queen coming forth into the great room, where all the company was, and being Seated in two chaires, Doctor Sheldon then Bishop of London perform'd the outward ceremony in publick, of declaring (*them*) to be man and wife. It may be wonder'd, why the Queen was not married by Proxy, and by My Lord Sandwich the King's Ambassador, before she left Portugall, as is usuall in such cases : Nor do's there appear any other reason for it, but that the Portugaises

are more scrupulous then other Nations, and would not have
the Ceremony perform'd in their own Country by a Protestant.

TOME II.

1662.
A matche between the King and C¹. Mazarin's Neice offer'd and refus'd on both sides at different times.

Many other proposalls and offers of Matches had been before
this made to the King; of which I shall only mention that of
Cardinal Mazarin's Neice, who was cryd up for the greatest
beauty in Europe; because it had this of particular in it, that it
had been at different times both offer'd and refus'd on both sides.
For in the time of the King's being abroad, and a litle before
the Treaty of S᷉ Jean de Luz, when there was a great alteration
and confusion in England, upon the Armys dissolving the
Rump Parliam᷉, and setting up their Comitee of safety; it
was thought by some of the King's freinds, that the Cardinal
would be glad to have such an honour done to his family, as
to have his Neice married to the King: On the other side,
considering how great he was in power and mony, they concluded, that if he would heartily imbrace the King's interest,
he might be able in a litle time to restore his Majesty. For
these reasons it was, that either Abbot Montague, or My Lord
Aubigny, took an occasion to propose the matter to him:
But the Cardinal it seems had an ill opinion of the King's
affaires, and thought them desperate, according to the notions
given him by Monsieur Bourdeaux the French Minister in
England, and therefore put it off with a compliment, and would
not enter into the Treaty. But when the King was restor'd
soon after, the Cardinal, not forgetting the proposall made to
him, had the courage to take it up again, and to make an offer
of his Neice to his Majesty with a vast Sum of mony for her
portion: And then, neither the charms of her beauty, nor so
much mony could prevaile with the King, who in his turn
also put it off with a compliment, and so the matter rested.

I have not much to Say from this time, till the beginning of
the Dutch War, all things then continuing quiet at least in
outward appearance both at home and a broad; Only I shall

T O M E
II.

1662.
Secret work-
ings of the
Republican's
Party against
the Govern-
ment.
observe, that the restless party of the Republicans were secretly working to destroy the Government, and for that end the Chief of them had privat meetings and consultations how to carry on their designs, wherein they could hardly agree amongst themselves concerning what sort of Government they should declare for, both in Church and State ; for their Councils consisted of all sorts of Protestant Dissenters, except the Quakers. Of all this his Ma^{ty} was from time to time advertis'd by some false brethren amongst them, and therupon he thought fitt to secure some of the old Officers of Cromwell's Army, and the

Wildman,
Bremen, and
Creed, Secur'd.
Cheif of the Nonconformists, such as Major Wildman, Major Bremen, Major Creed, and severall others that were likely to head them, and get together considerable numbers of disbanded Soldiers of the old Army, that were all good figthing men. These above nam'd, were kept in prison till the year 1667, when the Lord Chancellor Clarendon was layd aside. This however did not dishearten the Party from designing a Rising, one to be in London, and another in the North about York; both at the same time.

Bradford's
Conspiracy.
That in London was thus design'd ; that when his Majesty was to go to see one of the Militia Regiments, some of their gang, who were in it, should load their Muskets with bullet, and when they gave a voley to salute him, they should shoot at him ; And one Bradford a SerJeant of that Regiment, who was at this Consultation, when some of them said, What shall we do if we miss him ? answer'd, If you miss him with your shott, I will not miss him with my halbard : These words this Villain did not deny when he was taken, and brought in chains to his Ma^{ty}, who examin'd him himself ; and they were proved against him afterwards at his Tryall.

. Most of this Caball were Seised, and amongst the rest one Ridge a preacher, they were examin'd by the Secretarys and would confess nothing : wherupon his Ma^{ty} sent for Ridge, and

examin'd him himself, none being present but the Duke and
Lord Lauderdale. At first he would own nothing; but the
Duke asking him, if he were married, which he said he was
and had a wife and five small Children, and then pressing him
again, by letting him see that if he still persisted in his obstinacy,
and did not confess what he knew, he would certainly be
hang'd, and leave his wife and Children to starve, whereas
if he would be ingenuous and trust to his Maties mercy, he might
save his life and have wherwithall to provide for his family;
this so struck him, that he immediatly fell on his knees, ask'd
his Maties pardon, confessed the whole design, and serv'd as a
witness against the rest of them, who could not have been
convicted of Treason without him, there being but one Witness
besides himself; and he became So true a convert, that afterwards he was made a muster-master at Sea, and was slain in the
four days fight in 1666.

1662.
Ridge, one of
Bradford's
Caball, ex-
amin'd by the
King; the
Duke being
present, is the
occasion of his
confessing the
whole design.

T O M E
II.

As to affaires in the Government, and at Court, they at this
time went smoothly on, the Chancellor continuing Cheif Minister, and solely governing the matters of State. Lord Falmouth
was in great favour with the King from the beginning of the
Restoration; and none ever had it to such a degree, either in
this or any other Kingdom, that consider'd so litle his own
concerns, and so much his Masters; for when afterwards he was
kill'd at Sea, he dy'd without leaving any Estate behind him,
thō he was no ways extravagant in his expences : But he was
of so generous a nature, that when any projects of advantage to
himself had been brought to him, and that he had obtain'd the
King's promise for a grant of them, if some old suffering
Caveliers happen'd at the same time to put in for them, he
releas'd the King of his promise to himself and got them given
to the others, Saying, that for him, sooner or later the King
would provide. It were to be wished that all Favorites and
first Ministers would follow such an Example.

L^d. Falmouth
in great favour
with the King.
His Elogium.

1662.
E. Arlington
brought into
the favour by
the Chancel-
lor, but turn'd
afterward his
Enemy.

Sʳ W. Coven-.
try, the Duke's
Secretary, in
favour by
reason of his
great ability, yᵉ
Chancellor
and he jealous
of one another.

The Duke of
Buckingham
tho at first not
of the Coun-
cill, by degrees
comes into
favour, and
joins with the
Chancellor's
Enemies.

About this time the Lord Arlington being come from Spaine,
endeavour'd to insinuate himself into his Majesties favour, and
was at first supported by the Lord Chancellor, and his old
Master the Earle of Bristol, neither of which cared for Lord
Falmouth; But after his death, the Chancellor soon repented
the helping hand he had given to Arlington, and with good
reason, as will appear in the sequell of this history.

Sir William Coventry also, who was the Duke's Secretary,
and much in his favour by reason of his great ability, kept not
long well with the Chancellor; who finding him to be a very
industrious man in busines, and very capable, grew jealous of
him and secretly endeavour'd to keep him back, which the
other was clear sighted enough to perceive; and therfore when
the opportunity was offer'd, he fail'd not to give his helping
hand towards laying aside the Chancellor.

I must have also mention (of) the Duke of Buckingham;
who, thō when his Maᵗʸ came first into England, was not made
of the Councill (as all but himself were that had been of it
beyond Sea) by reason of several misbehaviours towards his
Majesty, when he came into England Some years before the
Restoration; yet being admitted to Court, and being of a very
pleasant and agreable conversation, he by degrees insinuated
himself again so much into the King's favour, as to be brought
first into the Councill and after some time to be made Master
of the Horse. Being thus advanced, he quickly joyn'd with
those other persons who design'd the Chancellor's ruine, and by
his railleries did by degrees use his Majesty to hear the
Chancellor spoken against: But that Minister was too well fix'd
to be easily shaken, thō he had many Enemies at Court who
had the King's hear, so that he made good his post against
them all for some years; till at last, finding that they could not
prevaile with his Maᵗʸ to lay him aside, they rais'd such a
faction against him in the house of Commons (a thing easy

enough to be brought about in that place against any first
Minister) as was at last the cause of his downfall, as will
heareafter appear.

But to return from this digression, to what more immediatly
relates to the Life and Actions of his Royall Highness. I (*It*)
must be remember'd that ever since his return into England,
he made it his busines, as being Lord High Admirall, to inform
himself of the condition of the Fleet; which, thō much
increas'd in number of Ships by the Vsurper's, was then by the
many changes and revolutions after the death of Cromwell,
but in an ill condition, the Navall Forces quite exhausted,
and the Magazins very empty; of which he gave a speedy
account to the King, who order'd matters so with the Parliament, that they voted him a sum of twelve hundred thousand
pounds, to be disposed of by him, as the necessitys of the State
should require: And his Majesty who understood the true
interest of the Nation, and had a particular inclination and
application to Maritime Affaires, appointed for the seruice of
the Fleet eight hundred thousand pounds of the sum, given,
which was most of it layd out in Navall Stores to fill the
Magazins, that it might be in his power at any time speedily
to sett out a considerable Fleet, when there should be occasion.

Besides the care which the Duke had of the Navy, he applyd
himself to understand the busines of Trade, which is the great
interest of England, and gave all encouragements to the severall
trading Companies; as those of the East Indies, Turky,
Hamborough, and Canary, and morouer he sett up a new one
for Guiny, which was absolutely necessary for the Support of
the Forcing Plantations, and for hindering the Dutch from
being absolute masters of the whole Guiny trade: to this end
he made use of the aduice and industry of Sir Richard Ford,
and some other Marchants, who had got the Secret which the

The Duke, as
Lord High
Admirall,
makes it his
busines to
inquire into
the condition
of the Fleet.

8ooooo^lb ap-
pointed for the
Fleet, most of
which layd out
in Navall
Stores.

The Duke
encourages
the Trading
Companies,

and sets up a
new one for
Guiny, w^ch
was call'd the
Royall
Affrican Com-
pany.

Dutch had, of dying the Sayes of such a coulour as the Blacks liked, and of giving them the Smell in the packing them up, like that which was used at Leyden, from which place formerly all the Sayes were brought that were sent into Guiny.

The Duke sends Sir Rob: Holmes wth two Ships to support the Aff: Company against the increchements of the Dutch.

And whereas the Dutch, during the Civill Wars in England, had every where increashed much upon the English Trade, and had dispossessed the English of the Castle of Cormentin on the Gold Coast; the Duke at his first setting up the Guiny or Royall Affrican Company, borrow'd two Ships of his Ma^ty, and sent Sir Robert Holmes with them, and with some other Ships belonging to the Company and some few land men, with which according

Sir Rich: Holmes seizes the Fort of Cap de Vert and the Castle of Cormentin.

to his orders he seiz'd the Fort of Cap de Vert in Affrica, and took the Castle of Cormentin from the Dutch, leaving garrisons in both of them, and settling Factorys for the Company all allong that Coast.

The King gives the Duke a patent for Long-Island.

Some time after this, the King gave the Duke a Patent for Long Island in the West Indies, and the Tract of Land between New England and Mary Land, which always belong'd to the Crown of England since it was first discover'd; upon which the Dutch had also incroached during the Rebellion, and built a Town, and some Forts, to secure the Bever-trade to them-

The Duke borrows two Ships from the King, and sends Sr Rich: Nicholas to take possession of Long Island, afterwards call'd New York.

selves: Wherfore the Duke borrow'd two men of war of the King, in which he sent Collonel Richard Nicholas (an old Officer and one of the Grooms of his Bed-chamber) with three hundred men, to take possession of that Country; which the Dutch gave up upon composition without stricking a Strok, most of the Dutch inhabitants remaining there, together with the old English Inhabitants, and some other Nations who had first planted there with the English; So that Collonel Nicholas remain'd in peaceable possession of that Country, which was then call'd New York, and the Fort up the River nam'd Albany. And as the Duke did all on his side to advance Trade, the Parliament press'd on to it by the King were no

less active to make it flourish, which they chiefly did by the
Act of Navigation, and other Bills for the encouraging of
Trade, and building of Ships.

These proceedings and the Severall complaints of our
Marchants of the injurys they received from the Dutch, by
their depredations of them during the late disturbances in
England, were a sort of preamble and introduction to the
war which soon after follow'd against Holland; for it now
grew to be the Sense of the whole Nation, and of the House
of Commons in particular, that Satisfaction ought to be given
to our Marchants for the injuries and losses they had sustain'd
by the unjust incrochements of the Hollanders, which losses
were represented to amount to seven or eight hundred thousand
pounds. These Complaints being at last brought to the
Parliament, both Houses resolved, That the indignities and
dammages done to Vs by the Dutch, were the greatest obstructions to Foreign Trade, and that his Ma^{ty} should be moved
to take Speedy course for the Redress thereof.

Notwithstanding all this, the Dutch still refused to give that
reasonable Satisfaction which was required of them ; beleeving,
and with some colour of reason, that the Nation would not
easily engage in a new and expensive war at Sea, having been
but lately settled in peace at home. In the next place, their
Embassador Van-Gough perceived, that the King himself was
not much inclin'd to a war, and that the Chancellor was wholy
adverse to it ; which gave him a wrong aim in this matter, and
made him conclude that nothing would be carried in oposition
to the sentments of the first Minister. This so misled him,
that he would not beleeve the Duke when his R. H. told him
plainly in the way of freindship, That unless his Master's the
States gave such reasonable Satisfaction as was requir'd, for

1664.
The Severall
occasions of
the first Dutch
war.

The whole
Nation, and
particularly
the Parlia-
ment, bent for
having Satis-·
faction given
by the Dutch
for the injuries
received from
them.

The Dutch
refuse to give
Satisfaction to
the English,
beleeving that
the King and
the Chancel-
lor were not
for a war.

The Dutch
Ambassador
so misled by
his opi'n'n,
that he would
not beleeve
the Duke him-
self, when in

T O M E
II.

1664.
freindship his
R. H. endea-
vours to disa-
buse him.

the injuries done to the English by his Contrymen, a war would certainly break out: He took it, as said only to fright him, and so deceived both himself, and his Masters, by his too great cunning.

This admonition of the Duke finding no good effect, the King was in a manner necessitated by the generall outcry of the Nation, to declare open war against the Dutch about the beginning of the ensuing February; cheifly occasion'd by the

Instead of
giving Satis-
faction, the
Dutch sent
privat orders
to de Ruyter
at Cadiz, To
Sail to Affrica
and dispossess
the English of
Cormantin,
&c.

privat orders sent to De Ruyter their Admirall, then in the Streights with twelve men of war, to take in a sufficient supply of victualls at Cadiz, and from thence to make the best of his way to the Coast of Affrica, to dispossess again the Englis of Cormantin Castle, and to ruin all our Factories therabouts, which had been lately establish'd by the particular care and directions of the Duke.

S^r Jo. Lawson
meets De
Ruyter at
Cadiz, and
suspects his
design; but
having no in-
structions to
attack him,
he only gives
notice to the
Duke.

Now when De Ruyter came into the Bay of Cadiz to fit himself for the intended Voyage, he found Sir John Lawson there, who was newly come with a Squadron of our Ships from concluding a peace with the Algerines; and Sir John perceiving, by the Sort of Victualls which De Ruyter took in, that his design was indeed for the Affrican Coast to destroy the establishment of our New Company there, he forthwith advertized the Duke thereof by letters: for after calling a Councill of his Captains together, and reading his Instructions, he found he had no power to proceed to any Act of hostility.

Upon notice
of DeRuyter's
being sail'd to
the Coast of
Guinea, P^ce
Rupert is
order'd with a
Squadron to
follow him in
October.

Upon this notice, and further news that De Ruyter was actually Sail'd from Gibraltar to the Southward, and that arriving on the Coast of Guinea, he had seiz'd all in his reach about Cap de Vert, the King resolved to send Prince Rupert to follow him with a Squadron of about twelve men of war, and six of the Company Ships, the least of which had forty guns. But by that time that this Fleet was fitted and come together, which was about the middle of October 1664, a further

account was brought, that the Dutch had prepar'd a more
considerable one under ᵗʰᵉ command of the Baron of Opdam,
with which he pretended in spight and contempt of Vs, to
force his passage through the Channel, in order to convoy the
Succours design'd for Guinea : In the mean time they had
sent before hand a Galliot to their Director general there to
give advice thereof.

T O M E
II.

1664.

The King, hereupon, layd aside the thoughts of having
Prince Rupert to go thither with the intended Squadron, and
in stead thereof, order'd a considerable number of more Ships to
be fitted out, amongst which were to be the ROYALL CHARLES,
the ROYALL JAMES, SWIFTSURE, and LONDON, of the 1ˢᵗ and
2ᵈ Rates, with others of the 3ᵈ and 4ᵗʰ; so as to make up about
fourty ; and resolved that the whole should be commanded by
the Duke, who accordingly parted at the beginning of November for Portsmouth, quickly after which he went abord,

Upon further
notice of the
Dutch fitting
out a Fleet
under Opdam,
'Tis resolved
that in stead
of P. Rupert's
Squadron, a
stronger one
be put out
under the
Command of
the Duke.

and joyn'd the Prince and the Earle of Sandwich. In the
mean time Opdam lay with his Fleet in the Goree, where after
all their bravado's, there arose great debates whither they
Should now go out, or no ; but the wind proving cross to
them all that month, determin'd their dispute, and gave them
no disagreable excuse for their staying still at home: For
about the beginning of December, when the wind came East,

In the begin-
ning of Nov :
the Duke go's
to Portsmouth
and soon after
abord the
Fleet with Pᶜᵉ
Rupert and
the E. of
Sandwich.

and consequently favorable to bring them out, their design
not to make use of it, continued the Same, and so they layd
up their Ships for this winter.

The Dutch
come not out
to Sea, but lay
up their Ships.

, The Duke knowing nothing yet hereof, but expecting rather
to meet them, cruised to and again for four or five days
between Dunnose, Portland, and Cape de Hogue, where by
reason of the narrowness of the Channel, he was obliged to Tack
every night ; and thō it was extreme dark still, and blew very
fresh, yet no ill accident happen'd either to himself or any of
the Ships.

The Duke
continues
cruizing in the
Channel, not
without dan-
ger.

TOME
II.

1664.
Seeing no ap-
pearance of
the Dutch
coming out,
he returns to
Spithead, and
from thence to
Whitehall.

But seeing now in all this time no appearance of any Dutch,
he return'd to the Spithead; where he met with the news, that
Opdam had received orders from his Masters to lay up, upon
their being inform'd that the Duke was ready and in expectation of them : Wherupon his R. H. after having encouraged
the Seamen by his presence and directions, return'd together
with Prince Rupert to Whitehall, about the beginning of
December; and left the Fleet, till he should return, under the
Command of the Earle of Sandwich, with orders to send out
the 4th and 5th Rates a cruising off the Isle of Wight, and to
bring in what Dutch Ships they met with, by way of Reprisals,
and this in pursuance of the King his Brother's directions.
His Highness gave order also, for the fitting out of the rest of
the Ships in harbour, that the whole Fleet with all the provisions
necessary might be ready to receive him again by the beginning
of Spring: Nor was he wanting to see all things perform'd
accordingly, and to hasten back to his charge, as soon as ever
the Season would permitt.

The Parlia-
ment meets in
November,
and gives the
King 2 millions
and a half for
the war
against the
Dutch.

The 24th of November the Parliament met, and the King,
in his Speech to both Houses, represented the present State of
Affairs, in relation to the United Provinces, and of the Navall
preparations he had made to bring the Dutch to reason :
Wherupon the House of Commons the very next day voted
his Majesty a supply of two millions five hundred thousand
Pounds. And on the 4th of March, the King's declaration of
war against the Dutch was solemnly proclaim'd.

1665.
The first
Dutch war
declar'd
March 4th.
The Duke go's
down to Gun-
fleet to take
the Command
of the Fleet,
March 23.

It was on the 23 of March following, that the Duke, attended
by severall eminent persons and Volonteers of the first quality,
parted from London to the Gunfleet, where the generall Ren-
devous of the Fleet was. And tho by his continuall directions
and presence, he hasten'd all he possibly could to have it com-
pletly equip'd to go out forthwith, yet with all his diligence it
could not be ready till some five weeks after: However his

Highness in the mean while employd his time to the best
advantage he could, by ordering all the Flag-Officers to meet
every morning on Bord him, and there to agree upon the
Orders of Battel and Ranck ; for thō in the late Fights in
Cromwell's time, the English behaved themselves bravely, yet
they minded not any set order, and their Victories were still
more owing to their valour, then method; so that this war,
begun now under the conduct of his R. H. was the first
wherein fighting in a Line and a regular Form of Battel was
observ'd.

In the beginning of May the Duke put to Sea with all his
Fleet, then which, the Nation never hitherto had seen one so
glorious and formidable, either in respect of the force and
number of Ships, or in regard of a Royall Admirall that commanded them, who had the greatest share both of danger and
glory in this Expedition.

. The whole Fleet was compos'd of about ninety eight men of
war of severall Rates : There were three of the first Rate,
eleven of the second Rate, fifteen of the third Rate, two and
thirty of the fourth Rate, eleven of the fifth Rate, and six and
twenty marchant Ships arm'd for war from forty to fifty
guns, besides fire Ships and tenders &c. The Fleet was divided
as usually, into three Squadrons, the Red, the White, and the
Blue : At the head of the first was the Duke, in the ROYAL
CHARLES, carrying, at the main top mast the Royall Standard,
which are the Arms of England. Sir John Lawson had the
honour to be his R. Hᵗ. Vice Admirall of that Squadron; and
Sir William Berkley his Rere Admirall. Prince Rupert was
Vice Admirall of the Fleet, commanded the White, and carried
the Vnion Flag at his main top mast : Sir Christopher Mynns
and Captain Sanson were his Vice Admirall, and Rere Admirall.
The Earle of Sandwich Rere Admirall of the Fleet, was
Admirall of the Blue, and carried the Blue Flag, at his main

TOME
II.

1665.

The Duke puts
to Sea with
the Fleet in the
beginning of
May.

The Fleet
consists of 98
men of war.

Division of the
English Fleet
wᵗʰ an account
of its severall
Commanders.

The Dutch
not yet ap-
pearing, the
Duke resolves
to visit them
on their own
Coasts.

top mast, his Vice Admirall and Rere Admirall wer Sir George Ayscue, and Captain Tyddiman.

His Highness being thus attended, thought the time long till he met with the Holland Fleet ; and they not yet appearing abroad, he resolved to visit them upon their own Coasts ; And for some time he cruised to and again between Scheveling and the Texel, and came so near the mouth of it, that he took a particular view of their whole Fleet then at anchor within the harbour ; which gave them so great an alarme, that they forthwith sett up beacons with great speed all along that Coast, so to give notice of any attempt of landing which they very much apprehended.

The Duke dis-
covering ten
Sail of Dutch
Marchantmen,
gives them the
chace and they
are all taken.

After this his R. H. stood off again some ten leagues, and there came to an anchor, expecting still their coming out ; but in Stead of them, he discover'd some ten sail of their Bourdeaux marchant men, convoy'd by two men of war ; wherupon, they being at about a league to windward of the Englis Fleet, he gave the signal to chace them, and thō it was a Fog, all the marchant men were taken, whilst the two Convoy men made a shift to Save themselves.

The Duke
returns with
the Fleet to
Gunfleet, to
repaire and
take in fresh
water.

The Duke seeing yet no appearance of the Dutch coming forth, remain'd however a few days longer on their Coast, till some of his Ships having their Masts come by the bord by foul weather, he thought fitt to return to the Gunfleet to repair and take in fresh water, so that it was now about the end of May, before he could be in a condition to return to Sea again ; however, as the winds stood, he knew at the same time that neither the Enemy could then come forth.

The Duke
go's out again
the 30th of
May.

But on the morning of the 30th, his R. H. order'd the signall for Sayling again ; and thō at the same instant the wind chang'd and came to the East, whereby it was very difficult to get clear of the Sand-bancks, he made all the use he could of the Tide, being sensible too, that the same wind would bring out the

Dutch, and that they might lickely make use of it to shew them-selves upon the English Coast, towards the Satisfying of their own people, and repairing a litle the credit they had lost by their late backwardnes; Nor was his Highness deceived in his conjecture. He therefore us'd all means possible to get out, So as to attend their motions : But with all his endeavours he could not, till the first of June, reach Southwold Bay, at which time he came to an anchor there, and about one a clock in the afternoon, the Dutch appear'd to windward of him.

TOME II. 1665. The 1ˢᵗ of June he reaches Southwold Bay where he first discovers the Dutch.

Their Fleet consisted of a hundred and thirteen Ships of war of all Rates, divided into Seven Squadrons, eleven Fire-Ships, and seven Yachts: The whole was commanded by Opdam, who (thō a man of quality and personall courage) was no great Seaman. The Officers under him, who carryd Flags at their main top mast, were Cornelius and John Evertson, (*Evertzs*) Stillingwert, Tromp, Son to the famous Tromp, Schram, and Cortenaer.

The Dutch Fleet consisting of 113 men of war. Their principal Commanders.

The two Fleets did not yet make up to one another, for the English require some time to put themselves in order of Battel, and besides they expected the return of some of their great Ships, which were gone but that very morning to make up their complement of men out of a great Fleet of Colliers then passing by, and bound for London.

The wind also which was still Easterly, fell much towards the evening, so that (*litle*) way could be then made : In the mean time both Fleets endeavour'd to get what wind there was.

The next day the Dutch were not to be seen, till about ten in the morning; when the Duke having a fresh gale stood towards them, with thirty of his best Saylers, but thought fitt to keep at about two leagues distance, till all his Fleet should be join'd and put in order : which being done, he advanced forwards, so that a litle before the close of the evening, both Fleets were gott within two litle leagues of one another. The

The 2ᵈ of June, the Duke makes up to the Dutch.

The great
Sea Fight
of the 3ᵈ
June 1665,
with the
Duke's con-
duct and dan-
gers therein.

Duke was at that time some eight leagues to the eastward of
Laystof, (which is about three or four leagues from Yarmouth)
and the weather was calm all night.

About two of the clock next morning the Dutch were
discover'd lighting their matches, and consequently preparing
themselves for the Fight; They had the same order of battel as
the English, all upon a Line. As the day broke there arose with
it a litle fresh gale at Southwest, which was a very proper one
for the approching Engagement, towards the better success of
which, the Duke with great care and labour made a shift to
get the wind; the White Squadron had the Van, and Sir
Christopher Mynns, who fir'd the first shot, led it: Whilst the
Dutch were led on by three Flag-ships, commanded by Tromp,
Courtenaer, and Stelingwart.

The Fight
begins at three
in the morn-
ing.

About three in the morning the Dispute begun briskly on
both sides, And when the Van of the Enemy was come up to
our Rere, the Duke commanded the signal to be given for
the tacking of his whole Fleet, so as to steer the Same course
with the Dutch; but the Sayler who was got up the mast to
give the Signall, happen'd to be so embarass'd and long about
it, that before he could let the Flag fly, Sir Christopher Mynns
had with the Van bore up round, (*round up*) ship after ship, and
brought his starbord tacks on bord; Which the Enemies Van
seeing, sprung their Luff hoping therby to weather most of the
White Squadron. The Duke, perceiving this, stopt the making
the intended signall, least it might have put his whole Fleet in
disorder; and in stead of bearing up round, as most of the White
had done, he tack'd only when it came to his turn; which litle
accident lost above six hours, for so long it was before the same
opportunity could be had: And then his R. H. thought fitt to
give the Signall, wherby the whole Fleet tack'd at once, So that
both Fleets had now their Star-bord tacks on bord, and lay as
close haled as they could: but the Dutch found great benefitt

by this accident; for had the Signall been made as soon as order'd, both the English and they would have had their Larbord-tacks on board, and have stood towards the Coast of England: so that when the Dutch should give way (as they afterwards did) they would have been more expos'd, by having a greater run to make towards their own Coast.

In these two first passes litle dammage was done on either side: Only the CHARITY of fifty guns, which was taken from the Dutch in Cromwell's time, and had been lately one of the Convoy to the Colliers (being a bad Sayler and unable to weather the Dutch) was retaken by them; thō not till Dickenson, her Captain with half his men were slain, whilst he did all he could to stand throw the whole body of the Enemy. Two other fourth Rates, and one fifth, 'that were coming up to join our Fleet, not being able to weather the Dutch, tack'd just before they came within cañon shot of them, and got in to our Fleet the next Tack.

By this time both Fleets had tack'd twice, and stood the same course, with their Starbord-tacks on board, the wind South West, and they left off firing for near an hour, thō they were within less then random shott of one another; for each endeavour'd now to make all the Sail they could, the English to keep the wind, and the Dutch to gain it: In the doing of which it fell out, that the Duke changed his order of Battel, as also Opdam did in his side; For the ROYALL CHARLES, in which the Duke was, being a very good Sayler, got on the head of the EARLE OF SANDWICH who was in the PRINCE, (a heavy Sayler, thō the stoutest Ship of the Fleet): had not the Duke done as he did, the Dutch had streach'd out on head, and might have weather'd him. So that now his R. H. with the Red had the Van, The Blue the Battel, and the White the Rere: And perceiving, that his Vice Admiral Lawson in the ROYAL OAKE had gott the length of the headmost of the

Dutch, he made him a signall to bear neerer to them ; Wherupon the whole Line did the same.

1665.
The heat of
the Engagment begins
not, till 10 in
the morning.

It was now about ten in the morning, when the heat of the Battel began. Never was seen a more proper day to dispute the Mastery of the Sea ; for it was very smooth, a fine steddy fresh gale at South West, not a cloud in the Sky, nor the least appearance of any alteration of wind or weather.

The Enemies Van was led by part of the Zealand Squadron, commanded by John Evertson with three fire Ships on head of 'em, Astern of whom was Opdam ; So the Duke bore down, and according to his Intention had to deal with Opdam : Nor did these two Admirals leave plying one another most furiously for some hours, till the Dutch began to give way

And now it was not long before that Sir John Lawson, one of the bravest Seamen of his time, was wounded in the knee with a great shott, which quickly after prov'd mortall; Who finding himself in that condition, and his Ship also disabled, sent off his Boat to acquaint the Duke therof, wherupon his R. H. order'd Captain Jordan, his own second and an old experienced Officer, to quitt the S^t. GEORGE where he was, and to command not only Lawson's Ship but his division also : But when he got on bord of the Ship which was the Royall Oak, he found her so disabled that he was forced to ly by to refitt her ; by which means (the fighting Instructions

Sir Jo: Lawson's Division
lying by, the
Duke is left
very much
expos'd.

not being then so well drawn as since they have been) all that Division lay by also to look after their Flag, So that the Duke was left very much expos'd, having now but four or five of his own Division on head of him, and Sir Thomas Allen in the PLIMOUTH led the Line.

Soon after this, three Dutch men of war which had been seen for some time to the windward of Vs, and were looking out for their own Fleet, bore down in order to join it. One of them was a great Ship of above eighty guns, which for want of some repairs had been left by Cornelius Evertson to his son, with orders to follow; the other two were not of the same force. These being to windward, endeavour'd to join the head of their Fleet, and young Evertson being a mettled man, and having a mind to distinguish himself, resolved to run on bord of the PLIMOUTH, hoping to bear her down; But Sir Thomas Allen perceiving by Evertson's working, what his design was, brought his Ship to at once, so that Evertson miss'd his aim, thō he came so near it that the yard-arms of both Ships touch'd, and they gave each other a severe broad-side in passing; after which Evertson, and the other two, made a shift to join their own Fleet, and Sir Thomas Allen continued still leading as before; till, finding himself extremely disabled, he was forced to ly by, as also were the FOUNTAIN, and the Mary, the first an Algereen prise of fourty guns, commande'd by Captain Do T'ile and the other was a Ship commanded by Sir Jeremy Smith, whose rigging was so cutt that he was forced to quitt the Line.

Soon after this, the old JAMES, a second Rate Ship commanded by the Earle of Marlborow, another of the Duke's seconds and just on head of him, sprung her Luff and got out of the Line; which Sir Allen Aplesy seeing (a great freind of that Earle) and not perceiving the Ship to be so much disabled as she was, said to the Duke, He was sorry to see his old Commarad do so ill; but his R. H. told him, He was confident the Earle was slain, and so it prov'd to be; for both he and his Nephew, the Earle of Portland who went a Volonteer with him, were kill'd. This Ship being gone, the Duke had only the HAPPY RETURN of fifty odd Guns commanded by Captain Lambert, on head of him; So that the Enemy had more leasure to ply his Royall Highness.

Much about this time it was that the Earle of Falmouth, the Lord Muskerry, and Mr Boyle, were all slain with one shott, as

TOME II.

1665.

Young Evertson endeavours to bear down the PLIMOUTH.

ThePLIMOUTH disabled, is forced to ly by, as also the FOUNTAIN and the Mary.

The E. of Marlborow being kill'd, his Ship the old JAMES lys by.

The Duke having now but one Ship on head of him, is in very great danger.

E. Falmouth, L. Muskerry, and M^r. Boyle,

3 G 2

1665.
killd with one
shott just by
the Duke.

they stood by the Duke on the Quarter-deck. The first of them
was Captain of his Guards, a very generous, bold man, and a
good horse Officer, who had Serv'd the Duke from the time he
first came into France to that moment, and had been with him
in all his Campagnes, both in France and in Flanders, and was
much esteem'd and intirely trusted, not only by his R. H, but
by the King, having never made a false step to either of them,
but allways minded nothing but their Seruice; and so litle his
own interest, that when he was kill'd he had nothing to leave to
his Wife and Daughter, So that if the King and the Duke had
not provided for them, they must haue starv'd : Such an Example
is hardly to be found amongst those who enjoy their Princes
favour.

The Lord Muskerry was Gentleman of the Bed-chamber to
the Duke, a very brave man and a good foot Officer. Mr Boyle
was a younger Son of the Earle of Burlington, who came a
Volonteer to attend his R. H, and never had been in seruice
before.

The Engagement still continued very warm on both sides,
till about two in the afternoon, when the fire of the Dutch
began to diminish; which encourag'd our men (if possible) to
increase theirs. Nor did Opdam himself now ply the Duke so
smartly as hitherto with whole broad Sides, but with two or
three guns only at a time, which made his R. H. conclude that
severall of them were dismounted, and many of his men lost.
This gave the Duke time to order his own Ship to forbear
firing, till, being some what clear'd from the great smoak, he
might see wherabouts he was, and in what posture both Fleets

The PLIMOUTH
and some
other English
Ships, that had
ly on a side to
refitt, rejoin
the Duke
again.

then stood: By which he discover'd, that the ROYALL OAK, the
MARY, and the PLIMOUTH, with some other disabled Ships,
were refitted and come on head of him, and the ROYALL
CATHERIN and SWIFTSURE on stern of him; which Seasonable
Rejoyning added such terrour to the Enemy, that those on the

11

Stern of Opdam began to give way, thō Opdam himself and
those on head of him (most of them Zelanders) still Venture to
keep their Luff.

The Duke therfore finding himself now much more at ease,
and but within muskett shott of Opdam, order'd his Master-
gunner to give him a salute in the usuall forme, Gun after Gun,
and to lay all the Guns himself, but to begin with those of the
lower Tire: The Gunner so well executed his office, that at
the third shott (which was plainly seen to take place as well as
the two former) Opdam and his Ship blew up. At which terrible
sight, the Enemy's Fleet all gave way, and ran for it putting
right before the wind, except the ORANGE, a stout Ship of
eighty four guns, which to the surprise of all kept still her Luff;
bẏ which and by her working, it was plain that the Captain,
who stood on the poap brandishing a two handed brod-sword,
intended desperatly to run her on bord the Duke; and so
boldly did the Ship advance all alone, that some about his
R. H. who were no great Seamen, cryd, She was a fire Ship;
but the Duke knowing her to be what she was, told them,
They would quickly find their mistake, by the brodeside she
was preparing to give them, which they had been sure of, had
not Sir Jeremy Smith in the MARY (one of the Duke's Seconds,
and just on head of him) happily interpos'd, and made up so
close to the ORANGE, that both their Yard-Armes touch'd,
and so gave her his own brode-side and received hers, which
kill'd and wounded no less then Sixty of his men. Presently
after this, another brode-side bein powred into the ORANGE by
the ROYALL CATHERIN, she found it high time to strike. The
men being taken out, according to the fighting Orders, she was
fir'd, and the Captain of her, call'd Sebastien Seaton, of Scots
parents a lusty proper man, did not stick to own, That he had
resolved to signalize himself by endeavouring to borde the Duke,
or to have the honour of being taken by him: But he had no
long time to please himself with that ambition, for in two or

Opdam blown
up by a shot
from the
Duke's Ship,
which his R.H.
order'd to be
level'd at him.

All the Dutch
Fleet run,
except the
ORANGE com-
manded by one
Sebastien
Seaton a Scots-
man.

The bravery of
this Captain
of yᵉ ORANGE.

He attempts to
bord the Duke,
but is hinder'd
by Sʳ Jer:
Smith.

TOME
II.

1665.
Four Dutch
men of war
burnt by one
fire ship, which
the Duke
order'd to be
clap'd upon
them.

three days after, he dyd of the bruises and hurts he received in his rash attempt.

It was now about half an hour after two, when the Duke, being in pursuit of the Enemy, saw four of their men of war (wherof one a Vice Admiral) fall foul of one another just on head of him : his R. H. finding them thus embarass'd, made a signal to one of the two fire ships that attended him, to clap them on bord, which was perform'd so successfully that they were in a moment all in a flame; Nor could there be a more lamentable spectacle, then to see the Sea about them cover'd with their men, who had no other refuge but to throw themselves into that Element to avoid the rage of the other. The generous temper of the English Seamen, which appear'd on this occasion, deserves to be taken notice of : for having by their valour reduced their Enemy to this Extremity, they did by their charity redeem most of them again, and with the hazard of Sinking themselves by picking them up, and overloading their shaloupes with too great a number of them.

Soon after this, whilst the Body of the English Fleet follow'd their advantages, there appear'd a fresh Squadron of the Dutch to windward of them ; which obliged the Duke to ly by a litle, and order a few Ships under the command of Sir William Berkley to bring up the Rere; and secure as well his own maim'd Ships, as those which were then taken from the Enemy.

His R. H. soon after made such way by the admirable Sailing of his Ship, that he quickly got on head of his Fleet again ; which he had no sooner done, but he saw three more of the Enemy fall foul one of another, of which the MARSEMAN of eighty four brass Guns, Jacob Rouse Commander, was presently boarded, and after she had struck was fir'd by one of our fire ships, without order and against the custome of war ; wherby the other two also suffer'd the same fate, and all so suddenly, that not one of the MARSEMAN's men could be Sav'd, and very few of the other two.

The Marseman
a ship of 84
Guns, and two
other Dutch
Ships burnt
without order
after they had
struck.

The next day the Duke order'd the Captain of the fire ship to be confin'd, in order to be tryd by a Court Martiall for what he had done without order and against the Rules of War; but before he could be further proceeded against, he dyd, and so prevented the punishment he had deserved.

TOME II.

1665.
The Duke orders the Capta'n of the fire Ship to be tryd.

It was now about six in the evening, when the English were still pursuing their chase, which they continued as long as the day held, wherby severall more of the Dutch Ships fell into their hands; and thō John Evertson, who was on the head of Opdam when he blew up, got clear, and stood away for the Meuse with twelve of the Zealand Squadron, yet few of those which stood for the Texel, which were the main Body of the Fleet, could in appearance have escap'd next day, had it not been for an accident that happen'd that night.

The English continue in pursuit of the Dutch as long as the day held.

For the Duke, when it began to grow dark, had order'd Captain Wetwang, in the NORWICH, to carry out lights, and to keep just on head of him all night, and close up to the Dutch; that in case they should alter their course, he should fire guns and make false fires, put up more lights, and steer the same course with them; that so, as soon as it should be light, they might again be sett upon.

The Duke orders to keep close up with the Dutch all night, in order to set upon them again next morning.

His R. H. after having given these plain and positive commands, remain'd still upon the Deck till it was quite dark, then he went down into his Cabin to take a litle rest; but before he layd himself down, he could not be satisfied without coming up once more to the Quarter Deck, to see how affaires went, and to reinforce his orders: Then he return'd back to his Cabin, it being eleven at night, when he layd him down upon a quilt in his clothes, so to be ready upon any occasion that should happen. But no sooner was he fallen a sleep, when Mr. Brunkerd, (*Brounker*) a Groom of his Bed-chamber who was in waiting, slipt up from him and apply'd himself to Captain Cox, who was Master of the ship, endeavouring to perswade him to shorten sails; that he might not expose the Duke by

Brunkerd's arguments to Cox and Harman, to perswade them to shorten Sail rejected.

running in amongst the Enemy in the night, the Ship being so good a Sayler, whereby he might be clapt on board by some fire ship, or find himself at break of day in the middle of the Enemies Fleet, expos'd to all their fire ; That he ought in these circumstances, to have a more particular care of the aparent Heir of the Crown, and the King's only Brother. To which, and many other arguments, Captain Cox very honestly answer'd, That he was but Master of the Ship; that the Duke had order'd him to make all the Sail he could, and that without a Countermand from his Highness, or at least from some Superior Officer, he neither could nor would shorten Sail. Brunkerd, finding he could not prevail upon him, address'd himself next to Captain Harman, the first * Lieutenant, with the like arguments ; But he, being an old experienced Officer, would not suffer himself to be so easily imposed upon, So that Brunkerd finding his Rhethrick could not prevail, went cunningly down between decks, and after some litle stay came up again to Harman, pretending to be just come from the Duke (thō he had not been so much as in his Caben) and told him with the greatest confidence imaginable, That he brought immediat commands from his Highnesses own mouth,

Harman at last
shortens Sail,
being impos'd
upon by Brun-
kerd's false
message from
the Duke. that he should forthwith shorten Sail. Captain Harman thinking it impossible for a Gentleman in his post to come with a Ly in his mouth of so dangerous a consequence, could not doubt the truth of the pretended Orders, and therfore did not only shorten Sail, but for some time brought to ; till, at last, fearing it might cause some considerable disorder in the Fleet, as indeed it began to do, he put before the wind again, and settled his top Sails a litle, and just as the day began to

---

* The Duke had two CAPTAINS on board, Sir W. Penn, who had the rank of a Vice Admiral, and Captain Harman, who is here consider'd in the capacity of first Lieutenant to H. R. H.

break, hoisted them a trip as they were when the Duke left
them, and this was done but just a moment before his R. H.
came up again upon the Quarter-deck; So that all things
appearing to him as he left them, he knew nothing of what had
thus pass'd during his repose.

By this means the Dutch were got a good deal on head of
the English, and the Duke when it grew light, found himself
about half a league a stern of the Body of the Dutch, and as
far on head of that of his own Fleet, having only the
CENTURION, a forth Rate, and two of his Yachts near him.
This posture of the Fleets contributed to keep his Highness in
ignorance of his own Ship having shorten'd Sail; for knowing
her to be a very good Sayler, he thought that was the reason of
his being so far on head of his own Fleet; and that the Dutch
had outsail'd him by reason of our going right before the wind,
and their drawing less water then we.

When it was broad day, the Duke found himself faire in
with the Coast of Holland, which he saw very plain. The Earle
of Sandwich was then about half a league still on stern with
the body of the Fleet, and Prince Rupert at some distance in
the offing. The Enemy, in the mean while, lost no time in
pursuing their Course for the Texel, with all the sail they could
make. However some of the English best sailing third and
fourth Rates fetch'd up and snap'd severall of the Sternmost of
them; all the rest were chaced to the very mouth of the Texel,
where the tide not serving then to get in, they came a while to
an anchor, but so near the Sands and in so shallow water, that
the Duke found it dangerous to Ventur neer them with his
great Ships, and they being above forty sail, were too strong
and numerous for his smaller ones; and what added to their
good fortune, was, that there were no fire Ships left to fasten
upon them; So that they got at last into their harbour.

TOME
II.

1665.
They get at
last into their
harbour, the
English having
no fire ships
left to fasten
upon them :
But 4 fire
ships in all, in
the English
fleet, wᵗʰ an
account how
they were im-
ployd.

We had in all but four fire Ships belonging to the Fleet ; Of the two first we have already given an account; The third was commanded by one Captain Balle, a small one made out of a sixth Rate, which being a good Sayler gavé chace to the Helverson, a Ship of sixty six guns, and at last ran up along her Brod-side, notwithstanding all the shott made at her by the Dutchman, and so clap'd him on bord, and fir'd his Ship, which oblig'd the Helverson to bring to, so to clear himself of her ; which he did, she being but a very small vessel : But by that means he fell in amongst some of our headmost Fregats, and was taken ; and the fourth of those fire Ships was dis-abled.

The Dutch
being got into
harbour, the
Duke stands
out to Sea
again, and so
ended this
great Engage-
ment.

Thus at last the Dutch being got into their harbour, the Duke thought fitt to stand out to Sea, to get a fair offing from the shore, that he might not expose his Fleet in case it should blow. And so ended this Engagement, the greatest and most considerable that had till then been seen : For the Enemy lost that day twenty men of War, the least of which was of forty

A short ac-
count of this
great Victory,
and of the
number of the
Ships lost by
the Dutch, and
of the kill'd
and wounded
on both sides.

guns ; Eight of the number were burnt and the rest brought away, together with four thousand prisonners. They had four of their Admiralls kill'd, Opdam who commanded in cheif, Courtenaer, Stillingwart, and Scram. It was reckon'd they lost in all ten thousand men, either slain, drown'd, burnt or taken prisonners.

Our Loss, as to common men, was inconsiderable for so great a Victory, The number of them not exceeding eight hundred Slain and wounded besides what were taken in the CHARITY, which was the only Ship we lost. Of Flag Officers we lost Sir John Lawson Vice-Admiral of the Red, who dyd some days after the Fight of a wound he had in the knee ; and Captain Sanson Rere Admiral of the White. Of persons of quality were slain the Earle of Marleborow, Captain of the

OLD JAMES, and on board of him, his Nephew the Earle of
Portland, The Earle of Falmouth, The Lord Muskerry, and
M^r. Boyle, son to the Earle of Burlington ; besides Sevarall
other Volonteers of less quality, and some of the Duke's under
Servants.

The Duke having taken an account of the condition of his
own Fleet, and of what he had taken and destroyd of the
Enemys, whose Fleet was got now safe into the Maze, the
Texel, and the Fly, he made the best of his way to the Buoy
of the Nore, in order to refitt and go out again as soon as
possible.

During his stay there, he took care to have his Scouts a broad,
which being usually of the best fourth Rates, went two and two
together towards the Texel, and other parts, so as to give notice
of the Enemies motions.   But after he had been thus Severall
days putting things in order with all expedition and success,
the King about the latter end of June thought fitt to send for
him and Prince Rupert up to London, to give a more particular Relation of what had pass'd, as well as an account of
the present condition of the Fleet, and what measures were
best to be taken for the rest of the Campagne; and in the
mean time order'd, that the Earle of Sandwich should be left
in chief.

We must not ommit before we proceed any further, to give an
account of what was perform'd by two of those Scouts, the
DIAMOND commanded by Captain Golding, and the YAR-
MOUTH by Captain Ayliff, sent out by the Duke to observe the
motions of the Dutch.   They happen'd to meet with two
Direction Ships (as the Dutch call them) belonging to Zealand,
of forty od guns each, The biggest Commanded by one
Masters, the other by youn Cornelius Evertson, who, thō
ours were somewhat better force, did not avoid engaging; at
the very first brod-side Golding was slain, but his Lieutenant

Davis managed the Fight so well, as also did the Captain of the YARMOUTH, that after some hours dispute both the Dutch Ships were taken, thō bravely defended; for they lost many of their men, and were very much disabled before they Struck.

Everstson, and Masters, the two Dutch Cap⁰. set at liberty by y⁰ Duke, because of their bravery.

The Duke gave Evertson his liberty in consideration of his Father Cornelius, who. had. perform'd severall Services for the King before his Restoration; and his R. H. freed also the other Captain for having defended himself so well, and made Lieutenant Davis Captain of one of those Prizes.

The Duke, at the King's Commands, leaves the Fleet under Earle Sandwich, and go's wᵗʰ Rupert to Court.

Resolv'd by the King, that the Duke, nor the Pᶜᵉ Rupert, should go no more to Sea that year.

In obedience to the King's Commands, the Duke left the Fleet under the Command of the Earle of Sandwich, and taking Prince Rupert along with him, went to attend his Majesty at London; By whom it was resolv'd, that neither the Duke nor Prince Rupert should go any more to Sea that year; but that the Earle of Sandwich should command the Fleet, since the busines to be done for the remaining part of the year would not be so much for seeking another battel, as endeavouring to intercept De Ruiter's Ships from Guinea, and other rich ones from the Straights and the East and West Indies, all which were expected to come homewards by the back of Ireland and Scotland : But those Ships by good fortune for them, got safe into Bergen in Norway.

The Duke's arguments to the King to let him go to Sea again. But can not prevaile.

The Duke did what he could to perswade his Majesty to let him go out again with the Fleet by many weighty arguments, to which the King return'd no other answer, but that he was resolved not to hazard his person again that year ; thō the Duke made it appear, the danger would be very small, since the Dutch could not be Strong enough to give another battel ; adding, That since he had begun that Campagne So Successfully, he desir'd to end it, and had vanity enough to beleeve, he could end it better then any body els, and that the care his Maᵗʸ now had of his person might possibly oblige him to send him out some other time at the head of the Fleet, when he should be more expos'd then he had yet been, for want of a vigourous prosecution of the advantages already gotten, which might oblige the Dutch to make such a peace as would be for the honour and advantage of England.

But the King remain'd fix'd to his first Resolution; and when the Fleet was ready to put out again to Sea, he went himself with the Duke, to the Buoy of Nore, to take a Revieu of the Fleet that was now left to the conduct of the Earle of Sandwich.

All this while the Duke had not heard one word of his Ship having shorten'd Sail, no body hauin given him the least notice of it; which happen'd well for Brunkerd, who had certainly suffer as he deserv'd, had the Duke been at that time inform'd A strange concurrence of accidents keep the Duke still in ignorance of Brunker's busines. of his misdemeanor; and it was by strange concurrence of accidents, that his R. H. was kept so long in ignorance of that which was so generally known and talk'd of: When the King and the Duke were coming back from the Buoy of the Nore, Captain Cox took an occasion of addressing himself to his R.H. with intention to purge himself in that matter, Saying to the Duke, That he beleev'd some thing might have been reported to his prejudice, but that he could very well clear himself when he should be examin'd, having done nothing but by order. The Duke not imagining what he meant, bad him explain himself, for no body had told him any thing to his prejudice: But just as Cox was going to begin his history, his R. H. was call'd away in all hast to the King, who was then staying for him in the boat just ready to go off. And the Captain being to go to Sea with the Earle of Sandwich, had no further opportunity of explaining himself.

After this, the great Plague increasing at London, the King The Plague in London, the King and the Duke remove to Hampton Court. and the Duke removed from thence, first to Hampton Court and in few days after to Salisbury; From whence the King thought fitt to send his R. H. to York, that he might have an eye upon The Duke is sent to York.

the Northern parts, there being at that time some apprehensions
of a Rising design'd by the Phanaticks and others of the old
Cromwelian and Republican Party, many of which hold correspondence with the Dutch, by whom they were incouraged, as
his Ma'ty was inform'd by some of his Spys amongst them ; and
to keep all things quiet in London, he left there the Duke of
Albemarle and the Earle of Craven with one half of the Foot
guards, and a Troop of the horse guards.

The Parlia-
ment meets at
Oxford.

A Present of
120000ᴸ pro-
pos'd by the
Paliamᵗ. for
the Duke, in
consideration
of his bravery
and conduct
in the late
Engagement.

The Parliament meeting at Oxford the Autumne following,
obliged the Duke to return thither to the King. At this
Session they gave a supply to his Majesty of 1256347ᴸ to
carry on the war, and at the same time beg'd leave to make a
present of about Six score thousand pounds to his R. H. in
token of the great sense they had of his conduct and bravery in
the late Engagement; and they also gave the King particular
thanks, for his care in preventing his Royal Brother from
exposing himself to any further danger at Sea.

The Duke at
last made ac-
quainted with
Brunkerd's
affaire, his
resentments
therupon.

It was about this time, that the Duke first heard what
Brunkerd had done in counterfiting his Orders at Sea, which
raisd in him no small indignation against the person so offending, not without his displeasure against those who so long had
concealed it from him. Prince Rupert and the Earle of Sandwich excus'd themselves to the Duke, by Saying, They realy
beleev'd he had known it, but was unwilling to take publick
notice of it, least he should have been obliged to punish
Brunkerd as he deserv'd. Those of his R. H. own family, who
were freinds to the person offending, beg'd pardon for their
silence, alledging that it was not their part to inform against a
freind and a fellow Servant; And they who were reckon'd his
Enemies, pretended it would have been look'd upon as malice
in them, to accuse him, since it might have cost him his life,
or at least might have ruin'd him for ever in all other respects.
Thus upon one pretence or other, all were faulty to the Duke,

in not advertising him in due time of what was of such
importance for him to know; And when he came to the knowledge of it, the house of Commons, of which Brunkerd himself
was a Member, took also cognisance of it, which hinder'd the
Duke from having him tryd by a Court Martial : By which
means he at last avoided the punishment he deserv'd ; for thō
his fellow Members seem'd at first violent enough against him,
he wisely, whilst the heat lasted, withdrew into France, and
during his absence some of his freinds prevail'd So far, as to
get the prosecution of him to be deferr'd till Sir John Harman,
the principall witnes against him, was return'd from his voyage
of the West Indies ; So that by length of time the prosecution
coold so, that Brunkerd was only turn'd out of the House, nor
could the Duke do any thing more at that time, then to turn
him out of his Service.

T O M E
II.

1665.

The various successes at Sea in that year, 1666, we shall not
much enter into, since his R. H. was permitted to have no further
share in them, but only to take a view of the Fleet before its
going to Sea. ⌊However to make things hang together in order
of time, It must be mention'd that the French King, having
endeavour'd by his mediation to procure a peace in favour of
the Dutch, without obtaining it, thought himself obliged by
vertue of an Alliance lately made with them, to joyn his forces
with them against Us⌋ and that when our Fleet was at Sea
under the conduct of Prince Rupert and the Duke of Albemarle,
thō We in the first Engagement that summer (by reason of the
Prince his being gone with his Squadron to seek out the French)
had somewhat the worst, yet we continued fighting on under
the Duke of Albemarle four days together, and for the first
three against double our number ; But that on the fourth day

1666.

This year the
French join in
war with the
Dutch against
the English.

The English
Fleet go's to
sea under
command of
Pᶜᵉ Rupert
and the Duke
of Albemarle.
In the first
Engagement,
which was on
——, the
English have
the worst, yet

424

TOME
II.

1666.
continue to
fight it out for
4 days to-
gether, and at
last after
Rupert's com-
ing in, they
oblige the
Dutch to
retire.
In the 2ᵈ
Engagement
of this year, on
the 25ᵗʰ July,
the Victory is
intirely on the
English Side.

The Fire of
London begun
the 2ᵈ Sepʳ.
and lasted 4
days.

The Duke ex-
pos'd to much
toyle and dan-
ger to quench
the Fire.

The Parlia-
ment meets,
and being in
an ill humour
they fall upon
the R: Catho-
licks, and en-
deavour to lay
yᵉFireonthem.

(our Fleet being then rejoin'd and we equal in number with them) the Dutch in four hours time gave way, and retir'd to their harbours.

After our Fleet had refitted at the Buoy of the Nore (for the Duke of Albemarle's Squadron was much damnifyd in their Rigging) and after the Hollanders had repair'd their losses, both Fleets put out again to Sea, and came to a second Engagement on the 25ᵗʰ of July which was Sᵗ James's day, in which we gain'd the Victory and drove the Dutch into their harbours; wher upon happen'd the Enterprise upon Schelling by Sir Robert Holmes, and the destroying there a hundred and fifty lesser ships, that lay there at Anchor, with the two men of war that garded them.

But there remain'd yet a terrible accident to make this year remarkable, which was the Fire which happen in London, consuming in four days time above thirteen thousand houses, eighty nine Parish Churches, with many other publick and magnificent Structures; and this happen'd in a time of war against Holland and France, and after the desolation caus'd the year before by the Plague. The Duke had no litle share of toyle and danger in exposing himself day and night to stop the rage of the Fire, much increas'd by the Easterly winds which then blew, which at last was effected by blowing up houses, that so the flames might have no matter to feed on.

The Parliament met again quickly after this, and severall of the Members finding the Nation under a Triple Scourge of Plague, War and Fire, were in an angry humour, and to vent themselves, they took occasion to fall upon the Papists; and whereas the Plague was evidently from the hand of God, and they themselves had engaged the King in the war, they at least endeavour'd, with a little reason as Christianity to lay the Fire on the Roman-Catholicks, and appointed a Comittee on purpose to make out an accusation against them upon that head;

thō at last they were forced with shame to give over the
Enterprise. And being also weary of the war, which they at
first so eagerly enter'd into, upon pretences of mismanagement,
they refused to give the Supplys necessary to carry it on. So
that the Lord Chancellor, the Lord Treasurer Southampton,
the Duke of Albemarle, and the other Ministers, perswaded
the King upon pretence of saving charges, to lay up the first
and Second Rate of Ships, and to send out such only as were
most proper to interrupt the Enemy's Trade, and only to make
a defensive war.

The Duke oppos'd all he could the taking of these measures,
urging, that our having no Fleet at Sea would raise again the
spirits of our Enemies, which now were very low, and give
them time as well as courage, to set out their Fleet again,
having a prospect of litle or no resistance; That what might
be sav'd by laying up our great Ships, according to the Counsell
given, would be spent in maintaining the Militia and other
necessary Land forces for the security of our Coasts and Ports;
and that we should suffer, not only in our interest, but in our
honour, by permitting the Dutch to ride masters of the Seas
just under our noses: Wherfor his R. H. frankly declared his
opinion, That the Expedient propos'd would prove but very
ill husbandry and be soon repented of. What follow'd, did
but too much confirm the reasons of his R. H. thō at that time
they did not prevaile.

For so it happen'd, that the Dutch came out with their Fleet
the Summer following, and were So far masters of the Sea, that
they came to the Buoy of the Nore, and so up the River of
Medway; where they burnt and destroyd several Ships, and
carryd away the CHARLES a first Rate, and had they push'd
vigourously they might have done much more mischief. This
was the last action of this war which gave the Dutch an

1666.
The Parlia-
ment weary of
the war, give
but weak Sup-
plys for carry-
ing it on.

The King to
Save charges,
is perswaded
by the Chan-
cellor and
others, to lay
up the 1ᵗ and
2ᵈ Rate Ships,
and make only
a defensive
war next
Campagne.

The Duke
opposes these
measures, and
gives his
reasons, but is
overruled.

1667.
The busines of
Chatham, June
1667, which
had not hap-
pen'd if yᵉ
Duke's advice
had been
follow'd.

The dissafec-
ted Party en-
couraged by
the ill Success
at Sea, grow
turbulent.

E. Northum-
berland's fac-
tious discourse
to the Duke,
concerning
laying aside the
Chancellor,
and disbanding
the Troops.

opportunity of ending the war with too much reputation, throu'
our own neglèct; for at this very time there was a Treaty of
Peace on foot at Breda, which was therè concluded the 9ᵗʰ of
July, and solemnly proclaim'd at London the 24ᵗʰ of August
following.

And now the timè drew near of the Parliament's next sitting,
which was to be on the 10ᵗʰ of October; and the disaffected
Party was so encourager by the ill Success at Sea of that
Summer, that they began to be very turbulent and bold: In
so much that Severall of the great ones amongst them had
privat meetings and Cabals, especially those of the Presbyterian
and Commonwealth gang, who never neglected any opportunity
of being troublesom to the Monarchy. To this purpose the
Earle of Northumberland, the Earle of Lester, the Lord Hollis
and others, who were for the Isle of Wight conditions, met in
consultation at Gilford, and what measures they there took
may appear by the discourse, which the Earle of Northumberland soon after held with the Duke before the Sitting of
the Parliament: for he coming to Sᵗ James's à day or two
after his arrivall in London, to wait upon his R. H. which was
his custom to do ; upon the Duke talking freely with him of all
things, and amongst the rest concerning the Lord Chancellor,
and the apprehension he had that his enemies at Court would
impeach him (for he took the Earle to be the Chancellor's freind)
contrary to his expectation, the Earle answer'd with a grave
face, That the laying aside of the Chancellor, who was very
much hated, was not sufficient to Satisfy the Nation, for they
also expected the disbanding of the Guards, and the redress of
severall other Grivences. At which the Duke interrupted him, ·
desiring him to have· care of talking at such a rate, for he
should be obliged to inform his Majesty of it; To which the
Earle answer'd, That he had said nothing to him, but what he
design'd to repeat to the King next day ; wherin he was as

good as his word, he and his party being imbolden'd by the resolutions taken at Court by the Chancellor's Enemies to impeach him, thinking the doing it might make some breach between the King and his Brother: However the Duke at that time calmly reason'd the matter with him, by letting him see the necessity of having Guards, for the safety of the King's person and quiet of the Nation, the want of which had prov'd so fatal to the late King and the whole government; But the Earle was of too inflexible a temper to be wrought upon by the Duke's reasons.

At this time it was that the King's consent was gain'd for the removall of the Chancellor, which for severall years before had been attempted by severall of his Enemies. The first that attack'd him was the Earle of Bristol, who impeach'd him in Parliament in the year 1664: But the King then Supporting the Chancellor, the Earle miscarried in his design, which incensed him so, as to make him break all measures of duty and respect to the King, and without leave obtain'd from the House of Lords, to apply himself to the house of Commons in a studyd speech full of Seditious reflextions upon his Majesty's proceedings. He had also at the same time the confidence to desire an audience from the King, and that My Lord Aubigny might be present at it; in which he express'd himself with So much insolence and extravagance, that had not the King more compassion of his folly, then consideration of his own dignity, the Tower, and some thing worse, would have been his just reward: For he had the boldness to tell the King (as the Duke was afterwards inform'd by the Lord Aubigny) that since he saw his Enemies had deprived him of his Majesty's favour, he would raise such a storm against them, that even his Majesty himself should feel the effects of it.

The rest of the Chancellor's Enemies went more temperatly and securely to work, by watching their opportunitys and

The King consents at last to the removall of theChancellor, wᶜʰ had been long before endeavour'd by his Enemies. The E: of Bristol was the first who had attack'd the Chancellor.

The E. of Bristol's insolent discourse to the King, after having miscarried in his Impeachment of the Chancellor in Parliament, in —64.

T O M E
II.

1667.
The Chancel-
lorinexcusable
in his misbe-
haviour to yͤ
King, in op-
posing a De-
claration of
Liberty of
Conscience,
which had
been before
agreed upon
in a Councill
held by yͤ
King, in the
Chancellor's
own lodgings.

insinuating by degrees a disgust in the King towards him. Nor
can I excuse the Chancellor of having given occasion by his
own misbehaviour towards the King, to make his down fall
more easily consented to by his Majesty. To ommit other
instances of his refractorines to the King's will, That of his
opposing the Resolutions taken by his Majesty, for an Indulgence to Dissenters in Religion about the year 1664, is too
memorable to be pass'd over ; For it having been propos'd and
solicited by the Lord Roberts, Lord Ashly Cooper, and others,
that by the King's Declaration a Tolleration should be granted
to tender consciences, in pursuance of, and grounded on the
Declaration at Breda, it was resolved by his Majesty in a
privat Councill held by him in the Chancellor's lodgings at
Worcester house, that a Declaration to that purpose should be
brought into the House of Lords, the Duke being also very
much for it : But when that busines afterwards came to be
debated by the Lords, the Chancellor speake violently against
it, and being seconded by the Bishops and others of the
zealous Church of England men, it was layd aside, which
did not a litle cool the King's warm heart towards the
Chancellor.

The Dˢˢ of
Cleveland
joins with the
Party against
theChancellor.

His Enemies were not wanting at proper times to revive the
memory of all his failings ; and the more to Strengthen their
Party, they gain'd the Dutchess of Cleveland to be on their
side, which they easily compass'd in regard of a former pique
she had against him, for having forbid his Wife to visit her
by reason of her scandalous life, thō formerly he had been a
great freind to her Father.

The Canary
Company
broke, meerly
out of Spite to
theChancellor.

The first publick attempt this Party made against him, was
their perswading his Majesty and instigating the House of
Commons, to break the Canary Company; for which he had
obtain'd a new Charter from his Majesty, which was done
merely out of Spite and to lessen his credit, to the great preju-

dice of Trade: For wheras that Company did and could oblige
the Canareans to take great Store of the manufactures of this
Kingdom, in part of payment for their wines, and also to sell
their wines at reasonable rates; so soon as the Company was
broken, the Canareans would take nothing but ready mony,
and at the same time rais'd the prices of their wines, which
prov'd a double loss to the Nation.

T O M E
II.
1667.

The Chancellor's Enemys having now prevail'd with the
King, to lay him aside before the Sitting of the Parliament,
which was to be on the 10th of October 1667 (as has been
already said) His Majesty acquainted the Duke with it, and
order'd him to let the Chancellor know it, telling him at the
same time, That it was not out of any dissatisfaction he had
against him, but that the necessity of his affaires requir'd it, it
being more for the dignity of the Crown for him to do it of
himself, then to suffer him to be torn from him by the Parliament: And therfore he order'd the Duke to tell him, he must
send the great Seal to him; and that, to shew he had still a
consideration for him, he would continue to him the privat
pension he formerly received.

The King
orders the
Duke, to ac-
quaint the
Chancellor, of
his being
oblig'd for
ye good of
his affaires to
lay him aside.

The Chancellor receiv'd the Message as became a good
Subject, and without delay sent the Seal to his Majesty; and
then told the Duke, That since his Enemies had prevail'd so
much, they would not stop there, but would prosecute him to
the last degree, and not mind the interest of the King and the
Crown, so they might ruin him. The Seal was given to Sir
Orlando Bridgeman as Lord Keeper, who was, till some time
after he had it, look'd upon as a very honest and able Lawyer,
but upon tryall prov'd to be too weak for so weighty an
Imployment.

The Chancel-
lor, in obedi-
ence to the
King's com-
mand, Sends
the Seals to his
Ma^{ty}, who gave
them to S^r
Orlando Bridg-
man, in quality
of Ld Keeper.

When the Parliament met, the House of Commons were
much out of humour by reason of our Losses at Sea, and the
expence of the war; and according to their usuall custom, in

The Parlia-
ment vote an
address to the
King, for turn-
ing out all
Catholicks out
of his Seruice.

T O M E
II.

1667.

the first place they vented their Spleen against the Papists, by voting an address to the King, that all such of them as were in his Troops, or in service at Sea, might be turn'd out; and that for their better discovery, the Oaths of Allegiance and Supremacy should be tender'd indifferently to all persons so imployd, and they should all by such a day take the Sacrament in the usuall forme of the Church of England.

They Vote an addre's of Thanks to the King, for having taken the great Seal. from Lord Clarendon.

This was done after they had voted the Thankes of the House to his Majesty for his gracious Speech at the opening of the Session, and they likewise order'd. (the motion being made by Sir Thomas Litleton) that particular Thanks should be given for having taken the Seal from the Earle of Clarendon, and remov'd him from the exercise of publick trust and imployment in affaires of State. It is to be observed, that this clause of Thankes concerning the Earle of Clarendon had hardly past, if his Majesty had not order'd his Servants in a privat manner to let it be known, that he desir'd it should be so; and had not the Earle charg'd his freinds in both the Houses, not to oppose it; as being resolved never to let any of his privat concerns obstruct the King's affaires: For if the Duke, with the Bishops, and other freinds of that Earle, had opposed it in the House of Lords, in all likelyhood it would not have been agreed to; and when it was put to the vote, the Duke and Severall of that Earle's freinds withdrew; for thō their obedience to the King would not permitt them to oppose it, they could not contrary to their judgment vote for it, not only in regard of their relation and freindship to the Lord Clarendon, but as thinking it an ill precedent for the Crown. His Majesty in answer to this Address, assured the two Houses, that he would never more give any Imployment of trust to the Earle of Clarendon.

Lᵈ Clarendon impeach'd in Parliament,

That Earle's Enemies being thus incouraged, thought it not fitt to stop here, but, to make all sure, resolved to impeach him:

The cheif Actor in this affaire was Sir William Coventry, who gave up his place of Secretary to the Duke, that he might be the more free to prosecute the Earle of Clarendon; Of all that Lord's Enemies he was the most dangerous, as having the best parts; Nor could the Faction perhaps have prevail'd, had not he been at the head of it. The House of Commons lost no time in preparing their Articles of Impeachment, to be prefer'd to the House of Lords; during which violent proceedings, the Duke had been very much put to it how to behave himself in that whole affaire, between his duty to the King, and what he ow'd in justice and freindship to the Earle, and to his own honour, had it not pleas'd God in the heat of this prosecution to visit him with the Small pox; so that before he was able to come abroad, this great busines was over, the Earle having by privat intimation from the King, to avoid a further storm, withdrawn himself out of England; wherupon there insued an Act of Parliament to banish him out of England during his life.

In both Houses of Parliament there was at that time a Presbyterian Party, not very considerable for their number but for their great industry in watching all opportunitys, if not quite to destroy, at least to bring low the Regall Authority. Some of the Cheif of them, thinking this a proper occasion for their purpose, and that nothing would more contribute therunto then a division in the Royall Family between the King and the Duke, applyd themselves privatly to the Earle of Clarendon, and sent him word, That they would all Stand by him, if he would stand by himself and join with the Duke to oppose the Violent and undue proceedings against him: Where it is to observ'd, that they made use of the Duke's name without the Duke's knowledge, who was all that time lay'd up with the Small pox. But the Earle was too honest and too wise to be caught in their snare, and they went off disapointed,

T O M E
II.

1667.
Sir William
Coventry a
Cheif Actor in
this affaire.

L. Clarendon's
prudence and
honesty in re-
jecting a pro-
posall, made to
him by a Pres-
byterian Party,
who design'd
thereby a
division
between the
King and the
Duke.

whilst the Earle, in conformity to his Maties will and pleasure, yeelded to the stream which ran so violently against him, and went over privatly to France, where he died in the year 1674, after seven years banishment.

He was born a privat gentleman of a good family, bred up to the Law, of good sense, and naturally eloquent, all which brought him into credit ; so that he was chosen a member of the House of Commons in that fatall Parliament of 1640, in which by his good parts he Soon brought himself into esteem, in so much that the King chose him to be a privat manager for him ; and therin he behav'd himself with so much dexterity and fidelity, that at the beginning of the Rebellion he was brought in to Court, and intrusted in the most Secret affaires, and for a reward of his good Seruice was made Chancellor of the Exchequer. When the Prince of Wales was sent down from Oxford into the West, he was one of his R. H. Councill appointed by the King to attend him, and was most relyd upon. When afterwards the King's affaires grew so desperat, that the Prince, for his safety, removed first to the Isle of Scilly, and thence to Jersey, and at last into France, Sir Edoward Hide always attended him. The murther of King Charles the first following soon after, the then present King sent him, together with the Lord Cottington, Ambassador into Spain, whence he return'd, and joynd the King at Paris soon after his Majesties escape from the battel of Worcester : From that time he had the entire confidence of the King, and began to act as a first Minister. He had the Sole management of the affaire of the Restoration with Generall Monk, and Admirall Montague, having been made Lord Chancellor some time before ; And when the King came into England, he was in such favour, that he carried all things before him, and none dared to oppose him. He got his grat freind the Earle of Southampton made Lord Treasurer, with whom, together with

the Duke of Ormonde and the Bishops (he being himself a very
zealous Protestant) being joyn'd in a strict league, .he ·was
feared and courted by the whole Nation. To this was added,
his having his Daughter married to the Duke of York, which
for the present was no small Support to him, thō at last it
probably rais'd So much envie against him, as to be the cause
of his ruine.

No Sooner was the Chancellor removed, when those who
had cheifly driven it on, began to disagree amongst themselves,
each of them pretending to succeed in the Ministry. Sir William
Coventry, without whose help Buckingam and Arlington
could never have brought it about, had most reason to expect
the place, as having most capacity and parts for it ; But the
other two, thō much inferiour to him in qualification, were
better Courtiers then he, and joyning together, they prevailed
to get him out of all his Imployments ; which having done, they
Strove each against the other, who should have most power and
credit with the King, whose affaires by their disagreement and
insufficiency suffer'd very much.

One thing there was, in which they, and all the Stickers for
the removall of the Lord Chancellor, agreed in ; which was, To
lessen as much as they could the Duke's interest with the
King, without which their guilty consciences made them apprehend they should be sooner or later exposed to the ressentments
of his R. H, for their behaviour in Lord Clarendon's busines,
and that he might prevaile hereafter with the King to bring
him back ; Which to prevent, they obtain'd his M^aties leave to
bring a Bill into the House of Lords (as has been said) to banish
him,. The Duke at that time was recovered of the Small pox,
and gave his reasons in the House for his voting against the

3 K

1668.
After the
Chancellor's
removall, the
Ministers disa-
gree amongst
themselves.

Sir Wil:
Coventry, tho
of more capa-
city, is outed
of all his Em-
ployments by
Buckingam,
and Arlington,
who were better
Courtiers then
he.

The Ministers
do all join in
endeavouring
to lessen the
Duke's interest
with ye King,
for fear he
should get
E. Clarendon
recall'd.

The Duke,
recover'd of
the Small pox,
gives his rea-
sons in Parl^t.
for voting
against E.
Clarendon's
banishment.

Banishment, as a thing unprecedented, there being no proof made of any of those Crimes layd to his charge.

1668.
The King is colder to the Duke then ordinary, upon this account. Malitious insinuations of the Duke's Enemies.

This made the King colder then usually to his R. H. which imbolden'd the Faction to venture one step farther; and under pretence of Duty and Zeal, to represent to the King, That the great power and credit of the Duke in the Nation was look'd upon as a lessening to his Majesty, and that in the present circumstance of affaires, it might be unsafe to have the entire command of the Sea, with a great part of the Land-forces, wholly at the Duke's disposall; considering the disgust he may probably have taken at the late Chancellor's disgrace, and the influence which his Party, and especially the Dutchess his Daughter, may have upon his R. H, to excite his ressentment.

The King can not be mov'd by any of those Sugestions ever to doubt of his Brother's fidelity.

These Suggestions, thō they deserved severe punishment, yet were taken by the King only as an overabundant Zeal in them, nor did they make any impression upon him, to the prejudice of the Duke; for his Majesties opinion of his Brother's fidelity was too firmly rooted in him to be shaken by any insinuations of that nature.

All the Chancellor's freinds remov'd, and the Creatures of Buckingam, and Arlington, preferr'd.

However, the now prevailing party would not be idle, but fell to work in removing all such as had been freinds to the late Chancellor, and putting in their room such as had been old Rebells, or notorious Opposers in the Parliament of the King's interest; Of the latter, were Sir Tho: Osburn, Sir Robert Howard, M'r Seymour, and Lord Vaughan, who were brought to Court and had good places given them by their Patron the Duke of Buckingham, as also Sir Tho. Littleton, Sir Rich: Temple, and Sir Robert Car, brought in by My Lord Arlington. Of the Republican and Cromwellian Stamp were Lord Roberts, Lord Orrery, Lord Anglesy, Secretary Trevor, and many others of the Same gang, who upon the defeat of the late Chancellor sooner or later came into Imployment.

They also, to gaine popularity to the hazard of the Crown, releas'd out of prison severall Republicans and old Officers of Cromwell's Army, such as the famous Major Wildman, Col: Salmond, Major Creed, Major Bremen, and others who were men of good Sense, very Stout, and had great credit with the disbanded Officers and Soldiers of that Rebellions Army, Of which very many had been in actuall possession of the Crown and Church Lands, at the time of the Restoration. These had been Secur'd by the advice of the Duke of Albemarle, as a thing which he knew to be absolutly necessary for the Safety of the Government, for the overthrow of which, that they might recover their unjustly acquir'd Estates, they had allways plots and contrivances on foot, which by the diligence of the old General were found out and disapointed.

T O M E II.

Wildman, Creed, and others, Cromwellian Officers, releas'd out of Prison.

After this, they fell upon removing the Duke of Ormonde from his being Lieutenant of Ireland; which was cheifly managed by the Duke of Buckingam, at the instigation of the Earle of Orrery, a person famous for having changed partys So often, and for his Speech made to Cromwell to take upon him the Title of King of England. The Earle of Arlington at first scrupul'd to joyn with them in putting out his old freind the Duke of Ormonde, but at last they threaten'd him into it. Nor had that Duke any that took his part but his R. H; who thought it very scandalous that one who had allways been so loyall, should be prosecuted and run down by men who had been most of them downright Rebells, or litle better ; meaning the Duke of Buckingam, who renounced the King his Master to gain the favour of Cromwell whose Daughter he would have married, But that Vsurper had at least so much of honour in him, as to say, He would never give his Daughter to one who could be so very ungratefull to his King : Having fail'd there, he (*with*) much ado and great Submission gott to marry the Lord Fairfaxe's Daughter, who had been General also of the

TOME
II.
_____
1668.

Sᵗ Tho:
Osburn, and Sᵗ
Tho:Littleton,
made Trea-
surers of yᵉ
Navy, without
acquainting
the Duke.

No disrespect
of the Mini-
sters hinders
the Duke to
joyn with them
for the King's
Seruice.

Buckingam,
and Arlington,
labour to
suppleant one
another.

D. Buckin-
gam's message
to the Duke,
offering him
his Seruice; to
wᶜʰ the Duke
answers

Parliament Army, Yet notwithstanding the endeavours of his R. H. the Faction prevail'd to out the Duke of Ormonde, and to put Lord Roberts in his place.

They also prevail'd to put in Sir Thomas Osburn, and Sir Thomas Littleton, to be Treasurers of the Navy, without so much as speaking or making the least i appl cation to the Duke about it, thō Such places never use to be disposed of without the concurrence and approbation of the Lord Admiral; and thō the Duke represented to the King the hardship done him, yet his Majesty order'd him to sign the Warrant for their admission; which having done, he afterwards lived very well with those two gentlemen, they being men of parts and executing well their office. They likewise obstructed for some time Sir Jeremy Smith's being made a Commissioner of the Navy, thō recommended by the Duke, as being an old Sea Commander and the fittest man in England for that employment.

Notwithstanding these disrespects and slights shewn by these new Ministers to the Duke, yet his R. H. never fail'd to join with them at the Cabinet Councill, or elswhere, in any thing that concern'd his Maᵗⁱᵉˢ Seruice; for no usage could ever prevaile upon him to be in the least wanting to his duty, and therin to give good Example to the meanest Subject. This his Maᵗʸ was so sensible of, that all the Duke's Enemys from first to last could never lessen the confidence he had in his R. Brother.

Thō these two Ministers, Buckingam and Arlington, agreed in mortifying the Duke, yet they were so far from being united in other matters, that they now labour'd to supplant and destroy each the other; In so much that the Duke of Buckingam sent a privat message to his R. H. by the Earle of Berkshire, one of his great confidents, to offer him his seruice, with great protestations of what he would do for him. To which his R. H. gave a plain answer, That he had formerly received such offers

from that Duke without any performance, and therfore could
not trust him; besides, that he look'd on it as below him, to
enter into any of their Cabals, being resolv'd to Serve the King
in his own way; And least any Story should be made of this
hereafter, and the thing misrepresented, his R. H. immediatly
gave the King an account of what had past, without naming
the person that brought the Message.

We must not omitt here an accidentall declaration, which
the King made of his mind concerning his Brother in presence
of three or four of his Bedchambermen; which happen'd upon
old Sir William Armorer's bluntly telling him, There was strange
news passing up and down in the Country, for it was said,
that his Ma⁷ intended to disband his Brother's Troop of Gards
and Regiment of Foot, and the reason given for it was that his
Ma⁷ had so disobliged him, that it was not safe for him to let
the Duke have such a body of men as they were under his
command, and to leave it in his power to revenge himself: To
which his Ma⁷ answer, That it was the greatest Ly in the
world, that it had never enter'd into his head, but that, on the
contrary, he had all the kindness imaginable for his Brother,
and were he master of more Kingdoms then those he had, he
would trust them all in his hands; and the King also added,
He had heard it reported, that he design'd to have the Duke of
Monmouth declar'd legitimate, which was a thought never
enter'd into his head, that he abhor'd it, and would endeavour
to find out the authors of so vilanous a report, and have them
Severly punish'd. Yet notwithstanding this so solemn a
Declaration, the factious Party desisted not to insinuate such
fancys into the Duke of Monmouth's head, who greedily
swallowed the poison, as will hereafter appear.

Now when this turbulent Party, that were Enemies to his
R. H. found they could not prevail with his Ma⁷ to entertain
any jealous thoughts of his Brother, and therby to out him of

TOME II.

1668. plainly, That he could not trust him.

Some remarkable expressions of the King's kindness for, and confidence in the Duke.

The Duke's Enemies fall upon another expedient to ruin him, which

1668.
was, that the
King should be
divorced from
the Queen.

D. Buckingam
and E. of Bris-
tol the cheif
promoters of
this project of
the Divorce.

The first hints
thereof come
from the old
Republican
party.

E. Bristol go's
incognito to
Parma, to find
out a new wife
for ye King.

The Duke,
advertis'd of
these Prac-
tices, cautions
the King
against them.

his Employments, they betook themselves to another expedient, no less effectuall for compassing their design, and more suitable (as they thought) to the genius and inclinations of the King; which was, that he should be divorced from the Quen (she not having had after so many years of marriage any children, nor being likely to have any) and be married again. Two of the cheif promoters of this, were the Duke of Buckingam and the Earle of Bristol, who very much pleas'd themselves with the invention and contrivance of it, and were heard to say, in discoursing about it, That if the Duke could be perswaded to consent to it, he would make himself be laught at, and dispis'd by all the world; and, if he oppos'd it, it would ruine him with the King. Many at Court enter'd into this Project, and there wanted not Lawyers and some Divines, that wrott papers to shew the lawfullness and reasonableness of it. There is reason to beleeve that the first hints therof came from some of the Old Republican Party, since nothing could be more for their turn, nor more likely to cause division in the Royall Family, and consequently the destruction of Monarchy.

Severall persons of different partys and professions, all joyn'd in this design, and none more active in it then the Earle of Bristol, who took upon him to find out a new wife fitt for his Majesty; and to that end he went privatly into Italy, upon information, that at the Court of Parma there were Daughters of that Duke, amongst whom might be found a fitt match for the King.

His Royall Highness was by his freinds advertis'd of all these practices, and thō he did not openly complaine to the King of them, yet he occasionally by way of discourse represented to him, That the Common-wealth-party and the Enemies of the Royall Family were still at work, in hopes of setting up again their beloved Idole of a Common-wealth, and seeing they could not bring it about by open force, they attempted to do it by Sowing division in the Royall Family, which they hoped might break out into a Civil-war and which would make the English Nation cast them off both, and even Monarchy itself, as destructive to the peace and happines of the people of England. It is to be presum'd, that such discourses as these had a good effect with the King, for thō he did permitt severall about him to argue with him upon that Subiect, yet they could not prevail with him to come to a resolution to do any thing in it.

Now to reinforce the Project of the above contrived Divorce, there was brought into the House of Lords a Bill for dissolving the marriage of Lord Rosse, upon the account of Adultery, and giving him leave to marry again, which Bill at last, after great debates, pass'd by the plurality only of two Votes, and that by the great industry of that Lord's freinds, as well as the Duke's enemies, who carried it on cheifly in hopes it might be a Precedent, and Inducement for the King to enter the more easily into their late proposalls : Nor were they a litle encouraged therein, when they saw the King countenance and drive on the Bill in Lord Rosse's favour ; But their hopes were again soon disappointed, for when his Majesty was inform'd of what was said, and what inference they made from his favouring Lord Rosse's Bill, he took an occasion to declare, That had he a conscience which would permitt him to be divorced, it would not Stick at taking a quicker and surer way (not unknown in history) of marrying again without giving the Parliament any trouble about it : And now that we are upon the point of Consciences, it is to be notted that when the Lord Rosse's pass'd the House, of eighteen Bishops that were there, only two * voted for the Bill, of which 'one doted throu' age, and the other was reputed a Socinian.

Now it was that the King began again outwarly to shew

Margin notes:

TOME II.

1668.

L⁴ Rosse's Divorce carryd on in Parliam¹. of purpose to be a precedent to the King's.

The King, thō he favour'd L⁴ Rósse's Bill, yet did soon after declare, that he was no ways dispos'd to follow his example.

* Dr. Cosens Bishop of Durham, and Dr. Wilkins Bishop of Chester.

The King begins again to

his former kindness and confidence towards the Duke, which for some time past had seem'd to cool by the instigation of those Enemies of his R. H, who had been taken into the Ministry upon Lord Clarendon's being layd aside; and espically of the Duke of Buckingam, who had so guilty a conscience of his misbehaviour towards the Duke, that he fancyd (thō without the least ground) that his R. H. had a design to have him murder'd; So that when he went out of Town any where, he had allways two Musketoons in his Coach, and many horsemen well arm'd to attend him. This came to the King's ears, who laught at the folly of that Duke's suspicion, and spar'd not to tell him how ridiculous he made himself therby. His Majesties eyes open'd every day more and more to convince him, that the Duke of Buckingam was not cut out for a Minister of State, who, thō very agreeable in his person and conversation, and full of flashy witt, had nothing of steady or solid in him.

It was about this time, in the beginning of the year 1669, that his R. H. (who had it long in his thoughts that the Church of England was the only true Church) was more sensibly touched in conscience, and began to think seriously of his Salvation. Accordingly he sent for one Father Simons, a Jesuite, who had the reputation of a very learned man, to discourse with him upon that Subject; And, when he came, he told him the good intentions he had of being a Catholick, and treated with him about his being reconcil'd to the Church: After much discourse about the matter, the Father very sincerly told him, that unless he would quitt the Communion of the Church of England, he could not be received into the Catholick Church; The Duke then said, He thought it might be done by a dispensation from the Pope, alledging to him the singularity of his Case, and the advantage it might bring to the Catholick Religion in general, and in particular to those of it in England, if he might have such dispensation for outwarly appearing a Protestant, at least till he could own himself publickly to be a Catholick, with more security to his own person, and advantage to them. But the good Father insisted, that even the Pope himself had not the power to grant it, for it was an unalterable doctrine of the Catholick Church, Not to do ill that good might follow. What this good Jesuite thus said, was afterwards confirm'd to the Duke by the Pope himself, to whom he wrott upon the same subject. Till this time his R. H. beleev'd (as it is commonly beleev'd, or at least said, by the Church of England Doctors) that dispensations in any such cases are by the Pope easily granted, But Father Simons's words, and the letter of his Holines, made the Duke think it high time to use all the endeavours he could, to be at liberty to declare himself, and not to live in so unsafe and so uneasy a condition.

Wherfor his R. H. well knowing that the King was of the same mind, and that his Majesty had open'd himself upon it to Lord Arundel of Warder, Lord Arlington, and Sir Thomas Clifford, took an occasion to discourse with him upon that subject about the same time, and found him resolv'd as to his being a Catholick, a very Sensible of the uneasines it was to him to live in so much danger and constraint; and that he intended to have a privat meeting with those persons above nam'd at the Duke's Closett, to advise with them about the ways and methods fitt to be taken for advancing the Catholick Religion in his Dominions, being resolved not to live any longer in the constraint he was under. This meeting was on the 25th of January, the day in which the Church celebrates the Conversion of St Paul.

TOME
II.

1669.

The Duke speaks of Religion to the King, and finds him resolv'd to be a Catholick.

The King appoints a privat meeting with Ld Arundel, Ld Arlington, and Clifford, at the Duke's clósett, to advise on the methods to advance Cath. Religion in his Kingdoms. They meet the 25 January.

T O M E
II.

1669.
The King
declares his
mind in the
matter of
Religion, with
great Zeal to
the Duke, and
the other 3
persons pre-
sent at this
privat meeting.

When they were met according to the King's appointment, he declar'd his mind to them in the matter of Religion, and repeated what he had newly before Sayd to the Duke, How uneasy it was to him not to profess the Faith he beleev'd, and that he had call'd them together to have their advice about the ways and methods fittest to be taken for the setteling of the Catholick Religion in his Kingdoms, and to consider of the time most proper to declare himself; telling them withall, that no time ought to be lost, That he was to expect to meet with many and great difficultys in bringing it about, and that he chose rather to undertake it now, when he and his Brother were in their full strength and able to undergo any fatigue, then to delay it till they were grown older, and less fitt to go thorow with so great a design. This he speake with great earnestness, and even with tears in his eyes; and added, That they were to go about it as wise men and good Catholicks ought to do.

Result of the
privat Con-
sultation about
Religion.
The work to
be done in
in conjunction
with France.

The Consultation lasted long, and the Result was, that there was no better way for doing this great work, then to do it in conjunction with France and with the assistance of his Most Christian Majesty, The House of Austria not being in a condition to help in it; and, in pursuance of this Resolution, Monsr. de Croissy Colbert, the French Embassador, was to be trusted with the secret in order to inform his Master of it, that he might receive a power to treat about it with our King. The doing of this took up much time, for the Treaty held on, not

Ld Arundel
sent to treat
with the King
of France.

only here, but also Lord Arundel was sent into France to conferr with that King, and to conclude the Treaty: Sir Richard Beling was intrusted to draw the Articles, and to do the part of a Secretary in that Negociation.

The Treaty
concluded in
the beginning
of 1670.
Articles of this

The Treaty was not finaly concluded and signd till about the beginning of 1670, The purport of which was, that the French King was to give two hundred thousand pounds a year

by quarterly payments, the first of which to begin·when the
Ratifications were exchang'd, to enable the King to begin the
work in England ; That when Catholick Religion was settled
here, our King was to joyn with France in making war upon
Holland ; That in case of success France was to have such a
part as was stipulated ; The Prince of Orange such a share,
And England was to have Sluce, Cassant, and Walkeren, with
the rest of the Sea-ports as far as Maesland-Sluce. The French
had a great mind to have begun with the war of Holland first,
but Lord Arundel being sent again over into France, convinced
that King of the necessity of beginning first with the Catholicity
here ; and so it was at last adjusted, and the first payments
began according to the Articles.

All this was translated with the last Secrecy ; and in preparation thereunto, Collonel Fitzgerald, lately come from Tanger
where he had been Governor, was to have a new Regiment
of Foot rais'd for him, and such Officers chosen for it as might
be confided in ; his Regiment was to be put into Yarmouth,
and he made Governor of that important Town : The Earle
of Bath was Governor of Plimouth, Lord Belasis of Hull,
Lord Widdrington of Berwick, all of them men in whom the
King might confide ; The Fleet and Portsmouth were in the
Duke's hands; nor was the Generality of the Church of England
men at that time very averse to Catholick Religion ; Many that
went under that name, had their Religion to chuse, and went
to Church for Companys sake ; The few Troops that were on
foot were look'd upon as well affected, and their Officers, all
except Collonel Russel, such as would serve the Crown without
grumbleing or asking questions. The rigourous Church of
England men were let loose and encouraged underhand to
prosecute according to the Law the Nonconformists; to the
end, that these might be more Sensible of the ease they should

Col. Fitzgerald
to have a new
Regiment, and
be made
Governor of
Yarmouth.

Plimouth,
Hull, Berwick,
and Ports-
mouth, in
hands of per-
sons to be
trusted.

The Troops
well affected.

1669.
The D. Buck-
ingam seeks to
support him-
self by the
favour of
Madame, with
whom he
manages a
Treaty with
France.

have when the Catholicks prevail'd. But how all this design came to faile, an account shall be given in its proper place.

The Duke of Buckingam finding himself every day sinking lower and lower in the King's esteem and confidence, and that his application to his R. H. by the Earle of Berkshire (who, as I should have said before, was introduced by the Earle of Peterborow) had no effect, and also finding that his Rivall, Lord Arlington, had in like manner made his addresses to the Duke with better success, and knowing with all the great credit which Madame the Dutchess of Orleans had with our King, he thought he could not be better supported or buoyd up, then by her favour towards him; And the better to introduce himself, he enter'd into a Treaty with Monsieur de Rouuigny (who was at that time the King of France's Minister in England and who mistakingly thought that Duke to be still in his former favour with the King) about a stricter Alliance between England and France, to be transacted with all secresy, only between that Duke on our King's part, and Madame for the King of France: In prosecution wherof, he sent over his great confi-

dent Sir Elis Leighton, with recommendations from Mons' de Rouuigny, to manage affaires with Madame. In the mean time the King kept the Secret, and suffer'd this mock-treaty to go on, that he might the better cover the reall one, of which neither Madame, nor that Duke, had the least knowledge; whose cheif drift in his own new project, was to keep himself up at the head of the Ministry.

This new
Treaty with
France, made
a Secret to the
Duke, and to
L⁴ Arlington.

This management was made a Secret to his R. H. and to Lord Arlington, But after Sir Elis Leighton was come back from France, and had settled a Correspondence with Madame, his R. H. came accidentally to the knowledge of it, and at last received a full account of the whole Transaction from Sir Elis Leighton himself; and then gave notice of it to Lord Arlington,

which serv'd not a litle to make the breach wider between him
and the Duke of Buckingham, and to make him more firm in
his R. H. interest (wherunto Sir Thomas Clifford, that Lord's
great freind, and a very stout and Loyall man, did very much
contribute) thō he still supported the creatures he had brought
in, in opposition to the Duke.

Of this there was an instance in the two Treasurers of the
Navy, Sir Tho: Osburn, and Sir Thomas Littleton, who
pretended to have discover'd great mismanagment in the
Commissioners of the Navy, who were persons put in by the
Duke, and depended on him, that so they might get in others
in their places of their own gang: This by a side wind reflected
on the Duke, and therfore he thought fitt to obtain of his Ma^{ty}
that the matter might be examin'd before him; and all sides
being heard, it appear'd that those accusations proceeded either
from malice, or from their ignorance in the affaires of the Navy,
and the proceedings of the Commissioners were fully justified.
They also attempted to perswad his Ma^{ty}, when a Squadron of
eighteen Ships were order'd in Councill to be got ready to go
against the Algereens, not to imploy Sir Thomas Allen a very
experienced Commander, in that Expedition, only because he
was the Duke's creature and recommended by him; and they
press'd to have that Command given to Sir Robert Holmes, a
creature of Lord Arlington's; who, thō very Stout in his own
person, had not the capacity of the other, nor temper enough
to govern such a Squadron: But his Ma^{ty} understood Sea-
affaires so well, and was so well Satisfied with his Brother's
managment of them, that notwithstanding the Suggestion of
others, he still follow'd his advice in those matters.

In the beginning of September, of this year, 1669, the King
and the Duke went to Southampton, to hunt in the New Forest,
where the news was brought them by an express of the death
of the Queen their Mother, who dyd at Colombe near Paris the

Sr Tho Osburn,
and Littleton,
pretend to dis-
cover great
mismanage-
ment in y^e
Commissioners
of the Navy,
but are disa-
pointed.

Sir Tho.
Allen's going
out against
Algereens,
oppos'd by the
Ministers,
becaus Sr.Tho.
was a creature
of the Duke's.

The Death of
the Queen
Mother at
Colombe.

latter end of August. ; She was youngest Daughter of the great
King Henry the 4th, of France, born the 28th Nouembre 1609.
N. S. and married to King Charles the 1st, in the year 1625.
After her great and many sufferings, God was pleas'd at last
to comfort her with the sight of her Son's Restoration to his
Father's Crown. She excelled in all the qualitys of a good
Wife, a good Mother, and a good Christian. She was buryd
with great magnificence at St Denis the buriall-place of the
Kings of France, in the same maner as the Queen Mothers of
France are us'd to be buried.

The Duke
regulates wth
the French
Embassador,
the Salutes at
Sea between
the English
and French
Ships in ye
Mediteranean.

Sir Thos: Allen being about this time to go out with a
Squadron of Ships under his command into the Streights, the
French Embassador propos'd to the Duke, the making some
regulation for the Salutes at Sea between the English and
French Ships which might meet there, his Master being then
about Sending out a Squadron, under the Command of
Monsieur du Quesne to treat with the Algereens; and at last
it was agreed, to avoid all disputes, That in the Mediteranean
they were not Salute one another; and the Duke took particular
care that in the agreement, the words, *In those Seas*, should be
inserted, that ther might be no consequences drawn from
thence as to other Seas.

On the 3d of January, of the year 1670, dyd the old General
The Duke of Albemarle, who was the cheif Instrument of the
King's wonderfull Restoration, and had received from his

The Duke
takes this
occasion to
advise the
King, not to
make any body
General, it
being too great
a Command for
any Subject.

Majesty honours and estate proportionable to his merite. Some
days before his death, his R. H. being inform'd that he could
not recover, speaking of it to the King, he took that occasion
to advise his Maty not to make any body General in his room,
for that it was too great a power and trust, as matters stood, to
be put in any one bodys hand, not excepting even himself; tho

if his Majesty would have a General, he hoped he would not
think of any other body for that place but himself, which
however he did not desire for the reason above given, and that
in time of peace there was no need of one ; and in case of a
war, his Ma^ty might make such General Officers as should be
fitt and proper for the occasion; And since the number of
his Troops at present was so small, it would look oddly, as an
unusuall thing, to have a General over them. For these and
other reasons his Ma^ty at that time resolved to have no new
General in the place of the Duke of Albemarle.

At the same time the Duke desired the King, that upon this
occasion of the Duke of Albemarle's death, his own Troop of
Guards might not lose their Rank of being the Second Troop
of Guards, which would be a hardship both to himself, and to
all the Officers of his Troop, who were very good men, to be
so postpon'd ; That when his own Regiment of foot was rais'd
call'd the Duke's Regiment, he did not then desire or expect
they should have their rank before Coldstream Regiment; they
being first rais'd ; and therefore since his Majesty saw he did
not desire to do wrong to others, he hoped that he should not
have wrong done to him nor to his Troop of Guards ; and his
Ma^ty was then so well satisfied with these reasons and the
justice of the Duke's desire, that he assur'd his R. H. that his
Troop should not lose their Rank of being the Second Troop of
Guards.

The Duke desires of the King, that his own Troop of Guards should n^ot lose t^heir Rank.

But so it was that upon the General's death, his Regiment
of foot called the Coldstream, was given to Lord Craven, and
made a Second Regiment of Guards, and his Troop of Guards
was the Queen's Troop ; and therupon the Queen who was not
of herself overkind to the Duke, was put upon it by some who
were glad of any occasion under hand to put any mortification
upon his R. H. to ask it of the King, That her Troop of Guards
might have the next rank to that of the King's ; which she

The Coldstream Reg^t. given to Ld Craven, and the old Generals Troop of Guards is call'd ye Queen's Troop.

T O M E
II.

1670.

The Duke
g^enero^uly he
dⁱspen e^s t
King from hⁱs
promise, and
acquiesces to
have hisTroop
of Guards lose
their rank of
2^d Troop,
which was
given to the
Queen's
Troop.

press'd so hard by herself and others, that his Ma^{ty} was very
much embarass'd what to do in it, remembring what he had
said to the Duke upon that subject: Of which his Royall
Highness being inform'd, he went to the King, and said, That
he saw his Ma^{ty} was teas'd by the women and others upon that
account, That for his own part he would be more reasonable
then they, and was content his Ma^{ty} should not stick to his first
resolution and promise (thō at the same time he could not (*but*)
think it a hardship upon him) but would quietly acquiesce to
what (*was*) easiest to his Ma^{ty}, For what ever others did, it was
his resolution never to make him uneasy for any concern of his
own; And so the Queen's Troop had the rank given it of the
Second Troop of Guards.

Madame
comes to
Dover in
May.

About the beginning of May, in the same year, Madame,
the King's only Sister now living, came to Dover to meet her
Brother, which she had long desird to do, and which was now
made easy to her upon the King of France's coming then into
Flanders to visit his new Conquests; But this her journy
prov'd to be unfortunat in many respects, and not only hurtfull
to our Kings affaires in generall, but particularly to those good
measures (*which*) had been taken as to the Catholick Religion.
I have already mention'd how the private Treaty was Signed
and exchanged between the two Kings, and that Some of the
mony in pursuance of it had been payd to the King; for thō
the French allways shew'd a strong inclination to have their
own work done first, and to begin with the war against Holland,
yet that King yeelded at last to the convincing reasons that
were given him to the contrary, as has already been said.
But now again, still looking upon it as more advantageous for
their own temporall concerns, to change those measurs then
taken, and knowing the great influence which in all likelyhood
Madame would have upon the King her Brother, it was
resolved by his Most Christian Majesty to make use of her to

bring that about which he so much desir'd ; For which reason
/ he consented to her journey, thō formerly he had been adverse
to her making a visite to her Brother in England, as also
Monsieur was for reasons of his own. She very willingly
undertook this Commission, hoping therby further to ingratiate
herself with that King, and to be more consider'd in France by
shewing the power she had over the King her Brother : She
had indeed a mind to Stay in England, not only out of love to
her Brother, but she presumed upon his temper and the
ascendant she should have over him ; and beleeved, that if
once she could compass her living with him, she might govern
all things here.

― When her coming over was first propose the Duke did not
like it, fearing the ill consequences it might have, and which
afterwards did happen ; and as dexterously as he could,
without appearing down right against it, he did his utmost to
hinder it, but without effect. Also an accident happen'd at
that time, which did very much facilitate Madame's prevailing
upon the King her Brother ; for a late new Act of Parliament
coming just at that time to be put in execution against
Conventicles, the King thought it necessary to leave the Duke
behind him in London, to prevent any disorder that might
happen upon the first Sunday in which the Conventicles were
to be shutt up and suppress'd, which fell upon the 10th of May;
So that Madame arrived at Dover three or four days before
the Duke could come thither. In which time she had so
prevail'd with the Kiug, that when the Duke arrived there
he found all the former measures broken, and the resolution
taken to begin out of hand with the War with Holland ; And
it was no litle Surprise to his R. H, that both Lord Arlington,
and Sir Tho. Clifford, being gain'd by Madame, had concurr'd
in it, who were the only two there present that knew of the
Secret Treaty. They meeting the Duke upon his first entring

The Duke
against his
Sister'scoming
to Dover,
fearing the ill
consequences
of it, as to the
privat Treaty.

Before the
Duke'sarrivall
at Dover,
Madame na̅d
already pre-
vail'd with the
King, to begin
first with the
Dutch War
and break all
the former
measures.
Ld Arlington,
and Clifford,
gain'd by
Madame, cou-
curr'd with her

1670.
to the great
Surprise of the
Duke, who was
concern'd to
See, that these
new methods
did quite ruin
the Catholick
Design.

The Duke's
reasons against
beginning with
the Dutch
War; But he
is overruled.

into Dover, before he had seen the King, told him what had been done; who answer'd them, He was very sorry for it, for he was sure, it would quite defeat the Catholick design; because when once his Ma^ty was engaged in such an expensive war as that would be, and was not absolute master of affaires at home, he unavoidably would run in debt, and must then be at the mercy of his Parliament, which, as matters had been order'd were not likely to be in very good humour; and, therfor, thō they had given very large Supplys for the former Dutch War, in all probability they would not do the same now, since that War was of their own proposall, wheras this is undertaken without their advice, and (in) conjunction with France; for which reason alone they would not approve of it, and besides it would give them a jealousy and suspicion of what was further intended. They answer'd, That, as to what his R. H. fear'd of the King's running in debt, there would be no danger of it, since his Ma^ty being to have fifty Ships out, to which the French were to joyn thirty, that charge might be easily supported by the Customes which they reckon'd at six hundred thousand pounds, and that such a Fleet, they thought, would be sufficient to deal with the Dutch; and that if the War succeeded, it was not much matter what people suspected. The Duke told them, He was sure they took wrong measures as to the Sea expence, for thō the number of Ships they mention'd might cost no more, and that he thought he should be able to look the Dutch in the face with eighty such Ships as those, and fire Ships proportionable, yet the necessary Convoys for the preservation of Trade, and the security of the Plantations, with a recruit of Ships which must be got ready to joyn the Fleet after an Engagement, would go near to cost as much more, not to reckon the Land forces which upon this occasion must of necéssity be rais'd. All this, and more, the Duke afterward represented to the King, but could not prevaile to get that fatal Dutch War put off.

Whilst Madame stayd at Dover, she prevail'd with the King to pass by his displeasure to the Duke of Buckingam, and got him restor'd again to his Majesties favour and trust; and when his R. H. found fault with her for so doing, she ingenously told him, She did it to make her court to the King, who she saw had a mind to be press'd to do it. She also made the Duke of Buckingam and Lord Arlington freinds; and had at that time so much credit with the King, by reason of the opinion he had of her good understanding and of his kindness to her, that she should have perswaded him to have done almost any thing she had a mind to. After about a fortnight's stay at Dover she was call'd back, the French Court being upon their return towards Paris; and a litle after her arrivall at her own house at St Cloud, she dyd of a sudden and violent distemper, which seiz'd her but the evening before to the great surprise and grief of all the Royall Family. The manner of her death gave some suspicion that she was poyson'd, but the Phisitians when she was open'd declar'd she was not.

TOME II.

1670.
Madame gets Duke of Buckingam restor'd to the King's favour, and made him and Arlington freinds.

This voyage of Madame's into England made a noise beyond Sea; and the Dutch were much alarm'd at it, whose jealousy was increased by the Duke of Buckingam's being sent soon after into France, In So much that Monsieur Vanbeuning, their Minister here, desir'd he might be impower'd to assure De Witt, that that Duke was sent upon nothing prejudiciall to his Masters.

Soon after Madame's death, his R. H. fell ill of a great cold, to that degree that it was fear'd it would turn to a consumption; so that he was oblig'd to go to Richmont for change of air, to get well of it; nor did he perfectly recover till almost the end of the Summer.

All things were now pretty quiet at Court, the two Cheifs Ministers having been lately made freinds. The winter

**T O M E
II.**

following there was some noise made upon a suspicion, that the
Dutchess of York was inclin'd to be a Roman Càtholick ; nor
was it without ground, for she that had been all her lifetime
very regular in receiving once a month the Sacrament in the
Church of England way, and upon all occasions had shewn
herself very zealous in her profession, but was of late observed
to have forborn so taking the Sacrament; and that which
confirm'd them the more in this suspicion, was, that during
all her great indisposition, of which she dyd, she had not
prayers said to her (as was usually) by any of the Chaplains ;

The Duke
owns the truth
to the King,
of the D^{ss}
resolution to
be a Catholick.

in so much that in December (*the King*) took notice of all this
to the Duke, who own'd the truth to him, That she was
resolved to be a Catholick, and was soon to be reconciled ;
Vpon which his Ma^{ty} charg'd the Duke to keep it as a great

None but F^r.
Hunt a Fran-
ciscan, Lady
Cranmore, and
Dupuy, privy
to her reconci-
liation.

Secret, which was accordingly done, for none but Father Hunt
a Franciscan who reconcil'd her, the Lady Cranmore, and
Depuy a Servant to the Duke, was privy to it. It was about
a twelve month before (as may be seen by the papers she left
behind her containing the motives of her Conversion) that she
began to doubt, and in August last she was fully convinced
and reconciled, thō the world knew it not till she dyd; which

The D^{ss} of
York's death,
31 March.

happen'd the last day of March, 1671, after she had received
all the last Sacraments of the Catholick Church. She dyd
with great devotion and resignation, and the morning before
her death, finding herself very ill that she could not long hold
out, she desir'd the Duke not to stir from her till she was dead;
and that in case Doctor Blanford Bishóp of - - - - - -,
or any other of the Bishops, should come to speak to her, he
would tell them the truth, That she was reconcil'd to the
Church of Rome, and had accordingly receiv'd already the
Sacraments ; But, if when so told, they still insisted to see her,
they might come in, provided they would not disturb her by
discoursing to her of Controvercy : And accordingly, when

Doctor Blanford soon after came the same morning to see her, being brought thither by her Brother Mr. Laurence Hide, now Earl of Rochester, (who did not certainly know that she was become a Catholick) The Duke meeting the Bishop in the drawing Room, told him what the Dutchess had charg'd him with; and being further satisfyd by the Duke, that she was reconcil'd, he said to him, He made no doubt but that she would do well (that was his expression) since she was fully convinced, and did it not out of any wordly end; and afterwards went into the room to her, and made her a short Christian exhortation suitable to the condition she was in, and then departed. Her Brother the Lord Cornbury, a violent Church of England man, came not near her when she was so ill, because he suspected she was become a Catholick.

It was not long after the death of the Dutchess, that the Duke was press'd by severall of his freinds, to think of marryin again, and they would have had him propose it to his Majesty; But he told them, It was as much the King's and Kingdom's concern as his own, and that if his Majesty had a mind to it, or thought it fitt, he would speak to him of it himself; which at last he did about six months after the death of the late Dutchess, and the person propos'd was the Princess of Inspruck, daughter to the Arch Duke of that place, who was of the House of Austria. This was done upon the information of Sir Bernard Gascon, a Florentin gentleman, who had long serv'd in the Army of King Charles the 1st, and had seen that young Princess, being well acquainted with the Dutchess her mother, who was of the house of Florence. The well wishers to the Crown were very desirous that the Duke should lose no time in marrying again, the King having no legitimate children, and the Queen likely to live long without hopes of having any; and the Duke having lost six of the eight he had by his first Wife, of which four were Boys, and only two

TOME II.

1671.

D^r. Blanford came to see her on her death bed, and tho he was told she was a Catholick, said, he made no doubt she would do well, since she was fully convinced.

The Duke press'd by severall of his freinds, to marry again. His Answer.

The King him-self speaks to the Duke of marrying, and the P^{ss} of Inspruck is propos'd.

1671.

S' Bernard
Gascogne,
after a long
delay, is sent
to negociate
the marriage
at Vienna and
Inspruck.

The Articles
sign'd, amongst
which one that
the D^{ss} was to
have a publick
Chappel.

E. Peterborow
is sent Embass'.
to marry the
P^{ss} of
Inspruck, as
Proxy for the
the Duke, but
stopt at Calais
with the news
of the Em-
presse's death,
and ye Em-
peror's reso-
lution to marry
that P^{ss} him-
self.

Daughters left. At last it was resolv'd, that Sir Bernard should be sent into Germany, to treat this Match both at Inspruck and at Vienna; yet the doing it was delayd for severall months, wherby we may conclude that the King was not very forward in it at that time. However, after a long delay, Sir Bernard was sent with necessary Instructions to both the above named Courts, for the treating and concluding this Marriage. This he effected after a tedious Negociation, and the Articles were sign'd and exchang'd privatly, between the Emperor and the King; one of which was, that a publick Chappel should be allowed the Dutchess in England. Hereupon the Earle of Peterborow was nam'd, and dispatched away as Embassador Extraordinary from the King to the Emperor, with the usuall Instructions upon such occasions, and with a power to marry that Princess by Proxy. But the said Earle was no sooner landed at Calais, when news came from Vienna of the death of the then Empress, and that the Emperor was resolv'd to marry that Princess himself, which did put an end to all this negociation.

1672.

Buckingam,
Lauderdale,
Arlington,
Clifford, and
Ashly Cooper,
E. of Shafts-
bury; These 5
call'd the
Caball were
now of the
Cabinet Coun-
cill, the last a
great stickler
for the Dutch
War.

THE year 1672 began with preparing the Fleet with as litle noise as might be, to have it in readiness to begin the War in the Spring with the Dutch, in pursuance of the Treaty above mention'd with France. Of the King's Cabinet Councill were then the Duke of Buckingam, Duke of Lauderdale, Earle of Arlington, Lord Clifford, and Ld Ashly Cooper, afterward Earle of Shaftsbury and Chancellor of England, and none more zealous then he for carrying on the War with Holland. Now thō none of them but Lord Arlington and Clifford had knowledge of the Secret Treaty with France, which gave the first Rise to this war, yet there were not wanting other specious reasons enough, to make the others enter into it, which were afterwards sett forth in his Maties Declaration of War published on the 28th of March of the present year. The War being thus resolved on, the first busines was to provide mony sufficient to carry it on ; for which they could find no other expedient but stopping all payments in the Exchequer, with an allowance of interest, of six per Cent to the persons unpayd, and this for the space of a year. In the next place it was thought necessary to procure, as much as might be, an Vnion amongst ourselves, before we fell upon our Enemies ; and in order therunto it was resolved, That his Ma^{ty} should put forth a Declaration for Liberty of Conscience, with due limitations for the preservation of the Church of England as it was by law establish'd, and for preserving the publick peace against any seditious practices in the meetings of the Non-Conformistes, which were to be in publick places to be allow'd them, where all should have liberty to come in ; But to the Roman Catholicks there was only exemption granted from the penal Laws, and liberty to exercise their Religion only in their privat houses.

Thō his R. H. was in his own Judgment against entering into this War, before his Ma^{tys} power and authority in England had been better fixed, and less precarious, as it would have been if the privat Treaty first agreed on had not been alter'd ; yet in obedience to the King's Commands, he lost no time and spar'd no pains in carrying it on with all the vigour imaginable, and with all the good husbandry that such an Vndertaking would permitt ; and therfore when it was propos'd in Councill to put an Embargo on all Ships outward bound, the better to man the Fleet, the Duke alone oppos'd it, because it would have put a stop to all Trade, and by consequence highly endammage the King in his Customes ; and, at the same time, he undertook to man the Fleet without so doing, for which he only desir'd that the Newfound Land Trade might be forbid for that Season ; And for the Main-Fleet which he was to command, he desir'd

T O M E
II.

1672.
The Publick
reasons for
this Dutch
War sett forth
in the Declar-
ation of y^e
28 of March.

The Duke
against enter-
ing into this
War before
the King's
authority was
better fix'd, as
it would have
been if y^e
privat Treaty
had been
follow'd.

The Duke,
alone opposes
the proposal
made in Coun-
cill, of an
Imbargo upon
all Ships, and
undertakes
without that
to man y^e
Fleet.

T O M E
II.

1672.
He desires
only 60 ships
of Line and 20
fire ships.

no more then Sixty Ships of Line English, with twenty fire Ships, and thirty French men of war with ten fire Ships, judging that force sufficient to deal with the Dutch. By this means there were Ships and men enough left for Convoys, so that the War would cause no interruption of Trade.

Sr Rob.
Holmes sent
out with a
Squadron to
intercept the
Dutch Smirna
Fleet.

The King about this time having advice that a rich Dutch Fleet was coming from the Straights throu' the Channell, convoyd by six men of war, sent orders to Sir Robert Holmes who was then at Portsmouth, to go out with what Ships could be got ready there, in order to intercept them; he had also orders to call to his assistance all such men of war as he should meet with in the Channell. Accordingly Sir Robert put out to Sea in the St MICHEL a second Rate, having with him the Earle of Ossory in the RESOLUTION, Sir Fretcheville Holles in the CAMBRIGE, Captn George Legge in the FAIRFAX, Captn John Holmes in the GLOCESTER, which four last were all third Rates, with about three or four smaller Ships of fifth and sixth Rates; and whilst he was cruising on the back of the Isle of

He meets Sr
Ed. Spragge at
the Isle of
Wight,but do's
not advertise
him to joyn
with him,as he
might to have
done.

Wight, he saw at some distance from him Sir Edward Spragge, sailing with about five or six men of war homewards, bound from the Mediterranean; but did not advertise him, as he had to have done, of the Orders he had receiv'd for all the King's Ships that he met to joyn with him; nor would he (allow) Captain Legge to go and speak with Sir Edoward, thō he much desir'd it: and this out of a privat pick and emulation, for he rather chose that the King's busines should suffer, then that Sir Edoward Spragge should have any share with him in the honour of that Enterprise; which was the cause why the Dutch came off with so litle loss, and we with so litle advantage upon this occasion.

Sir R. Holmes
attacks the
Dutch Smirna
Fleet. The
Dutch lose but
4 Marchand
men in this
Engagement.

Soon after the Dutch Smirna Fleet appear'd, and Sir Robert engaged them with more courage then conduct; for his own Ship was disabled in the Fight, and the Dutch gott off with the

losse only of four Marchant men, and but two of them of any
considerable Value.

·T O M E
II.

1672.

AFTER this Engagement the War against Holland was
immediatly proclaim'd, and the Generall Rendezvous of the
whole Fleet, both English and French, was appointed to be at
St Helens near the Isle of Wight; but notwithstanding all the
diligence that we could make, De Ruyter with about seventy
Ships of Line, besides fire-ships, gott to Sea before we and the
French could joyn. The Duke being advertis'd of this, and
also that the French Fleet were sail'd from Brest, and judging,
as the winds had been, that they must now be in the Channel,
he sail'd from the Buoy of the Nore with all the Ships of Line
which were then ready, which were only forty with twelve fire
ships; and having had all that day a fresh gale at West, which
carryd him down the King's Channel, by that time he was got
the length of the long-Sand-head, he had in the evening sight
of the Dutch Scouts, and by the Signals they made, he judged
they saw the Body of their own Fleet, thō he could not, it being
somewhat hazy towards the Eastward; and when he had got
about the head of the above mention'd Sand, he stood away to
the South; and as the night fell, the gale growing fresher, and
there being liklyhood of bad weather, he was obliged to come
to anchor, where he continued all night. At break of day it
prov'd litle wind, and the Duke had no sooner given the signall
for sayling, but that the wind came up East with a thick fog;
by which means he past by De Ruyter without seeing him, or
being Seen by him, and so stood away for St Helen's; had not
that Fog opportunly happen'd, the Duke could not have
avoided an Engagment upon Very unequall terms. About
eleven it began to grow clear, and the Duke found himself
somewhat to the West of Dover, fair in with the shore, and
continued on his course, so that early next morning he joyn'd

The Second Dutch War, proclaim'd.

The general rendezvous of the English and French Fleet at S^t. Helens.

De Ruyter with 70 ships of Line,gets to Sea before ye Junction of the English and French Fleets.

The Duke Sail'd from the Buoy of the Nore with only 40 ships of Line.

He discovers the Dutch Scouts in the evening.

The Duke passes by De Ruyter in a Fog without seeing him, or being seen by him, and passing by Dover joyns next morning the French at S^t. Helens.

T O M E
II.

1672.

The Duke
stays 2 days
at S'. Helens
to adjust all
things.

An account of
the Fleet.

The Duke's
Ship the
PRINCE of 100
guns, his
Squadron y*
Red.

His Vice
Admiral S' Ed.
Spragge in the
LONDON, his
Rear Admiral
Sir John
Harman in the
CHARLES.

C. d'Estreés
Adm. of the
White, his V.
and R. Ad-
mirals M'. Du
Quesne and
La Rabiniere.

E. Sandwich in
the R. JAMES
admiral of the
blew.

Sir Jos Jordan
in the
SOVERAIGN
V. Ad'. of the
blew and S'
John Kemp-
thorn R. Ad'.
in y* S'
ANDREW.

the French at St Helens (May 4th). As for De Ruyter, he came into * Dover road two hours after the Duke had pass'd by it, but thought it not convenient to Sail further West.

The Duke remain'd but a day or two at St Helens, only to settle the order of battel and to adjust all things with the Count d'Estreés, Commander of the French Squadron; which being done, he sail'd to look out for the Dutch Fleet, and to joyn the rest of his own Fleet which were not ready when he sail'd from the Buoy of the Nore.

Before we proceed, it may be proper to give some particular account of our Fleet, and how it was officer'd as to the Flags.

The Duke, as High Admiral of England, commanded the whole; his Squadron was the Red, and he was in the PRINCE a Ship of a hundred guns, this being her first voyage; Sir Edoward Spragge in the LONDON, a Ship of the same force, was his Vice Admiral; and Sir John Harman in the CHARLES of ninety Guns, was his Rear Admiral; The Count d'Estreés, Vice Admiral of France, in the St PHILIP of between eighty and ninety Guns, was Admiral of the White, and Vice Admiral of the Fleet; he carried his white Flag at the fore top mast head, none but the Admiral of France carrying it at the main Top mast head; his Vice and Rere Admirals were Du Quesne, and La Rabiniere, both in Ships of eighty guns and upwards. The Earle of Sandwich in the ROYALL JAMES of one hundred guns, was Rere Admirall of the Fleet, and Admirall of the Blew; Old Sir Joseph Jordan in the SOVERAIN of the same number of Guns, was his Vice Admiral, and Sir John Kempthorn in the St ANDREW of ninty od guns, his Rere Admiral. Sir

---

* According to Campbell, the Dutch Fleet was seen off Dover, May 9th, and on the 13th a Squadron of theirs chased some English Ships under the cannon of Sheerness. — EDITOR.

Robert Holmes in the St MICHEL of ninty od guns, and Lord
Ossory in the VICTORY of eighty od guns, were the Duke's
Seconds, which post Sir Robert had desir'd to have, since he
could not have a better Flag then Sir Edward Spragge.

1672.
Sr R. Holmes
in the S^t
MICHEL and
Ld Ossory in
ye VICTORY,
weretheDuke's
seconds,

When this Fleet sail'd from St Helens, the wind continuing
East, they were obliged to stop tides, So that it was some time
before they got the length of Dover, where they receiv'd notice
that the Dutch were without the banks of Flanders thwart of
Ostend ; Wherupon the Duke made the best of his way to find
them out, and was the next day joyn'd by Severall Ships of
Line from the River, that were not ready to saile with him
when he first Sett out. Vpon the (19th) of May about ten in the
morning he got sight of the Dutch, and having the wind of them,
it being West, he bore down right upon them : At which time
the Earle of Sandwich sent his Captain, Richard Haddoc, an
old Commander at Sea, to advertise the Duke, That by his
reckoning they should not be far from a Sand called the Rumble,
known by few of our Pilotes; and that he was confident the
Dutch were just to Leeward of it, designing to draw us upon it;
Wherfore the Duke examin'd all the Pilots on bord his Ship, and
they knew nothing of that Sand, it being out of the Tradeway
for the English ; But Captain Lecke master Gunner of his
Ship, who having cruis'd in Cromwell's time on that coast, knew
it as well as Haddoc did and was of his opinion : Wherupon the
Duke order'd some of the smallest fourth Rates to make saile
on head, to See if they could find out that Sand, which they
accordingly did, and found that what Haddoc and Lecke had
said, was true, and that the Dutch kept just to Leeward of
that Sand on purpose to draw the Duke upon it; That there
was but eighteen foot water in it, so that there could be no
engaging them that afternoon : And when he was come up
within allmost Cañon-shott of them, he brought to, the same
tacks on bord, and stood in with them towards the banks of

Capt Haddoc
advertises the
Duke of the
Rumble Sand,
on which the
Dutch design'd
to draw the
English Fleet.

3 N 2

T O M E
II.

1672.
stands in with
the Dutch
towards the
Banks of
Flanders.
Both Fleets
tack, and are
within less
then cañon
shot of one
another.

A Fog rises
next morning
and continues
till 8 or 9.

De Ruyter
stands in the
Banks, having
no mind to
ingage in the
morning and
so far from yᵉ
Banks.
The Duke
stands after
him, but the
gale fresheniug
he could not
ingage him.

The Duke, see-
ing the Enemy
avoided ingag-
ing, stood away
to Southwold
bay, to take in
water and pro-
visions.

Flanders till about ten at night; And then the Enemy first gave their Signals for tacking, which the Duke also did at the same time, and lay close haled to keep the wind : Both Fleets were then so near one the other, that some of their shot, when they fir'd for their signal of tacking, flew over our Line, wherupon the Duke stood towards the North till after midnight, at which time they tack'd again, and stood in towards the Banks of Flanders; which the Duke also did, and about two in the morning, finding the Soundings of those Banks, he tack'd, and stood out to the North.

Before day break, there fell a very thick Fog, which continued till about eight or nine; when it brake up, the Duke saw the Van of the Enemy led by a Vice Admiral, that was litle more then Canon-shot a stern of him, somewhat to windward of his own Ship and of some ten more that were next him, but to the rest of his Fleet that was in sight, they were Leeward; The Earle of Sandwich Admiral of the Blue, and his Division, were not in sight, he having come to an anchor in the Fog, but after it clear'd up he quickly joyn'd the Fleet.

When the Enemy saw themselves so near us, they tack'd and stood in towards the Banks, De Ruyter not having a mind to ingage so early in the morning and so far from the Banks, which appear'd by his working. The Duke tack'd at the same time, in doing of which three or four of his Ships brought their top masts by the bord; and the gale freshening, and being north west, there could be no ingaging, the wether not permitting to carry out the lower Tire, however the Duke waited on them towards their own Coasts; but towards sun set, seeing there was great likelyhood of more blowing wether, he stood off from the Banks. Seeing therfore that the Enemy avoided fighting, and that many of our Ships wanted water and provisions, occasion'd by our hasty coming out to joyn the French,

The Duke stood away for Southwold Bay, the wind continuing westerly, and the Ruyter stood in to his Coast, and came to an Anchor off of the Gorée. This sure was the first time that two Fleets were so near, and continued so long in presence of one another, and parted without engagin. De Ruyter had no mind to venture a battel, and with reason; for the loss of it might at that time have proved very fatal to his Country, considering the ill condition they were then in by the Conquests the Most Christian King in person had made upon them, and the great consternation they were then under. On the other side he was obliged to keep the sea, So to support the drooping spirits of his Countrymen, and to hinder the deserting of his men, and their getting the same fright amongst them, which was on shore: So that he had a hard game to play; And had he not been qualified as he was, he could not so well have fenced against all these difficulties as he did. He was indeed justly esteem'd the greatest Sea Commander of his time; he was bred up under old Van Tromp, and had been in all or most of the Cheif Engagements of the two first Dutch Wars; he had very good sense equall to his courage, which appear'd upon this occasion in so managing his Fleet, that altho they were so near one another for so long a time, the Duke could not come to an Engagement without great disavantage and hazard to his own Fleet ; for he posted himself so advantageously for his own Fleet, that drew less water then ours, neer the banks of Flanders, and serv'd himself so well of the wether, which was favorable to him, that the Duke could neither attack him in the morning so to make a decisive battel of it, nor far enough off from the Sands with which they were better acquainted then we.

When the Duke was come to an Anchor in Southwold Bay, he let such of his Ships of Line, as were in most want of provisions and water, anchor near the Shore for the quicker

**T O M E
II.**

1672.
AndDeRuyter stood into his Coast, and anchor'd off of the Goreé. De Ruyter's reasons for venturing a battel at that time.

De Ruyter the greatest Sea Commander of his time.

The Duke at anchor in Southwold Bay.

His care and
orders to pre-
vent being
surpriz'd.

De Ruyter's
reasons and
determination
to attack the
Duke in South-
wold Bay.

dispatch; which also severall of his fire Ships did to take in more balast, they having been fitted out in So much hast, that they had not time to take in all they wanted. This permission was given the wind being westerly, the Duke declaring at the same time, That so soon as it should come about to the East, he would stand a litle further out into the Sea, and anchor in his order of battel. He also order'd, That no light Colliers, or other trading-Ships should be permitted to go to the Northward, for fear of falling into the hands of any of the Enemies Cruisers or Privateers, wherby they might be advertis'd how his Fleet then lay. Notwithstanding which orders and precaution, a light Collier slip'd by in the night and was taken by a Privateer, and so carryd to De Ruyter, who therupon immediatly call'd all his Flag-men and Captains on bord, and the wind being just then come up East, he gave them an account of the Intelligence he had of the posture the English Fleet was then in, and propos'd to them to sail that night at Sun-set, so to be up with the Enemy by break of day, That in all probability they would not be in order, or in a condition to receive him, That having now the advantage of the wind for doing it, he could not hope to have so fair an opportunity again, and therfore thought he ought to make use of it. Notwithstanding all these reasons the Generality of the Officers seem'd not satisfied with them, but made severall objections against this proposall, Saying, That should the wind come Westerly when they were come up with the Enemy, they should be in an ill condition, It being very unsafe for them to ingage so far from their own Coast; And when De Ruyter saw he could not by reasoning bring them to be of his mind, he told them, That being convinced it was for his Master's seruice so to do, and being trusted by them with the Command of the Fleet, he was resolved to undertake it, and therfore order'd them to be ready to saile at the close of the evening which accordingly was done. The account of these particulars was afterwards given the Duke by Captain John Dick, Commander of the Josue, who was present at the debate.

As soon as the Duke saw the wind come up Easterly, he call'd for Sir John Cox, his Captain, and order'd him, in pursuance of what had been formerly resolv'd, to give the Signall for the Fleet to stand out, and be in order of battel to receive the Dutch in case they should be up with them the next day: Sir John represented to the Duke, that he was of opinion, there could be no danger of the Enemies coming upon him so soon, their Fleet being in the same condition as ours, taking in stores and provisions as we were; That Captain Finch, one of our Cruisers, come newly in from the Coast of Holland, had brought no news of the Enemies motion ; That the master of the Packet-boat was just come in also, who being brought in to the Duke, inform'd him, that he came the evening before throu' the Dutch Fleet, as they lay at anchor off the Gorée, That most of 'em had then yards and Top-masts down, and were taking in all sorts of provisions. Sir John therfore insisted, That by all this it was not likely that they could be So Soon in a sailing condition ; So that it would better for his R. H. to remain where he was at least for twenty four honres longer, in which time all his Fleet might be Supplyd with what was wanting, which it could not be in severall days should it stand out farther from the Shore: This advice was confirm'd by the French Major, and Captain Eliot his assistant, who were appointed to take the water and other necessaries for the French Squadron. Vpon all which the Duke was overperswaded to continue as he was. Sir John Cox was so fully perswaded that the Dutch could not come and attack us in twenty four houres time, that as soon as the Duke was gone to rest, without asking leave of his R. H, as he ought to have done, he brought his Ship, the Prince, on the Careen to

TOME
II.

1672.
The Duke
surpris'd at
Southwold
Bay.
The first
notice of the
Dutch Fleets
approaching,
given by one
Cogolin at 2
in the morn-
ing, May 28.

give her a ·Pair· of Boot-hose-tops. in order to her better sailing.

In this condition was the Duke·on the 28ᵗʰ· of May about two a clock in the morning, when he had the first notice of the approche of the ·Dutch; which was given by one Cogolin Captain of a French· fourth Rate, who had been out with Captain Finch a cruising on the coast of Holland, and his Ship being none of the best Sailers, could not· get into the Fleet the evening before, as the other had done; and therfore was obliged to come to an anchor a league and better to the East of the Fleet, that he might not be driven to the Leeward of it, the wind being north. east, and a Leeward tide. This happen'd well for us, for by that means we had quicker know-ledge of the approche of the Enemy; For this Captain inform'd that whilst he was getting under Sail to joyn the Fleet, two of their Scouts fell in with him, and thō they were each of them of equall force with him, they fir'd not at him, but brought to, and stood from him, which made him with reason judge that their Fleet was not far astern of them; Wherfore by way of signal to give notice of the approche of the Enemy, he fired all the way he stood in to joyn our Fleet, which instantly made us all prepare to receive them the best we could. As soon as it was day we perceiv'd the Enemy just to windward, bearing right down upon us. Such of our Ships of Line and fire ships that were nearer in with the shore then the Flag-men, .and some of the other great Ships, at the first alarme got under ·sail, to place themselves in their respective stations in order of

Not above 20
Ships of Line,
of the Red and
Blew Squad-
rons, bore the
brunt of De
Ruyter's and
Van Ghent's
Squadrons.
The Zeland
Squadron

battel; but by reason of the Leeward tide, and East·wind, few of them could get in when the Engagement began: So that of the Red and the Blew Squadrons there were not above ·twenty in all that. bore the brunt of De Ruyter's and Van ·Ghent's Squadrons.· The· Zeland Squadron commanded by Banker, had to do with the French commanded by the Count

D'Estreés, both of them standing to the Southwards, having their Larbord tacks on bord from the very beginning of the Ingagement, wheras the Duke and the Earle of Sandwich with theirs lay close hal'd with their starbord Tacks on bord. The Earle with his Blew Squadron led, and had to deal with Van Ghent and his Amsterdam Squadron, and De Ruyter, with his of the Maese ingaged with the Duke and his Red Squadron.

The better to avoid confusion or any sudden consternation, the Duke in the first place gave very seasonable and prudent Orders, That none who were about him should trouble the Officers of the Ship with unnecessary questions, and that no man whatsoever should so much as name a Fire Ship aloud; That if they perceived any such a bearing down upon him which neither he nor his Officers saw, they should whisper it to himself, or to ye Officer next to them.

Between seven and eight in the morning the Ingagement began with great fury, the Dutch having the advantage of the wind, of which De Ruyter thought to have made good use; for after that he and the Duke had given each other their Broadsides, hoping to make short work with his R. H. he sent two of his Fire ships to bord him. Sir Edward Scot formerly a Land Officer under the Duke, who now attended him as a Volonteer, happen'd first to discover them; but remembring what Command his R. H. had given, he gave notice of them only by a whisper to Sir John Cox, who stood then next to him: But scarce had Sir John call'd for an Officer to give him orders therupon, but a great shot struck him dead, and at the same time carried of the head of one M^r. Bell a Volonteer. Sir Edward then address'd himself to the Duke, who forthwith gave such directions that the Fire ship which came on first was quickly dispatch'd, and the other render'd useless for that bout.

TOME II.

1672. commanded by Banker, has to do with the French.

The Duke's Orders before the Fight.

The Fight begins about 8 in ye morning, the Dutch have ye wind. De Ruyter, after exchanging broadsides with the Duke, sends two fire ships to bord him. Sir Ed. Scot, the first that discovers the fire ships coming, and advertises. S^r. Jo. Cox slain.

By the Duke's directions the 2 fire ships are quickly dispatch'd.

T O M E
II.

1672.
The Duke first
Ship the
PRINCE so
disabled that
he's oblig'd to
leave her.

The Duke was all this while, with the few Ships that were with him, so plyd by De Ruyter and his seconds, that his Ship, the PRINCE, had before eleven of the clock her main-top-mast shot by the bord, her fore top Sayl, her Starbord main shrowds, and all the rest of her Rigging and fighting sails shot and torn to peices, and above two hundred of her men kill'd and wounded ; So that his R. H. finding his Ship unable to work any longer, was forced to leave her, after having privatly order'd his Captain to tow out of the Line and endeavour to refitt, or at least save her from the Enemies fire ships ; And to avoid noise and surprise, he went down between decks, as it were to order something there, and then slipping in to his Boat, he took with him only the Lord Feversham, M^r. Henry Savil, M^r. Ashton, Dupuy, and his

He go's abord
the S^t.MICHEL.

cheif Pilot ; His Shaloupe brought him to the St MICHEL, a Second Rate, Sir Robert Holmes Commander, that was on head of him somewhat to Leeward, and for that reason had not then been much damaged.

As soon as he was there got on bord, he put up his Flag that he carried with him, but there not being wind enough to spread it, he was fain to send his Boat to give notice to the Ship next him, where he was.

The French
standing away
to the South-
ward, are not
press'd by the
Zeland
Squadron as
they might
have been.

Whilst matters pass'd thus where the Duke in person was, the French, as I have already said, stood away to the Southward as close haled as they could ; but they were not at all press'd by Banker and his Zeland Squadron as they might have been ; for he hardly came neerer to them then half Cañon-Shot, which did not a litle diminish the reputation the Zelanders had gain'd in the two former wars, of being the briskest men amongst the Dutch ; so that neither of those two Squadrons were much endamaged : But it was not so with the Red, and the Blew, for they were press'd very hard by De Ruyter, and Van Ghent with their Squadrons ; And that which imbolden'd the Enemy the more, was, that there was not above twenty of the Red and

the Blew upon a Line that bore the first brunt of the two
above mention'd Squadrons, the rest of our Ships not being able
to get into the Line till the afternoon.

As soon as the Duke was on bord of the St MICHEL, he was
obliged to tack by reason of a Sand thwart of Laistoff, and
stood to the Southward as neer as he could ly ; And by that
means he wether'd De Ruyter and most of his Squadron, but
had the Amsterdam Squadron still to windward of him, which
had been obliged to tack for the same reason : So that now the The Duke
between two
Duke had them on both sides of him, and was forced to lead Lines of y^e
Dutch, and
for some time those of his division, that could get into his wake forced to lead
the few Ships
and tack after him, which were not many ; And the rest tack'd of his Division
that were with
Leeward of De Ruyter, so that the Enemy and we were much him.
mingled together.

Soon after that Duke had stood to the Southward, a gentle
gale sprung up at East, and being got clear of the Smoke he could
look a litle about him. The first thing he saw was the Earle The Duke
discovers the
of Sandwiche's Blew Flag some distance on head of him, E. of Sand-
wiche's Ship
appearing above smoke, which was so great about that place on Fire.
that one could not see any hulls. Whilst the Red was engaged The particu-
lars of the E.
with the Ruyter and his Squadron, The Earle of Sandwiche's of Sandwiche's
engagement
Division was no less hotly engag'd with the Squadron of Van with Van
Ghent and
Ghent, who with his Ship brought to on the broadside of the Brakell, and
how his ship
Earle ; whilst at the same time Captain Brakell, a bold hot headed the R. JAMES
was burnt.
Dutchman in a Ship of Seventy Guns, layd him on bord thwart
the hause, by which means raking him for and aft, they together
destroyd him a world of his men ; which obliged the Earle
(that he might be rid of so troublesom a neighbour) to order
his men to enter Brakell's Ship, which they did with their
swords, halfpikes, and pistols, and after some resistance they
master'd her. Thō this gave the Earle some ease, yet Van
Ghent and his Seconds so plyd his Ship the ROYALL JAMES,
and had slain and disabled so many of his men, that he was

obliged to recall those who had master'd and were in possession of Brakell's Ship; and then having sent to take the advice of his Captain, C. Haddoc an experienced Commander (who had been shot throu' the foot with a musket bullet and was then dressing in the Hold) by his advice he came to an Anchor by one fix'd for such accidents out of the Gun-room, which had the desired effect of being clear'd of Brakell's Ship, but prov'd in part the loss of the ROYALL JAMES; for besides that she was at the very beginning of the Ingagement somewhat to windward of her own Division, so by coming then to an Anchor, they drove farther from her, and the Enemy came nearer to her.

Van Ghent Slain.

About this time Van Ghent was slain by one of her shot, but that did not hinder the Enemy from still pressing her very hard; and they sent a fire ship upon her, which she sunk before she could reach her. The Earle was then no longer at an Anchor, for soon after he was got clear of Brakell's Ship, he cut the Cable that was out his Gun room, after which, when he had almost got clear off from amongst the Dutch, another fire ship came upon him, which he endeavour'd to bear up; but his Ship was so disabled, that she could not do it, and so the fire ship layd her on bord to windward on her larbord side, and burnt her.

The Duke Saw the R. JAMES blown up, but being to Leeward could not help it.

This the Duke beheld with Sorrow, but could not help, he being to the Leeward of her, thô he past close by her and saw the Sea all cover'd with her men, some sinking, some swimming, and others buoying themselves up upon what they could next catch hold of.

He orders the DARTMOUTH to ly by, and save all the men she could of the R. JAMES.

Hereupon he order'd the DARTMOUTH, which was just come up to him, to ly by, and save all she possibly could; So that she and some of the boats of the Line which followed the Duke, made a shift to pick up two or three hunderd, of which number

Cap. Haddoc, Lieu'. Majo,

were Captain Haddoc, Lieutenant Majo, the master Carpenter,

and one Lowd a Servant of the Earle of Sandwich, whom the King made Page of the Bedchamber so soon as he came to London. The Earle his Master had not the same good fortune, for being drown'd, his body was afterwards taken up, and honorably burried in Henry the Seventh's Chappell.

· Soon after this the PHENIX a small fourth Rate, Cap[n]. le Neve Commander, and not long after him the RESOLUTION a third Rate, Cap[ne] Berry Commander, and the CAMBRIDGE also the third Rate, Sir Fretchevill Hollis Commander, got on head of the Duke very Seasonably; for the S[t] MICHEL (where he then was) was between the two Lines of the Dutch, and had received so many shott between wind and water, that the water she made hinder'd her sailing; which the Duke perceiving sent down a Lieutenant, who brought him word, She had five foot water in Hold; yet by the care and diligence of the proper Officers, her leakes were soon stopt and she sufficiently clear'd of the water, without lying by, or forbearing to ply the Guns.

About this time, Van Ghent's Squadron of Amsterdam bore down nearer the Duke, as if they design'd more closely to press him, But on the sudden they brought to again, and contented themselves with plying him very hard with their great guns; the reason of this was (as the Duke was afterwards inform'd) that the Captain, who then Commanded Van Ghent's Ship, was kill'd at the time when this was doing, and that he who commanded after him, had not the resolution to do what the other design'd. Soon after this, Van Nesse the elder, who carryd a Flag in the main top, being to Leeward of the Duke, after he had tack'd and cut between De Ruyter's and the Amsterdam's Squadrons, he stretched out on head with some of De Ruyter's Squadron, and tack'd again and stood stem-lings with the Duke, designing to wether him, and bring up some fire ships he had with him; But when the STAVERN, one of his Seconds which led him, had got up with the broadside

TOME II.

1672.
and one Lowd sav'd, but the E. of Sandwich himself was drown'd.

The PHENIX, the RESOLUTION, and the CAMBRIDGE, come very Seasonably on head of the Duke.

The Duke's ship the S[t]. MICHEL so leaky, that she had 5 foot water in Hold.

Van Ghent's Squadron bear down upon the Duke.

Van Nesse the elder strives to wether the Duke and bring up some fire ships to attack him, but his heart fails him in the execution.

of the Duke, Van Nesse's heart fail'd him, and in stead of following his Ship on head of him, which was a ship of fifty odd guns, commanded by Captain Elzevire, he tack'd, and stood a way with his fire ships after him, and left the STAVERN behind him; which was so disabled by the broadside she receiv'd from the Sᵗ. MICHEL, and the rest of the Ships which followed the Duke, that she yeelded to the GREENWICH a fourth Rate, Captain Green Commander.

The Duke's Ship within musket shot of the Dutch, powers her broadside into their V. Adᵗˢ second, and raksher to and oft.

By this time the Sᵗ MICHEL had again so much water in Hold, that she made Leeward way, so that the Dutch being also to Leeward of her, she at last came to be within musket-shot of them; and as she pass'd by the first great Ship which was the Dutch Vice Admiral's second, some that were foreward on, cryd out, To forbear firing at her, for that she had struck: But the Duke quickly perceived by her working, that it was a mistake, and that the Enseigne suppos'd to have struck, was indeed shott down; wherfore the Duke order'd his broadside to be powr'd into her, which raked her fore and oft.

Now also Sir Edward Spragge with some of his Division was got on head of the Duke, when at the same time the Earle of Ossory in the VICTORY, who till then had kept in his Station a Stern of the Duke, was so disabled, that he was forced to bear away to refitt; Into whose place came Captain George Legge in the FAIRFAX, a third Rate. It being then above

The Duke's 2ᵈ ship no longer able to continue in the Line.

five in the afternoon, Sir Rob: Holmes gave the Duke an account, that his Ship the Sᵗ. MICHEL, was no longer able to continue in the Line, for besides her loss of men, which had been great, and the bad condition her sails, masts, and rigging were in, she had so much water in Hold, that if she did not very soon ly by, to stop the leakes, they should not be able to keep her above water; wherupon the Duke resolv'd to go on

He resolves to go on bord the LONDON, his Orders therupon.

bord Sir Edward Spragge in the LONDON, and at the same time order'd Sir Robert Holmes, not to strike the Standard, nor bear away out of the Line, till he saw the Standard flying on bord the LONDON, least the disappearing of it for any time, should discourage his own Fleet, which prov'd to be a necessary caution; for thō the Shaloup which carried him to the LONDON was a very good rower and had a good Crew, he was neer three quarters of an hour before he could reach the LONDON, she having got by the freshening of the gale so far on head of the Sᵗ MICHEL.

TOME II.

1672.
The Duke expos'd near an hour in his Shaloup, before he could reach the LONDON his 3ᵈ ship.

When the Duke came on bord the LONDON, he found her also much disabled, especially in her head sails; having had to deal with the Ship of Van Nesse the younger, a Rear Admiral, who was to windward of her, so that he swag'd apace down upon us. But at this time, it being now seven in the evening, De Ruyter made a signal for all his Ships that were to windward of him, to bear down to him, and he himself bore away to joyn the Zeland Squadron, which was to Leeward of him, and was still engaged with the French; In doing of which De Ruyter bore down upon the RAINEBOW, an old Second Rate, Captain Story Commander, (she was only of fifty six guns thō of three Decks) thinking she would give way to him; but seeing the sturdy Captain would not, De Ruyter brought to, and stood out on head of him, not thinking it safe for him to lay him on bord, there being of our Ships both to windward and to Leeward of him, and so he sheer'd away to joyu the Zelanders. This motion of the Dutch Fleet gave Sir John Jordan with the five or six Ships with him an opportunity to joyn the Duke, he having been to windward of him almost from the beginning of the Engagement: So that now the Duke had with him about five and twenty or thirty men of war, and some fire ships to windward of the Enemy. The rest of his Fleet bore away as De Ruyter did, and joyn'd the French, and so were to Leeward of the Dutch   But the

At 7 in the evening, De Ruyter bears away with all his Ships, to joyn the Zealand Squadron.

Capᵗ Story in the RAINBOW obliges De Ruyter to bring to, and stand out on head of him.

Sʳ Jo: Jordan joyns the Duke, who has now 25 or 30 Ships to windward of the Enemy at sun set.

The rest of the Fleet, having joyn'd the

T O M E
II.

1672.
French, were
to Leeward of
the Dutch.

Duke judg'd it best to keep as he was, just to windward of the Enemy, who by that time were all got together.

This was the posture of both Fleets just after Sun Set. And thus ended this memorable day, in which the Dutch, with all the advantage they could desire, of surprise, of wind, and of number of Ships that engaged, were far from Victory over the English; as their being the first to leave the Sea, and retreat into their harbours, will hereafter more fully appear. ·

·. But before we proceed to what followed the next day, (May 29th) we cannot pass by some remarkable actions not yet mention'd in this day's Engagement, without being unjust to English Valour. We have already taken notice, that the Dutch with great odds of number made their cheif effort upon that Division of ours where the Duke was in person; wherby not only his own Ship but his seconds, that were neer him, had the greatest share of the Enemies fire. Thus it was that when De Ruyter press'd so hard upon the Duke in the PRINCE, some of his Squadron

Sʳ Jo. Chiche-
lys Ship the R.
CATHERINE
taken by the
Dutch, but
releas'd again
by a brave
action of her
own men.

a stern of him attack'd no less warmly Sir John Chichely in the ROYALL CATHERINE, a large second Rate, who was somewhat to windward of the PRINCE, his wake, and was endeavouring to get in to his station, which was to be a stern of the Lord Ossory in the VICTORY, one of the Duke's Seconds, then just a stern of the Duke; But the ROYALL CATHERINE ply'd not her guns so fast as she ought, which was the master Guner's fault, in not having order'd his stores as he should have done; so that all under his charge was in desorder; and Sir John himself, being newly come from the Straights in the DREADNOUGHT a third Rate, went on bord the ROYALL CATHERINE only the day before the Engagement, and so had not leisure to examine and redress what was amiss. The slack fire made by the ROYALL CATHERINE imbolden'd the Enemy to press her the more, and to send some of their fire ships on bord her, the two first of which were put off by fire booms, but two more clapping her on bord, and one thwart her hause, the Seamen struck their Enseign against the Captain's order, and yeelded; wherupon the Dutch sent their boats on bord her, and carryd of Sir John with his Lieu^t., and severall of the men, and stow'd the rest in hold, all but the Master Gunner, the Carpenter, and Boat-swain; and they left one of their Lieutenants with a sufficient number of men to carry off the Ship. The Dutch left in the Ship, minding more the plundering of her then their other busines, did not keep her up so close to the Ships which had taken her, as they ought; so that at last, the Dutch Lieutenant having received orders to take out the men and fire the Ship, when he went to put them in execution, the Master Gunner, the Carpenter, and the Boat-swain, who had been left above deck, consulted together, and resolved as their men came up the hatches, to call to them to stand by them, and fall upon the Dutch, which they did, laying hand on hand-pikes, Iron-crous, and other trade on the deck, and soon overpowering the Dutch made them prisoners, and became again masters of the Ship. Hereupon Sir Edward Spragge who was in his station a Stern of the Duke, and had seen all that happen'd to the R. CATHERINE, but being to leeward of her could not help her, Sent his orders to those who had retaken her, to sail for the River, she not being in a condition to do any further Seruice that day.

Two of the Dutch fire Ships clapp'd also on bord the Edgar a third Rate of Seventy guns, but Captain Wetwang who commanded her So bestirr'd himself, that altho his main-sail was in fire, and that near eighty of his men leapt over bord, he at last clear'd himself of them.

Captain Francis Digby second Son to the Earle of Bristol who was Captain of the HENRY a second Rate, had six fire Ships that came on bord of him one after another; five of

Cap^n. Wetwang in the Edgar, clears himself of 2 fire ships, after his main Sail was on fire, and 80 of his men lept over bord.

The HENRY, Cap^n. Digby Commander, after having put off 6 fire

T O M E
II.

1672;
ships,the Cap*.
and Lieu*.
kill'd,is borded
by a Dutch
Ship of 70
Guns, but
releas'd again
by the bravery
of her own men
and y* Season-
able coming of
S.Rog: Strick-
land to her
releef.

which he put off, and as he had his hand on a fire boom to clear himself of the Sixth, he was shot dead with a small shot. Notwithstanding which that fire ship was also put off. Soon after which his first Lieutenant was kill'd, as was also Captain Bennet of the Duke's Regiment, together with his Enseign, whose Company was on bord that Ship: Hereupon a Dutchman of Seventy guns, seeing the Ship much disabled, and few men left on the Quarter deck and in the Wasts, borded her, and entering his men made himself master of all the Vpperdeck, with the Fore castle and great Cabine; But the remainder of the HENRY's men kept the lower Gun-deck, and Gun-room, and continued still plying their Guns; all which being observ'd by Sir Roger Strickland, who commanded the PLIMOUTH a small third Rate, he made sail to come to her releif: which the master of the HENRY perceiving (who had still continued on his post on the quarter Deck, either no minded by the Dutch who fell a plundering in the great Cabine, or perhaps taken by them for one of their own men, he being a fair hair'd burly man,) gave the word to the man at helm to bear up, which being done the HENRY gave the Dutch Ship such a jostle with her quarter, that she therby got clear of her; and Sir Roger coming up a moment after, gave the Dutchman Such a broadside, as obliged him to bear away, and leave his Lieutenant and men abord the HENRY to the mercy of those they thought to have master'd.

The night imploy'd on both sides to refitt the Ships.

But to return where we left the Fleet at Sun set: The night provd fair with litle wind, which both sides imploy'd in refitting their Ships, it being the Duke's intention to renew the Fight next morning. In the beginning of the night was seen from on bord the Duke, a great Ship on fire amongst the Dutch, which was fear'd might have been one of our disabled Ships that had fallen into their hands when they bore down to joyn the Zelanders; but it prov'd to be a great Ship of their own, which was so disabled that after having taken out their men they Set her on fire.

The next morning, being the 29th of May, at day-break the Duke found himself with the Ships already mention'd some half a league to windward of the Dutch, the wind continuing still a gentle gale Easterly, and the wether clear. At the rising of the Sun he could see none of the rest of his own Fleet, being windward of them, till towards nine of the clock, at which time he began to discover them to Leeward and somewhat a stern of the Dutch: upon which he bore down towards them, passing by the Enemy, who kept on their course without endeavouring to interpose or hinder his joyning his own Fleet, which he did before eleven at noon ; and then went on bord his own Ship the PRINCE, which Captain Narborow had refitted and put in a condition to engage again, having recruited her with the Crews of the two fireships, of which the one had been sunk and the other fir'd in the Engagement the day before. He then lay by, and made his signal to call all his Flag Officers on bord him, that he might have an account of the condition their Ships were in. Whilst this was doing, the Dutch continuing their Course to the Southward were got quite out of sight, and the Duke finding, that besides the loss of the ROYALL JAMES, some of his great Ships both first and second Rates, as the CHARLES THE 2^d, the St MICHEL, besides those already gone, were so disabled that they also must be sent to Sheerness to follow the rest, which were the VICTORY, the HENRY, and the ROYALL CATHERINE, third Rates, The FAIRFAX, the DUNKIRK, the YORK, fourth Rates, and the GREENWICH commanded by Captain Green, who carryd the STAVERN along with him without order, for which he was casheer'd ; and finding also, by the account given him, that very many of those who were in a condition to engage, had spent most of their ammunition, it was resolved by the unanimous

The Duke having joyn'd next morning the rest of his Fleet, he returns to his r^t ship thePRINCE now refitted.

TheDukecalls a general Councill of his Flag Officers, in which it was resolv'd the Fleet should return to be refitted.

TheDutch out
of a bravade
follow the
English, wher-
upon the Duke
turns upon
them again,
and pursues
them to their
own Coast.

consent of the Flagmen then present to make the best of their way to refitt at Sheerness, In order to which all the above Officers return'd on bord their respective Ships, to wait for the signal of the Admiral.

But Scarce were they got on bord, when from the Admiral's poop the Enemy's Fleet was seen standing after us, upon which the Duke thought it not fitt to pursue what had been resolved on, but, in stead thereof, to clap on a wind and stand with the Enemy, and accordingly he made the Signal for the Fleet to put itself into the order of Battel, which was accordingly done; having first order'd all the disabled Ships to make for the Nore and Sheerness, except two of them, the St MICHEL and the FAIRFAX, which made a Shift to stay thō very leaky, and in an ill condition. The Count d'Estreés with the French had the Van; The Blew then commanded by Sir Joseph Jordan the Vice Admiral, and Sir John Kempthorn Rere-Admiral, had the Rere. Sir John Harman who had sent his Ship away with the rest of the disabled ones, came himself on bord the Duke, who order'd him to go on bord the CAMBRIDGE, whose Commander, Sir Fretcheville Hollis, had been slain the day before, and there to put up his Flag of Rere Admiral of the Red.

In this good order the English Fleet stood with the Dutch, having the wind of them; but by that time that our Van had got the length of the Middle of the Dutch Line, De Ruyter made his signal to his Van for his whole Fleet to tack at once, which they did standing away close haled for their own Coast. Which the Duke seeing, made his signal to his Van to make what sail they could, his whole Line doing the same, edging down towards the Enemy; and as a soon he saw Mons'. du Quesne with his Flag in the fore top, who led the French, got on the broadside of the headmost of the Enemy, it being then about two in the afternoon, he made the signal for engaging and bore down upon the Dutch, we being then not above half

cañon shot to windward of them : But they seeing the Duke
thus in earnest, in stead of receiving him, or making a regular
retreat, they made all the sail they could, without staying to
secure their disabled Ships, of which the Duke told above
fifteen in their Rere, and had all the reason in the world to
beleeve he should be soon master of them ; but it pleas'd God
to order it otherwise, For at that very moment whilst things were
in this condition, from a clear sun-shiny day there fell all of a The Dutch
Sav'd by a Fog.
sudden so thick a Fog, that no body could see the length of the
Ship before him. The Duke Seeing it coming, took in the
signal (which was a Red Flag on the fore top mast head) and
brought to, and kept his Luf as close as he could, that during
the Fog the Dutch might not get to windward of him. The
Fog lasted above an houre, and when it clear'd up, we were
above cañon shot to windward of them, and the wind being
then about Northwest, the Duke let fly again the bloody Flag
(as the Sailers call it) and bore down once more to engage them,
But before he could begin with them, the gale freshen'd so, The Duke
again pre-
vented from
engaging by
foul wether.
that he could not carry out his lower Tyre ; Wherupon he took
in the bloody Flag, and kept to windward of the Dutch who
steer'd their course to the Weelings. About nine or ten at
night, the wether blowing still very fresh, his R.H. tack'd, having
reason to fear that he might otherwise fall in with the Bancks
of Flanders ; he stood off therfore close haled till midnight,
then tack'd again, and made after the Enemy till ten next The Duke still
pursues the
Dutch, but
they getting
within their
Banks, he
returns to the
Buoy of the
Nore to refitt.
morning, 30th of May. But then getting no sight of them, and
judging that by that time they have shelter'd themselves within
their Sands, whither it was not advisable to follow them, he in
fine found it requisite to tack about, and make (as he did) the best
of his way for the Buoy of the Nore, in order to refitt ; hoping
with reason, that he should be the first out at Sea again, as he
was the last that kept it.

. It was about the end of June before the Fleet was refitted. The King
comes down

TOME II.

1672.
to the Buoy of
the Nore, to
consult with
theDuke what
was further to
be done.

The Duke
proposes sail-
ing to yᵉ
Weelings, to
fightDeRuyter
there.

His reasons
against Shafts-
burys proposal
of going to in-
tercept the
Dutch East
India Fleet.

The Duke's
reasons over
ruled by the
King and his
Cabinet Coun-
cil.

The Duke go's
to Sea again,

Some days before they sail'd, the King came down to the Buoy of the Nore with some of the Committee of foreign affaires, of which number were the Earle of Shaftsbury, and Lord Clifford, to consult with the Duke and his Flag Officers, and to take his last Resolutions about what was to be undertaken for the rest of the Season: The Duke propos'd, the sailing straight to the Weelings, where De Ruyter then lay with the Dutch Fleet, to fight him, or oblige him to go in. The Earle of Shaftsbury and some others that came down with the King, perswaded his Majesty, that it would be more for his seruice to endeavour the intercepting of the Dutch East India Fleet, of which they had intelligence that they were daily expected home by the North of Scotland; That should our Fleet go to look after De Ruyter to engage him, those Ships in the mean time which were very rich, might get into the Vly or Texel: To which the Duke and other of the Flag-Officers replyd, That the surest way to be Masters of their East India Fleet, would be first to beat or drive into their harbours De Ruyter's Fleet, which they had reason to beleeve were not in a condition to stand us; That whilst their Fleet of men of war was intire and out at Sea, it would be dangerous so to spread our Ships, as would be requisite to intercept the EastIndia men, least the Enemy should come upon us on the sudden, and finding us so Scatter'd, might destroy our Ships before we could joyn into any order of battel; Nor was it to be doubted, that De Ruyter, either by their Privateers, their Advice-boats, or Fishermen, would be advertis'd from time to time of our Stations, and how we lay: But these reasons of the Duke and the Sea Officers were overruled by the King and his Cabinet Councill; and his R. H. was order'd to go and cruise in the most convenient and likely station to meet with their India Fleet.

In pursuance of this order, the Duke sail'd from the Buoy

of the Nore the ⠀⠀⠀⠀of July, and cruised between the Vly
and the Texel, so as only just to see the land from the top mast
head; but bad wether coming on he was obliged to come to
an anchor, and so to continue for a whole forthnight with his
yards and topmasts down. When the bad wether was over,
it was judged most convenient to go and cruise on the Soundings
of the Doggar bank towards the East of it; for the greater
conveniency of coming to an anchor when it should blow,
there being less water [in that side then to the Southward or
Northward of it, and consequently better riding at anchor
there: And it happen'd well that he did so, for by that means
he kept the Fleet together during all the time he continued in
that station, thō there was never four and twenty hours together
of fair wether all that time; But that did not hinder his having
Cruisers abroad the whole time, some of which as the CAMBRIDGE,
and another Fregate, met with the Dutch East India Fleet,
one of which was boarded by the CAMBRIDGE; but the Sea
went so high, she could not master her, being obliged to sheer
of, and the storm encreasing, they could neither keep company
with the Dutch, nor advertise our Fleet time enough; and so
they got by and put into the Ems.

Vpon this intelligence the Duke stood over to the Coast of
England, and came to an anchor near Burlington bay about
the ⠀⠀⠀of August, where he put a shore about three thousand
sick men, most of the Scurvy, which they contracted by reason
of the bad wether, which obliged us to have our ports shut and
calk'd, which did so heat the lower decks and so stiffle the men,
as to cause that distemper; Most of these did recover, but not
soon enough to get on bord their respective Ships before the
Fleet sail'd, so that some of ⠀⠀⠀great Ships, especially the
SOVERAINE, had harly hands enough to get up their Anchors.
After having taken in water and refretchments from shore, the
Fleet weigh'd, and made the best of their way for the back of

TOME
II.

1672.
and cruises
between the
Vly and the
Texel, to watch
for the East
India Fleet.
The Duke
changes
station, and
cruises to-
wards the
Doggar bank.

The CAM-
BRIDGE, one
of the Duke's
Cruisers, bords
a Dutch E.
India man, but
it blew so hard,
he could not
master her, and
the Storm
increasing the
whole Fleet
got by before
the Duke could
be advertis'd.

The Dutch
Fleet having
got into the
Ems, The Duke
returns to the
Engl: Coast,
and in Bur-
lington Bay he
puts a shore
about 3000
sick men.

After having
refresh'd at
Burlington
Bay, the Duke

**T O M E
II.**

*1672.
returns to the
Buoy of the
Nore.*

Yarmouth Sands, and came to an Anchor off of Lastoff about the beginning of September. Here the Duke had notice that some two days before, De Ruyter with his Fleet had appear'd in sight of that place, and was sayl'd back to the Weelings; wherupon it was judged convenient for the English Fleet, that had suffer'd much by the bad wether, to go to the Buoy of the Nore, the Season of the year being too far advanced to keep out the great Ships any longer in those Seas.

*The King
comes to the
Buoy of yᵉ
Nore.*

Some few days after the Duke was arrived with the body of the Fleet at the Buoy of the Nore, the King came down accompanied by Prince Rupert and Earle of Shaftsbury with some others of the Cabinet Councill to See the Duke, and informe himself of the condition of the Fleet. Those two Lords above nam'd had propos'd and very much urged to his Maᵗʸ, without the privity of the Duke, That the Fleet in the condition it was in, should go out again, and fight De Ruytèr in the Weelings where he then lay. Notice of this was given to the Duke by a privat freind, and that the King seem'd to enter into it; At the same time his R. H. observ'd that those two Lords were very busy in taking aside and whispering to some of the Flag-Officers; Of all which the Duke seem'd to take no notice, but let them go on in their own way till the proper time came of speaking. And when that evening, being the 16 of September, his Maᵗʸ order'd the Duke to appoint the Flag-men that they should attend him the next morning to consider farther what was to be done, his R. H. desir'd that some of the old Commanders of the Navy might also be appointed to attend, they having as much or more experience then the Flag-men: This was accordingly done, and when they were met, the King order'd the Duke to propose to them the going over for the Coast of Holland to look out for the Dutch Fleet to fight them or drive them into their ports, and that they should give his Maᵗʸ their thoughts upon it; which

*PᶜᵉRupert, and
Shaftsbury
urge the King
that the Fleet
should go out
again and fight
De Ruyter.*

they all did one after another in their ranks, the youngest beginning first, and at last the Duke deliver'd his own sense of it, which agreed with theirs, That the Season being so far advanced, it was by no means advisable to venture out the great Ships on the Coast of Holland, where if a Storm at West or Northwest should take them, they would run great risk of being lost, both men and Ships. In confirmation of this, Sir Jeremy Smith averr'd that in the Dutch war in Cromwell's time, near upon twenty Dutch men of war had been cast away in one night on that Coast. Captain Gunman, second Captain to the Duke, declared, He would not take care (*charge*) of his Ship, if they went over on that Coast; Capⁿ Sanders the Master said the same, but that they would both go along as Volonteers; These two were the boldest and ablest Pilotes in England for those Northern Seas. The King who had a good understanding in Sea Affaires, was hereby convinced of the unreasonablenes and danger of the proposall, thō Prince Rupert and Lord Shaftsbury would not recede from their first opinion; which his Ma^{ty} overruled, and order'd the great Ships should go out no more that year, but be sent to Chatam and their respective yards to be refitted against next year. And so ended this Summer Campagne at Sea.

Soon after the Duke's coming back to Court, the great Seal was taken from Sir Orlando Bridgman and given to the Earle of Shaftsbury, with the Title of Lord Chancellor of England. This alteration drew on another, for that Earle was one of the Commissioners of the Treasury, which place was now to be fill'd in case the King intended the Treasury should continue in Commission: But the Duke thought that his Ma^{ty} was inclin'd to have a Lord Treasurer; And therfore he desir'd the Lord Arlington to joyn with him in proposing to the King the Lord Clifford for that considerable Imployment: But he found Lord Arlington very cold in it, who endeavour'd to perswade

TOME II.

1672. The Duke's reasons against venturing out the Fleet any more that year, confirm'd by all the Experienced Sea Officers; wherupon the King orders the great Ships to be layd up. And so this Campagne ended.

After the Duke's return from this year's SeaCampagne, E. Shaftsbury is made Chancellor.

him, that the King had then no inclination to alter the way the Treasury was in; and the next day that Lord employd a freind of his to press the Duke that he would endeavour to get Sir Robert Car to be Commissioner in Lord Shaftsbury's room.

Ld Clifford
made Trea-
surer at the
Duke's recom-
mendation.
E. Arlington
discontented.

Some few days after, the Duke himself propos'd to his Majesty the Lord Clifford Treasurer, which proposall was well received by him, in so much that he said he would do it, as thinking no body fitter for it; he also told the Duke, That Lord Arlington had a mind to have that Staf, but he answer'd him, that he had too much kindnes for him to let him have it, for he knew he was not fitt for that Office, and that should he give it him, it would be his ruine and expose him to the malice of his enemies. A litle while after this, the King told the Duke, That he found Lord Arlington was angry with Lord Clifford upon his knowing that the Lord Clifford was to have the place; And he desir'd the Duke to perswade Ld Arlington, not to let the world see his discontent upon that occasion, and to endeavour to make them continue freinds; In obedience wherunto the Duke speake with them both, and they promis'd to live freindly together as formerly: But Ld Arlington kept not his word, but was ever after cold, if not worse, towards him.

The King
desires Lord
Clifford, and
Lord Arundel,
to perswade
the Duke to
receive the
Sacrament
with him, in
the Church of
England.

Christmas now coming on, the King spak to Lord Clifford and Lord Arundel of Warder, to perswade the Duke to receive the Sacrament with him at that time (which his R. H. had forborn to do for Severall months before thō he continued going to Church with the King) and that they should make his Brother Sensible of the prejudice it would do to both of them, should he forbear. So to do, by giving the world So much reason to beleeve he was a Catholick, and to that purpose he us'd

The two Lord's
Answer.

many arguments: to which they answer'd, That they beleeved it would be a hard matter for any body to prevaile with the Duke in so tender a point of Conscience; and that could they prevaile with him, it would signify Very litle, as to the making the world alter the opinion they had of his being what he really was, and instead of doing any good, it would make them have an ill opinion of his Christianity, by receiving in one Church and being of another, which would make him dispised by all good men : These and other arguments they us'd, with which the King seem'd to be Satisfied for that time, and so did not press them any further in that matter ; but upon the day before Christmas Eve, the King spake again to the Ld Clifford, desiring him to represente to the Duke what he had said before to him and his freind concerning the necessity of his receiving the Sacrament with the King; which the Lord Clifford did, but found the Duke not be mov'd in his resolution of not going against his Conscience.

T O M E II.

1672.

THE suspicion of the Duke's having changed his Religion, which his Enemies were not slow. in spreading about, gave them but too fair an opportunity of Venting with succes their malice against him, which hitherto had prov'd ineffectuall; for by this means they got him at last out of all his commands, and out of all busines, by procuring, (*March* 29th) under the pretence of securing the Protestant Religion, the forme of a TEST or Declaration to be passed in Parliament, such as no Roman Catholick in conscience could take or make ; and it was further inacted, That no person whatsoever should be capable of any Imployment Civil or Military, that did not take or make the said TEST, or Declaration. They also encouraged under hand the Duke of Monmouth to pretend to be legitimate, and consequently right Heir of the Crown, who of himself was ambitious and weak enough to give into their snare : But of this there will be occasion to speak more hereafter.

1673.
The Duke's Enemies get him at last out of all his Commands, by procuring The TEST to be pass'd in Parliament.

The Duke's Enemies also incourage the D. of Monmouth to pretend to be legitimate.

The Duke being disabled, by the above mention'd TEST from executing his Office of High Admiral of England, the Command

P^ce Rupert comands the Fleet in this Summer's Expedition.

of the Fleet in this Summer's Expedition was put into the hands of Prince Rupert, in which there past severall * Ingagements between the two Fleets, without any considerable loss or advantage on either side ; and what there was of advantage was on the Sight of the English: After which, the Parliament of England was wholly bent for a Peace with the Dutch, which was at last concluded at London the winter following.

L⁴Clifford lays down his place of Treasurer, upon yᵉ account of yᵉ Tᴇꜱᴛ ; and E. Danby, at the Duke's and L⁴ Clifford's recommendation, is made Treasurer.

This new Tᴇꜱᴛ had also the same effect upon the Lord Clifford, in outing him (*June* 19ᵗʰ) of the place of Lord Treasurer of England, and of being any longer a Privy Councellor ; who, thõ a new Convert, generously preferr'd his conscience to his interests. Upon his laying down his Staff of Lord Treasurer, it was given to Sir Thomas Osborne, newly created Earle of Danby, at the recommendation of the Duke, and also of the Lord Clifford who judged him the fittest person for it, as having given proofs of his capacity and diligence when he executed the office of Treasurer of the Navy. But this kindness of the Duke towards him, was ill requited on his part, as will hereafter be seen.

E. Peterborow is sent first to Neubourgh and then to Modena, to find a wife for the Duke.

The King being now sensible of the necessity there was, of his R. H. being married out of hand, order'd the Earle of Peterborow, (lately imployd in the Treaty for the Princess of Inspruck, which broke off upon the death of the Empress, and his Imperiall Majesty's resolving to marry her himself) to go incognito first to the Court of Neubourgh, and next to that of Modena, to see what Princess he could find that might be a fitt wife for his Brother ; And he not finding any to his liking at Neubourg, pass'd on to Modena, where having seen the Princess of Este, and judging that a better choice could not be made then of her person, he presently gave an account of it to the King and the Duke: Wherupon he was Commission'd by the King to demand that

---

* May 28ᵗʰ near Schonevelt, June 4ᵗʰ off Flushing, August 11ᵗʰ off the Dutch coasts. — Eᴅɪᴛᴏʀ.

Princess of her Mother (who was then Regent, her Son the
Duke being under age) in marriage for his Brother. It was
with no litle difficulty that the young Princess consented to it,
she being then but fifteen years old, and so innocently bred, that
till then she had never heard of such a place as England, nor
of such a person as the Duke of York. Besides she at that
time had a great inclination to be a Nun, in so much that the
Dutchess her Mother was obliged to get the Pope to write to
her, and perswade her to comply with her Mother's desires, as
most conducing to the Seruice of God and the publick good.
With much difficulty his Holiness and her Highness prevail'd
upon the Princess, and the Earle of Peterborow therupon
made his publick Entry at Modena, as Embassador Extraordinary from the King; and after having agreed all the
Articles of marriage, upon the 30th of September N.S. he
married her, by Proxy for the Duke his Master.

 The noise of this Match coming to the ears of the House of
Commons, who at time were mightily heated against that which
they call'd Popery, as they usually are when discontented with
the Government, enter'd into a hot Debate about it, and at
last resolved upon an Address to the King to break the Match,
because the Princess was a Roman Catholick, and that it was
promoted by France. It is to be observ'd, that altho the
meeting of this Parliament in October was only intended in
order to their further adjurnment or prorogation to January
following, yet by the dexterity of My Lord Shaftsbury, who
now (according to his usuall custome) had changed sides and
was at the head of the factious Party, Tricks were found to
delay the proroguing of the house, so to gain time enough for
the violent Party in the house of Commons to pass the above
mention'd address; which however had no effect upon the
King to break the Match so far advanced, and in which his
honour was so much engaged: Tho there wanted not at that time

TOME
II.
1673.

The Pope oblig'd to write to the P^{ss} d'Este, to perswad her to marry, as being most conducing to the Publick good and the Seruice of God.

The Articles concluded, the E. Peterborow on the 30th Sepr. marrys her by proxy for ye Duke his Master.

The House of Comons allarm'd with this match with a Cath: Princess, petition the King to break it.

T O M E
II.

1673.
L⁴ Arlington
advises the
King to stop
the Dutchess
in France.

The Dutchess
lands happily
at Dover yᵉ 21
of Nov: and is
there met by
the Duke, and
the marriage ..
declar'd by
Doctor Crew
Bᵖ. of Oxford.

They arrive at
Whitehall the
26 Nov.

The publick
Chappell
stipulated for
the Dutchess
by the articles
of the marriage,
is not allow'd
her.

some Councellors, of which My Lord Arlington was one, who
advised his Majesty to stop the Dutchess in France; which
shamefull advice was rejected by his Maᵗʸ, who therupon
prorogued the Parliament, whilst at the same time the Dutchess
was upon her journy from Paris to Calais. This address of the
house of Commons, thõ it had not its intended effect of
breaking the marriage, yet most of the Court were so frighted
with it, that few or none of them accompanied the Duke down
to Dover, when he went to meet his new Dutchess, who landed
there upon the 21 of November, and none of the Bishops, but
Doctor Crew Bishop of Oxford (afterwards Bishop of Durham)
offer'd to attend his R. H. to perform the part of declaring the
marriage, according to the usuall form in cases of the like
nature; which the Bishop perform'd in the manner following:
The Duke and Dutchess of York with the Dutchess of Modena
her Mother, being together in a room where all the company
was present, as was also My Lord Peterborow, the Bishop
ask'd the Dutchess of Modena and the Earle of Peterborow,
Whither the said Earle had married the Dutchess of York, as
Proxy of the Duke? Which they both affirming, the Bishop
then declar'd, it was a lawfull Marriage. After this their
R. R. H. H. arrived at Whitehall the 26 of November, having
been met by the King attended by the principall Nobility on
the River.

This late address of the house of Commons had caus'd so
great a fright at Whitehall, that even the King himself was not
wholly exempt from it : for wheras it was stipulated in the
Articles of marriage between the Duke and the Dutchess, that
she should have a publick Chappel, and namely that of
Sᵗ James's, formerly built by the late Queen Mother, yet his
Maᵗʸ was prevail'd upon by the Chancellors (*Counsellors*) then
about him, not (*to*) suffer the Dutchess to make use of that
publick Chappell, but only of a privat one they caus'd to be

fitted up in the house; and to give some coulour to this breack of Articles, they prevail'd with the Queen to claime a Right in the Chappell of St James's, she having formerly been possess'd of it, thō at that time she had no use for it, having her own at Sommersete house.

All these storms now rais'd, and which afterwards follow'd against the Duke in Parliament, bear their date, and had their origine from the suspicion they had of his being converted to the Catholick Faith, Nor could his privat Enemies till then gain any advantage of him. Before that time he was look'd upon as the darling of the Nation, for having so freely and so often ventur'd his life for the honour and interest of the King and Country, and for having been allways so active and industrious in carrying on every thing either as to Trade, or as to Navigation, that might tend to their advantage: But no sooner was the allarme given of his being turn'd Papist, when all these merites were blotted out of their memory, and he sett upon on every side as the common Enemy.

Many there were who at this time, under the pretence of freindship either reàll or feinsed, counsell'd his R. H. to withdraw himself for a while from the King's presence and all publick busines; Amongst the rest a certain noble Lord *, and he a Catholick; after many protestations of Zeal for his seruice, politickly advis'd him to write a letter from Dover to the King, and therin to desire his leave that for his own quiet, and to make his Ma^{ty} more easy in his affaires with the Parliament, he might retire with his new Dutchess to Audly end, or some such place in the Country remote from publick busines, where he might hunt and pray without offence to any, or disquiet to himself. All these advisers the Duke thanked for their good meaning, but told them that he was quite of another opinion and resolution; That untill his Ma^{ty} should command him to the contrary, he would allways personally attend upon him, and do him what

TOME II.

1673.

The Duke look'd upon as the darling of the Nation, till they Suspect him to be a Catholick; from hence it was, that all his prosecutions took their rise.

Many of the Duke's freinds advise him to withdraw.

* Lord Barkshire.

The Duke's answer to these pretended freinds, who advised him to retire.

The great Seal
taken from the
E. of Shafts-
bury, and given
to S⟨r⟩ Hen:
Finch.
E.Shaftsbury's
Charactere.

seruice he could, to which both his duty and his honour obliged him, and wherin he thought both his own and the King's security were concerned; That if his Enemies had already made so bold with him when he was present and could speak for himself, what would they not do in his absence? That in that case less could hardly be expected from them then their setting on foot another address from the house of Commons, (an Engine which seldom fails of doing execution, and is allways at hand upon such occasions) to have him banish'd, and perhaps excluded from Succession to the Crown. These reasons at least Silenced the givers of this advice if they did not convince them.

About the same time that the Duke was married, the great Seal was taken (*Nov.9*[th]) from the Earle of Shaftsbury, and given to Sir Heneage Finch with the title of Lord Keeper. That Earle (who in all the Revolutions this Nation has undergone from the beginning of the Rebellion in the time of King Charles the first, was famous for turning from side to Side and being still foremost in the severall turns of Government, thō never so contrary one to the other) had the great Seal in keeping not much above a year; in which time, none ever more boldly and warmly then he asserted the prerogative: He had the cheifest hand in his Majesties Declaration for Liberty of Conscience; It was he who promotted the second Dutch War, who, when the house of Commons was resty and would not grant Supplys sufficient to carry it on, advis'd the shutting up the Exchequer; and who, at the next meeting of the Parliament, in his speech to both houses, with Strong reasons maintain'd and justifyd all those proceedings, making use of that memorable Sayin, *Delenda est Carthago*: But when soon after, by the Clamour of the house of Commons, his Ma[ty] was prevail'd upon to recall his Declaration for Indulgence, he seeing which way the stream would run, all on the sudden dextrously turn'd

about, and clos'd in so intirely with the Republican Party, that
of a high prerogative man, he became an outrageous Enemy
even of the Crown it Self, and so continued to his death, as his
future actions will more fully shew.

ABOUT this time (*Feb.* 9th) the Peace was concluded between his
Majesty and the States Generall, which had been negociated inef-
fectually at Cologne; but by the interposition of the Marquis
de Fresno the Spanish Embassador here, who was arm'd with
a plenipotentiary power from Holland, all the Articles were
mutually agreed, and the Peace proclaim'd in London, (*Feb.* 28th)
as it was also at the Hague in the month of March. The House
of Commons, who formerly were so eager for a War with the
Hollanders, were now no less so for a Peace with him; and
soon after they press the King with address upon address to
enter into a War with France, whilst at the same time they
were very slow and backward in giving sufficient Supplys to
carry it on.

1674.
The Peace
concluded
between the
English and
the Dutch, in
February.

The House of
Commons
press the King
to enter into a
War with
France.

The Duke's Enemys having so far gain'd their point as to
make him quitt all his Imployments, still thought themselves
not secure enough, unless they also remov'd him from the
presence of the King, and even from his Succession to the
Crown, least he should have too good a memory of their behaviour towards him. In order to the first, it was projected in
their Cabals to have another TEST past in Parliament, more
comprehensive then the former one, that should contain a
renonciation of many other tenets in which the Catholicks
differ from the Protestants, and that none should be suffer'd
to come into the King's presence that did not take the said
TEST, without the leave first obtain'd under the hand of six
Privy Councellors. But when this new TEST was afterwards

The 2d TEST
contrived by
the Duke's
Enemys with
design to get
him removed
from the King's
presence,

T O M E
II.

1674.
The Duke's
freinds get a
Proviso added,
of exception
for his R. H. in
the Bill for the
SECOND TEST.

carryd by Vote in the House of Commons, (*Oct.* 30.) the Duke's freinds and the Loyall Party out of regard to the Blood Royall, had interest enough by a majority only of two Votes, to have a Proviso added of exception for the Duke's person, which put the litle Earle of Shaftsbury so out of humour, that he was heard to say, that he did not care what became of the Bill (about which they (*had*) taken so much pains) having that Proviso in it.

All endeavours
u͞'d by the
Duke's Ene-
mys to exclud
him from the
Succession to
the Crown:
First by per-
swading the
King to a
Divorce.

Then by setting
up the Duke of
Monmouth, to
pretend to be
legitimat.

E. Carlisle and
Shaftsburys'
proposall to
the King,
concerning the
Duke of Mon-
mouth.

Severall means at severall times were attempted by them, for excluding his R. H. from succeeding to the Crown. Their first enterprise of perswading the King to a Divorce, and to marry again, proving ineffectuall, they on the next place endeavour'd to make the Duke of Monmouth their tool to work with all, who had ambition enough to be wrought upon by them: To this they were not a litle encouraged by the great affection which the King shew'd towards that Duke, hoping from thence that his Ma^ty might be prevail'd upon to own him for his legitimat son. The Earls of Carlisle and Shaftsbury were two of the cheifest managers in this busines, and they had the confidence, not to say impudence, to tell the King, That if he would but consent to have the thing done, they would undertake to find witnesses to prove the Duke of Monmouth's Legitimacy; by which it appears, that (what is naturall to ill men) they thought the King's conscience as large as their own: But his Ma^ty received their proposition with indignation, and told them, That as well (*as*) he lov'd the Duke of Monmouth, he had rather see him hang'd at Tyburne then own him as his legitimat Son. However this did not discourage the party from pushing on their design, nor that Duke from prosecuting his ambitious thoughts which had taken possession of his brain, and were probably first instill'd into him by one Ross a Scotsman, put about him by the King to be his Governor when he first came out of France, who hoping therby to make his own fortune

The King
receives the
proposall with
indignation.

The Duke of
Monmouth's
ambition pro-
bably first
inspir'd in him
by his Gover-
nor, one Ross
a Scotsman.

put those high thoughts into his pupile's head; nor was the man
wanting on his part in industry to compass his design, for he
applyd* himself to the old Bishop of Durham, Doctor Cosens,
(Cosin) and told him, That he might do a great peice of Seruice
to the Church of England in keeping out Popery, if he would
but Sign a Certificat of the King's marriage to the Duke of
Monmouth's Mother call'd M". Barlow, thō her own name
was Walters, with whom that Bishop was acquainted in Paris
she then pretending to be his penitent, and to be converted by
him from her loose way of living. Ross also told the Bishop,
to make the thing more easy to him, that during his life the
Certificat should not be produced nor made use of: This in
time would have made Sure work, for according to the English
law the Bishop's Certificat is a legall proof of a marriage.
But the good old Bishop rejected his proposition, and afterwards acquainted the King with it; who then thought fitt to
keep it Secret, without making any noise about it, and only to
remove upon some other pretence the said Ross from his
Imployment; But afterwards, when the Tale of the Black
Box was spread about and began to gain ground, the King
incensed against the wickednes of these proceedings, divulged
this passage between Ross and the Bishop.

Thō all these machinations for setting up the Duke of
Monmouth as heire to the Crown, had nothing but forgery and
perjury wherby to subsist; yet in regard of the persons
concern'd in it, and of the great disturbances it rais'd in the
Nation from time to time, till at last it ended in open war,
it may not be amiss to trace here the birth, the education,
and progress of that Duke's actions and behaviour, when he
came to appear in the world.

His Mother's name was Walters, thō she took that of Barlow.

1674.
Ross proposes
to Bᵖ: Durham
to sign a cer-
tificat of the
King's mar-
riage to D.
Monmouths
mother Mⁿ.
Barlow.

Upon the
Spreding of
the Story of
the Black Box,
the King
divulges this
proposall of
Rosse's.

The history
of the birth
and education
of the Duke of
Monmouth.

his Mother's
true name
Walters, her
character
and loose
behaviour.

---

* The Duke's Biographer in this place, is retracing events which had occurred
prior to the Bishop of Durham's death, in Jan' 15, 1671-2: He had retired to
Paris in 1643. — EDITOR.

TOME
II.
She was born of a Gentleman's family in Wales, but having litle means, and less grace, she came up to London to make her fortune. She was very handsom, and thō she had no much witt, she had a great deal of that sort of cunning which those of her profession usually have. The famous Algernoon Sidney (thō at that time a Collonel in Cromwell's army of Samts) having got notice of her, enter'd into Treaty about her and came to an agreement for fifty broad peices, (as he himself related this Story to his R. H.) But being in that nick of time comanded hastily out of London to his Regiment, he miss'd his bargain. After this she travell'd into Holland, where she fell into the hands of his Brother Collonel Robert Sidney. who kept her for some time, till the King being then come to the Hague, and hearing of her, found means to get her from her Collonel, she not being averse to so advantageous a change; Wherupon that Collonel was heard to say, Let who's will have

Great reason to doubt whither D. Monmouth was the King's or Coll:Robert Sidney's Son, to whom he resembled even to a wort in the face.
her, she's already sped; and after her being with the (King) she prov'd so soon with child and came so near in time, that the world had cause to doubt whose child it was; and the rather, because when he grew to be a man, he so very much ressembled the Collonel both in stature and countenance, and even to a wort in his face. However the King own'd the child to a very high degree, as afterwards did appear. In the mean time his Ma'y was call'd away into Scotland, and during his absence she liv'd so loosely, that when he return'd from his Escape at Worcester into France, and she also coming thither in hopes of continuing in her former post, his Ma'y would have no further comērce with her, thō she made use of all her litle arts, with the help of freinds, to reingratiate herself; But when she found her hopes desperate, she afterwards so abandon'd herself at Paris, that at last she dyed of the disease incident to that profession.

Monmouth first bred up a Catholick by the name of Mr. Crafts.
As to her Son, he was first bred up a Catholick under the tuition of Father Goff, an English Oratorian, and went by the name of Mr. Crofts, and pass'd for a kinsman to the Lord of

that name; till afterwards, being sent for into England by the
King, who finding him well grown, and very handsom, took
so great a liking to him, that he resolved publickly to own him
and raise him in fortune and dignity; to which that there
might be no impediment, he had him instructed in the
Protestant Religion, which consists in renouncing Popery, and
which was easily brought about in one of his age by the
pleasurs of youth, and the prospect of preferment. Soon
after he created him Duke of Monmouth, and married him
with a rich Heiress in Scotland, the only child of the Earle of
Bucclugh, who brought him a fortune of about ten thousand
pounds a year. As he grew up in years the Kings kindnes
increased towards him, for thō he had no great capacity, he
had outward parts that make him very agreable; he was tall,
well shap'd, of a good air, of a civil behaviour, and none
danced better, and with all this he was very brave, which
made (*him*) much courted by both Sexes; Nor did he want
cunning and an insinuating behaviour where he had a mind
to please; and his R. H. amongst the rest had a reall kindnes
for him till he came at last to be convinced of his treacherous
designs, and even after that, the Duke continued to live fairly
with him, as he did with all those for whom the King had a
kindnes. Being then very young he accompanied his R. H.
in the first Dutch war, and was in the Engagement when
Opdam was blown up. Not long after, the King bought for
him Lord Macklesfeild's first Troop of Guards; and when the
second Dutch war came on, and his R. H. went again to Sea
in the year 1672, he was sent by the King into France to serve
by Land; where he had the honour done him by his Most
Christian Ma'y to let him serve as Lieutenant Generall (as
young as he was) at the Seige of Mastricke, at which place he
behav'd himself with distinction upon the retaking of a half-
moon. After that, having now gain'd reputation, he car'd not

Being very
handsom the
King takes a
great liking to
him, and owns
him pub-
lickly, makes
him turn Pro-
testant and
creates him D.
of Monmouth.

D: Monmouth
was very brave.

He accom-
panied the
Duke in y'e 1st
Dutch war,
and was in the
Engagement.

He behav'd
himself with
great dis-
tinction at

much for the fatigue of the War, and remain'd no longer in
the Army, neither that nor the next Campagne, then he needs
must, and then the King of France himself did, The pleasures
of the Court being more agreeable to him, then seruice in the
Feild.

His ambition
increases with
his years, and
to compass his
designs he at-
tempts to be
master of the
Troop.

The older he grew, the more his ambition encreas'd, nor did
he want Councellors about him to foment it. In order to compass his designs, he endeavour'd to make himself master of the
Troops that were in England, that in case any accident should
happen to the King, he might have a push for the Crown. To

He endeavours
to obtain a
Commission of
Gen¹¹. of all
the forces in
England.

this effect he endeavour'd to obtain from the King a Commission of Generall over all the Forces in England, and knowing
that in military affaires the King commonly advised with his
Brother before he resolved any thing, he thought it necessary
to gain his R. H. to be his advocat, and to propose what he
desir'd to the King, as a thing conducing to his Ma^tys Seruice,
not scrupuling to make use of the Duke's kindnes towards him
to supplant and destroy the Duke himself, and also presuming
that the secret of his design was wholly unknown to his R. H.

Addresses
himself to the
Duke, not
scrupuling to
make use of
the Duke's
kindnes to
him, to sup-
plant the Duke
himself.

And accordingly he came to the Duke to desire his favour in
this matter, representing to him the necessity of having a
Generall to command all his Maties forces within the Realm,
that in case any disorder or Insurrection should happen, the
Soldiers and Officers might know whom to obey warrantably
in the suppressing them; for he had been told by severall of
the Officers, that without such an authority it would not be safe
for them to obey him, nor to fire upon any in case of a mutiny;
That he desir'd such a Commission of Generall should be only
during pleasure, and not to be made use of at present, but to

ly by him in a readines against any such occasion. This proposall gave his R. H. ground to suspect there was more at the
bottom of it then the King's seruice as was pretended; But

without shewing any mistrust, the Duke answer'd him, That he did not see any necessity from the reasons he had given, of having a Generall, especially in a time of peace, over so few forces which could not be call'd an Army; That by his Comission of Captain of the first Troop of Guards, he was already impower'd to command any Forces that should be drawn out to quell an Insurrection, as much as he would be had he a Commission of Generall, since the words *kill, and slay,* would not be in it, as they were not in that of the late Duke of Albemarle's; That those Officers who gave him this advice and were so nicely scrupulous as to make a difficulty of obeying his orders upon any such occasion, deserv'd to have their Commissions taken from them, as being unfitt for military Imployment; That having at the time of the Duke of Albemarle's death already advised the King not to give a new Commission of Generall to any person whatsoever (not excepting his own) he could not so far contradict himself as now to perswade his Ma^ty to the contrary, there being no new reason for such an alteration of mind; and lastly he told him, That if such a Commission were fitt to be granted, he should think himself injur'd to have it bestow'd on any but himself; Wherfor he desir'd the Duke of Monmouth to desist from any such pretentions.

That Duke finding it in vain to press his R. H. any further in this matter, betook himself to other ways and means to compass his design; and at last by the assistance of his party, and cheifly by the great kindnes the King had then for him, he at last gain'd his point, and prevail'd upon his Ma^ty to depart from his former resolution which he declar'd upon the death of the Duke of Albemarle, of having no Generall, and to bestow that Charge now upon the Duke of Monmouth. Of all this his R. H. was a patient looker on, not being able to hinder it, and still carryd it fair even to the Duke of Monmouth himself without making any complaint about it to the King; for tho he well perceived that Monmouth aim'd at something

gives his reasons, why he could not approve Monmouth's pretentions, and advises him to desist.

Monmouth by the help of his party and the King's great kindnes for him, obtains at last his point.

The Duke bears all patiently what he could not hinder, and carrys fair even to the Duke of Monmouth himself, for whom the

11

T O M E
II.

King was then
in the hight
of his affection.

The D. of
Monmouth's
design of get-
ting his Com-
mission of
Generall to
pass the great
Seal with the
word *Son*,
ommitting the
word *Natural*,
prevented by
the Duke's
care, and how.

more then being Generall, and thō he knew that the King abominated the thought of that Duke's succeeding to the Crown, yet the proofs of his ambition were not as yet visible enough to work upon the King's mind, so much prevented not to say blinded with affection towards him: So that all his R. H. had then to do, was to be upon his guard; and in order therunto, having had notice that in some former Orders and Warrants signed by the King, the Secretarys at Whitehall had been so compleasant to that Duke as to put in the word *Son* and leave out the word *Natural*, he thought it time to look after it, now that his Commission for Generall was to pass the great Seal and go thorow all the Offices, that the ommission of the word *Natural* might be prevented: but not being willing to make complaint of it to the King without absolute necessity, he sent for Sir William Jones the Atturny Generall, who was to draw the Commission, and gave him caution about it, that according to the form of Law the word *Natural* should be inserted. He very honestly, thō the Warrant brought to him was with the word *Son* without *Natural*, however drew the Patent as it ought to be, with the word *Natural* in it; For greater security, the Duke also charg'd Sir Joseph Williamson, the Secretary of State, through whose hands the Commission was to pass, to let him see it before he brought it to the King to be sign'd. Notwithstanding all this, some few days after, when the King was rising from the Cabinet Councill, Sir Joseph layd severall Commissions before the King to be sign'd, which made his R. H. curious to see what they were; And when the King went down to walk in the Privy Garden, he stayd behind; and took up one of the Commissions, which prov'd to be that for the Duke of Monmouth's Generallship, and looking in it to see how it was drawn, he found the word *Natural* had been scrap'd out in all the places where it had been writt, and the word *Son* only left in; Vpon which the Duke reproched Sir Joseph for his breach of word, and want of respect to him, who made a shuffling insignificant excuse like one that had nothing to say for himself: But the Duke took the Commission and carryd it immediatly to the King then walking in the Garden, and acquainted him how Sir Joseph had behaved himself in that matter, and withall desir'd his Ma^{ty} that the word *Natural* might again be put into the Commission as it had been, and as it ought to be. Wherupon the King taking out his sizers, cutt the Commission in two, and order'd an other to be prepar'd for him to sign with the word *Natural* in it.

His R. H. press'd to have Sir Joseph Williamson punish'd for his misdemeanour in altering the Bill without the King's order, after it came out of the Atturney General's hands; But when the matter came to be examin'd, it appear'd that the rasures of the word *Natural* had been made by the Duke of Monmouth's particular order; who having sent to the Secretary's Office to see the Commission before it was sign'd, made his own Secretary Vernon do it in his presence, which as it was a great crime in them (thō unpunish'd) so was it no sufficient excuse for Sir Joseph Williamson: But this was a time in which that Duke's ambition, and the King's favour towards him, were both at the height; For he graspt at the same power in Scotland, and obtain'd a Commission of General in that Kingdom, which he would have had to be for life, and without the word *Natural*, but the Duke of Lauderdale refused to draw it otherways, then *during pleasure*, and with the word *Natural* in it, and so it pass'd.

I should have mention'd, that at the same time the King granted this Commission of General to the Duke of Monmouth, he also granted one of Generalissimo to his R. H., to make the other more easily disgested, it being much in his Maties nature, thō sometimes strongly byass'd by his affections, to keep measures with every body; which Commission of Generalissimo,

The Duke presses to have Sir Joseph, Williamson punish'd, for scraping out the word Natural without the King's Order.

Lauderdale refuses to draw Monmouth's Commission of General for Scotland, otherwise then during pleasure, and with the word Natural.

The King gives the Duke a Comm^{on} of Generalissimo, with which he was preparing to go to command his Maties troopes in Flanders for the defence of

TOME II.

T O M E
II.

that country,
but was pre-
vented by the
Peace.

The D. of
Monmouth
go's over to
Flanders, and
is with P.
of Orange in
the Engage-
ment at St.
Denis near
Mons, wch was
fought by ye
P. O. with the
Peace in his
pocket.

thõ of no present use in England by reason of the incapacitating Test, had never-the-less its force without restraint any where out of this Kingdom: So that not long after this the King by the importunity of the Parliament (whom nothing would content but a War with France) having withdrawn his Troopes out of the French seruice, and sent them into Flanders for the defence of that Country, wither more allso from hence were order'd to pass, his R. H. prepar'd to go thither to command those Forces in cheif. The Duke of Monmouth in the mean time went over, and came into the Prince of Orange's Army just time enough to be in the Engagement at St. Denis near Mons, which battel the Prince of Orange fought when he knew the Treaty of Peace between France and the States was sign'd, and had an authentique copie of it in his pocket. During this Voyage it was, that the Duke of Monmouth began to take his measures with that Prince, and to lay the ground work of what he under-took afterwards, using all his endeavours to gain his favour by promising him his faithfull seruice in England. At the same time also he applyd himself to gaine an interest in the English and Scotch Troopes, then in the States' Seruice, and with many of them both Officers he obtain'd his ends. After this, the Peace concluded brought him back into England, as it also stop'd the journy of his R. H. into Flanders.

This * Digression concerning the Duke of Monmouth, had let us forwards to the Relation of some publick transactions out of their due order of time, leaving some others unmention'd, which ought to have taken place, to which we must now go back.

We have already mention'd the King's firmnes in the busines

* During this Digression, The Secretary, whilst noticing events somewhat out of their due order, did not insert the date of the year in the margin of his MS. — Editor.

of the Duke's marriage, to have it accomplish'd notwith- standing the great heats about it in the house of Commons, and the timorousnes of some of his Ministers, who would have had it delayd, if not broke off: Nevertheless against the next meeting of the Parliament, which had been prorogued (*Feb.* 24th) to make way for that marriage, his Ma^{ty} was prevail'd upon by the suggestions of those Lords who were then at (*the*) helm, to issue forth severall Orders of Councill and Proclamations for putting the Laws in execution against all Nonconformists, and parti- cularly against Catholicks, forbiding them to come to Court, or any where near the Kings person: For it was the constant practice of these Ministers, that when ever any of them were affraid of the house of Commons for themselves, they presently exposed the Papists to the wooried, hoping therby to save themselves from being fasten'd upon. To this end it was, that in January, 1675, S. N. the Lord Treasurer and Duke of Lauderdale came to his R. H. (as they said) from the King, to let him know, That the Bishops had an intention to propose to his Ma^{ty} that the Laws might be put in execution against all Dissenters, and particularly that the Roman Catholicks might be speedily convicted, the doing of which had hitherto been negligently perform'd; That all the English Preists might be put from attending on the Queen, and that the King's naturall Daughters, as well as Sons, might be bred up of the Church of England. Having said this, they endeavour'd to perswade the Duke of the necessity there was in the present circumstances of his Maties affaires, that these things should be accordingly done; and further they endeavour'd to perswade his R. H. to concurr with them, in a thing so requisit at present for the King's seruice. But the Duke told them he could not be of their mind, for he thought it a dangerous thing to exasperate so numerous a Party as that of the Protestants Noncomformists; and as for the Roman Catholicks, he look'd upon it as a hard

The King is prevail'd on by his Ministers, to issue out Severall pro- clamations against all Non- conformists, and particu- larly against Catholicks.

1675.

The Ministers, when affraid of ye house of Commons, Sacrifice the Papists to sa^{re} themselves.

Danby and Lauderdale's conference with the Duke, upon the Sub- ject of putting the Laws in execution against Dis- senters.

The Duke reasons why he could not concur with these Lords proposalls.

thing for his Ma^ty to shew any new Severity against them, who had ventur'd their lives and fortunes for him and his Father, Especially there being no danger from them, since they were incapacitated from having any kind of Imployment, either Civil or Military ; That as to removing all English Preists from serving in the Queen's Chappel, and as to the breeding up the King's naturall Children in the Protestant profession, those were matters that concern'd others more than himself and therefore not fitt for him to enter into them, and so ended this Conference.

Wherupon the Duke went immediatly to the King to give him an account of what had been proposed by these Lords, hoping at the same time to diswade his Ma^ty from taking those

The Duke
endeavours to
diswad the
King from the
measures these
Lords had
engaged him
in, but in vain.

measures ; But he found the King allready determin'd to do what these Lords had propos'd, nor could his reasons to the contrary prevaile with his Ma^ty. He also found out that these two above mention'd Lords, together with the Lord Keeper and the two Secretarys, went to Lambeth house where they met the Arch-Bishop and some of the Bishops, and instead of being press'd by those Churchmen to any thing of this kind, they themselves press'd the Bishops very hard to make such proposalls to the King, to which at last they consented.

Another con-
trivance of the
Ministers to
pacify the Par-
liament, is to
have a Match
made up be-
tween the P^ce
of Orange and
P^ss Mary.

The King con-
sents to the
proposall, and
discourses the
Duke about
sending L^d
Arlington to
Holland to
sound the P^ce
of Or. inten-
tions to
Peace or War.

Amongst other contrivances which these Ministers had on foot to pacify the Parliament, they design'd to have a match concluded between the Princess Mary, the Duke's eldest Daughter, and the Prince of Orange, to which the King readily gave his consent; but the difficulty remain'd to gaine that of his R..H., to which his Ma^ty took an occasion to begin a discourse with the Duke about sending the Lord Arlington into Holland, telling him how necessary it was, during this Winter to be truly inform'd whither the Prince of Orange had a mind to have Peace or no, that he might take his measures accordingly ; and to that purpose he had thoughts of sending

the Lord Arlington into Holland, as the fittest person to sound
the intentions of the Prince of Orange. The Duke somewhat
surpris'd at this choice, represented to the King, That he
thought the busines might better be done by Sir William
Temple his Ambassador in Holland, for by so doing he
would give no jealousy to the French, wheras the sending Lord
Arlington one of his cheif Ministers, would certainly make
them suspect there was something secretly carried on to their
prejudice ; Besides, he thought that Lord so partiall to the
Prince of Orange, that it might be doubted whither he would
make a true report of that affaire, in case there should not be
that inclination to Peace as was desired : To this the King
reply'd, That as to what concern'd any jealousy which France
might take at it, he had already spoken about it to Monsr. de
Rouuigny their Minister, who approv'd of it, and for the other
objection, he was sure that Lord Arlington would give him a
sincere account of the Negociation. But the Duke further
urg'd, That it would look to the World like a too mean condescension and a too much seeking of the Prince of Orange, to
send such a person as Lord Arlington at upon such an arrand.
All the Duke's reasons made no impression upon the King, for
he had before hand resolved the matter, and what the King
now said was only by way of introduction to make way for
the main busines intended by his Ma^{ty}, For about two days
after this he told the Duke, he had forgett to say one thing
about the affaire he last spoke of to him, which was, that he
had likewise resolved to send Lord Ossory together with Lord
Arlington to say something, if need were, to the Prince of
Orange, which he knew the Duke would not be glad Lord
Arlington should have any thing to do with ; And this was,
that in case that the Prince of Orange should desire to know
what advantage he should receive, and what his Ma^{ty} would do
for him, in case he did consent to a Peace, and to what ever

TOME
II.

1675.
The Duke
against send-
ing of Lord
Arlington into
Holland,
represents his
reasons to the
King, but his
Ma^{ty} had al-
ready resolv'd
the matter.

The King tells
the Duke he
design'd to
send Ld Ossory
wth Arlington
to Holland, to
let the P. O.
know that if
he consented
to a Peace he
might hope to
mary the P^{cer}
Mary.

els his Ma^y should desire, that then Lord Ossory should be able to say, he knew the King and the Duke's mind so well, that if the Prince of Orange did what was expected of him, he might then pretend to marry the Princess Mary, and his addresses should be well received.

This Sudden proposall Very much startled the Duke, to see his Daughter. dispos'd of without his privity, and he told the King, He could not be of opinion to empower Lord Ossory with any such Comission, for he thought it a very undecent thing to have a matter of that nature proposed to the Prince of Orange, without his first seeking it; That to treat of such a matter before the Peace was concluded, would raise an incurable jealousy in France, and therfore not to be thought on at present: To which the King replyd, That there should be no Treaty about it till after the Peace, and that it should be only mention'd as an inducement to it, and hinted by Lord Ossory as a thing by him wish'd, and not as propos'd from the King or the Duke, till the Prince of Orange expressed his desire of it. In conclusion the King seem'd so resolved in the matter, that the Duke had nothing to do but to acquiesce, tho afterwards the success of this journy and privat negociation fully justified his sentiments of it; for the overtures and proposalls made both by the Earle of Arlington and Lord Ossory, were at that time as coldly received by the Prince of Orange as they were unwillingly consented to by the Duke.

ABOUT this time it was, that the Bishop of London Doctor Compton, very eminent for his zeal against Popery, came to the Duke and told him, that now his Daughter the Lady Mary began to be of an age, to think of preparing herself for receiving the Sacrament, and that in order therunto he was come to aske his leave that according to the rules of the Church of England, he might confirm her. The Duke answer'd, That since his conscience did not permitt him to communicate with them in any religious fonction himself, he could not for the same reason give his consent that his Daughter should; and that it was much against his will that his Daughters went to Church and were bred Protestants; and that the reason why he had not endeavour'd have them instructed in his own Religion, was because he knew if he should have attempted it, they would have immediatly been quite taken from him. To which the Bishop replyd, That he hop'd his R. H. at least would not take it ill from him, if he did the duty of his fonction in confirming his Daughter: To which the Duke's only answer was, That he could not give his consent to it; and so they parted. The next day the Duke meeting the Bishop, told him, He thought he would do well to inform the King of what had pass'd between them the day before; To which the Bishop answer'd, that he came with the design to ask his leave for his so doing: Wherupon he immediatly went in to the King, and received from him his Command to confirm his Neice. The Duke was willing it should pass so, because he perceiv'd the Bishop was resolv'd to do it; and since it was not in the Duke's power to hinder it, he thought it more decent it should be done by order from the King, rather then by the Bishop's own authority, and moreover that the world might see it was done by his Majesty's Command, without his consent.

ABOUT the beginning of June, 1677, The Prince of Orange sent hither Monsieur de Benting, the person he most confided in, to make great professions of duty and service to his Majesty, and to assure him he would wholly put himself into his hands, and follow his Counsell and directions both as to peace and war; but that he hop'd his Ma^{ty} would consider his honour,

TOME II.

1676.
The Duke answers, that his conscience not permitting himselfto communicat with them, he could not consent that his Daughter should.

1677.
Benting'sjourny to England. He makes great professions of duty and service to the King and the Duke, in his Master the P. Orange's name.

1677.
The Duke's
answer to the
great profes-
sions of kindnes
made to him
from his
Nephew the
P. O.

and not propose any thing which might be contrary to it. He also made great professions to the Duke from the Prince his Nephew, to which the Duke answer'd, That he should allways have that kindnes for his Nephew which both his own merit and the interest of the Royall Family, which cheifly consists in being well united, requir'd from him. Upon further discourse, he told Monsieur Benting, That he must not look on his Maties unwillingnes to enter into a war, as proceeding from any other reason but self preseruation; for he foresaw the absolute ruine of the Royall Family, if he should imbarke himself in a war in the condition he was now in, his magazins being empty, his Fleet not in a good condition, and above all the Parliament being in such a temper, that all he could do at present was to keep things quiet at home; which he might easily perceive by what so lately had been done by the house of Commons, in invading the Prerogative in so essentiall a point as that of Peace and War; That should his Ma^{ty} be ingaged in a forreign War, what would they not attempt when he should be so much in their power for maintaining it, and what would not the Republican Party then do when so fair an occasion for their purpose was offer'd them.

A Project set
on foot by L^d
Shaftsbury and
others of the
factious Party,
endeavouring
to prove that
the Parliament
was dissolved.

In this year the factious Party, in which the Lord Shaftsbury was now become the cheif Engeneer, thought they had found out arguments to prove by Law, that this present Parliament was dissolved, for not having had a Session in a whole year's time. This they were very fond of because they found their Party was not strong enough in this House of Commons to carry matters so far as they would have them carried against the Crown, which they hop'd upon a new Election of Members they might be able to compass. To this end, and to gain others to be of their mind, they printed and dispers'd a State of the Case with reasons for their opinion. They applyd themselves to all sorts of people, and amongst others to some of the Catholick

Lords, telling them, They would have fairer quarter and
better usage from a new Parliament then from this. The Lord
Shaftsbury had the confidence to send to the Duke to know if
he had read and consider'd any of the papers about the dissolution of this present Parliament, and what his opinion was
upon it; that if he pleas'd, he would send him another paper
with such convincing arguments, that his R. H. would by them
clearly · see this Parliament was absolutly dissolved, that if
he would be pleas'd to joyn with them, that point would certainly be carried.. To this the Duke answer'd, That he had
seen the Papers writt upon that Subiect, and was willing to
read any that should be sent him; but that he could not Say
what his opinion was, till he had heard what could be said on
both sides; that if the arguments were so convincing, they
would certainly appear so upon debate in the house of Lords,
and 'till then he could frame no judgment of them.

It is to be observed, that in one of their printed Papers upon
this Subject, there was a Clause inserted, in which it was
affirm'd that the Parliament had power to alter the Succession
of the Crown. That this might not alienate the Duke, the
Lord Shaftsbury sent to him the day before the meeting of the
Parliament, to assure his R. H. that without his knowledge that
Clause was put in. The Lord Wharton likewise send the same
excuse, adding, that it was the Lawyer whom they imployd
in the printing it, that put it in without their orders. The
Duke of Buckingham also sent to the Duke to assure him, that
Clause was not put in by his consent, but that it was the Lord
Shaftsbury who had drawn it, and caus'd it to be inserted;
which possibly was put in on purpose by them, hoping therby
to fright the Duke into a concurrence with them.

At the meeting of the Parliament the Duke of Buckingham
began with a long sett Speech to shew that the fifteen months
prorogation had dissolved this Parliament; wherupon the

T O M E
II.

1677.
Shaftsbury has
the confidence
to address him-
self to the
Duke, and to
desire his con-
currence, offer-
ing him printed
papers to prove
yᵉ Dissolution.

A Clause
added to one
of these Papers,
afferming that
Parᵗ. had
power to alter
the Succession.

Excuses made
to yᵉ Duke by
Buckingham,
Shaftsbury,
and Wharton,
all of them dis-
avowing the
Clause about
altering the
Succession.

The D. of
Buckingham in
a long Speech
in Parliament,
pretends to

TOME
II.

1677.
shew, that the
15 months pro-
rogation had
dissolved this
Parliament,
and is seconded
by the L.ds
Salisbury,
Shaftsbury,
and Wharton.

The 4 Lords
who had
motion'd the
dissolution, are
order'd to
withdraw ;
after which tis
resolved they
should beg
pardon of the
King and the
House.
D. Buckingam
sent for to
come in to the
House and beg
pardon, is not
to be found.

E. Salisbury
order'd to beg
pardon in his
place, upon
refusal is sent
to the Tower.

E. Shaftsbury
refusing to ask
pardon at the
Bar, is sent
likewise to the
Tower.
L.d Wharton
pretending he
had already
ask'd pardon,
and refusing
to ask it when
requir'd to do

Lord Fretchewill immediatly cryd, to the Bar! The Lords Salisbury, Shaftsbury, and Wharton, seconded the Duke of Buckingham's motion and assertion, and they were severally answer'd by some of the other Lords sitting in the House. At last it was mov'd, That the said Duke who had started, and the other Lords who maintain'd that opinion, should be call'd to the Bar. After a very long debate the question was carried, that the first debate raised by the Duke of Buckingham, should be layd aside. After which it was moved, that those four Lords should withdraw, which was warmly opposed by some, and this last debat was adjourn'd to the next day. Then the same debate was resumed, and at last the question was put for the four Lords to withdraw; the *Contents* were fifty three, *the Not Contents* thirty. In the next place they took into consideration what was to be done with them one by one; and first it was resolv'd, That the Duke of Buckingham should ask pardon of his Ma^{ty} and the House, at the Bar, and acknowledge his fault. The Gentleman Vsher of the Black Rod was sent to bring him in, but could not find him, he being slipt away; Wherupon the House order'd that the Black Rod should take him into Custody, and bring him to the Bar of the House next morning at ten of the Clock. The Earle of Salisbury's turn was next, who was order'd to come into his place, and there standing up bareheaded, to receive the reprehension of the House by the Lord Chancellor and to ask pardon of his Ma^{ty} and the House; which he being in his place, refused to do, wherupon he was sent to the Tower. The Earle of Shaftsbury was then call'd in to the Bar, and refusing, as the other had done, to ask pardon, was likewise sent to the Tower.

After this, the Lord Wharton was call'd into his place, and the same thing being said to him, as to the others, he answer'd That he had already ask'd pardon of the King and the House; the Lord Chancellor said, what he had done signified nothing;

11

he was to obéy the Lords, and do it now : Wharton answer'd, He had done it already : After the Lord Chancellor had thrice repeated the same thing, and the other the same answer, úpon his refusall to say more he was call'd to the Bar, there to receive his Sentence of being sent to the Tower. When he came to the Bar he would have obeyd the Lords, as he should have done in his place, but it was too late, and would not be admitted of, and so he foullowed the rest to the Tower.

TOME II.

1677.
it in his place, is not admitted to ask it after-wards at the Bar when he would have done it. And so is sent to the Tower.

The day following the Lords at their first meeting received an account from the Black Rod, that the Duke of Buckingham was not to be found at his lodging nor any where els ; upon which the House order'd, that in case he did not appear before the rising of the House, they should desire his Ma^ty to issue out his Proclamation to seize him wherever he could be found, and to stop the Ports ; But just before the House was ready to rise, he came in, and being required to ask pardon, as had been order'd, and he refusing it, he was likewise committed to the Tower.

D. of Buckingham at last comes into the House, when it was just ready to rise, and being requir'd to ask pardon, is upon his refusall sent to the Tower.

About this time the Duke of Ormonde (who contrary to the Duke's liking had been some years past removed from being Lord Lieutenant of Ireland, by the prevalency of the Duke of Buckingham at that time upon the King) adressed himself to the Duke to mediate with his Ma^ty for his being sent again Lord Lieutenant into Ireland ; which his R. H. willingly undertook, and procured his Maties agreement and consent to it, thō the Lord Treasurer secretly opposed it as much as he could. At the same time Lord Ranelagh put the Duke of Monmouth upon being Lord Lieutenant of Ireland, in opposition to the Duke of Ormonde, as not being his freind, and having a mind to get Lord Conway to be Deputy under the Duke of Monmouth. But this design was prevented, nor had his R. H. any knowledge of it, till he had first spoke to his Ma^ty for the Duke of Ormonde.

The D. of Ormonde who had been remov'd from the Lieuten-ancyof Ireland, against the Duke's will, is restor'd to that Imployment again by his R. H. mediation.

T O M E
II.
1677.
The P. of
Orange's
journy into
England in
Oct. after the
Campagne of
—77.
The design of
this journy to
concert a Plan
of a Peace, and
to propose his
marrying the
P⁽ˢˢ Mary the
Duke's eldest
Daughter.

.: In the month of October of this present year, the Campagne of Flanders being ended, the Prince of Orange came into England, and landing at Harwich went straight thence to Newmarket where the King then was. The cheif busines which brought him over was to concert with the King such a Plan of Peace between France and the Confederates, as might for the futur secure Flanders, and consequently Holland for being overrun by the French; And that in case France refused to submitt to it, his Ma⁽ᵗʸ should joyn his Forces with the Confederates to bring that King to reason. In the next place he came to propose his marrying the Lady Mary (which we formerly hinted) and very much insisted to have that concluded and dispatched before he enter'd into the discusion of publick affaires, pretending that otherwise his Confederates would beleeve he had made a hard bargain for them, to make a good one for himself. But the King, and much more the Duke, were of a contrary opinion, thinking it more expedient and decent that the Negociation should rather end, then begin with the marriage. This was opiniatred on either side for the first days, which were spent only in outward Ceremony of Entertainement, without falling into any busines; till at last the obstinacy of the Prince of Orange by the assistance of the Lord Treasurer (who from that time enter'd into the measures and interests of that Prince) prevail'd upon the flexibility of the King to let the

The P⁽ˢˢ of
Orange pro-
poses the
marriage to
the Duke.

mariage be first agreed and concluded: In order to which, the Prince in a visite he made to the Duke (having till then industriously avoided speaking of any busines) told his R. H. That he had something to say to him about an affaire, which was the cheif cause of his coming over, and which was to disire that he might have the happines to be yet nearer related to him by marrying

The Duke's
answer.

the Lady Mary. The Duke said, He had all the esteem for him that he deserved, or could desire, but till they had treated and brought to some ripenes the public affaire of War and Peace, it was not proper that a discourse upon any other matter should take place. Nevertheless the Prince of Orange still urged. that the busines of the marriage · might be first concluded, and the Duke remain'd no less firm in his opinion, and so the visite ended.

The same evening 'the Duke inform'd his Ma^{ty} of what had pass'd between him and the Prince of Orange; and the King said he had answer'd very well, but told him with-all, that at the great importunity of the Prince, he had given him leave to speak of marriage to the Duke, At which his R. H. was not a litle surpriz'd, and said, He could have wish'd his Ma^{ty} had been pleas'd to have acquainted him before with his mind, that he might have better known how to have carry'd it with the Prince when he made the proposall to him ; At which the King broke short off, and said, He would speak to him of it another time.

A day or two after the King calling to him the Duke, and the Lord Treasurer, fell into the discourse of the convenience of the Match, but not as of a thing positively resolved on, Vpon the Duke's desire that they might talk of it again the next morning; which they accordingly did, and then the Resolution was taken, his R. H. assenting to it, and receiving directions from the King to notify to the Prince of Orange both their consents to the marriage: That being done, his Ma^{ty} the next day sent for the Duke into the Councill Chamber, the Councill then sitting, and there declar'd, That the Prince of Orange having desir'd to have yet a more Strict Alliance with him by marrying the Lady Mary, he had consented to it, as a thing he look'd on as very proper to unite the Family, and which he beleeved would be agreable to his People, and shew them the care he had of Religion, for which reason he thought it the best Alliance he could make. After this, the Duke also declar'd his consent to the marriage, and said, He hoped that he had now ·

given a sufficient testimony of his right intentions for the publick good, and that people would no more say, he design'd the altering the Government in Church or State; for, what ever his opinion in Religion might be, all that he desired was, that men might not be molested meerly for conscience sake.

The P. of Orange's marriage with P^ss Mary declar'd in Councill, and ye Articles drawn by Ld Treasurer.
The Plan of the Peace.

After the Marriage had been thus declared in Councill, all the Articles relating therunto, by the great diligence and zeal of the Lord Treasurer, were in three days time drawn up and agreed to; which being done, they fell to work upon the Plan of the Peace. The cheif aime of the Prince of Orange was to ingage the King immediatly in the war against France in conjunction with the Confederates; And therfore, under the pretence of sufficient Frontiere for Flanders, and Barrière for Holland, he insisted upon termes that both the King and he himself knew very well the King of France would never consent to. On the other side, it was his Majesty's interest as well as inclination to get as good termes as he could without engaging in a War, so that some time and many debates passed, before they could agree upon a scheme of proposalls. At last it was resolved, That for a sufficient Frontiere and a Barriere, the Towns of Ath, Charleroy, Oudenarde Courtray, Tournay, Condé, Valenciennes, St Guilain and Binche, should be restor'd to the Spaniards, and that some person should be sent from the King with these proposalls to the French Court, and instructed to enter into no reasonings upon them, but to demande a positive answer in two days, and after that immediatly to return.

Ld Duras Sent to France with ye Plan of ye peace; ye French surpris'd with the proposalls carry it fair and give only a generall answer.

Lord Duras was the person pitched upon to carry this message, at the delivery of which that Court was very much surpris'd, both at the thing, and at the manner of it. However in appearance they took it gently, Saying, That the King of England knew very well he might allways be master of the Peace; but it seem'd hard that Tournay and some of the Towns in Flanders, upon

whose fortifications Vast treasures had been expended, should
be yeilded up without any consideration for them : However
they desir'd some short time to consider of a finall answer.
Lord Duras told them, he was tyd up to two days stay ; But
at the end of them, perswasion and good nature prevail'd upon
him to stay some few days longer, and at last to come away
with an answer in generall, which neither granted nor denied
the thing ask'd, but that the French Embassador in England,
should have power to finish the Treaty so as to satisfy his
Ma⁷ʸ.

T O M E
II.

1677.

Soon after this, the States of the Vnited Provinces thought
it their wisest course not to depend upon the Negociation on
foot in England, but to strike up a seperate Peace with France
upon termes agreed between them, leaving room for the rest of
the Confederates to come in to it within a time prefixt. The
knowledge of this caused the Prince of Orange to make that
rash attempt we formerly mention'd, upon the French Army at
Sᵗ Denis, out of meer spite, when he knew the Peace was
actually sign'd, hoping that if he could have made a thorow
Victory of it, the War might still be continued; especially
having for it on his side the Spaniards, and the Emperour, and
also the house of Commons, who were all of them feircely bent
against the Peace. The next day after the Battell the Express
arrived from the States to their General, to signify to him the
Conclusion of the Peace, of which it is said, he had the Articles
in his pocket before the fight began ; So that in conclusion,
the lives of four or five thousand men were sacrificed (I may
say in a time of peace) to the violent ambition of one
man.

1678.
The States
stricke up a
seperate Peace
with France.

The P. of
Orange out of
spite, attacks
the French at
St.Denis,when
he knew the
Peace was
actually sign'd.

Soon after, the King had concerted with the Prince of Orange
the project of a Peace between France and the Confederates;

The King, in
prosecution of
the Plan of a

1678.
Peace, raises
an Army of
between 20 and
30 thousand
men, in six
weeks time,
part of which
are sent over
into Flanders.
The Empe-
rour and
Spaine not
having yet
accepted of
the Peace, the
King proposes
to ye Parlia-
ment the keep-
up his Army
for the pre-
servation of
Flanders.

in prosecution therof, and to render it effectuall, his Ma^ty raised
an Army of between twenty and thirty thousand men in six
weeks time, of as good troops as any where were to be seen;
part of which were actually sent into Flanders for the defense
of that Country, and more were dayly transporting thither at
the very time when the Hollanders clapp'd up their separate
peace with France.   Now in regard that Spaine and the
Emperour had not yet accepted of the Peace, and that in
Holland a' great party, together with the Prince of Orange,
were wholy averse to it, and condemned their Deputys as
having exceeded their Commission in so hastily signing it, his
Ma^ty when the Parliament met propos'd to them the keeping on
foot his Army, as necessary for procuring a better and safer
Peace by force of Arms, if by Treaty it could not be done, and
allso for being a significant Garentee of it when procured;
especially since the Spaniards had declared, that by their single
Forces Flanders could not be preserved, and that they expected
constant succours from England and Holland, whose interest
it was, as well as theirs, to have it preserved: But the answer
and proceedings hereupon of the House of Commons made it

The House of
Commons
more jealous
of the King's
power, then of
that of France,
vote to have
the Army im-
mediatly dis-
banded.
The Factious
Party make it
their busines
to be rid of the
Duke, to pull
down the
Ministers, and
weaken the
Crown.
D. Monmouth
had several
private meet-
ings with L^d
Russell, &c. in

plainly appear, That they were in reality more jealous of the
King's power, then of the power of France; for notwithstanding
all their former warm addresses for hindering the growth of
the power of France, when the King had no Army, Now, that
he had one, they pass'd a Vote to have it immediatly disbanded,
and the Factious party which was then prevalent amongst them,
made it their only busines to be rid of the Duke, to pull down
the Ministers, and to weaken the Crown.

About this time, the Duke was inform'd of severall privat
meetings which the Duke of Monmouth had with Lord Russell,
M^r. Montague, Sir Henry Capell, and others of the Party, in
which was propos'd the removing of the Duke from Court, and
laying aside the Lord Treasurer; which Lord being informed

of the designs against him, endeavour'd to skreen himself by putting the King upon issuing out Proclamations and Orders of Councill from time to time, from (*for*) executing the Laws against Catholicks, banishing them from Court, and for searching after Preists with rewards to those that should take them; And at last, when he saw the storm coming neerer upon him, to shelter himself he stuck not to advise the King to send the Duke out of England: But all these litle Arts could not defend him from being at last not only turn'd out of the Ministry, but allso impeached in Parliament.

Here it ought to be observed in how different a manner the Duke carryd it towards the Lord Treasurer; for in April, 1678, a litle before the meeting of the Parliament, the Lord Russell and other considerable men of the party, sent to his R. H. to let him know, That if he would trust them, and joyu with them in what they should propose to him for the good both of his Ma^{ty} and of the Nation, they would undertake to remove the incapacity under which he lay of being high Admiral, or exercising any publick Office, and that they would do any thing els that might be for his Satisfaction; but that they expected from him his concurrence with them in prosecuting the Lord Treasurer, and removing him from his Imployment. To this the Duke's Answer was, That he willingly would joyn with them in any thing he thought was for the good of the King and the Nation, but that to fall upon the King's Minister without the King's consent, unless he were visibly guilty of some great misbehaviour (which to his R. H. did not appear) he thought to be very contrary to the good both of the King and of the Nation, and therfore could not joyn with them in it, but advised them to take other measures.

This unsettled temper of the Factious Party, which one while was for attacking the Duke and at other times called for his assistance to attack others, would easily have been crushed, or

have faded away of itself, had not a certain malicious contri-
vancé of an indigent wretch which happen'd at this time,
furnished them with an oppertunity of executing their designes;
which soon layd their enemies at their feet, and gave them a
fairer occasion then ever they could have hoped for, not only
of compassing their ends against the Duke, but of bringing the
King too to their termes, and of shakeing the foundation of the
Government itself: And as the greatest events oft times
dirive their origin from the Slightest accidents, tis certain
there was never so great a flame raised from one so trivial as this,
which not only occasioned the spilling of much innocent blood,
but had like to have sown the seeds of an other Civil War,
while the memory of that so lately quenched was still fresh in
the memorys of most men.

It fortuned that ones Oates a poor and despicable
Clergieman, either touched with scruples about Religion, or with
designe of doing what he afterwards put in execution, went over
to St Omers, where under pretence of becoming a Catholick,
(he) was admitted into the English College there in order to
study there and be instructed as others were in that place:
but the Fathers soon perceiveing his insincerity, and want of
due dispositions to execute what he pretended, thought fit to
dismiss him, who after some rambles returning to England,
either out of revenge to the Jesuits who he thought had used
him ill, or to gain a subsistance, being in the last degree of
povertie and contempt, pretended he had made a discoverie of
a Conspiracy, carried on amongst the Catholicks against the
King and Government, which he knew the Factious partie
would greedily grasp at, bein already in such terrours at the
Duke's being of that Religion out of whose hands, for that
reason, they had been long contriving to wrest all power and
command, and to create (if possible) a jealousie betwixt his
R. H. and the King.

The Duke, on the other side, was not insensible to what dangers and persecutions he expos'd himself by changeing his Religion, he knew he should ly open to those who would give him no quarter ; but he could never have imagin'd, nor indeed could the fury and malice of his Enemies ever have push'd their hatred so far as to banish him the Kingdome and almost exclude him from the Succession, had not this unfortunate pretended Popish Plot come into their assistance. **T O M E II.** 1678.

It is certain there was never any thing of that nature worse concerted in itself, nor more improbable in all its circumstances ; but meeting with a prodigious credulity in the people in relation to any thing which asperses Catholicks, and an implacable malice of some managers of it against the Duke, it rais'd such a storme as had like to have overwhelm'd both him and them ; and had not his Christian patience and magnanimity, his unshaken courage, and prudent conduct, gon beyon what we scarce have an example of in antiquity, he must necessarily have perished in it ; and not only he, but the King his Brother, and all the Loyal Partie been buried in the ruins of the Monarchy itself.

This pretended Plot or Conspiracy (which made so great a noise afterwards) had so perfect an air of the fabulous " reports which preceeded the late Revolution, that those who " remember'd it, thought themselves gon back to forty one, or " that the same —— and spirit was risen to life again : For " in stead of letters to Mr Pim, of horse and foot being muster'd " under ground, all people's ears were fill'd with dismall " rumours of a design to kill the King, and subvert the " Government to bring in Popery, and Arbitrary Power ; and " all this to be effected by an inconsiderable body of men, " who had neither numbers nor power, nor places of trust ; " but being charged upon the Papists and that the Jesuits " were the managers of it, all its motives of incredibility could "

KING JAMES 2^d. HIS OWN MEMOIRS, TOM. 7. p. 279, writ in his own hand.

T O M E
II.

1678.
The first dis-
covery of the
Plot.

" not hinder it from being greedely swallow'd downe, and
" beleived by the multitude.

" The first information was brought to his Ma^{ty} at Windsor
" in August 1678, by one Kirby a broken merchant, but his
" errand was only to prepare the way for one Tongue, who sayd,
" He had a great Plot to discover which concern'd his Ma^{ty} life,
" the Protestant Religion, and present Government, but desired
" to come privately in the night, for should he (be) knowne, the
" Papists, he say'd, who were the contrivers of it would knock
" him in the head.

" This man being introduced to the King, repeated the same
" Story, and left with his Ma^{ty} a bundle of papers for his further
" information, but they being long, he gave them to My Lord
" Treasurer to peruse: The substance of which was a most
" detestable Conspiracy against the King and Kingdom, sayd
" to be carryed on not only by his own Subjects, but that
" Monsr. Louuois the French King's Minister and Pere la
" Chaise his Confessor, were privy to it; that Don John of
" Austria encouraged it, and that the better to compass these
" wicked designes they intended to burn the City of London,
" and raise a Rebellion both in Scotland and Ireland; and

King James
Memoires
Tom. 8.
pag. 232.

" that one Doctor Oates had got knowlidg of this horrid
" Conspiracy, by conterfiting himself a Papist, and entring
" amongst the Jesuits, where to ingratiate himself the more
" with them, he confess'd and communicated once a week,
" thō he still remain'd a Protestant in his heart.

Tom. 7.
pag. 282.

" This surprising relation besides its other extraordinary
" circumstances, seem'd to afect his R. H. so much that My
" Lord Treasurer proposed the acquainting him with it
" immediately, but the King thought it more prudent first to
" examin it; to the end it might not be objected, that it had
" been communicated to any one what ever of that perswasion,
" before he had searched it to the bottom himself.

But the Duke came (*to*) the knowledg of it sooner than was
intended, by an other way : It seems upon the first discovery,
My Lord Treasurer had desir'd to see some thing under the
hands of those who were accused, because the Informer
pretended they trusted him still with the greatest Secretts, and
even their Letters themselves ; this was too reasonable a
request to be denyd, so he readily promised it, but being
dilatory in the performance was ernestely pressed over and
over again, till at last he writ a note to My Lord Treasurer to
tell him, That if he would send to the post house and intercept
certain letters directed to M^r. Bedingfeild who was the
Duke's Confessor, they will convince him of the truth of all
he had Sayd.

It fortuned that My Lord Treasurer was not at Windsor
when this note came, and M^r. Bedingfeild passing by the
Post Office just as the Mail arrived, call'd for his letters
himself, and had five deliver'd him made up in a thick
paket, which were sign'd Whitebread, Fennick, Ireland,
Blundel, and Fogarty ; the four first being Jesuits he was
acquainted with their hands, and soon perceiv'd these letters
were not writ by them, the last being a person he knew not
could say nothing to it, but finding treasonable expressions
in them all, suspected there was some Villany intended by
them, both against Catholicks in general and the Duke in
particular, so carryd them streight to his R. H. and he
immediatly to the King; whereby the person that was
marked out for the traitor, and the Duke who was
principally aim'd at in the contrivance, became by
Providence the first discoverers of this pretended Conspiracy.

. The first letter the King light on was signed Blundel,
which as soon as he read he tould the Duke he was of his
opinion, that there was some wicked contrivance in it, but

T O M E
II.

1678.
KING JAM:
MEM. TO. 8.
pag. 330.

The five
Letters sent
to Windsor.

KING JAM. M^m
TOM. 7. p. 283.
TOM. 8. p. 334.

T O M E
II.

1678.
K. J. M⁰⁰.
Tom. 8. p. 335.

" that he was confident he could find it out, having seen a
" hand not unlike it and would compare them togather.

" The Duke press'd the King and Lord Treasurer severall
" times that the letters might be produced and read, and the
" business examin'd into at the Committee of foraign affaires;
but that Lord, it seems, had conceiv'd some hopes that this
pretended Conspiracy might stand him in stead when the
Parliament met, and serve to skreen him from their displeasure
(which he much apprehended) by turning their eyes and atten-
" tion an other way; so the Duke could get nothing done in
" it, till a little before the King went to Newmarket, when at
" last the matter was carryd before the Councill.

The Examin-
ation of Oates
in Council.
Tom. 8. p. 231.

" As soon as Oates was brought in he tould the King, He
" had ventur'd his life for his Maᵗʸ at Sea, and his soul for him
" at Land, and was now come to discover a hellish Conspiracy;
" and then began his Narration with so much assurance, and
" accompanÿd it with such circomstances, as would have
" imposed almost upon any body, and did actually so, at first,
" upon severall there present, till by cross examination the
" vilany of it began to appear.

K. J. M⁰⁰.
Tom. 7. 286.

" One of the first things they asked him, was If he knew
" the hands of those persons, which the five letters were
" pretended to come from? Which he assured them he did, so
" a line or two of each letter was shewne him, and he imme-
" diatly tould whose it was, whᶜʰ proveing accordingly (that is
" to say as they were sign'd) gave him great credit at first; but
" afterwards when Mʳ. Ireland and Fennick's peapers, which
" had been seized, were compared with the letters pretended
" to be writt by them, there was not the least similitude: This
" put Oates a litle to shifts, who alledged they were their
" counterfeit hand. But when Mʳ. Ireland was brought before
" the Council himself, he proved, That whereas the letter bore

date from S'Omer's in August, that he was then in England, and　"
had not been beyond Seas of a long time, and when Blondel's　"
letter was compair'd with Tongue's depositions, it appear'd　"
to all present, to be the same hand writeing, and the other　"
four letters to be conterfeat also; So that Oates his telling so　"
readily at first sight whose letters they were, proved an　"
argument of their forgery, and that he and Tongue had been　"
both the contrivers and writers of them themselves: Nay Sir　" Tom: 8: p:336.
William Jones, thō afterwards so violent a prosecutor of　"
the Plot, being then Attorney-General, and Sir Robert　"
Southwell one of the Clarkes of the Council, tould the Duke,　"
upon comparison of the narrative and letters, they were　"
perswaded Oates writ every one of them himself; and their　"
never producing any of them at the Tryalls afterwards, was a　"
demonstration, they looked upon them as forged peapers,　"
that would have made against them: And it was a great　"
omission in those who were accused, that they made not more
use of them themselves; for all the five letters (besides what has
been sayd) were full of false spelling, neither point, comma,
nor marke of distinction in them, which had not the air' of
coming from men of business; and as to Oates' pretence, that it
was a common artifice amongst the Jesuits to writ in that maner
to avoid suspicion, and thought that a few faults in the writing
would hide it; or who can imagine, that five persons in
different places and even different Nations, should agree to write
their own names false (as they were in the letters) and false the
same way; should write the same false English, and writ upon
paper that had the same marke and same size, to agree in the
same cant and affectation, which upon examination was found
all to be so? Nothing less than an inspiration could worke this
miracle; whereas, on the contrary, whoever compares the
periods, the manner of expression, and even strokes of the pen,

T O M E
II.

1678.
Oates descrip-
tion of Don
John.
Tom:7. p:293.

Tom: 8. p.234.

Vol. of
Letters. p. 1.

King Jam. M⁹⁹
Tom:7. p: 294.
Oates's contra-
dictions.

Tom. 8. p.236.

with Oates' and Tongue's originall papers, will find they all came out of the same mint.

" But Oates is not discouraged with these rebukes, nor out of " countenance with the discovery of this forgery; but continues " his narration still persisting, That he was a great instrument " or agent of the Jesuits, to carry on their designes, not only " in England, but France and Spain too, that he had personal " conferences about it with the French King's Confessor, and " that in Spain Don John had admitted him into his presence, " where he saw the mony tould out for Sir George Wakeman " to poison the King; but this had as litle ressemblance to " the Spanish formes, as the description he made of him of his " person, for the King askeing him, what sort of man Don " John was? he sayd he was leane, tall, and black, whereas " the King and Duke knew him to be a litle, fat, and well " complexion'd man, thō he had browne hair; and when " afterwards Oates was blamed by M⁹ Kirkby for so gross a " mistake, he replyd by way of excuse, He might well give a " wrong description of a man he had never seen in his life.

" He was no less unfortunate in his answers in reference to " France; for being asked in what house that King's Confessor " lived, and where he spoke with him? He (replied in the) " Jesuits' house just by the King's house, whereas the Jesuits " have no house with in a mile of the Louvre: but neither " this could discompose his modesty nor interrupt his narra- " tion, so he goes confidently on accusing several persons of " quality; and when he named My Lord Arrundel and Bel- " lasis, the King tould him those Lords had served him and " his Father faithfully, and that unless the proofs against " them were very cleere, he would give no credit to them: To " which Oates replyd, God forbid he should accuse any one " unjustly, he did not say they knew it, but were to be

II

acquainted with it, thō afterwards he accus'd them posi- "
tively, which contràdictions My Lord Stafford urged with "
several others at his tryal, but My Lord's Chancellor's ill "
memory made it useless to him ; whereas if he had applyd "
to some others present, they both remember'd it and were "
willing to have born that testimony to truth, as would have "
manifested the Vilany of the wittnes, and might have saved "
that Inocent Lord's life. "

But, in reality, he did not positively accuse any Lord, "
till he had been before the house of Commons, and that he "
saw how they relish'd it ; nor did he till then, give them "
their different imployments, which how fit they were for, all "
the world might judge, nor did he make so much as a pro- "
bable story of it, till some Members of thatHouse had licked "
it into shape ; as if his Ma^{ty} might not be trusted with what "
concern'd his own life, or that the Parliament and wittnesses "
were more zealous for it than he himself : But there was no "
great Signes of that, since they did not accuse the Queen and "
Duke, till à considerable time after, who were certainly the "
most dangerous Plotters, if they were so at all ; and when "
they did, besides the improbability of that accusation, it had "
the misfortune to carry its contradictions along with it alsoe ; "
for when Oates gave in his information to the House of Lords, "
and had solemnly declar'd upon Oath, That he had no accu- "
sation against any person of quality soever but who he then "
named, yet a fortnight after he accused the Queen : but this "
indeed was a Christian liberty always allow'd him of contra- "
dicting at pleasure what he had sworne before, so he assured "
My Lord Chancellor when Colman was examin'd at Councill, "
that he never saw him before, but at his tryal he tould "
an other story : In fine he was trusted, he sayd, with their "
greàtest and most dangerous secretts, and yet, he con- "
fessed they would not trust him with mony for his coach "

Tom. 8. p.238.

TOME
II.

1678.

" hire, when he went to Dover, but sent Groue along with him
" to pay it ; he pretended to have deliver'd so many commis-
" sions, and kept not so much as one for a proof, thō he
" assured the King his intention was from the first to discover
" all ; he swore so many armes were brought, and yet none
" were ever found, Armys he sayd were rais'd, and yet none

K. Jam. Mem.
Tom. 8. p.251.

" ever appear'd ; nevertheless upon his testimony and his assis-
" tant Bedloe's (who att his first appearance too tould the two
" Secretarys he knew nothing of the Plot, onely Sir Edmond
" Bury Godfrey's murther) so many persons were imprison'd,
" prosecuted, and put to death, and rais'd such a furious com-
" motion as had like to have swallow'd up not only the Duke
" (against whom it was cheifly aim'd) but the King and
" Monarchy it self.

The designe of
the Plot was
the destruction
of the Duke.
Oate's Narra-
tive Fol. 9. 17.
19. 13. 16. &c.

There cannot be a greater proofe that this contrivance was
cheifly level'd at his R. H. then the injurious expressions which
were sowne and dispers'd thorough all Oate's narratives and
informations ; he makes no scruple of calling the Duke a
Rascal, a Papist, and a Traitor, he shall be hang'd, says he,
and I hope to live to see it, we will have no more regard for
him than if he were a Scavanger of Kent Street ; he hoped (he
sayd) to see him at the barr of the house of Commons, where
there were many better men than he, if the devil has a hotter
place in Hell than an other, he hop'd he would bestow it upon
him : These were the flowers of his eloquence, and such the
temper of the times as to suffer so infamous a Varlet to vomite
out these outrages against the King's own Brother, and a
Prince who was it not for his Religion, would have been the
darling and Idol of the People ; but it were as endless as unnecessary, to enumerate all his abuses, contradictions, and

* Sir Roger
L'Estrange's
Hist. of the
Times.

blunders, which are sufficiently layd open by *one who neither
injur'd him nor spar'd him : And the King himself was so fully
apris'd of the Vilany from the beginning, that he intended to

have nipp'd it in the budd, and hinder'd it from being made
publick, which he sayd would alarme all the Kingdom, and
put thoughts of killing him into men's heads who had no such
thoughts before, had he not been diverted from it by the
Treasurer, who foreseeing a Storme gathering against himself,
thought to cover his own head and elude the Parliament's displeasure, by throwing this pretended Conspiracy before the
house of Commons, assoon as they met; which otherwise, as
the Duke had earnestly press'd, might have been fully sifted
into, and the forgery detected by the Council it self, before the
Sessions, had not that Lord industriously delayd it. But such
was the infelicity of those times, and the people so ready to
take fire at the least rumour of a Popish Conspiracy, that when
it was communicated to the two Houses of Parliament, they
catch'd at it with such avidity, that all the contradictions, im-
probabitys, and even impossibilitys of the narration were swallow'd downe with greedyness, and the factious Party, which
was already but too much bent against the Duke on account
of his Religion, were overjoyd to find themselves possess'd of
so favourable a conjuncture of working his utter ruin.

The first step they made, was to petition the King to put
the penal Laws in execution; which they press'd with that
violence as he thought it necessary to yeeld a litle to the
current, and issued out a Proclamation for banishing Preists
&c. On which occasion the Duke met with a sensible
mortification from a hand he did not expected it, for when
it was moved in Council that the Dutchess's Preists might
be excepted, as well as the Queen's, and those of Forreign
Ministers, it was absolutely refused as a priviledge too great
for a Subject; but, as an expedient, proposed inserting them
into the Queen's List: But her Ma^{ty} (thō the Duke and King
himself desir'd it) would never consent, which was a great
tryal of their R. H.^{ses} patience, to find themselves soe soon

TOME
II.
1678.

The Parl^t.
petitions the
putting in
execution the
penal Laws.
Tom. 7. p. 297.

TOME
II.

1678.
It is moved in
Parl: that the
Duke should
absent from
Council and
busines.
TOM. 7. p: 302.

The King
desires it.
TOM. 7. p:303.

The Duke's
answer.

" abandon'd by one, from whom they expected the greatest
" favours and support.

" But this was only a begining of the evil, his R. H. must
" prepare himself for greater tryals, who soon after had intelli-
" gence of an intended banishment, which concern'd him much
" nearer. On the 2ᵈ of November the Earle of Shaftsbury
" moved in the Lord's House, that the Duke might be removed
" from all Councils and publick affaires. He had not yet the
" confidence to extend it to an exile from Court too; thō his
" Highness by this begining might easily see what it would
" come too. The next day the matter was taken into cousi-
" deration by his Maᵗʸ, who gave positive orders to all his
" servants and friends to oppose any motion of that nature,
" which might come into the house of Commons.

" But the King was not able to hould long to this resolution,
" the stream began to run so violently against the Duke, that
" he thought it impossible to defend him, unless he himself
" would temporise a little ; wherefore the next day after the
" Commitee for forreign affaires was risen, he call'd the Duke
" aside and tould him, That notwithstanding the foregoing
" order, it would not be in his power to support him against
" such addresses, as he foresaw would be brought in his dis-
" favour, unless he would yeeld him some ground to stand
" upon in his defence, and forbeare coming to the Commitee of
" forreign affaires, and decline meddling any more in publick
" busines ; which, he sayd, would give him a just pretence to
" reject and obviate any farther attempts of his Enemys.

" To this the Duke replyd, He was allways disposed to sacri-
" fice his person and interest to his Maᵗʸ's Seruice and ease,
" and would readily obey him when ever he commanded it,
" but could never do it willingly and of his own accord ; first,
" he sayd, Because in stead of stopping their mouths, it would
" on the contrary encourage his Enemys to press on farther, if

they saw his Ma⁷ once give ground ; Secondly, that he being ”
in a resolution to content the people in reference to Religion ”
and other things, it would give such as were not his freinds ”
some coulour to say, that now the world might see so soon as ”
the Duke was out of the Council all things were done to the ”
general Satisfaction of the Kingdom ; they would inferr from ”
thence, what a mighty influence he formerly had in the direc- ”
tion of affaires, and then by imagining that as soon as the ”
Parliament was up, he would infallibly reasume the same ”
again, if he remain'd at Court, they would raise from thence ”
an argument for his withdrawing from it too ; and he very ”
much apprehended the same reasons would then be urged ”
for his complyance to that, which were now made use of for ”
his absenting from Council. ”

. . It soon apear'd the Duke was not mistaken in his conjecture,
for within five days after, the House voted an Adress to be made
to the King, That his R. H. might withdraw from his Ma⁷ˢ
person as well as Councells ; but the King finding they run on
so fast, and that they already began to talke of excluding him
from the Succession, thought it necessary to stop their career :
He went therefore next day to the House of Lords in his Robes,
and calling up the Commons tould them amongst other things,
That he would pass any Bills they should devise in favour of, or
for the support of the Protestant Religion, both in his own time
and future ages, provided they went not about to impeach the
Succession or the right of the Crown in the true Line.

They vote that
the Duke
should with-
draw from
Court.
Jornal: Nʳ 8.
1678.

. When they saw his Majesty espouse his Brother's defense so
heartily, it check'd their prosecution of him a litle, So that ”
when the Bill for disabling Papists from sitting in Parlia- ”
ment, came up to the Lords, after a hot Debate it was ”
carryd at last in favor of a proviso to exempt the Duke from ”
the penalty of that Act. It was observed that the Duke of ”
Monmouth went out of the House before the debate ended, ”

The Duke
exempted from
the penalty in
the Act.
Tom. 7. p: 311.

" to avoid voteing, which the Duke could not refrain com-
" plaining of to the King, and tould him he fear'd not so much
" his open and his hidden enemys, especially one who had so
" great an interest with his Ma^{ty}; that for a long time he had
" suspected the Duke of Monmouth's friendship, he saw plainly
" he affected popularity, and was great with the Earle of Essex
" and Lord Wharton, and had reason to believe there was no
" ill understanding betwixt him and My Lord Shaftsbury
" himself; and that he frequently permitted his health to be
" drunk under the title of Prince of Wales: in fine, this
" complaint was too well grounded for the King to take amiss,
" nor did his affection to the Duke of Monmouth hinder his
" Ma^{ty} from blaming him for his cariage on those occasions.

Tom: 7. p: 313.

" This proviso in favour of the Duke sustain'd a hot Debate,
" when it was carryd back to the house of Commons; but
" thō the Presbiterians to a man, and those they term'd the
" moderate men amongst the Country Partie, voted against it,
" however by the helpe of the Lord Treasurer's friends, which
" some fancyd would have taken an other ply, the Court Partie
" carried it for the Duke, and on the 30th of November the Bill
" pass'd accordingly.

The credit of the Plot which hithertoo had but the support
of one witness, and that a blasted one too, seem'd very much
to abate; people began to lay things togather, and make use
of their eyesight and understanding which at first they were
haired out of; but the death of Sir Edmond Bury Godfrey
was so menaged (*Oct.* 17.) as not only to revive, but highten
the fury of it to a great degree.

Sr Roger
Estrange
Hist: the
Times.
part: 3: p:185.

This gentleman being a justice of peace was the first that
took Oates and Tongue's information, of which he made no
formal discovery, but on the contrary treated it as a ridiculous
Story; but finding afterwards he made such a noise, he was
terrifyd with the apprehensions of having committed a sort of

Misprision, which being highten'd with some threats from those who were displeas'd at his endeavouring to stifle the Plot, and most of all by his own melancholy, no one doubts but this unfortunate Gentleman layd violent hands upon himself.

T O M E
II.

1678.
Ibid. 181.

Bedloe's In-
formation.

But the People sufficiently disposed to charge the Papists with whatever was amiss, fail'd not to credit the rumour industriously spread a broad, That he was murther'd by them; and thereupon his Ma^ty was prevail'd with, to issue a Proclamation with a reward of 500*l*, for the discovery in what manner he dyd. Such a summe, and so great incouragement to informers, was sure to bring them another at least, which was much wanted; accordingly the Proclamation was no sooner out, but Bedloe came to one Brewer and told him, If he could possibly procure a description of Sir Edmond Bury Godfrey, he doubted not but he could get the 500*l*. and oft times consulted with his Brother (who had been his partner on like occasions) how to compass that affair : In fine his necessitys pressing, and 500*l*. quickening his invention, the matter was soon concerted, and on the 8th of November he depos'd before the Lords, " That " Sir Edmond Godfrey was murther'd in Sommerset house by " My Lord Bellassis' directions ; that he himself, with some " Jesuits had decoyd this Knight into the Court, where others " suddenly rushing upon him out of a door, forced him into the " house and there murther'd him; that his body remain'd " there two days, and was at last carryd to the place where it " was found : He made a long narration of the manner which " amazed people at first, but upon recollection the King " remember'd he was at Sommerset House himself at the very " time he swore the murther was committed ; this made his " Ma^ty doubt the truth of what he sayd, and to send the Duke " of Monmouth with Bedloe to Sommerset house, to shew him " upon the place where every thing pass'd. When the Duke " of Monmouth return'd, he tould the King the room, where

" Bedloe Sayd he saw the body ly, was the Queen's backstaires,
" which being the common passage for all the Queen's Servants,
" the place through which her meat was carryed, and where
" the footmen constantly waited, confirm'd the King in the
" beliefe of its being all a fiction ; besides his haveing been there
" at that time himself, made it impossible that a man should
" be assaulted in the Court, murder'd, and hurryd into the
" backstairs, when there was a Centry at every door, a foot
" company on the Guard, and yet nobody see or knew any
" thing of it.

The King, therefore, was as early aprised of the Vilany of his

Tom.7. p:331. information as he had been of Oates's which made him deny
" at first to prolong Bedloe's pardon, thō earnestly begg'd by the
" house of Commons ; and there is no doubt but all judicious
men would have been of the same opinion, had not the
violence of those factious men frighted people out of their
understanding, by flying into great heats upon this refusall,
charging it upon the Ministers and Chancellors, whose advice,
they sayd, had been always of fatal consequence to the Nation.
They found this ferment the world was in, a fit occasion to carry
on their darke designes against the Duke, and true or false
were resolved not to let it dye ; for in the bottom it was not so
much a Popish Conspiracy that frighted them, as a Popish
Successor, and their apprehentions were soon removed from
the Plot, to the Religion of those who were Sayd to be the
authors of it; it was not so much out of love for their present
Sovereigne, as the fear of him that was to come after, so that
under the notion of preserving one, they were resolved, if
possible, to prevent and ruine the other.

They begin to
project how to
disapoint the
Duke of
ye Succession.

Their first project, in order to this, was to put the King in a
capacity of having Children of his own to succeed him ; there
was no hopes by the Queen, and the readiest way to get rid of
her, was to bring her into the Plot : her dignity, they knew,

would be no discouragement to their Champion Oates, he was
too good a Christian to bear respect to Persons, but like a Son
of Thunder was ready to strike the lofti opt cedar, as well all
(*as*) the Lowest shrub, as his managers thought fit to direct him.

On the 25th of November, therefore, he repeated before the " Councel what he had sayd the night before to his Ma[ty], That " the Queen was privy to the whole designe and n one more " foreward to carry it on than herself; that he had heard her " Majesty say in Sommerset house, she was resolved to poison " the King for the injurys he had done her; they doubted not " but the King's inclinations to liberty would favour this " project: So they had sent one M[rs]. Elliot as from Oates " before hand, to acquaint him with this information; which " when the King seem'd to discredit, and urged the impossi- " bility of it, she told him, She thought he would have been " glad to have parted with the Queen on any terms. "

Tom: 7. p: 333.
The Queen is accus'd of the Plot.

Tom. 7. p: 309.

But this, instead of proving a temptation, made no other " impression on the King, than to give him a greater horrour " then ever of those infamous practices; for when My Lord " Ossory and Bridgwater were sent with Oates to Sommerset " house, to shew the place where he pretended to have heard " the Queen say those words he accused her of, he directed " them first to the guard room, then to the Privy Chamber out " of which, he sayd, went up a pair of backstaires into a great " roome; but unfortunatly for him, there were neither any " such staires there about, nor any large roome in that story. " But this unexhaustable fountain of impudence as well as invention, was not dejected, nor out of countenance at all these disapointments, nor would discover (thō earnestly press'd to it) who put him upon this detestable project.

Ibid. 333.

It was now perspicuous enough what all the management of the Plot tended to, The Duke saw plainly that all droue at his head, that his Enemys were resolved to move heaven, earth,

T O M E
II.

1678.

Tom. 7. 349.

Tom: 7. 325.

Ibid. 349.

and even hell itself to provent his comeing to the Crown ; this made it more necessary for him to arme against them, and endeavour to fix the King in his good resolutions and prepare him for the assault by representing the difficultys before hand, and what he knew would be urged against him ; he was not insencible of the King's ductile spirit, and the opinion his " Subjects had of him ; That Mr.May had sayd lately at a factious " meeting in reference to My Lord Treasurer, that they need " but opiniatre the matter and he was sure the King would " yeeld at last, which method he knew would not be neglected " by those who sought his destruction ; he begg'd therefore " of his Maty to take his condition into mature deliberation, " and weigh well with himself how far he was resolved to " support and stand by him, in case the Parliament press'd " to have him removed from his presence, and perhaps to have " his person secured : He acquaint him likewise with the " Cabals the Duke of Monmouth had of late with My Lord " Russell, Mr. Montague, Sir Henry Capel, and others of that " gang, where it had been proposed, that he should be " removed from Court and My Lord Treasurer layd aside ; " that the Duke of Monmouth proffer'd to joyne with them " in any thing for the attaining these two points, that they all " agreed to these resolutions except Mr. May ; that at all these " meetings they flattered the Duke of Monmouth with what " pleas'd him best, and that Sir Thomas Armestrong had sayd " upon Severall occasions, That the Duke of Monmouth had " assured him that the King had promis'd to declare him very " soon Prince of Wales ; but that if he did not, and that his " Maty should dy, he had four wittnesses ready to swear that " the King was marryed to Mrs. Barloe the Duke of Monmouth's " Mother.

The Lord Tresurer had already acquainted the King with these Scandelous reports, who had rebuked the Duke of

Monmouth for them, and therefore promis'd his R. H: he would
dóe what was.proper, to satisfy the world of the falsety of those
discourses, but those reprimands made no great change in
that young Duke's conduct ; the cunning managers who had
him now in their hands had dazled his eyes with the glimering
of a Crowne, they saw the King would not give into their
project of parteing with the Queen, so they resolved to try if
they could make the world belive he was marryed before, for
all ways were alike agreeable that lead them to the Duke's
destruction.

It is not to be wonder'd that the Duke of Monmouth, who
had more ambition than judgment and more adréss to Court
an interest than prudence to manage it, should fancy himself
within reach of a Scepter, when he saw the Duke (whom he
thought the only obstacle) Soe furiously batter'd on all hands,
especially being flatter'd in his folly not only by his great
freinds, and in privat meeting, but his very footmen began to " Tom.8. p.1.
talke publickly of the wittness that could prove the King's "
marriage with his Mother, and Collonell Birck a great leader "
in the house of Commons made no mistery of it, but ?? Tom.7. 361.
proposed it with other expedients to the Lord Treasurer, "
telling him it was in his power to bring that about which ?"
would make the Kingdom happy and endear his memory "
for ever to it, but the Treasurer tould him the King abhor'd "
the owning such an untruth ; whereby that project of "
tempting his Ma^ty to concurr with them in excluding the "
Duke, proved as unsuccesfull as the other. "

That Lord's credit with the King as yet was very great, The Ld Trea-
surer's ruin
proje^cted.
which made Collonell Birck think it in his power to persuade
him to any thing, but it was now nearer a period than either of
them imagin'd ; he had been long maligned by the factious "
party who in their privat meetings had projected his ruin, "
and commission'd the Duke of Monmouth to acquaint the ?"

" King, they would furnish him with whatever mony his
" necessitys require'd, on condition he would lay aside the
" Treasurer; for besides the common envy (which never fails
" to attend great favorits) they suspected him (thō very
" undeservedly) to be great friend of his R. H. This was not
the least of their motives to seeke his ruin, which these litle
contrivances would never have brought about in all probability,
had not another accident given a fitter opertunity to compass
their ends.

" Sir Lyonel Jenkins inform'd the King, that Mr. Montague
" when Ambassador in France had several private meetings with
" the Pope's Nuntio: this probably was only a pretence, but
" the King being otherwise ill satisfyd with his seruices a broad,
" and his carriage at home, thought fit to order his papers to
" be seiz'd, and Sr John Earneley was directed to acquaint
" the House of Commons with the reasons his Maty had to
" proceed in that manner against a Member of theirs; But it
" seems Mr. Montague had some apprehension of what was
" intended, and had secured those peapers elswhere, which the
" King designed to have taken; this he acquaints the House
" with, intimating at the same time they contain'd matters of
" consequence, which he knew was enough to rais their
" curiosity and make them be sent for out of hand.

This Gentleman, thō so lately imployd by the King, was now
linked with the discontented partie, whose study it was to
inflame the people; and these papers containing the substance
of a certain negociation with the French King, which he knew
would be no ways agreeable to the House and ruinous to the
Treasurer (which was an other of his aims) made him use this
contrivance to publish them, because the sole direction of that
affair had been in My Lord Danby's hands: nor was he
mistaken in his conjecture, for the Treasurer was soon after
impeach'd upon it. The King indeed staved it off for a time,

11

but was forced to leave him to the Law at last, and thō they wanted matter to bring him to a tryal, he endured severall years imprisonment, and had a long contest with the formalitys of Westminster-hall and Priviledges of Parliament ere he get clear of his accusation : But M^r. Montague will never clear himself of that infamous brand of treachery, that being trusted in a forreign Embacy divulged his Master's secretts to satisfy his own private malice against the Minister, and help on the prosecution against the Duke which he knew was so disagreable to the King his Master.

T O M E II.

1678.

In the mean time the credit of the Plot was supported by takeing up people of all ranks, and promises of reward to who Soever should make farther discoverys, which with a secure protection, and weekely pension could not fail of bringing in a recrute of Informers : Accordingly one Prance, Dugdale, Dangerfeild, Smith, and a numberless crew of indigent wretches offer'd themselves for that Seruice, who in the end became as burthensome to their Masters, as they were for a time to his Majesty's Treasury ; for notwithstanding the Parliament would not give the King a groat, yet forced him to maintain this rabble of wittnesses thō the tooles which he Saw were made use of to worke his own and his Brother's ruin.

Being now provided with So strong a body of Evidences, the Plot managers enter'd upon action ; and the King leaveing the Law to its course, they left likewise bloody markes behind them wherever they pass'd. The first object of their fury was M^r. Colman ; to be sure his haveing been of the Duke's family recommended him to the honour of his precedency, for it was there they strone to fix a suspicion and odium, he had been long look'd upon as a busy man, and formerly accused by one Luzansy, but being of ready wit and good tongue brought himself of ; however he was generaly hated, which the Duke perceiving had oft forwarn'd him to be careful how he

Colman condemned.
K. J. M^n.
Tom: 8. 381.

"
"
"
"
"
"

1678.

" carryd himself, not to be so busy and meddlesome, and that
" if he run himself again into troubles, he must (*not*) thinke that
" being the Dutchesse's Secretary would protect him; and
" indeed he was soon after discharg'd from that imployment
" by his Majesty's Command, so that he appear'd seldome at
" Court, but being known to depend on the Duke; Sir Edmond
" Bury Godfrey made choice of him, to send his Highness an
" account of Oates' and Tongue's depositions assoon as he had
" taken them. The Duke perceiving Oátes had named Colman,
" bid him look to himself, for he was sure to find no favour,
" and therefore if he had any papers that might hurte him, to
" secure them immediately; but he apprehending no danger,
" let them be seized, however kept close himself, and sent to
" advise with the Duke whether he should deliver himself up
" or not?. The Duke, replyd, He knew best what was in his
" papers; if they contain'd any expression which could possibly
" be wrested to an ill sence, he had best not apear, otherwise
" the surrending himself, would be an argument of innocency;
" he did accordingly, but found by experience that innocency

K. J. Mᵗ.
Toɴ. 8. 238.

" was no protection in such turbulent times, nor did Oates's
" having tould the Chancellor in Council he had never seen him
" before, hinder his being a Witness against him at the tryal;
" so he was condemned on the 27th of November and executed
" soon after." (*Dec.* 3.)

Haveing now dipp'd their hands in blood they run on with
greater fury, and cut themselves out more worke of the same
nature. Mʳ. Irelands, Pickeing and Groue were condemn'd,
and the House of Commons impeach'd the Lords Stafford,
Arundel of Vardor, Bellasis, Powis, and Petre, and were
running up higher, when the King thought it necessary to stop
their career, and take a litle time to breath: So prorogued them

167⁹⁄₈.
The Long
Parliament
dissolved.

till the 4ᵗʰ of February, and on the 24ᵗʰ of January dissolved
them quite: thus ended that Parliament which had sat 17 years,

and had been assembled to heal those National wounds which
had bled neare 20 years before; and thō it had then concurr'd "
with unexpressable joy to reestablish injured Monarchy, it "
was broaken for endeavouring with as much ardor and "
earnestness to pull it downe again. But who could have "
immagin'd, they had been capable of forgetting so soon the miserys
of the late Rebellion, as to run headlong into the same abbiss
again? and to fly with so much fury in the face of the Royall
Family, whose reestablishment had so lately been the worke
of their own hands, and to whose return they owed the Peace,
Laws, and Libertys of the Nation?

T O M E
II.

167⅞.
K. J. Mⁿ.
Toᴍ.7. 358.

The morning before the King prorogu'd the Parliament, "
Prance one of the Witnesses desired to be brought to him; "
where he fell upon his knees, and asked pardon for what he "
had done, and in the presence of Mʳ. Chiffins, and Captain "
Richardson, declare that all he swore about the Plot or Sir "
Edmond Bury Godfrey's death was false; but when he was "
reconducted to prison, the condemn'd hole and My Lord "
Shaftsbury's charitable exhortations so refresh'd his memory, "
that he stood to his first depositions, and remain'd as vallide a "
Wittness as ever. "

K. Jᴀ. Mⁿ.
Toᴍ:7. 369.
Prance recants.

These publick reproaches and the Parliament dissolution,
hinder'd not the tryals of those who were accused; so Green,
Bary, and Hill were soon after condemn'd and executed for Sʳ
Edmond Bury Godfrey's death, chiefely upon the evidence of
this very man that had made so sollem a recantation before,
and thō Bary always had lived, and now dyd a Protestant, and
to the last denyd the facts he was condemned for, as all others
did who suffer'd; nevertheless it made little or no impression on
the publick, no more than the innumerable Wittnesses as well
as Dyery from the beginning of August till the end of September,
That Mʳ. Ireland was travelling all that time in Staffordshire
when Oates deposed he was in Flanders and writt a letter from Sᵗ

Green, Bary,
and Hill con-
demned.

Lᴇᴛᴛᴇʀs,
Voʟ.I. pag:17.

T O M E
II.

1678.
K. Jam. M^{rs}.
Tom.8. 254.

M^r. White-
bread and
Fenwick con-
demn'd.

K. Jam. M^{rs}.
Tom:8. 13.

The Duke
considers his
condition, and
lays it open to
the King.

K. Ja. M^{rs}.
To: 8. p.19.

Omers; upon which he was notwithstanding condemned. (*Feb.*10.)
" M^r. Whitebread and Fenwick had been arrain'd at the same
" time, but there being no Wittness but Oates against them,
" they were remanded to Prison, for Bedloe then declared he
" had nothing to say against them, yet soon after upon pre-
" tended recollection he accus'd them, and they were condemned
" and hang'd upon his evidence: Such in fine was the prepos-
" session of all ranks of people in favour of the Plot, that the
" highest improbabilitys, the absurdest contradictions, the most
" apparent falsetys, the asseverations, of dying men, the infamy
" and manifest perjury of the Wittnesses, made not the least
" impression in behalfe of the accused, either upon Parliament,
" Judge, or Jury."

The disposition of the Parliament when dissolved and the
present temper of the people was such, as gave little hopes the
next would be better; so the Duke drew no great argument of
Safety from thence, but cast about how to shelter his head
" from the storme which both his Catholick and Protestant
" friends thought impossible for him to wether, and therefore
" agreed it would be as unsafe as difficult to remain'd any longer
" at Court, So My Lady Powis was deputed from the Lords
" in the Tower to beg of his Highness to withdraw into som
" neighbouring Country, France excepted.

But tho the Duke was sencible of his danger, he was
neither discouraged nor dejected; his inclinations rather lead
him to bear up against adverse fortune, than tamely to submitt,
he knew very well how to distinguish betwixt Christian patience
and pussillanimity, and whenever he gave way, it was his obedience, not his fear that caus'd it, for whatever his Ma^{ty} commanded, had always the force of a most sacred Law with him.

" About the middle therefore of February he lays open his
" condition and his heart again to the King; he tells him,
" That in obedience to his Commands he had withdrawn

T O M E
II.
·1671.

himself from his Councells, and the meddling in publick "
affaires, that neverthelesse whatever was ill relished by the "
people was still layd at his door; this did not Surprise him, "
he sayd, for he forsaw it would be so, and was always of "
opinion that his absenting from Councill and business would "
be of no advantage to his Ma^{trs} affaires, or his own, but only "
serve his Enemys for an argument to follow the blow, and "
have him removed from Court likewise, without which he "
knew they would never be Satisfyd, and therefore expected "
his Ma^{ty} would be press'd hard upon very speedily to doe it: "
He was not insencible, he said, in how ill a situation his Ma^{trs} "
affaires at present were, and how hard it would be for him to "
sustain such a battery as was raising against him, and "
therefore begged of him to consider well with himself how "
far he was resolved to stand by him, and that he would pleas "
not to flatter him with the beliefe that he would and could "
doe more for him than in effect he should be able to performe; "
that he saw clearly enough the odium he lay under, and "
therefore was fully prepar'd to make a sacrifice of his Country, "
Liberty, and Life itself, if necessary for his Ma^{trs} Seruice and "
ease. "

This discours as it confirm'd the King in the opinion he
always had of his Brother's sincere affection, and perfect
obedience, so it endear'd him the more; at the same time he
thought it impossible to keep him with him: but before he tooke
a final resolution in that matter he gave way to another
tentative, which if it had succeeded would not only he knew
calme the fury of his Enemys, but make him even the object
of the people's love whom now they Seem'd to hate and perse-
cute so grivously.

The Archbishop of Canterbury and Bishop of Winchester "
came one morneing and desired an Audience from the Duke, "
who being brought into his Closet, the Archbishop began a "

The Bishops
perswade y^e
Duke to
become a
Protestant.
K. Jam. M^r.
Tom: 8. 23.

TOME
II.
1671.

" well order'd discours representing the great trouble it was to
" him in particular, to his Breethren, and all the Nation, that
" his Highness should withdraw himself from the Communion
" of the Church of England, in which he was born and bred,
" and for which his Father of blessed memory had suffer'd so
" glorious a Martirdom; and enlargeing in commendations
" of its doctrine, sayd, It was not only more agreeable to the
" word of God, but more sutable to Monarchy than that of
" any other Church; that thō it had been always persecuted,
" it still florished like a lilly amongst thornes, so wonder'd
" his Highness could leave it, to embrace the communion of
" the Church of Rome, which if he would given leave to lay
" before him the arguments he was prepared with, he would
" convince him, held many doctrines contrary to the word of
" God; for which reason, he sayd, it was a standing artifice
" amongst the Priests, to hinder the people from reading the
" Scripture's bookes of controversie, that by keeping them in
" ignorance they might be govern'd the casilyer in that blind
" obedience, which was so pressingly imposed upon them : So
" beg'd his Highness would consider well a matter of so great
" consequence, and thō he knew he had too generous a soule,
" to be frighted into a change bay danger, or tempted by in-
" terest, yet he hoped truth would always prevail, and force
" him to return to his Mother the Church, which open'd her
" armes to receive him again.

The Duke's
reply.
KING JA: Mᵐ.
TOM.8. 25.

" This discours which lasted near half an houre his High-
" ness heard without interrupting him in the least; but when
" he had done, the Duke tould him, He was much surprised
" when the Bishop of Winchester some days before, desired
" they two might wait upon him as from the rest of their order;
" for thō he thought it not proper to refuse them, yet he look'd
" upon it as a thing of very ill consequence to him, to be moved
" on such a subject just before the meeting of the Parliament;

that he lay already under great pressures on account of his "
Religion, which this must necessairly agravate. So asked "
the Archbishop, if what he sayd was by his Ma^{tys} directions, "
or from the Bishops only ? He sayd, the King knew of it, "
but it was only by direction of his Breethren, The Duke "
then replyd, He doubted not but they two, and some others "
of their order meant well in it, but that he could not hinder "
himself from believing, that those who put them upon it "
intended his prejudice; That as to the discours they had "
made, it would be a presumption in him, who was an illitterate "
man, to enter into controversial disputes with persons so "
learned as they ; that nevertheless he would have acquainted "
them with the reasons of his conversion, did he think it "
proper at that time, or had leasure for it ; He assured them "
he had taken all the pains he could to informe himself in "
matters of Religion before he changed, that he did not doe "
it hastely, nor without a previous foresight of the inconve- "
niences which have already happen'd, and which were like "
to follow on that account; and, having Sayd so much, tould "
the Bishop they must not wonder, if by reason of the "
greater hurry of business, he was forced to dismiss them "
without entring into any farther debate about what they had "
urged. But for that reason, one of the first letters he writ "
after his departure was to the Archbishop, to tell him that "
his coming away was so sudden as well as unexpected, he "
had not an opertunity of speaking with him as he intended, "
to lay before him the motives of his conversion ; for thō he "
did not think it so proper, for the reasons he then alledged, "
to discours such matters at that time, yet he never refused "
speaking freely with any of his persuasion, and particularly "
himself, whom he allways looked upon as his friend, and had "
a great esteem for his person. He tould him therfore he had "
remain'd for many years a zealous son of the Church of "

The Duke
writes to the
Archbishop.
Tom. 8. 35.

TOME
II.

1675.

" England, in whose doctrine he had been educated and fully
" instructed by that worthy and learned man Doctor Steward:
" that during the (*time*) he was abroad, never any one speak
" to him about Religion except a Nunn, who, when he tould
" her he was too young to enter into disputes of controversy,
" she only desired him to pray that God would direct and
" enlighten him if he was not in the right; and that thō he
" receiv'd many civilitys from the Jesuits while he remain'd
" in Catholicks Countrys, yet never any one went about to
" perswade him to change his Religion; so that he might be
" assured it was both in his riper years, and a full conviction
" in all controversial points that forced him to embrace a
" Religion, he well foresaw would change his condition in this
" world, from one of the happyest Princes in Europe to that
" of the most unfortunate and abandon'd man upon earth.

The King
resolves to
send the
Duke away.
King Jam: M⁹.
Tom: 8. 29.

" Two days after this Conference the King asked the Duke
" what had pass'd betwixt him and the Bishops? Of which he
" gave him an account, whereby his Ma^{ty} found that project
" was ineffectual, and therefore thought no other way remain'd
" for quieting people's minds, but to give way at present to
" their importunitys; he would have been glad the Duke him-
" self had advised it, so asked his opinion what he thought
" proper to be done, but the Duke answer'd, It was hard for
" him to direct his Ma^{ty}, that knew not to dispose of himself;
" that if he gave moderate Councells it would be looked on
" as an argument of fear; if vigorous ones, the world would
" say, he cared not how he embroil'd the King, now his own
" condition was so desperate; besides he had little reason to
" presume, he could influence his Ma^{tys} Councels, when he saw
" those who were in the greatest trust and credit, steer a con-
" trary cours to his judgment, as well as interest, to affect
" popularity and court and esteem amongst his greatest
" enemys, and that therefore all he could doe was to be

entirely resigned to his Ma^{ys} pleasure, and would, as he had "
ever done, render a perfect submission to his orders. "

TOME II.
1679.

The Duke saw plainely enough wither all this tended, "
and that he must fall a sacrifice to the people's jealousys, but "
was resolved to make a merite of it in obeying the King's "
will, not following his own ; so reiterated his request to his "
Ma^{ty}. to consider well with himself how far he would stand "
by him in case his Enemys attack'd him in Parliament ; but "
the resolution was already taken : So the King tould him he "
was convinced it was absolutely necessary to yeeld to this "
torrent, accompanying his discours upon it, with great "
expressions of kindness for his Person and sorrow for the "
occasion, and in conclusion desired he would withdraw for "
some time out of England. The Duke who knew better "
how to obey the King than give way to his enemys, most "
readily acquies'd, never putting his own satisfaction or advan- "
tage in balance with his Ma^{ys} interests ; he only desired to "
have some thing to shew the world, what was the motive of his "
complyance, so begg'd a letter under his Ma^{ys} own hand "
expressing an order for his departure, which on the 28th of "
Febuary the King writ accordingly in these following "
termes. "

I have already given you my reasons at large why I think
it fitt that you Should absent from me for some time beyond
the Seas ; as I am truly Sorry for the occasion, so you may be
sure I shall never desire it longer than it will be absolutely
necessary both for your good and my Seruice ; in the mean
time I think it proper to give it you under my hand, that I
expect this complyance from you and desire it may be
assoon as conveniently you can. You may easily believe with
what trouble I writ this to you, there being nothing I am more
sencible of, than the constant kindness you have ever had for
me, And I hope you are so just to me as to be assured that no

The King's
Letter to the
Duke, to order
his leaving
England.
K. Jam. M^{rs}.
To: 9. p. 59.

TOME
II.

1679.
The Duke and
Dutchess goe
for Bruxelles.
K. Ja: Mⁿ.
Tom:8. 33.

absence nor any thing els, can ever change me from being truly and kindly your C. R.

The resolution being once taken, nothing remain'd on the Duke's part, but a ready performance without reasoning or " reply : Only a day or two after he tould the King, what " objections Several judicious and discreet persons had made " against it, but the King being fixed in his judgment as well " as resolution, no more was Sayd of the matter : So makeing " all necessary preparations for such a journey, with much " more expedition than could well be imagin'd, the Duke and " Dutchess (who was to bear a part in all his traverses and misfortunes) left England the 4ᵗʰ of March, went for the Hague and from thence to Bruxelles, to wait there the designes of Providence to which they always bore an entire submission.

The Lady
Anne not per-
mitted to go.

KING JAMES'S
Mⁿ.
To:8. 33.

It is more than probable that the Duke's Enemys haveing gain'd this point, fancyed they should be able to keep him all his life in banishment; for thō upon the first resolution for " his going, he asked the King leave to take the LADY ANNE " with him, which was readily granted, yet the Sunday " following the King tould him, many persons found it strange " that she should go, and accordingly obliged the Duke to " leave her ; whereas had they thought his return would have " been so speedy, they could never have deny'd him the " Satisfaction of her company, for fear of her Religion, " especially she haveing an elder Sister marryed, who would take place of her in the Succession.

Two days after the Duke's departure the Parliament mett (*March* 6ᵗʰ) and the King acquainted them with what he had done in order to calme people's apprehensions; that he had excluded the Popish Lords from Parliament, that Several executions had been made both for the Plot and Sʳ Edmond Bury Godfrey's death, that he had disbanded the Army as far as his mony would reach, and to the end all coulour of his being influenced by Popish Councells might be taken away, he had comanded his Brother to absent himself, and order the penal Laws to be put in execution against the Papists; so would now see whether the Protestant Religion, and peace of the Nation was as truly aim'd at by others, as they were realy intended by himself : This together with the rest of his Speech concerning the Navy, Traide, Subsidys &c, the Chancelor seconded and tould them, He hoped they would not overdo the business of the Plot, and in stead of making Laws for their security against Popery, hurry the Kingdom into confusion ; which, says he, are the only hopes the Papists have to see our Zeal out run our discretion, and that we our selves should be the unhappy occasion of rendring our own Councells abortive.

TOME II.
1679.

The King finding so many men of Estates were chozen Members of this Parliament perswaded himself they would be more moderated, and haveing such good Stakes to loose, would be very unwilling to throw Cross and Pile again, for all they had in the world ; but contrary to his expectation, this new Parliament was as far from any such healing temper, as that which went before it, they run as violently upon the Plot, as if nothing had been done in it hithertoo, and had not their malice to the Earle of Danby given him the honour of the first ranke in their intended prosecutions, the five Catholick Lords in the Tower had forthwith been tryd and in all probability sufferr'd too ; but the difficultys and delays which attended My Lord Danby's Tryal gave the Catholick Lords more time to prepare, and their Inocency to appear, whereby none but My Lord Stafford, to whom they gave no respit, felt the weight of that mercy less and bloody faction.

King Ch: Letters. p: 6.
Ibid. p. 10.

The Earle of Danby, then Lord Treasurer, finding himself under the displeasure of the Commons, after haveing endeavour'd his justification, surrender'd himself (*April* 15th) to the

The Earle of Danby surrenders himself.

T O M E
II.

1679.

Letters
Vol. I. p: 40.

The Duke's
opinion of yᵉ
Earle of
Danby.

King Jam. Mᵐ.
Tom. 8. 39.

Vsher of the Black Rod, and immediately after was committed to the Tower, and impeached; the King granted him his pardon, but the Commons questioning its velidity in cases of Impeachment, great debates and arguments were held upon it, and he press'd to declare whether he would stand to his pardon or plead to the Articles? He insisted on the former, but yet so as to leave room to justify himself too; this was so dissatisfactory to the Commons that it was believ'd they would have proceeded by Bill of Attainder, but the matter they had against him being insufficient, they could not go on in that method, and yet were resolved he should have the first lash of their displeasure which suspended for a time other prosecutions.

Had the Duke been capable of delighting in revenge this furnished him with a fit occasion; he was perswaded he owed his banishment to the Treasurer's advice, and one of the first things he heard after his arrival at Bruxelles, was the fall of that " great man, and that it was in great measure unpittyed: This " the Duke wonder'd at, because he had been free enough of " his Maᵗʸˢ treasure, where it could be applyd to make him " friends; he owned he always had a good opinion of him, as " a man of abilitys and resolution, till his late behaveour and " manner of quitting made him question his Loyalty, as well " as his judgment; the first thing, he sayd, that turned his " head as well as his heart was the readmission of the Duke of " Buckingham to Court, after his committment to the Tower; " the Treasurer had notice before hand of what was intended, " and thought he had diverted his Maᵗʸ from it, but soon after "' when he least expected such a thing, the Duke tould him, " he was inform'd the Duke of Buckingham had kiss'd his " Maᵗʸˢ hand at a privat supper at Mʳ. Chivin's: The Treasurer " was mightely surpris'd and struck when he heard it, and " burst out into complaints, How impossible it would be for him to serue the King, who published thus to the world how ”   T O M E

little credit he had with him ; that it would disincourage men ”   II.

from being Loyal and dutyfull, when they saw the King no ”   1679.

less kind to those who were not so ; that for his part he had ”

venter'd his fortune and life itself for his Ma^{tjn} Seruice, but ”

finding his pains thus render'd fruetless, he was resolved to ”

give up his staff and retire, rather than discredit and ruin ”

himself to doe his Ma^{ty} no good. The Duke did what he ”

could to appeas his passion, and tould him There was a ”

great intervale betwixt pardoning and trusting, he needed ”

not fear, that the Duke of Buckingham (who was so lost in ”

the opinion of the world as well as the King's) would ever ”

be in credit with him again, that he was sorry indeed the ”

King had done a thing which he granted would discourage ”

his true friends, but to throw up the game for one cross card ”

were to fly in his Ma^{tjn} face for a trifle, which became him ”

the least of all men, who had been so highly advanced and ”

favour'd by him.   ”

    With this discours the Treasurer was diverted from those ” *Ibid: 42.*

hasty purposes, however * the Duke with the same bouldness ”

and fidelity, but in all events kept a steadyer eye to his owne ”

security than his Ma^{tjn} interest ; which the Duke soon after ”

perceiving thought it his duty to advertice his Ma^{ty} of, cau- ”

tioning him not to confide so entirely in him as formerly he ”

had done ; but this it seems made no change in the King's ”

opinion, or at least in the trust and confidence he put in him ”

afterwards : Nevertheless the Duke was perswaded it was ”

this that stuck on the Treasurer's stomach, and made him ”

(when the informations were given in of the pretended Plot) ”

preferr his owne Security (or what he thought so) before his ”

---

* Some words appear to have been here omitted, perhaps, " however the Duke
" acted with the same boldness and fidelity ;" and, " but in all events *the Treasurer*
" kept," &c.

" Ma^{ts} apparent interest, by keeping the thing on foot till the
" Parliament met; which might easily have been made an end
" of before, and so prevented all the confusion, bloodshed, and
" hazard of a Rebellion, that ensued upon it.

   " Some were so malicious (thō the Duke never believ'd that)
" as to think him the first raiser of that Devil, but tis certain
" he might have laid him sooner if he had pleas'd; but on the
" contrary he opposed the Duke, My Lord Lauderdale, and
" all honest men, who advised the King to put of his journey
" to Newmarket in order to sift those informations to the
" bottom before the meeting of the Parliament, which would
" have laid open the Vilany of the first informers, and prevented
" the coming in of others, who were tempted by the great offers
" of reward. But My Lord Treasurer would not joyne with
" them in that advice, fancying by the helpe of his pretended
" Conspiracie and crying out against Popery he should pass
" for a Pillar of the Church, and ward the blow which he fore-
" saw was falling upon his shoulders; but My Lord Shaftsbury
" who soon found out his drift, sayd, Let the Treasurer cry as
" lowd as he pleases against Popery, and think to put himself
" at the head of the Plot, I will cry a note lowder and soone
" take his place; which he fail'd not to make good, and by
" that means turned to the Treasurer's poison what he tooke
" to be his only prerogative; so shallow and weake are the
" views of wisest men in the hands of Providence, whose
" designes are never frustrated whether theirs succeed or no.

   One would have thought the Plot managers had wanted no
spurrs, nor that the Duke's Enemys were too remiss in their
prosecution; but those it seems who desired to drive on more
furiously found means to have the Commitee of Secrecy
inform'd by My Lady Shaftsbury's buttler, that the French King
was to be on the Sea coast by the middle of June with an Army
of Sixty Thousand men, who were to be transported into Eng-

land to assist the Catholicks, and that the Duke, who was run away, they sayd, to save his head, was to return along with them: The House tooke fire immediately at this new discovery, and without farther doubt or examination (seeming to be in mighty apprehension) proposed sitting next day, thō Sunday, to provide for their Security.

T O M E
II.

1679.

Many set speeches and proposalls were made on this occasion, which at last ended (*April* 27) in this Vote, That the Duke of York being a Papist had being the principal encouragement to the Papists in their designes against the King; this was warmely prosecuted by many of that partie, and opposed at that time by none by (*of*) the Duke's friends but Mʳ Secretary Coventry: The reason they alledged for this Silence was, that those violent men would sooner come to Soberrer thoughts upon their own reflections, than by any thing that could be offer'd by private men whose interest might render them suspected to have consider'd that, more than the publick good; this was thought but a poor excuse for abandoning his cause on so urgent an occasion, but shew'd how violent the torrent run when his greatest friends durst not make the least head against it.

The Parliament Votes that yᵉ Duke's Religion gave rise to the Plot.

Ibid. 43.

But thō others trembled, his Highness had one powerfull support, which in this point at least stood immoveable; the King had often assured the Duke that nothing could alter him from the kindness he had ever for him, and that he would be watchfull on all occasions to defend him and all his concerns, and that thō he would be willing to doe any reasonable thing to please the people, he was resolved to stick firme to the Crowne; he saw whither this Vote tended and that the Duke's Succession was aimed at; he forthwith therefore call'd a Councel, and express'd himself with so much vehemence and energie against any such attempt, that had the Duke been present, he could not have inspired him with a greater resentment of that matter;

The King resolves not to abandon his Brother.
KING CH. LETTERS. p. 1.

KING CH. LETTERS p. 10.
LETTERS, V.I. p. 44.

TOME
II.

1679.

The King
offers an Ex-
pedient.
K. Ch. Let-
ters, p. 14.

Letters
Vol. 1. pag 46.

Various de-
bates against
the Duke.

he rebuked the Duke of Monmouth for the share he well knew
he had in those contrivances, and the hopes his Majesty had
(he Sayd) of reclaimeing him was the only thing that hinder'd
him from falling out with him for good and all.

He saw plainely they designed not only to fly at the Succession,
but were endeavouring to get a Vote that no Papist should ever
Reign, which he thought such a downe right rebellion, as that
the House would never be brought to it; but they were capable
of going much further, than he could then think possible, and
thō he lived not to see them make such an Act himself, the
Duke at least did. The King therefore thought no properer
means could be immagin'd, to put a stop to these proceedings,
than to offer the two Houses (*April* 30th) to agree to any Law
they could devise for the security of Religion, provided the
descent in the right Line were not defeated: he consented
that in case of a Popish Successor, all Spiritual and temporal
imployment should be given to Protestants, and none to be
displaced of the latter sorte, but by consent of the Parliament,
and if any further Security was necessary for Religion, he
would agree to it provided the Succession were not interrupted.

One would have thought such large offers might have contented
reasonable men, but nothing could do it, unless they had the
Duke at their feet, nor even then could they be secure against
him (said Mr. Sacheverell) unless the King would grant these
things he offer'd in his own life time. This put the House
upon various proposalls, and to shew how united they were in
their malice (thō they could not agree in what manner to
execute it) what ever any old manager moved, the new factious
Members still cryd up and applauded, like so many young
spaniels that run and barke at every larke that springs; some
were for destroying the Monarchie it self by setting up cross
titles in the Royal Family, and so make it necessary to rid

themselves of it, others were for a Bill only to exclude the
Duke, and for fear of a War have the Crown to go to the next
in succession, and if the Dutchess had a Son to have him
educated a Protestant; others were for setting the Duke aside
like an infant or lunatick, which they said alter'd no funda-
mentals: In fine it was generaly agreed, that unless they could
find means during the King's life to prevent the Crown's
descending to the Duke, it would be too late afterwards, which
in effect was strikeing at his life itself, and their intent undoubtedly
was to have proceeded to an Impeachment if not an Attainder,
for which reason a Commitee was appointed to search Colman's
letters, or what other information could be had to charge his
Royal Highness with the greatest crimes.

Vpon the Sunday following they reassumed this debate, and LETTERS,
VOL: I. p: 61.
thō they owned the King's proposalls were plausible, yet was
far, they said, from giveing England her wished Security, if
once the Crown fell to a Papist; For that no Parliament or power
could be of force to act without his consent, which, could not
be expected he would give against himself; no Oathes, they said,
which were the common cements of humain Society could bind
a Papist, that tyranny and arbitrary power must be its infallible
concommitants, and that thō a Popish Prince had bowells of
mercy for his people, it would not be in his power to act otherwise than by direction of the Priests, especially in all matters
wherein the Pope's authority and jurisdiction might be
advanced.

The Duke's friends finding how violently they run on, and The Duke's
friends reply.
that if no stop were put to these bitter and false insinuations,
it would soone be too late, venter'd at last to open their mouths
in his defence, now the King had shewne them the example;
they replyd, therefore, that thō many Attainders had pass'd to
barr the Lawfull pretender in former times, they only serued for
the most part to let out the best blood in the Nation, but sooner

T O M E
II.
—————
1679.

or later the Crowne still devolved to the true heire; and therefore how could it be esteem'd a providential care of the people's welfare, to intail an endless war upon the Kingdom? Many examples were brought how fruetless such precautions had always been, and amongst the rest the Settlement made by Henry the 8th, wherein after his own Children he gives the line of Suffolke preference to that of Scotland, and yet how litle

LETTERS
VOL.I. p.63.

it was regarded. But no argument was more insisted on, than the great probability that Scotland one of the antientest Monarchys in the world, would never joyn in changeing the . Succession which had continued in so long a descent, but, on the contrary, would catch at such an occasion to separate again from England, and have not only their Lawfull King, but a King that would live amongst them; the consequence of which needed no rethorick to convince the world how fatall it would be to England: But in spight of all the arguments that wit and reason could produce, faction and numbers carryd it; and

The Commons
Vote to ex-
clude the
Duke.

(*May* 15th) they Vote to bring in a. Bill to disable the Duke of York from inheriteing the Crowne of England, and that if his Maty should come by any untimely death they would revenge it upon the Papists.

The King dis-
pleas'd with
their Votes.

It was happy for the Duke that the King stuck so close to him in this dangerous conjuncture, but in reality their interests were as much united in this case, as their inclinations, which

LETTERS
VOL:I. p:65.

made the King so oft declare That he made no difference of friends betwixt him and his Brother, and that was the reason the Duke found so many, nor was it a small encouragement

Ibid: p.70.

to them, that the King never in his life apear'd more passionatly concern'd for his R. H, than in this occasion; but the King was sencible his own preservation depended upon it, and that his chief security lay in haveing a successor they liked worse than himself, otherwise in such turbulent times no one could answer what might be attempted upon his person, especially considering the late Vote about revenging his death: It was **TOME II.** apparent enough that thō the Duke was the first branch of the Royal Family they design'd to lopp off, the axe was layd **1679.** to the root itself, and Monarchy was to go down too, or bow exceeding low before the Almighty power of Parliaments. He resolved therefore to stick to the main chance, and suffer no diminution in the Prerogative during his time, and by consequence never to consent to any such Act; however (*he*) **KING CH: LETTERS p: 13.** thought it necessary to yeeld, as far as he could, to convince the world of his sincerity, and to put his enemys so much in the wrong (without parteing with any essential thing) as that if they forced him to breake he might have friends enough to assist him.

When the news of this Vote and the King's behaviour upon **The Duke's letter to the** it, was brought to the Duke, his pleasure was so great to see **King.** the King's kindness, that he took off all feeling of his own misfortunes. I can never (says he) sufficiently acknowledge " **KING JA. M⁰ᵖ. TOM: 8: 49.** the Sence of gratitude I have for your Maᵗʸˢ goodness to me, " I do assure you I can bear any misfortune with patience so " long as you are so kind; I have but one life to loos, and I " shall always be ready to lay it downe in your Seruice, and " at the rate the things now go there is too great a probability " an occasion may not long (*be*) wanting: They will never be " satisfyd, unless your Majesty unking yourself, and if you " deny them any thing they aske I am confident they will fly " out, especially if you permit the Militia of London and partes " ajacent to draw togather; I know there is danger and hazard " in makeing those steps that are necessary to keep your " Crowne, and more than would have been some months ago, " but you are utterly lost if it is any longer differr'd; let not " therefore knaves and mean spirited people flatter you into " an opinion, that you may be safe by yeelding and tempori- " seing, for nothing less than the destruction of your family and "

TOME
II.

1679.

" the Monarchy itself will content them : Now therefore is the
" time to breake in upon them before they are formed or have
" a man to head them ; and the only person capable (I think)
" of that imployment. (pardon mee for nameing him) is the
" Duke of Monmouth, for I am sure the same reasons and
" perswasions that has prevail'd with him to behave himself to
" you and me as he has done, will make him stick at nothing
" that favours his ambition ; and therefore I beg your Maᵗʸ
" will have a watchfull eye upon his actions for your own
" security ; and that you will please to give some signal marke
" of your displeasure to Sir Thomas Armestrong ahd young
" Gerrard, who were such ernest agitators against me in the
" House, for unless some thing of that nature be done, many
" will not think you in ernest. Suffer not Ireland or Scottland
" to be put in other hands as they are at present, you may
" count upon their assistance, and the Prince of Orange too
" has given me all imaginable assurance that he will stand and

KING JA: Mᵐ.
TOM 8. p: 58.

" fall by you ; wherefore I beg of your Maᵗʸ to make use of
" those partes and courage God has given you, and not rely
" upon concessions already made, or to make any more ; be
" pleas'd to use all possible diligence in provideing your fortes
" and garisons ; and certainly the speedyest way of breaking
" their measures, is to breake the Parliament itself, and pro-
" portion your way of liveing to your revenue, rather than to
" ly any longer at the Mercy of those men, who by that
" vilanous Vote to revenge your death upon the Papists, can
" have no other meaning, than to expose your life to the
" bloody hand of any desperate fannatick, who shall think
" fitt to attempt so unhumain an Act.

LETTERS
VOL. I. p: 79.

When this letter was given to the King it was further represented to him, that the Duke of Monmouth's ambition gave
life to all these commotions, as the only person capable of
being made a property by the Partie, who of late haveing

acted so bare faced, fancyd he could expect no quarter, and had therefore openly declar'd by his creatures, that he would do all he could to hinder the Duke's return.

T O M E
II.

1679.

The King read the letter with great attention and consider'd what was urged upon it, which one might see rais'd a sort of conflict in his breast betwixt his sincere affection to the Duke his Brother, joined with the reasons and necessity of self preservation; and the natural love he could not divest himself of in reference to the Duke of Monmouth: He sayd, he was sencible he had done amiss, but was not out of hopes he might be 'reclamed, and rather blam'd the Duke for begining too harshly with him, but his Ma^y being shewn the contrary, how kindly his Royal Highness had always treated him, how many faults he had pardon'd and forgot; the King, who was fixed in his resolution never to deserte the Duke, declared he would turn Armestrong out of all, and proceed with the like severity in respect of such as should apear against his Brother in the present debates, and that he would make the Duke of Monmouth the last man in the Kingdome if he persever'd in those ways: Nay such was the King's sollicitude in this matter, that while the Bill was passing the House of Commons, he tooke the pains to speake almost to every Lord himself, to diswade him from assenting to it when it came up to them; and tould them at the same time, let what will happen he would never suffer such a vilanous Bill to pass; he thanked the Duke for his advice and assured him he would stick firmely to him, and to himself; and that he was confident should that detestable Bill concerning the Succession pass the House of Commons, it would be thrown out by the Lords with indignation as it deserved.

The King in
some conflict-
with himself,
about falling
out with the
Duke of
Monmouth.

LETTERS
VOL. I. p. 70. 71.

KING CH:
LETTERS. p. 17.

But it went not so far this time at least, for on the 27th of May (which had been apointed for the tryall of the five Catholick Lords) they were brought to Westminster hall accordingly, where all things were in readyness for it, except an accord

4

554

TOME II.

1679.

betwixt the two houses; the Commons would not allow that the Bishops should be present at the tryalls, which the Lords opposed as contrary to use, only that they should withdraw when judgment was given; and the Bishops thinking to find a medium, desired leave to withdraw of themselves during the tryalls, with liberty to enter their protestation; but the Commons not satisfyd with that, would have the right itself decided, and insisted likewise upon haveing the validity of the Earle of Danby's pardon determin'd before they would move one step further.

The King prorogues the Parliament.
LETTERS
Vol. i. p.91.

..The King to put an end to this disput and not unmindfull at the same time of the Duke's advice, sends for the Commons up, and instead of proceeding to the tryalls, prorogued them (*May* 27th) to the 14th of August: He never speak better nor with greater energie, thō his speech was extempore as well as his resolution; this was so little expected, it struck them like thunder and left them all at a gaze, not knowing what way to turn themselves nor what measures to take.

The Duke is well pleas'd with the news, and desires the King to pursue that method.
KING JA: Mem.
To:8. 66.

.." When the Duke heard of it he beg'd of the King to
" follow his blow, he tould him they were stunn'd and dis-
" harten'd, that their measures were broaken, and if he gave
" them time to piece again and recover their spirits they
" would fall on with greater fury than ever; for which reason
" wishes the King if possible to put a stop to the disbanding,
" and call for him home; that after so much experience of his
" Matys kindness he might on this occasion expose his life
" again for his seruice, as the only acknowledgment worthy
" the favours he had receiv'd, and which the present posture
" of affairs gave too much reason to expect a necessity of.

He knew very well, that when the Parliament was up, those factious men had no other way to compass their ends, but by open force; which considering the flame they had blowne them-
" selves in too, was no ways improbable; wherefore he ceas'd

11

not conjuring the King, to pursue the method he now was
in, and not to imagin those men's good nature would be
wrought upon by complyance, which was the fatal rock on
which his Father miserably split, and which by that means
was so visible to him, that if he shunn'd it not, his fall would
be unlamented : Which representations thō they did not
worke his Ma^y up to those vigorous resolutions the Duke aim'd
at, they led him however by degrees to boulder measures than
it's believ'd his Councelors and Favorits at that time durst
venter to inspire him with.

"
"
"
"
"
"
"

T O M E
II.
1679.

But while his Highness preaches resolution to the King, the
Duke's friends preach a contrary doctrine to him, and if his
spirit had been capable of being broke with contradictions,
there was no circomstance or agravation wanteing to have
done it ; for besides the malice of his Enemys, he had the fears
and reproofs of his friends to struggle with ; they exhorte him
to be cautious in his expressions, and on all occasions to declare,
if ever the times comes, he will preserue the libertys of England
and the Religion as by Law establish, which, they said, he
might do, as well as other Princes who are of different Religion
from their Subjects ; they tould him the world complain'd he
was of an Arbitrary disposition, and loved the French government ; they wished him to remove to Breda to avoid the con-
cours of Papists, and suffer none about him, but such as by the
Laws of England are permitted to attend upon his person.
This caution no doubt was good, and what the Duke understood very well, nor was there ever any Prince in the world less
inclined to force others in point of Religion or to invade their
Libertys than he ; But for his friends to give soe readily into
every false and malitious insinuation, and to endeavour to toss
him from place to place, and add to his exile a banishment
from all his friends and fellow sufferers, was to deprive him of
the conforth whis is not denyd the greatest slaves, who in their

The Duke's
friends find
fault with his
conduct.
LETTERS
VOL. I, p. 33.

T O M E
II.

1679.

chains can tell their miserys to one another: But their zeal for his seruice, had a great mixture of personal views and advantages to themselves; as it appear'd in several of them afterwards; who, thō they had a mind to preserue him, it was for their owne sakes principally they endeavour'd it.

The Duke presses his returne.
KingJam:Mᵐ.
To:8. 62.

" The Duke nevertheless persisted in his opinion that if " his Majesty pleas'd to call him home it would quite dispirite " their enemys, and perhaps discourage them from attempting " any thing; but thō he press'd it ernestly it was still with " an entire resignation to whatever his Majesty thought best " for his owne seruice: Severall of the Duke's friends did the " same, but the King was still unresolved, he tould the Duke

Letters
Vol.1. p.95.
King Ch:
Letters.p.21.

he might easily believe the first thought he had after proroguening the Parliament (which he ownes were no longer to be sufferr'd togather) was relateing to him and what he should advise him to do, but as yet not being able to make any judgment what effect it might produce, must consider with himself and those he assured him (who) were his friends no less than his own, what was best, and would then give him his opinion.

Letters
Vol.1. p.95.

Ibid. 101.

But those friends were the men the Duke aprehended most, it was My Lord Essex, Halifax, Sunderland, and the Dutchess of Portsmouth, who had gain'd this credit with the King by apearing against the Exclusion, thō in the bottom they desired the same thing another way, and would therefore, he knew, certainly advise the King against his return; who they foresaw would ever oppose their timerous measures, and eclips them in the King's favour which now they soly possess'd; so under the notion that an insurrection was still to be aprehended, and that if his Highness return'd it would highten the present discontent, and drive those who had apear'd in opposition to him into some desperate action against the government, they did not only advise the King not to recal the Duke, but press'd him to promis never to doe it, till it was aproved of in Councel; but thō the

King yeilded to the first part of their advice, he rejected the later T O M E
with some sorte of indignation. II.

It was for the same reasons the Duke thought his return more 1679.
The King re-
fuses to lett the
Duke return.
seasonable, for if an insurrection happen'd, he hoped no one
could be better trusted at the head of his Majesty's forces, than
he, whose interest, as well as gratitude obliged him to venter
what was most deare to him in the King and Kingdom's
defence; But there was no such danger, but in their own *Ibid.* p. 100.
immaginations, on the contrary it appear'd, the people were
rather more displeas'd with those violent Members of Parliament,
than with the King for progogueing them; because the world
saw those turbulent proceedings tended more to the nurrishing
some faction, or the prosecution of some personal pique, than
the security and defence of the Nation; however the Duke's
friends gave into these reasonings against his return, and desir'd
him not to press it at present, and the King himself after *Ibid.* p. 30.
haveing fully consider'd the matter, thō he owned this prorogation had not produced any thing but blame upon the .
Commons, for doing those extravagant things which obliged
him to treate them so ill, yet, says he, I am sorry to tell you,
that the temper of the people is such in all places, especially
in London, that the Lords in the Tower being not yet tryd (by
which men's minds (*are*) as full as ever with the apprehension
of the Plot and Popery) that if you should come over at this
time, it would be of the last ill consequence both to you and
me. I am sure there is nothing troubles me more than to be
deprived of your company, nor can I write any thing more
against my heart than this, but when I consider it is the last
stake, I would not let my inclinations sway me so far as to give
a Councel so much to the prejudice of our intrest, as matters
stand at present.

This positive answer obliged the Duke to submit out of
obedience rather than conviction, till such time as his friends

T O M E
II.

———

1679.

were come off from those groundless aprehensions, who thought it not improper to move the King again upon that subject, but there were too many obstacles to be conquer'd at present considering what hands he had put himself and his affairs into.

The King formes a new Council.

Letters Vol.i. p.25.

His Majesty it seems had thought it necessary amongst other regulations, to model a new Council and place My Lord Shaftsbury at the head of it in quality of President; whom the King thought to keep from doeing hurt, by keeping him in his seruice: (a method which seldom succeeds) however when he opposed any motions which were made in the Duke's favour (which he never fail'd to do) the King had no regard to it, as knowing him his profess'd enemy; nevertheless being seconded in many

Ibid. 131.

things by Halifax, Sunderland, Essex, &c. who were supposed to be the Duke's friends, he gain'd upon the King in several points particularly this of keeping the Duke in banishment, thō the King was tould that such friends as would exclude the Duke from his native Country, would not stick in time to exclude him from the Throne too: But the King was not yet disposed to follow those vigourous Councells to the hight, which the Duke advised; he hoped by temporising a little to gaine upon his enemys, and in fine upon the more urgent

Letters Vol:i. p.133.

sollicitations of the Duke's friends, (and) tould them positively, there was no thinking of his return till after the tryall of the Lords in the Tower, with which, he sayd, the people would never be Satisfyd, if the Duke were here; that he was resolved first to have the Plot off his hands (the noise of which was now

Ibid. p.145.

somewhat abated) but that the Duke's comeing back would certainly give it new life, neither durst he answer that his person would be in safety, such was the hatred the people were in against Popery and him, as its cheife support.

The Insurrection in Scotland.

Nevertheless there happen'd an accident which might have fournished the King with a good pretence of recalling him, had

not the bent of his Council been so extreamly against it. Some
desperate fanaticks in Scotland haveing most barbarously assasi-
nated the Arch Bishop of S^t. Andrews (*May* 3.) and broken out
into open rebellion, it was necessary some forces should be
sent against them, and to be sure none could be better trusted
than the Duke; but in stead of that, he had the mortification
to see that honour conferr'd on his greatest enemy, and to serue
for an occasion of augmenting the credit and reputation of the
Duke of Monmouth, to whom that command was given. The
business being soon over, he return'd therefore with tryump LETTERS VOL.I. p.139.
leaving a mighty reputation behind him in Scotland, for the
clemency and indulgence procur'd by his means ; and in his *Ibid.* p.148.
way back, he was treated in many places with the title of
Highness which was no ways ill taken by him, and at his
return to Court receiv'd with great tenderness by the King,
even Armstrong himself found no markes of disfavour, thō the
King ceas'd not complaining of him. This gave the Duke's
friends too much ground to apprehend the worst, which they
fail'd not by long relations to advertice him of, so that to the
King's flat denyall to recall him, he had continuall accounts of
the Duke of Monmouth's advancing in his Majestys favour,
and of the mighty credit of Halifax, Sunderland, and Essex,
who undertooke the next Parliament should give the King full
satisfaction, mony, and what not, if the Duke were but kept
away ; in so much, that it was believ'd they would soon put it
out of the Duke's power to come back or even the King's to LETTERS VOL.I. p.151.
recall him ; which accounts following one on the back of
an other would have broken his spirit if any earthly consideration could have done it, but his letters to the King during
all these transactions, will be eternal monuments of his KINGJAM.M^m. TOM:8. p:49: 57.61.
Christian resolution in all these traverses of fortune ; If nature
suffer'd any thing on these occasions it was more for the King,
his friends, and his ungratefull Country, than for himself; he

T O M E
II,

1679.

The Duke's
friends press
him to change
his Religion.
LETTERS
VOL. I. p. 112.
136. 154.

was·So far.from wanting courage either to suffer with patience when there was no' remedy, or to bear up against his enemys where the case was not desperate; that under his great oppressions he would· comforth and encourage others when he seem'd most to want.it himself, and annimate his Majesty against that unsteddy and.yeelding temper which his own nature as well as his .chief Councellors inclined him too : But these were not all the difficultys his Royal Highness was. to fence against, his friends reláps.again into their.fears, which was more grievous to him than.all the rest, and had the bouldness to press him to change his Religion as the only resource he had left, and that without it both. himself, the King and Monarchy too, would infallebly be lost.

These menaces would have Staggar'd a Prince of less Christian. resolution, but no earthly motive could shake his perseverance when justice or.truth was concern'd, so he replyd with some " thing more asperity than ordinary,. That he wonder'd those " to whom he was known, could fancy him capable of so much " levity in a business of that high nature, as either to have " chang'd his Religion at first without full conviction or to " relinquish it now for temporal ends ; that what he had done " was upon full deliberation, and that he was resolved, let the " consequence.be what it will, to persever in the truth he had " already,imbraced.

Severall
executions for
the Plot &c.
and the Queen
and the Duke
accused again
of it.

But amongst all his contradictions, scarce any went more· to his heart, than the cruel treatment his friends met with in England, on account of this pretended conspiracy. On the 20th of June the five Jesuits, Mr. Whitebread, Harcourt, Fenwick, Gaven, and Turner were executed at Tyburne, and on the 14th of July Mr. Langhorne a. Barister of the Inner Temple; in· the different Countys the Catholicks suffer'd a grivous persecution by the Seizure of the therds of their estates or ·paying twenty pound a month, and the Priests by tedious imprisonments, amongst which one M^r. Poskett and M^r. Thwing suffer'd death at York, and M^r. Plesington at Chester. There were still new discoverys and the Duke himself render'd suspected by a Merchant in Venise averring that Sr Henry Tichburne had tould him, he was going to Rome by the Duke's orders, to prosecute the design in Cardinal Norfolke's letters; this the King himself thought might be of ill consequence, or at least was made use of as an argument against his returneing. The Queen too was brought again into suspicion upon the accusation of one Buss the Duke of Monmouth's cooke, who informed the Secret Committee, That being at Windsor in September last, he heard one Hankinson who had belong'd to the Queen's Chappel, desire Antonio the Queen's Confessor's Servant, to have a care of the four Irishmen he had brought along with him, who he sayd would do the business for them; the Committee had slighted it, but it being again sworn before the Recorder, Antonio was examin'd, and thō he denyd any such words, was committed for high treason: The King seem'd highly sencible of So injurious an aspersion on so vertuous a Princess, however nothing was done to vindicate her, in such awe did his Majesty stand of that popular rage, whose drift being to disapoint the Duke's Succession, there was no way of compassing it but by ruining him or the Queen; and therefore they would rather there had been no Plot than that they two should not be thought to be in it.

These were disincouraging relations to the Duke who could not expect much should be done for him, when the King durst not thoroughly vindicate the Queen; thō indeed the tryall and acquitting of Sr George Wakeman who was her Phisician, which follow'd soon after (*June* 18) did indirectly at least free her from that aspersion; but this gave the Duke no ease, on the contrary it served but to turn the fury of the partie more upon him, when they saw their other projects fail, and he had

T O M E
II.

1679.

LETTERS.
VOL.I. p.130.

Ibid. p.123.

The King still
positiue
against the
Duke's return.

TOME
II.

1679.
KING CH.
LETTERS. 33.

smal hopes the next Parliament would be more inclined to favour him, notwithstanding the King's fancy they would be better humour'd, that they were sencible of their late errours and that their eyes began to open in reference to the Plot, especially since Sr George Wakeman's tryal; but then least the Duke should lay hould of that for an argument to be recall'd, he obviates that inference by acquainting him That should he return, it would rais fresh commotions and renew the Plot which was now almost a ground, and which he conceiv'd would absolutely vanish after the tryal of the Lords; and if that busines, says he, be but well gon over the strength of the villenous partie will be much lessen'd and many arguments taken away against the Duke's return, which yet subsist and blind the understanding of many honest men; but that if on the other hand, things go worse and tend to a rupture, he aprehended the Duke's apeareing would raise more enemys, especially if the Plot were not at an end, for that tho what they have to say against him out of Colman's letters be weak and frivolous, yet, says he, I should be very unwilling to have a question brought upon the stage, whether or no you should be secured, and you at the same time present, considering how easy it is to have false witnesses, till Oates and Bedloe have their due.

This was the opinion the King had of the Plot and its wittnesses; while the seeming necessity of his affairs, made this unfortunate Prince (for so he may well be term'd in this conjuncture) think he could not be safe, but by consenting every day to the execution of those he knew in his heart to be most innocent; and as for that notion of letting the Law take its cours, it was such a piece of Casuistry as had been fatal to the King his father, and too shalow an excuse, to hinder him from a sencible remorce for those injustices and a hearty repentance of them when they were set in a trner light, which

it pleased God to doe some litle time after or at least before
his death.

And as (*to*) what related to the Duke's return, thō those reasons
were far from convinceing him, yet his dutifullness and never
failing obedience made him submit, and assure the King over
and over, he would rather sufferr an eternal banishment, than ”
bring the least detriment to his Majesty's affairs; but ”
haveing always had the liberty of speaking his mind freely ”
to him, could not forbear representing, he said, his opinion ”
in that matter, That he (*the*) riseing the King aprehended ”
could only be of the Green Riban Clubb (a factious marke ”
of distinction then brought up) who he was sure would do it ”
as soon as they were ready, whether he came or nò; and that ”
if the Lords in the Tower must first be tryd he doubted not ”
but the King's intention being known, would make that ”
Partie delay it only to keep him away; he was confident, he ”
sayd, the rebellion in Scotland was contrived to make the ”
King stand in greater need of his Parliament, and to deliver ”
him bound hand and foot into their power, but he begg'd ”
of him to catch them in the snare they had prepared for him, ”
and make use of those troops for his protection and security ”
against those very men, who by this insurrection had obliged ”
him to call them from Holland on whose fidelity he doubt'd ”
not but he might safely depend: The Duke knew very well ”
from what fountain these arguments sprung, and that so long ,,
as *Little Sincerity* (a cant word betwixt the King and him ”
for My Lord Shaftsbury) sat at the head of the Council, the ”
King would be eternally byased against him; but that factious
spirit could not smother, it seems, any longer his vilanous
designes, so that the King who had long suspected him, was at
last convinced he nurrished a snake in his bosome, and owned
he began to play the devil and could no longer be sufferr'd,
however he continued him in his station till the 15th of October

TOME
II.

1679.
The Duke
answers the
objections
against his
being recall'd.

KING JAM.M[r]
TOM. 8. p. 101.

KING JA. M[r]
TO: 8. p. 110.

KING CH:
LETTERS. 41.

4 c 2

TOME
II.

1679.
KING JA. M.
TO: 8. 133.

following, so fearfull the King was of breaking absolutely with so popular a man, his inclination ever leding him rather to flatter such sorte of people than to set them at defiance. And now that his Ma.ʸ found this corruption had crept into his Council, he began to apprehend the Parliament would not be so free from it, as he had flatter'd himself in the beginning; and therefore thought it necessary at all events, to have another string to his bow and try if from another source he could supply his pressing necessitys for mony, which was the main hank the Parliament had of him; and accordingly set up a Treaty with

LETTERS
VOL.I. p:111.

the French Ambassador promissing not to obstruct any of the King his Master's designes, provided they related not to Flanders or Holland, upon condition he might find his account in it, So far at least as to be able to live without other helpes. The French catch'd greedily at this overture, only were desirous that the Duke's consent might be had, because the year before some sharpe expressions of his against the French had given much disgust at that Court : For this reason My Lord Sunderland acquaints the Duke at large with the Project; advising mighty Secrecy, for that none he sayd but himself and another

KING CH:
LETTERS. p:41.

knew of it; the King likewise assures him, it was his kindness to him put him upon this method, that he might not ly so entirely at the mercy of the Parliament and be more at liberty to stick to the true Succession of the Crowne.

The King falls
ill, and sends
for the Duke.
LETTERS
VOL:I. p.178.

But before the Duke could make any answer, an accident happen'd which put an end for the present not only to this project, but to the great contest about the Duke's return : Upon the 22ⁿᵈ of August the King was taken ill at Windsor, he thought at first it was nothing; but finding himself wors, and more fevorish after Physick and letting blood, he order'd My Lord Sunderland to send away an Express to the Duke to come to him immediately but with as small a retenue as possible, and therefore to leave the Dutchess behind and likewise to be ready

to return when ever it should be thought proper; he was
directed likewise to give it out both at his parting from Bruxells
and arriuall in England, that he did it upon his own motion, so
fearfull his Majesty was of giveing the least disgust, and that if
any fault was found, it might fall upon the Duke's shoulders
which were more accustomed to such burthens, and this he
knew would make no great addition to what they already bore.

T O M E
II.

1679.
LETTERS
Vol. I. p. 190.

, Before the arrival of this express, the Duke finding he
stroue against the stream was resolved to submit to Providence
and press the King no more about being recall'd; which
made this news more unexpected, and thō it was very
agreable in one respect he was sensibly troubled for the occasion,
which doubled if possible his sollicitude and expedition; for
besides the great desire he had to return, the sincere and
Brotherly affection he always bore the King, made him uneasy
till he had the satisfaction of seeing how he was, and therefore
made little account of being censured by the world for disobedience in comeing without leave, provided he acted not against
his conscience, nor his Loyalty, he was not much in pain to
please the Publick which he knew was prejudiced against him,
and therefore generally judged blindly and unjustly, and were
not in a disposition to be gain'd that way.

" King Ja:Mⁿ
" To:9. 69.
"
"
"

Vpon the 8th of September he began his journey from
Bruxells acquainting no body but the Dutchess with his
intentions, and tooke only My Lord Peterborough, Mʳ.
Churchil, and a Barber with him, leaving orders with Sir
Richard Bolstrod to acquaint the Duke of Villa Hermosa
with the occasion of his sudden departure: The first night
he arrived at Armentiers, and the next at Calais, but the
wind blowing fresh and contrary, could not get out till the
10ᵗʰ in the evening, and the next morning landed at Dover in
a French Shallop, not being discover'd (by reason of the
disguise he had put himself in) neither by the Crew nor at

" The Duke
" partes from
" Bruxells.
" King Ja: Mⁿ
" To.9. 63.
"
"
"
"
"
"

TOME
II.

1679.

" Dover itself, except by the Postmaster who was an honest
" man and held his tongue; he tooke post from thence, leaving
" My Lord Peterborough behind, who was not able to go so
" fast, and arrived that night at London; Assoon as he light
" he call'd a hackney Coach and went first to M^r. Frowd the
" Postmaster to know what news, where he found to his great
" satisfaction the King was much better, from thence he went
" to S^r. Allen Apsley's house where he lay all night, and send
" for M^r. Hide and M^r. Godolphin to him; they tould him his
" comeing was still a secret, that neither the Duke of Mon-
" mouth nor any of his gang knew or suspected it, and there-
" fore they advised him to make all the hast he could to

KING JA. M^m
To: 9. 64.

" Windsor, while the thing was undiscover'd; accordingly
" he came thither next morning by seaven a'clock just as his
" Majesty was shaveing, and was himself the first man that
" adverticed him of his arrival.

Ibid. 73.
The King
receives the
Duke Very
kindly.

" The King tho seemingly surprised received him very
" kindly, and the Duke after his compliments and telling
" his Majesty how extream glad he was to find him so well
" recover'd, pursued his directions and speaking aloud, sayd,
" He hoped his Majesty would pardon him for comeing
" without his leave, considering the occasion, but that as he
" had already gon out of England in obedience to his Ma^{tys}
" commands, so now that he had the Satisfaction of seeing him,
" he was ready to go into any part of the world he should
" appoint. This Scene being over, all the Courtiers flock'd
" about him to make their compliments, his Enemys as well
" as his friends, for his presence always forced an awe and
respect even from those who were the worst affected to
him.

The Duke of
Monmouth
surpris'd and
troubled at the
Duke's come-
ing. Ibid. 65.

It required a resolution such as the Duke was master of, to
venter himself in this manner considering how all orders of
" people were set against him; the Ministers that had agreed

to his return he knew were not his friends in the bottom; and ”
My Lord Sunderland himself denyd positively to the Duke ”
of Monmouth that he approved of it, but on the contrary had ”
don all he could to prevent it; for it seems upon the King's ”
falling ill, the Duke of Monmouth aprehended what would ”
happen, and had press'd vehemently to have the Duke writ ”
too not stir, and therefore was the more surprised when he ”
saw him there; however could not avoid paying him his ”
respects, haveing the King's directions so to do. The Duke ”
received him civily, but discover'd a sort of disorder and ”
disturbed cariage in him all the while he remain'd at Windsor, ”
neither did the Duke of Monmouth nor his Wife (thō the Duke ”
had made her two visits) ever offer at any excuse for what ”
had pass'd, or imployd any body to bring them to a good ”
understanding; there was one indeed that wished well to ”
them both, who would have mediated an accommodation, ”
and proposed it to the Duke of Monmouth's chiefe adviser, ”
but he would never give any ear or incouragement to it. ”

His Royall Highness tooke care to return the Dutchess of ”
Portsmouth and all those Ministers thanks, who had been ”
privy to his being sent for; and finding the King had ex- ”
press'd so sencible a satisfaction in his presence, hoped he ”
would have parted with him no more; but those hopes were ”
short lived, for the very next morning the Earles of Sunder- ”
land, Essex, Halifax, M^r. Hide and Godolphin, comeing to ”
wait on him, My Lord Sunderland began a formal discours ”
to acquaint him, how upon his Majestys first falling ill they ”
judg'd it necessary his Royal Highness should be sent for, not ”
knowing what might happen, that they had taken care to ”
prepare the Lord Major and Aldermen, and the most con- ”
siderable persons in the Fleet and Army, who they found ”
well disposed in case of an accident (which indeed was true ”
but it was oweing to the care and endeavours of others who were ”

TOME II.
1679.
Ibid.

KING JA: M^r To. 9. 75.

It is resolved to send the Duke back.

TOME
II.
————
1679.

" more truly zealous for the Duke's interest than most of them)
" but that now, thanks be to God, the King being well again,
" those apprehentions and preparatives were at an end, and
" by consequence their sole business was to do all the pleasing
" things they could immagin, to put the Parliament in a good
" humour at their meeting which was drawing nigh, and that
" therefore it was thought necessary his Highness should return
" back to Bruxelles : However to take all manner of umbrage
" from him of the Duke of Monmouth's undermineing him in
" his absence, they tould him, They doubted not but the
" King would agree to the sending him out of England too,
" and take away his Commission of Captain General of his
" Ma.^tys forces ; and that his Highness should be sent for back
" immediately after the Sessions of Parliament was over ; and
" that if he approved of this they would propose it to the
" King, who they doubted not but would be well pleas'd with
" all the particulars of it.

Ibid. 76.
The Duke saw
it was in vain
to argue, Soe
Submitts.

" By this discours the Duke saw plainly his return was
" decreed, So thought it in vain to argue the point, but rather
" by a cheerfull complyance to make his court more gracefully
" to the King ; he left them therefore at full liberty (he say)
" to follow their own measures, who accordingly waited upon
" the King next day with the proposal, and found him willing
" enough to send away the Duke of Monmouth ; for besides
" his foolish and ambitious fancys, which the King was highly
" displeas'd at, he was well informed of his privat meetings with
" My Lord Shaftsbury, M.^r. Montague and other factious
" people, to the great prejudice of his Majesty's affairs.

It is resolved
the Duke of
Monmouth
Shall be sent
away too,

The credit that Duke had lately acquired in his expedition
against the Scottish Rebells, hinder'd him not from falling soon
after into his Majesty's displeasure ; who found out he had
managed those fanatticks, as if he rather intended to put himself
at the head of their forces, than repell them, and as if he had

10

more inclination to court their friendshipp, than punish their
rebellion, nor was the Duke after his arrivall at Windsor
wanting to his own preservation in makeing the King more
sensible of this danger; not out of ill will to the Duke of Monmouth (whatever might be maliciously insinuated), but purely
for the King's and his own Security, for so long as the Duke
of Monmouth's comportement was dutyfull or indeed Support-
able, he experienced all imaginable markes of kindness and
friendshipp from his Royal Highness, but when he set up to be
Prince of Wales and the head of the discontented partie, there
was no farther measures to be kept with him; the Duke knew
how to distinguish betwixt patience and a slavish subjection,
and thought it both just and commendable to stand up in his
own defence, when he could doe it without prejudice to his
Majestys affairs.

Before this Conference betwixt his Highness and those ”
persons above mention'd, they had sent one of their number ”
to him (to try his temper without doubt) by desiring him to ”
joyn with them in prevailing with the King to lay aside the ”
Duke of Lauderdale; but the Duke replyd, He had served ”
his Majesty a long time very faithfully, and was his particular ”
friend, of which he had given many testimonys during his ”
absence; that it would be a great discouragement to his ”
Majestys Servants, to see a person who had supported his ”
authority with so much zeal, so ill requited for it, and that ”
therefore he could by no means concur with them there in : ”
This person replyd, that their intention was only to lay him ”
gently aside, to sweeten things before the Parliament met, ”
who had a pique against him and would otherwise certainly ”
fall fowle upon him, so hoped upon that account his Highness ”
would pleas to be passiue at least in the matter; but he tould ”
them he could not promiss that neither, thinking it his duty ”

T O M E
II.

1679.

The Ministers
propose to the
Duke to joyn
with them in
getting the
King to lay
aside the Duke
of Lauderdal.
KING JAM. M^r.
To: 9. p.78.

TOME II.

1679.

KingJa:M^m To:9:80.

" to speak his mind freely and sincerly to his Majesty on " such occasions.

Tis not improbable but this answer gave a helping hand to the resolution of sending him back ; the Ministers immagined after the late favour.they had done him, the Duke would have thought himself obliged to enter blindfould into all their measures, but they found his spirit was not yet so broke with his adversities, as to hinder him from acting by those principles he ever thought his duty to be govern'd by, that he had the same firmeness wherever he thought justice, honour, or the King's interest engaged him, and they had reason to suspect that his credit with the King would always be too hard for theirs; therefore is it not to be wonder'd the sending him away again was so soon resolved on amongst them.

" The King indeed had promis'd he should be recall'd a few " days after the Parliament was up, but desired it might be a " secret as also what he had resolved in reference to the " Duke of Monmouth, till he thought fit to acquaint him with " it himself, which when he did surprized him extreamly. " He used many arguments against it, and press'd them with " more heat than well became him, and to shew his dissatis- " faction tould the King, since his Majesty thought him not " fit to command his troops as General, it seem'd improper he " should doe it as Captain of his Guards, and therefore desired " his troop might be given to the Duke of Grafton ; but after " he had slept upon the matter, he came next morning in a " more submissive manner, and acquainted the King, he was " ready to obey his orders, and accordingly went that evening " to London ; where instead of keeping to his promise, he had " a private meeting with Mr Montague and other factious " persons, telling them what had happen'd, and that he was " sent away for perswading the King to comply with his " Parliament, and for his zeal to the Protestant Religion.

II

When this resolution of sending back the Duke became
publick, many of his antient friends were hugely troubl'ed at
it, and particularly M^r. Secretary Coventry, who thought fitt
to represent his reasons to the King against it; but they not
prevaling, he urged at least the great unadvisedness of putting
the Heire of the Crowne into the power of a forreign Prince,
and that if his Majesty would not suffer him to remain in
England, it were more prudent to send him to Scottland:
this was the first time that designe had been named or thought
of; and appear'd so reasonable that My Lord Sunderland
and the King himself soon enter'd into it, only would have
him goe first back to Bruxells to fetch the Dutchess and
from thence streight into Scottland.

When the Duke found so many of his friends thus bent
against his leaveing them, (*he*) thought fit to discours that
matter again with those who first proposed it to him, but he
perceived they were all so positive for it (except M^r. Hide)
that he soon desisted : M^r. Godolphin sayd, should the Duke
not goe, after his consenting to it, upon condition of haveing
the Duke of Monmouth's Commission taken from him and
he sent away too, would looke like an artifice only to get that
done, whereupon the Duke assur'd them he would not move
his Majesty any more in that matter but rely on their words,
and comply exactly with what had already been resolved
on : But the Duke had underhand a pretty good assurance
from My Lord Sunderland and others, that when once he
was return'd to Court, he should remain there and not be
oblig'd to go to Scotland at all.

Before the King came back to London the factious partie
had got wind of this project, and as his Majesty was informed
by a spy he had amongst them, were hugely disturbed at it,
which made the Duke less avers to the journey; and so fear
of a counter order to remain at Bruxells when once he

TOME
II.
1679.
It is proposed
the Duke
should rather
be sent to
Scottland, than
to Bruxells.

King Ja. M^n
To: 9. 84.

" was there, desired to fix the matter so far at least as that he
" should be called from thence under pretence of goeing for
" Scottland, and therefore got the King to communicate it to My
" Lord Essex and Halifax. The former readily assented, the latter
" with some hesitation ; so then his Ma᷎ʸ declar'd it to all those
" five persons togather, who had been consulted with all along
" in those matters, viz. Essex, Halifax, Sunderland, Hide and
" * Godolphin, but would have it order'd so, as that he (it)
" should apear to be a thing of the Duke's own proposing,
" who was directed to write from Bruxells at his arrival there,
" to beg leave of his Majesty to goe for Scotland, and then
" under pretence of carrying his Daughters the Princess ANNE
" and ISABELLA (who had lately been permitted to make the
" Duke and Dutchess a visit to see their sister the Princess
" of Orange) he should goe into Holland, where the Yachts
" were to be sent to him, and some frigates to be ready in
" the Downes to carry him stright to Scottland ; but this

---

* The insertion of the Character which Bishop Burnet has drawn of this
Statesman, who continued to possess much influence in the succeeding reigns, may
not be deemed irrelevant. " The last of these was a younger brother of an ancient
" Family in Cornwall, that had been bred about the King from a page, and was
" now considered as one of the ablest men that belonged to the Court : He was
" the silentest and modestest man that was perhaps ever bred in a Court. He had a
" clear apprehension, and dispatched business with great method, and with so
" much temper that he had no personal enemies : But his silence begot a jealousy,
" which has hung long upon him. His notions were for the Court : But his
" incorrupt and sincere way of managing the concerns of the Treasury, created in
" all people a very high esteem for him. He loved gaming the most of any man
" of business I ever knew; and gave one reason for it, Because it deliver'd him
" from the obligation to talk much : He had true principles of Religion and
" Vertue, and was free from all Vanity, and never heaped up Wealth : So that
" all things being laid together, he was one of the worthiest and wisest men that
" has been employed in our time : And he has had much of the confidence of four
" of our succeeding Princes." (*Vol.* 2⁴. 8ᵗᵒ *Ed. P.* 113.) — EDITOR.

contrivance to keep it secret seem'd of no use, unless for the " T O M E
II.
greater ease in leaveing the Spanish Territorys, since the "
discontended partie had alredy notice of it in England. " 1679.
The Duke
returns to
Bruxells to
fetch tho
Dutchess.
King Ja: M^{rs}
To: 9. p. 66.

On the 25th of September the Duke therefore tooke his "
leave of the King, and by the way of Ostend arrived safe at "
Bruxells, where after a very little stay following the methods "
which had been agreed upon, pretended to goe and see the "
Princess of Orange, that the government there might not "
know of it till he was out of their Dominions, nor did he "
advertise them of his designe till the Yachts were come to the "
Hague; when his Highness sent a person of quality with his "
compliments and a letter of thanks to the Duke of Villa "
Hermosa, for his kindness and civility dureing his stay there, "
then went on board at Mesland Sluce, and from thence "
streight to London (after a little stop by the way) as the "
King had agreed underhand, without waiting for the frigates "
as was pretended he should. "

My Lord Essex and Halifax seem'd much concern'd at " The Ministers
are trobled at
the Duke's
coming to
London.
King Ja: M^{rs}
To: 8. 121.
this, but were tould, the Duke had leave only to take London "
in his way, the Season of the year being not proper to make "
the journey by Sea, whereas the Duke was all along assured "
underhand he should remain there, and not be obliged to goe
to Scottland at all. It is true there was a seeming mistery made
of permitting him to come to London, and the Duke and
Dutchess were obliged to wait in the Downes till leave was
sent, and till the Dutchess was fallen so ill as to vomit blood,
which furnished too reasonable an excuse for their been permitted to come a shore; but that juggle was understood by
the Duke, who was only caution'd for that reason to talke still
of goeing to Scottland, and the Dutchess herself desired to concur
in that little deceipt (as some of the Ministers term'd it) till it
were more seasonable to make the thing publick: But the
deceipt fall at last upon him who had been most accustomed

TOME
II.
_____
1679.
The Duke
after all is sent
to Scottland.
KING JA. Mⁿ
To: 8. 122.

to suffer them, so that about a week after the Duke's arrival
" My Lord Sunderland and M^r. Hide came to acquaint him,
" that his Majesty thought it for his seruice he should realy goe
" to Scottland, thō not to stay longer than the middle of
" January following.

The King's will was always a Law to His Royal Highness,
so without contesting the matter or complaining at these
" vexatious changes of Councells, and endless fatigues in
" traveilling, he sets out accordingly towards the end of the
" month (*Oct*^r 27) leaveing the two Princesses ANNE and
" ISABELLA at S^t. James's. The Dutchess notwithstanding
" her late illness and vomiting blood at Sea, the short time it
" was designed the Duke should stay in Scottland and the
" King's pressing her for that reason to remain at Court,
" would nevertheless accompany him; and thō she was not
then above twenty years old, chose rather even with the
hazard of her life, to be a constant Companion of the Duke
her Husband's misfortunes and hardshipps, than to enjoy her
ease in any part of the world without him, But it was a sensible
trouble to his Royal Highness to see the Dutchess thus obliged
to undergo a sort of martirdom for her affection to him, and
he to humour the peevish and timorous disposition of some
Councellors be thus sent a sort of vagabond about the world,
not only to his own, but to the King his Brother's visible
disadvantage; he was therefore much perplexed to guess from
" whence this new resolution arose, whether it was to content
" My Lord Essex and Halifax who were so ill satisfyd with
" his comeing to London and to make them believe it was
" never intended otherwise but that he should goe to Edinburg;
" or whether haveing at that time projected the violent pro-
" ceedings against Catholicks, which followed soon after, they
" had a mind the Duke should be absent while that was a
" doing; or whether they realy thought it the best to keep all

quiet in Scottland, especially since it cast such a dampe upon " **T O M E**
My Lord Shaftsbury and his gang when they first heard it : " **II.**
In fine whatever was the true cause, the Duke patiently 1679.
submitts without reply to the King, or expostulation with
those he thought the authors of it; for thō he was tould by LETTERS
some friends, that those two Lords were come over to his VOL.I. p.195.
interest, they advised him at the same time to menage them
ténderly, that their Stomachs were squemish and could not
disgest a great deal at once, that things must be communicated
to them by parcells, and it was hoped they would be brought
at last, to relish whatever should be offer'd to them for his
Highness's advantage and become stout and strenuous
assertors of his interest; but how much those advisers were
mistaken in one of those two Lords apear'd soon after, and
whether the other was ever sincerely the Duke's friend, is
still as great a mistery as the rest.

When the Duke arrived at York he met not so good a The Duke
reception as he had reason to expect; the people of that Towne arrives at
to cover their ill disposition found for an excuse, that formerly York.
upon the like occasion they had directions sent them, how to ʃbut: p.226.
behave themselves, which now not being done, they were
puzzled what respect to pay him. But this saved them, not
from being reprimanded for their neglect, wherein they were
the less to be excused, because others shew'd so good an
example, for in most other places on the road the gentry
express'd great duty and Loyalty, which his Highness fail'd not
to advertice his Majesty of; who in return assured him, they KING Ch:
could not have obliged him more, that his and their affections LETTERS.p:53.
were reciprocal, and therefore was resolved to stick to his true
friends, and old resolutions to the last.

Before his Royal Highness left London, he tould the King "
he thought it both just and reasonable that since he had been " KING JA:Mᵐ
always named of the Council of Scotland he should Sit in it " To:8. p.123.

" when he was there, which the King readily agreed too, and
" the Duke of Lauderdale was order'd to give directions
" accordingly; but My Lord Montrosse met the Duke at Yorke
" to tell him, there was difficulty made of his siting in Council,
" unless he took the Oath of Allegiance as it was called (thō in
" reality it comprehended the sence of the Oath of Supremacy
" too) and that some of the Council had writ to Court about
" it: The Duke thanked him for his advertisment, but tould
" him at the same time, that all the while he sat in the English
" Council no Oath had been ever tender'd him, that he had
" the same privilege in Scotland, and should not depart from
" it: Upon which the Marquis return'd and the Duke continued
" his journey, saying nothing of it till he came to Liythenton,
" the Duke of Lauderdal's house; where the Lord Advocate
" spoke to him of it again, insinuating as if this difficulty had
" been chiefly moved by the Lord Chancellor and the Duke
" of Lauderdal's friend; he confess'd it seem'd positive to him
" by the Act that the Oath was to be taken, and that My Lord
" Chancellor had sayd, both he, and the Lord Advocate might
" be question'd in Parliament in case the Duke sat in Council
" without doeing it: But his Royal Highness replyd, It was
" his priviledg as the King's Brother not to have Oathes re-
" quired from him as from other Subjects; that it had been so
" practiced in England and he saw no reason why it should
" be denyd him in Scotland. He acquainted My Lord Murray
" and Lord Hatton with this, who were of the same opinion
" and layd the blame chiefly upon the Lord Advocate himself.

  " Nothing more was say of this matter (only the Duke
" mention'd it to My Lord Argile) till his arrival at Edinburg,
which was on the 4ᵗʰ of December, where he was receiv'd with
all imaginable expressions of joy and gratitude, for the honour,
they say, the King and his Royal Highness did the Country, in
his comeing to reside amongst them. The Chancellor made him

a speech in the name of the Council, which his Royal Highness **T O M E**
replyd to in the most obligeing and affectionate termes imagin- **II.**
able, asureing them he would always make it his utmost   1679.
endeavours to promote the King's honour and Service together
with the interest of the Scottish Nation.

After this cerimony was over, the first thing was to adjust ” KING JA: MTH
the difficulty about this Siting in Council, for even before his ”   To:8. p.128.
arriual he met with letters both from the King and Duke of ”
Lauderdale, who upon Second thoughts were of opinion it ”
was necessary the Oath Should be taken ; his Majesty Sayd, ”
he Saw no more in it, than in the English Oath, and therefore ” KING CH:
advised the Duke not to boggle at one since he had taken ”   LETTERS 57.
the other : The Duke of Lauderdale endeavour'd to reinforce ” LETTERS
the same arguments ; but all this changed not his Royal ”   VOL.I. p.232.
Highnesse's opinion, he made the Act of Parliament which ”
enjoins it, be read ; upon hearing of which, he sayd, he was ”
more convinced than ever, for it appear'd manifestly to be ”
level'd against fanaticks, and such as had been in the late ”
Rebellion, which could no ways relate to him ; that he had ”
sat in the Scottish Council in England, had been Admiral of ”
Scotland ever since the Duke of Richmond's death, all which ”
was since the Act, and yet never any Oath was offerr'd to ”
him ; that indeed he had taken the Oath of Allegiance once ”
in the English House of Lords, because he found it in the ”
journal of that House, That the late King his Father when ”
Prince of Wales had done it, and that but once, and had he ”
not been in different circomstances then to what he was now, ”
he would not have done it all ; he confesses he layd done ”
his Imployments rather than take the Oath and Test made ”
in —73, but that was level'd directly against him, and so ”
maliciously penn'd that he could not have been obeyd, had ”
he kept his imployments without taking it : In fine these ”

T O M E
II.

1679.

The Duke of
Monmouth
returns from
Holland.

" reasons so far convinced his Majesty that at last he order'd
" the Duke to sit in Council, and that no oathes should be
" tender'd him at all.

But before this difficulty was adjusted his Royal Highness
had a more Sensible mortification in another point, for the
first news he heard from England, after his arrivall at Edinburg, was of the Duke of Monmouth's been return'd to
London ; he had left England about the same time the Duke
was sent back to Bruxells, and had been at Vtrecht, but made
no great stay in those partes, for whether he was jealous that
the Duke's journey to Scotland would breake his and his
partie's measures, or whether he thought he should have a
clearer stage when the Duke's back was turn'd, and was
resolved to profit by the occasion ; he arrived from Holland,
or at least appear'd publickly in Town the very next day after
the Duke set out for Edinburgh, at which the factious partie
shew'd great joy by ringing of bells bonefirs &c : he immediately sent M^r. Godfrey to beg leave to See the King, and that
he would pleas to permit him to offer what he had to say in
his justification, and to asure him at the same time that in case
it proued not satisfactory, he would most readily submit to his
Majesty's pleasure.

LETTERS
VOL.I. p.244.
The King
much Dis-
pleas'd at it.

The King was hugely surprised at his ventring to return
without leave, and sends to him to be gone immediately out of
the Kingdom. But instead of obeying, he goes streight to his
lodgings in the Cockpit, and it being late when he did it, the
King knew it not till next morning, who was then advertised,
where he was, and that all the people of his partie flocked to
him thither. This put his Majesty out of all patience, who
sent to him again that if he went not forthwith out of his
house, and the next day out of his Kingdom, he must never
expect to see his face any more, and as a farther mark of

KING CH.
LETTERS. p.61.

his displeasure order'd a Commission (*Nov:* 28th) to be drawne T O M E II.
out of hand to constitute the Duke of Albemarle Captain of
the troop of guards in his room. 1679. LETTERS VOL.I. p.236.

Vpon this message the Duke of Monmouth thought fit to
leave the Cockpit, but instead of goeing to Holland he went to
his house in hedge lane, and sent repeated instances by My
Lord Falconbridg, My Lord Gerrard, and at last by the
Dutchess of Monmouth herself to beg the King would pleas to
see him at least; but his Majesty stuck firme to his resolution,
and finding him not less firme in his disobediance, he took from
him likewise the Government of Hull and the Lieftenancys of
the Northrideing of Yorkeshire, which he gave to My Lord
Mulgrave, and that of Staffordshire to the Earle of Shrewsbury,
he order'd Sir Thomas Armestrong to be turned out of the KING CH: LETTERS.p.69.
Guards; so that nothing remain'd but the Master of the Hors,
which the King forebore depriveing him of for some time, that
he might not drive him to dispair, but soon after order'd
(*Dec:* 20) that employment likewise to be menaged by Commissioners.

All this severity made no impression upon him, he declar'd The Duke of Monmouth would not leave the Kingdom.
he would live upon his Wive's fortune, since the King took all
from him, and accordingly continued at his house, where all the
discontented party had free access to him, to project and cabal
without the least constraint; at one of their meetings in the LETTERS VOL. I. p. 253.
City, they layd a plan to prove the King was marryed to his
Mother, by means of a letter under the King's hand, owning
her to be his Wife, which letter they pretend'd was taken out
of her pocket, when she was carryed to the Tower, and in confirmation of this, affirmed they had a news book printed in
1652 which mentioned her under the title of Charles Stewart's
Wife.

No body could be more sensible than the King of this affront The Duke is not allarm'd at it.
and disobediance, however suffer'd him at his house, thō fixed

in his resolution not to see him. The Duke in the mean time had an account of all this from his friends, who advis'd him not to be allarm'd nor to come back upon it, for that would be improved by his enemys as a no less breach of the King's orders, than the Duke of Monmouth was new accus'd of; which the Duke readily submitts too, and seeming in great measure to slight it, gave his whole attention to the affairs of Scotland, where, by his industry, and application together with his affability and kind reception of the gentry and nobility, he gain'd such credit as did not only much better the King's affairs in that Kingdom, but acquired to himself such an universal love and esteem, that his enemys were hugely dejected at it, and Shaftsbury some time after bewaleing as it were the impotency of his malice, complain'd that the persecuteing of him in England, served only to make him reigne as it were in Scotland.

The Duke avoides enga-geing with any party in Scot-land.
Letters
Vol. i. p.268.

There was one Rock his friends apprehended he might split upon in that Country, which however he had the dexterity to avoid; no one doubted but the splendidness of the Duke's first reception there, was in great measure oweing to My Lord Lauderdal's care, which in gratitude might have ingaged his Highness to espouse his partie; but he soon found it necessary to keep a newtrality in those matters, for thô he might by generosity and affability, gain all parties to serve the King, and be friends to himself, he saw he could never make them so to one an other; wherefore he prudently shun'd any such par-tialitys, as would but have layd My Lord Lauderdal's burthen on his own shoulders, which were too hard loaden allready, and had no need of such an adition. But while the Duke gain'd friends in Scotland his absence made them fall away in England, the unsettledness of affairs in that Kingdom

Letters
Vol. i. p.224.

stagar'd many men of substance, and Some quite flew off both from him and the King. My Lord Essex had been long

wavering and at last surrender'd his place of Commissioner of **T O M E**
the Treasury ; he complain'd the Duke had not kept his **II.**
promise with him of doeing nothing without his advice, he *1679.*
apprehended, he Sayd, there was designes in the bottom
against Religion, and he was resolved to have no hand in such
Councells : Tis certain men of great fortunes may be allow'd
to be aprehensiue of ventering too far in such turbulent times,
and had he stuck there, no one could have blamed him ; but,
as the King observed, both he and My Lord Halifax hung $\underset{\text{Letters p.58.}}{\text{King Ch:}}$
after something he was in hopes they had forgot, and it soon
apear'd what it was the former drove at, the latter had the
good fortune to take both wiser and juster measures.

The Parliament had been prorogued to the 26th of January,
nor was it then designed they should meet; which assoou as
the factious partie got wind of, all hands were at work to
procure petitions to the King, they might then sit and do
business. The King foresaw this storme and sent to the Lord
Major to forewarne him not to encourage any such practices,
and issued out a Proclamation declareing it against Law,
threatening the utmost Severity to the transgressors ; but the
Earle of Shaftsbury and his partie laugh'd at such menaces,
and were as active and industrious in raising discontent, as the
King in endeavouring to apeas it; accordingly he and 9
Lords more gave the King a formal Petition to that purpose,
they had sollicited the Citie to joyn with them, but while the $\underset{\substack{\text{Vol.1. p.277.} \\ \textit{Ibid.} 272.}}{\text{Letters}}$
Parliament was up the King's authority was of some weight
there, which was one reason against their meeting, wherefore
notwithstanding this and several other petitions the King
resolved in his Council to prorogue the Parliament till the 11th *Ibid.* 280.
of November following, and took all necessary precautions by
forewarning the Lord Major very resolutely against any irregular practices, ahd by furnishing Portsmouth, Tilbury,
Sheerness, and all placcs of strength with a fit number of

T O M E
II.

1679.

troops and select Officers in case of an insurrection; which these tumultuous proceedings and the Duke of Monmouth's declaration, that he would not stirr from London, gave too much reason to aprehend; for besides his disobediance to the King's reiterated orders, he had given for a reason of his stay, that he knew the King's life was in danger, and therefore for his sake he would not leave the Kingdom, that he might be ready to revenge his Ma^{ts} death upon the Papists if any misfortune happen'd to him, which were dangerous insinuations, and made it more necessary for the King to look to himself.

LETTERS
VOL:I. p.280.

284.

. Immediately upon the King's resolution to prorogue the Parliament, the Duke had notice from his friends to prepare for his departure from Edinburgh, but not to doe it too hastely least the world might think he only waited for that, and in the mean time to be settling matters in Scotland, that the fruites of his journey might be not lost there; he goes about therefore to put the King's order in execution which his Highness had lately advised, and obtain'd leave accordingly that the Scotish troops might be exercised in the same manner with those in England, and that the fines and the defauters might be set apart for any emergent occasion.

KING CH:
LETTERS. 69.

The Duke
waits for the
King's orders
to returne,
which is
differ'd;

The Duke expected every day the King's orders without which he would not move, but instead of that his Majesty writ to him, That he thought it necessary he should not stir, till the prorogation was over, which could not be till the 26th of January; that he would send away the Yachts that very day for him, and hoped he would acquiess in what both he and all his friends thought equally necessary for both their advantage; that his being in Scotland had had so good an effect as to put a damp upon the discontented partie here, and no time being more to be aprehended than when the prorogation was made, his presence in Scotland would keep all quiet there, and his absence contribute very much to the same in England, whereas

LETTERS
VOL.I. p.300.

any change or motion (such as his coming especially) might create a new disturbance.

T O M E
II.

1679.

Though this fresh disapointment considering how his Royal Highnesse's patience had been exercised, was very mortifying; however it met with usual complyance, and thō he could not helpe being aprehensive what these frequent changes might end in, yet that made no so deep an impression upon him, as the resolution he heard was taken of exercising certain Severitys against Catholicks; this touch'd his Royal Highness more than what related to himself, so that he could not forbear complaining of it to the King, who assured him he was far from a persecuteing temper, especially when it must fall upon KING CH.
LETTERS, 77. persons who have deserved well of him, but in the present circomstances could not avoid doeing what indeed was very hard in it self, but hoped might prevent greater Severitys; it was conceiv'd the Nation would not be satisfyd, that by this long prorogation the further prosecution of the Plot should be suspended, if in the mean time this method were not used to remove the chief of the Catholick partie out of the Kingdom, that the people in the intrim might think themselves safe at least, and for that reason no passes were denyd to any LETTERS
VOL. I. p. 302. Catholicks who desired to go into forreign partes.

This fine spunn excuse which the Duke saw very well the The Duke is much con- cern'd for the intended pro- secution of the Catholicks. drift of, and which his Protestant friends gave so willingly into, made him tell them likewise he perceiv'd all sides concurr'd in oppressing those who had no ways deserved it, they replyd, that this method was necessary to open the way for his speedy return to Court, and his quiet abode when there; but his Highness's principles were not to build upon the ruins of inocent men, and (he) therefore expostulates so severely (at) their concurrence in this affair, that Mr Hide seem'd extreamly surprised at it, and sayd, He was no longer (he LETTERS
VOL. . p. 317. found) capable of serveing his Highness if he could not

preserve his countenance, protection, and even approbation in what he did ; expressing a desire rather to retire early, than by acting longer in his Highness's affairs draw a greater burthen of displeasure, where he expected to have merited most; but such was the Duke's generosity and justice that thō it had realy been for his advantage that the Catholicks should have laine under this persecution, he was resolved never to have it on such termes, as that those who had shared with him in his suffrings should have the like treatment procur'd them by his prosperity too.

1680.

THE 26th of January being come the King * prorogues the Parliament and writes to the Duke to return to Court, but as his life was made up of mortifications and crosses, so even the few satisfactions he had, were seldom without a mixture of disapointments; for thō the King had resolved to prorogue the Parliament till November, it seems he did it only till the 15th of April, and for reason alledg'd, that the French were useing all immaginable endeavours to engage the Dutch into an Allyance, that Monsr Davaux their Minister at the

T O M E
II.

1680.
The Parliament is prorogued, and the Duke order'd to return from Scotland.
KING CH.
LETTERS p. 81.

---

* RAPIN dates the rise of WHIG and TORY from this period. " At the time I am speaking of, we have seen Petitions sent to the King, to pray him to hold the Parliament; but as soon as the Parliament was prorogued, and the DUKE OF YORK at Court, a great number of contrary Addresses were presented in Abhorrence of the former, so that two Parties were formed called the *Petitioners* and the *Abhorrers*; and as the animosity between the two Parties gradually increased, they bestowed upon each other Names of reproach, and from hence came the so much famed distinction of WHIG and TORY. The Petitioners looking upon their adversaries as persons entirely devoted to the Court and the Popish Faction, gave them the name of *Tories*, a title given to the Irish Robbers, who were ready to act any daring or villanous Enterprize, these are the same that were since called *Rapparees*. The *Abhorrers* on their side considering the Petitioners, as men entirely in the Principles of the Parliament of 1640, and, Presbyterians in their hearts, gave them the name of *Whig* or *Sour Milk*, formerly appropriated to the Scotch Presbyterians and rigid Covenanters. These Names have been transmitted, with the Factions to which they were applied, down to our Age." (*Tindal's Translation.* — EDITOR.

VOL. I. 4 F

TOME
II.
_____
1680.

Hague partely by wheedling and partely by threats began to work upon them, and that in order to remove the main obstacle which ris from their union and dependance upon England, he insinuated they could expect no helpe from thence, pretending he had intelligence that the Parliament was to be prorogued for a long time, and that without it they knew the King could do nothing : The King therefore on the other hand thought it necessary both for the preservation of Flanders and the common peace of Europe to obstruct this Vnion, and had no way to perswade the Hollanders that he should be both

LETTERS
VOL.I. p.304.

willing and able (according to his Allyance) to assist the States if the French broke in upon them, but by letting them see, that he and his Parliament were not at such a distance but they could meet readily, and would in all probability, as readily concur, if need requier'd it, in a war against France, and for the support of Holland, as he and they could desire; so doubted not by this short proroguation and haveing the Parliament always at a call, he should keep France from invadeing Holland, and Holland from joining with France, which otherwise, that people's aversion to war would have forced the States to

LETTERS
VOL:I. p.319.

consent too. He resolved therefore (he sayd) to keep such a countenance in the matter as to perswade the world the difference betwixt him and his Parliament was not irreconciliable, that he durst meet them, and by that means keep his neighbours so well composed, that in reality he should not need to meet them at all, which was certainly the properest medium

LETTERS
VOL.I. p:224.

in this conjuncture, and what he most desired; for in the bottom the King never intended they should then · meet to do business unless the exegency of his forreign Allyances forced him to it.

The King's
reasons for
recalling him.

'This reasoning held upon so slender a thread, that the Ministers aprehended the Duke's comeing to Court might endanger the breakeing it, which put the King to his witts

again, to find an excuse for that too: so when he acquainted T O M E II.
the Council with his designe of calling his Brother out of
Scotland, he tould them, he found no such effect from his 1680.
absence as could perswade him to continue it longer, consider- LETTERS Vol. I. p. 332.
ing that probably the same questions might be put again in
Parliament not only of as high nature in themselves, but of so
great concerne particularly to him, that he thought it agreeable
both to reason and justice, the Duke should be present at the
next Sessions to make his own deffence, and in the mean time
assures them he will answer for such a complyance in him to
all things necessary for the general quiet and tranquility, as no
body should have reason to be alarmed at his return, or aprehended his presence might have the least ill influence upon the
publique; by which plausible turn the King made the Duke's
journey rather an argument for the Parliament's meeting than
a hindrance to it.

Assoon as the King's Letter pursuant to these resolves came The Duke takes leave of the Scotish Council. BAKER. p. 777.
to his Royal Highnesse's hands he acquainted the Lords of
the Privy Council of Scotland with it, assuring them that
though his joy was great to go to the King, yet he could not
part from them without a sencible trouble, and real reluctancy,
haveing met with such demonstrations of civility and kindness
from all ranks and orders, particularly the Council, as must
ever endear them to him, and make him bear a most greatfull
memory of their favours; that he would not fail to meet their
loyalty and affection, with all the services he should be capable
of doing them; that he would acquaint his Majesty he had in
Scotland a brave and Loyal Nobility and Gentry, a regular
and wise Privy Council, and the Judicatures fill'd with learned
and upright persons, that the disafected partie was not so considerable as those in England represented them; and then
haveing recommended peace amongst some Highland familys,
who he found firme to his Majestys interest, he tooke his leave

of them. The Chancellor in return assured his Royal Highness
they could never express the sence they had of the honour of
his presence, or of the advantage they had receiv'd from his
conduct and advice, declared how devoted they were and ever
would be to his Majesty's and Royal Highnesse's service, and
that they could not bear the trouble they had to part with him,
were it not for the pleasure he would have to be with the King,
and that they must always prefer his satisfaction before their
own; and to leave nothing undone which might testify their
gratitude on this occasion, The Privy Council sent a most
dutifull letter after him to the King fill'd with acknowlidg-
ments for the honour his Majesty had done them, by sending
the Duke thither, with huge commendations of his conduct and
prudence, as likwise all immaginable protestations of their
readiness to serve his Ma^{ty} and Royal Highness to the utmost
of their powers.

He comes
away by Sea.   Though the season of the year was improper for a journey
by Sea, yet the Duke and Dutchess too (who was now made
to hardships as well as himself) counted that for nothing, but
immediately went on shipboard and arrived happily at the
privy stairs on the 24th of February; he was no sooner there
but it apear'd who had Suffer'd most by his absence, and that
it was so far from being necessary for the King's affairs,
that nothing could contribute more to their advancement than
his being at Court again, which cast So great a damp upon
the discontented partie, that though My Lord Shaftsbury
stroue all he could to keep life in the Plot and in the Councells
of his factious Clubb, yet the credit of both grew faint and
Baker. 778. wavering, the very Townes and Countrys which had been most
active in promoteing Petitions, did publickely declare their
abhorrance of such practices, in which none were more zealous
than the City of Westminster it self, and the address from
Norfolke thank'd the King even for recalling the Duke.

This put a necessity upon those furious Zealots to redoubble their endeavours of keeping up (if possible) the jealouzys and ferment in the people, no accident could happen but it was immediately about to be some new designe of the Papists. One Atford was secured for certain undue practices in the " City, which Sir William Waller immediately proclaimes to " be a new Popish Plot, that the Guards were to join the " Papists to cut the Protestant's throats, and that the same was " intended in Ireland. "

T O M E
II.

1680.
The factious
Partie alarmed
at his returne.
KING JA: M⁰.
Tom.8.pag.135.

Soon after My Lord Shaftsbury acquainted the Council with an other Plot in that Kingdome said to be carryd on by Bishop Plunket the Catholick Primate and the reste of the Clergie for delivering it up to the French: The King bein then at Newmarket a Commitie of Lords was appointed to receive this information, and to send for whom and what they pleas'd, which was done it seems without acquainting the Lord Lieftenant of Ireland or his Majesty himself or so much as knowing the enformers names, which My Lord Shaftsbury thought not fit to trust them with; for no irregularitys were esteem'd dangerous in any proceedings against Catholicks, or the Duke himself who was brought into this Plot too, for they Saw well enough that So long as these accusations only affected private persons, it was but like lopping of the branches which would spring again, unless they could reach the head of the Cedar itself which would bring all downe along with it.

There could not be a boulder Stroke in order to this, than the pretence of a Black Box, in which was sayd to be found a writing, importeing a contract of mariage betuixt his Majesty. and the Duke of Monmouth's Mother; the King was resolved to serch into the bottom of it, and Sʳ Gilbert Gerrard who was sayd to have seen it, was carryed before the Council, but he positively disowned that he had either seen or knew any.

such thing; this insolence however stuck upon the King's
" stomach, and therefore in May following when his Majesty
" was indisposed haveing two or three ague fitts, the Duke of
" Monmouth it seems writ to him to enquire of his health
" signeing at the bottom your dutifull Monmouth, and inclosed
" it, in one to Mʳ. Godolphin ; which when he deliver'd to the
" King his Majesty bid Mʳ. Godolphin tell him, That if he
" would make his actions answerable to the conclusion of his
" letter and obey his orders, it was the only way to a recon-
" ciliation, but that if he flatter'd himself with the Support of
" the factious partie, or that the Parliament might interpose
" for him, he should find it would but make things worse;
and accordingly about a month after perceiving no change
in the Duke of Monmouth's conduct published a declaration
(*June* 3) protesting upon the word of a King and faith of a
Christian, that he was never marryed to Mʳˢ. Barlow, alias
Walters, the Duke of Monmouth's Mother, no to any other
woman but the Queen, which together with the Oath of all
the Lords present was registred in Chancery.

The discovery of this Mine hinders not My Lord Shaftsbury from driveing on an other, the Success of which he thought
would not be so easily prevented. On the 16ᵗʰ of June therefore accompanyd with severall Lords and Commoners, he came
to the grand Jury at Westminster, where after haveing represented the mighty dangers of Popery, and spoke with great
bitterness against the Duke, he * indicted him for being a

The Duke is
preseuted for
recusancy.
Kɪɴɢ Jᴀᴍ: Mˢˢ
Tᴏᴍ.8.pag.145

Lᴇᴛᴛᴇʀs
Vᴏʟ.ɪ. p.364.

---

* Tɪɴᴅᴀʟ, in his translation of Rᴀᴘɪɴ, gives the names of those persons
who attested the bill, " the Earls of Huntington and Shaftsbury; the Lords
" Grey of Werk, Brandon Gerard, Russel and Cavendish; Sir Gilbert Gerard,
" Sir Edward Hungerford, Sir Scroop How, Sir William Cooper, Sir Thomas
" Wharton, John Trenchard, Thomas Thynne, and William Forrester Esquires.
" By the sudden dismission of the grand jury, the matter had no consequence in
" the forms of the court." — Eᴅɪᴛᴏʀ.

Recusant, accompanying his information with proof of his TOME
haveing heard Mass, and desired them to present him as such II.
to the end two therds of his estate might be Seized, thinking 1680.
it of dangerous consequence, he sayd, that the Plot office
should remain in such hands, and then (to put him in good
Company) he desired at the same time, the Dutchess of
Portsmouth might be presented too as a common neusance:
The formalitys of the Law required some time ere this could
be brought to an issue in reference to the Duke; but the
Dutchesse of Portsmouth stayd not so long ere she was frighted
into a reconciliation, and did it so effectually as to become
even a Patron to her pretended prosecutors, to give them King Jam: M^r.
Tom:8.pag.157.
private meetings, and particularly the Duke of Monmouth;
and in order to shew her new friends her Zeal for their seruice,
did all she could to enforce those Councels which were for
removeing the Duke from Court again; and alledged for a
reason of her coudness to him, that the Dutchesse had not shewn
her so much respect or markes of kindness as she thought her
due: This was but a frivolous excuse, the true motive was
security, and * interest (which generally are the only Idols such

---

* BURNET says (vol: 2ᵈ.) " She was hearty for the Exclusion: Of which, adds
" he, I had this particular account from Mountague, who I believe might be the
" person that laid the bait before her. It was proposed to her, that if she could
" bring the King to the Exclusion, and to some other popular things, the Parlia-
" ment would go next to prepare a Bill for securing the King's person; in which
" a clause might be carried, that the King might declare the Successor to the
" Crown, as had been done in Henry the eighth's time . . . . Mountague
" assured me, that she not only acted heartily in this matter, but she once drew
" the King to consent to it, if she might have had 800,000l. for it: And that was
" afterwards brought to 600,000l. But the jealousies upon the King himself were
" such, that the managers in the House of Commons durst not move for giving
" money till the bill of Exclusion should pass, lest they should have lost their credit
" by such a motion: And the King would not trust them." (8ᵛᵒ: Ed.) — EDITOR.

TOME
II.

1680.

The Dutchess
of Portsmouth
brought over
to the factious
partie, upon
which they
think of send-
ing the Duke
away again.

KING JAM. M᷍.
TOM:8.pag.149.

Ibid. p.159.

persons offer incense too) that influenced her in that affair, for those generous principles of supporteing oppress'd inocency make but a weak impression upon people of that Character.

Shaftsbury's cunning therefore on this occasion deceiv'd him not, thō hers did in the end; for he by seeming to declare war against this mercenary woman, frighted her into an Allyance with him against the Duke, and she haveing the greatest influence over the King was the enemy of all others that wrought his Royal Highness the greatest mischief. Nor is it to be wonder'd that when the partie got such a reinforcement, they began to shake the King's resolution, which assoou as the Ministers were " aware of, they turn likewise with the wether and fall into " expostulations with his Highness himself, telling him, That " all the misfortunes that have befallen the King and him too, " were to be charged to his account, that the factious Partie " could never have rais'd such a storme against the Govern- " ment had not his declareing himself a Catholick given them the first handle: This was perpetually buss'd also in his Majestys ear by those who had greatest credit with him, which made the Duke think it necessary to justify himself, and shew the true origin from whence all those misfortunes sprung. It is " true, says he, one day to the King considering how low the " Monarchie is now brought, it has not vigour enough left to " crush those who rise in opposition against it, and therefore " such attacks as these make a sencible impression upon it; " but had those persons who now complain most, or their " greatest friends, who had the management of affairs at the " Restoration done their duty, the Crowne had been out of the " reach of such attempts as now shake it So grievously. A " weake distemper'd body is sencibly affected with any light " accident, which makes not the least impression upon one in " perfect health; it was they therefore, who brought the " Crowne so low who ought to bear the blame of its present

agony; for had that oportunity been prudently managed "
which the Restoration afforded, the Crowne might have had "
such a revenue settled upon it as would have answer'd all its "
expences, and so cut the ground from under the Republikan's "
feet, who have no other to stand on when they invaded the "
Throne. The next fault was the engageing the King in a "
war with Holland; which is not, says he, to be layd at my "
door, all the world knows it was the House of Commons "
and the Merchants that press'd it, on account of the injurys "
they had suffer'd from the Dutch in the Indies, on the Coast "
of Guinia, and els where, and I was not lead into it any "
otherwise than by the cry of the people, and the desire of "
being at the head of such a force, which considering 'my "
temper and education could not be wonder'd at. And thō it "
had not the Success that might have been expected, no fault "
was ever found with my conduct or management. But the "
most fatal blow (says he) the King gave himself to his power "
and prerogative was, when he sought aid from the House of "
Commons to destroy the Earle of Clarendon, by that he put "
that House again (*in mind*) of their impeaching privilege, "
which had been wrested out of their hands by the Restoration; "
and when Ministers found they were like to be left to the "
Censure of the Parliament, it made them have a greater "
attention to court an interest there than to pursue that "
of their Princes from whom they hoped not for so sure a "
Support. "

But notwithstanding all the Duke could say to shew from "
what spring all these troubles flowed, still the cry went against "
him, as the Jonas for whose sake these stormes were rais'd; "
and therefore the King had no sooner declared in Council on
the 18th of August, that the Parliament should sit on the 21st of
October, but all the world cast about to save themselves, and
the Duke like that Prophet must be sacrificed for the publick

TOME
II.
———
1680.
KingJam.M^rs.
Tom.8.pag.151.

"quiet. Some of his friends informed him that an Impeach-
"ment would certainly be brought against him for High
"Treason, others tould him they would drive at a bill of
"Limitation, which once pass'd, they would look upon a
"Common wealth in a manner settled, others sayd they would
send him away again; in fine their was no evill that malice or
envy could contrive but by some hand or other it was levell'd

Ibid. 143.

"at his head: However none of these informations troubled
"him so much as an account he had, that the Ministers them-
"selves had resolved to have a bill brought in the next Parlia-
"ment, to banish all Catholicks out of the Kingdom; he
"knew My Lord Halifax had long meditated this project, but
"thought it would never have gon farther, whereas now he
"found it was both embraced and advised by those in greatest
"power, thinking to make their court to the Nation by it, and
"settle all things at quiet: but he (was) astonished that men
"of sence did not see that Religion was only the pretence,
"and that the real contest was about Power and Dominion,
"that it was the Monarchie they designed to banish, without
"which the other banishments would give them little Satis-
"faction.

The King pre-
vail'd upon to
send the Duke
again into
Scotland.
King Jam.M^rs.
Tom:8.pag.165.

However as yet no new measures were taken in reference to
the Duke, the Ministers had some courage left, till a Parlia-
"ment stared them in the face; and had the King been able
"to live without the assistance of that Assembly, the Duke
"had found more friends and he himself better served, but
"when once the time of its siting aproached, all eyes were
"fixed upon it, and every head turned by its influence: In
"October following while the Court was at Newmarket, the
"Duke began to find the effects of this, his being sent away
"again began to be more discours'd of than ever: Upon
"which his Highness spoke to My Lord Sunderland and M^r
"Godolphin who assured him there was no alteration of

measures, and that his Majesty thought of no such thing, " **T O M E**
but their couldness soon after to the Duke's friends made " **II.**
him suspect there was more in it than they pretended, and " 1680.
(*he*) was at last convinced of the change when the day after "
the King's arrival in Town, they both came to Mr Hide and "
tould him they thought it for his Majestys service that the "
Duke should go again out of England and the next day "
tould the Duke himself the same thing; who upon discours "
found they had determined to this by My Lord Essex and "
Halifax, the first where of was for his going to Flanders, the "
latter only for his absenting from Court: The Duke say he "
was not astonished that those two Lords should give such "
advice, but that My Lord Sunderland and Mr Godolphin "
should concur with them in it, surpris'd him to the last degree, "
especially since they never gave him the least advertishment "
thereof, but on the contrary bore him in hand with continual "
assurances there was no such thing intended; he tould them "
he was not conscious to himself to have given them any reason "
to treat him so, but had used a greater condescention to them "
than ever he had done to any in their Station before. "

These supportes failling him so unawares struck him with " The Duke's
a wors aprehention, and made him suspect the King himself " discours to
began to waver, and accordingly he soon found by discours's " this occasion.
on that Subject that his Majesty now doubted whether he " King Jam. M^m.
could stand by him or no: The Duke represented to him his " Tom.8.pag.171.
constant and late engagement to the contrary, but found him "
So changed, that it gave him great reason now at last to "
aprehend what he had been oft tould but never believed, "
That his Majesty would abandon him in the end. He put "
(*the King*) therefore in mind how My Lord Shaftsbury had "
given his Majesty's instability for a land marke, as he call'd "
it, to disswade all men from trusting or relying upon him, "
and that he was pleas'd to reply to it, He was glad that Lord "

" had put such marke upon him, for he would prove him a
" Lyer and so turn it against himself: His Maᵗʸ could make
" no reply to this, nor to the complaint his Highness made of
" his two Ministers' conduct towards him. Nevertheless the
" Duke tould him if his Majesty thought his absence would
" be for his seruice he would go to any part of the world, but
" believ'd it would have a quite contrary effect, that it would
" discourage his friends, hearten his enemys, and ruin his
" credit; wherefore he begg'd of him before he came to a
" positive resolution, to advise with those who were no ways
" byas'd in their Councells, whereas My Lord Sunderland and
" Mʳ. Godolphin were influenced he fear'd, one by his three
" Uncles, the other by his Brother in Law; that My Lord
" Essex his principles as to government was too well known,
" and his late reconciliation with Myᵈ Shaftsbury made it
" without doubt; that My Lord Halifax was an Athist and
" had hithertoo been no good friend to Monarchie: In con-
" clusion the King promised he would take the advice of his
" Privy Council, which accordingly he did, and a much
" greater part was against it; but the King and those who
" had most credit with him continuing in their former opinion,
" cunningly moved such questions in Council, as they saw
" would both distract and terrify the rest, as whether the
" King should break the Parliament if it should impeach the
" Duke and such like perplexing suppositions, which diverted
" their comeing to any resolution in reference to the matter in
" hand, and made those who were against the Duke's going
" be silent: Whereupon his Majesty proposed his returning
" again to Scotland, as the best expedient, and sayd he would
" advise him to it, which he did accordingly the Sunday
" following; but the Duke had the same answerd ready he had
" formerly made him, That he neither thought (it was) for his
" Maᵗʸˢ seruice, nor had he any business of his own in that

Country, but that if his Majesty thought fit to command "   **T O M E**
him, his obedience was the Same it ever had been, and if "   **II.**
so desired he would pleas to write a letter to the Council "   1680.
of Scotland, acquainting them he had commanded his repair "
thither to look after his affairs in that Kingdom, which was "
done accordingly. "

There was one thing his Highness thought might be of use "   The Duke
to him before he went, which was to have a Pardon and "   desires a Pardon, which is
therefore asked it of his Majesty as a thing that would take "   denyd.
KingJam: M^{re}
away all grounds of impeachment ; the King Sayd, that had "   Tom.8. p.177.
been already proposed to him by Secretary Jenkins, but he "
conceiv'd it would be better (if the Parliament went to that) "
to break them, than to give him a Pardon, wch he conceiv'd "
would create as much tumult and disorder as the other ; and "
when the Duke replyd, It was a favour had scarce ever been "
refus'd any Minister and hoped it would not be denyd him ; "
the King nevertheless persisted in his resolution of not doing "
it, which gave his Highness but a melencolie apprehention
of what his future fate might be, when he Saw his enemys so
furious against him, those he tooke to be his friends so treacherously abandon him, and the King himself so unsteddy in his
resolutions of standing by him : This made him lay aside the "
thoughts of absconding for awhile about the Town to see "
how matters would go, which some had advised him too, "
and think it even necessary for his preservation to be gone "
haveing reason to believe it was his life they aim'd at now. "

However he did not so abandon himself to Providence as   The Duke's
to neglect all reasonable endeavours for his own support, he   discours to
ye King at
was always resign'd but never despair'd, so fail'd not at his   parteing.
parteing to represent to the King the danger his Majesty "   KingJam. M^{re}
Tom.8. p.179.
run in following the Councells of unsteddy, weak and "
treacherous men ; and forwarn'd him not only with the "
example of several of his predecessors, but particularly with "

TOME
II.

1680.

" that of the late King his Father ; that Zeal for Religion was
" the pretence now, just as it was then, but that the drift and
" designes of the Parties were the. same, and therefore not to
" credit those who were so ready to undertake for the good
" Success of such complyances they moved him too; which
" might perhaps put off the evil day, but would make it much
" more formidable when it came. He then fell upon what
" methods his enemys might probably take against him, as
" Impeachment, bill of Attainder, or Exclusion, that it was
" to guard him from the first he had desired a Pardon, because
" if once an Empeachment were lodged in the House of Lords,
" the Commons would certainly press his Majesty to issue out a
" Proclamation, for his apearance at such a day, which if he
" complyd not with, he should be declar'd a Traitor, and then
" if he dyd before his Majesty, his blond being tainted, his
" Children could not be restor'd but by Act of Parliament :
" The King sayd there was no danger of their takeing that
" method, but that if they did, he would never consent to any
" such Proclamation ; he sayd he would tell them, to make
" what Laws they pleas'd for security of Religion, where in he
" would concur, but not in the pursute of their malice against
" the Duke his Brother, and if they press'd hard upon him
" would certainly break them ; but he rather thought they
" would prosecute him by bill, and then he should have more
" time to fence against it, and let what will happen was

King Jam. M^{rs}
Tom.8. p.184.

" resolved (he sayd) never to consent to any unreasonable
" demande either in reference to him, the Militia, their time
" of sitting, or in fine any thing that lessen'd his power or
" prerogative.
" This resolution, the Duke Sayd, he was glad to hear, but
" still apprehended the same reasons and reasoners, who had
" prevail'd thus far might stretch out his Majesty's complyance
" even to yeildeing any of the points he mention'd ; that he

fear'd when his back was turn'd, there would be no one "
found, who would venter to advise resolute Councells, espe- "
cially haveing so fresh an example of his Majesty's mutability, "
in sending him away after haveing so positevely resolved the "
contrary; and lastely he enlarged upon what methods he "
thought necessary for the King's own preservation, where in "
he left nothing unsayd which was fit for a Loyal Subject and "
a most affectionate Brother to say. "

There was more reason for the Duke's endeavouring to fortify
the King in his good resolutions, seeing in what hands he left
him and what artes had been used to influence him, and which
would always be ready on the like occasions; he was now "
fully Satisfyd that those Ministers which formerly he took so "
much for his friends, were the very first projectors of this, and "
had consulted and layd the matter together with the Dutchess "
of Portsmouth, long before they acquainted the King with it; "
and to prepare him by degrees and bring him over to their "
opinion, represented his Majesty's condition to be much "
worse than in reality it was, that the heartes of the People "
were quite alienated from him, that the Fleet would abandon "
him, and that the very Guards themselves began to be "
poison'd, and could not be depended on. This was tould "
the King by each separately as if it were their single opinion, "
with which he was so terrifyd he could hould out no longer "
but at last agreed to send the Duke away. "

There is no doubt but the Dutchess of Portsmouth had "
made her conditions with My Lord Shaftsbury and the "
factious Partie; she had been Several times at London that "
Summer from Windsor, in one of which journeys she had a "
Conference with My Lord Howard of Escrike, which when "
the King tould her of, She sayd it was to bring him over, "
but it soon apear'd who was brought over by it, for besides "
her picking quarrels with The Dutchess that she was "

The continuance the Ministers had to bring the King to consent that the Duke should be sent away.

TOME
II.

1680.
"not So kind to her as formerly, nor shew'd her so much
"respect as to Mad⁰ Mazarine, she took likewise occasion to
"complain of the Duke, that dureing the King's late sickness
"he made her no offers of kindness, whereas in effect she
"could not but be Sencible it had been highly improper for
"him to have done it, had his Majesty's distemper been more
"dangerous than in reality it was: She knew very well (and
"so did those who caball'd with her) that the Duke never
"abandon'd his friends, in which they might have rested
"secure, had they been realy so; however both he and the
"Dutchess used all the artes they could to pleas her, but that
"not being the true cause of her disgust, such applications
"wrought no cure.

The Parliament meets.

The day after the Duke's departure bein the 21ᵗʰ of October,
the Parliament met. The King acquainted them in his Speech
of his haveing made Allyances with Spain and Holland, that
Tangier had been very expensive of late for which he demanded
a supply, that he would not have them meddle with the
Succession but was ready to concurr in any thing els for
security of * Religion, and therefore minded them to proceed
in the discovery of the Plot and the Tryalls of the five Lords
in the Tower.

The Bill of Exclusion brought in.

The Commons gave litle attention to what his Majesty proposed, but running quite counter to his directions fell immediately upon the Succession, and therefore what pass'd in the
House was of little moment till the 11 of November, when
they were ready with a Bill to exclude his Royal Highness
from the Throne and to make him incapable of inheriteing and
possessing the Crowne of England or Ireland, and that if he
ever clam'd or made any attempt to possess himself thereof,

**Letters
Vol. i. p.429.**

---

* The fact of Charles the second having abjured the Protestant Religion before
his Restoration, is stated by Rapin when noticing this Speech. — Editor.

or exercise any such power, Jurisdiction &c, that he should be deem'd a Traitor, and suffer as such ; that who soever should assist him in any such clame, or by word or writeing assert his haveing a Right, should incur the like guilt, that if he the said Duke of York should after the 5th day of November, 1680, enter into any of the said Dominions, or those who were aiding to him therein, shall be guilty of High treason and that neither he nor they should be capable of any pardon or *Noli prosequi* allowed, but that it should be lawfull for all Magistrates, Officers, or other Subjects to resist the said Duke of York if he attempt'd to return, and were thereby required to do it, and to apprehend or subdue him by force; but in the end (*they*) insert a proviso that this Act should not affect the next, or any other heire to the Crowne, who may succeed as if the Duke of York were dead, and then orders it to be read twice every year in all Churches and to be given in the Charge at every Assise or Session during the life of the Said Duke of York.

The Debate (*Oct*: 26.) concerning this Bill was so solemn and the case So extraordinary that it seems necessary to give an abstract of the particulars of it, not only for the honour of those who durst in opposition to all the terrours and threats of those violent men discharge their duty and conscience in the defence of justice, but also to shew how fury and malice hurryd men (otherwise of good partes and learning) to outface the common maximes of reason, justice, and Religion itself under pretence even of defending it.

My Lord Russell first open'd the matter by telling them that since they were assembled to consult and advise about the great affairs of the Kingdom, that he conceived none to be of greater consequence than the preservation of the King's life together with their Libertys and Religion, all which were in eminent danger from Popery, so that if the Parliament did not supress the growth of Popery, Popery would soon suppress it

T Ö M E
II.
———
1680.

and therefore moved they might begin with considering how to prevent that and a Popish Successor in the first place. ... ..

Sr Henry Capel seconds him and makes the Papists to have been the chief instruments of all that was ever done or happen'd amiss of late: It was their diabolical Councells, says he, that made war be declar'd with Holland that the Protestants might destroy each other, it was they brought division into the Fleet under Prince Rupert and General Monk with design to ruin it, and were the occasion of the Shipps being burnt at Chattam It was they set the City on fire and by their Councell those who were taken in the fact pass'd without tryal, and a Papist that confess'd he was one of them, was hang'd in hast, that the business might be huddled up; it was they caus'd the violation of the triple league, and sacrificed the King's honour by perswading him to make an Allyance with France, and to seize the Dutch Smirna Fleet before war was declared; that in Ireland the Papists contrary to Law wore armes, that in Scotland they had chang'd the Government, there being now a standing force and almost no Parliaments in that Kingdome; that the French Ambassador's frequency at Court look'd as if he were one of the King's Cabinet Council rather than a Minister of a forreign Prince, that the truth of all this appear'd by Colman's Letters, and that it was the hopes of the Duke's Accession to the Crown, that gave life and encouragement to these enormitys, and therefore it behouded them to prevent it. Severall other Members concured in chargeing all the misfortunes and mismanagements they could think on, upon the back of the Papists as the main authors of them, So that if it had not looked too * little the power of the Prophet Elias (which would have suted ill with a Religion they decryd at such

---

* Here the word *little* appears to have been inserted by the Secretary for that of *like.* " if it had not looked too *like* the power," &c. — EDITOR.

a rate) they would undoubtedly have charged them with the
irregularitys of the Season, as they did the Christians in the
primitive Church, and that they hinder'd the rain from falling,
or the Sund from shining upon the earth; and truly they might
as well have arraign'd them for governing the influnces of the
heavens, as that a handfull of men in no credit or imployment
(the Duke only excepted) should govern that of State; however
this pass'd for good and solid reasoning, and a sufficient argument to take into consideration how to prevent a Popish
Successor, preferable to all other business.

That point being therefore determined Coll: Titus stood up
and said, He had observed from the cours of the evidence concerning the Popish Plot, that it was the expectation of the
Duke's Accession to the Throne that had given life and encouragement to those designes, that it was not to be hoped, their
interest could be lessen'd while his expectancy stood, and
therefore moved that a Bill might be brought in to exclude
him. My Lord Russel sayd, There apear'd no other means to
prevent the certain miserys which would otherwise infallebly
fall upon the Nation; and Mr Harbord sayd, The Duke
influenced all Councells, as to Peace and War, forreign
Allyances and domestick affairs, that the meeting, sitting
and dissolveing of Parliaments depended on his pleasure, that
the prosecution of the Plot had been discouraged by him, and
that thō he bore a great respect to his person, he could not
think the King and Kingdom safe without his exclusion and
therefore press'd it might be brought in accordingly.

Mr Granvill then stood up, and agreed that the dangers
from Popery were great, but hoped however other means
might be found for their security than so extraordinary a
method; that the King had offer'd to agree to any other, provided it impeached not the Succession, so that to proceed upon
such a bill would disoblige the King and obstruct all other

business, which might be of ill consequence both at home and abroad; and therefore moved a bill might be brought in to banish Papists, and another for frequent Parliaments and good Magestrates, which he hoped would do the worke as well, and not proceed with severity against the Duke without hearing him in his own defence.

Sr Henry Capel sayd in answer to the first objection That it was no new thing for Parliaments to give advice contrary to the King's directions, that it was his great Council and could not be restrain'd; that there were precedents where Kings have had advice offer'd to them by the Parliament, which thō not gratefull at first, yet upon further consideration they have enter'd into and aproved of, as it happen'd, he sayd, in the case of the late tolleration, which at first the King declar'd he would not departe from yet afterwards thought fit to recall it: Coll: Titus, in answer to the expedient, sayd, That banishing the Papists without the Duke would signify nothing, that it would be in his power alone to do any thing when once he was on the throne, for that it had been found by sad experience that the strength of the Laws was not sufficient to defend them from Popish Tyrants, that no Prince of that Religion ever thought himself bound to keep faith with Hereticks.

Mr Hyde in opposition to this, sayd, He was concern'd for the honour of the House's equity, not to condemn a person without hearing him or any process against him, he questioned whether such a Bill would be binding, that he believed many Loyall persons as well as himself would be of that opinion, and so it might occasion a Civil War, the King, he sayd, might well out live the Duke, and why should they   * to prevent a thing they could never answer for? He did not

---

* Here some words seem to have been omitted, thō no vacant space was left in the MS. — EDITOR.

aprehend the cause was so desperate but that they might secure
themselves without overturning fundamentalls.

Sr Lyonell Jenkins seconds this and was of opinion let the danger be what it would, it was more eligible to try expedients than to run at first to so desperate a remedy as he tooke the bill to be, which was so manifestly against both Law and Conscience that nothing less than an Army could maintain it; he therefore moved for a tryal of expedients, and that it was time enough to proceed to extremity when all ordinary ways and means were found insufficient.

Mr Bennet in answer to this, wonder'd, he sayd, any one could doubt of the legality of such a proceeding; that the Legislative power was unlimited, that the Commons could offer what they thought proper to the Lords, and so to the King, and surely, says he, they want not a Law to make Laws. Nor can any Law be against the Laws they make; and as for the arguments from conscience, he slipp'd that over with a slight piece of sophistry too, that he saw no conscience against it, unless they were in conscience obliged to introduce Popery; the expedients he fear'd, when they came to be examined would be found insufficient, that no Law would bind Papists who never thought themselves obliged to keep either Law, word, or promis, to Protestants any longer than it was necessary to compass the cutting of their throats, and as for the danger of Civil Warrs, he fear'd it not, in favour of Idolatry, especially if they were once backed with a Law to defend the Protestant Religion.

This way of reasoning agreed not with Mr Seymour's sentiments, who thought it very unbecomeing the modesty of the House, to fall upon that which was the only thing the King had prohibited; he Saw no such danger of Popery as to have recours forthwith to so desperate a remedy, they were secure while the King lived; and the Duke's affection to the Nation, his love of justice and moderation, made it as litle to be

apprehended should he survive him : He had not only shewn
as great respect to Protestants as others, but as a marke of his
moderation, let his Children themselves to be bred up in that
Religion ; besides, he sayd, it would be so desperate an attempt
to offer at changing the Religion so well established by the
Laws, that it was highly improbable a Prince of his prudence
and wisdom should endeavour a thing so impossible to be
afected; that this Law, if made, would not be counted binding
by all in England, by few in Ireland, and none in Scotland;
which must needs occasion a fatal seperation and a Civil War
in the end ; it were to act on the papists' principles to dis-
enherit for Religion and by declaring that the ground of the
quarrell, engage all Catholick forraing Princes against them,
and by consequence require a standing Army for its support,
which would not only endanger the Religion but the Libertys
of the Kingdom much more than any Popish Successor or
King could doe.

. To this Sr William Jones replyd, That expedients in Politicks
was like Mountebank's tricks in Phisick which oftener doe hurt
than good, that a Government is too weighty a building to be
supported by pillars that have either flaw or crack, and he
fear'd no expedient would be free from them. He saw more
reason to apprehend their Religion and Liberty should they
not exclude the Duke than Civil War if they did, he gave it
for granted a Popish King would have a Popish Council,
Popish Judges, and Justices of Peace, Popish Commander at
Sea and land, and Popish Bishopps too; and since none even
now, have any imployments given them, but who are for a
Popish Successor, what an influence will a Popish King have!
and therefore inferr'd they must be very credulous and inconsiderate to trust their Religion and Liberty to the good will of a
Prince who will be in subjection to the Pope and influenced
by Priets and Jesuites ; he believ'd it would rather unite
Scotland and Ireland more strictly than occasion separation ;

that the major part of Scotland, and the Protestants of Ireland
hated Popery as much as they, and as for forraign Princes,
he sayd, by that bill, England would become more formidable
to their Enemys and usefull to their Allys; and lastely for the
conscientious part sayd the Duke was not excluded for his
Religion but for his incapacity of governing according to the
English Laws, which incapacity whether it proceed from
Religion or any other cause was all one to them.

These answers thŏ shallow and superficial, especialy in reference to the main objection of conscience arriseing from the
Oath of Allegiance which binds to the Successor without exception as much as to the present possessor, as also on account of
the Standing Law of the Land by which the Crown was always
declared to be Monarchical and hereditary, and that all Subjects by the force of natural Allegiance were tyd to the observance of it; however, faction and number overpower'd, and the
bill is brought in accordingly. After the first reading Sᵣ
Lyonel Jenkins stood up and sayd He thought it contrary to
nature, and justice, they should condemn any one not only
before conviction, but before the Partie is heard or witness
examined in his defence, and to doe this by a new Law, while
there arc old ones in force to punish that crime, he conceived to be extreamly severe and against the right of every
English man. 2ᵈˡʸ He sayd it was against the principles of the
Church of England to dispossess any man of his right because
he differs from it in faith, unless it were a doctrine universally
receiv'd; that Dominion is founded in grace, for his part, he
sayd, he thought there was more Popery in the Bill, than could
possibly be in the Nation without it, for none but Papists and
fift Monarchy men did ever go about to desinherit men for
their Religion, that the Kings of England have their right from
God alone, and no power on earth can deprive them of it. So
hoped that House would not go so manifestly against both the

Law of God and the Land too by changeing the Monarchy
and making the Crowne elective, for by the same reason that
this Parliament disinherits this Prince for Religion other
Parliaments may doe the like upon other pretences, and by
such exclusions elèct whom they please; in fine it was against
the Oath of Alegiance, he sayd, which they had all tàken in its
litteral sence without Jesuitical evasion, whereby they were
bound to the Duke as Presumptive Heire, and he knèw no
law could dispense them from it; and thō he was cautious in
disputing the power of Parliament, yet he was of opinion the
Parliament could not disinherite the Heire of the Crowne and
if Such an Act should pass it would be invalid in itself, and
therefore thought it his duty to oppose it.

Mr John Hampden replyd to the first That there were
precedents more than sufficient, of persons being condemned
by bill without being heard, that the government would be too
weake to subsist without such a power in the legislative
authority of the Nation. To the 2nd he answer'd, It (was)
manifest that the Papists aim was to introduce Superstition and
Idolatry togather with a forraign power, and that it was folly
to think the useing the only means for the preservation of their
Religion was inconsistant with the principles thereof. To the
3rd he sayd That nothing but the like cause could have the
like efect, and that since the Succession of the Crown had been
often changed and yet continued hereditary, why must it be fear
now? And to the last he sayd This Bill was no such unreasonable expedient, for that if the Dauphin of France or Infanta
of Spain, should become Protestant he doubted not but those
Kingdoms would be more impatient than we for this remedy.

These replys fell mightely short of giveing that satisfaction,
which sincere and judicious persons loked after, they saw no
such danger of Popery, as that this should be the onely means
to prevent it, or if there were, they agreed not to that principle

that it was lawfull to use any means whatsoever for the preservation of their Religion; for by that rule rebellion, murther, or
any other crime would be justifyd, if but conceived necessary
for that end, and so in efect abollish all Religion and
morality, under pretence of supporteing it: and thō men
of calmer spirites were ashamed of such horrid positions and
doctrine, yet nothing could bring the majority of the House to
their right witts in this matter, so long as the Phantom of
Popery hover'd in their imagination, So the bill was order'd to
be engross'd, and then Mr Vernon desired it might be read
again; upon which Sr Lyonel Jenkins repeated what he had
formerly Sayd, alledging there had never any direct answer
been made to it, and added It was a very hard case that the
Duke, who had so many excellent endowments which he had
imployd in the Service of the Nation and had venter'd his life
in fighting its battles, should be so used by those people he had
merited so well of. Mr Hide spoke much to the same effect,
and sayd The Duke had harder measure than the late King's
murtherers, who had fair tryalls and liberty to speak for
themselves: Upon which Sr William Hickman stood up for
the Bill, but first enumerated all the objections, as that it was
against natural justice to condemn a man unheard, and too
severe a judgment for so small a crime; 2dly that it was
against the Oath of Allegiance and the Principles of the
Protestant Religion, and by consequence would be a scandal
upon the Church; 3^{ly} that it would be void in it self and that
there would be a Loyal partie that would never obey it;
4^{ly} that it would make the Crowne elective and occasion a
Civil Warr; and Lastly that the proviso in favour of the
Duke's Children was not strong enough: As to the first, he
answer'd it by beginning (*begging*) the question, and supposeing
that the safety of the King and Kingdom depended upon
it, and therefore inferr'd, they were bound to preserve them

by rules of justice and Religion before any man's right or intrest whatever; to the Second, he admired, he sayd at such an objection, for he never heard the Oath of Allegiance pleaded in favour of Popery, nor ever conceived that Oath extended to a Successor during the King's life, and by consequence no dispensation was needed, and that it was no discredit to the Church to secure it self against Popery by all lawfull means: This gave as little satisfaction to the Duke's friends as the rest, for the Oath to be sure would oblige, when the case happen'd whether it did now or no, or otherwise the Swearing to a Successor are words that have no signification, and by pretending it was no dishonour to the Church to seek its security by all Lawfull means, was supposeing the means Lawfull, which was the point in question again; to the Therd and Forth, he Sayd It was a Strange argument to doubt whether the Legislative power of the Nation could make Laws to bind its Subjects, and therefore it could not be supposed, that any person would not acquiess to it; that it would rather be a means to avoid a Civil War by encourageing the Protestant Partie to stick together in defence of their Religion when it was backed by a Law. This answer was as unsatisfactory as the rest, for their being a Law already which enjoins the takeing of an Oath, which in itself is just and had been complyd with accordingly, what future Law made by men can absolve them from it? Nevertheless these answers pass'd current amongst the partie, and to make the fallacy of them less discernable, St Francis Winnington endeavours to cover them over with his usual flowers of eloquence, by telling them That these arguments against the Bill were only proper to lull them into a fatal negligence and security, as if it were needless or to no purpose to oppose Popery, that the great endeavours used thereby to reconcile the world to Popery made it more necessary to pass this Bill to obstruct it; the decay, he sayd,

of the Monarchy in its grandure, honour and reputation, the
destruction of the Navy in Sixty Six, the litle apearance of
being able to restore it to its former strength and splendour,
the doubble dealing of the Ministers in forreign Allyances in
order to keep up an intrest with France was all owing to their
machinations, that from being Umpire to this part of the
world we were grown the most despicable Nation in Europe,
that the Government was weakened no less by divisions and
debaucherys, than fears and Jealousies, that we most narowly
escaped ruin when the City of London was burnt, when the
Tolleration pass'd, when the Army was on Black Heath, and
lastly when the Popish Plot was discover'd ; so that nothing
stood betwixt them and utter destruction but the King's life,
all which dangers, says he, past and present, are oweing to
Popery, nor are there any hopes of their being less while there
is a Popish Successor: So I wonder, says he, any one can offer
such arguments against the Bill, since natural justice obliges us
to it for our own defence and self preservation, that it would
be of dangerous consequence to pretend the Oath of Allegiance
binds to the next Heire in case he should thing fit to rais
rebellion, nor was it a scandal to the Church to take care it be
not destroyd ; and therefore all these arguments, says he, weigh
nothing with me : the King indeed hath his right from God,
and can doe no wrong, but if we should give these qualifications
to a Successor it would make strange confusion ; a man, says he,
cannot have a greater clame to any thing than to life, and yet
upon forfeitures that is sometimes taken away for the publick
good ; the same may be sayd in reference to right too, when
the Prime Legislative thinks it necessary for securing the
Government, do's not the therteeth of Queen Elizabeth make
it treason to say that the Parliament cannot alter the Succession? And in Henry the eight's time were there not many
instances of it as well as in other reignes?

In fine the Duke's friends saw there was no possibility of driveing them from those groundless and ujust Suppositions, that all the ills that either had already happen'd or might possibly fall upon the Nation must be charged upon Popery, and that if the Duke suceed'd Popery must of necessity follow. at his heels, nor to make them distinguish betwixt what was due to an Heir during his expectancy and what they swear to observe when the Crown descends upon him ; for thō the Successor is not to be ranked with the present possessor, yet by the oath they were obliged to defend his right which now they went about to annull, and if ever he fortuned to succeed, then natural Allegiance and the Oath (thō formerly taken) would be binding to him then, as much as to the other now, and oppugne point blank the Law which now they labour'd so much to establish. It was true indeed (they owned) that life and Liberty might be taken away for the publick good, but that it was not lawfull to doe it without just cause and a fair tryall, and thō the Statute of Queen Elizabeth made it treason to say the Parliament cannot alter the Succession, yet that and such like precedents had been in soberer times looked upon as incroachments upon the Prerogative, and litle or no regard had to them, because the King held his Crown from God alone and therefore no power upon earth had authority to dispute it.

Their reply to the last objection was something more plausible, where it was urged that if the Duke had a Son hereafter, he would be excluded by the Bill ; but to that they answer'd, It would be as wne the King dys without issue, the next heir is proclaimed to prevent an interregnum, thō the Queen Mary possibly be with child, to whom the right in the first place do's belong. In fine all argument was to be resolved at last into Votes, and those being govern'd more by faction than reason, that Partie was sure of Victory, so the Bill pass'd accordingly.

However they would not so easily have carryd their point, hat they not used all mañer of artes to cleere the passage and leuel those rubbs they knew would obstruct it. Their craft and spite went hand in hand, and were of mutual assistance in perfecting their designs, they had shewn their utmost malice in contriveing and wording this Act, and did no less their cunning in prepareing the way for it. They had not only purged the House of many well affected Members for haveing discouraged Petitions in their respective Countrys, but struck such a terrour into all the rest by their houghty Votes, threats of being brought into the Plot and by sham informations, that many who desired to serve the King and wished well to the Duke durst not open their mouths in opposition to it. The Duke's haveing been so lately sent away in such manner, made many fall off too, they saw they must expect no quarter from the House if they concur'd not with it, and they dispair'd of being supported by the King if they were prosecuted by the Parliament; for who (thought they) could expect protection being the Duke found it not? This therefore made most men think of nothing but how to cover their own heads, and be passive at least in all those critical debates.

As soon as the Duke hear what had pass'd, he fail'd not to remind his Majesty of the ill consequence both in respect of himself, and his Successors, if he suffer'd the hereditary Monarchy to be made Elective, as also to permit honest men to be torn from him or terrifyd from their duty by the imperious treatment, pretended Plots, and malicious contrivances of his greatest Enemys, that new Villains apear'd every day who accused not only his friends in England, but in Ireland too, as the Duke of Ormonde, Lord Chancellor, and others; that if he gave way to this contrivance, it would run like wild fire, that besides the unjustice of letting innocent men

" The Duke's
" Sence there-
" upon.
" KING JAM. M^{rs}
" TOM: 9. p. 71.
"
" Ibid. p. 87.
"
"
"
"
"
"
"

T O M E
II.

1680.
KING JAM. M⁰
TOM. 9. p. 90.

". suffer, he would soon be destitute of all support if he sacri-
" ficed good men to appeas the fury of the ill. He again
" reminded him of the late King his Father's mistake in the
" like condesentions, and that since sooner or later he must
" make head against them, he better doe it while he had ground
" left to stand upon and friends to depend on, then when all
" was lost; that Scotland and Ireland were both firme to his
" intrest, and that there were many thousands yet in England
" who had not bow'd their knees to Baal, and by consequence,
" that there were still enough to stand by him, if he would stand
" by himself : He sayd not this (he assured him) that he doubted
" his Majesty's kindness and steadfatness in his resolution and
" promis in reference to himself, never to consent to any act
" that should exclude him, but only to press him not to loos
" any time, seeing his Enemys lost none, and to put some stop
" to these endless accusations of his best friends, who could
" alone secure his eas and happiness, and not depend upon
" finding it in a forced complyance with the disorderly

KING JAM. M⁰
TOM. 9. p. 93.

" pretentions of his Parliament, remembring in what manner
" they made good to the late King his Father that so oft
" repeated protestation, That they would make him the most
" glorious King in Christendom.

The King
sends to the
House, that
he will never
pass the Bill.

LETTERS
VOL. I. p. 400.

These remembrances were not lost upon the King, they
quicken'd his apprehentions and sollicitude and made him in
a message to the Commons repeat what he had sayd in his
speech concerning the Succession, which he tould them again
he was resolved never to alter ; this was not done So much out
of hopes to stop it, as to destroy a report (*that*) had been industriously spread abroad that the King in the bottom was consenting to the Bill.

It was on occasion of the King's proposing this message in
Council, that My Lord Halifax first manifested his zeal against

the Bill to his utter separation from the other partie ; and that
My Lord Sunderland and M⠂ Godolphin did as treacherously
desert the Duke's interest, and underhand countenance it as
much as they durst ; and therefore when the King declared
his resolution in Council likewise, to endeavour its being thrown
out at the first reading in the House of Lords, those two and
My Lord Essex opposed it, pretending that though it was not
reasonable the Bill should pass as it was, yet in the Commitee
it might perhaps be modifyd with limitations, and turn'd to a
temporary banishment or the like, and so much they thought
necessary to prevent an utter breach betwixt the King and the
Parliament ; whereas they well foresaw that if once it were but
lodged there, by addresses from the Lower House, petitions
from the City, publick clamours, and all manners of threats,
the Commons would be sure of Victory at last : but the King
was aware of their cunning and malicious contrivance, and
resolved to let it linger as litle as possible when once it came to
the Lords, and therefore he wen about himself to sollicite
against it, and tould amongst every Lord he met with, That
nothing could be more for his service and the public quiet than
to throw out the Bill at the very first reading.

It is not to be wonder'd it had soe quick a passage through
the Lower House where the Current runn with such violence,
nevertheless after it was ready it lay dormant there 4 or 5 days
because they thought the Lords were not sufficiently prepared for
it ; during which time the factious Members endeavour'd to terrify
them and the King himself, with Addresses from the Common
Council, and the House of Commons's answer to his Majesty's
message, but most particularly with continual allarmes sent up
to the Lords of new discoverys, and terrible treasons, all which
reflected on the Duke and his friends ; and just before the Bill
was brought up, in comes two Lords and acquaints the rest,
There was a man at the door had the most desperate treason to

T O M E
II.
1680.

The Commons
delay sending
up the Bill, till
the Lords were
prepared for it.
LETTERS
Vol. I. p. 437.

LETTERS
Vol. I. h. 454.

TOME
II.

1680.
Dangerfeild
accuses the
Duke before
the Lords.

revail that ever was heard within those walls; who being order'd to come in proved to be Mr Dangerfeild, a face they were not unacquainted with, nevertheless he impudently accused the Duke, that he had proposed to him to kill the King, and to the end this accusation might strick more terrour into the Duke's friends, he sayd My Lord Peterborough was present and that My Lord Privie Seal was acquainted with it.

LETTERS
VOL.I. p.387.

They had made use of the same stratagem in the House of Commons when the Bill was first brought in there too, where Dugdale arraign'd the Duke most dreadfully, and one Francisco Peris sayd he had been hired to kill My Lord Shaftsbury, Oates &c : Dangerfeild also gave in then the same information against the Duke he now repeated, but that House needed not such provocatives to swallow the Bill, they did it but too greedely of themselves, wherefore his evidence was scal'd up for a more pressing occasion, and now made use of for a vehicle to the House of Lords, whose stomacks were found to be much more squemish upon the point.

They thought
to lesten the
Votes for the
Duke, by accu-
sing his friends.

Their main designe in this, was by accusing the Duke's friends to cause their being order'd at least to withdraw while the Bill was debateing, and by that means deprive him of so many Votes, and to stricke terrour into others, which effect he (it) had upon My Lord Privy Seal, who being otherwise well affected to the Duke, however gave his voice for the Bill; but My Lord Peterborough sayd so much in his vindication (particularly that this very man had accus'd him formerly before the King and Council of an other fact, and then sayd he had

LETTERS
VOL.I. p.440.

no more against him) that the Lords thought it not proper so much as to commit him ; whereas had this stratagem succeeded, others would have been accused, no matter of what, so it had but suspended their sitting till the worke had been done.

The Bill is
carryd up to
the Lords.
Ibid. 402.

This debate being rather suspended than finished, the Bill of Exclusion (which had been presented by My Lord Russel just after Dangerfeild had given in his evidence) came upon the stage, that Lord it seems had gotten it into his hands, and though many of the Commons opposed his going up with it then, as not thinking the House of Lords sufficiently prepared, however his impetuous temper and exceeding ardour on this occasion hurryd him on with such violence, that he run away with it in spight of all opposition; so when they could not withould him, a great number of Members accompanyd him and it, and as soon as it was deliver'd, gave a mighty shout, which tumultous and barberous way of proceeding, had too great a ressemblance of forty one, not to convince all judicious persons, that this would prove a prelude of the Same Tragedie if not timely prevented: Of which the King himself became so sencible, that it was none of the least motives to his firmness in the matter, not only to break their force at the first attack, but because he saw the more aversion they shew'd to the Duke, the less reason they had to attempt any thing against his own person, so long as the Duke was to succeed him; by which means his Royal Highness whom the Parliament would have made pass for the man in the world that gave most encourage-ment to Plots against the King's life, the King on the other hand, look'd upon him, as his principal Bulwark and security against any desperate attempt of that nature, which soon after apear'd to be no vain aprehension.

And now it was come up to the House of Lords, before they enter'd upon it, great artifice was used by the malignant partie to prolong the debate about My Lord Peterborough, that the Bill might be put off till next morning, and in the mean time by terrours and perswasions they hoped to draw many persons to their side; but the Duke's friends aprehended nothing so much as delay, so press'd vehemently, and at last prevail'd to have its fate tryd off hand. Assoon as the Bill was once read, the House turn'd into a Committee which lasted till nine at

It is cast up by the Lords.

LETTERS VOL.I. p.442.

T O M E
II.

1680.

night : it is not possible to represent with what fierceness and malice the one side press'd it, and with what eloquence and learning the other opposed it, it was on this occasion that My Lord Halifax distinguished himself no less for his great capacity and ready wit, than his zeal and Loyalty; he answer'd most fully and off hand all that Shaftsbury and Essex had studyd and concerted together, and spoke no less than fifteen or sixteen times for his share; the rest of the Duke's friends were not wanting to their duty neither, so that after the most solemn debate that ever had been heard in that noble assembly, the question was put Whether the Bill should be rejected or no? and it pass'd in the affirmative by a majority of thirty three voices.

This signal Victory gave great life and vigour to his Royal Highness's cause, it layd open many darke purposes and made colours more distinguishable than hithertoo they had been; it shew'd some people's Loyalty who had been till then suspected, and made a plain discovery of those ill designes which others had long smother'd under pretence of friendshipps, amongst which My Lord Sunderland manifested the corruption of his heart which he had hitherto plastered over with fawning pretentions of duty and affection, but no one was more displeas'd and surprised than the King at this Lord's voteing for the Bill, and sayd he would soon tell him his mind upon it.

They propose
the King being
divorced.

LETTERS
VOL. I. p. 443.

But though the wether clear'd up little there were still heavy clouds flying about; for no sooner was the Bill rejected, but the Lords go upon means for securing Religion, and such was their aprehension on that head, that those methods which were counted moderate would in a manner have wrought the Duke's ruin as effectually, as those they had rejected: and My Lord Halifax who had so signalized himself against the Bill of Exclusion, immediatly proposed one of banishment, and that for life too; but in this conjuncture the malice of his Royal

T O M E
II.
1680.

Highness' enemys was more beneficial to him, than the mistaken good will of his friends, for the factious partie by good fortune being no ways satisfyd with what would have been as fatal to the Duke, and which probably might have pass'd, as men were then hayr'd and frighted out of their senses; but by aimeing at something still more extravagant, threw them upon methods which the King would never agree too, which in the end proved the Duke's chiefe preservative: for My Lord Shaftsbury laughing at this proposal as a thing that could never hould (and perhaps that was My Lord Halifax his thought too) said being the Bill was rejected, there remain'd no other means, but to have the Queen divorced and the King to marry a Protestant W$_i$f$_e$; which extravagance, though seconded by many, the King shew'd so much horrour of, that he went himself from man to man as he had done the day before in reference to the Duke, that he might if possible stifle this wicked project in its birth too.

The Commons areashtonished at the news of the Bill's being cast out.
LETTERS
VOL. I. p. 423.

The news of the Bill's being rejected struck the Commons like thunder, and as men in that condition, they remain'd for some time without motion ; till at last Sr John Hotham proposed their adjourning to the next day, which was agreed too as necessary after such a Blow to recolect their spirites and recover their strength, and to come to some resolution what was now to be done : This method was something particular, for what place could be so proper to regulate matters as where they then sat? but they made no scrupule of publishing by this means to the world, that House itself was not be trusted with their projects till they had been concerted and model'd in private Caballs, and then brought thither to be pass'd only for method and order sake, by which means they devolved the government not only from the King to the Parliament, but from the Parliament it self to the Sunn Taverne and King's head Clubbs.

T O M E
II.

1680.
The Commons
refuse Succors
for Tangier.
LETTERS
VOL. I. p.469.
Ibid. p.470.

·The next day which was the 17th of November had being appointed by order of the House to consider his Majesty's Speech in reference to Tangier; that place of late had been extreamly press'd by the Moors, they had taken several out workes though after a most vigorous resistance particularly at Charles's fort where Cap: Jones made a long defence, and when it was quite undermined he with his small garrison cut their way thorough the besiegers to the Town, from whence by a generall Sally in October following they had repuls'd the Enemy, killing above 500 of them, took two cannons, five colors, and several prisoners, and fill'd up their trenches, but was now so weaken'd with continual attacks that without Supplys of all sortes, it would be impossible to hould it out any longer.

LETTERS
VOL. I. p.470.

This was fully represented, but made litle impression upon them, they could think, nor talke, of nothing but Popery; which they pretended hung so dreadfully over their heads ; it obsessed them like a specter, and wherever they turn'd their eys they fancy'd it stared them in the face ; so that, though one would have thought Tangier had little relation to Religion or the Duke's Succession, however they wrest all to that, and presently cry out, It was a nursery not only for Popish Soldiers, but for Priests and Religious too of that perswasion, and that there had been sometimes a Popish Governor of the place, so that to succour it was but to augment, they Sayd, their present evils ; and declar'd in fine against giveing mony either on that, or any other account till they knew what they were to have for it; and till there was a thorough change from one end of the State to the other ; mony, they sayd, was like food to the Stomack which if in health turns to nurrishement, but if out of order breeds more ill humours : in fine such was their fury against the Duke, and rage for this disapointment, that no bitter or extravagant thing was left unsayd. My Lord Russell amongst the rest, declared That if his own Father had been against the

Bill he would have voted him an Enemy to the King and
Kingdom, and that if he could not live a Protestant he was
resolved to dye one at least. Mr Lenson Gower sayd Some
men perhaps will endeavour to make their peace with the Duke,
but I will perish first; wherefore my opinion is we should
breake up, and each man return to his Country and let the
People see how we are used, and I doubt not but they will
soon join with us, their swords in their hands, and hen we'l let
the Duke know we defy him, and all his Popish adherents.

These unmannerly threats the Duke knew how to dispise,
but the King could not so easily recompose himself and his
affaires, when instead of Supplys he got nothing but representation, and addresses (which they plyd him with at this time)
and instead of succours for Tangier was threaten'd with a
Rebelion.

There had indeed one argument been made use of against
the Bill of Exclusion by My Lord Halifax, which gave a handle
to these factious men to highten the aprehensions of danger,
and served them particularly for a pretence against the relieving
Tangier; it had been urged by that Lord, how imprudent it
would be to declare the Duke an enemy to the State, who was
actually at the head of a powerfull Nation, where there was an
Army too; that in Ireland his power was no less considerable
where there was 10, or 15 Papists for one Protestant, that he
had great interest in the Fleet and credit with the English
Troops, all which Mr Hampden repeating sayd, And if we ad
to that, his being Admiral of Tangier too, surely there is good
reason to supply that place? The Court Partie thought to have
moderated this heat by assureing them the King would concur
in any other methods for secureing Religion; but they replyd
all other methods would be of no force when once a Popish
Prince was in possession of the Throne, because the King's
example had always influenced the Nation to a complyance.

TOME
II.
1680.

LETTERS
VOL. I. p. 472.

Ibid. p. 469.

Ibid. p. 512.

TOME
II.

1680.

When Henry the 8ᵗʰ says Mʳ Titus, was for the Supremacy, the Kingdom was for it, when he was against it, the Kingdom was so too. When King Edward the 6ᵗʰ was a Protestant, the Kingdom was Protestant. When Queen Mary came to the Crowne, it was Papist again: And when Queen Elizabeth succeeded her, her Religion succeeded too, and so gave it for granted should a Papist Prince come to the Crown, Popery would come along with him: This carryd some apearance of reason which served to raise people's aprehentions, who consider'd not the different circomstances of those times, and the temper and power of Princes in those days; the Protestant Religion was then new, and though the liberty it encouraged made many embrace it, yet in Queen Mary's time the memory of what they had been was not So entirely forgot, but that by the example and authority of the Prince they were easily brought back again; whereas now after a long settlement of a Religion which had layd aside all those hard points of Doctrine, either as to faith or practice, which the Church of Rome obliges too, it was not reasonable to presume the people would be so susceptible of a change, and return to a Religion which besides its opposition to their liberty, they were so prejudiced against by Education, as to look upon it with detestation and horrour.

They fall upon the Duke's friends.

LETTERS Vol.I. p.474.

LETTERS Vol.I. p.404.

In this confusion of speeches and reasoning, thō they could not come to a resolution how to renew their assaults against the Duke, however to shew they would have no peace with him, they fall upon those who had lately espous'd his intrest or had not at least so heartely concurr'd with them as they expected; upon this score they impeach Sʳ Edward Seymour for misaplying 600000ᵗ given for building 30 shipps, and vote an adress to the King for removeing My Lord Halifax from his presence and Council, their pretence was for haveing advised the late dissolution, and thō Sunderland and Godolphin had

un equal share with him there in, their late behaviour had
washed them clean, so no notice was had of them in their
address. The Lord Chief Justice Scroggs too, thō formerly so
usefull a servant in the prosecution of the Plot, is now fallen
under their displeasure, because he had discharged the Grand
Jury in June before, some 4 or 5 days sooner than usual,
whereby he prevented an intended presentement against the
Duke which otherwise would have been ready before the end
of the terme; so they voted him an obstructer of publick
justice, a violator of his oath, and of the fundamental Laws of
the Kingdom ; in fine whatever had an apearance of a fault,
if it was done in favour of the Duke it was mortall in their
eyes : But Sr Edward Seymour with his dexterity and eloquence
warded the blow aim'd at him, and My Lord Halifax though
he offerr'd to withdraw, the King would not suffer it, but his
Majesty was forced to yield up Scroggs so far at least to their
malice, as to discharge him from his imployment, but recom-
penced it afterwards with a pention.

By this time they had rowl'd many different projects in their
heads but found none so effectual as their beloved Bill of
Exclusion, so they labour'd mightely to procure a short
prorogation, and then to bring it in a new; but the King was too
well satisfyd with haveing thus broaken their measures to put
them in a way of peiceing them again ; however to keep up
their odium against the Duke till they were ready for a new
attack, great encouragement was given for witnesses to come
in against him, whereupon one Lewis deposed, That Mis
Celier had engaged him to burn the Shipps at Chattam, that
the French were then to land, that he was to have been join'd
with Gowe in endeavouring to kill the King, and that for all
this and several other services of the like nature he was assured,
the Duke would both stand by him and be his paymaster ; one
Zeile apear'd also who concurr'd in this evidence, upon which

They bring
new accu-
sations against
the Duke con-
cerning the
Plot.

LETTERS
Vol.I. p.500.

LETTERS
Vol.I. p.472.

T O M E
II.
1680.

They dispute about wording the pardon for the wittnesses.
LETTERS VOL:I. p.474.

the Attorney General indicted M^{ia} Celier of high treason : Thus they layd about them on all hands, hopeing by some of these random Strokes to reach his Royal Highness' head at last.

It was the practice of the House of Commons upon the first apearance of any witness, to adress the King for a pardon and maintenance for him; which being done for these two, the King tould them by M^r. Secretary Jenkins, that he would grant them pardons for all crimes, perjury excepted; but the House was not satisfyd with this, and their reason was pretty odd; the witnesses, they sayd, were sworne allways to Say the whole truth, whereas it might not be proper for them at certain times to tell all they knew, and by that means might be lyable to be perjured, so they persisted in their Sollicitation that the Pardons might be for perjury too, but this Scurvy reason was not likely to make his Majesty change his resolution, tho the Attorney General who was to draw them was forced to strecth his authority in another point, to give the House Some satisfaction in this matter.

LETTERS VOL:I. p.493.

It seems he had been complain'd of for not drawing Dangerfeild's pardon full enough, and feareing he might incur the same fault again, came to Lewis and asked him, Whether he was guilty of any other crimes, than what was mentioned in the King's warrant, which was for treasons, misprisions, felonys, outlarys &c. To which he conscientiously answer'd, good man, that he was guilty of forgery too, which it Seems was not express'd there, So care was taken to have it inserted and then all was right; for it matter'd not how wicked they were, or had been, provided they were but made legal witnesses, and that their past Vilanys might not hinder them from committing more.

The Commons present an Address.

By this time the Commons were ready with an Address they had been long meditateing, and on the 29^h of November present it accordingly; which, to fill the people with terrour, and support the credit of the Plot, contain'd a narrative of the whole fiction, which they represented as a cloud that still hung over their heads and threaten the Land with a storme of ruine and confusion ; the Papists are there Sayd (as was usual) to be the chiefe influencers of all Councells in reference to the State and Government, that all imployments Civil and Military in Court or Country were disposed of at their discretion, that they either corrupted all who had any hand in the Administration of affairs, or destroyd whom they could not corrupt, that they had credit enough to make Parliaments be prorogued at pleasure, and to aply the mony given by it to what uses they thought fit, that their credit and interest was such, as to be able to attempt any change in the Religion, or Government ; in fine that there was no design they were not able to execute, nor any wickedness they were not ready to performe, So that no security could possibly be hoped for, but by preventing the Succession of the Duke to the Crown ; and they further prayd that none but persons of known fidelity, and true Protestants might be put into imployments, and then his Majesty might expect supplys for Tangier, and other occasions, when they can be assured, their aids shall not be imployd to strenghten their Popish adversarys, and encreas their present dangers.

T O M E
II.

1680.
LETTERS
VOL. I. p. 517.

In future times it will not be credited that so numerous an assembly of persons chozen for their wisdom and abilitys to compose the representitive of the People of England, could either have believed such follys, or have the confidence to impose upon the world that they did, as to think that a handfull of men, not makeing by computation the hundreth part of the Nation, under the oppression of severe Laws, kept out of all imployments, and at this time persecuted, imprisoned, and even many put to death, should be able to strike such terrour into the whole Kingdom, that all attention of affairs both forreign and domestick must ceas and ly unregarded, till some means

The Duke's friends terrifyd with the violent proceedings against him.

T O M E
II.

1680.

LETTERS
Vol:I. p.433.

The Duke's
friends
renew their be found to secure them from this pretended mountain's falling upon their heads.

But all this Cant was througly understood, the Duke alone was the person they fear'd, and for him alone was this Storme raised, all their severitys to others were but so many platformes to rais their batteries against him, which now again struck such terrour into his Highness' greatest friends, that they trembled with aprehention what the consequence might be, and seeing no other resource, recur to their old sollicitations in reference to Religion, which upon this occasion they press'd him with, more violently then ever; but to introduce it gently, began with adviseing him to moderation upon the throwing out of the Bill, that his enemys being numerous it would be dangerous to add dispair to their malice, that it had been a common artifice in that partie; to make those who had voted against him believe, that haveing now drawne their swords they must cast their scabords away, that he was an implacable man and would give no quarter, they assured him many were brought in by a real terrour of Popery, and the dradfull rumours that the Religion and Government were on the brink of ruin; that such men might be brought back with clemency and moderation, and by convincing the world in spight of their malice, that his Royal Highness could forgive, and that the Religion and Government had nothing to fear from him.

All this the Duke heartely concurr'd in, and never Prince gave greater testimonys of moderation in Success, or of magnanimity in suffring; but when his friends renew'd their assault in point of Religion it was grievous to him beyond expression, yet in that too his temper failed him not, he knew how to distinguish the motine from their advice, and their good will from their arguments.

They represented to him therefore the weak condition the Government was in, the confusion, terrour and aprehentions.

people were come too by this pretended Plot, and which had T O M E II.
life (they said) only from his Highnesse's Religion, that .the
King being straighten'd for mony and the Parliament refrac- 1680. solicitations about Religion. LETTERS VOL.1: p.405.
tory, he would be in strange agonies how to supply, his neces-
sitys, and preserve his prerogative, and most especially his
Highness's pretentions, the Duke of Monmouth haveing gain'd
many about the King; that the factious partie would certainly
break upon his Highness's friends, who yet indeed supported
the King in his vigorous Councells, but by impeachments or
accusations would soon be removed both from Court and
Councills, and then there would be no hopes to prevent all
from going to ruin, unless the Duke were present to assist his
Majesty with his advice, strengthen his resolutions, and support
his own creatures; that it would be impossible for his friends
to helpe him long, if he did not helpe himself: So that as his
Highness's Religion was the ground of all the fears and aprehentions the Nation was in, and origin of all the present
troubles; so it kept him at a distance from his Majesty, who in
the end would infallibly give way to the torrent, for want of
his support and assistance; they tould him it was impossible
the Popish Religion could ever take footing again in England, LETTERS VOL.I. p.418.
that if it did, it must be cemented in blood, and therefore
thō they know him to be too generous to be moved to change Ibid: pag. 637.
through fear, or his owne misfortune, they begg'd of him
however, that the King's safety at least, the wellfare of the three
Kingdoms, might have a share in his considerations; they
threaten'd him with dangers from abroad if the French should
invade Flanders, in how ill condition the King would be to
contest matters with the Parliament; that all measures of
parsimony and frugality would soon be broke, for want of his
presence to support the King in those resolutions, whereby his
Majesty would infallebly be delivered up into the power and
disposition of the House of Commons, who would only relieve

his necessities ; that thō the Bill was cast out, yet the revival of it was vehemently contended for by all sortes of people, and his Highness loaded with all the ills that have either hithertoo happen'd, or can possebly befall the Nation, that one way or other his ruin was inevitable, which would not only affect himself, but his Children too, for that the same power and interest which prevail'd to determin who should not reigne, will soon say who shall, and they would never think themselves secure under the Government of those, whose Father they have excluded. They tould him it was resolved to have all his friends removed from Court, and his revenue seized, so that he would be reduced to the faint assistance of some forreign Prince : in fine that the King had done and sufferr'd so much he would at last be forced to new resolutions. This, his greatest friends assured him was the true State of his case, and that their was no remedy under the Sun but to embrace the Protestant Religion, from which he had unhappily departed, that his Highness was not a private person, nor by consequence. tyd up to the strickt rules that obliges others; that the publick clamed share in his resolution, and that if ever it were Lawfull to depart from an opinion, thō never so good, this was the time, not only for his own sake but his Majestys who lay under such intollerable pressures, for the people's. sakes, for the preventing the efusion of so much blood, which his perseverance in the Religion he was in, would be the inevitable cause of, for the sake of his Children that they may not be deprived of their right, and for his Dear Dutchesse's sake, whose. qualifications as well as her right had destined to a Throne, and lastly for the sake of Monarchy and the three Kingdoms which could not be preserved from utter ruin by any other means upon earth.

It was not possible to say more to shake his constancy ; and yet to give a greater force to their argument, they used the,

same litle artes to draw the Duke from his Religion, which his
enemys used to draw the King from supporting him, for as they (to terrify his Majesty the more) were accustomed to tell him seperately each one the same thing, as if they had concerted it together, so the Duke's friends to make the greatest impression, represent all these dangers each as from himself, assureing him that as his return to the Protestant Religion would make all those troubles and persecutions drope like an autumnal leaf, so without it, he must infallebly expect all the calamitys they had painted out in such dreadfull colours, must fall upon him, the King, and the people.

Nothing could be more dismal to his Royal Highness than such representations not only of his own dangers, but the King's uneasiness and hard circomstances, the suffrings of the Catholicks, and confusion the Nation was in; and that all this should be charged to his account, not only by his enemys but his friends too, that if this was the fruite of his late Success and Victory over the Bill, what must be expect when thing went cross: however all they could Say, and more if it had been possible, was not capable of casting the least mist before his eys, or staggering him in any kind, either in reference to his faith, or former resolutions.

He tooke the pains to write a long letter from Edinbourg in answer to this arguments and solicitations. He was in hopes, " he sayd, never to have been press'd again to that, which he " was sure he never gave the least reason to believe he should " be brought too, that by the Grace of God he hoped to live "' and dye a true Sonn of the Catholick Church, and to suffer " with Christian patience whatever might be fall him on that " account, that it would be too long for a letter to lay before " them the reasons and motives of his Conversion, so would " content himself with representing the manner only, and to " let them see it was not done hastely nor was it the efect of a "

" Childish immagination, or the fruite of perswasion when he
" lived in Catholick Countrys, never any one (as he had tould
" them before) speaking to him of that, during his banishment,
" but a Nunn, and that in efect was only to desire him to begg
" of Almighty God to direct him, but that on the contrary he
" (*had been*) thoroughly instructed in the tenets of the Church
" of England by D^r. Stuard, and so zealous therein, as to be
" fully as instrumental as any one to have the Duke of Glocester
" brought away from the Queen his Mother, for fear of his
" being influenced by her in that point; that the first origin of
" his doubts proceed'd from a treaty which a learned Bishopp
" of the Church of England had writ, and desired him to read
" while he was in Flanders ; the drift of which was to clear
" the Church of England from the guilt of Schisme by sepa-
" rateing from the Church of Rome, which being the first
" writeing he had ever read of that kind, instead of confirmeing
" him in that beliefe had quite the contrary efect, especially
" after he had seen the answer to it, which that Bishopp likewise
" recommended to him : this made him more inquisitive after
" the grounds and manner of the Reformation, so he read
" all the Historys he could relateing to that Subject, and thō
" at that time he confess'd he lived not so regularly as he ought,
" yet had some good intervals which he employd that way;
" that after his return to England, D^r. Heylin's History of the
" Reformation and the preface of Hooker's Ecclesiastical Policy
" thoroughly convinced him that neither the Church of England,
" nor Calvin, or any of the Reformers, had power to do what
" they did, and he was confident, he sayd, that whosoever reads
" those two books with attention, and without prejudice, would
" be of the same opinion : nevertheless he rested not satisfyd
" there, but made all immaginable enquiry into that matter,
" not only by reading but by discours with several learned
" Bishopps, not forgetting the danger and persecution it would

inevitably draw upon him; when once it should be known; "
but that being fully convinced he could resist no longer, so "
in the year 1672, before he went to Sea, he withdrew from "
the Communion of the Church of England, yet for some "
time continued to wait upon the King to Cheppel ; that even "
then such was the aprehention of his best friends before the "
thing was known publickly, that the Duke of Ormonde, "
Secretary Coventry, and several others, perswaded him to "
withdraw before the meeting of the Parliament, as not thinking "
it possible for him to stand the shock and fury of that Assem- "
bly ; by which it apear'd he was sufficiently forwarded of the "
danger before he exposed himself to it, but thanked God it "
had no efect upon him, so as to draw him from his duty, on "
the contrary that he layd down all his Commissions rather "
than take the Test, and prepared himself for the storme which "
he saw comeing upon him, and had felt sufficiently ever "
since : so it could not be denyd (he hoped), but that his "
Conversion was sincere and puerely for the sake of Truth, "
since he had all the temporal discouragements immaginable, "
which by the grace of God he was resolved to suffer with "
patience, let the malice and machinations of his enemys run "
to what exess it would.

Haveing given this short account of his Conversion, he
thought it necessary to answer the other motives they press'd
him with, as the great advantage it would be to the King's
affairs should he return to the Protestant Church ; his "
Majestys eas (he sayd) and well fare was ever more dear to "
him than his own, and in an other case would have been a "
more powerfull argument than self preservation ; but besides, "
that no hearthly consideration could ballance that of "
Eternity, he did not perceive (he sayd) as the Case now "
stood, that changing his Religion would have any such efect "
as they proposed ; all the world, says he, sees that it is not "

T O M E
II.
1680.

His answer to
their reasons
of State.

KING JAM: M⁷ˢ
TOM. 8. p. 205.

" Religion they drive at so much as the destruction of
" Monarchy, and if this handle were taken away an other would
" soon be found ; besides, if he should conforme they would say
" it was by vertue of dispensation, and so immagin him a more
" dangerous enemie, for by entring into all his imployments,
" they would fancy his power greater and his will the same to
" do mischief: that by the helpe of negligent Protestants, and
" Papists in Masquerade, nothing would be impossible for him
" to bring about, and from thence would ground a pretence
" of haveing more concessions for their security, and ty up his
" Majesty's hands straighter than ever now they aim'd at, and
" whoever opposed them would immediately be branded as
" one of that number, which by consequence would forward
" rather than retard their design of bringing the Nation to a
" Common wealth; that the King therefore would reap no
" advantage by it, as he did no disadvantage by his being a
" Catholick, it hinder'd not those who were truly Loyall from
" continuing so, and those who were for changing the Govern-
" ment, no change but that would content them. He owned,
" that his absence from the King might make things go wors,
" but saw no reason why he should be kept from him, haveing
" done nothing to deserve such a punishment ; that it argued a
" great weakness in the Government not to be able to protect
" the Inocent, and that such a procedure was a great dishearte-
" ning to Loyall men, as well as a great concurrance to the
" aims of trecherous ones *, who haveing begun with him
" would end with the King, to court a popular intrest, and to
" have the reputation of being heads of the Protestant Religion,
" thō they have none at all ; he thought it hard he should be
" sacrificed to make those men's fortunes, who had done him
" all the mischief they could in this world, and were angry he
" would not abandon the hopes of being happy in the next too,
" to be capable of returneing to Court only to be their Slave

to forward their designes, and establish their greatness; he ”
should be as ready, (he sayd) as ever to venter his life for ”
his King and Country's Service, but could not make his ”
Majesty the same compliment which D^r. Oates did, that he ”
had venter'd his life for him at Sea, and his soul for him at ”
Land : He desired them therefore to be carefull especially in ”
discours with the King, not to agrave this point by laying all ”
the present disorders to the Duke's Religion, for that it ”
would be a means to ruin him entirely with his Majesty, it ”
was enough that his enemys made use of this argument for ”
his destruction, he hoped his friends would not do it too ; ”
it was not, he sayd, so much from his Religion that those ”
mischiefs sprung, as from mutability in Councells and want ”
of steddy resolutions ; for that notwithstanding the great ”
terrour some Statesmen were lately in, affermeing there would ”
certainly be a rebellion if the Duke returned from Flanders, ”
yet how was he receiv'd both times ? and in his journey to ”
Scotland treated with all immaginable respect ? that at his ”
last return to England things were more quiet than ever, and ”
if the same Councells had been pursued might have continued ”
so still, for at that time almost all the Countrys shew'd their ”
detestation of the late rebellious proceedings, and rejected ”
the petitions both in City and Country for the Parliament's ”
sitting, thō the Lord Major Clayton was deficient in his duty ”
in that point ; so that it was not his presence at Court that ”
rais'd this storme, but his being sent away that heartened ”
the King's enemys when they found him quit ground, whose ”
spirites were broken and dejected with his presence ; and ”
therefore thought it highly unreasonable that he must bear ”
the burthen which ought to be layd upon other men's ”
shoulders; but his condition, he sayd, put him in mind of ”
the publick odium Cardinal Mazarin lay under when he lived ”
in France, what ever went amis was layd at his door, if a ”

" hors did but stumble they would cry out, LE DIABLE DE
" MAZARIN; in fine he begg'd of them to press him no more
" with those arguments which he had clearly proved were not
" the real causes of the present evills, nor to teaz him to do
" what his conscience would never allow of, desireing them
" rather to use their skill and Rethorick in his defence, than
" to possess his Majesty with an opinion that all would do well
" if he were a Protestant, or make the King believe it is the
" Duke's stubborness that brings all those troubles upon him,
" which in reality were owing to the irresolution and
" unsteadyness of those Councells he ever endeavour'd to fix
" with all his credit, when he was in a station to do it; and
" that thō he be the only person that feels the smart of that ill
" conduct at present, his Majesty in the end would find
" himself too affected by them, and be convinced that those
" methods ever have and ever will be pernitious to his
" interest.

The Duke is
presented
again for
recusancy,
the Bill of
Limitation
and Articles of
treason framed
against him.

Though his Royal Highness thus sollidly and judiciously
defended himself against the arguments of his friends, it
hinder'd him not from lying as much open as ever to the assault
of his enemys who were as insatiable in their malice as inde-
fatigable in the pursuite of it; The Chief Justice Scroggs had
eluded one process where his Royal Highness was presented
for being a Papist (for which that Judge had been call'd to an

LETTERS
VOL.I. p.531.

account by the House of Commons) so to repair that, the
Grand Jury of Westminster was directed to present him again,
which thō it could have no immediate effect, was a preparatory
to an Impeachment, and in the mean time the Bill of Limitation

LETTERS
VOL.I. p.553.

was brought into the House of Lords, into which certain clauses
wer put no (less) prejudicialle to him, than what had lately
been rejected; as that in case of the Duke's accession to the
Crown, the whole power of Government should be vested in a
Council of 41, that all forreign treatys and negociations should

be transacted by Commissioners taken out of the said Council, that Ireland should be governed by it also, and that it should have power to fill up all vacancys, or remove any out of their imployments, subject nevertheless to the disalowance or aprobation of the Parliament, which when sitting, was to exercise all this authority which was granted to others only dureing the intervalls of their Sessions; that the Duke of Yorke was to be banished during the King's life, to some place five hundrd miles from England, to forfeit his revenue if he came nearer, and his life if he return'd into any of his Ma^{tys} Dominions, and that whosoever receiv'd him either in England or Ireland should be guilty of High treason likewise; and least this should not do the work, they framed 34 articles of High treason against him, where in, all the mischiefs that either actually had, or possibly could fall upon the Kingdom were charged (as they modestly termed it) upon his hellish practices: When the Duke heard of this he acquainted his Majesty, he thought this Limitation project wors, if possible, than the Bill of Exclusion, " and would give a greater shock to the Monarchy by vesting " the power in the Parliament and to drop the Government " more gently into a Commonwealth, that Algernoon Sidney " and his partie had express'd as much; and that My Lord " Shaftsbury's seeming to be dissatisfyd with it, as insufficient, " as but a wheedle to draw it on the faster, so forwarned his " Majesty never to listen to it; but it seems the Parliament " it self was not at leasure to drive on these projects to a head at " present, but was forced to let them ly like so much seed in the " ground (in hopes of a fruitefull product afterwards) till they had dispatch'd My Lord Stafford's tryall (which was now apointed) and in which his Royal Highness was not totally forgoten neither.

That Lord was chosen out of the five then in the Tower, as one whose age and infirmitys would render they thought least

Ibid. pag. 543.

King Ja. M^n
Tom. 9. p. 100.

The Lord
Stafford tryd
and con-
demn'd.

4 m 2

TOME
II.

1680.
LETTERS
VOL:I. p.536.

capable of a vigorous defence, which they knew their evidence. would not bear. However during the whole time of his tryal (which began on the * 20th of November) he was so far from being dejected that he never looked better in his life, he behaved himself with respect but assurance, and appear'd more concèr'd to have such crimes layd to his charge, than that they were like to be so fatal to him; so that thō he did not perhaps make so good use as he might of those advantages, which the blunders and contradictions of the witnesses gave him, yet he did it sufficiently to manifest his own inocency and the malice of his prosecutors to all upright and impartial men, had the Major part of those who sat upon him been such; but their votes being governed by other motives, he found (as well as the Duke whom they strone to wound through this Lord's side) that inocency was but a weak defence against false witnesses, an enraged people, and prejudiced Juges.

LETTERS
VOL.I. p.537.

Ibid. pag.578.

The tryall lasted five days, where all that malice could invent, was made use of to take away this inocent man's life, nevertheless the witnesses against him were sufficiently bispater'd and falsifyd in almost every point; but alas, what could such a defendant do in opposition to such sharp managers, and the prepossession of the greatest part of his Judges, who made a National cause of it, some thought nothing unlawfull against a Papist, others were so fearfull they durst not be guided by their reason, So that thō all conscientious men who durst speake their minds, declared, they would not condemn a dog upon three such evidences as were brought against him, yet of the 86 Lords that sat upon him, 54 voted against him; it is certain, he lay under great disadvantages from the fury of the factious partie (*who had*) the

---

* Convicted of High Treason, Dec: 7th. — EDITOR.

possession of the world in favour of the Plot, their main aim in that, and in all their other prosecutions (*was*) to cast an odium upon the Duke, in order to which they thought nothing unpermitted; yet those who wish'd him (*Lord Stafford*) well, were of opinion, that had he managed the advantages which were given him with dexterity, he would have made the greatest part of his Judges asham'd to condemn him; but it was his misfortune to play his game worst when he had the best cards, or rather the will of God to shorten his life a few days, to Crown him with the blessing of dyeing for his Religion, and accordingly accompanying his execution as he had done his tryall, with all immaginable protestations of his inocency, and a most Christian comportment, his head was cut off upon the Tower Hill the 29ᵇ of December following.

It is neither necessary, nor to the present purpose to give a full relation of this sollemn tryall which is printed at large, any further, then to shew, that thō this good Lord was sacrificed with many more to the fury of the faction, yet that blow by which he fell as well as most others were level'd at his Royal Highness's head, it was his birth right, liberty, and life itself, they hunted through these bloody paths, and counted all for nothing so long as he kept his ground : At the very first opening therefore of the evidence at this tryall, Sʳ Francis Winnington sayd, It was the prospect of a Popish Successor that gave life and encouragement to the designes of destroying the Government and introduceing Popery. Oates swore that upon perusal of his papers, which he had overlooked before, he found that the Duke's guards had releas'd several persons who were taken up on suspicion of haveing fired the Citty; that Father Bedingfeild had given the Society great assurances of his Royal Highness's readiness to advance the designe of killing the King; Godfrey's murther was likewise layd at his door, Dugdal deposeing that the Duke sent to Colman when he was

T O M E
II.
1680.

Letters
Vol: 1. p. 616.

The Duke is aim'd at in this and all other prosecutions.

Letters
Vol: 1. p. 537.

Letters
Vol. 1. p. 537.

T O M E
II.

1680.

Ibid: p.595.

in custody not to confess, and that Colman replyd, he had
already reveal'd part of what he knew of Sr Edmond bury
Godfrey ; upon which he had notice however not to confess,
and that care should be taken that Sr Edmond bury Godefrey's
evidence should do him no harme : in fine their intention
was to blacken the Duke, and establish (as they thought) the
credit of what they layd to his charge by the death of this
Lord, and My Lord Arrundel whom they designed to try next,
and by that means be able to get the Bill of Exclusion brought
in again, which the tottering condition of the King's affairs
gave small reason to hope he should be able to resist ; All those
about him were indeed so terrifyd with this blow, and so settled
in their opinion, that nothing but the Duke's Conversion or
ruin could set things to rights again, that the former being
dispair'd of, it was fear'd most people about the King would
advise him to yield to the latter ; for those who had most
authority at Court were well grounded in a wholesome piece
of casuistry, That in such cases it was not only Lawfull, but
the highest act of Religion, if they could save the King, the
Monarchy, the Nation, and Government only by giving up
one (thō the greatest man in it) and so according to Caiphas's
principle, thought it a cheap bargain, if by such a sacrifice
they could save the efusion of so much blood, which they
fancyd must otherwise of necessity be shed ; but what was
worst, this Doctrine began to get footing amongst his Royal
Highness's friends too, some of which sayd, Since he was so
obstinate in his own Faith he could not expect others should go
beyond the Alter to Serve him.

They dare not
venter to try
My Lord
Arrundel.
LETTERS
Vol:1. p.616.

Nevertheless the factious partie, thō highly exalted by this
victory, found the Lords had been more carefull and nice in
the examination of matters than they expected, which had
plunged them a litle, and put a stop to their bringing on My
Lord Arrundel's tryal, thō next in their project ; for the

evidence (*not*) being quite so full in reference to him (and for the same witnesses to bring new matters after so many examinations would be scandalous) and his abilitys too well known to think he would loos that advantage, made them suspect the success; and on the other hand to be baffled in that, would have knock'd all on the head again; so they contented them-selves at present with the weapons already in their hand, which they managed the best they could to drive on their designes against the Duke, which was the main scope of all those other prosecutions.

It was suspected, that was the drift too of My Lord Carlisle and Howard of Escrik's pretended kindness to their kindsman; they had with Crocadil tears in their eys, voted him guilty, and then thinking in some measure to repair their reputation, moved the House, to have his sentence (*changed*) to a per-petual banishment; but that being soon rejected, they desired leave to see him at least under pretence of carrying Divines to him; one would have the Bishopp of London, the other D^r. Burnet, but no body believ'd either of them were so sollicitons about his soule, or had any hopes he would change his Religion, or turn Informer to pleas them, which he had not done to save his life. People therefore conjectured their intention was to see, if by cross examinations they could make him let fall any words which they might wrest against the Duke, and such witness would have found room enough in their consciences to turn and twist the most inocent expression to their malicious purposes, but by God fortune the Lords would not allow them leave to see him alone, without the presence of a Warder, So that project (whatever it was) was happely disapointed, to the great Satisfaction of his Royal Highness's friends, who expected no good from Such an interview.

My Lord Carlisle and Howard of Escrik endea-vour t^o see their kindsman.

Letters Vol. i. p. 616.

Whatever the King's motive might be, to leave the Law in this conjuncture to it's cours, and every man to his own

The King was ill advised to behave himself as

TOME
II.

1680.
newter in
this tryal.
LETTERS
VOL. I. p.623.

judgment, it is certain that as most of his Majestys servants run
into this Lord's destruction, so by the least pervious care it was
believed they would have done quite otherwise: and there is
no doubt but had he been acquited, it would have given the
King much more eas, and ridded his hands of the Plot
infinitely sooner, than this passiue comportment, which gave
his enemys a fuller scope to pursue their projects, and by
hightening the storme droue still more and more into the deep:

Ibid: pag.619.

Accordingly he was tould by those who remember'd the year
40, that the present Parliament which had sat but two months,
had made greater advances to his and the Government's Sub-
version, than that other did in two years, and it was the
opinion of many judicious persons, that the Faction was got
so far on their road that they would not now stay till the
Duke's time came to try their strength for the Supreme
Dominion.

The dismal
prospect of the
Duke's affairs,
all men in
power being
against him.
LETTERS
VOL. I. p.631.

Amongst all these ill omens of forbodeing mischiefs the
Duke had not the least glimps of hopes from those who had
most credit with the King, the Dutchess of Portsmouth who
had so great an influence in affairs, had made mighty court of
late to the Parliament men, she had placed herself near the

Ibid: pag.539.

KING JA: M
TOM:8.pag.209

Commons at the tryal dispenceing her sweatmeats and gracious
" looks amongst them, and haveing formerly tould the Duke
" to his face That the changing his Religion was the ground of
" all the present evills, it was not to be doubted, but she now
used the like arguments to the King: The Duke of Monmouth
left no stone unturned to regain his Majestys favour, M.
Crofts had acquainted him that Duke was ready to give all
immaginable assurances of his fidelity and obedience, if he
might be readmitted to his Majestys presence and esteem;
but the King had so much resolution still, as to persist in his

LETTERS
VOL: I. p.396.

former answer, That he should be very willing provided
he took Edinbourg in his way to Whitehall. My Lord

Sunderland who yet remain'd in his place of Secretary of State run along with Shaftsbury, not only in the Bill of Exclusion, Association, Limitation, that against the Queen, &c; but even went to their clubbs and encouraged the Partie to persever in pressing the King, assureing them, if they did it he would yield to the Exclusion at last; on the other hand the King's necessitys were great, which the Parliament men being asprised of a hundred of them had publickly sayd, and even sworne, they would never give him a farthing till he consented to the Bill; infine there was such artes and industry used that forreign States were brought into this Batterie too, the Dutch and Spanish Ministers were prevail'd upon to represent to his Majesty, that unless he complyd with his Parliament, there was no hopes of his ever being easy at home, nor any grounds for his Allys abroad to depend upon his former engagement and necessary assistance.

This stratagem was so well layd, that Mr Sidney the King's Envoy at the Hague had been prevail'd upon to write what terrours the States were in, at the news of the Bill of Exclusion being cast out, he sayd they came running to him in the greatest consternation immaginable, declaring they had rejected all other offers for their good, resolveing to depend wholy upon England and that now they Saw no reason to hope for either Support or assistance from thence; the people (he sayd) were in the last confusion, and Mr Van Beningham almost out of his witts. It is true upon the Duke's complaint of this, the Prince of Orange assured him the States were far from pressing the King to pass the Bill of Exclusion, that they were only Sollicitons to hear of a good understanding betwixt him and the Parliament, on which depended (he sayd) the Support or ruin of the Republique; but their own Memorial contradicted that, and goes much farther, it represents how the King had induced them not only by arguments, but threats, to rely

Side notes:
TOME II.

1680.
Ibid: pag. 631.

Ibid: pag. 616.

Ibid. p. 633.

The Spanish and Dutch Ministers are brought in to perswade the King to pass the Bill of Exclusion.

LETTERS Vol: I. p. 719.

Ibid: pag. 775.

upon his protection, rather than engage in an **Allyance** with France, which was conceiv'd to be So disavantagious to the publick peace of both Nations; that he had as an assurance, promis'd to call his Parliament, that they had thereupon depended on his Royall word, which had hithertoo put a stop to the French King's encroachments, but that now he would find no difficulty in executing his designes, when he Saw this irreconciliable difference betwixt the King and the People, and accordingly was armeing powerfully; whereas Spain being in no condition to help it self, they expected nothing but inevitable ruin; and in the end they take upon them to tell his Ma^{ty}, he may find by experience, that these frequent dissolutions did but exasperate more and more both people and Parliament, and therefore could not but lament their misfortune to be ruin'd because his Majesty would not comply with them in reference to the Succession, a contingency that perhaps might never happen, and should it come to pass, he knew very well how little regard had been given to such exclusive Acts in former times.

But this stratagem so plausebly couched under the colour of a forreign Allyance, the King soon discover'd had its origin from home, nor did he make any secret of what he suspected, but order M^{r}. Sidney to be reprimanded for takeing upon him to send such Memorials, and to intermeddle in things which were out of his Commission.

The Duke's
Councel on
this occasion.
KING JAM. M^{rs}
TOM.9. pag.105.

" Assoon as his Royal Highness heard of it, he observed " to the King how industrious his Majesty's enemies were to " move heaven and earth against him, and that therefore it " behou'd him to be the more watchfull and resolute himself; " he did not (he sayd) blame the Dutch and Spaniards for doing " what they thought necessary for preservation of their own " Countrys, but thought it a good example for his Majesty to " follow and that he ought to do the same, he begg'd of him

therefore to consider well ere he engaged in a War for the "
defence of the Dutch, who after haveing ruin'd him at home, "
would serve him as they did their Allies at Munster at "
Nimeghen, that neither the Emperour nor Duke of Bran- "
denbourg had given any promis of joining with him or them "
against France, so that if he engaged in this quarrel purely "
for the sake of the Dutch, he would deliver himself bound "
hand and foot into the power of the Parliament; who would "
infallibly insiste upon disposeing not only of what mony they "
gave, but nameing the Officers too, an incroachment not to "
be borne, só beggs of him to be aware of such Councellors "
as would advise him to it. "

Nevertheless some Lords of the Council, grounding their
arguments upon this Memorial press'd the King to call the
Parliament into the Banqueting house, and there represent to
them, That the States of Holland had quited the friendship
of France at his sollicitation made by their advice, and therefore desired to know what he and the Dutch may depend on
if France should fall upon them; but others easily convinced
his Majesty it would be to no purpose, unless he were disposed
to deliver up the Duke to their mercy, without which no
complyance or consideration could be hoped for, whatever the
consequence might be either at home or abroad.

In this manner was his Majesty batter'd on all hands, thō
the only bulwork the Duke had in this extremity, the King's
own occasions for mony, the peace of Christendom, his
forreign Allyances, allmost all the people about him except
two or three of the Duke's friends never let fall their sollicitations that he would not prefer his Brother before himself, to
that extremity things were now come; nor was the King in
his own nature impregnable: nevertheless he was so true to his
own, and the Duke's intrest, as not to abandon him in the
main point at least.

TOME
II.

1680.
The Duke
gains ground
in Scotland,
while he is
persecuted in
England.

LETTERS
VOL: I. p. 399.

Ibid: pag. 513.

LETTERS
VOL. I. p. 394.

" During this persecution of his Royal Highness in England, the Scotch charm'd with his presence were as Zealous to support his right and reputation in the world as the English were to invade it; his generosity, affability, and great aplication to business mixed with an unbyaced fidelity and Love of Justice had so won the heartes of the Nobility and Gentry of that Country, who being of a temper rather to court the Prince's than the people's favour, they placed him in a manner on the Throne before his time in Scotland, while the Parliament endeavour'd to dispossess him of his right before he came to it in England: This encouraged the Duke to procure a petition from thence against his being banished, if the Parliament in England should press it, which they were readily disposed to do, or to give any other marke how much they abhor'd those factious proceedings of the Parliament there; nor was his Highness the only gainer by his residence in Scotland, the King had an equal share of advantage by it; he stifled at its first birth a commotion of the fanatical partie which then happen'd to break out, whereof some were taken and made examples of, but many more won over by the great esteem his presence had gain'd amongst them; he regulated many things relating both to Civil and Military affairs, he placed and displaced Officers according as he found them disposed and qualifyd for his Majestys Seruice, and did it in so winning and obligeing a manner, that even those who lost their imployments, lost not by it their respect for him nor dutyfulness to the King; of which there could not be a more convincing example than in the President of the Sessions comportment on that occasion, who being gon up to London to Sollicite what the Duke aproved not of, was no sooner tould that his Highness thought it not fit he should so much as speak to the King, but he presently answer'd, His Royal Highnesse's orders shall be obeyed, and without moveing the King even underhand or seeing any of the discontented partie, return'd

privately back into Scotland; so great an influence had his T O M E
II.
Highness gain'd over them as to force esteem and obedience
even from enemys themselves. 1680.

All this while the King was infinitely perplexed with the LETTERS
VOL.I. p.647.
impertinence of the Parliament, however was persuaded to
continue their Sessions under pretence, that their extravagances
would at last render them odious to the people; but when the
Duke heard of this wheedle, he tould the King, He not only." KING JA: M⁰
To.9. pag.111.
exposed his prerogative, but his person too, if he let them sit "
any longer; that never such an Address as the last was "
presented to a King on the Throne, or by subjects that were "
not in open Rebellion, that their endeavouring to take away "
his power of pardoning, was an argument they were not "
unprepair'd to take away his libertie too; and that therefore it "
behoved him to look well to himself; he was out of patience, "
he sayd, to See his Majesty prevail'd upon by weak and "
intrested men to continue the Sessions after such insolent and "
insupportable carriage. "

In other circomstances these arguments would have had The Dutchess
of Portsmouth
their weight, but those who advised the contrary were so well sides with the
Factiouspartie.
backed as to overbalance any thing the Duke could say. The LETTERS
Dutchess of Portsmouth who had need of mony as well as VOL.I. p.737.
protection, seconded these Councels with all her credit, she was
tould the House would not forget her amongst the reforms, and
threaten'd to throw her in to the lump of grievances; this they
knew would fright her intirely into their measures, to which
she had shewn so great a disposition already: Accordingly she
sticks at nothing to court an intrest amongst the Parliament
men; this open'd the doors of her apartement, not only to many
of the violent partie, but to My Lord Shaftsbury himself, who
in a jesting manner bragg'd publickly of it, but others found
their friends were so scandalized at this new Allyance, that
Several were forced to purge themselves of the aspersion, which

occasion'd many reflection and no litle mirth during those debates. But My Lord Essex had tould them plainly at last, that the Kingdom would neither suffer popish Favorites or popish Ministers, and that like Samuel he must aske, What meant the bleating of that kind of cattel? To which he hoped the King would make the same answer with Saul, That he only kept them with his other evil Councellors to be offer'd up in sacrifice, to pleas the people.

But notwithstanding this puritanical grimace, these parties were not so disperate, as not to unite heartely enough against the Duke, nor did all this juggling open the King's eyes, nor give him a due suspicion of those peoples advice, who he saw were saveing stakes with the oposite side; but by a criminal patience, gave the malignant partie great advantage over himself
LETTERS
VOL. I. p.647.
and his real friends, whom they either terrifyd into a complyance, or defamed and blancken'd them if they persever'd in their duty, and had this publick Coitering continued much longer, they would not have left an honest man about him.

Great endea-
vours used to
remove the
Duke's friends
from the King.
This was what the Parliament aim'd at, and therefore many violent speeches were made in both Houses against whatever they thought had been advised the King in oposition to their designes, with intent to blacken the advisers; and thō no one was named, nor an impeachment offer'd at (there being no crime aledged sufficient to ground an impeachment upon) they hoped nevertheless to fright his Majesty by their clamours, and force him to abandon those they chifly aim'd at, and My Lord Essex quoted Precedents where persons for publick reports only, had been displaced; on which occasion his Royal Highness observed to the King, That the Lord who
KING JAM. M⁹
To.9. pag. 115.
" press'd to have evil Councellors removed upon Common fame " and cited examples of it, could have found in the same Reigns " Precedents likewise for laying violent hand upon their King.
LETTERS
VOL. I. p.644.
However this made M⁹ Secretary Jenkins withdraw for a time,

and My Lord Shaftsbury following the blow made all the others Stagger ; the Duke, he sayd, thō absent, govern'd the Councels as much as ever, that no imployment was disposed of either Civil, Military, or even Ecclesiasticall it self, but by his approbation, and therefore press'd vehemently that such persons might be removed, as either owed their advancement, or had any relation to the Duke; which sawey expression the Duke of Monmouth took pleasure in repeating frequently, immagining to cast a blamish upon his Highness by it ; So that had this libertie of declameing continued much longer, his Majestys friends would have been torn or frighted from him, and he left as a Captive in the hands of his enemies before he had been aware ; as apear'd by Sr Robert Payton's treatment, who, because it was discover'd that he had formerly some correspondence with the Duke, was expell'd the House upon it, nor would his speaking scorrelously of his Royal Highness when he made his defence, save him from that punishment, the ever haveing been his friend was in their acceptation like the irremissible sin against the Holy Ghost.

It was thought reasonable, by these firy patriots, that the destruction of Popery should go hand in hand with that of a Popish Successor, in order to which there was no end of projects and proposals; as wild some of them, as they were unnatural and cruel : Some times the Papists were to change habitations, those who lived in the North of England were to be transplanted into the South or West, and so with the others ; then they were for banishing them quite, and supplying their place with a better generation by naturalizing all Protestant strangers ; an other contrivance was to have them register'd both Priest and Layity, that their numbers might be known ; but they soon perceiv'd that project would produce a quite contrary efect to what was aim'd at, and by discovering how few they were, take away that aprehention they labour'd so

TOME
II.

1680.

Ibid: pag.701.

Ibid. pag.693.

LETTERS
VOL.1. p.653.

Projects for destruction of Popery.
LETTERS
VOL:1. p.601.

Ibid: VOL: 2.
p. 6.

Ibid: VOL.
p.763.

much to establish; and as to a Popish Succcessor they thought
an association the best expedient, not such an one as was made
in Queen Elizabeth's days against the Queen of Scotts, that,
they sayd, would no more fit the present circomstances of
affairs, than a coate made for a Child of fouer year old, would
fit him when he came to be forty; that the dangers of Popery
from the Duke, were now much greater than they were then
from that Queen; so they took care to draw it accordingly:
but by making it so strong against him, it had in reality the
same force as the Bill of Exclusion, which gravell'd them a

litle, because they were loath to part with any article in it, and
yet to bring in the same thing twice in one Sessions was against
the Parliamentary Laws; but they now were above formalities,
and fancyd the Lords would be no nicer than themselves, in
the matter, especially since many of those who had been against
the Bill, had since voted My Lord Stafford guilty, for which
it was immagin'd (or at least great endeavours were used to
perswade it) that the Duke would never pardon them; which
by consequence might change their conduct in reference to
him: But this dareling project by the multeplicity of others,
and some intervening disputes fell for the present; however
My Lord Shaftsbury would not let it dye, but tram'd an association pursuant to these resolves, which was afterwards seized
in his closet, containing a promis of mutual assistance in
resisting the Duke of York's Succession, and a resolution to do
that by force, the King would not be brought to establish by a
Law.

The Lords and
Commons had
like to have
quarter'd
about privi-
ledges and
Imployments.

Many people were astonished that the King's patience
was Still proof against all these licentious proceedings, his
only excuse was, they might perhaps fall out amongst
themselves; and there happen'd indeed a dispute during
these debates which might probably enough have brought it
about.

The Lords it seems had pass'd a Bill in their own favour in reference to the tryalls of Peers, which when it came down to the Lower House some Members moved that since the Lords expected the Commons should concur to the inlargeing of their priviledges, it was but reasonable to have some regard to their own, and immediately proposed that the Act against Scandalum Magnatum might be repeal'd: This motion was hugely opposed by the leading members; they aprehended that should they put the Lords out of humour, they might miss this opertunity of getting them to pass the Association Bill, but the yong members being fond of the exemption, and having got the bitt in their mouths, run away with it in spight of all their haranging; but when it came up to the Lords they rejected it, and by that time the yong Commoners grew cooler in the matter: so it created no *mis*understanding nor gave any obstruction to their other designes, thō an other bone of division had like to have been thrown in amongst them soon after, in which the grandees of the House shew'd their weakness too, and that they were not above the temptation of averice and interest, no more than their Neibours.

There had been great talke of a bargain or certain conditions to be offer'd to his Majesty, in which, it seems, many of the heads of the partie like the prudent Steward in the Gospel had the grace not to forget themselves; it was sayd My Lord Russel was to be made Governour of Portsmouth, Sʳ William Jones Chief Justice, Titus Secretary of State, and that they had articled also for My Lord Shaftsbury to make him Lord Hight Treasurer, thinking it dangerous to leave him out, but he (good man) as soon as he heard of it, fel into a mighty passion they should think him capable of sacrificeing the publick good to his private interest; this made others ashamed too, and forced them to take great pains in clearing themselves since they found it would not take, and carryed on their

TOME II.

1680.

LETTERS Vol.:1. p. 659.

LETTERS Vol. 2. p. 2.

LETTERS Vol. 1. p. 738.

TOME
II.

1680.
The Parlia-
ment were for
articleing with
the King.

LETTERS
VOL. I. p. 669.

Ibid. p. 679.

More projects
to disable the
Duke.

hipocrisy so far, as to pass the selfe denying Vote as a standing security against any such attempts for the future.

Haveing purged their project thus from all its dross, they prepared the reste, which was of more refined mettal, and the King thought it worth his while to see what this pretended bargain would produce; the Duke's friends without much study, saw plainly enough what it would tend too, but found it impossible to stop the experiment, so at last out of it comes, with an assurance That in case his Majesty would pleas to redress some crying grievances only, he should find them afterwards as tractable as he could wish; and to let him see how moderate they were, limited them to these few heads: First, that the Privy Council might not judg of *meum* and *tuum*, that the corruption of Judges might be remedied which they conceiv'd came from their Commission being revocable at pleasure, and therefore desired they might run, *quamdiu se bene gesserint*, that Justices of Peace, Deputy Leiftenant, and all imployment both Civil and Military, not excepting the Fleet, might be in the hands of men who were known to be good Protestants, that he would confirme the Act of Association, and exclude the Duke of York, and then they promis'd upon their words they would relieve Tangier and suply his Fleet.

This they knew was but part of the King's necessitys, and undoubtedly were but part of their demands neither, they had more ready on the first occasion, and other methods a brewing to driue on their aims in reference to the Duke, in case the King's squemishness should still boggle at a point blank Exclusion. In the project therefore of an Act for secureing the Protestant Religion, they repeal'd the clause which exempted the Duke of York from the Test, they disabled him from being Admiral of Ireland, Tangier, or the Indies, or from bearing any imployment in his Majestys Dominions, and that if he succeeded to the Crowne they tooke care he should be a nominal King only, and therefore provided that in case of the King's death the Parliament then in being, or the last before, should assemble and sit for six months of their owne accord, that the two Houses should fill up the vacant imployments, Ecclesiastical, Civil and Military, that it should not be in the power of the said Duke of York to controwle any thing done here in, so long as he continued a Papist, nor have the power to dispose of any place or benefice belonging to the Crowne, that he should not have a negative voice in Parliament, nor have the power to raise any forces without its consent. T O M E II. 1680.

These were the lowest terms they could come too, in reference to the Succession: which was no comfortable alternatiue to his Royal Highness, and thō all this was but part of their wares and the King saw plainly enough what a bargain he was like to have of them all together, however he still powsed upon the matter, which gave them great encouragement they should prevail at last, and afforded them time likewise to try all the fords and even untrodden paths to arive at what they drove at: The Lord Major, the Sheriffs, and some others had a priviledge of making each a freeman of London, which they were used to sell for mony, but now had some thing in view of much more precious esteem; so one of the Sheriffs proposed the Duke of Buckingham to be made free, but the Court of Aldermen by good fortune hesitated a litle upon it, which gave time to discover and prevent the project, which was to have made the Earle of Shaftsbury free man by the same method the day following, then immediately have chozen him Aldermand and Lord Major the next election; by which means they would not only have been masters of the Citty, but given great encouragement to a Commonwealth disposition in the people, when they saw Noblemen of the first order willing (*to*) Rank themselves with tradsmen and Citizens. A contrivance to have made Shaftsbury Lord Major. LETTERS Vol: i. p. 684.

TOME
II.

1680.
The Parlia-
ment impeach
the Duke's
friends.

LETTERS
Vol: 1. p.672.

Besides all these irregularities and exorbitant pretentions, the King saw a tendency in the Parliament to unite all Sects and Religions except Popery, and that a renoncing of it alone should be sufficient to procure a tolleration and protection ; that a man might be what he pleas'd provided he were not a Papist, and thō this would have let in Atheisme and all sorts of immorality, they were not frighted at it, they were disposed to destroy all Religion rather than not destroy the Duke for the sake of his.

One would have thought the King had now seen enough of their voteing to have put an end to it, but his curiosity or necessitys still gave him more patience to wait, and see if they would yet offer him any thing worth his acceptance, in which the King lost much ground ; but they lost not the time which this loitering gave them of playing all their Engins against the

LETTERS
Vol. 2. p. 6.

Ibid: pag. 60.

Ibid: pag. 9.

Duke ; they spread a report that the Duke himself had writ to the King, rather to yeeld to his Exclusion than expose his person and Government any longer by resisting the inclinations of his Parliament, and to prevent any one's giveing a contrary advice, they fell upon all those they imagined favour'd him, whom hitherto they had so much modestie as not to name, but now desire bouldly My Lord Halifax, the Marques of Worcester, the Earle of Clarendon, the Earle of Feversham, Mr Hide might be removed from all places, and his Majestys presence, for haveing councell'd him against the said Bill : They

Ibid: p.33.

impeached for the same reason the Lord Cheef Justice * Scroggs ; but when it came up to the Lords, because it contain'd no special matter (which had been an old dispute) they

Ibid; pag.29.

rejected it ; and that no Stratagem might be wanting to alarme and amuse the people, new informations were brought concerning

---

* Jan' 5. 16⅚. — EDITOR.

the Irish Plot, and several imprison'd upon it, to perswade T O M E
the Kingdom, that so long as the Duke had an expectancy   II.
of comeing to the Crown, they must never hope to see an   1680.
end of plotting ; and to give the King himself a cast of their
office too, they pass'd a * Vote, that whosoever should lend or
advance him mony, upon any branck of his revenue, should be
responsable for it in Parliament as a hinderer of its sitting.

The Duke of Monmouth seeing his Royal Highness so
furiously batter'd on all sides, and the King so passive in the
matter, thought it a fit occasion to attempt his own readmission *Ibid: pag. 19.*
to Court, and to make his pretentions more plausible fain'd a
repentance, which he knew the King's tenderness for him
would not be proof against ; and as it fortun'd, some of the
Duke of Yorke's friends themselves, had like to have given a
helping hand to his endeavours here in : It seems My Lord LETTERS
Halifax thō vehement against the Bill of Exclusion, had been   VOL. 2. p.40.
always as positiue against the Duke's return, or his being ever
suffer'd near the King's person ; but now seeing it would almost
be impossible to keep his Majesty steddy in his resolutions, if
the Duke was not at his elboe, and that no one had, or could
pretend to that intrest with him, began to wish his Highness
back, and thought the readmission of the Duke of Monmouth
to Court, would be a good pretence to have him likewise
recall'd ; but others thought it better to run any hazards than
to suffer that Star to blaze again, especially considering to what
a low ebb his Royal Highnesse's credit was reduced when the
meanest man in the Kingdom could aspers and vilifie him with
impunity ; Oates had sayd publickly The Duke was possess'd LETTERS
with a devil, and that for the love he bore the Nation, he would   VOL. 2. p.23.
make no Scruple to kill him with his own hand if he could *Ibid: p.35*

---

* Jan' 7. 16⅞. — EDITOR.

1681.

come at him, yet no notice was taken of it, and My Lord Shaftsbury thinking that his being in Scotland gave him too much ground to stand upon his defence, press'd mightely to have him sent into some foreign Country; and to make merry with his misfortunes, sayd, If he were in Italy, he and Cardinal Norfolk might probably govern the Pope.

The King prorogues the Parliament, before which they make certain violent votes.
LETTERS
VOL. I. p: 727.

These insolencies without the House and exorbitant demands within, convinced his Majesty at last, there was no compromising matters by means of expedients, thō many of his false friends still press'd him to it, and were for haveing mony at any rate (proposeing without doubt to find their own convenience in it full as much as his) endeávouring therefore to perswade him that thō he yeelded too far at present, measures might be found to set his affairs to rights again in more temperate times; but he was too well aprised of (the) character of the Commons to think they were to be trick'd by such artifices, and that by consequence whatever mony he got, it would cost him more prerogative than it was worth, without hopes of redemption; he was sencible the King his Father was much in the wrong by endeavouring to put the Parliament still more and more in the wrong, that the destruction of the Monarchie was as much aim'd at now as then; and that the Exclusion of the Duke would but be a warning piece to the present possessor to provide for himself: Wherefore on munday the 10th of January he prorogued the Parliament to the 20th, resolveing at the same time, not to let that Parliament sit any more, which had offer'd so many indignities in their speeches and Addresses; and accordingly it was soon after disolv'd (Jan': 18) and another apointed to meet at Oxford the 21st of March following, but to keep forreign States in awe, particularly the French, a pretended short prorogtion was thought necessary. The Commons suspecting the King's intentions even before the Vssher of the Black Rod came to call them up,

LETTERS
VOL: 2. p. 41.

they voted (*Jan*ʸ: 10ᵗʰ) That whosoever advis'd the King against
passing the Bill of Exclusion, was as betrayer of his Majesty
and the Protestant Religion, a promoter of French intrest, and
a pensioner of France.

These hard words at parteing did not diminish the Duke's
satisfaction when he heard they were dismiss'd, for besides,
that his all was at stake in England, he began to feel their
influence even at Edinburgh it self; the great intrest and
esteem he had gain'd there, hinder'd not the Factious partie
from finding a way of affronting him, they had stir'd up the
Scolars and aprentices of that Town to enter into a sort of bond
or combination to burn the Pope, which was thought a proper
way of begining an atack upon his Royall Highness himself,
but by the care and vigilance of the Magestrates it was timely
prevented; for thō the rabble might be gain'd on such an
occasion, it was impossible to moue the substantial part of
the City in his disfavour, he got such an awefull esteem
wherever he personally resided, that the most invenomed malice
of his enemies was not able to anoy him : even in England
it self, (while he was suffer'd to remain at Court) the King's
affairs went infinitely better, and many of those who barked so
furiously at him when his back was turn'd, cring'd and faun'd
upon him when he was present.

This was so manifest that the Duke had rais'd one argument
from it even while the Parliament was yet siting, why the King
should call him back, that his being on the place always
damp't their malice rather than increas'd it, that thō "
many might be found who wished his Majesty well, yet "
such was the terrour of these prosecutors, that none but "
he durst give bould advice when they saw how Ministers "
were used; that others had fortunes to make or to secure, "
and might hope to preserve themselves, thō the King and "
Monarchie itself should fall, but that he was firmely linked "

The Fanaticks attempt affronting the Duke at Edinburg. LETTERS VOL: 2. p. 38.

The Duke's arguments for being recall'd.

KINGJA:Mⁿ To: 9. p. 126.

Ibid: 110.

TOME
II.

1681.

" to both, and must share in their fate whatever it proved;
" that others might have private ends, dependances, and
" relations, which might sway their Councels, flatter their
" hopes, and make them suffer those changes with patience
" they had not courage to oppose; but that he alone was
" equally concern'd with his Majesty if possible to prevent
" them; that as to the danger they pretended Religion would
" be in, should he come to the Crown, or have the management
" of affairs, he hoped, he Sayd, his friends would not imagin him
" either so weak as to think it possible to force a change upon
" the Nation, or so insincere as to endeavour a thing he had
" so oft declar'd to be against his judgment; for thō he wish'd
" all men like himself as to Religion, yet thought it unlawfull

King Ja. Mⁿ
To:9. p.119.

" to force any man much less a whole Kingdom to imbrace it;
" that he always thought it the intrest of the Monarchie to
" preserve the Church of England as by Law establish'd,
" and that he constantly join'd with the Bishops and Loyal
" partie in the Parliament, and was in admiration how men
" could aprehend danger from Popery, which was so incon-

Ibid. p. 121.

" siderable a body and forclosed from all imployments, while
" they overlook'd the imminent danger of being swallow'd up
" by Presbitery and Fanatysisme, which already had over-
" spread the face of the Kingdom, and had the impudence to
" propose in Parliament the repeal of the Act of the 35ᵗʰ of
" Queen Elizabeth and the Corporation Act, and indeed all
" such Laws as have been counted the Church of England's
" only bulworks against them; he begg'd therefore of his
" friends not to aprehend the imaginary dangers of Popery, not
" so far to dread the authors of the real ones, as not to give

King Ja. Mⁿ
Tom. 9. p.125.

" their best advice to his Majesty and to endeavour his
" readmission to the management of affairs, which the Bishops
" themselves had owned (when he came last from Scotland)

that not only the King, but the Church of England itself had " TOME
'found the good effects of. " II.

But all this arguing was so far from prevailing with the King, 1681.
while the Parliament sat, that he durst not permit the Duke's
return   it was broke, but put him off til after the Sessions
of the Parliament at Oxford, which now he tould the Duke he
was prevail'd upon to let meet in order to sit and doe business. LETTERS Vol. 2. p. 93.

There could not be greater argument how much his Royal They press the Duke to change his Religion.
Highness was above fear or dejection, than thus to content
(*contend*) as it were for Empire when Hannibal was at the walls
of Rome, yet his friends were far from being either govern'd
by his reasons, or confirm'd by his example, they were in such
aprehentions notwithstanding the late dissolution, that they
would not let him injoy this litle glimps of sunshine, but by LETTERS Vol. 2. p. 48.
renewing their old sollicitations assure him it would be impossible & 74.
to keep his head above water, or for any of his friends to abide
by him, unless he did the only thing which could extricate
himself, the King, and all his friends from inevitable ruin;
but nothing of this, made the least impression upon him, he
knew (he sayd) his obligations and duty both to God and the
King, which he was resolved not to confound, and left the
success to the disposal of Him, who is not tyd up to the rules of
humain foresight, and could bring that to pass which seems
impossible to men, but that if Providence thought not fit to
redress his misfortunes in this world, he was content to wait for
his reward, which he was sure (if he did his duty) would not
fail him in the next.

But what griev'd his Highness most was to see the King
himself enter into the same aprehentions ; he had sent for
Mr. Hide before he had resolved to dissolve the Parliament, to
tell him it would not be in his power to protect the Duke any LETTERS Vol. 2. p. 81.
longer, if he did not conforme and go to Church and that he
design'd to send him to Edinbourg to let him know as much.

TOME
II.

1681.

M' Hide was hugely surprized, as well as troubled at this resolution; for thō it was, what, not only he, but all the Duke's Protestant friends both wish'd and had press'd with more vehemence, than the respect due from them could well alow of, yet he knew so well the Duke's tempér and steddyness, when he either wàs; or thought himself in the right, that all the dangers in the world would never move him, and by consequence (*he*) must be wholly abandon'd if the King persisted in that resolution; all therefore he could do, was to contrive some delay, and being sick of Commission he had no great difficulty of pretending to be realy so, which put off his journey till the Parliament was dissolved, after which the King cooling a litle in his aprehentions, and other expedients being proposed (thō more absurd if possible then the former) served at least to let it drop for the present, and any shifting or alteration in a lingring distemper gives present eas, thō it no way forward the cure.

This project therefore was, that in case the Duke survived the King, he should be regarded as a Minor, and put under the tuition of his own Children; this, how rideculous soever it apear'd, wanted not fomenters both at home and abroad, and the Prince and Princess of Orange who were to have that Province confer'd upon them, were not altogether passive in the matter.

Some changes
in the family.

While the Factious Partie were thus moulding their projects against the ensuing Parliament, it behoved the King to make preparations of his part likewise, which was not to be done LETTERS
Vol.1. p.707. efectualy till he had made certain reformes in his Family and Councel, he saw plainly that if he cleans'd not his own nest, LETTERS
Vol. 2. p.73. he should soon be forced to abandon it: My Lord Salsbury gave the first occasion by desiring to withdraw, thereby to express his greater dissatisfaction when the King declar'd in Council he was resolved to brake the Parliament, and the

Earles of Essex, Sunderland, and Sr William Temple were
order'd to bear him company, and thō My Lord Conway who
succeeded in the Secretaries office was litle known, yet it
being so hard to find a trusty man and capable of that
imployment, the King accepted of him upon Mr Seymour's
recommendation, and for the same reason the Duke, thō he
had proposed an other, was very well satisfyd with the choice.

But no one had more need than the Duke to prepare
antidotes against the intended Parliament, his letters had
hithertoo been infectual to perswade the King to recall him
home, or to pursue such measures as he thought necessary for
their mutual preservation ; he resolved therefore to send one
up to Court to reinforce his arguments, and propose some
expedients which he hoped would be much more for the King's
ease and advantage, than those which were now in agitation, and
of which he was sure his own ruin was to make the main
ingredient.

Mr Churchill being pitched upon for this service he was "
commission'd in the first place to press the King not to suffer "
the Parliament to sit, at least till those popular heats were "
abated, and by that means convince the world that he would "
be King and steddy to his resolutions ; 2^{ly} that he should "
diswade his Majesty all he could from any such Allyances "
with Spain and Holland, as would ingage him in a War with "
France, for that would but enslave him to his Parliament "
and they might probably leave him in the Lurch at last, the "
behaveour of the Ambassadors of both those Countrys haveing "
been such of late, as gave no encouragement to rely much "
upon them ; 3^{ly} that an Allyance with France was the only "
means to support the King and preserve the Monarchie and "
even the Church of England itself, by affording a supply "
without a Parliament, which aim'd manifestly at the ruin of "
them all ; that matters were come to such a head that the "

T O M E
II.
1681.

The Duke
sends M^r.
Churchill to
the King with
proposalls.

KING JA: M^{rs}
To. 9. p. 131.

" Monarchy must be either more absolute or quite abolished,
" that France would be Sorry to see England a Commonwealth,
" that Spain desired it, and Holland would not be displeas'd
" at it, and that since his Majesty was so kind as to resolve not
" to abandon him, nothing but an Allyance with France could
" support him in that resolution, considering how he had been
" used by others even the Prince of Orange himself; 4ly to
" Sollicite his return, for which there needed (he sayd) no other
" argument than the dejection and trouble of the old Cavaliers
" and all honest men, together with the joy of the other partie
" at his being sent away, and how much quieter things were
" while he remain'd at Court, thō the aprehentions of a contrary
" efect had always been the pretence for keeping him from it.
" In fine he directed him to press the King to resolute
" Councels, which the last Summer's experience convinced
" him to be his only security, but cautions Mr Churchill to be
" carefull how he communicats these matters to My Lord
" Halifax, as not likely to enter into such measures ; and that
" if the vain aprehention of troubles were still objected against
" his return, to begg permission at least, that he might come
" and wait upon his Majesty for a week or a forthnight, and
" if that be also denyd, and he by consequence condemned to
" remain still in exile, to insist that his power at least might
" be increased where he was, and he made General of the
" forces of the Kingdom of Scotland.

When Mr Churchill arrived at Court he found the King as
deaf to his arguments, as he had been to the Duke's letters, only
he gave some ear to the Allyance with France, but for the
rest, being fixed in his resolution of the Parliament's meeting,
it served him for an answer to all the other demands ; so that
the Duke's own friends seeing the King immoveable, thought
it not proper his Royal Highness should come and be in
England while the Elections were a makeing, least his suposed

intrest might exasperate the people, for that should the King TOME
thwart or cross the measures of those Councellors who under- II.
took for the Parliament's good behaveour and promis'd such 1681.
mighty matters from it (thō they aim'd at nothing but an
accomodation betwixt the King and them let it cost what it
will) would all be charged upon the Duke; for men of most
credit about the King began now to have litle regard to his
Royal Highnesse's intrest, nay many of them proposed it as the
first step or preliminary in order to settle the King's afairs, or
indeed their own advancement, and thought any advantage
cheap that could be purchased at so easy a rate.

Tis true My Lord Halifax and Mr Seymour confess'd, that
neither measures of vigor nor good husbandry could be con-
stantly pursued (thō both So necessary) without the Duke's Letters Vol. 2. p. 119.
presence, and yet declared his presence could not be supported;
this was such a paradox, that his Royal Highness could not
forbear expostulateing that matter, when he heard it, To King Ja: M^n To. 9: pag. 219.
pretend, says he, that what is for the good of the Service ″
cannot be supported, is to throw up the game, for when ″
good measures and good men are not stood by, it is the ″
worst simptom a Government can have, and shews that if it ″
is not at the last gaspe, it cannot avoid dying a lingring ″
death. ″

But it was in vain to argue against a settled resolution; a The Prince of Orange complains of the Parliament's prorogation, and is for the Bill of Exclusion.
Parliament was necessary, they sayd, (thō no good could be
hoped from it at home) to make things more easy abroad and
avoid clamours from forreign partes, that otherwise Spain and
Holland would cry out The King abandon'd all to the French Letters Vol: 2. p. 118.
which they still presumed a Parliament would oppose: The
Prince of Orange was so full of this, that he could not forbear Ibid: p. 122.
writeing to the Duke himself That every body was wonderfully
allarm'd at the Parliament's being prorogued, for thō he owned
they flew very high, yet, he Sayd, unless the King and they

T O M E
II.

1681.

agreed, all the States of Europe which were linked in the same intrest with England must necessarily be ruin'd ; nay he went farther to others, Sʳ. Gabriel Silvius when he came from Holland, made no mistery of owneing that the Prince of Orange was for haveing the Bill of Exclusion pass, which, he sayd, would give great satisfaction to Christendom, and doe the Duke no prejudice, their being no probability of it's takeing efect more than other Acts of the like nature in former times, and that the Duke himself had own'd he liked it better than any other expedient ; but the snake which lurked under this compliment upon the Prerogative, was not invisible no more than his other darke designs, which now b𝚎𝚐𝚊𝚗 to be suspected by more than the Duke alone, who therefore answer'd that false suggestion

King Ja: Mᵗ.
To. 8. p. 225.

" by shewing That to suffer the Parliament to meddle with the
" Succession was in efect to turn an Hereditary Kingdom into
" an Elective one, and that thō such attempts have formerly
" been disapointed, yet it was dangerous to suffer them again.
" A man that has parryd one thrust may be kill'd at the next,

Ibid: p. 226.

" that it had been always observed, when ever the Parliament
" was allow'd to meddle in any matter of State, they ever after
" claim'd it as a priviledge, the King made use of their
" assistance to destroy the late Earle of Clarendon, and they
" have grounded a pretence from it of inspecting the conduct
" of States men, and indeed have fallen upon almost every
" Minister since, and should they be suffer'd to doe the like in
" this case, they would clame it as their due for the future to
" appoint a Successor to the Crown : Tis true the Prince of

Letters
Vol: 2. p. 215.

Orange denyd his haveing given rise to that report, or to have ever sayd any such thing himself, but his conduct during all these transactions gave too much ground to suspect his sincerity in that, as well as his views in all the rest ; but nothing was able to alter the opinion of the refined reasoners, who govern'd the present Councels ; they hoped, they sayd, by a Parliament

to stop peoples mouthes _{on} one side, and prevent forreign T O M E II.
attempts on the other; that if France were not kept quiet
abroad, no quiet must be expected at home, that hithertoo it 1681.
had the good efect to preserve the peace, but should France
atack Flanders and there be no hopes of a Parliament, all the
world would be in an uproar; so when Mr Churchill return'd,
the King assur'd his Royal Highness that thō he could not King Ch: Lett: p. 92.
promise himself much good by it, yet his ingagement to forreign
Ministėrs and severall usefull friends at home, oblig'd him to try
the experiment.

But it was these usefull friends the Duke suspected most, and
shew'd plainly why the King in reason ought to doe so too;
he could not but be sencible their arguments were strung upon
too slender a thread to hang long together, but what startled
him most, was how the King could immagin that those " King Ja: M^{re} To.8. p.220.
Ministers who had been attack'd by the last Parliament, and "
were perswaded this would prove no better, could be for "
haveing it to meet, unless they proposed to make their peace "
by throwing up all, or so much at least as would bring all the "
rest after it; for who ever, says he, saw any Minister escape "
who was once impeach'd, but by giveing away some essential "
part of the Prerogative, or by betraying the King and the "
trust he put in him, as My Lord Danby and Sunderland had "
done, that for his part he had raison to aprehend, that those "
who were in this Situation design'd to make him the Sacrifice "
of reconciliation, and that the King himself had sufficient "
cause to be jealous of them upon the same account; wherefore "
he wished his Majesty to chuse some Councelors and "
confidents as went upon sollid principles of honour, Loyalty, "
and conscience, which are always found to be the Safest "
methods in the end. "

It is certain nevertheless that many who meant well to the
Duke concur'd in these measures, for thō they had no design

TOME
II.

1681.

to hurt him by it, the confusion things were in made them act blindfould, and the Duke was forced to have patience till by more mature reflexion those men could get the better of their false notions and groundless aprehensions; and therefore he made use of such instruments as far as they would go, and had the caution not to move with too much Violence those wheels which seem'd to stop, for fear of breaking all in pieces; as yet he saw they were at such a gaze, that nothing was discern'd by them in its due proportion, that in a litle time probably objects would apear more distinct, and then it was hoped they would act more rationally; the King indeed had

LETTERS
VOL:I. p. 143.

assur'd his Royal Highness that he would never consent to the Bill, and that upon the first irregular Vote he would breake the Parliament, but his Highness had found the King exceeding wavering of late, he saw him so dilatory in executing any good purpose, that if it was not quite layd aside, it lost halfe its force by the lingring manner of performance: So it had

LETTERS
VOL.I. p. 127.

fared with his resolution of weeding his family and Council, which like many others had dwindled to nothing; the only hopes he had, was the King being sencible that those people who press'd so violently for the Duke's Exclusion, would still

Ibid: p. 121.

think themselves so unsecure during the King's owne life, as not to stop there, and the King being fully resolved never to suffer any change in his own time, was the only foundation on which his Royal Highness's security seem'd to rest.

The King agrees to a Treaty with France.

KING CH:
LETT" p. 91.

As to the other Expedient of an agreement with France which was part of M' Churchill's Commission, the King gave so far into it as to permit the Duke to endeavour to bring it about, but would not (he sayd) be the first mover of it himself, being desirous to know what termes he was like to have, ere he exposed his honour too much, since the French Ambassador upon the first overture of it by M' Churchill gave nothing but

LETTERS
VOL. 2. p. 141.

fine words; but cautions the Duke not to consent to any article

which might foreclose him from calling a Parliament if he
thought it fitting, and to press, that the present payment in
hand might be more considerable thō the succeeding ones were
less; and lastly, that the person whom the Duke should think
fit to send, might come streight to London and there deliver
his letters to Mr Hide, to be shewn the King: The pretence for
this was to prevent the delay which going about by Scotland
would unavoidably occasion; but the true reason was some
insinuations that the Duke might perhaps treat of matters the
King was not privy too, which jealousie the Duke was under a
necessity of haveing so much regard too as to obviate the
thing without seeming to suspect it.

Notwithstanding this Treaty was kept exceeding secret and The Dutchess
of Portsmouth
the Dutchess of Portsmouth herself (thō too much in the intrest pretends
friendship
of France) not made privy to it, yet it is probable she got some which comes
to nothing.
intimation what was a doing, being she took a fancy to shift sides
again, and endeavour a reconciliation with the Duke at a time Lɛᴛᴛᴇʀs
Vᴏʟ.ɪ. p.398.
he seem'd most abandon'd; it had been indeed long the opinion
of some of his welwishers, that the Duke haveing no hopes but
in a treaty with France, and she likewise haveing no other
foundation of security but from thence, they could not long be
other than friends: Whatever in fine was the motive that
brought her to it, Mis Wall came to ask a conference with M^r
Hide, where fair overtures were made towards a reconciliation,
if his Highness (she sayd) thought her friendship worth Lᴇᴛᴛᴇʀs
Vᴏʟ.2. p.143.
the courting; tis certain he had no great reason to ground
much upon a person who made such quick turnes, and seem'd
to be govern'd by nothing but intrest and ambition, however
he thought it not prudent to slight any offer of kindness
especially from one in so much power, and which might be of
so great advantage to him in this conjuncture, but it was the
Duke's misfortune that Mr Hide (who was his Agent in this

TOME II.

1681.

affair) was one of the Commissioners of the Treasurie, and had in the management of that imployment, shewn greater regard to the King's necessities, than to support his credit, with that Lady, which whether it made them clash in their negociation, or her natural fickleness, join'd with some new discoverys of better termes from the other side, chang'd her mind, tis certain all came to nothing in the end; the Duke was realy concern'd for it, not that he built so much upon her friendship as he fear'd her enmitie on so critical an occasion, just before the Parliament was to meet, when all the world was arming with thunder against him.

The Duke pretended for recusancy.
LETTERS Vol. I. p. 175.

As a mark of this, his Royal Highnesse's enemys were far from being idle even during this short interval of Parliament; for since they could not make new Laws to his prejudice, they found means to stretch the old ones beyond their natural extent in order to convict him as a Papist, for which being Straighten'd in time, the Justices of the old Bailie sent for the Grand Jury of Middlesex after they had been discharged at the Sessions at Hick'sshall, and swearing them a new, deliver'd the presentment against the Duke of York, which upon Mr Oates his affidavit, That he had seen his Highness at Mass and receive the Sacrament according to the rites of the Church of Rome, they

Ibid. p. 170.

found it *Billa Vera*. This was certainly very irregular, however some of the Duke's friends fancyd an advantage might be made of it, in case the King had realy a mind to have his Brother with him; for under a pretence of makeing his apearance after the proclamation came out, as the Duke of Norfolke and some others had done, it would have been a good excuse for letting his Royal Highness come to London; but upon a more mature consideration of all its consequences, and the bitter animosities against him, it was thought neither safe for his person, nor

LETTERS Vol. I. p. 191.

practicable in itself, so they chose rather to remove it by *certiorari* to the King's bench, and if it could not otherwise be eluded, to stop it by a *Noli prosequi*, which was not doubted but the King would grant (if necessary) in the end.

T O M E II.
1681.

The time now drawing near for the Parliament's meeting at Oxford, the preparations which were màde on all sides, looked, as if the debates were to be managed rather by force, than argument ; for which reason the King took care, not only to be accompanyd with a good number of his Guards, but had order'd the greatest part of My Lord of Oxford's regiment, to be quarter'd on the road, to secure his return, and left a good body of men to be an awe upon the Citie in his absence : His Majesty was only perplexed about Coll: Russel whose fidelitie he doubted, and therefore had proposed to My Lord Thanet to buy his regiment, which he at first agreed too, but after declin'd on pretence, that the King's not going on with the reforme at Court as had been projected, was a desincouragement for honest men to venture ; the Duke would have recommended the Earle of Mulgrave, but the King was preposses'd against him, so was forced to respite that matter for the present; but leaveing the chief command with my Lord Craven, he hoped there could be no great danger in his absence, he writ to all the Lords not to fail being there, in whose Loyalty he had more confidence than in the Commons, after which he went to Windsor, and on the 14ᵇ of March arrived togather with the Queen at Oxford.

Preparations against the meeting of yᵉ Parliament. LETTERS VOL. 2. p. 184.

Ibid. p. 171.

Ibid. p. 175.

There had been great endeavours used to diswade the King from chusing this place for the Sessions, My Lord Essex and several other Lords had presented a petition against it, alledging they could neither be so commodious, nor safe, but exposed (as they termin'd it) to the swords of the Papists, and their adherents ; which thō it was no argument to the King to change his measures, who knew very well whose swords it was that threaten'd him, however the factious partie (which in this new Election was more numerous than ever) for a pretence,

LETTERS VOL. 2. p. 108.

T O M E
II.

1681.

·at least to .come thither very ; well armed, and much ·better attended than was usual on such occasions ; and · that no industry might be wanting to rais a ferment in the people ·and support the hatred against the Duke, they had sprung up.a new Plot againot the meeting of the Parliament, of. which .Sir William Waller (a most active and fiery Partizan of the faction) had been the informer himself.

He tould the King that one Fitzharris an Irish man had

FitzharrisPlot.

LETTERS
VOL: 2. p.196.

fram'd a. malicious libel to alianate the peoples afections from him, to which he had .been encouraged by the French Ambassador, but that he himself being acquainted with one Everard who pretend to helpe Fitzharris, was brought privately by him into his chamber, whereby he made this discovery : Upon this .Fitzharris was committed, and a few days. after Sheriff Cornish came up to acquaint the King, that Fitzharris denyd what he was aćcused of, but Sayd if he might havé a pardon, he knew a Plot of· a much higher nature than. any yet mention ; upon which the two Secretaries were sent to examin him, to whom he deposed That Mons Montecucully before he went out of England, had offer'd .him ten thousand pound to kill the King, but refuseing to undertake it, he urged him to it, saying, It might easily be done at Mad Mazarine's by poison, when his Majesty eat there; he. sayd the Duke of York was privy to this designe, and that ·assoon as the ·work . was done, an Armie was to. come from France and Flanders to support his Royal Highness ; that a great many Parliament men were to be boil'd to death to make a Saint Ampoul to anoint him and the succeeding Kings of England at their Coronation, and that mony was rais in Italy by the Dutchess .of Modena's means for· the carrying on this design, she being privy to 'it likewise.

The. King was soon aware what was aim'd. at, by this foolish storie, and thō he resolved, if possible, to disapoint them, yet he perceiv'd that neither the gross improbabilitys of such incoherent stuff, was sufficient to dampe the credit of it, nor his purpose of not granting a pardon sufficient security against its being extorted from him, if great care was not taken to prevent it; he foresaw that upon his denyal, the Parliament would press for the pardon, and so by the cry and terrour of a new Plot carryd on by the Duke not only against the life of the King, but the Parliament men too, they might more easily drive on their beloved Bill of Exclusion, which the late Elections in the Citie shew'd they were more earnestly set upon than ever, haveing thanked their Members for haveing press'd that Bill in BAKER 781. the late Parliament and besought them never to give a penny of mony, till that, and other Laws were pass'd for securing them from Popery and arbitrary power.

But the King was resolved to cross bite them if possible, and therefore order'd a Commission of Oyer and Terminer to try Fitzharris forthwith for his Libel, there being three witnesses LETTERS to prove it, for Sr William Waller had already given evidence, VOL.2. p.199. togather with Everard and one Smith who concurr'd with them in all particulars, the only difficulty was the want of time to execute this commission before the Parliament met, whose importunity it would be hard to resist; but the King left that to Providence, and before he quitted the Towne order'd the prosecution to be follow'd with all imaginable expedition; but thô the King's caution and foresight was good as to the main, yet it was the Duke's misfortune to ly so open on all hands, that every assault or random shot took place still on one side or other: His Royal Highness had long press'd the King for a pardon, imagining it would shelter him from some of the Parliamentary proceedings, and now that the King was on the Ibid. p.203. point of granting it, his friends thought better to wave it upon this foolish storie, rather than give the malicious world occasion to say, He had more than ordinary need of such a security by

TOME
II.

1681.

reason of this pretended discovery : It pleas'd God likewise to send him and the Dutchess an other sencible trouble at this time by the death of the Lady Isabella their youngest Daughter at London, which was the more aflicting because they had not the satisfaction of seeing and assisting her in her sickness ; but those hardshipps were unavoidable sequels of the uneasy banishment and cruel persecution, they were both so unjustly condemn'd too.

The factious
Partie tempt
the King with
mony.
LETTERS
Vol. 2. p. 208.

Before the King left London the factious partie had tempted him with mony too, and had offer'd him Sixty thousand pound upon condition he would pass the Bill, but thō the King's necessities were great, they did not overballance his honour and true intrest ; so finding they could not compass their aim by composition were resolved to carry it, if possible, by high hand in Parliament, and certainly never any Assembly of that nature met with wors dispositions against the King, or more fury against the Duke, breathing nothing but his ruin and destruc-tion, which struck such a terrour into many who had hithertoo Stood by him, that they fell off a pace: My Lord Halifax indeed still was against the Bill, but proposed expedients fully as pernitious ; in fine most people thought they should come off at an easy rate, if they could make their peace with the Parliament at the expence of his Royal Highness' birth right, which now began to be made litle account of by men of greatest credit ; so he waits with impatience the event of this meeting from which so much harme was to be feared, and so litle good to be hoped for or expected.

The Parlia-
ment meets
at Oxford.

On the 21th of March the King open'd the Sessions by a Speech, where in he tould them in reference to the Duke, That the just care they were to have of Religion, ought not to be improved into such unnessary fears, as to be made a pretence for changing fundamentalls of the Government ; that he hoped the example of the ill success of former heates would dispose

them to a better temper, and that they would not lay so much
weight upon any one expedient against Popery, as to count all
others infectual, that he could not depart from what he had
so often declared about the Succession; but to remove all
reasonable fears from a Popish Successor, if means could be
found out, that in such a case the administration of the
government might remain in Protestant hands, he should be
ready to hearken to any such expedient, by which the Religion
might be preserued, and the Monarchy not destroyd.

When the Duke heard of this last clause he gave all for lost,
unless the reasty temper of his enemies, who loved no ways but
those of their owne invention, should hinder their acceptance of
that which would have fetter'd and degraded him as much as
the Bill of Exclusion it self; but, it seems, they were not so
stubborn as was expected, and by consequence the Duke had
fallen a sacrifice to their malice, had not Providence thrown
another bone of dissention amongst them, which was no ways
foreseen or expected : The first motion indeed was for bringing
in the Bill of Exclusion, but Mr Birch, Mr Hampden, and
many others of the most violent and cunning Members opposed
it, saying, The King had made an offer of agreeing to any other
expedient, and that they thought it but reasonable to harken
at least to such an invitation ; the King on the other side who
thirsted after this accommodation, had consulted before hand
with his friends, whether he should expect the Parliament's
offring particular expedients, or do it first himself, and thō the
latter was sure to ambarrass and entangle him much more than
the other, (for he would ever be held fast to what he had offer'd,
whether they accepted of it as full satisfaction or no) however
to foreward the matter, it was resolved the King's Servants in
the House should begin the debate by proposeing other means,
to see if they could divide the Members by it, and wean them
at least from their fondness of the Bill.

TOME
II.

1681.

Expedients
proposed as
bad as the Bill.
LETTERS
VOL. 2. p. 213.

This method would have proved as pernitious to the government as fatal to the Duke, had not those implacable spirits by
grasping at too much, lost the hould they had already got;
they were resolved it seems to wrest Fitzharris out of the King's
hands, and those of justice too which was ready to pass upon
him, in order to mould him to their own shape and designes,
he proveing a thorow paced evidence to their purpose; for
besides the crimes he had already charged upon the Duke, he

had brought the Queen again into the pretended Plot of
poisening the King, which he sayd Don Francisco de Melo
had assured him of: Now the readyest way to bring their ends
about, was in the first place to impeach him themselves and by
that means put a stop to all other prosecutions, and prevent his
conviction and punishment for the Libel.

. This therefore was done out of hand, and the Bill of
impeachment sent up to the Lords; but the King as watchfull

as they, in a thing on which so much depended, had used all
imaginable arguments to induce the Lords to reject the
Impeatchment and leave him to the Law, which had its success,
and they did accordingly when the Bill of Impeatchment came
up to them: This put the House of Commons into such a .fury
that casting off all former thoughts of moderation or agreement,
they refused with indignation and contempt all offers of
expedients, and order'd the bringing in the Bill of Exclusion
immediately, voteing at the same time, That it was the
undoubted right of the Commons to impeach either Peer or
Commoner, and that the Lords not receiveing it, was a manifest
breach of government, and that whatever Court or Judge should
try Fitzharris, should be proceeded against as an enemie to the
King an Country.

This was on Saturday night, and on Munday morning assoon

as they met, the Bill of Exclusion was read a first time
and order'd a second reading, when the King sent up for them

to the House of Lords, and there, to their great surprise, apeared in his robes, thō the Lords (not knowing any thing of it neither, were not in theirs.) He tould them he perceived such heats and animosities ariseing betwixt the two Houses, that he saw no speedyer way of apeasing them, than by dissolveing the Parliament, which he directed the Chancellor to doe, and haveing before hand order'd relays on the road, took coach immediately and arrived that night at Windsor.

This unexpected vigor in the King struck them like thunder with confusion and amazement, and gain'd his Majesty exceeding great reputation, his friends now began to take courage again, and those turbulent and fiery men were left in the last degree of rage and despair, not only vext at their disapointment, but asham'd after so much undutifull behaveour to be thus exposed and baffled ; for they saw there was no more hopes of a Parliament in hast, without which, all their well laid projects were like to vanish into smoke.

The King was resolved to be the first that should informe the Duke of this agreeable news, so sends an express with it, telling him, He found it necessary tó be very quick with them, it apearing from their votes and carriage that nothing but violence could be expected from such men : The Duke was overjoyd at it, not only because the King was at last come to those methods of resolution and vigor he had so long press't him too, but to see an end of that expedient which was as terrible to him as the Bill of Exclusion it self. The King indeed liked it as litle as he, but was overpower'd by the advice of others, and thought it necessary to justify himself in the opinion of many who concurr'd with the factious partie, not that they realy were so themselves, but out of a pannick fear for Religion, which they fancyd in mighty danger ; besides the King foresaw it would give a good colour to the Declaration which he design'd to publish for the Kingdom's satisfaction,

T O M E II.

1681.

The King dissolves the Parliament at Oxford.

KING CH: LETTERS pag: 99.

LETTERS VOL.2. p.245.

T O M E
II.

1681.

However the Kingstilldenys to let the Duke return.

King Ch: Letters pag. 100.

Letters Vol:2. p.26.

That it was not either his want of care for Religion or the people's quiet, but the turbulent temper and rebellious practices of ill men, that forced him to this sudden resolution.

But as it was his Royal Highness's destiny that those few comforts he had, should never be without some bitter ingredient; so now that he thought all obstacles and arguments removed which could hinder his return, and that his greatest enemies could not immagin a reasonable pretence to retard it, nevertheless the King tells him, he must have patience for that, till he saw further how matters were like to go, and that it might not seem as if this sudden dissolution had been only made for his convenience and to clear the way for his return to Court: This was a mighty check to his satisfaction as well as expectation; for if such wide and general reasons could serve the turn, they would never be wanting he knew, and the same pretext would subsist without end, which gave him a more heartless prospect of his afairs than any thing that yet had happen'd, he found it extream hard he should still be the main sufferer in all ill conjunctures, and receive no benifit by the good; however his friends advised him to submitt, they tould him, that till the reformes were over which the King was resolved on, both in the Leiftenancy of the City, Justices of Peace, and Militia of the whole Kingdom, the Duke's presence would give some obloquy as if it were done by his instigation; so he was forced to smother his resentment for the present both in his letters to England and his discours in Scotland, and especially in his thanks to the King for his steddyness in sticking to him, taking all to himself, without hinting at the necessity of his Majestys doing what he did even for his own preservation; nor did he so much as mention the aprehention he was in, by the offer of the expedient, hopeing by that method to gain much more upon his Majestys good nature, who liked well to have his favours relished; and indeed nothing was 'more uneasy to him, than to be pressed with too much violence, even to things never so reasonable in themselves; which made some people fancy the King might be the less inclined to the Duke's return upon that account, who by driveing him on formerly, beyond his natural pace, had render'd his Councells (thō aproved of in the King's judgment) uneasy to his temper.

T O M E
II.
1681.
LETTERS
VOL. 2. p. 315.

Assoon as the factious partie had recover'd their spirits a little, the Duke found that thō their measures were broke by this unexpected blow, yet their malice was not deminished, and therefore they neglect'd none of those methods they were yet masters of to prosecute and molest him; the time was nōw come for removeing his late presentment by *certiorari* to the King's Bench, where they found means contrary to custome and the constant practice of the Courts of Justice, to rais arguments against granting it, by one Smith a Lawier imployed by DᵗʳOates: This was such a surprise upon the Duke's Councel, who were no ways prepair'd to answer reasons they had no notion of, and in oposition to a thing that had never yet been disputed, that the Duke had certainly been convict of recusancy by this trick, had they not prevail'd with the Court to make an adjournment, which gave the Duke's Councel time to frame answers to the objections, and they proveing satisfactory, the *certiorari* was at last obtain'd ; but it hinder'd not the ashtonishment the world was in, to see the impudence his enemies were arived too, when so infamous a fellow as Oates, durst hould up his head against the King's Brother, and pretend to have him denyd a common benefit in the Law, which the meanest Subject in the Kingdom had never yet been refused.

The Duke had like to have been convicted.

Ibid. p. 264.

But notwithstanding that these angry and artefull men put the best countenance they could upon their late disadvantage, their credit nevertheless declined so visibly that the Duke of Monmouth himself began to waver, finding his projects faded

New obstacles to the Duke's return.
LETTERS
VOL. 2. p. 104.

TOME
II.

1681.
Ibid: p.321.

Ibid: p.366.

Ibid: p.272.

Ibid: p.271.

LETTERS
VOL. 2. p.273.

a little in their hands; they had given him vast hopes while they promised themselves the spoiles of the government, but were now brought too low to make other peoples fortunes; this made him think of courting an other intrest and try again if by a fawning cariage, and pretence of reclaiming he could regain the intrest he had lost with the King: At the first overture of this matter the Duke's friends had credit enough to put a check to it, but the Dutchess of Portsmouth comeing into his intrest and the King's natural afection runing before, it was hugely fear'd the Prodigal Child would be brought home again, before he left eating huskes, or even the Company of the Swine, the only obstacle was the manifest hardship of keeping the Duke in banishment, were he admitted to Court; and that being still resolved against, was the main impediment to the other, which was the only advantage his Royal Highness drew from his misfortunes; for thō the daily benefit which acrued to the government by the late vigorous proceedings began to remove the objections hithertoo insisted upon against the Duke's return, yet others sprung up in their room as his Royal Highness well foresaw; the common topick hithertoo for keeping him away, had been, the boisterousness of the weather and the unsettledness of the times: but now it was urged, that things being much quieted, should he return, it would disturb the calm, so that what way soever the wind blew it was still in his face.

However some of the Duke's friends advised him to temporise stil, and submit to these reasons, others were for his pressing the King in this matter, which pussled him the more because his inclination as well as reason prompted him to the latter; but the King's tenderness in that point (least by being urged too hard he might throw up all) made the other more prudent: at last they proposed this, That his Highness should beg leave for the Dutchess to come to the Bath or Tunbridg for her

health, which had been much impared by liveing in a Country
so contrary to that she was born in, and that for himself he
would be well contented to live at Audley end, or any other
seat his Majesty should apoint, so that he might have the
satisfaction of seeing him now and then, and even at those times
would not pretend to meddle the least in any publick business
They councel'd him likewise to express an entire resignation Ibid: p. 304.
of his own intrest to his Majestys pleasure and quiet, and that
if he did not think fit to grant him that, he was ready to submit
to any termes yet more uneasy, if his Majestys occasions
required it ; for nothing they sayd would more conduce to
obtain leave for his being nearer the King, than shewing a
willingness to go further off if necessary ; he was desired to
send Mr Churchill with his letter, and at the same time to-write
to all the persons in credit with the King, assuring them of his
being resolved to be entirely guided by their Councels.

These persons were the Chancellor and President, My Lord
Halifax, the two Secretaries, Mr Seymour, and Lord Hide,
(the King haveing lately given him the patent of a Viscount). LETTERS VOL. 2. p. 296.
Tis certain the greatest part of these persons had a dread of the
Duke's return, fearing his presence would make ciphers of
them all, the two first were so bent against it, that they
pretended withdrawing from business upon a rumour of his
being recall'd ; My Lord Halifax was no less an enemy to it,
and Mr Seymour alledged that things were not yet so well
composed, as that should he come, he would be secure not to Ibid. p. 295.
be sent away again, that it was necessary the King should be
fixed and settled in a habit of going on resolutely in good
measures, that the Sheriffs of London were now to be elected,
that Fitzharris his tryal was not yet over, on the success of
which muoh would depend ; so that he could not be of opinion,
he sayd, it was proper for the Duke to press a return till winter,
and even then he could not answer for any but himself : This being

TOME
II.

1681.

his opinion, and by consequence My Lord Conway's too (who was always guided by him) there remain'd only My Lord Hide and Secretary Jenkins who realy wished his Highness at Court again, who were much too weak a partie for the rest; especially considering the jealousie that now was got amongst them, That My Lord Hide stood fair to be Treasurer and that then under the Duke's direction, and protection (were he

Ibid: p.299.

present) he would run away with his Majestys favour, and business, from them all, and extinguish their credit and usefullness about the King; by which means that Lord's avowed duty to the Duke, was likely to bring a prejudice to his service.

LETTERS
VOL: 2. p.302.

This advice was heard (*hard*) to be digested, because the Duke was of opinion that if he were not speedely recal'd he never should, and that if he could not return with all the credit and intrest too which he ought to have in the King's business, he had rather stay where he was; the only reason against that, was, that if once he was admitted to Court again, many things could not be done without his privity and advice, and insencibly that restriction would fall away of it self; but infine without weighing consequences he was forced to submit, for the King

KING CH.
LETT. 104.

himself being positiue in the matter, tould him, He was fully perswaded their enemies wished for nothing more than such a handle as his return to create new troubles, which now by steddiness and patience he hoped to master at last, and thō he confess'd the Duke had great need of that vertue, he assured him his absence exercised it no less in himself, and that nothing but the consideration of both their goods, could make him endure the thoughts of that seperation any longer.

These kind expressions sweeten'd a little the harsh usage they carryd along with them, but could not hinder the Duke from lamenting his condition; for when he weighed the present situation of afairs on one hand, the disposition of the Ministers, the King's orders, and the advice now given him on the other, he was fully perswaded the King himself began to be jealous of him ; otherwise his friends, he fancyd, would never have councel'd him to refrain from business, which must of necessity be fatal to both, as being so necessary to their mutual support : besides (says he) if notwiths the entire submission and resignation I have always for the King's commands, he can be so far imposed upon, as to entretain such a suspicion, what may he not be brought too in a little time more? Had I affected popularity or consider'd only my own well-being in the world, I had not trodden the paths which I now am so intangled in, I could without doing any thing but what his Majesty himself press'd me too, have been above the malice of those false and mean spirited men, who now seek my ruin ; but I thank my God I have ever had a horrour of those base methods of obtaining my ends, and hope I shall still continue to make my duty to God and the King, the only rule of my actions.

T O M E II.

1681.
KING JA. Mr.
To. 9. p. 141.

But that was not the case, the King was far from being jealous, for besides that the Duke had never given the least occasion for such a mistrust, it was not in the King's temper to be so, it was the Ministers that suspected the Duke would never concur in their measures, and yet be too powerfull for them to contest with ; and therefore it was hoped, that this complyant cariage, and his Royal Highness's declining publick business, seconded by so reasonable a pretext as the Dutchesse's health, would worke upon his Majestys good nature too power-fully to be obstructed by any favorit : Wherefore the Duke dis-patches Mr Churchill immediately, with letters and Instructions pursuant to the method and advice of his friends, assuring his Majesty, that if he pleased to grant him the Satisfaction of waiting upon him, and that he may not be the only Subject who after haveing had so great a share in his troubles should

Mr Churchill sent to Court to beg leave for the Dutchess to go to the Bath. KING JA: Mr. To. 9: p. 143.

KING JA: Mr. To. 9. p. 149.

" be debar'd tasting the sweet of that quiet his Majesty now
" enjoy'd, he would not only refrain medling or speaking to his
" Majesty, or his Ministers, of any business relateing to England,
" but even as to Scotland too, if his Majesty desired it, so soon
" as he had given him a relation what condition that Kingdom
" was in, notwithstanding that he might see his afairs had
" not suffer'd or worsen'd there by his acting hithertoo in them;
" and that the generality of the Nobility and Gentry were
" extream desirous he should continue the direction of them,
" by which they knew they would escape such hard usage
" as they had experienced formerly, from many of their own
" Country men.

It was natural to believe that by removeing in this manner
what was conceiv'd to be both the King's and Minister's main
aprehention, other difficulties would have fallen of themselves ;
but thō the King heard Mr Churchill with patience, and
express'd all immaginable tenderness for the Duke, he tould
him nevertheless he could do nothing in it without adviseing
with those he trusted, and thō no sollid reason could be brought
against it, only general aprehentions, however Mr Churchill

acquaints his Royal Highness, he found both from his Majesty
and those of his Council who were then at Court, there was
very litle hopes of success; it could not be beaten out of their
heads, but that the Duke's comeing would endanger a rebellion,
and My Lord Sunderland had left behind him a dangerous
impression, that it was what the Duke wished, as being desirous
to come to a tryall of skill with his enemies in the King's life
time, by whose assistance he might better hope to master them
then when he should be left to himself ; which thō the wildest
and the worst grounded immagination in the world, was
improved by cunning men to work upon the King's excessive
love of eas, so as to make him aprehend danger even where his

own judgment tould him there was none: The King indeed

confess'd his inclination was at strife with his reason on this occasion, which togather with My Lord Halifax's absence in the Country (whose advice the King waited for) gave My Lord Hide leasure to create what friends he could, and if possible to gain the Dutchess of Portsmouth, to whom the Duke had order'd him to make some little court of late ; for thō he was perswaded honorable ways were the best, and that no great confidence could be expected betwixt him and her, however he hoped by that means, to keep her from obstructing so reasonable a thing, and by force of civilitie put a necessity upon her of being so at last to him : In order to this, a contrivance was made for Mr Churchill to wait upon the King to her lodgings, and My Lord Feversham had engaged to prepare her before hand to discours him about it, but when he came thither, she never took the least notice of him, but on the contrary when the King with the Queen (*went*) soon after to Sheerness and Chatam, she went to Altrop to give her dear friend My Lord Sunderland a visit, and at her return from thence had her private meetings with the Duke of Monmouth, My Lord Shaftsbury, and that gang; which considering her great intrest with the King was astonishing to all the world and a scurvy omen to the Duke's afairs in general; the least that could be aprehended from it, was, that if the Duke's return was allow'd of, the Duke of Monmouth's must go hand in hand with it, the King having gone a good way towards a reconciliation with him already, and thō it was a great degrading of his Royal Highness to be ranked thus upon equal termes with the Duke of Monmouth in this Controversie, yet if it had come to that, the Duke was disposed to overlook this humiliation with the rest, and fight with any armes rather than be worsted ; but when My Lord Halifax came up, he, My Lord Hide, and Mr Seymour soon brought the King off from that panty at least.

T O M E
II.

1681.
Ibid. p.327.

Ibid: p.284.

Ibid: p.404.

Ibid. p. 401.

TOME
II.

1681.

LETTERS
VOL. 2. p.408.

It was with those three persons the King debated this afair, against which the main objection was a pretended necessitie of trying first what a Parliament would do; but the King was soon convinced that nothing was more improper than the thoughts of a Parliament's meeting at all, nevertheless they agreed the King's afairs would not yet bear the Duke's return, but that when it did, it must be without the restriction of not medling with business : because it would be necessary (they sayd) he should lay his shoulder to the burthen, and helpe to support the King in the measures he was now upon, and countenance those who were imployd, and particularly themselves who advised his return; so that thō a delay was at last resolved on, it was accompanyd however with some mollefying circomstances, which made it the less distastfull to him, and finding the Ministers were come off their mighty aprehention of his medling in business, hoped they might change in other points likewise.

The Duke
being denyd
to return, the
Princess Anne
goes for
Scotland.
LETTERS
VOL. 2. p.475.

It was always his Royal Highnesse's principle to contend for what he thought just and reasonable, as far as decency and respect to the King would allow of; but when once a determination was made, he not only receiv'd all sort of denyalls and disapointments with submission, but without the least complaint of his hard usage to the King, or seeming distrust of his Ministers; so he writ to them all to shew he was well satisfyd with their conduct, hopeing by that means also to take away that aprehention of his partialitie to My Lord Hide, which had slacken'd on occasions their Zeal for his Service ; and now he settled himself entirely to the business of Scotland : Princess Anne likewise came to him, whose journey had hithertoo hung upon uncertainties, for even while there was still some hopes of the Duke's being allowed to come to Court, it was thought *Ibid.* p. 414. nevertheless very proper not to contermand the Princesse's going to Scotland (which the Duke had desired and the King

consented too) that it might be a blind upon his return, and
hinder any disturbance upon the peoples immagining it, which
was stil. aprehended would be a necessary consequence; but
that being now at an end, she went a broad a yaught the
begining of July and arrived safe at Edinburg soon after.

Besides what has been mention'd of Mr Churchill's commission, the Duke (immediately after he was sent) writ to desire
another favour of the King, which was the easalyer granted
that he might not seem to deny him every thing: His Royal
Highness it seems had been advised by many of the chief "
men in Scotland, that it would (be) both for the King's "
Seruice and his advantage, that a Parliament were call'd in "
that Kingdom; the Duke sends their reasons to the King, "
and withall proposes himself to be his Commissioner, not "
thinking it fitting either for the King's Seruice, or the dignity "
of his own person, that any body els should represent his "
Majesty, if he were then on the place; but least it might be "
used as a pretext for keeping him there, he gave orders that "
this matter should not be open'd to his Majesty unless the "
other was denyd; when therefore it was proposed the King "
gave more readily into it, to soften in some measures the "
harsh treatment his Royal Highness had received in all the "
rest.   "

It was not doubted but the Loyal disposition of the greatest
part of the nobilitie and Gentrie, together with the Duke's
presence and winning behaviour, which had gain'd such an
influence over that Kingdom, would make a Parliament not
only contribute to the quiet and advantage of Scotland, but
by running counter to that of England, be a check and bar to
such violent proceedings as hithertoo distracted that Nation; "
the only aprehention was of My Lord Lauderdal's being "
influenced by his Lady to oppose it, for fear least a Parliament "

Marginal notes:

TOME
II.

1681.

Ibid. p. 511.

The Duke
disire a Par-
liament may
be call'd in
Scotland.

Ibid. p. 433.

KING JA. M^{rs}
To. 8. p. 273.

T O M E
II.

1681.

" should look a little too narrowly into certain methods she
" had lately found out of geting mony for herself.

" The designe of it therefore was no sooner made publick,
" but the factious partie there (who foresaw the consequence) in
" conformetie with their breethren in England used all manner
" of endeavours to obstruct what ever should be offer'd for the
" King's service, and particularly the Duke's being his
" Commissioner ; they pretended that the Statute made in the
" first parliament of King James the 6th, admitted of none to bear
" any office that did not conforme to the established Religion ;
" this was proposed to the Duke of Hamilton, which, thō he
" rejected it, as it deserved (the Act not extending to a
" Commissioner) however he was a little stubborn when the
" Duke first spoke to him ; and thō his Highness offer'd to have
" him readmitted into the Council, out of which he had been
" put by My Lord Lauderdal's means, he declin'd it at first,
" till within a day or two being better advised he came to an
" esayer temper. But these objections and difficulties made

LETTERS
VOL.2. p.435.

no impression upon his Majesty, so he order'd My Lord
Murray, Secretary for that Kingdom, to dispatch away his
proclamation and letter to the Council of Scotland, nomeing
the Duke his Commissioner in the Parliament which he
apointed to meet on the 28th of Jully following.

Fitzharris tryd.

The same day these dispatches went for Scotland Fitzharris
was tryd, which put the King in a track of unraveling all the
wicked misteries of the Cabal ; thō no industry had been
wanting on their part, to ward this blow, and preserue if
possible a life on which so many depended : In order to this
they had contrived to have him accuse My Lord Danby and
some others, of Sr Edmond Bury Godefrey's death, and means

LETTERS
VOL.2. p.381.

was found to bring him (thō prisoner) to the King's bench bar
fo this end, where, upon his information, the Bil was found by

the Grand Jurie, and My Lord Chancellor so far gave into the TO M E
trap, as to move for that Lord's being tryd for it immediately ;
but it apear'd so ridiculous and scandalous to question a Peer
upon an information of a man who had been so offt examin'd
before the Secretaries and Council, and thō stil pretending to
declare all he knew, never mentioned My Lord Danby before,
that at last all thoughts of it was layd aside, and those sly
managers disapointed of their aim ; which was to have got his
own tryal differ'd on that pretext, then by bringing on some
other information have done the like again, and by that means
reprived him in effect as long as they thought needfull ; which
had they succeeded in, their cunning had gon beyond the
power of Parlimentary votes or addresses, which had declared
it a high breach of priviledg to try any person (who lay under
their Impeachment) for the same crimes for which they stood
impeached; which, thō it was vehemently urged at his tryal,
and the pannel, a pack of the worst men the Citie could afford,
yet the plea was overruled, and he found guilty upon the information of Sʳ. William Waller and the other two witnesses,
much against their wills; who were thus forced to execute
justice upon a wicked instrument of their own and hang a man
they had accused, only to lead into a method of hanging others,
and by that means have kept up the credit of the Duke's being
stil in a plot, without which they saw, he would soon be in a
situation aboue the reach of their malice.

This trick failing so scurvily, My Lord Shaftsbury tryd
another ; he comes to the Chancellor and tould him, That there
was a gentleman of good fashion who could make a further
discovery of Sʳ. Edmond Bury Godefrey's death, if he might
have a pardon ; and prevail'd with him to write to the King
(who was then at Windsor) about it : but My Lord Hide and
Mʳ. Seymour soon convinced his Majesty how scandelous it
would (*have*) apear'd, after so many pardons, and three years

T O M E
II.
1681.

LETTERS
VOL. 2. p. 443.

My Lord
Shaftsbury
trys another
trick to keep
up the Credit
of the Plot.
LETTERS
VOL. 2. p. 393.

T O M E
II.

1681.

The Dutchess
of Ports-
mouth's prac-
tices layd open
by Fizharris's
trayall.
LETTERS
VOL. 2. p.430.

Ibid. p.444.

elapsed since the thing happen'd, to give way to fresh accusations, so that this project was quashed in like manner: Nevertheless they were not yet discouraged, and since they saw there was no supporting of the credit of the Plot in England, they endeavour'd to receive it however in Ireland; in order to which one Dennis, Hethington, and Macnamara, three Irish witnesses were put upon hireing others to corroberate their testimony against the Queen, the Lord of Ormonde and Lord Chancelor of that Kingdom; but their practices being discover'd, and they clapt up upon an action of subordination, this contrivance was stifled in its infancy too; so that now the strugglings of the partie were like those of a man in his agonie, which are rather simptoms of aproaching death, than helps to recover life and strength again.

Amongst other advantages which the Court gain'd by thus countermining the Plots of the faction, especially in Fitzharris's tryal (which made both sides put such stress upon it) was the bringing many hidden things to light which otherwise would probably never have been discover'd: Fitzharris it seems at his tryal had subpena'd the Dutchess of Portsmouth, Mrs Wall, and My Lord Howard of Escrek, to prove he had been imployd by her Grace to bring eminent persons over (to) the King's intrest, thinking to make a merit of haveing been so serviceable to the Court, and that My Lord Howard had had a conference with her accordingly; so when that Lord gave in his testimony, he sayd, Their conversation would (was) chiefly upon endeavouring to procure a good understanding betwixt the King and his Parliament, and that the Dutchess of Portsmouth's intentions were very good in that matter, and used her endeavours to take off his Majesty from adhereing so fast to the Duke: so now his Royal Highness saw, what a special friend she had been to him all along, and how extraordinary a providence it was, that a person who had so great a credit with the King (considering

how hard other matters press'd upon him) had not prevail'd
with him to abandon his Brother long before; but the Duke
was forced to overlook all this, that he might give no ombrage
to the King of being like to live uneasily with her, who now
seeing the wind came about, and her other friends failing her,
began to wheedle with the Duke not only receiv'd with all
markes of kindness but return'd his too by the same hand ; and
considering how necessary this complyance was to give the
Duke's friends a greater credit not only with her, but the
King too, the Duke and Dutchess writ to her also, but had
no mind indeed their letters should be deliver'd unless it
were thought absolutely necessary; so Mʳ Churchill's verbal
compliment doing the work, they were burnt as had been
directed.

But this was not all the misteries which Fitzharris' tryal
discover'd, it seems My Lord Howard had other dealing with
him than he thought fit to mention ; for he was no sooner found
guilty, but Fitzharris's wife and maid came and accused that
Lord himself to have had the greatest share in composing that
Libel for which her husband was condemn'd, and that most of
it was writ in his own hand; upon which his Lordship was
seized and sent to the Tower, and immediately after Fitzharris
was executed : But that the pretended Popish Plot might not
seem to dy with him (the King being desirous to trim a little)
Bishop Plunket the Catholick Primat of Ireland haveing been
most falsely acused and condemn'd as guilty of that pretended
conspiracy, was executed the same day, which those who
wished the King well were very sorry had been so hastely
done ; for besides that his last speech convinced all men of
his innocency, My Lord Shaftsbury the very next day was
committed to the Tower upon the information of Six Irish
witnesses, five of which were Protestants ; which did so plainly
manifest the real vilanie that had been cover'd under this

T O M E
II.
1681.

LETTERS
VOL. 2. p. 478.

Ibid: p. 531.

Lord Howard
of Escrick sent
to the Tower.

Bishop
Plunket
executed.
LETTERS
VOL: 2. p. 491.

TOME
II.

1681.

LETTERS
VOL. 2. p.492.

The Earle of
Shaftsbury
commited to
the Tower.

Ibid. p.506.

LETTERS
VOL. 2. p.495.

Ibid: p.505.

SIR ROBERT
L'ESTRANG
HIST: TIMES.
123.

pretended Popish Plot, and particularly the wicked combination to take way that holy Bishop's life, that My Lord Clarendon sayd, All honest men trembled when they reflected how much inocent blood had been spilt upon it.

The commitment of this Lord produced a mighty change in peoples judgments and affections, and was exceeding usefull to the Duke's friends, and to convince the world how unjustly he had suffer'd under the long persecution of such wicked and treacherous contrivances : So that this great Patriot instead of being rescued as he hoped to have been by the Citie, was houted at for a traitor, as he went through it to the Tower, which shew'd how willing the people were to be of the King's side, if endeavours had been used to make them so ; and thō at his first apearance at Council several Lords there seem'd more afraid of him, than he of his accusations, yet when the warrant was sign'd for his commitment, he sunk on a sudden with aprehention, and look'd as dejected then, as he had done impudently before.

Tis fitting this age should be acquainted with the Character of a man, that had so great a hand in the confusions of the last, and had been so industrious a prosecutor of all those wicked contrivances against His Royal Highness : We are tould therefore by one who knew him well, that in all revolutions from his first apearance in the world, he had the cunning to keep the wind on his back and to swim continualy with the tide, so that in all changes from the year fourthy to sixty, he came sailing down before it ; he had a ready tongue and a great adress in business, without those barrs of honour, shame and conscience, which are so obstructive to ambitious designs ; while matters went successfully with him his good humour keept pace with his good fortune, never any man run higher in commendation of the King, nor stood up more for the Prerogative than himself while he was Chancellor, but when the wind came about to the popular partie, he turu'd tail to the government, and proved the most envenomed cnemic the King and Duke ever had ; as to his last change some thing might be sayd for his excuse, that he deserted not the King til his Majesty deserted himself by recaling the declaration for Libertie of conscience; so that finding he could not be supported at Whitehall, he was resolved to seek it at Westminster ; he had rather a subtil wit than a solid judgment, and was better at pulling down than building up, never any incendiary had a quicker invention and a more protesting face, without faith or truth, with which he imposed upon mankind, as apear'd by his perswading the Kingdom into two contradictions in the space of a year : for in his speech when he was Chancellor, he convinced the world that the State was never in a happyer Situation (because in reality he was so himself) that there was no danger from Popery nor any thing els, and before the year's end without any visible change (except in his own condition) he made the Kingdom believe their was no liveing for fear of it.

But thō his heart fail'd him (as was sayd) a little at the first upon his commitment, he had still his witts about him ; and by demanding the benefit of his Habeas Corpus before the Attorney Generall was aware of it, both he and My Lord Howard had like to have got out.; but they prevented that, and found means to hould them fast for a while, thō at last he slipt through their fingers by a stratagem, which gravel'd the Court more than any thing that had happen'd during the whole course of these troubles.

When the news of Shaftsbury's being sent to the Tower came to Edinburg, the Duke was no less pleas'd to see the King at last pursue those methods heartely which were only capable of relieveing him, than to see so evenomed an enemie humbled, and his villanies detected : He begg'd therefore of

" King Ja. Mᵗ
To. 8. p.281.

" his Ma^{ty} to follow the blow now that they were stunn'd, as
" the only way to master a faction which by long experience
" he had found was never to be gain'd by concessions nor
" indulgence, that the hand of God was visibly in it not only
" in bringing their villanies to light, but by turning their own
" malicious designes upon themselves, and had cast them into
" the pit they had dug for others, that it was a good prelude
" to the Parliament of Scotland, and gave good grounds to
" hope in that Kingdom likewise the Partie would be so
" discouraged as not to attempt any thing which might hinder
" the happy issue of that Sessions.

The P^{ce} of
Orange comes
for England.

LETTERS
VOL. 2. p. 522.

But the Duke had scarce leasure to reflect upon this
advantage, before news was brought him of the Prince of
Orange's desire to make the King a visite, which he press'd
with so much earnestness and hast (on pretence of being obliged
to be back on such a time) that the King was under a necessity
either of denying him (which he could not in civility doe) or
permiting him to come before he was prepar'd to weigh well
the consequences of it, or have the Duke's therein; who dreaded
the effects of that intervew, and fail'd not to advertice his
Majesty of several visible objections against his comeing ; as

KING JA. M^{rs}
To. 8. p. 288.

" that it would give great heart and a new life to the factious
" partie at this critical time, when the King had them in a
" manner under his feet, that it would create great jealousie at
" the court of France, which would be of the worst consequence
" in the present circomstances, but above all it was manifest
" his business could beno other, than to worke the (King) to an
" agreement with his Parliament, which would lead him back
" into the Laberinth he had now found the only way out of,
" and quite blast the Duke's expectations of even seeing an

LETTERS
VOL: 2. p. 541.

" end of his miseries : but leave being given before these
reasons could be writ, much less consider'd, the Prince of
Orange made great hast over and arrived the 24th of July at

Windsor; he carryd fair at first, but it soon apear'd his aims
wefe such as gave all immaginable reasons of jealousie to his
Royal Highness, for thō his prentence was only succours for
Flanders and Holland, yet it was easily understood, that
succours could not be obtain'd but by a Parliament, and to be
sure the Duke would be sacrificed as a preliminary, before
one penny could be hoped for.

When therefore he press'd for a Parliament, the King asked
him, Whether in case it should propose again·the Bill of
Exclusion, he would advise him to pass it? He abhor'd it: *Ibid.* p.542.
Then, says the King, but if they proposed a Limitation? he
answered, The Crowne could not be tyd: Put (*the*) case,
says his Majesty, they insist upon haveing such Officers in all
imployments as they can confide in, and so take the Militia,
Navy, Sea Portes, Judges &c, out of my power! He replyd,
he disclaim'd it, Why then, sayd the King, it being manifest
that the Parliament has, and consequently will insist upon
these things, and that if notwithstanding all this, a Parliament
be necessary; it behoues you to offer some measures to aecom-
modate these contradictions; to which he desired time to
consider, and leave to speake with whom he pleas'd about it;
which being given him, he immediatly return'd to London,
where he was no sooner arrived, but My Lord Russell waited upon
him, and the two Sherifs doing the same, invited him to diner *Ibid.* p.553.
in the Citie, which he readily accepted; and when My Lord
Halifax, My Lord Hide, and Mr Seymour diswaded him from
it, he replyd, He had been twice in England and had dined in
the Citie both time, and knew no reason he might not doe
it now; but they tould him the Citie was then in a fair
correspondence, but now in a direct opposition to the King:
At which he growing angry turn'd from them, and sayd, He
had promis'd, and he would go; but Mr Seymour posting
upon it to Windsor to acquaint the King with what had pass'd,

T O M E
II.

1681.

LETTERS
VOL. 2. p.560.

his Majesty writ to him to come immediately thither, which he durst not but comply with, thō he made no difficulty of owneing how much he was troubled to break his word with his beloved Citizens.

At his return to Windsor he renew'd his sollicitations that a Parliament might be speedily call'd, that the delaying of it had never made them more tractable, and that without it his Majestys Allys abroad would be overrun: The King sayd, It would doe them no service to assemble a Parliament and brake it immediately, which he was sure he should be necessitated to doe ; but promis'd (if that would satisfy him) that in case the French invaded Flanders, he would then call one, thō he was convinced they would not give him a farthing but on the conditions he had already mention'd : notwithstanding this assurance, the Prince still urged his Majesty would pleas to try them at least, for thō he believ'd they would propose the Bill of Exclusion, yet he hop'd they might be brought to consent to other expedients for security of Religion ; but the King being sencible that no good could come of their meeting, and that he should loos by it all the advantage he had already got, was positiue against it ; upon which the Prince desired a Conference might be had at least with the Spanish and Dutch Ambassadors, which was done accordingly, and their request and reasons fully answer'd, which put an end to this negociation.

The Pᵉ of
Orangereturns
disatsfyd.

It was visible enough from all these proceedings, that thō perhaps the concern the Prince was in for Flanders and Holland, might be one motine of his comeing; yet it was not the chief ; he was not stranger to the temper of English Parliaments, who had ever (he knew) a much greater attention to their own priviledge and encreas of power, than to support the King's honour in forreing Wars and Allyances, thō of their own adviseing ; and therefore had the King by the Prince's perswasion been again intangled in that net, he saw very well the Duke must fall in the end, and the Monarchy itself be grievously plumed, ere any thing considerable could have been squees'd from them; and thō he had so good a share in the expectancy, which the King tould him would be ill policy in him to postpone to an Electiue title, yet it is probable he was too impatient to wait for his turn, and that without doubt he aim'd at that unnatural usurpation at least upon his Vuele and Father in Law, which Seaven years after he found means to accomplish; but being disapointed for this time and finding all his artes and arguments unsuccessfull, he went away as ill satisfyd with others as others were with him; for thō he was far from being able to answer particulars, yet he would never submit; for as the King observed, he loved not to be convinced: however he parted fair in apearance, with many protestations of affection and defference to the King at least.

T O M E
II.
1681.

KING CH:
LETTERS
p. 112.

The Duke had seemingly a fair delivrance of the P^ce of Orange's journey; but the dreggs of it which he left behind, rais'd such a ferment after he was gon, as made his Royal Highness aprehend that notwithstanding all his struggling he should fall a sacrifice in the end either to the malice of his enemies or the King's necessities. The disconted partie were at last convinced that by contending with the King they had always come by the wors, so changed their method and resolved to see what wheedling and a seeming complyance would do; several therefore of the hottest members pretended to be so aprehensive of Flanders, that they profer'd, in case the King would call a Parliament, they would give a supply for that end, without insisting upon the Bill of Exclusion, the Limitation, or the displaceing of any Minister; this train (which was of the P^ce of Orange's laying) was by being so plausible, much more dangerous for his Royal Highness, than their rough and haughty way of proceeding; it staggar'd many people of distinction, particularly My Lord Chamberlin,

The disconted
Partie profer
expedients
which were
ruinous to y^e
Duke.

LETTERS
VOL. 2. p. 574.

Ibid: p. 584.

TOME
II.
—————
1681.
Ibid: p.588.

and there was great caballing about it; but those who had better insight into the drift and wiles of that Partie, were not to learn that if the King were once fetter'd again with a Parliament, and a War, they could lead him by more ways than one to the wilderness he had been so lately lost in, and the last errour would have been harder to remedy than the former. So by good fortune for the Duke, his Majesty was above the temptation, and stuck to the measures he had already taken.

The Parliament meets in Scotland.

The Parliament in Scotland was by this time assembled, where the King's letter being read, his Royal Highness made them this following Speech.

KING JA: Mⁿ
To: 9. 158.

" As I have had the honour to serue his Majesty in other
" capacities, so I esteem it none of the least, to be made choise
" of as his Commissioner in this his antient Kingdom, since
" it shews to all the world as well his kindness to me, as the
" trust and confidence he has in me, by putting me not only
" in a capacity of serving him as becomes a dutyfull and loyal
" Subject, but also by giveing me an opertunity of letting you
" all see the real concerne I have for the good of this Country,
" and my readyness to serve it and promote its intrests.

" I doe not doubt but this will be a happy meeting, and
" give satisfaction to his Majesty and all his Loyal Subjects;
" which I say with the greater confidence, haveing by my long
" residence amongst you, found so great and universall a
" readiness in advanceing whatever was for his Majestys
" Seruice.

" You have heard in his Majestys letter the reasons for his
" calling you together at this time, and what he does and may
" expect from this his antient Kingdom, of whose loyalty and
" affection he has so little reason to doubt.

" He has commanded me to assure you, that he will inviolably
" mentain and protect the Protestant Religion as now established
" by Law, and the Church government by Arch Bishops and

Bishops, and will take all your other concernes into his " TOME
Royal care and protection; and seriously recommends to you " II.
to fall upon such courses as shall be necessary for suppressing " 1681.
those seditious and rebellious conviticles, from which proceeds "
so much disorder and confusion, and all those horrid and "
extravagant doctrines, which are such scandall to Christianity, "
and so manifest a subvertion of all publick and private intrests· "
in this Kingdom. "

I am also to declare to you in his name, that it is, and "
always was his intention, that the Laws should have their "
due cours for the security of his Subjects, their rights, and "
properties, and that he will discountenance all courses "
inconcistant with them, no one being more concern'd in "
their due observance than himself: "

He does also expect on your part, that you will not be "
short of the Loyalty of your Ancestors in aserting and "
clearing his Royal prerogative, and declareing the rights of "
the Crown in its natural and legal cours of descent; and that "
you will take care to provide and settle such necessary and "
seasonable supplys, as the intrest and the support of his "
government calls for; and I hope also, that as the Council "
has already done their part in promoting the trade of this "
Kingdom, you will likewise do yours too, by endeavouring "
to make it still flourish more and more. "

MY LORDS AND GENTLEMEN: The inclination I have "
to serue and promote the intrests of this Kingdom, has been "
the chief inducement to his Majesty to give me the opertunity "
of convincing you of it; so you may be sure I shall not fail "
in any thing which conduces to that end; and I hope you "
will have the same consideration and kindness for me, as to "
enable me to performe what shall be most for his Majesties "
service also. "

TOME
II.

1681.
LETTERS
VOL. 2. p. 471.

This augmentation of power, thō it was beneficial to the Duke in some kind, yet it gave a handle to many of his greatest and slyest enemies to create jealousies in the King, which thō it was a distemper his Majesty was not much subject too, however it being so naturall to Princes, it put an obligation upon his Royal Highness of being exceeding cautious, and to act in his station of Commissioner with an entire regard to the King's intrest, and not to give the least surmise he had any hidden, or by ends of his own; and indeed never any Commissioner, whose fortune might seem to depend upon the success of his management, could be more vigilent, zealous, and active in his Majestys service, which made the success answerable to both their expectations.

LETTERS
VOL. 2. p. 587.

The question about the Bourroughs was the first tryall of Skill; which being carryed for the Court, was a good omen that all other matters would go on answerable to its wish, they readily agreed to send a most loyal and dutifull adres to his Majesty, and concurr'd to what ever was proposed to them for the support of the King's preragative, as well as what related only to the common benefit of the Nation; and to convince the world that the Duke was not so blindly zealous in his Religion, as that if ever it were in his power he would force

Ibid: p. 617.

those who would not go to Mass, to go to Smithfeild (as his enemies industriously gave it out) he not only concurr'd too, but took great pains to conquer all oppositions in passing such Acts as were for the security of the established Religion, and got an Oath or Test to be enacted, which all Officers in Church and State, or Graduates in the Vniversities, were to take for its further support, and prevail'd for the same reason to have all field conventicles suppress'd.

The Parlia-
ment in
Scotland
declare highly

The Parliament likewise on their part were not wanting neither in markes and expressions of duty to the King, or

affection and gratitude to his Royal Highness; and therefore
pass'd an Act to assert the rights of Succession, where in they
declared that the Crown of Scotland, as well by inherent right
and nature of the Monarchy, as by the foundamentall and
unalterable Laws of the Kingdom, does descend by lineal
Succession according to proximity of bloud, and that no
difference in Religion nor Act of Parliament itself could alter
or divert the said right of Succession, and lineal descent of the
Crown to the nearest heire, and declared it high treason either
by word or writeing to endeavour the alteration, suspention, or
divertion of the Right of Succession.

The world was surprised at this testimony of the dutyfullness
and Loyalty of the Kingdom of Scotland, which haveing been
always looked upon as the fountain of Presbiterie, should so
strenuously assert the Preragative of the Crown, when England
it self flew so furiously in its face; and therefore it was not to
be express'd how wonderfully the news of these proceedings
ashtonished the Duke's enemies in England: they had thought
it at first impossible he should be able to serve the King there,
and had fram'd a thousand lyes for that purpose as it was
customary with them on such occasions; and therefore were
the more dejected, when they found that the Duke had master'd
all opposition which they fancyd he would have sunk under, and
not only encreas'd his intrest, but augmented his reputation
by his great adress and dexterity in business, whereby he
had dashed all their hopes, detected their falceties, and reduced
their power and credit to the last gaspe.

My lord Conway therefore and Lord Hide thought this a
fit time for his Royal Highness to renew his sollicitations to be
recall'd to Court, not doubting but so much patience, So
perfect an obedience, and so much pains in his Majesties
business would receive its due reward at last; and to the end
it might be the easilyer granted, his Highness was advised to

TOME
II.

1681.
in favour of
the Preroga-
gative, and the
descent to the
true Line.

LETTERS
VOL: 2. p. 591.

The Duke's
friends renew
their sollicita-
tion for his
return.
LETTERS
VOL: 2. p. 477

T O M E
II.

1681.
Ibid: p. 572.

desire only leave to come for a few days, that he might give his Majesty an account of the transactions during the Parliament, and what was necessary for the future quiet and good of that Kingdom, and particularly about chusing a new Chancellor, with a proffer to return when ever the King pleased; and as a greater argument of it, not to desire leave for the Dutchess to come along with him.

Considering how prosperously things had gon of late not only in Scotland but in England too, it was believ'd nothing could be objected against it: Colledge had been found guilty at Oxford, who haveing been a violent partizan of the factious tribe was accused of several crimes, but acquitted by a shamefull ignorant Jurie in the Citie of London, but being sent to Oxford where part of his vilanies had been committed, he received there a due reward for them all; and the Court was so far in hopes to prevent the like packing of Juries in the Citie again, as that My Lord Shaftsbury might have as much justice as the Law would give him; but fortune was as cross to the Duke as his enemies were malicious, for an accident happen'd which did not only disapoint this, but drew an other persecution upon his R. H. which was more grievous than all the rest and at a time he expected it the least.

My Lord
Halifax
opposes it.
LETTERS
Vol: 2. p. 589.

Ibid. p. 592.

My lord Halifax it seems was conceiv'd to be less inclined than any of the cabinet Council to the Duke's return, and therefore this project about his writeing to desire it, had not been communicated to him; but when M^r. Oglethorpe arriv'd from Scotland with the Letters concerneing it, My Lord Conway without reflexion shew'd My Lord Halifax his Royal Highnesse's letter; at which he was hugely surprised, that such a thing should be negociated without his privitie, and gave him such a jealousie that the Duke put not an entire confidence in him, that tho My Lord Hide used all immaginable artes and asseverations to remove that uneasiness, it is still remain'd

even so far as to influence his advice against it, of which he T O M E II.
made no secret to the Duke himself; assureing him that nothing
could be more unvellcom to him in the world than to have the 1681.
Ibid: p.608.
honour of his commands, and at the same time the misfortune
of thinking it not for his Highnesse's seruice that they should
be complyd with; and his opinion bore so much weight with
the King, that instead of his Royal Highness's obtaining leave
to come to Court (of which he thought himself secure) My
Lord Hide was order'd to go to Scotland with the most
ungratefull message he could possebly be charged with, it being
to tell his Highness, That his Religion was still an invincible
obstacle to whatever good or favour his Ma^y design'd him, and
that without a complyance in that point all other tentatives
would be inefectual.

Whether the Duke's complyance in being present when the My Lord Hide is sent to Edinburg to pèrswade the Duke to change his Religion.
LETTERS VOL. 2. p.585.
prayers were read in the Parliament, as the Commissioners
were always used to be, and his concurrance in passing the
Acts about Religion, made people fancy he might possebly
make a further step, and that those things were only design'd
as preparatives; or whether it was My Lord Halifaxe's opinion
(hightened perhaps by the late disgust,) that had prevail'd upon
the King, My Lord Hide infine was sent to Edinburg (there
being no means of eluding it now) to tell the Duke in plain
termes, That unless he would conforme and go to Church he " KING JA: M^n To. 9: p. 167.
must expect no leave to return to Court, nor could his "
Majesty, he sayd, support him any longer but on that "
condition, that he had struggled hard to defend him hithertoo, "
but that now, without his complyance herein, not only he, "
but the King himself must be inevitably ruin'd. "

The Duke was amazed to find himself (he knew not how)
blown farther back than ever, just when he thought he had
wether'd the storme, and was entring into a secure harbour;
had he not been formed to these traverses of fortune, and

TOME
II.

1681.
KINGJA:M™
To:9. p.168.

prepared for such contradiction, he must have sunk into dispair " with the very reflection on such a treatment; nor did My " Lord Hide fail on his part, by reason of his own inclination ". as well as the King's order, to press his Royal Highness with all manner of arguments to swallow if possible this bitter pill: for tho no man could serue the Duke with more zeal and fidelity than that Lord had done, yet he was ever so disponding in that point, as to tell his Royal Highness continually, That he must expect to see no other signes of his Stedyness to his intrest, than in his sinking with him, unless he himself would make that step which alone could save both hims and all those who depended on him.

It was easy to be immagin'd that all the Duke's friends would run into this cry, he always stood alone in this debate, in which friends and enemies join'd hands against him : My

LETTERS
VOL. 2. p. 610.

Lord Halifax tould him That all the good part of England, seconded My Lord Hide's errand with their wishes, and tho it was a tender point which no one durst venter to press home, yet (he sayd) he could not hould (out of the abundance of his zeal for his prosperitie) from assureing him, he should think it a greater miracle than had happen since the Apostles time, to wether the storme which his enemies had rais'd against him, without takeing away the armes he had put into their hands; that the hopes of this, had been hithertoo the support of his friends, and preserved them in his intrest, but that if once they dispair'd of it, he must expect all men would desert his cause, as they would a towne that can no longer be defended, and that his enemies would triumph for a victory not of their gaining, but his giveing.

KING JA. M™
To:9. p.168.

" In this strain run all their sollicitations and arguments; " and My Lord Hide in two or three days conversation and " discours on this subject, made a full representation of the " dismal situation his Royal Highnesse's afairs were in, if he

did not acquiess to the King's request and resolution in this " TOME
matter; but to their grief, as well as his immortal glory, and " II.
happiness, all those temptations could not shake him in the 1681.
least, which made them lament that generosity, which they
could not deny but suited so well with his character and which LETTERS VOL. 2. p.612.
they loved and admired so much on other occasions, should
now (as they imagin'd) be so fatal to him and them; but
finding him impregnable, My Lord Hide as the last efort " KING JA: Mⁿ To. 9. p. 160.
and lowest conditions he must ever expect, pull'd a paper "
out of his poket writ by the King himself, profering, That in "
case he would promis to go to Church without doeing more, "
he should haue libertie to come to Court so soon as the "
Parliament in Scotland was up: But the Duke persisting in "
a constant denyal, My Lord Hide left him with the comfortless
view of being abandon'd by all the world, charged with the
ruin of the King's affairs which went nearer his heart than that
of his own, and of ending his days in the most uneasy banishment and afflicting circomstances that fortune could possebly
reduce him too.

Tis certain never man gave higher proofs of true Christian
resolution and constancy, nor underwent a harder tryall, than
this Pious and generous Prince on this occasion; which might
much better have become those primitiue times My Lord
Halifax spoke of, than such a desolate age in which so much
suffring for the sake of Truth was generally counted as great a
scandal and follie as to the Jews and Gentils in the Apostles
time, which in some measure verifyd his Lordship's prophesie
about it; and thō it is to be fear'd he will have few followers,
he will never want admirers, amongst which even those very
persons who threaten'd to throw all up, if he persisted in his
resolution, could not forbear from ranking themselves, by
commending what so much displeas'd them, and even acting
as formerly in his business; so prevalent is true Christian

generosity to force an esteem even from those, who are most offended by it.

As all this sollicitation made no alteration in the Duke's Judgment, neither did the hardships he underwent make any change in his affection and dutifull comportment to the King, nor in his sedulous attention to the affairs committed to his charge; which he managed with so much prudence and conduct, and govern'd the debates in Parliament with such adress, that he brought it at last to a happy conclusion : and least the people might object, that their well being had no share in his concern, and that his attention was only to doe the King's business or his own, he permitted them to sit on, after all the publick bills were pass'd, till they had finished severall Acts relateing only to the Country business, so that no one could accuse him of partiality; for haveing prevail'd to gain a precedency to the King's business (a thing scarce ever done in an English Parliament) he let them see, they fair'd not the wors for their civilitie and confidence; so that all sides were pleas'd, and only he who was the main instrument of this good accord, was left groaning under the pressure of disfavour and persecution, and no prospect left of ever seeing an end of his misfortunes.

The Duke sends his Scheme for the future government of Scotland.

But the King's natural afection as well as love of justice, would not let him persever in so harsh a resolution, especially after he had heard from My Lord Hide, that thô his Royal Highness was immoveable in his Religion, he had been no less zealous and indeed no less successfull in his Majestys business; which mollefyd him a little, and incouraged My Lord Hide to renew his sollicitation, that his Highness might be permitted to come and acquaint his Majesty at least with the state of his affairs in Scotland now the Parliament was ended, and also to lay before him a certain Scheme for the future government of that Kingdom, and the disposal of severall offices vacant at that time.

The King seem'd not avers from so reasonable a thing, but objected, It was not yet to be thought of, till the tryalls of the two Lords Shaftsbury and Howard were over ; which he repeated several times, and so put a stop to any further sollicitation for the present, but being resolved not to dispose of the Chancellor of Scotland's place nor any other but with the Duke's advice, he writ to him to send the Scheme he mention'd ; to which the Duke replyd, That not being " permited to deliver it by word of mouth, he would do it in " the best manner he could by writeing, thō it must needs be " much more imperfect, in regard he could not obviate such " objections as might be made by those, who were not so " perfectly instructed in the affairs of Scotland ; and which it " would be impossible to foresee, but were he present could " easily answer. "

He acquainted the King therefore, that the great mis- " management in that Kingdom of late had risen chiefly from " private animosities, many of those whom his Majesty had " intrusted of late haveing govern'd their actions more by that, " than the views of his intrest ; which had so dissatisfyd the " generalitie of the Nation, that it was absolutely necessary " such men should be layd aside. "

This the King had been convinced of some time before, and finding the Parliament willing to joyn with him in that reforme, was fond enough of granting a Commission for that purpose, with designe to have it reinforced with a parliamenty power to take off the odium of that ungratefull ofice from himself. But the Duke thought it no good policy in his Majesty, to " call for aid from a Parliament to execute what he had " authority of himself to doe ; that it was proper only for him " to punish and reward, which convinced the King of his " mistake, and prevented the Parliament's intermedleing in a " matter which belong'd purely to his prerogatiue ; he advised "

TOME II.
1681.

KING JA: M'*
To.8. pag.233.

LETTERS
VOL.2. p.623.

KING JA: M'.
To.8. pag.295.

" him likewise to make choice of such as had given proofs of
" their fidelity and were of Loyal familys, it being such his
" Majesty was to depend on both in England and Scotland,
" and that the extraordinary favours and partialities formerly
" shewn to the Lord Argile, could neither be answer'd nor
" without much difficulty amended, since that that family had
" been so much advanced and so much power put imprudently
" into their hands.

" The King, he sayd, knew so well the temper and consti-
" tution of that Kingdom that he needed say the less to him
" of it, nor tell him, that being sure of the affections of the
" Nobilitie and Gentry, there was no need of fearing the
" rest, who had so great a dependance on them especially
" northwards; that he found the generality well inclined and
" scarce any that had power or even will to disturbe his affairs,
" that it was their intrest as well as duty to be Loyall and
" preserve the present government, that they dreaded nothing
" more than to see presbitery and de Covenant restored, or a
" Commonwealth in England, either of which would make
" them as great Slaves as in Cromwell's time, there being but
" one or two Noblemen in Scotland that he suspected to be of
" republickan principles; so that tho the West and some of
" the South partes were fill'd with Commoners of the refined
" Presbiterian doctrine, and were all for a Commonwealth, yet
" that it would be no hard matter to keep the Country quiet ;
" but that as for the union and good understanding which was
" so much desired amongst the people of qualitie, he thought it
" very hard to be compass'd, the King he Sayd knew their
" disposition and the piques they had to one another, never-
" theless, it was an easy matter enough to unite them so far,
" as that all sides might agree to serue his Majesty as they
" ought; but that it was not to be efected by laying any one
" man aside, and puting in an other in his station, no particular

person being so universally beloved as that all sides would "
be pleas'd with him ; that whosomever for example, should "
be put in the Duke of Lauderdal's place and have the sole "
management of affairs committed to him, would make himself "
be felt as much as he had done before by those who were not "
his friends or of an other intrest. "

What he had to offer therefore, he sayd, was, that the "
King would have two Secretaries of State for that Kingdom, "
one to reside in Scotland, the other in England, through "
whose hands all the business might pass, that they should "
take their turnes and chang every year or halfe year, and to "
prevent these two takeing too much upon them, and running "
into the same errours and partialities others have done before "
them, he advised that five or six of the Scotch Privy Council "
might always attend at Court too, and be changed in like "
manner every year; through whose hands likewise the "
business passing would hinder the Secretaries from shewing "
partialities, and obviate that common clamor of one man's "
engrossing the whole governing part, as if he were King of "
Scotland. "

The standing forces, he sayd, were in no good condition "
for want of experienced Officers, very few of them haveing "
seen any seruice, or knew any thing of their duty, that most "
of them owed their imployment to some friend in power, "
without regard to personal merite, who likewise protected "
them against the Lt General's complaints, so that without "
punishing those who were faultie, and puting good Officers "
into all vacancies, litle service could be expected from those "
troops.; and that the Captains of the two foot Companys who "
were pay'd to prevent the Highlanders from plundring, were "
very unfit Subjects for that seruice, that they had scarce a "
man in constant pay, but put most of the mony in their own "
pockets. "

" As to the Revenue considering how small it was, he thought
" it proper as any of the Lords of the Treasurie dy'd, not to
" fill up his place, seaven being more than needed to manage
" sixty thousand pound a year ; and that when the farmes of
" the Customes and Forreign Excise expired, he was of opinion
" it were better to collect them as in England, which by
" experience was found the best : besides the people complain'd
" of the Custommers for letting prohebited goods come in, and
" suffring the manufactures of other Nations to be imported,
" paying only two or three per cent, which by the law should
" pay ten ; that these practices hinder'd the vent of their own
" manifactures, which were it in the King's own hands would
" not be permitted, that his Majesty would infallebly gain by
" that method, for that those who had now them in farme
" were growne very rich, thō poor and necessitous before ;
" and that as to the other branches of the Revenue he was
" informed, he sayd, there might be several discoveries made
" of Lands which (had) fallen to the Crown and still lay in
" private men's hands.

" What he had to offer in reference to the Highlanders was,
" That if the King would pleas to pay what was due to My
" Lord Argile, he might preserue that antient and Loyal Clan
" of the Maclanes ; that means might be found to make it easy
" to his Majesty, and that it would be a great support to his
" intrest there, for should the Earle of Argile haue the
" Maclanes estate, he would be greater than it were fit for a
" Subject to be ; and then to prevent the plundering the low
" Lands by the Highlands in general, the only way would be
" to distribite the mony (which now went to the payment of
" the two Companies which doe not their duty there in)
" amongst the fouer great men there, to wit, the two Marques
" of Huntley, and Athol, and the Earles of Argile and Seaford,
" which would come too about Seaven hunderd pounds a piece,

and oblige them to answer for the Highlands, and to make T O M E
II.
good whatever any of their dependants should take from the 1681.
Low Lands; by this means those great men would have more "
dependance upon the King, and Secure the peace of those "
Countrys without puting his Majesty to more charge than he "
was allready at. "

This was part of what his Royal Highness had a mind to The King
aproves the
Duke's
lay before his Majesty in reference to Scotland, and the King reasons and
was so thoroughly satisfyd with the Duke's judgment and management.
LETTERS
integrity therein, that he seem'd to aproue of each particular, VOL: 2. p.663.
and for the present readily complyd with whatever changes he
proposed; would never dispose of any imployment without his
advice, nor refuse any person his Highness offer'd to fill it.
And thō My Lord Lautherdale seem'd much astonished Ibid. p.665.
at the exceptions his Royal Highness made in the new
regulations against the Lord Register, the Earle of Argile, and
President of the Sessions, and used many arguments to
convince his Majesty they were all well disposed to his seruice,
he reply'd, He was informed from his Brother of their
behaviour and principles on which he intirely relyd, and
would not permit the last, who was then in Towne, so much as
to apear in his presence, because he had come away without
the Duke's permission.

But notwithstanding the King's countenance and aprobation, The Duke
finds opposi-
the Duke found he had many difficulties and stubborn spirits tion and
troubles about
to deal with; amongst other regulations the Parliament had the new Test
in Scotland.
framed a Test, which many refuseing who were injoin'd the LETTERS
taking it, particularly the Duke of Monmouth, Duke Hamilton VOL. 2. p.679.
Ibid. p. 689.
and several Ministers in Edinburg, made some troubles be
aprehended; but the reception the Lord President of the
Sessions had found at Court, gave a check to complaintes, and
the King had that consideration for his Royal Highness as not
to let him be persecuted in England and Scotland too, for Ibid: p.767.

TOME II.

1681.

since he was not disposed to content him in one place, he was resolved to support him in the other; thō that argument was not needed to induce the King to aprove of his Royal Highnesse's conduct and management which had been exercised with so much judgment, fidelitie, and zeal for his seruice, that unless he abandon'd himself he must sustain the Duke, who labouring for his Majestys ease and advantage bore all the odium as well as fatigue of what apear'd either harsh or disgustfull, while his Majesty had the advantage: for now My Lord and Lady Lautherdale as well as many others began to grumble at severall proceedings, so that when the Duke found it necessary for the King's service and peace of the Kingdom to make examples of some great men, he had great men likewise to oppose him.

The Earle of Argile prosecuted for refusing the Test. LETTERS VOL. 2. p. 689. KING CH: LETTERS, 131.

The Duke of Hamilton had misbehaved himself all along and particularly in refusing to take the Test, and thō the King had denyd to give any dispensations on that account, yet his Son My Lord Arran's protestations of adhereing in all things to his Majestys intrest, and obediance to the Duk's commands, made some compensation and put a stop to any prosecution there: but it was thought proper to go farther with My Lord Argile for equivocateing upon the point in this Test; the partie solemnly profess's the Protestant Religion as established in the first year of King James the Sixt, and promises never to consent to any change or alteration contrary thereuntoo, he swears to the King's supremecy, renounces the Covenant &c; the Earle of Argile had taken it as a privie Councellor, giveing a certain explanation or sence of his own, which the other Lords of the privy Council not attending too, it had pass'd upon them, but being to take it again as Commissioner of the Treasury, the Duke order'd him to shew his explanation; wherein amongst other things, he sayd, It was not his meaning to bind himself up, from making any alterations he should

think fit for the advantage of the Church and State: The TOME
Council was no ways satisfyd with this gloss, but he persisting II.
in it, they thought fit to commit him and indict him upon it, 1681.
of which they advertised the King, who aproved of what they
had done, only order'd them, not to prenounce Sentence til
they had transmitted an account of what had been proved
against him; upon this they proceed'd to a tryal, in which after
a sollem hearing he was found guilty of treason, Leasing
makeing, and Leasing telling, but not of perjury, for there had
been several indictements preferr'd against him; however
pursuant to the King's directions, sentence was respited, til
farther orders: My Lord Argile complain'd of this, as exceeding
harsh usase, pretending it was an unusal stretch put upon the
Law, and the Dutchess of Lautherdale concern'd herself much Letters
in his behalf, and thō neither she, nor her Duke durst deny Vol. 2. p. 749.
the resonableness of such a prosecution, however they expostu- Ibid. p. 757.
lated in some measure (at) his Royal Highness's insensibility, of
the kindness he had receiv'd from that Duke, at his first going
down into Scotland, by his being of opinion his Royal Highness
should sit in Council there withóut takeing the oaths; but thō
the Duke was not forgetfull of any kindness (nor did he owe
that to him) he would not be deverted, to make friends to
himself, from pursuing the King's intrest wherever he thought
it concern'd.

It was neither the King's nor the Duke's intention to take The Earle of
away the Earle of Argil's life, but make use of this occasion Argile escapes
out of prison,
to get him more into their power, and forfeit certain Juris- upon which
Sentence is
dictions and superiorities which he and his predecessors had pass'd upon
him.
surreptitiously acquir'd, and most tyranicaly exercised; and
therefore when the King sent his letter in forme for passeng King Ch:
Letters
Sentence upon him, he order'd execution to be stop'd and in pag. 129.
the mean time desired the Duke's advice how to dispose of those
Superiorities and Offices which he thought too much for any

T O M E
II.

1681.

one Subject, and was glad (he Sayd) he had got them out of so
ill hands. But it seens this Lord's aprehention would not let
him trust to the King's mercy, So he found means to escape
out of prison by the help of his Daugter, who haveing got
leave to see him, he changed cloaths with her footman, and
carrying up her train as she went out, pass'd undecern'd by all
the guards, and soon after got secretly out of the Kingdom;
upon which, Sentence being prenounced against him, his armes
were reversed and other markes of dishonour put upon him
according to the custom and Laws of the Country; nay some
of the Council were for haveing his Daughter (by whose means
he escaped) whipped through the streets of Edinburg, but the
Duke prevented it by saying, they were not used to deal so
cruelly with Ladys in his Country, but notwithstanding his
mercifull temper and that he design'd no real harme to My
Lord Argile himself, yet his enemies were too watchfull to let
slip any pretence of decrying his conduct; so great endeavours
was used to mitigate this Lord's crime to the King, and to

LETTERS
VOL.2. p.78.

insinuate as if some ill might come of the Duke's pressing
things too far, that the greatest part of the orthedox Clergie of
Edinburg it self refused to take the Test, but the King was
soon convinced of the falsetie of those reports, and the litle

Ibid. p.828.

disturbance which the Whiggs made at Lanrick was so soon
quell'd, that it was scarce heard of in Town; however the King

Ibid. 802.

thought fit to issue out a proclamation for aprehending My
Lord Argile, that if it miss'd his person it might convince the
world at least he was satisfyd with the Duke's management,
and silence thereby the discourses industriously spread abroad,
as if he had been prosecuted more out of a pique by the Duke,
than by reason of any guilt to the King.

My Lord and Lady Lautherdale who had a great share in
these reports, intrested themselves very much for the family;
and thō they had little to say in justification of My Lord

Argile himself, they interceded vehemently in behalfe of My
Lord Lorn his Son; this the Duke was no less ready to concur
in, than the King to grant, only desired that in the settling of
the estate upon him, a due regard might be had to the debts,
and provision made for his yonger children; but My Lady
Lautherdale press'd hard to have all the offices likewise
confirm'd to My Lord Lorn (except that of Justiciar which
she owned was to great for any Subject) but the King would
by no means restore that family to any powers, and was once
in a mind not to part with them to any body at all, but keep
them undisposed of in his own hands; and thō his Majesty
afterwards signed new Commissions for those and severall other
hereditable jurisdictions which were fallen likewise to him by
refusal of the Test, he made them all dureing pleasure only;
and to such as his Royal Highness recommended; notwithstanding the interposition of others, and the great endeavours
used to stop those made by My Lords Dalhousie and
Roxborough, instead of the Duke of Monmouth, but his
Majesty notwithstanding signed them with the rest: My Lord
Arran was dissatisfyd too, that his Father's offices had been
disposed of without regard to him, but he was tould that should
he fall off for that, it would look as if he had differ'd from his
Father only to have his imployments, that new converts must
be tryd a little ere they are trusted too far; which satisfyd
him in appearance, and he continued in his former professions
of a perfect obedience to the Duke's orders, resolveing, he
Say, to go immediately to Edinburg to renew them to him in
person.

The affairs of that Kingdom and particularly this of My
Lord Argile's, gave the Duke much more trouble by My Lord
Halifax's meddling in them: he perceiv'd the Duke sent his
directions in that matter to My Lord Hide, whose encreas of
credit he was allways jealous of, and besides looking upon

TOME II.

1681.
LETTERS
Vol. 2. p.784.
Ibid. p. 794.

Ibid. 846.
Ibid. p.812.

Ibid. p. 811.

Ibid. p. 815.

LETTERS
Vol.2. p.818.

himself as the priuie Minister thought nothing ought to be done without his priuitie, It not being possible, he sayd, to govern one ship if he knew not what cours the other Steer'd; and thō he was tould, the affairs of Scotland had always been under a distinct management, and that My Lord Hide was acquainted with them, as servant to the Duke, not as Minister to the King, nevertheless he prevail'd with the King to admit him into those Councels; which put the Duke upon a necessitie either of breaking with him, which he had no mind to doe, or of communicateing those matters to him for the future, which besides the addition of trouble gave him new opposition instead of ease in the management of them.

The Lord
Lorn has
leaue to come
up and plead
for himself.

The chief matter yet in debate in reference to the Lord Argile, was the Signature or disposition of his estate for payment of his just Creditors, and some moderate donatives to such as his Father had ruined for their fidelitie to his Majesty; the surplusage being intended to descend to his family; this the Duke sent up for the King to confirme, but great objections were made against it by My Lord Halifax as well as others : My Lord Lorn likewise desired leaue to come

and plead for himself, whis his Majesty refused unless the Duke consented; but his Royal Highness was too indulgent to refuse it, only desired, his Majesty would pleas to determin

nothing till he had heard his answer to the objections, which was readily agreed too, and when they came gave the King so much satisfaction, that there was no material alteration made, only that the actings of the Commissioners might be

lyable to appeals; but this hinder'd not My Lord Lorn and his friends from pressing hard to haue the Superiorities restored him, pretending they were but a Sort of chief rents, or an authoritie over his Tenants, but My Lord Middleton shew'd the King the difference betwixt Common Tenants and Vassells who are obliged to follow their Lord on all occasions, which

was a power the King thought not fit to trust in such hands, so
that he positively refused it, thō he agreed to restore My Lord
Lorn in blood; which the Duke approued of also, but advised
his Majesty, for fear of some trick, not to signe the restitution in
blood before the Signature, which he thought a prudent caution
and did accordingly, signing at the same time My Lord
Queensbury's patent upon the Duke's recommendation: So that
all those oppositions and obstructions either at Court or els
where which came from his Royal Highnesse's enemies, serued
only to gine his Majesty a higher opinion of the Duke's
management, and convince the world, that he acted not only
pursuant to his inclinations but most agreeably to reason and
justice when he suffer'd himself to be guided by the Duke's
advice in all matters relateing to that Kingdom.

Whilest the affairs of Scotland went successfully enough where
the Duke managed himself, they were not so prosperous in
England where he was not permited to be, thō that was stil
used for a pretext to keep him away; the King had indeed
some hopes of an honester Lord Major's being chosen than the
year before, that the Citie would come by degrees to its duty,
that better Juries might be got, and justice haue its due and
natural cours, which by the perjurys of the fanatical partie had
been so impudently obstructed hithertoo; but it seems those
people were not so easily put out of their road, for the bill
against one Rous a partizan of theirs, being pretended to the
Grand Jury thō the evidence was full beyond exception they
brought it in ignoramus.

·· This made the Court dispair of any better success against
the Earle of Shaftsbury, unless some part of his crime haveing
been committed in Westminster,· they could haue a Jurie
return'd by the Bailif of that Citie; but (besides that it was a
moot point amongst the Judges whether practicable or no) they
found upon examination that all they could charge him with

TOME
II.
1681.
Ibid. 875.

Ibid. 889.

LETTERS
Vol. 2. p. 788.

The Earle of
Shaftsbury
acquited by
an ignoramus
Jury.

KING CHAR.
LETTERS 123.

LETTERS
Vol. 2. p. 681.

Ibid. p. 688.

T O M E
II.
────────
1681.
LETTERS
Vol. 2. p.699.

there, was only words spoken long ago, which were no more within the Act; so they were forced to venter a Citie Jurie again, which the Sheriffs. took care to chuse so fit for their purpose, that thō the evidence was beyond exception and given in open Court, yet Sr Samuel Bernadiston the foreman return'd

Ibid. 729.

the Bill ignoramus, upon which the Bells rung, bonefires were made, and such publick rejoiceing in the Citie, that never such an insolent defyance of authority was seen before.

This so disharten'd the Court that they knew not which way to turn for redress, it was under consideration whether a *Quo warranto* might not be brought against that part of the Citie's

Ibid. 688.

Charter whereby they chuse their Sheriffs, but that was a thing of time, and in the mean while the Earle of Shaftsbury, and Lord Howard, were admitted to bail the last day of the terme, the King no ways obstructing the due cours of Law, notwithstanding those fanaticks were not asham'd of doing it even in so impudent a manner as obliged them to own their perjurie and unjustice in the face of the Sun.

Notwithstanding this disapointment there was still some

Ibid. 730.

lingring hopes of the Duke's return, and some persons advised it that the King might not seem dejected with this blow, nor as if the fear of the partie had kept his Majesty in awe; but the King's dilatoriness and irresolution join'd with the timorous councells of many about him, particularly My Lord Halifax, made him differ'd this intended favour to the Duke, till an other cross accident dampt all such hopes, and threw his Royal Highness more back in his expectations than ever.

The P^{ce} of
Orange renews
his endeavours
to make the
King unite the
Parliament
and desert the
Duke.

The Prince of Orange it seems finding his endeavours unsuccessfull in England, tryd if by forreign ingagements he could force the King into an union with his Parliament, and a breach with France; and thō he knew well enough that such a good agreement could not be cimented but in the Duke's ruin, that

LETTERS
Vol. 2. p.638.

hinder'd him not from driveing on (in order to it) a sort of

Protestant League with the two Northern Kings, the Elector of Brandenburg, the house of Lunebourg, and all the other Princes, who were jealous of the peace of Nimighen's being broke, and at last communicated it to the King, whose conjunction was only wanting (they sayd) to make it perfect; and this· they press'd with so much importunitie, that the King was hard put to it, to avoid either giveing a harsh denyal to their clamerous demands, or falling out with France which would have quite broke the measures he was in.

T O M E II.

1681.
Ibid. 668.

The King's necessities had been long so great and the Parliament so refractory and insolent, that he had no way left of relieving one (without consenting to the unreasonable demands of the other) but by a private Treaty with France; the Duke first put the King in the way of it, which the French at first answer'd only by compliments and in general termes, but at last it was concluded they should give the King fifty thousand pound every quarter, the first paiment to be at the end of June 1681, without any condition on the King's side but that of friendship, but promises on the French part not to disturb Flanders nor Holland.

The King's private agreement for a Pention from France.

Ibid. 247.

But his most Christian Majesty (who could not it seems long be idle) thought it (tis probable) no breach of his engagement to take Strasbourg, and Cazal, and soon after burnt the Tripolin Ships at Scio a port of the Grand Segniors, setting as it were at defyance at one and the same time, the Pope, the Emperour, and the Turke; this made the Spaniards and Hollanders grumble a little, but· when he came so ·near them as to block up Luxembourg, they cryd out aloud, and the King to pacify their former complaints haveing engaged he would call a Parliament in case the French prosecuted their intentions *par voy de fait*, the Spanish and Dutch Ambassadors pretended now the case was come; so ·that the King was forced to giue in a Memorial to the King of France, That unless he

The French motions had like to have forced the King to call a Parliam', and that had like to haue turn'd to the Duke's advantage. LETTERS VOL.2. p.639.

Ibid. 736.

TOME
II.

1681.
Ibid. 700.

would suffer provisions to be brought into Luxembourg, he must necessarily call a Parliament, the consequence of which was well understood by every body, but by none better than his Royal Highness, who by these ebbings and flowings in his expectation, was kept in a more uneasy situation than a settled banishment would have been ; it put him upon continual anxieties how to ward himself from the malice of his enemies, and reward the fidelitie of his friends, how to keep fair with those who were teped, without disobliging those who were warmer in his seruice, how to make new friends and keep his old ones from falling off; but what was more perplexing than all the rest, was his not realy knowing in such confused Councells and unsettled times, what made realy for him, and what made against him.

Hithertoo the least seeming necessitie of a Parliament, was counted an unanswerable argument to keep him away, which now being thought unavoidable by reason of the King's promis, and the French proceedings, the Duke's hopes by consequence was never lower; when by I know not what mutabilitie of judgments and capricious fancys of Ministers, it had quite contrary effect, and was like to haue brought his Royal Highness back when he and all the world expected it least.

LETTERS
VOL. 2. p. 710.

Mr Seymour it seems tould the King, that should he suffer a Parliament to meet, and not permit the Duke to be there, would be a yelding back the advantages he had got, and proue in effect his and the Monarchys ruin; that all the Loyal adresses which of late had been presented to him so strenously asserting the right of the Crown, and the Succession in the true line, meant plainly the Duke's return, and that all honest men would be dejected and disharten'd if it fell out otherwise.

Ibid. 724.

These reasons were not without their weight; but the true one was his and the other Ministers own preservation ; they consinder'd the united malice of their enemies and the disunion

which increas'd every day amongst themselves, both in their
opinions and actions; whereas the factious partie were still firm
and uniforme in pursut of theirs, and to be sure would neither
forget nor forgiue those Councells nor Councellors, who had
hitherto disapointed their malice; which with the hidden
intrigues of the woemen and the King's unsteddy temper,
convinced them, that without the Duke they should all return
into their original Cahos, and that none but he could keep
them from falling to pieces, nor the King from sliding back
upon the first rub or disapointment.

This made My Lord Halifax himself acquaint his Royal
Highness, that hitherto it had been an uspeakable trouble to
him, that he could not get the better of his own thoughts when
they stood in opposition to his Highnesse's commands, but that
now he was so happy as to think nothing more reasonable, than
what he so much desired, and that he should be present when
the Parliament met, to answer for himself in case they had the
confidence to lay any thing to his charge.

However the King was not so easily brought over to this
opinion, aprehending that if the Parliament proceeded to an
Impeachment, he should be hard put to it to avoid puting the
Duke under restraint, which he thought would be wors than
to stay where he was; but they answer'd, there was no danger
of the Commons running to that height, but if they did, the
Lords, to be sure would make a great difference betwixt his
Majestys Brother and an other Peer; that it was a hard case
for the Duke, and disadvantageous to his Ma^ty himself, that
the Plot which was dead to every body els, should still be kept
alive in him; in fine the King who realy desired to do what
was best for the Duke, if it did not prejudice himself, gave at
last into their arguments, and the French motions makeing
every body look upon a Parliament as unavoidable, it was

TOME
II.

1681.

Ibid. 746.

LETTERS
VOL: 2. p. 716.

Ibid: 723.

T O M E
II.

1681. expected every day when his Royal Highness would be Sent for.

When this news came to Edinburg the Duke scarce knew how to credit it, but waited a confirmation and the event, without stirring in it himself; not only because he was yet in the darke as to the true origin of this unexpected change, but also, for that he was advised the King would have the pleasure of makeing it his own act, and that it must either doe of itself or not at all: but as it sprung up like an untimely plant, so it withered and faded away as suddenly, and in a few days, no more markes or foot steps apear'd of it than if it had never been at all.

My Lord
Halifax
crushes this
project. This quick relaps was oweing to my Lord Halifax's refin'd arguing, who was always for cleaving a hair in his advice, he remain'd still of opinion the Duke should be present if the Parliament met, but pretended he ought, by no means, to come before; it was urged against this, that such a return would look liker a summoning of him to answer in Parliament than a recalling him from banishment, and indeed My Lord Hide and Mr Seymour were so ernest against it, that they thought it better he remain'd where he was than to come in that manner; for if things went ill which was much to be fear'd, it would, they sayd, be layd at his door, and he have no other benefit by it than to screen others from danger by LETTERS
VOL. 2. p.801. drawing all the Jury of the Partie upon himself, as if God had made him a Prince only to cover the failings of Ministers, and the iniquities of the People; but my Lord Halifax had so much credit with the King, that his opinion overballanced the others, and by some new scheme (as it was thought) he so LETTERS
VOL. 2. p.751. changed his Majesty in that matter, that now a thousand difficulties were started against it, which made the other Ministers Ibid. 759. suspect his Lordship look'd back to his old politicks, and the

makeing himself popular again ; and his declareing at this time
against prosecuteing dissenters was no small Simptom of it:
infine Mr Seymour acquaints the Duke he finds his Royal
Highness must be made a sacrifice once more, to attone for the
Sins of the Ministers, and was so dissatisfyd in the main, that *Ibid. 751.*
he left the Court a little abruptly and went discontented into
the Country.

But no one had more reason to be discontented and melancoly
upon the matter than his Royal Highness himself, for besides
this balke upon his expectation, he saw his friends quitting the
list, and which way to keep them togather was a task he knew
not well how to go about : On one hand My Lord Halifax
sayd, he hop'd his Highness would believe that whatever *Ibid: 716.*
opinion he had concerning his return, it sprung from no other
motiue but his aprehention that it was neither for the King's
seruice, nor his own, to come at an unseasonable time ; nor
would he allow himself to suspect, he sayd, that those with
whom he differ'd in this matter had gain'd any advantage
upon him in his Highnesse's opinion, but that he will pleas to
let him have the same place in it he ever thought fitt for him,
when he was most satisfyd with his endeavours to serue him
and his zeal for his right ; My Lord Hide on the other hand
was no ways satisfyd with his triming, and Mr Seymour
displeas'd with them both, which gave his Royal Highness a
more comforthless prospect of his affairs than all the rest, and
made his presence more necessary (as the Ministers themselves
had judged) at the same time it was render'd almost impossible,
and to compleat his danger, the aprehentions still encreasing
least France should break the peace, and the clamours on that
account of the Spanish, and Dutch Ministers that a Parliament
might be calld for their deffence, embarrassed the King and
threaten'd the Duke, if possible, more than ever.

1682.

TOME
II.

1682.
LETTERS
VOL. 2. p. 78.

THE promis his Majesty had made of calling a Parliament in case the King of France should pursue his designes by acts of Hostility, intangled and gravel'd him exceedingly, for it required a nice distinction to shew that the blockade of Luxembourg was not in the case, and the Spanish and Dutch Ministers were no ways satisfy.d with the profer of leting fifty cart loads of corn enter into it (which had been the product of the King's late Memorial at the French Court) and were so fully perswaded there was no other safety but in a Parliament, that they declared they would rather loss Luxembourg than that a Parliament should not be call'd ; which made the King despair of eluding it any longer, he only resolved with himself to meet them with such a resolution as became their King, and to dissolve them forthwith if they offer'd any. thing against the Prerogative; he was casting about what place was most convenient for their meeting, and pitched at last upon Cambridg, that in the intervals of business he might be near the place of his pleasures, and in the mean time expected with impatience what answer the King of France would give to the Memorial, which the English and Dutch Ministers had orders to present jointly to that Court.

But instead of an answer his Majestys Envoy was tould that their Memorial could not be receiv'd in the manner it was deliver'd, that his Most Christian Majesty could not hinder Princes and States from entring into what leagues they pleas'd at home, but that he would not suffer them to do it in his own Court and against himself, but that they might propose what they pleas'd seperately, and then should have his answer. Nothing could be well objected against this, which delayd the matter till orders were sent to his Majestys Minister there, to propose the same things seperately ; to which the French replyd, They would quit their pretentions to whatsoever was then in possession of the Spaniards, provided Luxembourg might be deliver'd to them in three months.

When this was communicated to the Dutch Ambassadors, they flew out in great passions and abusiue expressions, even against the King, accusing him of Briberie from France, and manifest breach of his promis in not calling a Parliament, from which, they sayd, no ill could be aprehended, but some little hardships to the Duke of Yorke whom it seems they made no great account of ; but the King nevertheless tould thèm, He saw no reason why he should be press'd to call a Parliament, when propositions were made from France (not so unreasonable) but that a treaty might be grounded upon them, which could not be call'd acting in a hostile manner, and therefore required them to communicate the matter to their Masters, til when they were like to have no other answer.

When they saw the King had too much reason on his side to be chang'd, and too much resolution to be frighted, they became something calmer and owned there was ground indeed given for a treaty, but sayd there would be much more hopes of success, if a Parliament were sitting at the same time, and therefore ceased not solliciting for it ; but those violent efforts both at home and abroad to force the King to a Parliament in spight of his teeth, made him more avers to it than ever, he was not well pleased with those who had advis'd him to make that conditional promis, which now perplexed him so grievously,

T O M E
II.

1682.
LETTERS
VOL. 2. p. 791.

LETTERS
VOL. 2. p. 83...

The French
made propoˢᵃˡˢ.

Ibid: 847.

LETTERS
VOL. 2. p. 848.

Ibid. 851.

T O M E
II.

1682.

Ibid: 892.

LETTERS
VOL. 2. p. 907.

The Duke
at last is
brought back
to Court.

and much less with the Prince of Orange to whose intregues abroad, and his last visite in England, these troubles were oweing; as indeed it was afterwards owned by some of the States themselves to the King's Resident there, that all those vehement sollicitations by the Dutch Ministers for a Parliament, came from that Prince, and two or three more of the States that join'd with him, and that the late answer sent to the King had been dispatched by the same persons without the privitie of the rest, or that otherwise it had never been done : but his Majesty found means to make the Prince of Orange sencible at last, that these cobwebb stratagems were too weak and transparent, either to blind or fetter the world, or that they would contribute to his own advantage, or the publick peace of Europe, which he pretended to take so much to heart.

All these changes of Councells made no change in the Duke's prospect of being recall'd whether a Parliament was to sitt or no, there never wanted some reason of State against his comeing, or at least for delaying it, which in the end proued the same; he had only more reason to dispair than ever, because he found he could count upon few men's friendship, most of the Ministers were for playing their own game, which made cautious and timerous Councells always prevail ; and that amongst so many different measures at Court, none of them had turn'd to his advantage : wherefore the best he could hope for, was to continue the remainder of his life, an honourable banishment as the only reward of his duty, obediance, and signal seruices, when an unforeseen accident brought him back by the means of a person he least expected it from ; nor indeed was it done for the Duke's sake, so that had he not managed the occasion with incomparable cunning and dexterity it had proued as unsuccessfull as the rest.

It was infine the Dutchess of Portsmouth without intending it, that put an end to the Duke's long and undeserued Exile, as

well as to the King's troubles and uneasiness, for without his **T O M E**
Royal Highnesse's assistance and advices, he could never haue **II.**
got so perfect a victorie over those implacable spirits which had *1682.*
haunted him so long, thō that he had served for a standing
reason against allowing them that mutual happiness.

No body doubted but that Ladys power was great enough
to haue done it sooner if she had pleas'd, but hithertoo it had
been turned against, not only the Duke, but in some measure
the King himself; she had courted the Rebellions partie, " Kɪɴɢ Jᴀ. Mⁿ.
when she aprehended their prevailing, she had been a busie " To. 9. p. 173.
instrument in endeavouring to reconcil the Duke of Montmouth 266.
with the King, had frequent intervews with Shaftsbury, Lord
Howard of Escrick, &c. and My Lord Sunderland after he Lᴇᴛᴛᴇʀs
had been discharged from his imployment, ceased not to be Vᴏʟ.2. p. 79...
every day in her lodgings til the King positively forbid her to
see him; who at last growing out of patience with her double
dealing gave her so many markes of his displeasure, that it " Kɪɴɢ Jᴀ: Mⁿ.
is believ'd he would haue gon further, had he not already " To: 9. 172.
owned her Son the Duke of Ritchmond in so publick a "
manner. "

When she found therefore those deceitfull measures were not The Dutchess
to be pursued, and that her wheedle of pretending to bring project to rais
those angry men over to the King's intrest, would no longer the Duke back.
pass upon him, she Set herself to worke to regain her credit with
his Majesty, which [* by her credit with his Majesty, which]
by her usual artes she still found means to succeed in; and
when she had brought it to as high a pitch as ever, she wisely
set her head to work how to profit by the fair weather while it
lasted, and procure some certain fund for a future settlement
let what will hapen, prudently enough forseeing that another

---

* The words between crotchets seem to have been inadvertently left by the
Secretary in turning to a new page. — Eᴅɪᴛᴏʀ.

TOME
II.
—————
. 1682.
LETTERS
Vol: 2. p.809.
popular commotion in the Kingdom, or even a little time
without any other accident, might bereave her of it again ; so
she resolved to rais a great summe of mony and place it in a
forreign Country as a secure retreat and subsistance, if the
weather should grow cloudy again in England.

The King's necessities were to great to comply with her
expectations out of his revenue, so the only Shift she could
think of, was to prevail with his Majesty to propose to the
KING JA: M^{ty}.
To.9. 173.
" Duke, to settle upon her a rent charge of five thousand
" pounds per annum out of the Post Office for fifty years, and
" to promis his Royal Highness an equivalent out of the
" hereditary Excise, and then she proposed raising a hundred
" thousand pounds upon it in present, being the summe she
" wanted for her intended project. The Duke was always too
" complyant to refuse any thing the King desired, and too
" sencible of the Dutchess of Portsmouth's power to think he
" could purchass her favour too dear ; so answer'd immediatly,
" That since all he had in the world was from his Majesty, it
LETTERS
Vol. 2. p. 810.
should always be at his disposal, and was therefore ready to do
whatever was proposed, but believ'd it not feazable unless he
were personally present in Town, both to consult the manner
and performe what was necessary for such a conveyance ;
which he knew if the Dutchess of Portsmouth were once
convinced of, she would move heaven and earth to bring it
about.

KING JA. M^{ty}.
To.9. 174.
" All this while, the Duke knew Very well his revenue was
" so settled, that nothing but an Act of Parliament could
" alienate any part of it ; which he took care not to mention to
" any liveing soul, least that might have made the King lay
" the thoughts of it aside, or made her sollicite for a Parliament,
" which would have given that project a mischievous turn, and
" done him hurt instead of good ; and by great fortune none
" of the Lawiers about Town who were studying which way to

bring it about, light upon that difficulty, thō they found out " T O M E
others' which they endeavoured to obviate by proposeing to II.
have it surrended into the King's hands, and the King to 1682.
surrender it to her: But at last S' George Greffreys who was LETTERS
VOL. 2. p. 81...
the Dutchess of Portsmouth's Councel, assured her, it might be Ibid. 859.
done by le ving a fine upon so much of the profits of the
Post Office as was necessary for that end, which put her upon
pressing the King with all immaginable earnestness for the Duke's
return, his presence being necessary for that, and was the more
urgent in it, because being extreamly subject to fitts of the
Collick she was advised to go to Burbon waters in France,
and she long mightely to see the matter finished before she
went.

‹ This made many things be turn'd into arguments for his
Royal Highness's comeing to Court, the very shadow of which LETTERS
before were capable of blasting any such thought: My Lord VOL. 2. p. 730.
Shaftsbury being acquited by an Ignoramus Iurie, which had
thrown the Court so much back, she sayd, made it the properest
time in the world tō recall the Duke, to convince the factious
partie that the King was not terrifyd with their insolence; but
his Majesty who was not so easily led by people, that could
blow in his manner hot and could as their intrest serued, was
very reasty upon the point, and indeed before this matter was Ibid. 737.
started was never less disposed to do it thant at this time; My
Lord Halifax had so terrifyd him with dangers if the Duke
were there before the Parliament met, and the King on the
other hand being in a manner determined to have none, made
his comeing desperate, but at last her importunitie overcame
all obstacles and objections, and the King promised her
he would recall him whether there were a Parliament or no;
but the Season of the year and her indisposition forceing her
away before that could be brought about, She writ full of
kindness to the Duke begging of him not to neglect her

TOME
II.

1682.
Ibid. 727.

LETTERS
VOL: 2. p.893.

KING JA. Mᵐ
To.9. 174.

KING CH:
LETTERS
pag. 185.

LETTERS
VOL. 2. p.904.

business in her absence, and that if he was not recall'd to Court before her return, she would go upon her knees to the King to obtain it, which should she do now would look too sordid, as if intrest were the only motiue: This seem'd a contradiction, to beg of him to do what she desired and that then he should be recall'd, because his presence was supposed necessary to make the conveiance; but the reason was, it had been resolved at last, that the Duke should meet the King at Newmarket to dispatch this business there and then go back into Scotland again, where he was to leave the Dutchess and Princess Anne as a pledg of his return: so the matter being settled to her likeing, she set out the same day for France which his Majesty did for Newmarket; by this means the Duke's great hopes dwindled into a piece of harder usage than ever, he was to be sent for indeed, only to divert himself of part of his estate to oblige the Dutchess of Portsmouth; of whose assistance he could make Small account, when once her own business was done; however he readily accepts it, without capitulation, thinking it prudent to take what he could get, and leave the rest to his own conduct and behaveour, when once he had the hapiness to see the King again. But before it came to that, the King's good nature went farther than the Dutchess of Portsmouth's averice, and he resolved with himself the Duke should come for good and all, and that haveing done so much for her satisfaction, was determin'd to do the rest for his own and be no longer deprived of the conversation, assistance, and comforth of a Brother, whose obediance and submission to his will, his constancy and patience in his suffrings, and fidelity in his business had render'd him if possible more dear and necessary to him than ever; he therefore dispatch'd away M. Legg to Edinburg, desiring the Duke to meet him at Newmarket, and order'd My Lord Hide to acquaint him that for expedition sake he should come alone, but that his intention

was he should return back with him to London where he was
resolved that the Dutchess who was then bigg with child should
come to ly in.

Assoon as the Express arriued the Duke lost no time, but
going on board the fourth of March on the Henrietta Yacght
that lay ready at Leith, he made the best of his way to
Yarmouth, where after a rough passage he arrived the tenth
and went that night to Norwitch, at both which places he
was very well receiv'd and the next day came to Newmarket,
where the King receiv'd him with all imaginable demonstrations of kindness, which his Royal Highness answer'd with
no less tenderness and affection, Assureing his Majesty, he
should find him as obedediant for the future as he had
hithertoo been; and haveing private notice given him that
his declining business would be agreeable to the King, some
two or three days after his arrival, he tould his Majesty That
when he had given him an account of his affairs of Scotland,
he would abstain from any further medling in what related to
the publick, and thō he acknowledged it would be an
uneasiness to him, who had been bred in business from his
infancy, to live an idle life, yet he was desirous to contribute
in every thing to his Majestys quiet, and disproue the
allegations of his enemies, who to create a jealousie in the
King, and aprehention to the people, had blazed it about, That
now the Duke was return'd all Councells would be govern'd
by him; he was therefore resolved to wave all business unless
his Majesty expresly order'd the contrary, and wish'd that all
his Subjects would shew the same submission to his will and
concern for his eas and satisfaction. The King was well
pleas'd with this declaration and said it would contribite to
the quiet and peace of them both, and without all dispute
it contributed to keep the King steddy and fixed in his
resolution of takeing him back with him to London

TOME
II.

1682.
The Duke
comes to
Newmarket,
to meet the
King.
KING JA: Mⁿ.
To. 9. 174.
and 183.

TOME
II.

1682.
My Lord
Halifax and
M^r. Seymour
oposes the
King going
back with the
Duke to
London.
KING JA. M^m.
To:9. pag. 181.

KING JAM.M^m
To.9. pag.181.

" notwithstanding the earnest sollicitations of My Lord
" Halifax and M^r. Seymour to the contrary.

" My Lord Halifax came not downe to Newmarket till some
" days after the Duke's arrival, and thō he knew he had been
" exceeding scruiceable to him in many cases; yet in others he
" was sencible of his haveing disgusted him; he asked him
therefore at his first intervew, whether he was to apear before
him as a criminal or no? but the Duke receiv'd him so
graciously, and seem'd by his great attention to his good offices
not to remember the ill ones, that my Lord was rassured, and
shew'd to be entirely satisfyd with his reception, thō in the
bottom he was neither changed in his opinion nor his conduct.

" He and Mr Seymour were the two prevailing Ministers
" and neither wanted wit nor eloquence to second their
" intentions, which they had made good and bad use of as
" their privat intrests or natural inclinations guided them, but
as those changed, their Councells did the same; they had wished
the Duke's presence to protect them from the fury of the
Parliament, but now that danger being over and the forreign
clamours in great measure apeas'd, other considerations and
jealousies succeeded in their place, they fear'd notwithstanding
the Duke's promising not to meddle in business, yet one day
he would eclips them in it, and that My Lord Hide would
outstrip them too in the King's favour, by vertue of the Duke's
countenance and protection, which by his assiduous and faithfull
seruice during the whole cours of the misfortunes, they were
" sencible he had merited beyond them all; so that thō they
" were at the same time convinced that the Duke's presence
" was necessary to keep the King steddy to the very measures
" they themselves had advised, yet intrest blinding their
" judgment on this occasion, they press'd earnestly that the
" Duke might dispatch what he came for at Newmarket, and
" so return to Scotland again: But the King after he had

once seen his Brother could not be prevail'd with to part "
from him again, was resolued to give him some satisfaction "
after so much suffring, so pretending the Dutchess of "
Portsmouth's business could not so well be executed there, "
in spight of all their intrigues and Sollicitations, brought "
him back to London.

Where he was no sooner arrived but the Attorney general "
was order'd to prepare such writeings as was necessary to "
make the conveyance, but upon a stricter enquiry into the "
matter and a full perusall of all the acts relateing to the Duke's ".
settlement, he found out at last what the Duke knew from the "
first, that nothing but an Act of Parliament could make it valid "
or impower the Duke to alienate any part of his revenue. "

This was a mighty disapointment both to the King and "
Dutchess of Portsmouth, but the Duke kept his councel and "
never mention'd his haveing been aprised so long before of "
this impossibilitie, which he had managed so dextrusly as "
to procure his return without being obliged to dismember his "
estate, which (thō he could deny the King nothing) would "
have been a great trouble to him ; tis true his Majesty "
designed to give him an equivalent out of his hereditary "
revenue, but his Royal Highness would have been very loath "
to let his former settlements be ravel'd into by Acts of "
Parliament, for when once any thing belonging to him had "
come into such hands, he knew not what disposal might have "
been made of the rest ; but their being other reasons against "
calling a Parliament the King and Dutchess of Portsmouth "
were forced to be satisfyd, and could be no ways displeased "
at the Duke, who had shewn all imaginable readiness to do "
whatever had been required from him. "

Haveing thus turn'd the Dutchess of Portsmouth's averice
to so signal an advantage, without any damage to his estate,
and yet warded himself from her anger, he had the less to
aprehend from her mighty credit with the King, which after "

TOME
II.

1682.
KING JA: Mᵉ
To: 9. 176.

" her return from France was grown greater (if possible) than
" ever; and therefore being disapointed of her aime this way,
" was resolved to do it an other, and prevail'd at last with his
" Majesty to make her a grant of ten thousand pounds a
" quarter out of his private French fund till a hundred
" thousand pound was run up, tho it was the King's main
" Support to defend him from the tyrany of a Parliament; but
" there was no resisting her importunities, when once she (*had*)
" knowlidg of it, which til then, had been kept a secret from
" her, and indeed communicated to none but the first Com-

Ibid. p. 177.

" missioner of the Treasury and Mᵣ Churchill (by whom it
" had been negociated) otherwise tis probable both her eys and
" hands would have been sooner upon it, and her payments
" have commenced before they did, the last quarter not being
" satisfyd when the King dy'd.

His Royal Highness remain'd with the King til the 3ᵈ of
May, which day he parted from Windsor where the Court then

The Duke
returns to
Scotland
to fetch the
Dutchess, and
had like to
have been
drown'd in
his passage.

was, to fetch the Dutchess bigg with child out of Scotland; he
chose to go by sea in the GLOCESTER frigat with several
smaller vessells to attend him, which, thorough the unskil-
fulness or treachery of Captain Ayres the Pilot (who was tryd
and condemn'd afterwards) was lost, and the Duke himself in
great danger of being so too; Captain Ayres his intention was
it seems, to follow the Colliers' road, betwixt the Cost and the
Sand banks, but the Commanders being against it, order'd
him to go out to Sea thinking to clear them all, but he still
pressed to tack fancying he had time enough to go within the
banks and at last he had leave given him, when the Commanders
thought themselves far enough out at Sea to go beyond them
all; but it seems both were deceiv'd, for a little while after, the
ship struck upon the Lemon (*and*) oar in Yarmouth road*, where

---

* In a small Volume of *Some Historical Memoires of the Duke of York to the year*
1682, published in 1683, Sir John Berry's Letter, Captain of the Glocester, is
inserted, giving a Relation of this Loss. — EDITOR.

she stuck for some time, and had not too much hast* been
saved, assoon as she came into deep water immediately sunk
and at least a hundred persons in her ; but his Royal Highness
as soon as they dispair'd of saveing her, got into his shallop
and from thence went a board the Yacght, on which occasion
such was the modesty and respect of those who attended him,
many whereof were persons of quality, as the Earls of Perth,
Middleton, &c, that no one whatever offer'd to go into it, but
whom his Highness pleas'd to call himself, which was only
Mr Churchill and one or two more; but other boates comeing
to their rescue, most of the persons of quality and his Royal
Highnesse's Servants got off also, and many more might have
been saued, had not the timorousness of the boatmen hinder'd
their comeing near the ship when they thought her about to
sink, for fear of sinking with her; those therefore who were
thus abandon'd (thō ready to be swalloud up) gave a great
huzza assoou as they saw his Royal Highness in safety, to the
no less honour to the English Seamen for their intrepiditie and
zeal, than the Duke's for haveing gain'd so great an esteem
amongst them, when such endeavours were used to render him
the object of all men's hatred.

Haveing escaped this danger he got safe a shore to Scotland,
where pursuant to the King's directions he declar'd the Lord
Haddo then Lord President of the Sessions, to be Lord
Chancelor, the Earl of Queensbury Lord Treasurer, and the
Earl of Perth Lord Justice General ; after which makeing as
little stay as possible he return'd for England with the Dutchess,
the Lady Anne, and the rest of his family, nor did the late
disaster hinder him nor her Royal Highness from venturing to

---

* Here some words would seem to have been omitted, perhaps — hast been *made*,
might have been saved, &c. — EDITOR.

Sea again, dangers and suffrings was now grown so habitual
to them both, and they so resigned to providence, that they.
never disputed or delayd any orders for their own convenience
or safety, the ships were ready and apointed for that Seruice,
which the Dutchess without hesitation venters to go on board
of, thō there was no disincouragment wanting to deter her from
a Sea voyage; she was then bigg with child, and the fresh idea
of the Duke's late escape which upon any accident would
Strike them all with aprehention and terrour must needs be of
most dangerous consequence in the condition her Royal
Highness was in, which so discouraged those about her, that
My Lady Peterborough begg'd leave to go in another ship;
least she should communicate her aprehentions and frights to
the Dutchess herself, and contribute in spight of her will to
what of all things she desired to avoid; the Duke had his
share in all these sollicitudes, but his satisfaction in returning
to Court made some compensation, whereas that was not the
thing that charmed the Dutchess, on the contrary she had
always chozen to accompany him in his banishment, thō
intended for never so short a time, rather than live at eas where
he was not: it was therefore the passionate affection she had
for him that made her neither desire to go by land, nor stay
behind, till she was brought to bed, but thought herself happyer
in any danger or trouble with him than in any security or eas
without him; so they imbarked accordingly, and this Voyage
proveing happyer than the last, they arrived without any ill
accident on the 27ʰ of the same month at Whitehall, whither
the King came on purpose that day from Windsor to meet
them, to the unspeakeable joy of them all: It was hard to say
who had most pleasure in their return, it is certain the King's
share was not the least, for besides the tender affection he
bore his Brother, he had a mighty loue and esteem for the
Dutchess, he did not only honour her personal merit, but

commiserated in some measure her suffrings more than the
Duke's, because she went a whole sharer with him in all his
misfortunes, and had over and above some private grivances of
her own in which his Royal 'Highness bore no part ; her
passionate love for the Duke her husband made their joint
afflictions easy to her, but render the other the more
insuportable, for as yet all these adversities had not washed
him clean from certain personal disorders, which had all along
been so grievous to her ; but she lived not much longer before
she had the satisfaction of seeing him not only become a perfect
rival of her vertue, but a most exemplar and fervent penitent
for the Sinns of his former life.

What made this meeting still more comfortable was the
good condition the King's affairs were in ; his Majesty had at
last taken those vigorous councells, and resolute methods the
Duke had so long press'd him too, and was convinced by
experience of what his Royal Highness had continually
inculcated, that there was no compounding matters with that
sort of people, and that the only way to be served faithfully
and dutifully in his Court and Council, was not to suffer either
his person, dignitie, or prerogative, to be infring'd or reviled,
nor the lines, liberties, and properties of his Subjects to be
invaded and ruin'd under the notion of preserveing them ; and
that those unparalell'd attemps upon his Government which had
so encouraged the ill men and terrifyd the good, were no longer
to be born with : that he must Support his friends if he would
have them continue So, for that no one thō never so loyally
disposed durst march faster than his leader ; thō the Duke
himself was in some measure an exception to this rule, for
notwithstanding he was a persecuted, banished, and abandon'd
Prince, he did not only keep peace with his Majesty in this
career, but enter'd it in great measure first himself, and thō
still accompanyd with so much prudence as never to put the

TOME
II.

1682.

King to the inconveniencie of defending an indiscreet zeal; thus he shew'd by his management in Scotland, a good example of the doctrine he preached, which when his Majesty followed, it set him at rest the remainder of his days; he had often tould him that the wrack which the Crown had suffer'd in his Father's time was so fresh in the memorys of most men, that he wonder'd any prudent person could run into the same errours, or the malicious partie think to play the same game so soon again, that the Rocks indeed which he split upon, lay hid to him, but were so visible now that should not his Majesty avoid them he would perish rather derided than pitied.

These were the measures the Duke had long advised, and now being with his Majesty, as much as his engagement of not meddling in business would permit, kept him steddy too; by which at last he so worsted the enemies of his government that none who ris up against it now were call'd by any other names than Rebells: It was by these methods he master'd the

BAKER 786.

stubborn temper of the Citizens, and gain'd his point in the Election of the Sheriffs notwithstanding the tumultuous and rietous opposition of the factious partie, and forced them from that scandelous retrenchment of Ignoramus Juries, under which they had long lurked with so much security and acted any sort of treason without fear or shame.

The Earl of
Shaftsbury
sues for
pardon.

When this strong hould therefore began to be in danger of being reduced, it brought My Lord Shaftsbury on his knees and made him sue for pardon from the Duke; the message was

KING JA. Mᵐ
To. 8. 315.

" something ambiguous, which made his Royal Highness return
" him this answer; That he knew him too well to trust him in
" any thing relating to himself, but if he would make such
" submission to his Majesty as became him, and give
" convinceing proofs of a true conversion, he would take him
" willingly by the hand; for that if the greatest enemie he had
" in the world (which he tooke him to be) would become a

loyal and dutifull Subject to the King, he could easily " T O M E
II.
1682.
overlook the injuries done to himself, and readely forgive "
them with all his heart. "

But it seems that Lord was not so well disposed to aske The Earl of Sunderland does the like.
pardon as the Duke to givé it, so no farther step was made in
that matter ; however other great men began to shift for them. "
selves, the Duke of Monmouth waver'd a little, and My Lord "
Sunderland who was made of plyebler mettal than the rest, "
and who by keeping still in with the Dutchess of Portsmouth, "
had never qùite left his hóuld of the Court, now at her "
return out of France used all her credit, which was very "
great, to be readmitted to his employment again ; he had "
been long meditateing that matter, at least ever since he saw
the faction began to decline, and had open'd his desires to My
Lord Hide, of being reconcil'd to the Duke while he was yet Lᴇᴛᴛᴇʀs Vol: 2. p. 853.
in Scotland, accompanying his request with all imaginable
assurances of sorrow for what was past and promises of future
good behaveours, and begg'd of him to acquaint his Royal
Highnéss with it, and as a marke of his sinceritie chose to
make aplication, he say'd, first to the Duke, ere he did it to
the King: But thō My Lord Hide thought it good policy in
the Duke to encourage repentance, yet he knew it was
dangerous to trust so faithless a man ; so tould him, He
durst not venter to make any such proposal to his Highness in Ibid. 850.
his absence, but that being so soon expected he would not
only then acquaint him with it, but accompagny his request
with all the good offices he was capable of, by which he
neither disencouraged his hopes nor engaged the Duke, which
was submitted to it, and promised he would not so much
as move the King in the intrim. However My Lord Hide Ibid: p. 890.
writ to the Duke about it, the answer to which miscarryed,
which put him into some axiety and suspicion, and not without

T O M E
II.

1682.

cause, since that was the only letter which was known to have fail'd during his Highness' stay in Scotland.

But when the Dutchess of Portsmouth was come back again, he had a surer card to play than the Duke's intrest, he had always been her favorit, and her late kindness to the Duke began to souren a little; She had got a grant of her money without being behoulden to him, and she could not blame him, that it was not done in the manner she first projected, yet she was not pleas'd that the fund out of which it was now to be pay'd, had been so long made a secret to her, this gave her a jealousie of the Duke's presence at Court might be a means to make more things so, she likewise observed that the King

King Ja: M^m
To. 9. 171.

" and the Duke had long and frequent conferences together,
" in privat, which she concluded were upon matters of State,
" thō in reality they were concerning Religion, which the
" King at that time had great scruples about; all this made
" her aprehend there was no depending upon the Duke's
" engagement not to meddle in business, and therefore she was
" resolved, if possible, to get it into her own hands, or those of

King Ja: M^m.
To. 8. p. 215.

" her creatures; which made her press so vehemently My Lord
" Sunderland's readmission, that the Duke who stood upon so
" ticklish a point himself durst not openly opose it, much less
" did he venter to meddle (whatever her Grace might think) in
" any business but what related to Scotland, infine thō My Lord
" Halifax did what he could to hinder it nothing was proof

King Ja: M^m
To. 9. 176.

" against her importunitie, and My Lord Sunderland was
" made Secretary of State in My Lord Conway's room who
had been so in his; so that now she thought herself well enough armed for any attempt, thō it were even to send the Duke back again into banishment, which she began to entertain some thoughts of, and if his Majesty had lived much longer, tis probable she might have efected it.

The Duke of Monmouth's inclinations to follow this example were too weak to withstand the Sollicitations of his factious friends, who kept him fixt in his engagments to them : all the Dutchess of Monmouths' long importunity could doe, was to give her leave at last to tell the King, that if he would pleas to pardon his past follies, he would for the future keep company with none but such as his Majesty should apoint ; but, repenting immediately of what he had done, tould her next day, She might say what she pleased for herself, as a thing she believ'd he would do, but not to engage for him, it seems he aprehended some thing more would be required of him which he was resolved never to consent too; so that, thō she press'd him all she could, he was not to be prevail'd upon any further : The report however of it allarmed all sides, the Duke's friends aprehended a seeming reconciliation might put him in a capacitie of doing more mischief, and the other partie were affraid to loos the main handle of their faction ; so My Lord Shaftsbury, Russel, Mr Montagu &c, at their next meeting charged him with what they had heard, but he confidently denyd he had any designe to reconcile himself with the Court, that he could not hinder the foolish words and wishes of his wife, and to convince them how firme he was in their intrest, made a sort of progress, as had been resolved amongst them, into Cheshire and the neih-bouring Counties to rais the people into a factious temper in order to future designes ; but thō in some places he got a few forced acclamations from the Rabble, in others he met with afronts, so that neither he nor his partie reaped any great good from that contrivance.

TOME II.

1682.

The Duke of Monmouth makes some offers towards a reconciliation.

KING JA. Mⁿ To: 8. p. 517.

ON the other hand the King got every day more and more advantages over these pretended patriots, by fineing the late

1683.

The Quo Warranto

TOME
II.

1683.

brought
against the
Cities'Charter.
Sheriffs of London and other fiery sticklers for their riotous
proceedings, and at last subdued entirely that Stubborn and
rebelleous Citie, by bringing a *Quo Warranto* against its
charter and franchises, which after a long and solemn debate
was by judgment of the Court of King's Bench seized in the
King's hands. The Duke began to call his enemies to account
too, and thō his inclinations always lead him to mercy and
pardon, he thought it necessary to terrifie others by making an
example of the late Sherif Pilkington ; who having Sayd upon
the Duke's return, He had fired the Citie and was now come to
cut their throats, he caus'd him to be indicted, (*May* 8th) and
the words being proved by two Aldermen, the Court assign'd
his Royal Highness a hundred thousand pounds for damages.

Nothing now was wanteing to make the King perfectly easy
in his affairs but the Duke's assistance in the management
" of them ; and therefore at his return from Newmarket
" acquainted him with his design of admitting him again
" into the Commitee of forreign affairs, and of consulting
" him in all other matters as well as what related to Scotland,
" but thought it proper, he Sayd, to delay it a little till he Saw
" what bent his Neibours took in order to peace or war, which
" might force him perhaps to certain measures not so agreable to
" the people, and he was willing to spare the Duke the odium of
" haveing it charged to his account; but the discovery of a
" cursed Conspiracy, which in Part they had already providen-
" tially escaped, but still in great measure hung over their
" heads, hasted the Duke's readmission into business for their
" mutual security, sooner perhaps than otherwise it might have
" been done.

The King had in a manner entirely conjured downe those rebel-
leons spirites which had haunted him so long; but as their quitting
a body they haue long possess'd, is generally accompanyed
with great convultions and strugglings, so, as a làst effort of

their malice, they framed a most detestable Plot not only to subuert the Government, but to murther both the King and Duke at a blow, and amongst other Hellish contrivances to compas their wicked ends, had a designe of lodging armes, men, and all other necessaries for such an attempt, at a place called Rye house belonging to one of the Conspirators in the road from Newmarket, with design to murther both King and Duke in their late return from thence: but by an extraordinary prouidence a great fire happening there, put an end to the diversion of that place sooner than was intended, and forced the King and Duke back to London some days before the time which had been apointed for it, and before the Conspirators were ready; which most happely disapointed that execrable vilany, and preserved them both from the most barberous attempt the malice of men was capable of inventing.

It was towards the end of Trinity terme ere any discovery was made of this Conspiracy, and thō So many persons were privy to it, no one had the bowells or remorse to acquaint the King or his Royal Highness with the danger they had escaped and were still threaten'd with; it is true the Duke of " King Ja: Mⁿ. Tᵒ.8. pag. 345. Monmouth about the end of April had desired the Dutchess " of Portsmouth, to obtain leave for him to see the King in " order to make his submission, which perhaps was with " design to discover the Plot; but if that argued an earlyer " remorse than that of any other, it render'd him more guilty, who after such an inspiration to his duty coul relaps into his former obdurateness, and say nothing of it, till one Keeling came in and reveal'd the design, which was then soon unravel'd to the Bottom.

The Earle of Shaftsbury, who had been the first kindler of this fire, wanted patience and courage it seems to wait its blazing out, and was so disharten'd upon a disapointment or two, that complaining the numbers to whom the matter was

T O M E
II.

1683.

communicated were too few to do the work, and too many to conceal it, on the 19th of November, one of the days apointed for a general insurrection, skulked downe the river and went with Walcot and Ferguson to Holland; the case was changed to what it had been when he lay under the cover of those shamefull ignoramus Juries, he then pretended he would walke the King out of the Kingdom, as he arrogantly express'd it, but now durst not allow his own wicked councells leasure to come to tollerable maturity : However this disharten'd not the other fiery spirites, the chiefe of which were the Duke of Monmouth, Earle of Essex, Lord Gray, Lord Howard of Escrick, Lord Russel, Colonel Algernoon Sidney, M. John Hampden, Armstrong, Romsey, Rumbald, Sheppard, Walcot and Ferguson, who soon return from Holland and many others all deeply concerned, some in the intended insurrections, others in the assasinations, and many in both; they went on therefore with their wicked consultations and apointed a Council of Six to haue the priuie direction with inferiour classes under them, who had meetings without end to forme their preparations, both in order to a general insurrection, in which it was sayd near fourty thousand men were engaged,

Bishop of
Rochester's
Hist. of the
Conspiracy,
pag. 50.

and to contriue in what manner they might assasinate both King and Duke, which sometimes they were for executing in St James's park, or when they should be going down the river, or to Hampton Court, or to Windsor, or in the Play house, but at last pitched upon Rye house; and thõ they saw by what had happen'd; that Providence so visibly watched over the persons of the King and Duke, yet they were rather enraged than deterr'd by that disapointment, especially when Rumbald came up from Rye house, and tould them, how slenderly attended the King and Duke had pass'd by there: they met therefore and consulted with more freedom than ever, n'ay (such was their horrid barbarity) they would wantonly make

their jests upon that bloudy business, and in their canting
language sport with the most hellish contrivance that could
possebly enter into the hearts of men, they resolved all loyall
persons of distinction should accompany their Prince in this
cruel massacre, Officers of State, privy Councellors, Judges;
in fine who ever was supposed to be truly affection'd to the
King or Duke were inserted into the bloody List, nor was
there any opposition made to whatever was proposed of that
nature, their only difficulty or disagreement was what to set
up, not what to pull downe, and in this point the Scotch and
English had like to have divided. In this manner therefore
were they laying about them with all the infernall malice that
generally attends the pretended conscientious zeal of such fiery
patriots and implacable men, when the discovery of the whole
Conspiracy overtook them on the 4ʰ of June, and justice
followed, thō mixed with mighty clemency close at its heels.

It is not necessary to enter into the particulars of this cursed
Plot, the history of which has been so accurately and elegantly
writ by the Bishop of Rochester; it is only worthy observation
that the undenyable conviction and voluntary confession of
many of the Conspirators, the witnesses not only credible but
one of the Nobility, the innumerable concurring papers and
depositions, My Lord Essex cutting his own throat in the
Tower, the same day My Lord Russel was tryd and found
guilty of it, are other sort of proofs of its reality than the
disagreeing testimonys of such indigent Varlets, as composed
the evidence of the pretended Popish Plot, made up of contradictions and even impossibilities, disowned by the last breath
of every one that dyed for it, not one paper produc'd to prove
it, nor one tittle of it ever believ'd by the King himself and
therefore were as manifest demonstrations of the falsety of the
one; as the foremention'd circumstances were undenyable proofs
of the other.

However the King's generous caution not to be imposed upon again by pretended Plots, and not immagining the worst of Subjects could harbour so hellish a design against him, made him yeild a slow credit to the first relation, which gave leasure to many of tho chief managers to take the alarme, and by that means scatter and withdraw themselves beyond the Seas: The Duke of Monmouth, upon the first discovery of it, absconded a while, but a proclamation comeing out against him, he was forced at last to do for his own security what his good nature could not bring him too, he writ therefore to the King in a most humble manner to beg pardon for his fatal errours, his crimes appear'd to him, he sayd, in so terrible a shape, that he prefer'd even death it self before the present sence of them; in fine he press'd so vehemently for pardon, that the King was not proof against his sollicitations, but admits him to his presence at Mr Secretary Jenkins' Office; who being withdrawn,

" and none present but the King and Duke, he freely
" owned his knowledge of the whole Conspiracy except what
" related to the intended assasination, with which he aver'd he
" never was acquainted, he named all the persons concern'd
" with him in it, and did not contradict any thing My Lord
" Howard had Sayd, except one particular which was not
" material, he very well remember'd what Rumney had Say'd
" of My Lord Russel, who when Trenchard had fail'd him,
" sayd he would put on his boots and go to Taunton himself,
" and make the people rise, he wonder'd no more witnesses
" had come in against Wildman, since no man, he Sayd, had
" been more active in the Conspiracy then he; that the
" Councel of Six had given fifteen pound a man to send Aron
" Smith downe into Scotland, that Sir William Courtney,
" S^r —— Drake, and other Gentlemen knew of it in the West,
" that Booth was the man they depended on in Cheshire, and
" Sr John Hotham in Yorkshire, he owned his haveing visited

the Guards in order to a surprise, that D⟨r⟩ Owen, M⟨r⟩ Mead, "
and all the chief of the Nonconformist Ministers were both "
privy and actine in the Conspiracy, that Major Hurst of "
Chichester undertook to surprise Portsmouth, which, he sayd, "
might easily be done because the Guards, he sayd, were "
drunk every night ; and being asked by the King, If they "
had a correspondence with any of his own Guards, or any "
of the Court ? he positively denyd they had ; he Sayd, Monro's "
and S⟨r⟩ John Cockram's comeing up upon the account of "
Carolina was but a pretence, their real business being to "
adjust matters so, that their riseing there might be at the same "
time with that in England, that Rowallen Baily and other "
Scotch in hould were all engaged, that they complain'd they "
wanted arms, but not good wills to the business ; and Sayd, "
that My Lord Argile would bring a great aid to the Western "
men, who had layd a designe to surprise Sterling Castle by an "
old gate towards Ballinquith, where they Sayd no guard was "
kept, that they were to seize the Chancellor and Treasurer "
in Edinburg which they thought might be easily efected "
by 40 or 50 horse, and doubted not but they could get so "
many into the Town without any notice being taken. "

All these particulars his Royal Highness set downe, and was
the more exact in doing it, because assoon as the Duke of
Monmouth had got his pardon, he began to heard as formerly
with his factious Councellors, which made the King aprehend
the evil spirit was enter'd again ; he was not content with his
Majestys promis of being exempt from Wittnessing against his
old friends, but he began again to be their Patron too, the
truth of it was, they had got such a dominion over his unstable
mind, that they soon overthrew all his new made vows of
Loyaltie ; but haveing left a letter in his Majestys custody,
wherein he owned all his knowledge of the Conspiracy, which
the King had required not only as a ty upon him, but for

T O M E
II.
1683.

publick satisfaction, it being so hard to stifle the groundless
suggestions of those false and factious men against the plainest
matters of fact in the world ; his business was therefore to get
it back, which he press'd so ernestly, that his Majesty when he
saw him positiue, was so good as to tell him, He would not
keep it against his will, and so return'd it to him, upon which
he flew back immediately and denyd every word he had sayd :
By this Stratagem, he had wash'd himself clean in the eye of
the Law, and had preserued his head from the block without
contributing to bring others to it, and was so ungratefull as to
make no other use of his Majestys gracious pardon than to draw
from thence an advantage of entring more securely into a new

King Ja. Mᵐ.
To. 8. pag. 355.

" cours of disobedience ; the King was exceeding angry to find
" his indulgence thus abused, but all he could do was to
" banish him the Court, upon which he withdrew privately beyond
" seas with one Gentleman and a Seruant took shiping at
" Greenwitch in a fisher boat, and landed soon after in Zealand.

" Before he went went away some persons would have per-
" suaded him to have gon and serued the Emperour in Hungary,
" but, he sayd, that would draw him too far of; wherefore he
" only made a turn to Bruxelles and from thence to Holland,
" where he saw the Prince of Orange; and whether he Satisfyd
" him or no (as he pretended he could with a quarter of an
" hour's discours) it argued no great respect in that Prince,
" to the King and Duke, to admit a visite from a person who
" had own'd himself capable of entring into so horrid a
" Conspiracy against them both, and who still endeavour'd to
" keep up his credit with that rebellious partie and his vain
" pretences to a Crown; this the Duke in some measure
" expostulated with his son in Law, and forewarn'd him not to
" credit a person who had so infamously denyd what he had so
" solemnly declar'd, nor to countenance one who had so
" lately done his best to destroy them all and involve the

Kingdom in blood and confusion. But that Prince's darke designes were not under the tyes of honour and duty, so he then began to give the Duke of Monmouth such encouragement as hinder'd his hopes from extinguishing with his friends, who now were every day found guilty and executed.

BY this discovery and the punishment of several of the chief Conspirators, his Majesty had at last crushed those rebellious snakes, which had so long infested his Royal Throne, and gave him leasure to think of supporting it by forreign Allyances now it was in securitie at home, in order to which a Mariage was treated betwixt the PRINCESS ANNE and PRINCE GEORGE, Brother to the King of Denmark; there could not be a greater argument how averse the Duke was, from forceing any one in point of Religion, than his submission to the King's pleasure in marrying his second Daughter to a Protestant Prince too, thō the late comportement of the Prince of Orange was no great encouragement to try what another Son in Law might proue of the same Religion, but no command or desire of his Majesty, that was not manifestly against the Law of God was ever so much as ballanced by the Duke; so the Marriage was solemnized on the 23th of July, and not long after the King in recompence of his Royal Highnesse's dutifull complyance in this and in all other matters, restored him to his former imployments of High Admiral and Privy Concellor, and made him some sort of reparation likewise for the publick calumnies and aspertions cast upon him, by the conviction of Oates both for *Scandalum Magnatum* and perjury ; extending also his kindness to others for his sake, the Prisoners for Oates's pretended Plot were discharged upon bail, and a general pardon intended them, but for some formalitys of Law was for a time delayd.

And now the King had brought his affairs to a more happy
situation than ever they had been since the Restoration; he
saw his enemies at his feet, and the Duke his Brother at his
side, whose indefatigableness in business took a great share of
that burthen off his shoulders, which his indolent temper made
uneasy to him, and this his Royal Highness performed with
such a perfect conformety to his Majestys inclinations and
obedience to his will, as made his seruices as free from jealousie
and unsuspected, as they were affectionate and usefull, both to
confirm his happyness at home and establish his reputation
abroad; which two points being attain'd to a great degree, the
King had a pleasant vew of future tranquility for the reste of
his days, and to enjoy the frutes of his late toils, the memory
of which gave a higher relish to his present eas; when it pleas'd
God to shew on how sandy a foundation all temporal happiness
in this world as well as the best layd projects are built, by
calling him out of this life, when he seem'd most secure of
enjoying it by the mastery he had got over those restless,
crafty, and implacable spirites that had so long and furiously
sought it.

" It was on the 2ᵈ of February that the King was seized with
" a violent fit of an apoplexy just as he came out of his closet
" where he had been for some time before he was dress'd:
" The Duke was immediately advertised of it, but before he
" could get to his Majestys bed chamber, one Doctor King
" being in the withdrawing room was called in, and had let
" him blood; and then by aplication and remedys usual on
" such occasions (which was done by his own Phisicians) he
" came perfectly again to his sences, so that next morning there
" was great hopes of his recovery: but in the forth day he
" grew so much wors that all those hopes vanished, and the
" Doctors declared they absolutly dispair'd of his life, which
" made it high time to think of prepairing for the other world;

accordingly two Bishops came to doe their function, who "
reading the prayers apointed in the common prayer book on "
that occasion, when they came to the place, where usually "
they exhort the Sick person to make a confession of his Sinns, "
the Bishop of Bath and Wells who was one of them "
advertised him, It was not of obligation: so after a short "
exhortation asked him, If he were sorry for his Sinns? "
which the King saying he was, the Bishop pronounced "
absolution, and then asked him, If he pleas'd to receive the "
Sacrament? To which he made no reply, and being press'd "
by the Bishop several times, gaue no other answer but that "
it was time enough, or that he would think of it. "

The Duke, who stood all this while by his Majestys "
bed side, and seeing that notwithstanding the Bishop's "
sollicitation he would not receive the Communion from "
them, and knowing the King's sentiments in matters of "
Religion concerning which he had lately had frequent "
conferences with him, thought it a fit oportunety to remind "
him of it, and therefore, desireing the company to stand a little "
from the bed, Sayd, He was overjoyed to find his Majesty in "
the same mind he was when he spoak lately to him in his "
closet about Religion, at which time he was pleas'd to shew "
him a paper he had writ himself of controversie, and "
therefore asked him, if he desired he should send for a Priest "
to him? to which the King immediately replyd, For God's "
sake Brother doe, and pleas to loos no time; but then "
reflecting on the consequence, added, But will you not expose "
yourself too much by doing it? The Duke who never thought
of danger when the King's Seruice call'd, thō but in a temporal
concern, much less in a eternall one; answer'd, Sʳ, thō it cost "
me my life I will bring one to you, and immediately going "
into the next room, and seeing never a Catholick, he could "

send but the Count de Castel Machlor; he dispatched him "
on that errand, and thŏ other Priets were sent for, yet it "
fortuned none could then be got but Father Huddleston a "
Benedictin Monk who had been so assistant to his Majesty "
in makeing his escape after the battle of Worcester, who "
being brought up a pair of backstairs into a private closet, "
the Duke advertised the King where he was, who thereupon "
order'd all people to withdraw except the Duke; but his "
Royal Highness thought fit that My Lord of Bath, who was "
Lord of the Bedchamber then in waiting, and My Lord "
Feversham the Captain of his Guards should remain in the "
room, telling the King, it was not fit he should be quite "
alone with his Majesty considering the weak condition he was "
then in; and assoon as the room was clear'd, accordingly "
call'd Mr Huddleston in, whom his Majesty received with "
great joy and satisfaction, telling him he desired to die in the "
faith and Communion of the Catholick Church; that he "
was most heartely sorrie for the sins of his past life, and "
particularly for haveing differ'd his conversion so long, that "
he hoped nevertheless in the merits of Christ, that he was in "
charitie with all the world, pardon'd his enemies and begg'd "
pardon of those he had any ways offended at that if it "
pleas'd to God he recover'd, was resolved by his assistance to "
amend his life; then he proceeded to make a confession of his "
whole life with exceeding tenderness of heart, and pronounced "
an act of Contrition with great piety and compunction: in "
this he spent about an hour, and haveing desired to receiue "
all the succours fit for a dying man, he continued makeing "
pious ejaculations, and frequently lifting up his hands, cryd, "
Mercy Sweet Jesus, mercy, till the Priest was ready to give "
him extreme unxion; and the blessed Sacrament being come "
by that time this was ended, he asked his Majesty If he "

desired to receiue it? who answer'd, He did, most ernestly, "
if he thought him worthy of it: Accordingly the Priest after "
some further preparations going about to giue it him, he "
rais'd himself up, and sayd, Let me meet my heavenly Lord "
in a better posture than lying on my bed ; but being desired "
not to discompose himself, he repeated the act of contrition "
and then receiv'd with great pietie and devotion, after which "
Father Huddleston makeing him a short exhortation left "
him in so much peace of mind that he looked approaching "
death in the face with all immaginable tranquilitie and "
Christian resolution. "

The company then being call'd in again, his Majesty "
express'd the greatest kindness and tenderness for the Duke "
that could possebly be conceiv'd, he owned in the most "
publick manner the sence he had of his Brotherly affection "
during the whole cours of his life, and particularly in "
this last action, he commended his great submission and "
constant obedience to all his commands, and asked him "
pardon alowd for the rigorous treatment he had so long "
exercised his patience with; all which he sayd in so affec- "
tionate a manner, as drew floods of tears from all that were "
present, he spoke most tenderly to the Queen too, and infine "
left nothing unsaid, or undone, that so small a time would "
allow of either to reconcile himself to God, or to make "
satisfaction to those he had injured upon earth, disposeing "
himself to dy with the pietie and unconcernedless becomeing "
a Christian, and resolution becomeing a King; and then his
sences begining to fail him, (which had continued perfect till
about an hour before his death) he expired betwixt eleaven
and twelve a clock in fryday morning being the Sixt of
February, 168⅘.

His death was universally lamented, as in his life he had
been generally beloued, for even the malignity of those who

TOME
II.

1684.

KING JAM.
PAPERS
CONCERNING
KING CH: HIS
DEATH.

750

TOME most molested his reign, sprung more from a hatread of his
II. power and character than from any aversion to his person.

1684. He wanted no qualification that could make a Prince glorious
and a Nation happy, thō mixed with some disorders and
infirmities which ſullyd those shineing natural partes, which
were otherwise the admiration of his Neibors, as well as the
delight and security of his subjects; he was so exceeding
ingenious in his conversation, So affable in his nature and so
easy of access, as endear'd him beyond expression to all who
had the honour to be about him; thō some abused that
benignity to a contempt as they did his mild disposition and
mercifull temper, to the great disturbance of his government,
which he bore with So long, as made his judgment and
courage be call'd in question for a while, but shew'd in the end
he neither wanted cunning to countermine those who dispised
him, nor resolution to break those stubborn spirits, who
thought to have run him on the same rock on which his
Royal Father so miserably perished, thō his excessive love of
ease made him loiter so long about it as to suffer many
irregularities in his government, and a most unjust oppression
of the inocent, particularly in Oates's Plot, till awaked by the
dayly admonitions of his Brother, he shook off his fetters at
last, and made the Regal power apear in its natural vigour and
luster again, in which it continued till his death.

HERE ENDS THE SECOND VOLUME OF THE MANUSCRIPT.

Printed by A. Strahan,
Printers-Street, London.